Unitet States Office of the Comptroller of the Currency

Annual Report Of The Comptroller Of The Currency

Unitet States Office of the Comptroller of the Currency

Annual Report Of The Comptroller Of The Currency

ISBN/EAN: 9783741125362

Manufactured in Europe, USA, Canada, Australia, Japa

Cover: Foto ©knipser5 / pixelio.de

Manufactured and distributed by brebook publishing software
(www.brebook.com)

Unitet States Office of the Comptroller of the Currency

Annual Report Of The Comptroller Of The Currency

OF THE

COMPTROLLER OF THE CURRENCY

TO THE

FIRST SESSION OF THE FORTY-SEVENTH CONGRESS

OF THE

UNITED STATES.

DECEMBER 5, 1881.

WASHINGTON:
GOVERNMENT PRINTING OFFICE.
1881.

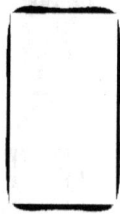

TABLE OF CONTENTS.

[A full index will be found at page 215 of this volume.]

TREASURY DEPARTMENT, }
Document No. 228. }
Comptroller of Currency. }

REPORT

OF

THE COMPTROLLER OF· THE CURRENCY.

TREASURY DEPARTMENT,
OFFICE OF THE COMPTROLLER OF THE CURRENCY,
Washington, December 3, 1881.

I have the honor to submit for the consideration of Congress the nineteenth annual report of the Comptroller of the Currency, in compliance with section 333 of the Revised Statutes of the United States.

Eighty-six national banks were organized during the year ending November 1 last, with an aggregate authorized capital of $9,651,050, to which $5,233,580 in circulating notes have been issued. This is the largest number of banks organized in any year since 1872. Twenty-six banks with an aggregate capital of $2,020,000, and circulation of $1,245,530, have voluntarily discontinued business during the year. National banks are located in every State of the Union except Mississippi and in every Territory except Arizona, the total number in operation on October 1 last being 2,132. This is the greatest number of banks that has ever been in operation at any one time. The total number of national banks organized from the establishment of the national-banking system, February 25, 1863, to November 1 of the present year is 2,581.

From the establishment of the system to November 1 last, 340 banks have gone into voluntary liquidation by the vote of shareholders owning two-thirds of their respective capitals, and 86 have been placed in the hands of receivers for the purpose of closing up their affairs. The total amount of claims proved by the creditors of these insolvent banks is $25,966,602, and the amount of dividends paid to creditors is $18,561,698.

The estimated losses to creditors from the failures of national banks, during the eighteen years since the passage of the act, is $6,240,000, and the average annual loss has therefore been about $346,000, in the business of corporations having an average capital of about $450,000,000, and deposits averaging about $800,000,000. Twenty-one of these insolvent banks have paid their creditors in full, and forty of them have paid more than 75 per cent. each. The individual liabilities of shareholders of insolvent banks has been enforced in fifty three instances, and about $2,700,000 has been collected from this source. During the past year dividends have been declared in favor of the creditors of insolvent national banks, amounting to $929,059, and the affairs of twelve such banks have been finally closed, nine of which have paid their creditors in full.

There were no failures of national banks during the period from June 19, 1880, to November 1 of the present year. Since that date the Mechanics' National Bank of Newark, and the Pacific National Bank of Boston, to which reference will be made hereafter, have suspended, and the former bank has been placed in the hands of a receiver.

The following table exhibits the resources and liabilities of the national banks, at the close of business on the 1st day of October, 1881, the returns from New York City, from Boston, Philadelphia and Baltimore, from the other reserve cities, and from the remaining banks of the country, being tabulated separately:

	New York City.	Boston, Philadelphia, and Baltimore.	Other reserve cities.*	Country banks.	Aggregate.
	48 banks.	102 banks.	87 banks.	1, 895 banks.	2, 132 banks.
RESOURCES.					
Loans and discounts	$246, 757, 659	$211, 814, 653	$134, 406, 498	$576, 043, 493	$1, 169, 022, 303
Overdrafts	143, 733	55, 507	386, 307	4, 188, 143	4, 773, 780
Bonds for circulation	22, 991, 500	57, 290, 800	27, 847, 100	255, 206, 100	363, 335, 500
Bonds for deposits	820, 000	625, 000	3, 848, 000	10, 247, 000	15, 540, 000
U. S. bonds on hand	7, 854, 050	2, 518, 050	6, 302, 000	24, 298, 350	40, 972, 450
Other stocks and bonds	13, 413, 567	7, 386, 271	4, 614, 456	36, 482, 409	61, 896, 703
Due from reserve agents		20, 866, 093	19, 767, 054	92, 335, 036	132, 968, 183
Due from other national banks	19, 917, 055	14, 143, 191	10, 479, 467	33, 965, 733	78, 505, 446
Due from other banks and bankers	3, 278, 155	1, 496, 037	3, 775, 495	10, 757, 140	19, 306, 827
Real estate, furniture, and fixtures	10, 760, 828	6, 739, 161	4, 593, 197	25, 235, 915	47, 329, 111
Current expenses	1, 089, 101	792, 083	844, 553	4, 006, 199	6, 731, 936
Premiums	1, 061, 797	247, 164	360, 495	2, 469, 130	4, 138, 586
Checks and other cash items	2, 513, 144	1, 337, 655	1, 048, 504	9, 932, 577	14, 831, 879
Exchanges for clearing-house	146, 597, 213	27, 198, 422	14, 592, 607	834, 013	189, 222, 256
Bills of other national banks	1, 580, 588	1, 802, 778	2, 019, 871	12, 329, 475	17, 732, 712
Fractional currency	37, 964	40, 426	54, 971	240, 585	373, 946
Specie	51, 524, 768	17, 584, 343	17, 256, 624	27, 969, 001	114, 334, 736
Legal-tender notes	8, 983, 371	6, 934, 070	10, 767, 998	26, 473, 002	53, 158, 441
U. S. certificates of deposit	1, 915, 000	2, 150, 000	2, 055, 000	620, 000	6, 740, 000
Five per cent. redemption fund	1, 016, 807	2, 543, 414	1, 194, 348	11, 361, 183	16, 115, 752
Due from U. S. Treasurer	395, 180	218, 485	136, 165	607, 014	1, 356, 844
Totals	542, 651, 490	383, 783, 603	266, 350, 800	1, 165, 601, 498	2, 358, 387, 391
LIABILITIES.					
Capital stock	51, 150, 000	79, 398, 330	40, 401, 500	292, 872, 155	463, 821, 985
Surplus fund	10, 947, 316	21, 954, 102	12, 208, 793	74, 030, 407	128, 140, 618
Undivided profits	12, 832, 315	6, 287, 274	5, 779, 776	31, 472, 826	56, 372, 191
National bank notes outstanding	20, 112, 590	50, 632, 029	23, 513, 195	225, 942, 155	320, 199, 969
State bank notes outstanding	47, 472	35, 614		161, 932	245, 018
Dividends unpaid	246, 228	1, 356, 702	172, 542	2, 060, 455	3, 835, 927
Individual deposits	295, 692, 013	163, 432, 337	120, 094, 419	491, 778, 762	1, 070, 997, 531
U. S. deposits	437, 422	366, 243	2, 262, 560	5, 410, 465	8, 476, 690
Deposits of U. S. disbursing officers	89, 934	107, 140	844, 813	2, 580, 916	3, 631, 803
Due to national banks	104, 089, 161	45, 523, 222	34, 048, 738	22, 201, 825	205, 862, 946
Due to other banks and bankers	38, 007, 039	13, 926, 472	24, 885, 452	12, 228, 508	89, 047, 471
Notes and bills rediscounted			364, 393	2, 726, 772	3, 091, 165
Bills payable		764, 138	1, 774, 619	2, 125, 320	4, 664, 077
Totals	542, 651, 490	383, 783, 603	266, 350, 800	1, 165, 601, 498	2, 358, 387, 391

*The reserve cities, in addition to New York, Boston, Philadelphia, and Baltimore, are Albany, Pittsburgh, Washington, New Orleans, Louisville, Cincinnati, Cleveland, Chicago, Detroit, Milwaukee, Saint Louis, and San Francisco.

The following table exhibits, in the order of their capital the sixteen States having an amount of capital in excess of $5,000,000, together with the amount of circulation, loans and discounts, and individual deposits of each, on October 1, 1881:

States.	Capital.	Circulation.	Loans and discounts.	Individual deposits.
Massachusetts	$96,177,500	$71,267,089	$205,248,480	$125,198,324
New York	85,780,160	47,946,726	330,257,556	372,853,780
Pennsylvania	56,518,340	42,429,247	138,869,386	138,046,152
Ohio	29,389,000	21,468,480	66,518,608	60,960,674
Connecticut	25,539,630	17,966,332	43,475,312	25,761,231
Rhode Island	20,065,000	14,718,956	28,496,882	11,317,358
Illinois	15,199,600	8,165,189	61,555,795	72,972,402
Maryland	13,603,030	8,605,433	30,205,683	26,117,350
Indiana	13,093,500	8,767,700	24,899,023	23,206,436
New Jersey	12,960,000	10,386,784	29,243,480	28,250,618
Kentucky	10,435,100	8,885,111	17,774,891	9,145,739
Maine	10,385,000	8,211,247	17,305,908	9,325,083
Michigan	9,435,600	5,614,979	24,329,000	23,127,184
Vermont	8,151,000	6,442,899	10,899,272	5,191,352
Iowa	5,950,000	4,414,103	13,456,065	15,770,134
New Hampshire	5,830,000	5,158,159	7,518,017	4,292,687

COMPARATIVE STATEMENTS OF THE NATIONAL BANKS FOR ELEVEN YEARS.

The following table exhibits the resources and liabilities of the national banks for eleven years, at nearly corresponding dates, from 1871 to 1881, inclusive:

	Oct. 2, 1871.	Oct. 3, 1872.	Sept 12, 1873.	Oct. 2, 1874.	Oct. 1, 1875.	Oct. 2, 1876.	Oct. 1, 1877.	Oct. 1, 1878.	Oct. 2, 1879.	Oct. 1, 1880.	Oct. 1, 1881.
	1,767 banks.	1,919 banks.	1,976 banks.	2,004 banks.	2,087 banks.	2,089 banks.	2,080 banks.	2,053 banks.	2,048 banks.	2,090 banks.	2,132 banks.

RESOURCES.

	Millions.	Millions.	Millions.	Millions.	Millions.	Millions.	Millions.	Millions.	Millions.	Millions.	Millions.
Loans	831.6	877.2	944.2	954.4	984.7	931.3	891.9	834.0	878.5	1,041.0	1,173.8
Bonds for circulation	364.5	382.0	388.3	383.3	370.3	337.2	336.8	347.6	357.3	357.8	364.3
Other U. S. bonds	45.8	27.6	23.6	28.0	28.1	47.8	45.0	94.7	71.2	43.6	56.5
Stocks, bonds, &c.	24.5	23.5	23.7	27.8	33.5	34.4	34.5	36.9	39.7	48.9	61.9
Due from banks	133.2	128.2	149.5	134.8	141.7	146.9	129.9	138.9	167.3	213.5	230.8
Real estate	30.1	32.3	34.7	38.1	42.3	43.1	45.2	46.7	47.8	48.0	47.3
Specie	13.2	10.2	19.9	21.2	8.1	21.4	22.7	30.7	42.2	109.3	114.3
Legal-tender notes	107.0	102.1	92.4	80.0	76.5	81.2	66.9	64.4	63.2	56.6	53.2
Nat'l-bank notes	14.3	15.8	16.1	18.5	18.5	15.9	15.6	16.9	16.7	18.2	17.7
C. H. exchanges	115.2	125.0	100.3	109.7	87.9	100.0	74.5	82.4	113.0	121.4	189.2
U. S. cert. of deposit		6.7	20.6	42.8	48.8	29.2	33.4	32.7	26.8	7.7	6.7
Due from U. S. Treas				20.3	19.6	16.7	16.0	16.5	17.0	17.1	17.5
Other resources	41.2	25.2	17.3	18.3	19.1	19.1	28.7	24.9	22.1	23.0	26.2
Totals	1,730.6	1,755.8	1,830.6	1,877.2	1,882.2	1,827.2	1,741.1	1,767.3	1,868.8	2,105.8	2,358.4

LIABILITIES.

Capital stock	458.3	479.6	491.0	493.8	504.8	499.8	479.5	466.2	454.1	457.6	463.8
Surplus fund	101.1	110.3	120.3	129.0	134.4	132.2	122.8	116.9	114.8	120.5	128.1
Undivided profits	42.0	46.6	51.5	51.5	53.0	46.4	41.5	44.9	41.3	46.1	56.4
Circulation	317.4	335.1	340.3	334.2	319.1	292.2	291.9	301.0	313.8	317.3	320.2
Due to depositors	631.4	628.9	640.0	683.8	670.4	666.2	630.4	668.4	736.9	887.9	1,083.1
Due to banks	171.9	143.8	173.0	175.8	179.7	179.8	161.6	165.1	201.2	267.9	204.9
Other liabilities	8.5	11.5	11.5	9.1	11.8	10.6	10.4	7.9	6.7	8.5	11.9
Totals	1,730.6	1,755.8	1,830.6	1,877.2	1,882.2	1,827.2	1,741.1	1,767.3	1,868.8	2,105.8	2,358.4

The following table shows, at corresponding dates for three years, the increase of loans, deposits, circulation, capital and surplus, the amount of United States bonds on hand, and the movement of money in the national banks of the country, arranged in three groups—viz, those in the New England and Middle States, those in the Western and Northwestern States, including Kentucky and Missouri, and those in the remaining States and Territories:

NEW ENGLAND AND MIDDLE STATES.

	Oct. 1, 1881.	Oct. 1, 1880.	Oct. 2, 1879.
	No. of banks, 1,202.	No. of banks, 1,187.	No. of banks, 1,168.
Loans and discounts	$843,092,901	$773,916,399	$654,037,648
United States bonds on hand	27,373,650	21,076,400	41,983,650
Capital	335,009,700	333,363,300	331,646,630
Surplus	96,046,995	90,827,648	86,749,498
Net deposits	749,303,734	689,604,705	548,757,240
Circulation	233,132,972	229,826,416	227,824,388
Specie	82,209,124	89,074,603	32,977,600
Legal-tenders and United States certificates	33,828,596	36,485,314	66,097,350

WESTERN AND NORTHWESTERN STATES.

	Oct. 1, 1881.	Oct. 1, 1880.	Oct. 2, 1879.
	No. of banks, 748.	No. of banks, 729.	No. of banks, 715.
Loans and discounts	$264,703,034	$212,796,017	$179,161,250
United States bonds on hand	11,502,450	6,578,500	9,551,100
Capital	99,769,000	95,597,500	94,013,150
Surplus	25,708,901	24,191,511	23,034,727
Net deposits	295,520,514	227,994,373	170,119,124
Circulation	66,442,810	66,957,403	66,376,624
Specie	23,085,587	15,118,278	6,229,429
Legal-tenders and United States certificates	21,170,992	23,491,204	24,465,934

SOUTHERN AND PACIFIC STATES AND TERRITORIES.

	Oct. 1, 1881.	Oct. 1, 1880.	Oct. 2, 1879.
	No. of banks, 182.	No. of banks, 174.	No. of banks, 165.
Loans and discounts	$66,000,148	$54,464,852	$45,304,199
United States bonds on hand	2,096,350	1,138,500	1,407,350
Capital	20,043,285	28,593,185	28,408,185
Surplus	6,384,632	5,490,424	5,002,303
Net deposits	66,804,503	50,342,345	41,008,042
Circulation	20,624,287	20,566,217	19,585,330
Specie	6,477,845	3,988,508	2,966,703
Legal-tenders and United States certificates	4,891,016	4,415,410	5,392,678

Similar tables in reference to a number of the States in different sections of the country are given in the Appendix.

EXTENSION OF THE CORPORATE EXISTENCE OF NATIONAL BANKS.

Section 11 of the National Bank Act of February 25, 1863, provided that—

Every association formed pursuant to the provisions of this act may make and use a common seal, and shall have succession by the name designated in its articles of association and for the period limited therein, not, however, exceeding twenty years from the passage of this act.

Section 8 of the act of June 3, 1864, provides that each association—

Shall have power to adopt a corporate seal, and shall have succession by the name designated in its organization certificate, for the period of twenty years from its organization, unless sooner dissolved according to the provisions of its articles of association, or by the act of its shareholders owning two-thirds of its stock, or unless the franchise shall be forfeited by a violation of this act.

The act last named, as well as that which preceded it, contains the following provision:

Copies of such [organization] certificate, duly certified by the Comptroller, and authenticated by his seal of office, shall be legal and sufficient evidence in all courts and places within the United States, or the jurisdiction of the government thereof, of the existence of such association, and of every other matter or thing which could be proved by the production of the original certificate.

Section 5136 of the Revised Statutes of the United States provides that—

Upon duly making and filing articles of association and an organization certificate the association shall 'become, as from the date of the execution of its organization certificate, a body corporate, and as such and in the name designated in the organization certificate, it shall have power, first, to adopt and use a corporate seal; second, to have succession for the period of twenty years from its organization, unless it is sooner dissolved according to the provisions of its articles of association, or by the act of its shareholders owning two-thirds of its stock, or unless its franchise becomes forfeited by some violation of law.

From these sections it appears that the period of existence of an association, as a body corporate, commences from the date of its organization certificate, and not from that of the certificate of the Comptroller, authorizing the association to commence business, as provided for in section 5169 of the Revised Statutes. The corporate existence of the national bank first organized will, under this limitation of law, expire on January 1, 1882, and that of the second bank on April 11 following. From the date last named to February 25, 1883, the number of banks whose corporate existence will terminate is 393, having a capital of nearly 92 millions, and circulation of nearly 68 millions, as follows:

Date.	No. of banks.	Capital.	Circulation.
1882.			
In May	11	$3,900,000	$1,781,500
In June	16	4,205,000	3,452,500
In July	24	4,385,000	3,591,500
In August	10	1,205,000	863,000
In September	11	3,532,500	1,577,500
In October	5	550,000	494,100
In November	5	850,000	770,000
In December	5	570,000	505,000
1883.			
In January	9	1,250,000	1,080,000
On February 25	297	71,538,450	53,740,810
Totals	393	91,985,950	67,855,910

The number of national banks organized under the act of June 3, 1864, the term of whose corporate existence will cease during each year prior to 1891, is 1,080, with capital and circulation as follows:

Years.	No. of banks.	Capital.	Circulation.
1884	248	$80,034,390	$62,740,950
1885	728	186,161,775	119,266,745
1886	19	2,560,300	1,780,100
1887	6	1,100,000	976,500
1888	10	950,000	692,100
1889	4	650,000	567,800
1890	65	9,415,500	6,557,790
Totals	1,080	280,871,965	192,581,085

Bills will undoubtedly be brought before Congress during its present session for the extension of the charters of those banks whose corporate existence is soon to expire.

The principal reason urged by those who favor a discontinuance of the national banking system is, that money can be saved by authorizing the government to furnish circulation to the country; in other words, that the profit to the banks upon their circulation is excessive. Sixteen years ago the banks had on deposit, as security for circulation, 276 millions of dollars in United States bonds, of which amount nearly 200 millions was in six per cents and 76 millions in five per cents. The banks now hold 32 millions of four and a half per cents; 92 millions of four per cents; 241 millions of three and a half per cents, converted from five and six per cents; and also 3½ millions of Pacific railroad sixes. The remaining five per cent. bonds held by them, amounting in all to $758,900, have ceased to bear interest. The average premium borne by the four per cent. bonds during the last six months has been about sixteen per cent., and at this price they net to the holders less than three and a half per cent. interest. During the same period the three and a half per cents also have, for a considerable portion of the time, been worth a premium in the market of from one to two per cent., so that the banks do not at the present time, and it is probable that they will not, for a long time to come, receive an annual average rate of interest as great as three and a half per cent. upon the United States bonds deposited by them as security for their circulating notes. Until the year 1877 the banks continued to receive interest upon the par value of their bonds at the rate of either five or six per cent., while the net interest now received, as already stated, does not exceed three and one-half per cent. On ten per cent. of the amount of bonds thus deposited by the banks, amounting to 39 millions, they receive no circulation; and from this portion of their bond deposit they derive no benefit or advantage not possessed by any other class of bondholders. They pay a tax of one per cent. upon the amount of their circulating notes outstanding; keep on deposit with the Treasurer an amount of lawful money equal to five per cent. of their issues, as a permanent redemption fund; and also reimburse to the United States the expense of redeeming their notes at the Treasury. The actual net profit upon circulation, based upon a 4 and a 3½ per cent. bond, and with rates of interest on bank loans varying from five to ten per cent., is estimated to be as shown in the following table:

Class of bonds deposited.	5 per cent.	6 per cent.	7 per cent.	8 per cent.	9 per cent.	10 per cent.
	Per ct.	Per ct.	Per ct.	Per ct.	Per ct.	Per ct.
4 per cent. bonds, at 16 per cent. premium	1.49	1.39	.88	.58	.27	.03
3½ per cent. bonds, at 1 per cent. premium	1.74	1.59	1.43	1.28	1.12	.96

The profit upon circulation is seen to be greatest where the rate of interest for the loan of money is least; and this arises from the fact, already stated, that the bank receives in circulating notes ten per cent. less in amount than it deposits in bonds. Thus, if the bonds deposited are three and one-half per cents, and the commercial rate of interest is ten per cent., there is a loss to the bank of six and one-half per cent. upon the ten per cent. margin of bonds deposited. If the commercial value is six per cent. only, then the loss upon the margin mentioned is two and one-half per cent., instead of six and one-half per cent., as in the previous case.

The profit on circulation varies, therefore, from one and one-eighth per cent., where the interest on loans is nine per cent., to one and one-half per cent. where the rate of interest is six per cent.

The proportion of taxation, National and State, imposed upon the banks has been shown to be much greater than that upon any other moneyed capital, being in the aggregate equal to an average rate of four per cent. upon the amount of their issues. The amount of interest received by the banks upon the United States bonds held by them has in late years gradually decreased, and the profit upon circulation has thereby been reduced almost to the minimum. Such profit cannot now, at least, be said to be excessive.

But if the National Bank Act has conferred upon the associations organized thereunder the right to issue circulating notes, it has placed them all under the operation of a uniform system, and has surrounded them with numerous restrictions, among which are the following:

The capital stock must be fully paid in, and a portion of this capital, not less in any case than $50,000, must be invested in United States bonds and deposited with the Treasurer. If the capital stock of an association becomes impaired at any time, it must be promptly restored. Their circulating notes must be redeemed at par, not only at the place of issue, but at the Treasury of the United States.

The banks must lend on personal security only, and not upon that of real estate, and only ten per cent. of their capital may be loaned upon accommodation notes, or other than actual business paper, to any one person, company, firm or corporation. They cannot lend money on their own circulating notes, or upon shares of their own stock, and must take the notes of every other national bank in payment of debts due to them. The rate of interest charged must not be greater than the rate provided by the laws of the several States in which they are located. They must pay taxes or duties to the government upon their capital stock, deposits and circulation, and to the States they must pay such taxes as are imposed on other moneyed capital. They are required to keep on hand as a reserve, in coin or other lawful money, a certain proportion of their deposits. There must be no preference of creditors in cases of insolvency.

Shareholders are held individually responsible for all contracts, debts and engagements of the association, to the extent of the par value of their stock, in addition to the amount invested in such shares. The banks are required, before the declaration of any dividend, semi-annually to increase their surplus fund by an amount equal to one tenth of their net earnings for the preceding six months, until it shall equal twenty per cent. of their capital. Losses and bad debts must be charged to profit and loss account before dividends are paid. In other words, dividends must be earned before they are declared. Full statements, accompanied by schedules, of their resources and liabilities must be made to the Comptroller several times in each year, and must also be published at the expense of the association making the same. Other statements, showing their semi-annual profits, losses, and dividends, must also be returned, and statements in reference to the business of any association making the same may be required at any time, a penalty of $100 per day being prescribed for each day's delay to comply with the call therefor. The banks are subject to personal examinations, and if a bank becomes insolvent a receiver may be at once appointed. If the directors knowingly violate, or permit to be violated, any of the provisions of the act, all the rights and privileges of the bank are thereby forfeited; and the directors are held-personally and individually responsible for all damages sustained by any person in consequence of such violation.

It is recommended that an act be passed during the present session, authorizing any national bank, with the approval of the Comptroller, at any time within two years prior to the date of the expiration of its corporate existence, to extend its period of succession for twenty years, by amending its articles of association. The bill may provide that such amendments must be authorized by the votes of shareholders owning not less than two-thirds of the capital of the association, the amendment to be certified to the Comptroller of the Currency, by the president or cashier, verified by the seal of the association, and not to be valid until the Comptroller's approval thereof shall have been obtained, and he shall have given to the association a certificate authorizing it to continue its business under such extension. Responsibility for the extension of the corporate existence of the banks will thus, in a measure, rest with the Comptroller; and he can require such an examination of its affairs to be made, prior to granting the extension, as may seem to him proper, in order to ascertain if the capital stock is intact, and all the assets of the bank in a satisfactory condition.

It is unquestionably true that many national banks would greatly prefer the abolishment of the national system, if it were accompanied by a repeal of the provision of law imposing a tax of ten per cent. upon State bank circulation; and there is little reason to doubt that such repeal would speedily follow the abrogation of the National Bank Act. The laws in many of the States authorize the issue of State bank notes, based upon the deposit of State bonds as security therefor. The repeal of the tax law referred to would result in re-establishing the State bank systems in many parts of the country, the issues of which would be far more profitable to the banks themselves than is the circulation now issued under the national system; while in other sections circulating notes, put forth without any security whatever, would prevail as formerly. The notes of these various systems would be redeemable, not at any common center, as at present, but at the chief city of each State or section of country issuing the same; and the price of exchange would thereby be enhanced to rates certainly not less than the cost of transporting gold from the places of redemption to the commercial center of the country. In many parts of the country these rates would necessarily be oppressive, resulting in great loss to the people, which loss would steadily increase with the growth of business.

As another consequence of the abolition of the present system, the large surplus which the national banks have now accumulated, amounting to $128,140,618, and which adds greatly to their strength and safety, would doubtless be divided among their shareholders; while many of the safeguards and restrictions of the present law, which experience has shown to be valuable, will be either abolished or so changed by the varying legislation of the several States, as to be practically of little value in comparison with the present homogeneous system.

If, on the other hand, the corporate existence of the national banks shall be extended, all the advantages of the existing system will be preserved, subject to such amendments as may be hereafter found necessary; while the circulation of the banks, which is the principal objection urged against the system, will, under existing laws, diminish in volume as the public debt shall be reduced.

The whole number of national banks in operation on October 1 last was 2,148. Of this number 393 were associations having a capital of $50,000 each; 164 had a capital of over $50,000 and less than $100,000, and the capital of 829 banks ranged from $100,000 to $150,000 each. The minimum amount of bonds required to be deposited by banks of the capital named is one-third of their capital, but not less in any case than $30,000. The minimum amount required by all other banks is $50,000, and the least amount of bonds which, under existing laws, may be deposited by the 2,148 banks now in operation, is about $82,400,000. It is probable that from 100 to 150 millions of United States bonds would be sufficient to supply the minimum amount necessary to be deposited with the Treasurer by all the banks which may be established during the next twenty years. It is therefore evident that the national banking system may be continued without change in this respect for many years, even if the bonded debt of the United States shall, during that time, continue to. be reduced as rapidly as it has in the past year. The discussion of the question as to the kind of circulating notes which will be substituted for the national-bank notes, if the latter are retired, is postponed for the. present, as it is impossible to forsee the events which may occur to affect that question within the next few years.

If, for any reason, the legislation herein proposed shall not be favorably considered by Congress, the banks can still, under the present laws, renew their existence if they so desire; and in the absence of prohibitory legislation many of them undoubtedly will, on the expiration of their present charters, organize new associations, with nearly the same stockholders as before, and will then apply for and obtain from the Comptroller certificates authorizing them to continue business for twenty years from the respective dates of their new organization certificates. Such a course of procedure will be perfectly legal, and, indeed, under the existing laws, the Comptroller has no discretionary power in the matter, but must necessarily sanction the organization, or reorganization, of such associations as shall have conformed in all respects to the legal requirements.

The passage, however, of a general act directly authorizing an extension of the corporate existence of associations whose charters are about to expire would, in many instances, relieve the banks from embarrassment. As the law now stands, if the shareholders of an association are all agreed, the process of reorganization is simple; but if any of the shareholders object to such reorganization, they are entitled to a complete liquidation of the bank's affairs, and to a *pro rata* distribution of all its assets, including its surplus fund. In many instances executors and administrators of estates hold national-bank stock in trust; and while they might prefer to retain their interests in the associations which issued the stock, they would perhaps have no authority to subscribe for stock in the new organizations. While, therefore, the legislation asked for is not absolutely essential, yet its passage at an early day would be a great convenience to many of the national banks, and especially so to the class last referred to.

SUBSTITUTES FOR MONEY.

For a long period in their early history, bills of exchange were in fact what their name implied—namely, bills drawn in one country to be paid in another. The common law of England, which inflexibly forbade the assignment of debt, was a bar to their early introduction into that country; but they eventually forced themselves into use there, through the facilities which they afforded in the conduct of trade with other nations. It was long before the transfer of inland debts was sanctioned in England; but the practice at length prevailed, being first adopted in the intercourse between London and York, and London and Bristol. By the gradual striking off of one limitation after another, bills of exchange,* after the lapse of several centuries, became what they now are, simply an order from one person to another to pay a definite sum of money. The convenience of trade gradually overpowered the narrow restrictions of the common law, until it became lawful to transfer an obligation from one person to another, in the form of a bill of exchange, while at the same time it remained unlawful to do so in other forms, such as by a simple acknowledgment of the debt by the debtor.

About the end of the sixteenth century the merchants of Amsterdam and Hamburg, and of some other places, began to use instruments of credit among themselves; and, as their intercourse increased, these instruments naturally assumed the form of an acknowledgment of the debt by the debtor, with a promise to pay to the bearer, on demand, or at a specified time. Such instruments are now called promissory notes. They first began to be used by the goldsmiths, who originated the modern system of banking soon after 1640. They were then called goldsmiths' notes, but they were not recognized by law. The first promissory notes issued in England, under the sanction of law, were those of the Bank of England, in 1694, and which were technically bills obligatory, or bills of credit. By the act founding the bank its notes were declared to be assignable by indorsement, although this privilege was not then extended to other promissory notes. But by an act passed in 1704, promissory notes of every kind, including those of private bankers and merchants, as well as of the Bank of England, were all placed on the same footing as inland bills of exchange; that is to say, they were all made transferable, by indorsement on each separately. With respect, however, to the Bank of England notes, as these were always payable on demand, the practice of indorsing soon fell into disuse, and they passed from hand to hand like money. In the case also of the notes of private bankers of great repute, the indorsement was often omitted.

Until near the year 1772, this method of making exchanges by the issue of promissory notes, made payable to bearer on demand, was generally adhered to by bankers. But about that time the practice in this respect became changed. When the bankers made discounts for their customers, or received deposits from them, instead of giving as before promissory notes or deposit receipts, they wrote down the amount to the credit of their customers on their books. They then gave them books containing a number of printed forms. These forms were called checks, and were really bills of exchange drawn upon the banker, payable to the bearer on demand.

Prior to the period when checks were introduced, the issue of promissory notes by the London bankers was very extensive; but the method of doing business by the use of checks was found by them to be so convenient, and it possessed so many practical advantages over that by way of notes, that issues of the latter were soon generally discontinued, and that of checks adopted in their stead. The bankers, however, were never forbidden to issue such notes until the bank act of 1844.

For many years the English courts held that a check is binding on the banker, having assets of the drawer, without acceptance; but more recently these earlier decisions have been overruled, and it is now the established doctrine of the highest English tribunals that a check is not binding upon a bank until accepted, notwithstanding the fact that the bank has assets of the drawer. In a case in which the First National Bank of New Orleans was defendant, where certain holders of its drafts on a Liverpool bank attempted to recover from the latter bank the amount of the drafts out of an ample balance to the credit of the New

*Much of the information regarding bills of exchange is gleaned from Macleod's Theory and Practice of Banking.

Orleans bank after its failure, the House of Lords affirmed the decision of the Lord Chancellor, and held that the drafts were not even equitable assignments of any part of the drawer's funds.*

PROPORTION OF BANK CHECKS, BANK NOTES, AND COIN USED IN LONDON, FROM DATA PREPARED BY SIR JOHN LUBBOCK.

The first information given to the public as to the amount and proportion of checks, bank notes, and coin used in the business of banking, was by Sir John Lubbock, an eminent scientist and banker, and president of the London Institute of Bankers, and was based upon the business of his own bank during the last few days of 1864. His statement, given below, is copied from a paper read by him before the London Statistical Society, in June, 1865, entitled "Country Clearing," and published in the journal of that society for September, 1865, to whose tables I have added the proportions of checks, bank notes, and coin:

In order to give the proportion of the transactions of bankers which passes through the clearing house to that which does not, I took the amount of £23,000,000, which passed through our hands during the last few days of last year, and found that it was made up as follows:

Clearing	£16,346,000	70.8 per cent.
Cheques and bills, which did not pass through the clearing	5,394,000	23.4 "
Bank notes	1,137,000	4.9 "
Coin	139,000	0.6 "
Country notes	79,000	0.3 "
Total	23,095,000	100.0 "

It would appear from this that out of each £1,000,000, rather more than £700,000 passes through the clearing. The second amount given above, £5,394,000, includes, of course, the transfers made in our own books from the account of one customer to that of another. These amounted to £3,603,000, the remainder, £1,791,000, representing the cheques and bills on banks which did not clear.

In order to ascertain the proportion of payments made in bank notes and coin, in town, I have taken an amount, £17,000,000, paid in by our London customers. This was made up as follows:

Cheques and bills on clearing bankers	£13,000,000	77.4 per cent.
Cheques and bills on ourselves	1,600,000	9.5 "
Cheques and bills on other bankers	1,400,000	8.3 "
Bank of England notes	674,470	4.0 "
Country bank notes	9,570	0.1 "
Coin	117,960	0.7 "
Total	16,802,000	100.0 "

The above amount of bank notes, small as it is, must, I think, be still farther reduced. All the clearing bankers have accounts at the Bank of England, and, as we require notes to supply our till, we draw them from the Bank of England, crediting the bank in our books. Out of the above amount of £674,470, £266,000 were notes thus drawn by us from the bank to replenish our till, and did not represent an amount paid in by our customers to their credit. This amount must, therefore, I think, be deducted from both sides of the account. On the other hand we must add the amount of notes paid in for collection and discount, and loans on security, which pass through a different set of books and which represented a sum of £2,460,686.

Making these alterations we find that out of £19,000,000 credited to our town customers, £408,000 consisted of bank notes, £79,000 of country bank notes, and £118,000 of coin:

Cheques and bills	£18,395,000	96.8 per cent.
Bank notes	408,000	2.2 "
Country notes	79,000	0.4 "
Coin	118,000	0.6 "
Total	19,000,000	100.0 "

* House of Lords, p. 352, June 17–19, 1873.

In an article on bank notes, published in the Journal of the Institute of Bankers, London, for March, 1880, Mr. John B. Martin gives a table showing the percentage of bank notes, coin and checks used in banking transactions, which was compiled by him from several sources. This table is given below:

	Robarts, Lubbock & Co.		Morrison, Dillon & Co.		Manchester and Salford Bank and another local bank.			Martin & Co.	
	Received 1864, London.	Received 1864, general.	Received.	Paid.	1859.	1864.	1872.	Received 1878-'79.	Paid 1878-'79.
	Per cent.	Per cent.	Per cent.	Per ct.	Per ct.	Per ct.	Per ct.	Per cent.	P. ct.
Bills and cheques ...	96. 8	94. 1	90	97	47	58	68	96. 5	96. 9
Notes..............	2. 6	5. 3	7	2	} 53	38	27	2. 6	2. 1
Coin................	. 6	. 6	3	1	}	4	5	. 9	1. 0
	100	100	100	100	100	100	100	100	100

The first two columns of percentages are obtained from the data contained in the table previously given, and show the ratio of checks, notes, and coin received by the firm of Robarts, Lubbock & Co., in payments made to them during the last few days of 1864; the first column showing the percentages of the items named above, in the receipts from London bankers alone, and the second, the percentages in the receipts from all sources. The next two columns are derived from an analysis of the receipts and payments of the firm of Messrs. Morrison, Dillon & Co. The next three columns show, for the years 1859, 1864, and 1872, respectively, the percentages of checks and cash derived from an estimate made of the total transactions of the Manchester and Salford Bank, and published in the Journal of the Statistical Society for March, 1873, at page 86. In reference to these transactions of the Manchester banks, it is stated that the amount of cash shown is very remarkable, and that it is believed the proportion of coin in it very largely exceeds that of England, taken as a whole, because the statement proceeds from a great wage-paying district. The last two columns of the table show the results of an analysis of the receipts and payments of Martin & Co. To obtain these percentages, the transactions of Mr. Martin's own firm were observed for six working days in each month, from the 20th to the 26th, for a period of several months, covering the latter part of 1878 and the first part of 1879.

In each instance in this table, it is to be observed, the transactions are those of one bank or firm only, and in making up the aggregate, from which the percentages are calculated, the business for several days has been taken; differing in these respects from the returns hereafter given from the national banks in this country, which are results obtained from combining the transactions upon one day, and for the most part of the same day, of a large number of banks doing business in widely different sections of the country.

PROPORTION OF BANK CHECKS USED, FROM DATA PRESENTED BY PRESIDENT GARFIELD.

The first information ever given upon this subject in this country was compiled by the late President Garfield, who was well known as a careful investigator of economic subjects.

In his speech on resumption, delivered in the House of Representatives on November 16, 1877, he said:

In 1871, when I was chairman of the Committee on Banking and Currency, I asked the Comptroller of the Currency to issue an order, naming fifty-two banks which were to make an analysis of their receipts. I selected three groups. The first was the city banks. The second consisted of banks in cities of the size of Toledo and Dayton, in the State of Ohio. In the third group, if I may coin a word, I selected the "countriest" banks, the smallest that could be found, at points away from railroads and telegraphs. The order was that these banks should analyze all their receipts for six consecutive days, putting into one list all that can be called cash—either coin, greenbacks, bank notes or coupons, and into the other list all drafts, checks, or commercial bills. What was the result? During those six days $157,000,000 were received over the counters of the fifty-two banks; and of that amount, $19,370,000—12 per cent. only—in cash, and eighty-eight per cent., that vast amount representing every grade of business, was in checks, drafts, and commercial bills.

RECEIPTS IN MONEY AND CHECKS OF ALL THE NATIONAL BANKS.

In order to obtain the fullest possible information on this subject the Comptroller recently issued two circular letters to the national banks, asking for classified returns of their receipts and payments at different dates. The first circular requested a return to be made for June 30, which date marked the close of the fiscal year; and the second one asked for a return on September 17, which was the middle of the third month following. It was believed that a comparison of returns made for dates so dissimilar would be a substantial test of their accuracy, and would present a fair average of their operations for the current year. Returns for June 30, were received from 1,966 of the 2,106 national banks then in operation, and in response to the request for statements for the date of September 17, returns were received from 2,132 banks, being all of the banks in operation at that date. A few of these later returns, about fifty in number, were for a day subsequent to September 17, but their relative number being small they have been tabulated as being of that date

The total receipts of the 1,966 banks, on June 30 last, were 284 millions of dollars ($284,714,017). Of this amount there was less than two millions ($1,864,105) in gold coin, about half a million ($440,997) in silver coin, and eleven and one-half millions ($11,554,747) in paper money; the remainder, amounting to 270 millions ($270,854,165), being in checks and drafts, including nine millions ($9,582,500) of clearing-house certificates. The gold coin equaled 0.65 of one per cent. of the total receipts; the silver coin was 0.16 of one per cent.; the paper money 4.6 per cent.; while the checks and drafts constituted 91.77 per cent. of the whole amount; or, including the clearing-house certificates, they were equal to 95.13 per cent. In other words, the total percentage of coin and paper money received was 4.87 per cent. only, while that of checks and drafts was 95.13.

The receipts of all of the national banks, 2,132 in number, on September 17, were $295,233,779. Of this sum $1,078,044 consisted of gold coin, $500,301 of silver coin, and $13,026,570 of paper money. The remainder, amounting to $277,628,862, consisted of checks and drafts, and $6,592,337 of clearing-house certificates. The gold coin equaled 1.38 per cent. of the total receipts; the silver coin 0.17 of one per cent.; the paper money 4.36 per cent., and the checks and drafts 91.85 per cent., while the checks, drafts and clearing-house certificates, together, were equal to 94.09 per cent. of the whole. On September 17, therefore, the total percentage of cash was 5.91 per cent. only.

TOTAL RECEIPTS OF MONEY AND CHECKS BY THE BANKS IN NEW YORK CITY AND IN FIFTEEN OTHER PRINCIPAL CITIES, AND BY THE REMAINING BANKS.

The receipts of the forty-eight national banks in New York City, on June 30, were 167 millions ($167,437,759), of which less than one-half million ($460,993.67) was in gold coin, $15,996.95 in silver coin, and $1,706,604.06 in paper money; the remaining 165 millions ($165,254,164) being in checks and drafts, including nearly four millions ($3,835,500) of clearing-house certificates.

The banks in New York City, on September 17, reported receipts amounting to $165,193,347, of which $805,588 was in gold coin, $7,857 in silver coin, and $1,071,315 in paper money, the remainder, $163,-308,587, being in checks and drafts, including $3,792,000 of clearing-house certificates.

The receipts of the 187 banks in the fifteen reserve cities, exclusive of New York, on June 30, were seventy-seven millions ($77,100,705), of which $581,070 was in gold, $114,485 in silver, $3,631,710 in paper money, and seventy-two millions ($72,773,450) in checks and drafts, including $5,747,000 of gold clearing-house certificates.

On September 17 the receipts of 189 banks in fifteen reserve cities, exclusive of New York, were $77,922,246, of which $1,448,415 was in gold, $138,248 in silver, $4,486,045 in paper money, and $71,849,538 in checks and drafts, including $2,734,378 in clearing-house certificates.

The total receipts of the banks outside of the cities, 1,731 in number, on June 30, were forty millions ($40,175,542), of which $822,041 was in gold coin, $310,516 in silver coin, six millions ($6,216,433) in paper money, and nearly thirty-three millions ($32,826,552) in checks and drafts.

On September 17 these banks, 1,895 in number, received $52,118,185, of which $1,724,040 was in gold coin, $354,197 in silver coin, $7,469,210 in paper currency, and $42,570,738 in checks and drafts.

TOTAL RECEIPTS AND PROPORTIONS OF GOLD COIN, SILVER COIN, PAPER MONEY, AND CHECKS AND DRAFTS.

In the following tables are shown, both for June 30 and for September 17, the proportions of gold coin, silver coin, paper money, and checks and drafts, including clearing-house certificates, to the total receipts, in New York City, in the other reserve cities, and in banks elsewhere, separately, and also the same proportions for the United States:

JUNE 30, 1881.

Localities.	Number of banks.	Receipts.	Proportions.			
			Gold coin.	Silver coin.	Paper currency.	Checks, drafts, &c
			Per cent.	Per cent.	Per cent.	Per cent.
New York City	48	$167,437,759	0.27	0.01	1.02	98.70
Other reserve cities	187	77,100,715	0.76	0.15	4.71	94.38
Banks elsewhere	1,731	40,175,542	2.04	0.77	15.47	81.72
United States	1,966	284,714,016	0.65	0.16	4.06	95.13

SEPTEMBER 17, 1881.

New York City	48	$165,193,347	0.54	0.01	0.65	98.80
Other reserve cities	189	77,922,247	1.86	0.18	5.61	92.35
Banks elsewhere	1,895	52,118,185	3.31	0.08	14.27	81.74
United States	2,132	295,233,779	1.38	0.17	4.36	94.09

On June 30 the proportion of gold coin to the whole receipts in New York City was 0.27 of one per cent.; of silver coin, 0.01 of one per cent.; of paper money, 1.02 per cent.; and of checks and drafts, including clearing-house certificates, 98.7 per cent.

The percentage of gold coin received in the fifteen other cities was 0.76; of silver coin, 0.15; of paper currency, 4.71; and of checks and drafts, 94.38. The percentage of gold coin received by the banks not included in these cities was 2.05; of silver coin, 0.77; of paper currency, 15.47; and of checks and drafts, 81.71.

Taking all the banks together, the relative proportion of gold coin received was 0.65, of silver coin 0.16, of paper currency 4.06, and of checks and drafts 95.13 per cent.

On September 17 the proportion of gold coin to the whole receipts in New York City was 0.545 of one per cent., and of silver coin, 0.005 of one per cent.; of paper money, 0.65 of one per cent., and of checks and drafts, including clearing-house certificates, 98.8 per cent.

The percentage of gold coin received in 15 other cities was 1.86; of silver coin, 0.18; of paper currency, 5.61; and of checks and drafts, 92.35. The percentage of gold coin by the remaining banks in the country was 3.31; of silver coin, 0.68; of paper currency, 14.27; and of checks and drafts, 81.74. The receipts of the 2,132 banks together show a relative proportion of gold coin, 1.38; of silver coin, 0.17; paper currency, 4.36; and of checks and drafts, 94.09.

CHECKS AND DRAFTS IN THE PRINCIPAL CITIES.

The following table shows, for June 30 and September 17, the number of banks, the total receipts, and the ratio to such total of the checks and drafts received, in New York City and in fifteen of the other principal cities:

Cities.	June 30, 1881.			September 17, 1881.		
	No. of banks.	Receipts.	Proportion of checks, drafts, &c.	No. of banks.	Receipts.	Proportion of checks, drafts, &c.
			Per cent.			Per cent.
New York City	48	$167,437,759	98.7	18	$165,193,347	98.8
Boston	54	33,088,080	96.5	54	24,091,061	93.7
Albany	7	1,417,704	93.8	7	1,486,315	96.5
Philadelphia	32	18,061,565	96.0	32	17,830,648	96.4
Pittsburgh	22	2,149,067	90.4	22	3,126,749	86.2
Baltimore	16	3,875,255	92.9	16	4,425,113	93.9
Washington	5	206,601	60.0	5	226,783	45.8
New Orleans	7	1,206,759	89.8	7	1,620,771	80.2
Louisville	8	742,330	92.8	8	775,304	83.4
Cincinnati	8	2,965,355	88.0	10	3,876,785	90.0
Cleveland	6	1,751,037	94.0	6	2,618,064	95.1
Chicago	9	8,141,189	92.0	9	13,926,835	90.3
Detroit	4	806,211	87.5	4	1,219,481	93.5
Milwaukee	3	417,244	88.3	3	670,172	94.9
Saint Louis	5	1,940,053	82.3	5	2,627,045	81.5
San Francisco	1	332,265	91.8	1	298,121	77.4
Total, excluding New York City	187	77,100,715	94.4	189	77,922,247	92.3
Total, including New York City	235	244,538,474	97.3	237	243,115,594	96.7
Banks elsewhere	1,731	40,175,542	81.7	1,895	52,118,185	81.7
United States	1,966	284,714,016	95.1	2,132	295,233,779	94.1

2 C C

PROPORTION OF THE RECEIPTS IN THE FOUR PRINCIPAL CITIES.

The table below exhibits the total receipts, on June 30 and September 17, of the 48 banks in New York City, the 54 in Boston, the 32 in Philadelphia, and the 9 in Chicago, and the proportion which the receipts in each city, and the aggregate of all of them, bear to the receipts of all the banks in the United States on the same dates. It also shows the receipts, and proportion to the whole, of the banks in twelve other cities, and the same as to the remaining banks of the country:

Banks in four principal cities, and elsewhere.	June 30. 1881.			September 17, 1881.		
	Number of banks.	Amount.	Per cent-age to total receipts.	Number of banks.	Amount.	Percent-age to total receipts.
New York City	48	$167,437,759	58.81	48	$165,193,347	55.95
Boston	54	33,088,080	11.62	54	24,094,061	8.16
Philadelphia	32	18,061,565	6.34	32	17,830,648	6.04
Chicago	9	8,141,189	2.86	9	13,026,835	4.41
Totals	143	226,728,593	79.63	143	220,144,891	74.56
Twelve other cities	92	17,809,881	6.26	94	22,970,703	7.78
Totals of cities	235	244,538,474	85.89	237	243,115,594	82.34
All other banks	1,731	40,175,542	14.11	1,895	52,118,185	17.66
United States	1,966	284,714,016	100	2,132	295,233,779	100

From an examination of this table it will be seen that the receipts of the 48 banks in New York City on June 30 were nearly three-fifths (58.81 per cent.) of the whole, and on September 17 about 56 per cent. This fact shows how closely connected is the business of all the national banks with the great commercial center of the country, nearly every bank and banker in the Union having deposits, subject to sight-drafts, at that point. The receipts of the Boston banks on June 30 were nearly 12 per cent. of the whole, and were 8 per cent. on September 17; while those of Philadelphia were about 6 per cent. at the latter date, and of the banks in Chicago about 4.5 per cent. The receipts in these four great cities comprised nearly four-fifths of the total receipts on June 30, and nearly three-fourths of the total on September 17; while the receipts of the sixteen reserve cities on June 30 were more than 85 per cent., and on September 17 more than 82 per cent., of the whole amount. The receipts of 1,731 banks located in the districts outside of these cities on June 30 were but 14.11 per cent., and of the 1,895 banks on September 17 but 17.66 per cent., of the whole.

TOTAL RECEIPTS AND PROPORTIONS OF CHECKS AND DRAFTS IN STATES AND TERRI-
TORIES.

The table next given shows, for the same dates, the receipts of the banks in each State and Territory, exclusive of those located in the cities named in the previous table, with similar percentages. Attention is called to the remarkable coincidence shown in this table, in the percentage of checks and drafts for the two dates named, it being 81.7 per cent. in each instance. The percentages of the cities for the same dates, as given in the next preceding table, also correspond very nearly, the small difference between them being principally due to the change in the city of Boston from 96.5, on June 30, to 93.7 per cent.

on September 17. The slight variation in the average ratios for the two dates is evidence of the general accuracy of the returns:

States and Territories.	June 30, 1881.			September 17, 1881.		
	No. of banks.	Receipts.	Proportion of checks, drafts, &c.	No. of banks.	Receipts.	Proportion of checks drafts, &c.
			Per cent.			Per cent.
Maine	67	$1,167,284	82.3	69	$1,016,018	79.8
New Hampshire	45	509,594	75.3	47	500,318	75.7
Vermont	41	405,256	79.2	47	407,423	74.3
Massachusetts	182	4,246,968	83.5	190	4,047,688	81.3
Rhode Island	58	1,235,886	87.9	62	1,486,144	90.5
Connecticut	79	2,533,108	87.4	85	3,536,106	88.1
New York	226	5,059,233	83.1	243	5,634,586	83.3
New Jersey	62	3,907,471	92.0	67	4,412,620	91.0
Pennsylvania	179	3,934,436	84.8	191	5,718,088	84.9
Delaware	14	313,628	86.3	14	381,077	89.0
Maryland	20	278,008	83.7	22	252,470	77.8
District of Columbia	1	27,983	64.0	1	41,699	76.4
Virginia	18	1,518,480	89.5	18	1,439,571	87.2
West Virginia	16	112,415	65.0	17	180,627	72.4
North Carolina	12	344,720	85.0	15	391,965	78.3
South Carolina	9	395,441	85.9	13	728,573	80.4
Georgia	11	281,995	69.5	12	738,926	77.3
Florida	2	23,026	23.7	2	40,739	77.8
Alabama	8	100,177	72.0	9	293,226	85.7
Texas	14	292,786	67.8	15	832,923	76.8
Arkansas	2	53,220	66.2	2	51,183	76.7
Kentucky	37	446,275	76.7	42	688,199	87.0
Tennessee	21	702,408	63.9	25	893,058	73.3
Ohio	142	2,825,066	80.0	161	3,150,787	76.1
Indiana	80	1,321,819	74.6	93	2,092,531	72.7
Illinois	120	1,411,907	70.6	130	3,332,447	80.0
Michigan	70	988,890	73.5	76	1,423,241	77.1
Wisconsin	30	543,935	80.8	31	545,019	64.3
Iowa	68	975,956	68.2	76	1,552,481	71.4
Minnesota	25	1,227,770	80.8	27	1,784,146	78.1
Missouri	13	163,481	67.3	17	566,861	82.3
Kansas	10	421,744	78.1	13	395,885	65.6
Nebraska	11	511,723	76.0	12	815,481	80.1
Colorado	13	1,185,387	81.1	17	1,533,504	85.1
Nevada	1	6,543	52.8	1	7,559	8.2
California	8	235,384	48.2	10	260,637	52.5
Oregon	1	165,420	71.8	1	171,526	72.6
Dakota	5	48,474	68.6	8	257,442	64.3
Idaho				1	17,924	51.2
Montana	2	19,662	88.6	3	75,716	54.1
New Mexico	4	117,306	82.5	4	119,972	79.3
Utah	1	92,969	49.8	1	112,761	80.5
Washington	1	15,526	37.4	2	38,242	30.0
Wyoming	2	6,782	33.6	3	144,796	87.8
Totals	1,731	40,175,542	81.7	1,895	52,118,185	81.7

PROPORTION OF RECEIPTS WHICH REPRESENT LEGITIMATE BUSINESS.

If all of these receipts represented legitimate business, the means for merchandising and for manufacturing would be most abundant. It would be an interesting subject for investigation to determine what proportion of the checks received by the banks in New York City, on any given day, represent operations at the Stock Exchange, and what proportions of these operations represent legitimate and what speculative transactions. In taking as a basis for such an estimate the posted sales of the Stock Exchange, a difficulty arises from the fact that these sales on any one day do not by any means include all the transactions at the board. In the opinion of the most experienced brokers, not more than one-third of the purchases and sales are recorded in the printed list. Even in the case of those recorded, the number of shares bought or sold, assumedly at par, is not an indication of the money value of the transactions as they appear in the bank clearings, on account of the different par value of the various shares dealt in. The par is usually one hundred dollars per share, but the average price of sales would not probably exceed sixty dollars per share.

The checks received by the banks in New York City, including both State and National, on the 30th of June, 1881, and which were cleared on the following day, amounted to 141 millions. Of this amount, 113 millions were cleared by twenty-three banks, all of which have relations to a greater or less extent with brokers. From an examination of the clearings of each of these twenty-three banks, it was found that the total of certified checks on that day amounted to about 80 millions, of which it is probable that at least 90 per cent., or 72 millions, represented stock transactions. About ten per cent. of this amount should be allowed for the daily payment and reborrowing of loans by brokers, which is accomplished by means of certified checks. It is therefore estimated by those who are conversant with these subjects, that of the 141 millions of exchanges, about 65 millions represent stock exchange transactions.

There are really no data upon which a conclusion can be obtained as to what proportion of these large stock transactions are speculative, and what legitimate, or for investment. It is estimated, however, by those who have had long experience in the business, that not more than five per cent. of all purchases and sales at the stock board are for investment account. Assuming that these estimates are reasonable, it would follow that about 60 millions of the 141 millions of clearings upon June 30, or about three-sevenths of the whole, represent the speculative transactions of the stock board, and that 81 millions, or four-sevenths, represent legitimate business transactions.

PROPORTION OF CHECKS WHICH PASS THROUGH THE CLEARING HOUSE.

The checks, drafts and certificates received by the national banks in New York City on June 30 amounted, as has been seen, to $165,233,164. The gold clearing-house certificates amounted to $3,814,500, which were received by the banks in payment of balances due them on the morning of June 30. The remainder consisted of checks and drafts alone. The clearing-house statement shows that on the morning of July 1 $126,937,110 of the before-mentioned checks and drafts were paid through the clearing-house. The remaining $34,381,554, which did not pass through the clearing-house, consisted probably of checks, which had been used in payments made by one depositor to another, in the same bank, and were consequently settled by simple transfers of accounts on the books of such banks. On Saturday, September 17, the total amount received by the banks in checks, drafts, and certificates was $163,208,586; of which $3,792,000 were in gold clearing-house certificates, received by the banks in payment of the balances due them at the clearing-house on the same day, leaving $159,416,586 of checks and drafts received. Of this latter sum, $139,881,760 consisted of checks, &c., which were paid through the clearing-house on the morning of Monday, September 19 (the next business day), by the same banks, as shown by the clearing-house statements of that day. Of the checks and drafts received by the national banks of New York City on September 17, about 20 millions were settled without passing through the clearing-house; and, as was remarked in reference to similar checks and drafts shown by the statement of June 30, they were probably settled by transfers of accounts on the books of the banks on which they were drawn.

It was about eighty years after the first issue of promissory notes by the Bank of England that the London clearing-house was established, and the organization of the New York clearing-house dates eighty years still later, in 1853; so that it may be said that the clearing arrangement now in use in this country, and so familiar to all bankers, has been in operation but twenty-eight years. The assistant treasurer in New York has been a member of the clearing-house but three years, and the large payments to the clearing-house banks, averaging two and a quarter tons of gold coin daily during the past year, which would be about thirty-six tons daily if paid in silver, are transferred in bags, or upon drays from the Treasury to the banks. If these balances could be paid in gold certificates instead of coin, the system of bank machinery in New York would be complete.

Checks, certificates of deposit, and drafts, or bills of exchange, which are now used so largely as substitutes for money, are the most important and useful parts of the machinery of the bank. The issue of circulating notes is not an essential feature of banking, for there are many banks in this country, chiefly incorporated under State laws, which do not issue such notes. But checks and drafts are almost as indispensable to the successful conduct of the business of banking as capital or deposits.

USE OF CHECKS IN FRANCE. ENGLAND, SCOTLAND, AND IRELAND, AND IN THE UNITED STATES.

In England, banks and bankers are numerous, and large numbers of such instruments of exchange are used, particularly in the principal cities. In France, on the other hand, their use is much more infrequent, for except the Bank of France, with its 90 branches, there are no incorporated banks in that country, and thirteen of these branches were conducted in 1880 at a loss of more than $30,000.

Victor Bonnet, a well-known French writer, says:

The use of deposits, bank accounts, and checks is still in its infancy in this country. They are very little used, even in the great cities, while in the rest of France they are completely unknown. It is, however, to be hoped that they will be more employed hereafter, and that here, as in England and the United States, payments will be more generally made through the medium of bankers, and by transfers in accounts current. If this should be the case, we shall economize both in the use of specie and of bank notes; for it is to be observed that the use of bank notes does not reach its fullest development, except in countries where the keeping of bank accounts is unusual, as is evident by comparing France in this respect with England. M. Pinard, manager of the Comptoir d'Escompte, testified before the commission of inquiry, that the greatest efforts had been made by that institution to induce French merchants and shopkeepers to adopt English habits in respect to the use of checks and the keeping of bank accounts, but in vain; their prejudices were invincible; it was no use reasoning with them, they would not do it, because they would not.

It would seem, however, from the following extract from the report of the Bank of France for 1880, that an effort is being made to overcome this prejudice:

Since the end of the operations of 1879, we have endeavored to give new advantages to those who had current accounts with us, and we have granted them facilities for transfer from one place to another, free of cost, for all sums proceeding from discount operations, or the encashment of documents on demand. We have desired to proceed further with this plan, and we have just completed this first arrangement by giving to all those who had current accounts with us, without exception, the means of disposing by open cheques of the whole of the sums which stand to their credit. These cheques, which are subject to a commission when they represent a simple deposit of funds, will, on the contrary, be delivered gratuitously when they are drawn against the proceeds of discounts or drafts on demand encashed by the bank, and they will be made payable in all our establishments indifferently. The cheques will thus become a powerful and very convenient means of exchange, which will simplify all transactions, and which will probably reduce, in considerable proportion, the need for the note circulation. In addition to this we have authorized the use of cheques within the town itself for the withdrawal of funds which do not require the displacement of capital. We are certain that when the use of cheques is thoroughly understood it will be of great service to commerce.

There are now in this country 6,796 banks and bankers located in all its principal cities and villages, and the number of checks and drafts in daily use by our own people is consequently larger, in fact, far greater, than anywhere else in the world. In some countries a charge is made to the depositor for keeping his account. In others, bank accounts are refused unless the depositor comes well introduced and it is believed that his account will be of considerable pecuniary benefit to the bank. In this country the bank is in many instances a convenience to the depositor, rather than the depositor of benefit to the bank; for the latter keeps the cash account of the depositor, and pays out amounts upon his order, and at his request returns to him his checks properly indorsed, which are then held by the depositor as vouchers or receipts for the payment of his debts.

It is evident that the amount of coin and paper currency used in any country depends largely upon the number of banks and bankers it contains, and upon the method of doing business; and no theory is more absurd than that which has been so frequently urged during the currency discussions of the past few years, that the amount of money required is in proportion to population. Tables showing the per capita of coin and currency in use in any country are curious and interesting, but almost valueless in determining the amount of paper money required. Through the machinery of the bank, with its system of checks, bills of exchange and clearing-houses, large amounts of business may be settled without the use of coin or circulating notes. Coin and currency are but the small change used in trade. Checks and drafts are substitutes for money, and in every case, if these were not used, the latter would be required. Yet, notwithstanding the almost exclusive use of these substitutes for money in large business transactions, all payments, great and small, depend for their integrity upon a true measure of value, and that measure is a piece of gold coin of standard weight and fineness. All other coins, not subsidiary and intrinsically worth less than the general standard recognized at commercial centers, and all kinds of paper money which are not immediately redeemable in gold coin, are not only not needed, but are worse than useless, for they disturb values.

The London Bankers' Magazine for November, which has just been received, contains an abstract of a paper recently read by Mr. Pownall before the London Bankers' Institute, from which the following table has been compiled. The percentages of the receipts in the city of New York on September 17 have also been added to the table:

Localities.	Coin.	Notes.	Checks.
	Per cent.	Per cent.	Per cent.
New York	.55	.65	98.80
London	.73	2.04	97.23
Edinburgh	.55	12.67	86.78
Dublin	1.57	8.53	89.90
Country banks in 261 places	15.20	11.94	72.86

It will be seen that the proportion of checks and drafts used in London does not vary greatly from that of the same items shown in the receipts of the banks in New York City. The proportions used in the banking business of the country districts is less, as in the United States it is less in the banks outside the cities; but the use of checks and drafts in the country districts in the United States is nearly nine per cent. greater than in the corresponding districts in England.

Through the courtesy of Mr. E. Dayrell Reed, secretary of the Institute of Bankers, London, the Comptroller acknowledges the receipt of a "rough proof" of an important paper read by Mr. George H. Pownall before the Institute, on October 19 last, on "The proportional use of credit documents and metallic money in English banks," and regrets that it was received too late for use in the preparation of this part of the report. The paper is elaborate, and gives, in addition to the table already quoted, many others; among which are tables showing the proportion of gold coin, silver coin, bank notes and checks used by banks located in agricultural places, in the metropolitan area, and in the cotton, woolen, iron, pottery, and silk manufacturing districts. The entire paper will greatly interest the economic student; but under the circumstances the Comptroller is compelled to content himself with the following extracts:

There is a certain grim satire in these figures, when one thinks of the libraries filled with blue books full of weighty arguments, all curiously wrought out, to help in the settlement of the great note question. It is clear that the cheque and the clearing system are the main lines upon which banking is destined to run. Dead theories respecting notes and the right of issue belong to the generation to which they were living verities. To us the living fact is the substitution of a new instrument of credit. For the present generation the improvement of the cheque and the clearing system, the mechanical details of office organization, those details of bookkeeping which save time, are, from the enormous number of documents passing through the hands of bankers, of more weight than the most learned treatise on notes and note makers.

*   *   *   *   *   *

Banking statistics, gathered with due patience, would play a great part in industrial statistics. They represent trading totals, they rise and fall with prices, they expand with commercial prosperity, they contract in the day of bad trade. Systematically collected, they would furnish constant lessons. From no other source could we gain so much and so valuable information as to trading currents as from bankers. In their books the trading world is photographed. It has been calculated that 97 per cent. of the transactions of British wholesale commerce pass through the hands of the bankers of the United Kingdom. The sources of that commerce and its distribution must in the broadest way be marked in the totals of the banking world. The cottons of Lancashire, the woolens of Yorkshire, the shipping of Liverpool, the commerce and finance of London, are all represented there.

The tendency of this generation is to seek to place its theories upon an exact basis. How much would the social and trading life of England be illustrated if we could mark out, though only at intervals, or even for a single day, the magnitude of our great industries as they are represented in the books of bankers.

The conversion of the mode of settlement of claims from payment by coin and notes into payment by cheque and clearing is not merely a local, or even a national, movement. The American statistics, so opportunely published, demonstrate the wide-reaching influence of the causes working in that direction.

Wherever the English race has planted itself and founded a community, there the tendency towards a common financial organization has shown itself. We see this at home, we see this in America, it is repeated in Australia. There is, therefore, in despite of much diversity, much that is common to all these systems.

In the Appendix will be found tables giving the amounts and ratios of gold and silver coin and paper money, as well as that of checks and drafts, in each of the cities, States, and Territories of the Union.

TRANSACTIONS OF THE NEW YORK CLEARING HOUSE.

The New York Clearing House Association is composed of forty-five national and twelve State banks, and the assistant treasurer of the United States at New York.

Through the courtesy of Mr. W. A. Camp, its manager, a statement of the transactions during the year ending October 1, 1881, has been obtained, which shows that the total exchanges were more than $18,000,000,000, while the balances paid in money were less than $1,800,000,000. The daily average balances paid were nearly $6,000,000, or about 3.5 per cent. of the amount of the settlements. The balances paid in money during the year consisted of $1,394,966,000 in clearing house certificates of the Bank of America, legal-tenders amounting to over $8,633,161, and $372,119,000 in gold coin, weighing 6864½ tons. If, instead of gold coin, silver had been used, the weight would have been nearly 11,000 tons. The largest transactions for any one day were on the 28th of November, and amounted to $295,821,422.37. The total transactions for the year exceed that of any previous year, by $11,643,-269,121.43. The following table shows the yearly transactions of the New York clearing house for the twenty-eight years since its organization in 1853, and the amounts and ratios of currency required for the payment of daily balances:

Years.	No. of banks.	Capital.	Exchanges.	Balances paid in money.	Average daily exchanges.	Average daily balances paid in mony.	Ratios.
							Pr. ct.
1854	50	$47,044,930	$5,750,455,987	$297,411,494	$19,104,505	$988,078	5.2
1855	48	48,884,180	5,362,912,098	289,694,137	17,412,052	940,565	5.4
1856	50	52,883,700	6,906,213,328	334,714,489	22,278,108	1,079,724	4.8
1857	50	64,420,200	8,333,226,718	365,313,902	26,968,371	1,182,246	4.4
1858	46	67,146,018	4,756,664,386	314,238,911	15,393,736	1,016,954	6.6
1859	47	67,921,714	6,448,005,956	363,984,683	20,867,333	1,177,944	5.6
1860	50	69,907,435	7,231,143,057	380,693,438	23,401,757	1,232,018	5.3
1861	50	68,900,605	5,915,742,758	353,383,944	19,269,520	1,151,088	6.0
1862	50	68,375,820	6,871,443,591	415,530,331	22,237,682	1,344,758	6.0
1863	50	68,972,508	14,867,597,849	677,626,483	48,428,658	2,207,252	4.6
1864	49	68,586,763	24,097,196,656	885,719,205	77,984,455	2,866,405	3.7
1865	55	80,363,013	26,032,384,342	1,035,765,108	84,796,040	3,373,828	4.0
1866	58	82,370,200	28,717,146,914	1,066,135,106	93,541,195	3,472,753	3.7
1867	58	81,770,200	28,675,159,472	1,144,963,451	93,101,167	3,717,414	4.0
1868	59	82,270,200	28,484,288,637	1,125,455,237	92,182,164	3,642,250	4.0
1869	59	82,720,260	37,407,028,987	1,120,318,308	121,451,393	3,637,397	3.0
1870	61	83,620,200	27,804,539,406	1,036,484,822	90,274,479	3,365,210	3.7
1871	62	84,420,200	29,300,986,682	1,209,721,029	95,135,074	3,927,666	4.1
1872	61	84,420,200	32,636,997,404	1,213,293,827	105,964,277	3,939,266	3.7
1873	59	83,370,200	33,972,773,943	1,152,372,108	111,022,137	3,765,922	3.4
1874	59	81,635,200	20,850,681,963	971,231,281	68,139,484	3,173,958	4.7
1875	59	80,435,200	23,042,276,858	1,104,346,845	75,301,558	3,608,977	4.8
1876	50	81,731,200	19,874,815,361	1,009,532,037	64,738,812	3,288,381	5.1
1877	58	71,085,200	20,876,555,937	1,015,256,483	68,447,724	3,328,710	4.9
1878	57	63,611,500	19,922,733,947	951,970,454	65,106,974	3,111,015	4.8
1879	59	60,800,200	24,553,196,689	1,321,119,298	79,977,839	4,303,320	5.4
1880	57	60,475,200	37,182,128,621	1,516,538,631	121,510,224	4,956,009	4.1
1881	60	61,162,700	48,565,818,212	1,776,018,162	165,055,201	5,823,010	3.5
		†71,403,745	‡584,440,115,759	‡24,448,833,204	68,181,783	†2,843,647	4.2

The total amount of transactions for the twenty-eight years given in the table is $584,440,115,759, and the annual average is $20,872,861,277.

The clearing-house transactions of the assistant treasurer of the United States at New York, for the year ending November 1, 1881, were as follows:

Exchanges received from clearing-house $358,193,774
Exchanges delivered to clearing-house 92,748,620

Balances paid to clearing-house................................... 270,966,495
Balances received from clearing-house 5,521,341

Showing that the amount paid by the assistant treasurer to the clearing-house was in excess of the amount received by him 265,445,154

A table compiled from statements made by the New York clearing-house, giving the clearings and balances weekly for the months of September, October, and November, of the year from 1872 to 1880, will be found in the appendix, and may be valuable for purposes of comparison.

DISTRIBUTION OF COIN AND PAPER CURRENCY.

The reports for 1879 and 1880 gave valuable tables of the amount of coin and paper money in the country on January 1, 1879 (the date of resumption), and on November 1 in 1879 and 1880.

* The capital is for various dates, the amount at a uniform date in each year not being obtainable.
† Yearly averages for twenty-eight years.   ‡ Totals for twenty-eight years.

The imports of gold in excess of exports, from the date of resumption to November 1, 1881, have been $197,434,114, and the estimated gold production of the mines is $104,150,000. The amount received from these two sources during the year ending November 1, 1881, has been $114,749,390.

The stock of standard silver dollars is also increasing at the rate of about two millions three hundred thousand monthly, the amount coined during the year having been $27,824,955. Tables are again given herewith showing the amount of coin and currency in the country on January 1, 1879, and on November 1, 1879, 1880 and 1881:

	January 1, 1879.	November 1, 1879.	November 1, 1880.	November 1, 1881.
Gold coin*	$278,310,126	$355,681,532	$453,882,692	$562,568,971
Silver coin*	106,573,803	126,609,537	158,320,911	186,037,365
Legal-tender notes	346,681,016	346,681,016	346,681,016	346,681,016
National bank notes	323,791,674	337,181,418	343,894,107	360,344,250
Totals	1,055,356,619	1,165,533,503	1,302,718,726	1,455,631,602

The amount of legal-tender notes has remained the same since May 31, 1878, in accordance with law. The increase of national-bank notes during the year ending November 1 last was $16,510,143. This, together with the increase of the gold coin, $108,686,279, and of silver coin, $27,716,454, makes a total increase of coin and bank notes of $152,912,876. The statement below gives the amount of coin and currency in the Treasury at the same dates as in the previous tables, and the amount in the national banks on the dates of their returns nearest thereto—viz. January 1 and October 2, 1879, and October 1, 1880 and 1881, respectively. The amounts given for the State banks, trust companies and savings banks, are for the nearest comparative dates of their official reports:

	January 1, 1879.	November 1, 1879.	November 1, 1880.	November 1, 1881.
GOLD.				
In the Treasury, less certificates	$112,703,342	$156,907,986	$133,679,349	$167,781,909
In national banks, including certificates	35,039,201	37,187,238	102,851,032	107,222,169
In State banks, including certificates	10,937,812	12,171,292	17,102,130	19,901,491
Total gold	158,680,355	206,266,516	253,632,511	294,905,569
SILVER.				
In the Treasury, standard silver dollars	17,249,710	32,115,073	47,156,588	66,576,378
In the Treasury, bullion	9,121,117	3,824,931	6,185,000	3,424,575
In the Treasury, fractional coin	6,048,191	17,854,327	24,635,561	25,984,687
In national banks	6,460,557	4,986,492	6,495,477	7,112,567
Total silver	38,879,908	58,780,823	84,472,626	103,698,207
CURRENCY.				
In the Treasury, less certificates	44,425,675	21,711,376	18,221,826	22,774,830
In national banks, including certificates	126,491,720	118,546,369	86,139,925	77,630,917
In State banks, including certificates	25,944,465	25,555,280	25,828,794	27,391,317
In savings banks	14,513,779	15,880,921	17,072,680	11,782,243
Total currency	211,375,639	181,693,946	117,563,225	139,579,307
Grand totals	408,935,902	446,741,285	485,668,362	537,583,083

*Estimate of Director of the Mint, which includes bullion in process of coinage.

If the amount of coin and currency in the Treasury and in the banks be deducted from the total amount estimated to be in the country, the remainder will be the amount then in the hands of the people outside of these depositories, as follows:

	January 1. 1879.	November 1. 1879.	November 1, 1880.	November 1, 1881.
Gold	$119,629,771	$149,415,016	$200,250,181	$267,663,402
Silver	67,693,895	67,228,714	73,848,285	82,939,158
Currency	459,097,051	502,168,488	542,951,898	567,445,959
Totals	646,420,717	718,812,218	817,050,364	918,048,519

The gold in the Treasury, including bullion in process of coinage, has increased during the year $34,102,560, and in the banks $7,170,498. The paper currency in the Treasury has increased $4,553,004, and in the banks it has decreased $13,727,914. The increase of gold, outside of the Treasury and the banks, is $67,413,221, and of paper currency $241,494,061.

In the foregoing tables the silver certificates issued by the Treasury have not been included, but the standard silver dollars kept to redeem them on presentation form a portion of the silver coin in the Treasury. The silver certificates in the hands of the people and the banks, at dates corresponding with those given in the preceding tables, were as follows:

January 1. 1879.	November 1, 1879.	November 1, 1880.	November 1, 1881.
$413,360.	$1,604,370.	$19,780,240.	$58,838,770.

It will be seen that the amount of these certificates in circulation has increased $39,058,530 during the past year. Of the $58,838,770 circulating on November 1, 1881, a large portion are constantly in the hands of the people, being paid out by the banks in preference to gold coin or legal-tender notes.

The total amount of silver dollars coined up to November 1, 1881, was $100,672,705, of which, as stated in one of the foregoing tables, $66,576,378 was then in the Treasury, although an amount equal to $58,838,769 was represented by certificates in the hands of the people and the banks, leaving only $7,737,609 actually belonging to the Treasury. Of the $100,672,705 coined, $34,096,327 were therefore circulating in the form of coin and $58,838,769 in the form of certificates. The remainder of the silver, $85,364,660, is in subsidiary and trade dollars and bullion, of which $29,409,262 is in the Treasury, and $55,955,398 is in use in place of the previous fractional paper currency, which, on March 23, 1874, was at its highest point, and amounted to $49,566,760. The increase since the date of resumption of gold and silver coin and paper currency outside of the Treasury and the banks, is thus estimated to be $271,627,802, and the increase during the year ending November 1, $100,998,254. Or, if the amount of silver certificates in circulation be added, the total increase in the circulating medium since resumption would be $330,053,217, and during the past year, $140,056,782.

AMOUNT OF INTEREST-BEARING FUNDED DEBT OF THE UNITED STATES
AND THE AMOUNT HELD BY THE NATIONAL BANKS.

The report for 1880 contained tables exhibiting a classification of the interest-bearing bonded debt of the United States, and of the bonds held by the national banks, for a series of years. These tables are again presented, and now exhibit also the amount of the outstanding bonds of the government, and the amount held by the banks, on November 1 of the present year.

The operations of the Secretary of the Treasury, in continuing the 5 and 6 per cent. bonds which matured during the year 1881, give them increasing interest. On March 1, 1881, 5 per cent. bonds amounting to $469,320,650 were outstanding, redeemable at the option of the government after May 1, 1881, and 6 per cent. bonds amounting to $202,266,550 were then outstanding similarly redeemable after July 1, 1881. The refunding bill, authorizing the sale of 3 per cent. bonds, with the proceeds of which, if sold, the maturing bonds would have been paid, did not receive the signature of the President, and failed to become a law. On April 11, the whole amount of 6 per cent. bonds were called for payment on July 1, 1881; but to the holders of all the 6 per cent. loans (except the Oregon war debt, amounting to $688,200) permission was given to have their bonds continued, at the pleasure of the government, with interest at 3½ per cent. per annum, provided they should so request and the bonds should be received by the Treasury for that purpose on or before May 10, 1881, which time was afterwards extended to May 20. Of these bonds there were presented for continuance the amount of $178,055,150, and the remainder, amounting to $24,211,400, has, since March 1, 1881, been either paid from the surplus revenues or has ceased to bear interest.

On May 12, a like privilege (for continuance at 3½ per cent.) was given to the holders of the five per cent. bonds, if presented on or before July 1, 1881; and on the latter date notice was given for the payment on October 1, 1881, of the registered fives not continued. The total amount of five per cent. bonds continued under this arrangement was $401,504,900, and of 6 per cent. bonds $178,055,150. The remaining 5 and 6 per cent. bonds outstanding March 1, 1881, amounting to $92,027,150, were paid upon presentation, or now remain outstanding without interest. There has also been paid during the year ending November 1, $123,969,650 of interest-bearing bonds, making a saving in interest of $6,352,240. The total interest saved during the year, by continuance and payment of the bonds, was $16,826,192.

The following table exhibits the classification of the unmatured, interest-bearing, bonded debt of the United States* on August 31, 1865, when the public debt reached its maximum, and on the 1st day of July in each year thereafter, together with the amount outstanding on November 1 of the present year:

Date.	6 per cent. bonds.	5 per cent. bonds.	4½ per cent. bonds.	4 per cent. bonds.	Total.
August 31, 1865	$908,518,091	$199,792,100			$1,108,310,191
July 1, 1866	1,008,388,469	198,528,435			1,206,916,904
July 1, 1867	1,421,110,719	198,533,435			1,619,644,154
July 1, 1868	1,841,521,800	221,588,400			2,063,110,200
July 1, 1869	1,886,341,300	221,589,300			2,107,930,600
July 1, 1870	1,764,932,300	221,589,300			1,986,521,600
July 1, 1871	1,613,897,300	274,236,450			1,888,133,750
July 1, 1872	1,374,883,800	414,567,300			1,789,451,100
July 1, 1873	1,281,238,650	414,567,300			1,695,805,950
July 1, 1874	1,213,624,700	510,628,050			1,724,252,750
July 1, 1875	1,100,865,550	607,132,750			1,707,998,300
July 1, 1876	984,999,650	711,685,800			1,696,685,450
July 1, 1877	854,621,850	703,266,650	$140,000,000		1,696,888,500
July 1, 1878	738,619,000	703,266,650	240,000,000	$98,850,000	1,780,735,650
July 1, 1879	310,932,500	646,905,500	250,000,000	679,878,110	1,887,716,110
July 1, 1880	235,780,400	484,864,900	250,000,000	739,347,800	1,709,993,100
July 1, 1881	196,378,600	439,841,350	250,000,000	739,347,800	1,625,567,750
	Continued at 3½ per cent.	Continued at 3½ per cent.			
November 1, 1881	161,876,050	401,504,900	250,000,000	739,347,800	1,552,728,750

*The Navy pension fund, amounting to $14,000,000 in 3 per cents., the interest upon which is applied to the payment of naval pensions exclusively, is not included in the table.

These operations of the Secretary during the present year have largely reduced the amount of interest receivable by the national banks upon the bonds held by them.

During the year 1871, and previous thereto, a large portion of the bonds bore interest at the rate of 6 per cent.; and until the year 1877 all of the bonds bore interest at either five or six per cent. At the present time, more than 65 per cent. of the amount pledged for circulation consists of bonds bearing interest at the low rate of 3½ per cent., and nearly 35 per cent. of them bear interest at the rate of 4 and 4½ per cent. This will be seen from the following table, which exhibits the amounts and classes of United States bonds owned by the banks, including those pledged as security for circulation and for public deposits, on the first day of July in each year since 1865, and upon November 1 of the present year:

Date.	United States bonds held as security for circulation.					U. S. bonds held for other purposes at nearest date.	Grand total.
	6 per cent. bonds.	5 per cent. bonds.	4½ per cent. bonds.	4 per cent. bonds.	Total.		
July 1, 1865.....	$170,382,500	$65,576,600			$235,959,100	$155,785,750	$391,744,850
July 1, 1866	241,083,500	86,226,850			327,310,350	121,152,950	448,463,300
July 1, 1867.....	251,430,400	89,177,100			340,607,500	84,002,650	424,610,150
July 1, 1868.....	250,726,950	90,768,950			311,495,909	80,922,500	422,418,400
July 1, 1869.....	255,190,350	87,661,250			342,851,600	55,102,000	397,953,600
July 1, 1870.....	247,355,350	94,923,200			342,278,550	43,980,600	386,259,150
July 1, 1871.....	220,497,750	139,387,800			359,885,550	39,450,800	399,336,350
July 1, 1872.....	173,251,450	207,189,250			380,440,700	31,868,200	412,308,900
July 1, 1873.....	160,923,500	229,487,050			390,410,550	25,724,400	416,134,950
July 1, 1874	154,370,700	236,800,500			391,171,200	25,347,100	416,518,300
July 1, 1875.....	136,955,100	239,359,400			376,314,500	26,900,200	403,214,700
July 1, 1876.....	109,313,450	232,081,300			341,394,750	45,170,300	386,565,050
July 1, 1877.....	87,690,300	206,651,050	$44,372,250		338,713,600	47,315,050	386,028,650
July 1, 1878.....	82,421,200	199,514,550	48,448,650	$19,162,000	349,546,400	68,850,900	418,397,300
July 1, 1879.....	56,042,800	144,616,300	35,056,550	118,538,950	354,254,600	76,603,520	430,858,120
July 1, 1880.....	58,056,150	139,758,650	37,760,950	126,076,300	361,652,050	42,831,300	404,483,350
July 1, 1881.....	61,901,800 Continued at 3½ per cent.	172,348,350 Continued at 3½ per cent.	32,600,500	93,637,700	360,488,400	63,849,950	424,338,350
Nov. 1, 1881.....	53,741,600	187,634,550	31,981,650	92,005,800	369,608,500	56,512,450	426,120,950

The banks also held $3,486,000 of Pacific Railroad 6 per cents., and $738,900 of 5 per cents., upon which interest had ceased, which latter amount has since been reduced to $229,000.

AMOUNT OF UNITED STATES BONDS HELD BY COMMERCIAL BANKS, TRUST COMPANIES, AND SAVINGS BANKS ORGANIZED UNDER STATE LAWS.

The amount of United States bonds held by banks organized under State laws is ascertained from such reports as have been received by the Comptroller, through the courtesy of State officers who have responded to his request for copies of their official returns at the latest dates. From such returns it is found that these institutions held, at different dates during the year 1881, the following amount of United States bonds:

Held by State banks in twenty-one States..................... $12,048,452
Held by trust companies in five States..................... 15,631,573
Held by savings banks in fifteen States 210,845,514

Total 238,525,539

The amount held by geographical divisions in 1880 and 1881 was as follows:

Geographical divisions.	1880.	1881.
Eastern States	$45,230,098	$40,468,340
Middle States	157,563,757	176,573,889
Southern States	956,470	1,673,460
Western States	2,672,242	5,735,518
Pacific States	7,240,835	14,874,332
Totals	213,665,402	238,525,539

This amount is $3,201,340 less than that returned to the Commissioner of Internal Revenue, who receives semi-annual reports, for purposes of taxation, not only from banks organized under State laws, but also from private bankers, giving their average capital and deposits, and the amount of such capital invested in United States bonds. From these returns the following table has been compiled, showing, by geographical divisions, the average amount of capital invested in United States bonds for the six months ending May 31, in the years 1879, 1880, and 1881:

Geographical divisions.	By State banks, private bankers, and trust companies.	By savings banks.	Total.
Capital invested in United States bonds.			
May 31, 1879:			
New England States	$3,669,967	34,941,378	38,611,345
Middle States	25,686,469	123,818,148	149,504,617
Southern States	3,593,179	86,021	3,679,200
Western States	8,326,402	2,164,668	10,491,070
Pacific States and Territories	5,015,948	1,372,845	6,388,793
United States	46,291,965	162,383,060	208,675,025
May 31, 1880:			
New England States	3,737,093	37,693,200	41,430,293
Middle States	20,564,834	146,301,155	166,865,989
Southern States	2,541,991	1,000	2,542,991
Western States	8,137,554	2,474,557	10,612,111
Pacific States and Territories	3,883,816	2,717,904	6,601,720
United States	38,865,288	189,187,816	228,053,104
May 31, 1881:			
New England States	2,985,496	36,640,795	39,626,291
Middle States	21,908,703	168,617,049	190,525,752
Southern States	1,707,702	21,689	1,729,391
Western States	6,714,948	2,689,447	9,404,395
Pacific States and Territories	5,004,313	6,911,198	11,915,511
United States	38,321,162	214,880,178	253,201,340

The above table gives the average amount of capital invested in United States bonds, from which should be deducted the amount of premium paid at the time of purchase, which cannot be ascertained.

The amount of United States bonds held by the national banks on October 1, 1881, was $426,120,950, and the average amount held by the other banks and bankers of the country, during the six months ending May 31 last, was $253,201,340. The total amount held by all the banks and bankers during the last two years is thus shown to be considerably more than one-third of the whole interest-bearing funded debt of the United States, as follows:

	1880.	1881.
National banks	$403,369,350	$426,120,950
Savings banks	189,187,816	214,880,178
State banks and trust companies	24,498,604	21,650,668
Private bankers	14,366,684	16,670,494
Totals	631,422,454	679,322,290

LOANS AND RATES OF INTEREST.

The following table gives the classification of the loans of the banks in the city of New York, in Boston, Philadelphia, and Baltimore, and in the other reserve cities, at corresponding dates in each of the last three years:

OCTOBER 2, 1879.

Classification.	New York City.	Boston, Philadelphia, and Baltimore.	Other reserve cities.	Country banks.	Aggregate.
	47 banks.	90 banks.	82 banks.	1,820 banks.	2,048 banks.
On U. S. bonds on demand	$8,286,525	$2,017,226	$4,360,523		$14,664,274
On other stocks, bonds, &c., on demand	78,062,085	22,605,795	11,445,079		112,112,959
On single-name paper without other security	22,491,926	13,136,911	7,150,230		42,779,076
All other loans	87,011,366	118,267,128	65,023,494	$435,154,810	705,456,798
Totals	195,851,902	156,027,060	87,979,335	435,154,810	875,013,107

OCTOBER 1, 1880.

Classification.	47 banks.	101 banks.	83 banks.	1,859 banks.	2,090 banks.
On U. S. bonds on demand	$3,915,077	$525,445	$1,378,168		$5,818,690
On other stocks, bonds, &c., on demand	92,630,982	30,838,692	16,558,260		140,027,934
On single-name paper without other security	27,755,152	22,542,776	10,402,295		60,700,223
All other loans	114,127,290	137,405,246	75,687,334	$503,294,724	830,514,594
Totals	238,428,501	191,312,159	104,026,057	503,294,724	1,037,061,441

OCTOBER 1, 1881.

Classification.	48 banks.	102 banks.	87 banks.	1,895 banks.	2,132 banks.
On U. S. bonds on demand	$2,539,928	$415,164	$468,496	$2,661,256	$6,084,841
On other stocks, bonds, &c., on demand	97,249,162	39,251,526	24,227,158	35,423,896	196,151,742
On single-name paper without other security	26,935,878	34,465,661	12,904,338	73,114,405	147,420,282
All other loans	120,032,691	137,682,302	96,806,506	461,843,937	819,365,436
Totals	246,757,659	211,814,653	134,406,498	576,043,494	1,169,022,304

In the table below is given a full classification of the loans in New York City alone for the last five years:

Loans and discounts.	October 1, 1877.	October 1, 1878.	October 2, 1879.	October 1, 1880.	October 1, 1881.
	47 banks.	47 banks.	47 banks.	47 banks.	48 banks.
On indorsed paper	$92, 618, 776	$83, 924, 833	$81, 520, 129	$107, 058, 860	$112, 049, 004
On single-name paper	15, 800, 540	17, 297, 475	22, 491, 926	27, 755, 152	26, 935, 878
On U. S. bonds on demand	4, 763, 448	7, 003, 085	8, 286, 525	3, 915, 077	2, 539, 928
On other stock, &c., on demand	48, 376, 633	51, 152, 021	78, 062, 085	92, 630, 982	97, 249, 162
On real-estate security	497, 524	786, 514	670, 021	1, 336, 513	236, 100
Payable in gold	4, 319, 014	6, 752, 181			
All other loans	2, 786, 456	2, 670, 371	4, 821, 216	5, 731, 917	7, 747, 587
Totals	169, 162, 391	169, 585, 980	195, 851, 902	238, 428, 501	246, 757, 659

The following table exhibits the amount of loans, capital, surplus, net deposits, specie and paper money in the banks in New York City, in the other reserve cities, in the States and Territories, and in the Union, on October 1, 1881:

Assets and liabilities.	New York City.	Other reserve cities.	States and Territories.	United States.
	48 banks.	189 banks.	1,895 banks.	2,132 banks.
Loans	$246, 757, 659	$346, 221, 151	$576, 043, 494	$1, 169, 022, 304
Capital	51, 150, 000	119, 799, 830	292, 872, 155	463, 821, 985
Surplus	19, 947, 316	34, 162, 895	74, 030, 407	128, 140, 618
Net deposits	268, 769, 373	335, 669, 226	507, 200, 770	1, 111, 639, 369
Specie	50, 627, 368	34, 535, 367	27, 509, 821	112, 672, 556
Legal tender notes and United States certificates	10, 898, 371	21, 899, 231	27, 093, 002	59, 890, 604

The loans of the banks on October 1 were $1,169,022,304, which is an increase of $132,000,000 over the corresponding date in last year. The total individual and bank deposits, not deducting the amount due from banks and the clearing-house exchanges, have increased $225,725,496, and amount to the unprecedented sum of $1,381,852,887. The ratio of the total loans to capital, surplus, and net deposits was then 68.9 per cent.; in 1880 it was 67.3 per cent.; in 1879 65.3 per cent. The proportion of cash to net deposits was 15.5 per cent. on October 1, 1881, and for the corresponding dates in 1880 and 1879 it was 17.9 and 18.0.

In his report for last year the Comptroller gave tables showing the ratios of loans to capital, surplus and net deposits, and of cash to net deposits, of the banks in New York City, in other reserve cities, and of those elsewhere, on or near October 1 of each year, from 1870 to 1880, inclusive, and he then remarked as follows in reference thereto:

If the ratios of the loans of the banks in New York City to their capital, surplus and net deposits be examined, it will be found that in October of 1879 and 1880, they were 70.8 per cent., in 1878 but 65.4 per cent., in 1877 but 68 per cent., and in 1876, 65.4 per cent.; and that the loans are now proportionately higher than at any time since 1873. The means of the banks in Boston and the other reserve cities were more fully employed in October than they were at the corresponding dates for the two previous years, though the business of the banks was not as much extended as it was during the four years following the crisis of 1873.

The ratios of the loans of the banks in the country districts were, on October 1, last,

7.3 per cent. less than at the corresponding dates in 1875, and 5.2 per cent. less than in 1877. The opportunities for using money in this group of banks are not in proportion to the increase of deposits, and their balances in other banks have by no means diminished.

It will surprise those whose attention has not heretofore been called to the subject to find how closely the means of the banks in the commercial cities have been employed during the last eleven years, notwithstanding the variations in rates of interest, and particularly during the last two years, when money has been so abundant and the deposits have so rapidly increased. It will be seen that prior to 1876, with the exception of a single year, the loans in New York exceeded the net deposits, while since that time, though there has been considerable variation, the net deposits have been somewhat in excess of the loans at the dates given. In the other principal cities, which continually keep large amounts of money in New York subject to demand, and thus diminish their own net deposits, as given in the above table, the loans have always largely exceeded their deposits. The same remark is true of the banks in the country districts which have in New York, as well as in other cities, large amounts of money on deposits subject to call. The capital of this class of banks is also much larger as compared with their deposits than is that of the banks in the large cities, and their loans therefore relatively greater.

The same comments apply with equal force to the ratios shown by the returns for October 1 of the present year, as may be seen from the following table:

Dates.	New York City.	Other reserve cities.	States and Territories.	United States.
	Per cent.	Per cent.	Per cent.	Per cent.
October 1, 1881	72.6	70.8	66.4	68.9
October 1, 1880	70.8	67.7	65.7	67.3
October 2, 1879	70.8	65.4	63.9	65.7

The ratios of cash to net deposits for the same dates were as follows:

Dates.	New York City.	Other reserve cities.	States and Territories.	United States.
	Per cent.	Per cent.	Per cent.	Per cent.
October 1, 1881	22.9	16.8	10.8	15.5
October 1, 1880	26.4	18.5	12.1	17.9
October 2, 1879	24.7	19.4	12.7	18.0

In reference to reserves the Comptroller last year remarked as follows:

The amount of legal cash reserve required of the banks in New York City is 25 per cent. of their deposits, of the banks in the other reserve cities one-half of this ratio, and of the banks in the country districts 6 per cent. of their deposits.

The banks in the interior, if we consider their large deposits elsewhere, are as a rule found to be much stronger in available means than the banks in New York City; while the reverse of this should always be true when such large balances, amounting to more than 100 millions of the funds of other banks, are constantly on deposit in the latter city subject to demand.

The amount of legal reserve required to be held by the banks was largely reduced by the act of June 20, 1874, the provision requiring reserve on circulation having been repealed, and the percentage held in the larger cities has been greatly diminished during the past few years. The sudden and enormous increase of individual and bank deposits in the commercial centers should be accompanied, not only by the reserve required by law, but by a much greater percentage of coin and a much smaller expansion of loans, if the banks would check unhealthy speculation, and keep themselves in condition for an adverse balance of trade and for the legitimate demands of the depositors and correspondents who confide in them.

On October 1 of the present year the aggregate reserve held by the New York City banks, including the five per cent. redemption fund, was 23.3 per cent. only, falling below the amount required by law, and similar deficiencies were shown by previous statements of the clearing-house: but the returns of the banks to the clearing-house for the weeks ending October 27 and 29 following, show a contraction of loans and reduction of liabilities, and a slight excess of reserve over the amount required by law. The reserves in the other reserve cities, which include the amount held by agents in New York, were considerably less than at the corresponding date last year, although still in excess of the amount required by law, being 30 per cent. of deposits; while the total reserves of the banks in other localities were, as usual, very strong, amounting to 31.2 per cent. of the net deposits.

The loans and deposits for each year since resumption day, on January 1, 1879, have increased largely in each group of banks, while the *cash* reserves in each are being gradually reduced. It is evident that these deposits consist, to a much greater extent than usual, of the avails of loans placed to the credit of dealers. This exhibit shows that the banks are rapidly expanding; and there are many indications that this rapid increase is not the result of legitimate business, but of venturesome speculation, largely consequent upon the importation of coin and increased issues of silver certificates and bank notes. The increase in the amount of United States bonds held by the banks has been 13 millions during the last year, but it is 15 millions less than at a corresponding date in 1879. This is somewhat surprising, when it is considered that $3\frac{1}{2}$ per cent. bonds can be purchased at about par, and that the rate of interest paid on deposits in New York City is from two to three per cent. only.

The attention of Congress has previously been called to section 5200 of the Revised Statutes, which places restrictions upon loans, and to the difficulty of enforcing its provisions. In cities where large amounts of produce are received and stored, it is represented that it is impossible for the banks to transact this class of business, if restricted to loans for an amount not exceeding in any instance one-tenth of their capital. It is true that the limitation does not apply to loans upon produce in transit, where the drafts are drawn on existing values; but if produce is stored instead of being shipped, large loans cannot be made except in violation of law. In such case the Comptroller has no means of enforcing the law, except by bringing a suit for forfeiture of charter, and this course might result in great embarrassment to business, as well as loss to many innocent stockholders of the banks. It is evident that the law should be so amended as to exclude from the limitation mentioned legitimate loans upon produce or warehouse receipts, as well as loans upon United States bonds.

Large loans are also continually being made upon other stocks and bonds, and these loans are largely made to stock-brokers, the result being to assist and promote speculative operations upon the stock board. The provision of law mentioned is valuable, so far as it affects banks outside of the large commercial centers, as it provides for a just distribution of loans; but it is recommended that the limit be increased to ten per cent. upon the combined capital and surplus, and that loans upon United States bonds be not limited in amount. It is also recommended that the limit for loans upon stocks and bonds be increased to fifteen per cent. upon capital and surplus, and that such penalty be then imposed for exceeding this limit as would make a violation of the provision unprofitable if the penalty were collected. It is important that some amendment of this kind be enacted, or that means be provided for enforcing the provisions of the section as it now stands.

3 C C

RATES OF INTEREST IN NEW YORK CITY, AND IN THE BANK OF ENGLAND AND THE BANK OF FRANCE.

The average rate of interest in New York City for each of the fiscal years from 1874 to 1881, as ascertained from data derived from the Journal of Commerce and The Commercial and Financial Chronicle, was as follows:

1874, call loans, 3.8 per cent.; commercial paper, 6.4 per cent.
1875, call loans, 3.0 per cent.; commercial paper, 5.6 per cent.
1876, call loans, 3.3 per cent.; commercial paper, 5.3 per cent.
1877, call loans, 3.0 per cent.; commercial paper, 5.2 per cent.
1878, call loans, 4.4 per cent.; commercial paper, 5.1 per cent.
1879, call loans, 4.4 per cent.; commercial paper, 4.4 per cent.
1880, call loans, 4.9 per cent.; commercial paper, 5.3 per cent.
1881, call loans, 3.8 per cent.; commercial paper, 5.0 per cent.

The average rate of discount of the Bank of England for the same years was as follows:

During the calendar year ending December 31, 1874, 3.69 per cent.
During the calendar year ending December 31, 1875, 3.23 per cent.
During the calendar year ending December 31, 1876, 2.61 per cent.
During the calendar year ending December 31, 1877, 2.91 per cent.
During the calendar year ending December 31, 1878, 3.78 per cent.
During the calendar year ending December 31, 1879, 2.50 per cent.
During the calendar year ending December 31, 1880, 2.76 per cent.
During the fiscal year ending June 30, 1881, 2.74 per cent.

The rate of interest in the city of New York on December 2, as derived from the Daily Bulletin, was, on call loans, from 4 to 6 per cent., and on commercial paper from 6 to 7 per cent.

During the present year the rate of discount of the Bank of England has been changed six times, as follows: On January 13, increased from 3 to 3½ per cent.; February 17 reduced to 3 per cent., and on April 28 further reduced to 2½ per cent.; on August 18 increased to 3½ per cent.; August 25 to 4 per cent.; and again increased on October 6 to 5 per cent.

The rate of the Bank of France has been changed but twice during the present year, and in each instance there was an increase, as follows: On August 25 from 3½ to 4 per cent., and on October 20 from 4 to 5 per cent., which is the rate at the present time. The bank rates of discount for the week ending November 12 were, in Berlin, 5½ per cent., Amsterdam, 4 per cent., Brussels, 5½ per cent., Vienna, 4 per cent., and St. Petersburg 6 per cent.*

DUTIES OF DIRECTORS AND EXAMINERS.

The recent failure of The Mechanics' National Bank of Newark has called the attention of the public directly to the duties of bank directors and of examiners of national banks.

Section 5147 of the Revised Statutes provides that each director, when appointed or elected, shall take an oath that he will, so far as the duty devolves on him, diligently and honestly administer the affairs of such association, and will not knowingly violate or permit to be violated any of the provisions of this act. Section 5136 also provides that the association shall have power to prescribe, by its board of directors, by-laws not inconsistent with law, regulating the manner in which its stock shall be transferred, its directors elected or appointed, its officers appointed, its property transferred, its general business conducted, and the privileges granted to it by law exercised and enjoyed.

---

* The Economist, London, November 12, 1881.

In accordance with the provisions of this last named section, by-laws
are generally adopted by national banks soon after their organization,
which usually contain, among other provisions, sections similar to the
following:

There shall be a standing committee, to be known as the "Exchange Committee,"
appointed by the board, every six months, to continue to act until succeeded, who
shall have power to discount and purchase notes and bills and other evidence of debts,
and to buy and sell bills of exchange, and who shall, at each regular meeting, make a
report of the notes and bills discounted and purchased by them since their last previous
report.

There shall be appointed by the board every three months a committee, whose duty
it shall be to examine into the affairs of the bank, to count its cash, and to compare
its assets and liabilities with the balances on the general ledger for the purpose of
ascertaining that the books are correctly kept and the condition of the bank corre-
sponds therewith, and that the bank is in a sound and solvent condition: the result of
which examination shall be reported to the board at its next regular meeting.

The object of these by-laws is, first, to keep the board of directors continuously informed what notes and bills are discounted, and to furnish
them with a detailed account thereof; and secondly to establish a check
by the directors upon the cashier, teller and bookkeeper of the bank,
to whose immediate custody and control the assets and accounts of the
bank are committed. A method is thus provided by which the diligent
and continuous administration of the directors, which is required by
their oaths, shall be performed.

It is thus seen that both the laws of the United States and the by-laws
adopted by the directors themselves, under the law, in clear terms define their duties. The men employed by them in the banks are under
their supervision, the law providing—

That the bank shall have power to elect or appoint directors, and by this board of
directors to appoint a president, vice-president, cashier, and other officers, define their
duties, require bonds of them and fix the penalty thereof, dismiss such officers or any
of them at pleasure, and appoint others to fill their places.

The duties of the board of directors are plainly defined, and however
innocent they may be of any intention of wrong, they are responsible
for the safety of funds committed to their care. If it can be shown that
any of them had notice of illegal transactions, it is a serious question
whether they are not legally bound to make good the loss which may
occur; and it is a question whether they are not also liable for losses
which may occur from neglect of duty, even without notice. If this is
not the just and proper construction of the present law, then it becomes
a subject for the consideration of Congress, whether additional legislation upon this point is not required. The National Bank Act is full
of restrictions, to which reference has already been made in another portion of this report, such as those requiring an adequate reserve; the
enforced accumulation of the surplus; the method of increasing and
reducing the capital stock and its prompt restoration if impaired; the
prohibition against making loans on real estate and on the security of
their own shares of stock, or of accommodation or other loans than business paper in excess of one-tenth of the capital of the bank; the prohibition against the declaration of dividends unless earned; against certifying checks without the necessary deposit; and many other similar provisions. These restrictions are intended to protect these institutions,
by imposing upon them general rules, which experience has shown may
be properly done by the government *without its thereby becoming the
guardian of the bank, or of the moneys of its depositors or stockholders, or
being in any way responsible for the management of its funds.* It is the
duty of the examiner to ascertain whether the officers of the bank
and its directors are complying with the requirements of the law

and whether they are in any way violating any of its provisions, to the end that in such case they may be enforced by the proper authority..

The stockholders elect the directors, who are usually men not only of high character and well known in the community where the bank is located, but are generally also large stockholders in the bank, and having therefore each a personal interest in its prosperity and good management. The depositors confide in the bank because they believe the directors will manage its affairs honestly and diligently, and will employ honest and faithful servants for that purpose. They know that the bank is organized under laws which contain wholesome restrictions, and that it is the duty of the Comptroller, so far as he can through his corps of examiners, to inform himself of the condition of the bank, and to require that its business shall be conducted in conformity with law.

The examiner can have but a limited knowledge of the habits and character of those employed in the bank. If the teller is making false entries, and daily abstracting the funds of the bank; if the bookkeeper is keeping false accounts and rendering untrue statements; if the cashier is placing forged paper among the bills receivable and upon the register book, and transmitting such paper to distant places where it is purported to be payable, it is not possible for an examiner, in a day or two, to unravel this evil work, which may have continued for months, and obtain a correct balance sheet. A full and complete examination of the bank necessitates not only counting the cash, proving the bills receivable and stock ledger, comparing the individual deposit accounts with the general ledger, and ascertaining if the business of the bank is conducted in accordance with law; but, also, the thorough examination of all accounts, the verifying of accounts-current, and ascertaining by telegraph or letter the correctness of such verification, the calling in of every depositor's book, and correspondence with every bank or banker doing business with the bank.

Examinations should be periodically made by a competent committee, selected from the board. The directors have abundant means at their command, and if they have any reason to suspect dishonesty or fraud, it is their business to investigate thoroughly, and they should employ experts to assist them in so doing. The national bank examiners have, in fact, been frequently called upon by the directors of both national and State banks for this purpose; and if it is the intent of the law that the national banks shall be thus searchingly examined, it should be so amended as to make this intent clear, and should also make provision for the necessary compensation for such service. The small compensation now provided does not contemplate a yearly auditing of all the accounts of a bank by the examiner, as the pay is entirely inadequate for such a work—the amount allowed for the examination of banks of like capital being the same, without reference to the difference in the volume of their business. The inspection by an examiner of a small bank is usually completed in a day; of larger banks, through the aid of an assistant, in two or three days. But a thorough analyzing and scrutiny of everything would require one or two weeks; and if fraud were suspected it might continue for months without entirely satisfactory results.

The reports of the bank, as made to the Comptroller five times in each year, are each published in a newspaper where the bank is located, and every stockholder has, therefore, an opportunity to scrutinize these statements, and to make inquiry of the directors in reference to the affairs of the association.

The detection of embezzlement may occur as an incident, but it is not the principal object, of the system of bank examinations. It is peculiarly the business of the directors, who are daily or weekly in session, to keep themselves informed of the habits and characters of their employés, to see that their time is given to the service of the bank, and that they are not engaged in speculations, and thus, by continuous watchfulness, to prevent defalcations on the part of their servants; while it is the business of the examiner to detect frauds so far as in his power, and in his occasional visits to see that the directors are loaning the funds, and, with the other officers, managing the affairs of the bank strictly according to the provisions of the law. The examiner's visits are usually made about once a year, while the directors are at hand at all times. Faithful performance of the duties of each gives assurance of almost absolute safety. Lax performance of duty on the part of either invites disaster. The directory must continuously look after its own servants. The examiner looks after the acts of the directors.

The report of the examiner is confidential. It is for the use of the Comptroller's office only, and is in no sense a certificate of the good condition of the bank. In many instances the capital stock of a bank has thus been found to be impaired, and the deficiency has been made good without the knowledge of the general public. In other instances banks have been obliged to pass their usual dividends, using their earnings to liquidate all bad and doubtful debts—the number of banks passing dividends during the present year being 175; in 1880, 230; in 1879, 304; and in 1878, 343.

Hundreds of instances have occurred annually, and many are occurring daily, wherein the banks, under the reports of the examiner, are notified of violations of the act and are brought under the discipline of the law. The betterment of the condition of the banks, and the enforcement of the requirements of the law, are part of the continual and ordinary supervision exercised by this Office. It is a supervision and labor not seen or known of by the general public, whose attention is only arrested when some sudden or unexpected failure occurs; and this simply illustrates the fact that, with the best endeavors, and the most careful supervision by this Office, such disasters may happen in the many contingencies of administering difficult and extensive duties, if directors neglect to exercise that continuous vigilance for which they were elected, and which they have sworn to perform.

The Mechanics' National Bank of Newark was placed in the hands of the receiver on November 2 last. It had a capital of $500,000, a surplus of $400,000, and deposits of over $2,500,000. The capital and surplus are lost, through the criminal conduct of the cashier, and the stockholders are personally liable for an amount equal to the capital stock. The depositors will, it is estimated, receive at the outcome from 60 to 80 per cent. of their claims, depending upon the amount collected from the stockholders and that received from the estate for whose benefit the funds of the bank are alleged to have been abstracted, which estate is also now in the hands of a receiver appointed by the court. This bank was many times examined by skilled accountants of great experience, but it cannot be denied that some of them were misled by the criminal cashier, who, through his apparently high character and standing, so long deceived not only the directors, but every one with whom he had business relations. The examination of August 14, 1879, was conducted by two experienced experts, but was, as I am informed, rendered useless by a forged telegram purporting to be from the correspondent of the bank in New York. The examiner, on August 16, 1880, verified the accounts of correspondents, as he was specially instructed to do in a letter from the Comptroller in June previous; but he also was deceived by a forged letter from the New York correspondent, skillfully planned for this purpose, addressed to the examiner, received through the mail, and bearing the New York post-mark. Either of these examinations would have disclosed the robbery of the cashier, if the examiners had not been deceived by forgeries which would have been likely to mislead the most thorough expert.

It is, however, far from correct to represent that similar defalcations in national banks have not been previously discovered. The greatest defalcation in the history of the government, of eleven hundred thousand dollars, in the office of the assistant treasurer of New Orleans, which had certainly existed, in whole or in part, for more than a year, was discovered nearly fifteen years ago by an officer of this bureau, which discovery also resulted in the disclosure of a large deficiency in the First National Bank of New Orleans, and the placing of that bank in the hands of a receiver. Since that time many of the other banks which have failed have been placed in the hands of receivers through the vigilance of bank examiners; and in many other instances officers of solvent and insolvent banks have, through the same means, been indicted and convicted for criminal acts. The bank examiners in New York City and Boston are nominated by the clearing-houses of those cities, and many other examiners now employed are men of the highest character, who have for years rendered excellent service. It is of the greatest importance that all men employed in this branch of the public service shall be well-trained and fitted for their work. It is not claimed that every examiner employed is a first-class expert—the compensation authorized is not sufficient for that purpose in many small districts. If State lines can be disregarded in the appointment of examiners, and men be selected for these positions upon merit alone, and kept well employed, a corps of skilled examiners would soon be engaged in this work, who would reflect the highest credit upon this branch of the public service. The records of this office show, however, that only one among all the examiners ever appointed has been found guilty of wrongdoing, while in no branch of the government service have men performed more faithful duty than those who have been engaged in the examinations of the national banks.

Such disasters do not exhibit the weakness of the banking system, but rather the weakness and wickedness of human nature. The system is strong, and carefully and elaborately guarded. Private companies and individuals are continuously suffering from embezzlements and forgeries. It is scarcely to be expected, if a robber or a forger is placed in control of all of its assets, that a national bank can be saved from disaster by the occasional visits of an examiner. Some additional legislation will be required; but there is not so much necessity for additional restrictions as there is for increased care upon the part of examiners, and increased diligence and sagacity on the part of directors who are in charge of great trusts.

The Pacific National Bank of Boston suspended on November 18 ultimo. The last report of the examination of this bank gave what seemed to be a thorough exhibit of its affairs. A long communication was addressed by the Comptroller to the directors of the bank on February 19 last informing them of such irregularities as then existed in the conduct of its business. They were specially informed that the irregular and illegal practice of loaning the credit of the bank by the issue of certificates must be discontinued. In reply to this communication a letter from the president of the association was received on February 28, explaining the irregularities referred to. In regard to the issuing of the certificates he said that "never in a single instance has any stipulation been made by us in regard to any certificate issued to any party. They are issued in regular form, and are payable at any moment upon presentation." To this it was replied by the Comptroller on March 3 that—

The examiner distinctly stated in his recent report that "loans are sometimes made by the issuing of demand certificates, and parties obtaining loans in this way indorse the certificates and pledge them as collateral, or stipulating the time of payment for them, have them regularly discounted, and thus raise money indirectly from other parties and banks." If this statement be correct, the bank is lending its credit, which it is not authorized by law to do, and the practice must, as stated in my letter of the 19th ultimo, be discontinued.

That this information was brought to the attention of the directors is evident from a letter received since the date of suspension, on the 25th instant, from the person who made the examination, which says:

Had your letter, which you wrote after my last examination, which was read by Mr. Benyon, the president, to the board, as you requested, been heeded, the present condition of things would have been avoided.

Such a letter, in any properly-conducted bank, addressed by the Comptroller to a board of directors composed, as was the case in this instance, of prominent merchants and business men, should have been sufficient to correct the abuse and save the bank from the disaster which has occurred.

The examiner also informs me that during the examination, and subsequent thereto, he called special attention of the directors to the hazardous manner of doing business, and urged them to follow closely the president and examine loans made by him and the way in which his business was conducted, and was promised by more than one director that close attention would be given to the whole matter. The directors thus had full information in reference to the irregular and illegal methods of the bank which have since caused its ruin.

The law should certainly be so amended as to make it a criminal offense for an officer of a bank clandestinely to make loans, either by the use of certificates, as in this case, or otherwise.

RETIREMENT OF NATIONAL-BANK NOTES AND WITHDRAWAL OF BONDS HELD AS SECURITY THEREFOR.

The only legislation in reference to the national banks during the last session of Congress was contained in section 5 of "the funding act of 1881," which was as follows:

SEC. 5. From and after the first day of July, eighteen hundred and eighty-one, the three per centum bonds authorized by the first section of this act shall be the only bonds receivable as security for national-bank circulation, or as security for the safe-keeping and prompt payment of the public money deposited with such banks; but when any such bonds deposited for the purposes aforesaid shall be designated for purchase or redemption by the Secretary of the Treasury, the banking association depositing the same shall have the right to substitute other issues of the bonds of the United States in lieu thereof: Provided, That no bond upon which interest has ceased shall be accepted or shall be continued on deposit as security for circulation or for the safe-keeping of the public money; and in case bonds so deposited shall not be withdrawn, as provided by law, within thirty days after interest has ceased thereon, the banking association depositing the same shall be subject to the liabilities and proceedings on the part of the Comptroller provided for in section 5234 of the Revised Statutes of the United States: And provided further, That section four of the act of June twentieth, eighteen hundred and seventy-four, entitled "An act fixing the amount of United States notes, providing for a redistribution of the national-bank currency, and for other purposes," be, and the same is hereby, repealed: and sections 5159 and 5160 of the Revised Statutes of the United States be, and the same are hereby, re-enacted.

This act was vetoed by the President.

The number of national banks, which deposited legal tender notes for the purpose of obtaining possession of their bonds, in anticipation of the passage of this bill, was 141. These banks were located in twenty-four States, and the amount of legal tender notes deposited by them was $18,764,434, as follows:

States and cities.	No. of banks.	Amount.	States and cities.	No. of banks.	Amount.
Philadelphia	6	$2,590,800	New York City	9	$2,843,849
Pennsylvania	14	2,083,300	New York	23	1,934,600
Boston	4	1,034,100	New Jersey	5	837,000
Massachusetts	2	81,000	Indiana	10	1,080,000
Connecticut	10	1,675,400	Missouri	3	164,745
Montana	1	36,000	Virginia	1	45,000
District of Columbia	1	72,000	Ohio	19	1,402,630
Rhode Island	2	385,200	Minnesota	3	135,000
Nebraska	2	171,900	Kentucky	1	310,900
Kansas	2	81,000	Michigan	1	27,000
Illinois	10	845,900	Iowa	4	100,460
Maine	2	135,000	Vermont	3	463,560
North Carolina	1	135,000	Wisconsin	1	21,150
Maryland	1	72,000			
			Totals	141	18,764,434

Only about one-third of the bonds which were thus released were subsequently redeposited, and for some months thereafter the total amount of bonds redeposited by the 141 banks which reduced their circulation was less than 7 millions. The Third National Bank of New York, which withdrew $840,000 of bonds, soon thereafter disposed of the same to the Government, and has not since made any deposit whatever. The same statement may be made in reference to eight other large banks, which withdrew bonds amounting to over two millions of dollars, and also to many other smaller banks—thus showing that they withdrew their bonds because they desired control of them, and not for the purpose of arbitrarily reducing circulation. The Comptroller has been unable to obtain any evidence that there was a combination on the part of the banks to deposit legal-tender notes and withdraw bonds for the purpose of deranging the money market.

Since the adjournment of Congress, only $2,394,545 of legal-tender notes have been deposited under the act of June 20, 1874, for the purpose of retiring circulation, and these notes have been redeemed without any expense whatever to the Government of the United States—the cost thereof having been paid from the five per cent. redemption fund. The bonds now held are chiefly 3½ and 4 per cents, there being 241 millions of the former and 92 millions of the latter. The amount of interest received from an investment in either class of these bonds is nearly the same, and there is but little disposition to deposit legal-tender notes for the purpose of withdrawing them. Some banks take occasion to withdraw their 4 per cents, for the purpose of realizing the large premium of 16 per cent., which they now bear, as this premium can be used for the purpose of liquidating any losses which may occur in their business. The 3½ per cent. bonds are being frequently called by the Secretary, and the banks may therefore have occasion to withdraw them after interest has ceased, and it is important that they continue to have this privilege, upon a deposit of lawful money as now provided by law.

The amount of loans of the national banks in New York City on October 1, 1881, was 246 millions, and 97 millions of this amount was payable on demand; the total amount of loans of all the banks was 1,169 millions, of which 196 millions was demand loans. It is probable that the proportion of demand loans held by the State banks is fully as great. Any proceeding which would tend to bring on a panic, or erange the money market in New York, would, first of all, affect the value of the stocks and bonds held by the banks as securities for these loans. It would be directly against the interest of the bank to pursue such a course, and it is a new principle in banking to assume that banking institutions will so conduct their business as to depress the value of securities which they themselves hold. If the banks, however, either National or State, or private bankers, should at any time desire to derange the market, they could do so, independently of any legislation by Congress, by calling in their demand loans. Such a course would be much more simple and easy of accomplishment than the depositing of legal-tender notes in the Treasury, and it would be much more effective. If, however, Congress shall consider it advisable to prevent the banks from depositing in the Treasury for this purpose large amounts of coin or other lawful money, then section 4 of the act of June 20, 1874, may be so amended as to require those desiring to withdraw bonds to give a reasonable notice of their intention to do so, before completing the transaction.

When bonds deposited to secure the circulation of the national banks are called for payment by the government, it is necessary that the banks should withdraw them for redemption. This they can do, either by substituting other bonds or by depositing, under section 4 of the act of June 20, 1874, lawful money, to retire the circulation secured by the bonds which they desire to withdraw. The most convenient method for the banks is to avail themselves of the provision of section 4 referred to, as in many cases they desire permanently to withdraw bonds, without substitution. Prior to May 23 last, the Treasurer of the United States, and his predecessors in office, had, as a matter of convenience both to the banks and the government, permitted the redemption of called bonds by the following method: The banks sent a power of attorney, authorizing the Comptroller to withdraw the bonds, and the Treasurer of the United States to assign them to the Secretary of the Treasury for redemption on account of the bank, as much of the proceeds as might be necessary being used to retire the circulation secured by the bonds. The bonds were never out of the hands of the officers of the Treasury Department. The banks were thus relieved from the necessity of first sending in the money to retire their circulation, and the Government was enabled to get in its called bonds with more promptitude. On May 23, however, the Treasurer declined longer to allow this method of withdrawal and redemption, alleging that the proceeds of these bonds were coin, and not legal-tender notes, and that section 4 of the act of June 20 requires deposits for the retirement of circulation to be made in legal-tender notes only.

On June 1 the Comptroller addressed a letter to the Secretary of the Treasury, in which he stated the position taken by the Treasurer, and "that he declined to receive gold coin, which is a legal tender in payment of all debts, and insisted upon a deposit of United States notes, which are but promises to pay coin on demand." The Comptroller dissented from this ruling of the Treasurer, and held that the act, properly construed, authorized the receipt of "lawful money," which includes gold and silver coin as well as United States notes, and requested that the question be referred to the Attorney-General for his construction of section 4 of the act of June 20, 1874.

On the 6th of June the Secretary referred the matter to the Attorney-General, and on the 14th of the same month the latter officer decided that "the banks may withdraw their bonds upon the deposit of the requisite amount of any kind of lawful money." He said, further, that—

The language of section 4 is almost too unambiguous for construction, as it expressly confers upon national banking associations the right to deposit sums of not less than

$9,000 in lawful money, and to take up the bonds deposited for security of circulating notes; and that these words, as here used, possess their ordinary signification is apparent from the phraseology of concomitant and other provisions of law, and from considerations touching the general subject.

He also quoted a decision of his predecessor on a similar point, in confirmation thereof. On the same date that this decision was rendered by the Attorney-General, the Secretary of the Treasury addressed another letter to him, in which two additional questions in reference to this matter were asked: First, whether, under section 3 of the act approved June 20, 1874, chapter 343, a national banking association may deposit any lawful money other than United States notes for redemption of its circulating notes; and, second, whether the holders of the notes of any solvent national banking association may demand of the Treasurer, under the provision of sections 3 and 4 of that act, redemption of such notes in United States notes?

On June 30, 1881, the Attorney-General replied, and, as to the first question, decided that a bank may deposit coin for the purpose mentioned in the 3d section as above quoted. In answer to the second question, he said:

I think the Treasurer, while having the privilege, under sections 3 and 4 of said act, to redeem bank circulation in United States notes, has the right to pay them in coin. The government notes are promises to pay dollars, and for such promises the thing promised may properly be substituted by the promiser, and that the act of June 20, 1874, chapter 343, was not intended to repeal or affect the general provisions of the law (Revised Statutes, section 3585, *et seq.*) making the coin of the United States legal tenders in *all* payments.

This decision removed all the distinctions which had been previously insisted upon by the Treasurer of the United States, as to the kind of lawful money that might be received or paid in these transactions.

NUMBER, CAPITAL AND DEPOSITS OF NATIONAL BANKS, STATE AND SAVINGS-BANKS, AND PRIVATE BANKERS.

The capital of the 2,115 national banks in operation on June 30, 1881, as will be seen by a table in the Appendix, was $460,227,835, not including surplus, which fund at that date amounted to more than 126 millions of dollars; while the average capital of all the State banks, private bankers and savings banks, for the six months ending May 31, 1880, was but $210,738,203. The latter amount is but little more than one-third of the combined capital and surplus of the national banks.

The following table exhibits in a concise form, by geographical divisions, the total average capital and deposits of all State and savings-banks and private bankers in the country, for the six months ending May 31, 1881:

Geographical divisions.	State banks and trust companies.		Private bankers.		Savings banks with capital.		Savings banks without capital.	
	No.	Capital.	Deposits.	No.	Capital.	Deposits.	No.	Capital.	Deposits.	No.	Deposits.
		Mill's	Mill's		Mill's	Mill's		Mill's	Mill's		Mill's
New England States....	41	7.26	20.97	80	4.70	5.16	1	.02	.19	424	402.86
Middle States	218	39.28	189.78	938	55.40	94.11	7	.61	4.68	174	428.40
Southern States	240	24.71	42.43	258	5.59	17.32	6	.44	.84	3	1.24
Western States and Territories..............	479	41.94	132.44	1,762	27.64	125.26	22	3.15	31.90	28	20.86
United States......	978	113.19	385.62	3,038	93.33	241.85	36	4.22	37.61	629	862.36

The table below exhibits the capital and net deposits of the national banks on June 30, 1881, together with the aggregate average capital and deposits of all classes of banks other than national, for the six months ending May 31, 1881:

Geographical divisions.	State banks, savings-banks, private bankers, &c.		National banks.		Total.	
	No.	Capital.	Deposits.	No.	Capital.	Net deposits.	No.	Capital.	Deposits.

		Millions.	*Millions.*		*Millions.*	*Millions.*		*Millions.*	*Millions.*
New England States	546	12.0	429.2	552	165.9	208.6	1,098	177.9	637.8
Middle States	1,337	95.3	717.0	664	171.7	599.7	2,001	267.0	1,316.7
Southern States	507	30.7	61.8	184	31.1	59.5	691	61.8	121.3
Western States and Territories	2,291	72.7	319.4	715	91.5	272.1	3,006	164.2	591.5
United States	4,681	210.7	1,527.4	2,115	460.2	1,139.9	6,796	670.9	2,667.3

From this table it will be seen that the total number of banks and bankers in the country at the date named was 6,796, with a total banking capital of $670,966.043, and total deposits of $2,667,343,595.

In the Appendix will be found similar tables for various periods, from 1875 to 1881, where will also be found other tables giving the assets and liabilities of State institutions during the past year, so far as they could be obtained from the official reports of the several State officers.

A table arranged by States and principal cities, giving the number, capital and deposits, and the tax thereon, of all banking institutions other than national, for the six months ending May 31, 1881, and for previous years, will also be found in the Appendix.

The following table exhibits, for corresponding dates nearest to May 31 in each of the last six years, the aggregate amounts of the capital and deposits of each of the classes of banks given in the foregoing table:

Years.	National banks.			State banks, private bankers, &c.			Savings banks with capital.			Savings banks without capital.		Total.		
	No.	Capital.	Deposits.	No.	Capital.	Deposits.	No.	Capital.	Deposits.	No.	Deposits.	No.	Capital.	Deposits.
		Mill's	*Mill's*		*Mill's*	*Mill's*		*Mill's*	*Mill's*		*Mill's*		*Mill's*	*Mill's*
1876	2,091	500.4	713.5	3,803	214.0	460.0	26	5.0	37.2	691	844.6	6,611	719.4	2,075.3
1877	2,078	481.0	768.2	3,799	218.6	470.5	26	4.9	38.2	676	843.2	6,579	704.5	2,120.1
1878	2,056	470.1	677.2	3,709	202.2	413.3	23	3.2	26.2	668	803.3	6,456	675.8	1,920.0
1879	2,048	455.3	713.4	3,639	197.9	397.0	29	4.9	36.1	644	747.1	6,360	656.5	1,893.5
1880	2,076	455.9	900.8	3,798	190.1	501.5	29	4.0	34.6	629	783.0	6,532	650.0	2,219.9
1881	2,115	460.2	1,139.9	4,016	206.5	627.5	36	4.2	37.6	629	802.3	6,796	670.9	2,667.3

PRIVATE BANKERS.

In the Appendix will be found a table giving by geographical divisions, and by States, Territories and principal cities, the number of State banks, savings banks. trust and loan companies and private bankers of the country. together with the amount of their capital and deposits, and the amount invested by them in United States bonds. The first official information of this character ever published in regard to the private bankers of the country was contained in a table in the Comptroller's report for 1880. From the table in the Appendix, mentioned above, the following information in reference to the private bankers in sixteen of the principal cities has been separated, it being thought that it will prove of special interest:

Cities.	Number of banks.	Capital.	Deposits.	Invested in U. S. bonds.
Boston	47	$4,065,697	$2,570,068	$1,003,243
New York City	508	45,482,515	45,414,576	9,670,751
Albany	3	550,000	1,611,470	351,000
Philadelphia	52	1,890,614	6,174,785	224,208
Pittsburgh	7	563,910	2,025,477	20,374
Baltimore	19	773,657	2,389,632	195,384
Washington	6	394,000	3,747,763	287,029
New Orleans	5	32,000		
Louisville	2	178,000	728,464	
Cincinnati	8	812,167	3,863,817	280,205
Cleveland	4	55,000	963,938	8,967
Chicago	24	2,004,197	10,455,063	172,589
Detroit	7	181,256	945,069	7,333
Milwaukee	4	64,667	550,047	350
Saint Louis	11	261,302	304,976	44,405
San Francisco	9	1,275,918	8,271,059	104,074
Totals	717	58,534,300	89,996,545	12,370,012

The following table gives similar information for the thirty-one States and Territories, exclusive of the cities in the above table, having an amount of capital in excess of $100,000. In this table the number of private bankers is 2,255; the aggregate amount of capital, $34,169,435; and of deposits, $148,178,652, the average capital being $15,152, and the average deposits $65,711:

States and Territories.	Number of banks.	Capital.	Deposits.	Invested in U. S. bonds.
Illinois	310	$4,183,346	$21,656,149	$1,245,738
Pennsylvania	172	4,140,679	19,078,585	288,461
Ohio	213	4,119,220	19,931,774	656,222
Indiana	106	3,130,268	11,870,164	571,999
Iowa	276	2,975,737	10,388,843	67,287
Texas	107	2,580,951	7,033,240	14,000
New York	163	1,551,347	12,699,067	304,268
Michigan	137	1,213,796	5,218,413	74,464
Missouri	81	1,129,244	6,843,267	134,142
Kansas	135	1,001,172	4,076,393	32,600
Wisconsin	79	848,746	4,901,883	111,960
Minnesota	89	679,227	2,772,567	45,848
Nebraska	86	675,300	2,053,586	14,070
Alabama	21	564,085	1,372,342	800
Colorado	51	547,827	2,705,441	15,000
Montana	14	512,706	904,498	
Georgia	30	478,910	1,308,131	7,000
Oregon	12	436,500	973,519	250,000
California	22	387,709	1,022,592	
Virginia	18	369,792	2,102,077	35,000
Kentucky	23	368,731	1,926,815	80,000
Rhode Island	7	358,181	462,268	32,613
Mississippi	11	314,579	838,326	48,280
Nevada	9	292,851	617,530	100,000
Washington	9	284,050	657,015	
South Carolina	8	239,956	73,921	
Dakota	37	216,263	484,335	
Connecticut	12	168,500	1,359,079	8,063
Utah	10	157,225	1,484,710	
Louisiana	3	146,329	35,812	30,000
Wyoming	4	135,208	421,310	
Totals	2,255	34,169,435	148,178,652	4,227,815

The remaining fifteen States and Territories, not enumerated in the above table, contain 66 private bankers, with an aggregate capital of $620,120, and aggregate deposits of $3,670,357. Massachusetts has only three private bankers, outside the city of Boston, with an aggregate capital of $50,000, and aggregate deposits of $539,028. Maryland has but two private bankers, outside of the city of Baltimore. The State of Maine has but seven private bankers. North Carolina four, New Hampshire four, New Jersey five, Delaware and Vermont only one each, Florida six, and Arizona five. The average amount of capital held by each of these 66 private bankers is $9,244, and of deposits $57,127.

The total number of private bankers in the foregoing cities is 717, with an aggregate capital of $58,534,300, and aggregate deposits of $89,996,545 —the average capital being $81,637, and the average deposits $125,518. About 70 per cent. of these private banks are located in New York City, representing nearly four-fifths of the aggregate capital and more than one-half of the aggregate deposits. The average amount of capital and deposits of each private banker in the city of New York is about $89,000; and the bankers in that city also held $9,670,751 of United States bonds, which is more than one-half of the amount of such bonds held by all of the private bankers of the country.

The following table shows, by geographical divisions, the number of private bankers in the United States, with the aggregate amount of their capital, deposits, and investments in United States bonds, for the six months ended May 31, 1881:

Geographical divisions.	Number of banks.	Capital.	Deposits.	Invested in U. S. bonds.
New England States	80	$4,698,782	$5,162,708	$1,067,652
Middle States	938	55,397,130	94,104,980	11,401,808
Southern States	258	5,588,828	17,323,504	263,780
Western States and Territories	1,762	27,639,115	125,254,362	3,937,254
United States	3,038	93,323,855	241,845,554	16,670,494

The table below is a recapitulation of the foregoing, showing by groups the aggregates for the bankers in the sixteen principal cities, in the thirty-one States and Territories having a private banking capital in excess of $100,000, and in the fifteen remaining States and Territories:

RECAPITULATION.

	Number of banks.	Capital.	Deposits.	Invested in U. S. bonds.
Principal cities	717	$58,534,300	$89,996,545	$12,370,012
Principal States and Territories	2,255	34,169,435	148,178,652	4,227,815
Remaining States and Territories	66	620,120	3,670,357	72,667
United States	3,038	93,323,855	241,845,554	16,670,494

STATE BANKS, SAVINGS BANKS, AND TRUST COMPANIES.

The act of Congress of February 19, 1873, section 333 of the Revised Statutes, requires the Comptroller to obtain from authentic sources, and to report to Congress, statements exhibiting under appropriate heads the resources and liabilities of such banks and savings banks as are organized under the laws of the several States and Territories. In compliance with this act he has presented annually in the appendices to his reports the resources and liabilities of these corporations, so far as it has been possible to obtain them.

Through the courtesy of State officers, returns of State banks, savings banks, and trust and loan companies have during the past year been received from twenty-three States. Many of the States and Territories, including Illinois, Nebraska, Dakota, Oregon, Virginia, and Tennessee, do not require periodical returns of the condition of the different classes of banks organized under their laws.

STATE BANKS AND TRUST COMPANIES.

From these returns the following abstract has been compiled, showing the resources and liabilities of State banks and trust companies for the last two years, the number reporting in 1880 being 650, and in 1881 683:

	1880.	1881.
RESOURCES.		
Loans and discounts	$281,496,731	$352,725,986
Overdrafts	597,690	1,407,695
United States bonds	26,252,182	27,680,025
Other stocks, bonds, &c	35,661,792	42,330,957
Due from banks	40,340,345	54,662,829
Real estate	19,489,086	21,396,772
Other assets	7,374,037	11,941,741
Expenses	979,492	1,136,427
Cash items	11,176,592	16,900,762
Specie	6,905,977	17,925,628
Legal tenders, bank-notes, &c	51,500,226	27,301,317
Total	481,774,159	575,500,139
LIABILITIES.		
Capital stock	109,318,451	112,111,325
Circulation	283,308	274,941
Surplus fund	25,008,431	27,857,976
Undivided profits	10,774,731	12,237,320
Dividends unpaid	486,094	576,413
Deposits	298,759,619	373,632,632
Due to banks	18,613,936	19,105,664
Other liabilities	18,530,189	30,303,868
Total	481,774,159	575,500,139

The foregoing table was prepared from returns from five New England States, exclusive of Maine, which has but one State bank in operation; from four Middle States, not including Delaware; and from all the Western States excepting Illinois, Kansas, and Nebraska. The only Southern States represented therein are South Carolina, Georgia, Louisiana, Texas, and Kentucky. The only Pacific State is California. There is but one State bank in New Hampshire, six in Vermont, and none in Massachusetts. There are, however, five trust and loan companies in the latter State, and ten in Connecticut.

SAVINGS BANKS.

The following table exhibits the aggregate resources and liabilities of 629 savings banks in 1880 and in 1881:

	1880.	1881.
RESOURCES.		
Loans on real estate	$315,273,232	$307,096,158
Loans on personal and collateral security	70,175,090	95,817,641
United States bonds	187,413,220	210,845,514
State, municipal, and other bonds and stocks	150,440,359	153,819,912
Railroad bonds and stocks	20,705,378	27,069,018
Bank stock	32,225,923	33,249,203
Real estate	39,038,502	41,987,674
Other assets	27,053,452	37,408,163
Expenses	216,423	135,572
Due from banks	22,063,091	40,663,641
Cash	17,072,680	13,758,106
Total	881,677,350	967,790,662
LIABILITIES.		
Deposits	819,106,973	891,961,142
Surplus fund	51,226,472	60,289,905
Undivided profits	4,740,861	10,325,800
Other liabilities	6,603,044	5,213,815
Total	881,677,350	967,790,662

The foregoing table includes the returns from the six New England States, from four Middle States, not including Delaware, from the State of California, and from three other States and the District of Columbia. The aggregate of loans in the New England States is $230,239,027, and of deposits $403,304,135. In the Middle States the aggregate of loans is $130,204,828, and of deposits $424,212,944.

Some of the largest savings banks in the city of Philadelphia, organized under old charters, are not required to make reports to any State officer. Returns received directly from four of these banks, having deposits amounting to $26,895,295, are included in the returns for the State of Pennsylvania.

The savings-bank deposits given in the foregoing table for 1881, based on reports made to the State authorities, are $891,961,142, and the deposits of the State banks and trust companies were $373,032,632. These deposits do not include bank deposits. The deposits of the national banks on October 1, 1881, exclusive of those due to banks, were $1,086,942,470. These deposits of the national banks bear to those of the savings banks the proportion, nearly, of 55 to 45, to those of the State banks and trust companies the proportion of 74 to 26, and to the combined deposits of both the proportion of 46 to 54.

The total population of New England, according to the census of 1880, is 4,010,529, and the number of open deposit accounts in the savings banks is 1,227,899; which is equal to 30.6 accounts to each one hundred of the entire population. The average amount of each account is $328.45; and if the total deposits were divided among the entire population, the average sum of $100.56 could be given to each individual.

The deposits of the savings banks in the State of New York were $353,629,657, while the population is 5,082,871; showing that an equal distribution of the savings-bank deposits among the entire population of the State would give $69.57 to each individual.

Tables showing the aggregate resources and liabilities of State banks, trust companies and savings banks, in each State from which returns turns have been received from the State authorities, appear in the appendix.

SECURITY FOR CIRCULATING NOTES.

During the past year there has been much change in the classes of United States bonds which the national banks have on deposit to secure their circulation, owing to the redemption or continuation of the five and six per cent. bonds of 1881. The classes and amount of these bonds held by the Treasurer on the 1st day of November, 1881, are exhibited in the following table:

Class of bonds.	Authorizing act.	Rate of interest.	Amount.
Ten-forties of 1864 (interest ceased).	March 3, 1864	5 per cent.	$50,000
Funded loan of 1881 (interest ceased).	July 14, 1870, and January 20, 1871	5 ...do	708,900
Funded loan of 1891	......do.........	4½ ..do	31,981,650
Funded loan of 1907	......do......do.........	4 ..do	92,005,800
Loan of July and August, 1861, continued.	July 17 and August 5, 1861	3½. do	36,040,650
Loan of 1863, continued ($1s)	March 3, 1863	3½ ..do	17,700,950
Funded loan of 1881, continued	July 14, 1870, and January 20, 1871	3½. do	187,634,550
Pacific Railway bonds	July 1, 1862, and July 2, 1864	6 ..do	3,486,000
Total			369,608,500

The total amount of bonds held for the purpose of securing circulation on October 1, 1865, was $276,260,550, of which $199,397,950 was in 6 per cent. and $76,852,600 in 5 per cent. bonds. On November 1, 1880, the banks held $56,605,150 of six per cents, and $147,079,750 of 5 per cents.

On November 1, 1881, all of these bonds had been called, and, with the exception of $758,900, on which interest had ceased, had been redeemed, or extended at the rate of 3½ per cent. The banks now hold $31,981,650 of 4½ per cents, and $92,005,800 of 4 per cent. bonds. They hold also $3,486,000 of Pacific Railroad bonds, and $758,900 called bonds on which interest has ceased. The remainder, $245,601,050, consists of bonds bearing interest at the rate of 3½ per cent. The average rate of interest now paid by the United States upon the bonds deposited as security for circulating notes is about 3.7 per cent. upon their par value. The amount of interest paid is equal to about 3½ per cent. only of the current market value of the bonds.

SPECIE IN BANK AND IN THE TREASURY OF THE UNITED STATES, AND ESTIMATED AMOUNT IN THE COUNTRY—SPECIE IN THE BANK OF ENGLAND, AND IN THE BANK OF FRANCE.

The following table exhibits the amounts of specie held by the national banks at the dates of their reports for the last eight years, the coin and coin certificates held by the New York City banks being stated separately:

Dates.	Held by national banks in New York City.				Held by other national banks.	Aggregate.
	Coin.	U. S. gold certificates.	Clearing-house certificates.	Total.		
Oct. 3, 1872..	$920,767 37	$5,454,580	....	$6,375,347 37	$3,854,409 42	$10,229,756 79
Dec. 27, 1872..	1,396,091 05	12,471,940	....	13,778,031 05	5,209,305 40	19,047,336 45
Feb. 28, 1873..	1,958,769 86	11,539,780	....	13,498,541 86	4,279,123 67	17,777,673 53
Apr. 25, 1873..	1,344,950 93	11,743,320	....	13,088,259 93	3,780,557 81	16,868,808 74
June 13, 1873..	1,442,097 71	22,139,080	....	23,581,177 71	4,368,909 01	27,950,086 72
Sept. 12, 1873..	1,063,210,55	13,522,600	....	14,585,810 55	5,282,658 90	19,868,469 45
Dec. 26, 1873..	1,376,170 50	18,325,760	....	19,701,930 50	7,205,107 08	26,907,037 58
Feb. 27, 1874..	1,167,820 09	23,518,640	....	24,686,460 09	8,679,403 49	33,365,863 58
May 1, 1874..	1,530,282 10	23,454,660	....	24,984,942 10	7,585,027 16	32,569,969 26
June 26, 1874..	1,842,525 00	13,671,660	....	15,514,185 00	6,812,022 27	22,326,207 27
Oct. 2, 1874..	1,291,786 56	13,114,480	....	14,406,266 56	6,834,678 67	21,240,945 23
Dec. 31, 1874..	1,443,215 42	14,410,940	....	15,854,155 42	6,582,605 62	22,436,761 04
Mar. 1, 1875..	1,084,555 54	10,622,160	....	11,706,715 54	4,960,390 63	16,667,106 17
May 1, 1875..	930,105 76	5,752,600	....	6,683,325 76	3,937,035 88	10,620,361 64
June 30, 1875..	1,023,015 86	12,642,180	....	13,665,195 86	5,294,386 44	18,959,582 30
Oct. 1, 1875..	753,904 90	4,201,720	....	4,955,624 90	3,094,704 83	8,050,329 73
Dec. 17, 1875..	860,436 72	12,532,810	....	13,402,246 72	3,668,659 18	17,070,905 90
Mar. 10, 1876..	3,261,131 36	19,086,920	....	22,348,051 36	6,729,294 40	29,077,345 85
May 12, 1876..	832,313 70	15,183,760	....	16,016,073 70	5,698,520 66	21,714,594 36
June 30, 1876..	1,214,522 92	16,872,780	....	18,087,302 92	7,131,167 00	25,218,469 92
Oct. 2, 1876..	1,120,814 34	13,404,760	....	14,576,574 34	6,785,079 69	21,361,654 03
Dec. 22, 1876..	1,434,701 83	21,602,900	....	23,037,601 83	9,962,046 06	32,999,647 89
Jan. 20, 1877..	1,669,284 94	33,629,660	....	35,298,944 94	14,410,322 61	40,709,267 55
Apr. 14, 1877..	1,930,725 59	13,889,180	....	15,829,905 59	11,240,132 19	27,070,037 78
June 22, 1877..	1,423,258 17	10,324,320	....	11,747,578 17	9,588,417 89	21,335,996 06
Oct. 1, 1877..	1,538,486 47	11,409,920	....	12,948,406 47	9,710,413 84	22,658,820 31
Dec. 28, 1877..	1,955,746 20	19,119,080	....	21,074,826 20	11,832,924 50	32,907,750 70
Mar. 15, 1878..	2,428,797 44	35,003,220	....	37,432,017 44	17,290,040 58	54,722,058 02
May 1, 1878..	2,688,092 06	25,397,640	....	28,085,732 06	17,938,024 00	46,023,756 06
June 29, 1878..	1,905,705 22	11,954,500	....	13,860,205 22	15,391,264 55	29,251,469 77
Oct. 1, 1878..	1,779,792 43	11,514,810	....	13,294,602 43	17,394,004 16	30,688,606 59
Dec. 6, 1878..	4,009,299 01	12,277,180	....	16,286,479 01	18,068,771 35	34,355,250 36
Jan. 1, 1879..	5,421,552 49	12,739,544	....	18,161,092 49	23,338,664 83	41,499,757 32
Apr. 4, 1879..	5,312,966 90	12,220,040	....	17,533,006 90	23,614,656 51	41,148,563 41
June 14, 1879..	6,058,472 34	12,291,270	....	18,349,742 34	23,983,545 10	42,333,287 44
Oct. 2, 1879..	7,218,967 69	12,130,900	....	19,349,867 69	22,823,873 54	42,173,731 23
Dec. 12, 1879..	20,096,249 64	8,366,140	$21,569,000 00	50,031,389 64	28,981,651 95	79,013,041 59
Feb. 21, 1880..	12,252,541 44	7,464,650	35,855,000 00	55,572,191 44	33,869,860 31	89,442,051 75
Apr. 23, 1880..	12,505,720 49	6,914,250	25,458,000 00	44,867,970 49	41,461,761 72	86,329,732 21
June 11, 1880..	16,682,226 40	7,810,200	33,337,000 00	57,829,426 40	41,677,078 86	99,506,505 26
Oct. 1, 1880..	16,104,855 28	7,489,700	36,189,000 00	59,783,555 38	49,562,954 11	109,346,509 49
Dec. 31, 1880..	19,773,859 01	6,709,900	28,246,000 00	54,729,759 01	52,443,141 91	107,172,900 92
Mar. 11, 1881..	15,924,683 90	4,825,300	30,809,000 00	51,558,983 90	53,607,211 36	105,156,195 26
May 6, 1881..	26,242,108 60	4,625,900	34,176,000 00	65,044,008 60	57,584,553 48	122,628,562 03
June 30, 1881..	20,822,790 87	4,513,400	41,858,000 00	67,194,190 87	61,444,736 63	128,638,927 50
Oct. 1, 1881..	15,317,168 04	4,486,600	31,721,000 00	51,524,768 04	62,809,968 08	114,334,736 12

The issue of gold certificates was authorized by the fifth section of the act March 3, 1863, and they were used for clearing-house purposes soon after the passage of the National Bank Act. The first issue was made on November 13, 1865. On June 30, 1875, there were outstanding $21,796,300, of which the national banks in New York City held $12,642,180. The issue of these certificates was discontinued on December 1, 1878, and the amount outstanding had decreased on June 30, 1879, to $15,413,700, and on October 1, 1880, to $7,480,100. The issue of these certificates having been discontinued by the government, and the amount of gold coin having rapidly increased, the banks in New York found it necessary to establish a depository of gold coin, for the convenience of the clearing-house. This depository, at the present time, is the Bank of America, by which bank certificates of deposit were first issued on October 14, 1879. The amount of such certificates outstanding on November 1, 1879, was $9,155,000, on January 1, 1880, $25,610,000, and on June 1 following, $39,550,000. The amount held by the national banks in New York City on June 30, 1881, was $41,858,000; and on October 1, $31,721,000.

The clearing-houses of Boston, Philadelphia and Baltimore have organized similar depositories, in order to utilize their gold coin, and to save the risk and inconvenience of handling and transporting it. The total amount of such certificates held by the national banks in New York on October 1 was $31,721,000; by those in Philadelphia, $5,325,000; in Boston, $4,919,000; and in Baltimore, $1,095,000; total, $43,090,000.

The national banks held silver coin amounting, on October 1, 1877, to $3,700,703, and on October 1, 1878, to $5,392,628. On October 2, 1879, the amount held was $4,986,493, and on October 1, 1880, it was $6,495,477, including $1,165,120 in silver treasury certificates. On October 1, of the present year, the official reports of the State banks in New England, New York, New Jersey, Pennsylvania, Maryland, Louisiana, Ohio, Indiana, Iowa, Wisconsin, Missouri, and Minnesota, show that these banks then held specie amounting to $9,019,500, of which the banks in New York City held $4,985,820. The official returns from the State banks of California do not give separately the amount of coin held by them; but the bank commissioners of that State estimate that of the total cash reported, amounting to $11,276,000, $10,846,672 consisted of coin. The amount of coin held by State banks in the States before mentioned, including California, was, therefore, $19,866,172.

The Director of the Mint, in his report for 1880, estimates the amount of coin in the country on June 30, 1880, at $501,555,711, of which $358,958,691 was gold and $142,597,020 was silver. His estimate for the fiscal year ending June 30, 1881, is as follows:

Amount of coin in the country June 30, 1880	$501,555,711
Net gold coinage for the year	78,293,087
Net silver coinage for the year	27,642,660
Net importation of gold for the year	5,824,975
Net importation of silver for the year	1,295,086
Total amount of coin June 30, 1881	614,611,519

Of this amount the Director estimates that there was used in the arts $3,300,000 of gold, and $75,000 of silver, making a total of $3,375,000. If this be deducted from the total given above, it will make the amount in circulation on July 1, 1881, $611,236,519, of which $439,776,753 was in gold, and $171,459,766 in silver. From July 1, 1881, to November 1, the Director estimates that there was added to the coin $28,716,474 of gold

4 C C

and $9,640,858 of silver, making the stock of coin in the country at the latter date $649,563,851, of which $468,493,227 was gold and $181,070,624 was silver.

The amount of bullion in the mint and in the New York assay office on November 1 is stated to have been $94,075,744 of gold and $4,966,741 of silver, making in all $99,042,485; which, added to the estimated amount of coin stated above, gives $748,606,336, of which amount $562,568,971 was gold and $186,037,365 was silver.

The following table shows the amount of gold and silver, including the amount held to protect gold and silver certificates, and the percentage of each, in the Treasury of the United States, on September 30 of each year from 1876 to 1881, and on November 1, 1881:

Period.	Silver.			Gold coin and bullion.	Total coin and bullion.	Per cent. of—	
	Standard dollars.	Other coin and bullion.	Total silver.			Silver.	Gold.
September 30, 1876	$6,029,367	$6,029,367	$55,423,059	$61,452,426	9.8	90.2
September 30, 1877		7,425,454	7,425,454	107,039,529	114,464,983	6.5	93.5
September 30, 1878	$12,155,205	15,777,937	27,933,142	136,036,302	163,969,444	17.0	83.0
September 30, 1879	31,806,774	21,173,023	52,979,797	169,827,571	222,807,368	23.8	76.2
September 30, 1880	47,784,744	30,878,286	78,663,030	135,641,450	214,304,480	36.7	63.3
September 30, 1881	66,092,667	28,945,297	96,037,964	174,361,343	269,399,307	35.3	64.7
November 1, 1881	66,576,378	29,409,262	95,985,640	172,989,829	268,975,469	35.7	64.3

The bullion in the Bank of England for each year from 1870 to 1881 is shown in the following table, the pound sterling being estimated at five dollars:

1870	$103,900,000	1876	$143,500,000
1871	117,950,000	1877	126,850,000
1872	112,900,000	1878	119,300,600
1873	113,500,000	1879 *	150,942,980
1874	111,450,000	1880 †	141,637,000
1875	119,600,000	1881 †	115,221,870

Below is a similar table, giving the amount of gold and silver, and the percentage of each, in the Bank of France, on December 31 of each year‡ from 1870 to 1880, and on November 10, 1881, five francs being estimated at one dollar:

Years.	Silver coin and bullion.	Gold coin and bullion.	Total.	Per cent. of	
				Silver.	Gold.
December 31, 1870	$13,700,000	$85,740,000	$99,440,000	13.8	86.2
December 31, 1871	16,240,000	110,680,000	126,920,000	12.8	87.2
December 31, 1872	26,520,000	131,740,000	158,260,000	16.8	83.
December 31, 1873	31,260,000	122,260,000	153,520,000	20.4	79.6
December 31, 1874	62,640,000	204,220,000	266,860,000	23.5	76.5
December 31, 1875	101,000,000	234,860,000	335,860,000	30.1	69.9
December 31, 1876	127,720,000	306,080,000	433,800,000	29.4	70.6
December 31, 1877	173,080,000	235,420,000	408,500,000	42.4	57.6
December 31, 1878	211,620,000	196,720,000	408,340,000	51.8	48.2
December 31, 1879	245,520,000	148,320,000	393,840,000	62.3	37.7
December 31, 1880	244,360,000	110,480,000	354,840,000	68.9	31.1
November 10, 1881	236,895,452	124,440,284	361,335,736	65.6	34.4

* London Economist, November 8, 1879.

† London Bankers' Magazine, October, 1880 and 1881.

‡ The Bulletin de Statistique, as quoted in the Bankers' Magazine, New York, vol. xiii, page 740; except the items for 1879,'80 and '81, which were obtained from the London Banker's Magazine for August, 1880, page 661, and September, 1881, page 716, and the last item from The London Economist, November 12, 1881.

NATIONAL-BANK FAILURES AND DIVIDENDS TO CREDITORS.

During the year ending November 1, 1881, no national banks have failed; but since that date, the Mechanic's National Bank of Newark, N. J., and the Pacific National Bank of Boston, Mass., have suspended, and the former bank has been placed in the hands of a receiver.

The affairs of twelve banks which failed prior to November 1, 1880, have, during the year, been finally closed, and final dividends have been paid to creditors. These banks with the total dividends paid, are given below :

	Total dividends.
Bethel, Conn., First National Bank	100 per cent. and interest.
Brattleboro', Vt., First National Bank	100 per cent. and interest in full.
Delphi, Ind., First National Bank	100 per cent. and interest in full.
Duluth, Minn., First National Bank	100 per cent. and interest in full.
Fort Scott, Kans., Merchant's National Bank	60 per cent.
Franklin, Ind., First National Bank	100 per cent. and interest in full.
Kansas City, Mo., First National Bank	100 per cent.
New Orleans, La., Crescent City National Bank	84.83 per cent.
Poultney, Vt., National Bank	100 per cent. and interest in full.
Saratoga, N. Y., Commercial National Bank	100 per cent. and interest in full.
Warrensburg, Mo., First National Bank	100 per cent. and interest in full.
Winchester, Ill., First National Bank	63.6 per cent.

Attention is called to the fact that nine of the twelve foregoing insolvent national banks, whose affairs have been closed during the past year, have paid in full the principal of the claims proved against them, and that eight of the nine have paid principal and interest, seven of them paying interest in full.

The following banks whose affairs are still in the hands of receivers paid dividends during the past year, as follows, the total dividends paid by them up to November 1 being also given :

Bozeman, Mont., First National Bank, 15 per cent.; total, 85 per cent.
Butler, Pa., First National Bank, 10 per cent.; total, 40 per cent.
Charlottesville, Va., Charlottesville National Bank, 5 per cent.; total, 55 per cent.
Chicago, Ill., City National Bank, 7 per cent.; total, 77 per cent.
Chicago, Ill., Third National Bank, 10 per cent.; total, 100 per cent.
Chicago, Ill., German National Bank, 25 per cent.; total, 80 per cent.
Fishkill, N. Y., National Bank, 15 per cent.; total 100 per cent.
Georgetown, Colo., Miners' National Bank, 30 per cent.; total, 65 per cent.
Helena, Mont., Peoples' National Bank, 15 per cent.; total, 30 per cent.
Lock Haven, Pa., Lock Haven National Bank, 10 per cent.; total, 90 per cent.
Meadville, Pa., First National Bank, 35 per cent.; total, 100 per cent.
Newark, N. J., First National Bank, 10 per cent.; total, 90 per cent.
Norfolk, Va., First National Bank, 4 per cent.; total, 49 per cent.
Saint Louis, Mo., National Bank of State of Missouri, 5 per cent.; total 95 per cent.
Scranton, Pa., Second National Bank, 25 per cent.; total, 25 per cent.
Washington, D. C., German-American National Bank, 20 per cent.; total, 40 per cent.

It will be noticed that three of the above banks have already paid the principal of their claims to creditors, and it is believed that they will also pay interest, either in part or in full. Of the banks given which have not paid 100 per cent., it is expected that many will do so, and they will perhaps pay interest, in addition.

The total amount of dividends paid by the Comptroller to the creditors of insolvent national banks during the year ending November 1, 1881, was $929,059.16. The total dividends paid to creditors of the 86 banks placed in the hands of receivers prior to November 1 amount to $18,561,698, upon approved claims amounting to $25,966,602. The dividends paid equal about 70 per cent. of the proved claims. Assessments amounting to $7,601,750 have been made upon the shareholders of insolvent national banks, for the purpose of enforcing their individual liability, of which about $3,000,000 has been collected, and nearly $400,000 of it within the past year.

A table showing the national banks which have been placed in the hands of receivers, the amount of their capital, of claims proved, and the rates of dividends paid, and, also, one showing the amount of circulation of such banks issued, redeemed, and outstanding, will be found in the Appendix.

TAXATION OF NATIONAL BANKS.

The Comptroller again respectfully repeats his recommendation for the repeal of the law imposing a tax upon bank capital and deposits, and the two-cent stamp upon bank checks.

The receipts of internal revenue show an increase of $10,447,763 for the fiscal year 1880, and a still further increase of $11,447,996 for 1881, the total increase during the whole period being more than twenty-one and a half millions. The increase of the receipts of the government from customs, internal revenue, and other sources during the year 1880 was $59,699,426, and for the two years named it was nearly 87 millions ($86,955,108). The expenditures of the government during the last fiscal year were less than for either of the two previous years, and the surplus revenue during the same period was more than 100 millions. The receipts for the four months ending November 1 last show a still further increase, and it is probable that the surplus revenue for the present year will be much greater than for any one that has preceded it. The whole amount of internal revenue collected by the Commissioner during the last fiscal year was $135,229,912, all of which, with the exception of $11,520,704, was derived from the tax on spirits, beer, and tobacco.

The amount paid by the national banks to the Treasurer of the United States, for taxes on capital and deposits, during the year ending June 30, 1881, was $5,372,178.22, and the amount paid by banks, other than national, to the Commissioner of Internal Revenue, under the law taxing bank capital and deposits, was $3,757,912. The value of the two-cent check stamps issued during the fiscal year was $2,366,081. The total amount of bank taxes which it is recommended should be abated is $11,496,171, which amount is much less than the annual increase of the internal revenue during the past two years. The receipts from taxes are largely increasing, while the expenditures of the government are largely decreasing, through the reduction of the public debt and of the interest thereon. The reason that has heretofore been urged against the abrogation of these laws—namely, that the amount produced was necessary for the support of the government and for the payment of the public debt—has long since lost its force. Their repeal has already been recommended, both by the Secretary of the Treasury and the Commissioner of Internal Revenue.

While in many of the States there may be a necessity for taxing banking capital and deposits, for purposes of revenue, this reason for retaining a war tax, in the case of the United States Government, has passed away. The rates of interest for money are gradually lessening, and the State taxes which the banks are compelled to pay are as much as should be imposed upon these great agencies for developing the manufacturing and commercial interests of the country. The Comptroller herewith presents tables which give, as far as can be ascertained, the amount of the banking capital of the country, the amount of United States and State taxes, and the rate of taxation paid by the national banks in every State and principal city in the Union for the year 1880.

The following table shows the amount of United States and State taxes, and the rate of taxation paid by the national banks, in every State and principal city of the Union for the year 1880:

States and Territories.	Capital.	Amount of taxes.			Ratios to capital.		
		United States.	State.	Total.	United States.	State.	Total.
					Per ct.	Per ct.	Per ct.
Maine	$10,435,000	$124,884	$228,263	$353,147	1.2	2.2	3.4
New Hampshire	5,827,830	70,523	97,720	168,243	1.2	1.7	2.9
Vermont	8,355,683	93,745	141,678	235,423	1.1	1.8	2.9
Massachusetts	44,995,010	569,299	819,389	1,388,688	1.3	1.8	3.1
Boston	50,500,000	813,080	943,219	1,756,299	1.6	1.9	3.5
Rhode Island	20,009,800	210,778	255,850	466,628	1.0	1.3	2.3
Connecticut	25,556,933	308,612	400,797	709,409	1.2	1.6	2.8
New England States	165,680,256	2,190,921	2,886,916	5,077,837	1.3	1.8	3.1
New York	32,847,771	561,912	590,085	1,151,997	1.7	1.9	3.6
New York City	50,650,000	1,580,926	1,459,209	3,040,135	2.1	2.9	6.0
Albany	1,800,000	55,398	57,124	112,522	3.1	3.2	6.3
New Jersey	13,147,917	225,397	241,937	467,334	1.7	1.9	3.6
Pennsylvania	28,969,856	465,380	182,124	647,504	1.6	0.7	2.3
Philadelphia	17,180,580	405,834	115,377	521,211	2.4	0.7	3.1
Pittsburgh	9,850,000	161,365	72,288	233,653	1.7	0.7	2.4
Delaware	1,761,677	28,573	7,423	35,996	1.6	0.4	2.0
Maryland	2,306,815	37,263	31,538	68,801	1.6	1.4	3.0
Baltimore	10,891,830	153,847	162,505	316,352	1.4	1.5	2.9
District of Columbia	252,000	4,837	3,910	8,747	1.9	1.6	3.5
Washington	1,125,000	16,513	4,428	20,941	1.5	0.4	1.9
Middle States	170,781,946	3,697,245	2,927,948	6,625,193	2.2	1.8	4.0
Virginia	2,866,000	55,892	51,270	107,162	2.0	2.0	4.0
West Virginia	1,780,795	25,033	26,835	51,868	1.4	1.7	3.1
North Carolina	2,501,000	34,459	32,477	66,936	1.4	1.4	2.8
South Carolina	2,324,900	32,299	55,185	87,484	1.4	2.5	3.9
Georgia	2,201,500	31,418	36,776	68,194	1.4	1.7	3.1
Florida	75,000	1,195	1,975	3,170	1.6	2.0	3.6
Alabama	1,518,000	20,054	32,754	52,808	1.3	2.2	3.5
New Orleans	2,875,000	56,992	4,851	61,843	2.0	0.2	2.2
Texas	1,267,042	19,248	17,548	36,796	1.5	2.0	3.5
Arkansas	205,000	3,546	2,750	6,296	1.7	1.3	3.0
Kentucky	7,151,135	92,417	41,088	133,505	1.3	0.6	1.9
Louisville	3,008,560	49,604	18,608	68,272	1.7	0.6	2.3
Tennessee	3,055,300	57,396	80,975	138,371	1.9	2.7	4.6
Southern States	30,829,178	479,613	403,092	882,705	1.6	1.4	3.0
Ohio	18,699,746	296,403	325,047	621,450	1.6	1.9	3.5
Cincinnati	4,225,000	96,157	94,722	190,879	2.3	2.3	4.6
Cleveland	3,700,000	54,013	60,362	114,375	1.4	1.6	3.0
Indiana	13,236,452	213,989	272,963	486,952	1.6	2.2	3.8
Illinois	10,714,600	199,573	180,842	380,415	1.9	1.8	3.7
Chicago	4,250,000	203,049	107,447	310,496	4.8	2.5	7.3
Michigan	7,384,851	114,968	115,216	230,184	1.6	1.7	3.3
Detroit	2,100,000	46,326	36,446	82,772	2.2	1.7	3.9
Wisconsin	2,425,000	48,903	43,332	92,235	2.0	1.9	3.9
Milwaukee	650,000	26,048	19,409	45,457	4.0	3.0	7.0
Iowa	5,793,813	103,810	121,676	225,486	1.8	2.1	3.9
Minnesota	4,901,552	76,613	81,289	157,902	1.6	1.8	3.4
Missouri	1,416,667	25,024	25,673	50,697	1.8	2.3	4.1
Saint Louis	2,650,000	62,407	64,089	126,496	2.4	2.5	4.9
Kansas	865,694	19,903	13,899	33,802	2.3	2.2	4.5
Nebraska	854,121	28,071	20,381	48,452	3.3	2.5	5.8
Colorado	1,070,000	51,853	28,645	80,498	4.9	2.8	7.
Nevada	30,874	340	184	524	1.1	0.4	1.5
California †	1,680,073	23,955	16,369	40,324	1.4	1.0	2.4
San Francisco †	1,500,000	17,325	102	17,427	1.2	0.0	1.2
Oregon	250,000	8,660	3,688	12,348	3.5	1.5	5.0
Dakota	376,722	7,587	5,430	13,017	2.0	1.7	3.7
Idaho	100,000	1,564	3,111	4,675	1.6	3.1	4.7
Montana	200,000	6,622	2,078	8,700	3.3	2.1	5.4
New Mexico	400,000	6,857	8,655	15,512	1.7	2.2	3.9
Utah	200,000	4,513	3,350	7,863	2.3	1.7	4.0
Washington	150,000	2,662	1,440	4,092	1.7	1.0	2.7
Wyoming	150,000	3,160	3,021	6,190	2.1	2.0	4.1
Western States and Territories	89,975,165	1,750,324	1,658,866	3,409,190	1.9	2.0	3.9
Totals	457,266,545	8,118,103	7,876,822	15,994,925	1.8	1.8	3.6

* The capital of the banks that reported State, county, and municipal taxes on stock and real estate
× $144,773,085.
† California banks pay no State taxes on capital, except on such as is invested in real estate.

Like tables for the years 1867 and 1869, and for the years 1874 to 1879, inclusive, may be found in the Appendix.

In order that the great inequality of the percentage of the United States and State taxes to the capital of national banks in the different geographical divisions of the country may be seen, tables have been prepared for the years 1879 and 1880, in which the capital stock invested and the percentage thereto of taxes paid is given, as follows:

1879.

Geographical divisions.	Capital.	Amount of taxes.			Ratios to capital.		
		United States.	State.	Total.	United States.	State.	Total.
New England States.....	$165,032.512	$1,942,269	$2,532,004	$4,474,213	1.2	1.5	2.7
Middle States............	170,431,205	3,190,113	2,936,269	6,126,382	1.9	1.7	3.6
Southern States..........	30,555,018	425,997	383,927	809,924	1.4	1.3	2.7
Western States and Terr's.	90,949,769	1,457,812	1,751,032	3,208,844	1.6	2.0	3.6
United States	456,968,504	7,016,131	7,603,232	14,619,363	1.5	1.7	3.2

1880.

New England States.....	$165,680,256	$2,190,921	$2,886,916	$5,077,837	1.3	1.8	3.1
Middle States............	170,781.946	3,697,245	2,927,948	6,025,193	2.2	1.8	4.0
Southern States...	30,829,178	479,613	403,092	882,705	1.6	1.4	3.0
Western States and Terr's.	89,975,165	1,750,324	1,658,866	3,409,190	1.9	2.0	3.9
United States......	457,266,545	8,118,103	7,876,822	15,994,925	1.8	1.8	3.6

The inequality in the percentages in United States taxes, which appears in the foregoing tables, arises from the fact that, while the United States tax is imposed on the three items of circulation, deposits, and capital, the percentages given in the tables are those of the total tax, derived from these three sources, to capital only. Where deposits and circulation are large in proportion to capital, the percentage of United States tax in the table is therefore greater; where the deposits and circulation are proportionately smaller, the percentage is less. The inequality in State taxes originates in an actual difference in the rates. The table below shows for the years 1878, 1879, and 1880 the great inequality in the rates in State taxation paid in the principal States in the country.

Cities.	1878.			1879.			1880.		
	United States.	State.	Total.	United States.	State.	Total.	United States.	State.	Total.
	Per ct.	Per. ct.	Per ct.	Per ct.	Per ct.	Per ct.	Per ct.	Per ct.	Per ct.
Boston	1.3	1.3	2.6	1.3	1.3	2.6	1.6	1.9	3.5
New York...............	2.2	2.9	5.1	2.6	2.9	5.5	3.1	2.9	6.0
Albany...................	2.8	2.8	5.6	2.9	2.5	5.4	3.1	3.2	6.3
Philadelphia	2.0	0.7	2.7	2.1	0.7	2.8	2.4	0.7	3.1
Pittsburgh	1.3	0.5	1.8	1.4	0.6	2.0	1.7	0.7	2.4
Baltimore	1.2	1.8	3.0	1.2	1.3	2.5	1.4	1.5	2.9
Washington	1.4	0.6	2.0	1.4	0.4	1.8	1.5	0.4	1.9
New Orleans	1.5	1.0	2.5	1.7	0.5	2.2	2.0	0.2	2.2
Louisville................	1.4	0.5	1.9	1.5	0.6	2.1	1.7	0.6	2.3
Cincinnati	1.5	2.7	4.2	1.9	2.4	4.3	2.3	2.3	4.6
Cleveland................	1.1	2.0	3.1	1.3	2.0	3.3	1.4	1.6	3.0
Chicago..................	2.5	2.6	5.1	3.4	2.4	5.8	4.8	2.5	7.3
Detroit..................	1.7	1.5	3.2	1.8	2.2	4.0	2.2	1.7	3.9
Milwaukee...............	2.4	2.6	5.0	2.8	2.5	5.3	4.0	3.0	7.0
Saint Louis	1.6	2.4	4.0	1.8	2.1	3.9	2.4	2.5	4.9
Saint Paul	1.3	1.5	2.8	1.5	1.5	3.0	1.7	1.8	3.5

The tables already given indicate the necessity of some precise rule of State taxation. The States in which the rates of taxation were most excessive during the years 1878, 1879, and 1880 are given in the following table:

States.	1878.			1879.			1880.		
	United States.	State.	Total.	United States.	State.	Total.	United States.	State.	Total.
	Per ct.	Per ct.	Per ct.	Per ct.	Per ct.	Per ct.	Per ct.	Per ct.	Per ct.
New York	2.0	2.6	4.6	1.5	2.0	3.5	1.7	1.9	3.6
New Jersey	1.4	1.8	3.2	1.5	1.8	3.3	1.7	1.9	3.6
Ohio	1.3	2.2	3.5	1.4	2.0	3.4	1.6	1.9	3.5
Indiana	1.3	2.1	3.4	1.4	2.1	3.5	1.6	2.2	3.8
Illinois	1.7	2.1	3.8	1.5	1.8	3.3	1.9	1.8	3.7
Wisconsin	1.7	2.2	3.9	1.6	1.8	3.4	2.0	1.9	3.9
Kansas	1.6	2.6	4.2	2.1	2.7	4.8	2.3	2.2	4.5
Nebraska	2.3	2.6	4.9	2.6	2.6	5.2	3.3	2.5	5.8
South Carolina	1.0	2.1	3.1	1.2	2.0	3.2	1.4	2.5	3.9
Tennessee	1.6	2.1	3.7	1.7	1.8	3.5	1.9	2.7	4.6

The national banks, under present law, pay to the United States a tax of one per cent. upon the amount of their notes in circulation, one-half of one per cent. upon the amount of their deposits, and the same rate upon the average amount of capital beyond the amount invested in United States bonds. These taxes are paid semi-annually by the national banks to Treasurer the of the United States.

The following table shows the amount annually paid under this law, from the commencement of the national banking system to July 1, 1881, showing an aggregate of taxes paid to the United States, by national banks, of $108,855,021.90:

Years.	On circulation.	On deposits.	On capital.	Total.
1864	$53,193 32	$95,911 87	$18,432 07	$167,537 26
1865	733,247 59	1,087,530 86	133,251 15	1,954,029 60
1866	2,106,785 30	2,633,102 77	406,947 74	5,146,835 81
1867	2,868,636 78	2,650,180 09	321,881 36	5,840,698 23
1868	2,946,343 07	2,564,143 44	306,781 67	5,817,268 18
1869	2,957,416 73	2,614,553 58	312,918 68	5,884,888 99
1870	2,949,744 13	2,614,767 61	375,962 26	5,940,474 00
1871	2,987,021 69	2,802,840 85	385,292 13	6,175,154 67
1872	3,193,570 63	3,120,984 37	389,356 27	6,703,910 67
1873	3,353,186 13	3,196,503 29	454,891 51	7,004,646 93
1874	3,404,483 11	3,209,967 72	469,048 02	7,083,498 85
1875	3,283,450 89	3,514,285 30	507,417 76	7,305,134 04
1876	3,091,795 76	3,505,129 64	632,296 16	7,229,221 56
1877	2,900,957 53	3,451,965 38	660,784 90	7,013,707 81
1878	2,948,047 08	3,273,111 74	560,296 83	6,781,455 65
1879	3,009,647 16	3,309,668 90	401,920 61	6,721,236 67
1880	3,153,625 63	4,058,710 61	379,424 19	7,591,770 43
1881	3,121,374 33	4,910,945 12	431,233 10	8,493,552 55
Aggregates	49,062,536 26	52,611,319 23	7,148,136 41	108,855,021 90

The amount of tax paid upon circulation alone is $49,062,536, while the whole cost to the government of the national system, since its establishment in 1863, has been but $5,148,649.01.

The banks, other than national, pay taxes to the United States on account of their circulation, deposits and capital, at the same rates as are paid by the national banks; but these taxes, instead of being paid to the Treasurer, are collected by the Commissioner of Internal Revenue.

The table below exhibits the taxes which have been paid by these banks for the years from 1864 to 1881, inclusive. The amounts given under the head of tax on circulation have, for a number of years, been principally derived from the tax of ten per cent. upon State bank circulation paid out. The whole amount of tax paid by these banks is $61,540,471.63:

Years.	On circulation.	On deposits.	On capital.	Totals.
1864	$2,056,996 30	$780,723 52	...	$2,837,719 82
1865	1,993,661 84	2,043,841 08	$903,367 98	4,940,870 90
1866	990,278 11	2,099,635 83	374,074 11	3,463,988 05
1867	214,298 75	1,355,395 98	476,867 73	2,046,562 46
1868	28,669 88	1,438,512 77	399,562 90	1,866,745 55
1869	16,565 05	1,734,417 63	445,071 49	2,196,054 17
1870	15,419 94	2,177,576 46	827,087 21	3,020,083 61
1871	22,781 92	2,702,196 84	919,262 77	3,644,241 53
1872	8,919 82	3,643,251 71	976,057 61	4,628,229 14
1873	24,778 62	3,009,302 79	736,950 05	3,771,031 46
1874	16,738 26	2,453,544 26	916,878 15	3,387,160 67
1875	22,746 27	2,972,260 27	1,102,241 58	4,097,248 12
1876	17,947 67	2,999,530 75	989,219 61	4,006,698 03
1877	5,430 16	2,896,637 93	927,661 24	3,829,729 33
1878	1,118 72	2,593,687 29	897,225 84	3,492,031 85
1879	13,903 29	2,354,911 74	830,068 56	3,198,883 59
1880	28,773 37	2,510,775 43	811,436 48	3,350,985 28
1881	4,295 08	2,946,906 64	811,006 35	3,762,208 07
Aggregates	5,483,323 05	42,713,108 92	13,344,039 66	61,540,471 63

From returns heretofore received, the following condensed table has been prepared, which shows the taxes, both National and State, paid by the national banks during each year from 1866 to 1880, inclusive, and their ratios to capital:

Years.	Capital stock.	Amount of taxes.			Ratio of tax to capital.		
		United States.	State.	Total.	United States.	State.	Total.
					Per ct.	Per ct.	Per ct.
1866	$410,593,435	$7,949,451	$8,069,938	$16,019,389	1.9	2.0	3.9
1867	422,804,666	9,525,607	8,813,127	18,338,734	2.2	2.1	4.3
1868	420,143,491	9,465,652	8,757,656	18,223,308	2.2	2.1	4.3
1869	419,619,860	10,081,244	7,297,096	17,378,340	2.4	1.7	4.1
1870	429,314,041	10,190,682	7,465,675	17,656,357	2.4	1.7	4.1
1871	451,994,133	10,649,895	7,860,078	18,509,973	2.4	1.7	4.1
1872	472,956,958	6,703,910	8,343,772	15,047,682	1.4	1.8	3.2
1873	488,778,418	7,004,646	8,499,748	15,504,394	1.4	1.8	3.2
1874	493,751,679	7,256,083	9,620,326	16,876,409	1.5	2.0	3.5
1875	503,687,911	7,317,531	10,058,122	17,375,653	1.5	2.0	3.5
1876	501,788,079	7,076,087	9,701,732	16,777,819	1.4	2.0	3.4
1877	485,250,694	6,902,573	8,829,304	15,731,877	1.4	1.9	3.3
1878	471,061,238	6,727,232	8,056,533	14,783,765	1.4	1.7	3.1
1879	456,968,504	7,016,131	7,603,232	14,619,363	1.5	1.7	3.2
1880	457,266,546	8,118,103	7,876,822	15,994,925	1.8	1.8	3.6

These statistics show that during the fifteen years covered by the table the average amount annually paid by the national banks to the States and to the United States was $16,589,199, or more than 3½ per cent. upon their capital stock; during the last year given, the total amount paid was $15,994,925, or more than 4 per cent. upon the amount of the average circulation of the banks then in operation.

STATE TAXATION OF NATIONAL BANKS.

The United States Supreme Court, in the case of The People ex rel. Williams vs. Weaver, at the October term in 1879, decided that the States have no right to assess the shares of national banks located within their borders, for purposes of taxation, at a greater rate or valuation than other moneyed capital in the hands of individuals is assessed; and that an individual in New York, holding bank shares, has the same right to deduct his just debts from the amount of his bank shares as he would have to deduct them from his personal property, including his moneyed capital. The Supreme Court also pointed out the method of relief for national banks to pursue when taxes are assessed upon them at a greater rate than is assessed upon other moneyed capital in the same State, such method being to enjoin the collection of excessive taxes.

In November, 1880, it was decided by the United States circuit court of the northern district of the State of New York, in the case of the Albany Exchange Bank vs. Charles A. Hills et al., that the law of the State of New York, under authority of which taxes had been assessed for fourteen years upon bank shares, was void and invalid, for the reason that this act did not permit the owners of bank shares to reduce their assessment by the amount of their debts, while owners of other moneyed capital possessed that privilege under the general statutes of the State. As soon as this decision was known, injunctions were obtained by nearly every bank in New York City, restraining the collection of taxes imposed by State authority upon the shareholders of those banks. The collection of over $1,700,000 was thus enjoined. The question involved was appealed to the Supreme Court of the United States.

Since my last annual report, two acts have been passed by the New York State legislature, to establish a system of taxation. One of them expressly permitted the deduction of debts, in the assessment of shares of banks organized under the authority of the State or of the United States. In the second act the taxation of corporations generally was provided for, excluding banks and some other corporations.

Although the first act apparently removed the objection which existed to the former State law taxing National and State banks, yet it did not provide against the unjust and discriminating valuation of the shares of banks, as compared with the valuation of real estate and of other personal property. After considerable discussion the majority of the banks in the Clearing-House Association of New York have decided to pay the tax imposed under this law for the year 1881, notwithstanding this objection to it.

During the year there have been two important decisions in reference to taxation of national-bank shares rendered in the United States circuit court for the northern district of the State of New York. The first was in the case of the New York State National Bank of Albany vs. W. J. Maher, where the court held that the assessments against the shareholders of the bank were absolutely void, for the reason that the assessors did not place the names of the shareholders, with the number of their shares and the assessable value of the same, upon the regular assessment-roll, but upon a list separate therefrom.

The second decision was in a suit brought by the First National Bank of Utica against the State tax-collector, to test the effect of the acts which provided for the taxation of corporations generally.

The amount of the tax imposed by the law mentioned, in all cases other than those of banks and certain specified corporations, was at a rate much less than the rates of local taxation in many parts of the State, and less than that imposed upon the shares of banks. In this suit it was decided that Congress did not intend to prohibit the State from taxing its own corporations more lightly than shares in national banks, provided that the latter class of property was not assessed more heavily than other moneyed capital in the hands of individuals.

A suit was brought by the Evansville National Bank, in the United States circuit court of the State of Indiana, in order to test the validity of the statutes of that State, directing the assessment of bank shares. It was held by the bank that these statutes are void, because they do not grant to the owners of bank shares the privilege of deducting their just debts from the assessed valuation of such shares, while under the general statutes of the State that right was granted to the owners of other moneyed capital. Justice Harlan, of the United States Supreme Court, recently decided in this suit that the law of Indiana "enforces in certain cases a rule of taxation inconsistent with the principle of equality underlying the legislation of Congress, and conformity to which is essential to the validity of State taxation of national bank shares." He decides that every shareholder of a national bank, who, at the time of assessment, had debts, and no credits from which he could deduct the same, except national bank shares, from which the State laws did not permit him to make such deduction, is entitled, through the bank, to an injunction against the tax assessed upon the shares.

As it is in the power of the States, under the present law of Congress, so to legislate that through unequal valuations bank shares may be discriminated against as compared with other moneyed capital in the hands of corporations or individuals, a necessity appears to exist that, in order to avoid protracted and expensive litigation, Congress shall so amend the present law that there can be no doubt as to the precise amount of taxation which may be imposed by the States on national bank shares.

In my last annual report a suggestion was made in reference to the amendment of section 5219, Revised Statutes of the United States. It is now again recommended that the section named shall be amended to read as follows :

But the legislature of each State may determine and direct the manner and place of taxing the shares of national banking associations located within the State, subject to the following restrictions, namely: That the maximum rate of tax shall not exceed —— per cent.; that the rate, and the valuation upon which such rate is calculated shall not exceed the least rate and valuation to which other moneyed capital, in the hands of individuals, or of corporations of any class, in such State is subjected, and that the shares of any national banking association, owned by a non-resident of any State, shall be taxed in the State or town in which the bank is located, and not elsewhere.

If such an amendment becomes a law it will, in a great measure, prevent the various forms of discrimination which have been exercised in the imposition and collection of taxes upon national bank shares, under State authority. The Supreme Court of the United States has decided that, without the permission of Congress, the States would have no right to impose any taxes whatever upon national banks, and that in enacting the law under which the States now exercise this right, Congress was conferring a power on the States which they would not otherwise have had. This court also decided that it was the evident intention of Congress to protect the banks from anything beyond their equal share of the public burdens. Congress has therefore the power wholly to rescind the right granted to the States to tax national banking associations. This, however, is not asked or desired. But, inasmuch as it has been the tendency of legislation in different States to disregard, or render inoperative, the provisions of the act of Congress permitting and restricting State taxation of national bank shares, it is certainly not too much to expect that Congress will regard it as due to themselves to pass such amendments as will carry out the intention of their original act, clearly defined and sustained as it has been by the decisions of the Supreme Court of the United States.

LOSSES, SURPLUS, EARNINGS AND DIVIDENDS OF THE NATIONAL BANKS.

During the year ending September 1, 1881, the national banks charged off losses amounting to $12,691,349.75. Of this, $5,889,761.19 was charged off during the six months ending March 1, 1881, and $6,801,588.56 during the similar period ending September 1, 1881. The following table shows the number of banks that charged off these losses, and the amount so charged off by them, in each State and reserve city throughout the United States, for the two semi-annual periods ending March 1 and September 1, 1881, respectively. The total losses charged off in each of the four preceding years have been added to the table. Full tables for the five previous years may be found in the Appendix:

States and Territories.	March 1, 1881.		September 1, 1881.		Aggregate.
	No. of banks.	Losses.	No. of banks.	Losses.	
Maine	37	$77,806 40	39	$81,689 17	$159,495 57
New Hampshire	24	99,725 42	29	123,014 54	222,739 96
Vermont	23	126,093 71	29	155,990 86	282,084 57
Massachusetts	96	240,971 17	108	439,978 14	680,949 31
Boston	35	280,815 43	34	420,239 30	701,054 73
Rhode Island	27	566,227 60	25	247,484 81	813,712 41
Connecticut	43	193,035 40	54	238,940 77	431,976 17
New York	128	441,955 39	136	579,034 66	1,020,990 05
New York City	36	989,797 57	38	1,331,205 05	2,321,002 62
Albany	6	40,960 64	6	46,262 49	87,223 13
New Jersey	47	211,657 61	49	217,217 23	428,874 84
Pennsylvania	120	398,222 91	121	356,224 18	754,447 09
Philadelphia	27	175,251 05	26	230,998 11	406,249 16
Pittsburgh	16	152,358 84	18	105,729 25	258,088 09
Delaware	6	21,076 93	4	513 49	21,590 42
Maryland	11	15,713 42	10	36,429 10	52,142 52
Baltimore	9	51,336 66	10	47,843 10	99,179 76
District of Columbia	1	436 60	1	109 45	546 05
Washington	5	49,435 34	5	23,543 63	72,978 97
Virginia	13	53,809 45	13	58,828 98	112,638 43
West Virginia	10	24,596 12	9	8,851 42	33,447 54
North Carolina	7	30,522 29	9	89,067 00	119,589 29
South Carolina	7	63,772 53	8	138,042 71	201,815 24
Georgia	6	10,544 64	8	55,418 00	65,962 64
Florida	1	1,070 16	1	2,155 64	3,225 80
Alabama	3	10,270 81	5	56,027 38	66,298 19
New Orleans	6	15,137 27	7	59,782 98	74,920 25
Texas	9	39,264 53	11	71,519 97	110,784 50
Arkansas	2	5,925 33			5,925 33
Kentucky	24	51,239 83	25	59,876 67	111,116 50
Louisville	8	35,232 24	8	122,638 43	157,870 67
Tennessee	16	43,222 31	15	75,024 21	118,246 52
Ohio	86	189,875 45	91	215,348 17	405,223 62
Cincinnati	4	37,435 88	5	39,178 05	76,613 93
Cleveland	6	98,097 39	5	45,975 31	144,072 70
Indiana	52	197,352 79	51	200,483 52	307,836 31
Illinois	71	185,954 89	69	110,410 73	296,365 62
Chicago	8	49,189 62	8	36,201 75	85,391 37
Michigan	47	143,548 67	46	97,721 86	241,270 53
Detroit	3	28,208 26	3	10,599 86	38,808 12
Wisconsin	10	14,595 30	12	21,397 92	35,993 22
Milwaukee	3	15,556 79	2	21,091 99	36,648 78
Iowa	35	75,411 39	42	89,239 76	164,651 15
Minnesota	22	101,230 17	19	68,889 50	170,119 67
Missouri	7	20,294 95	7	16,410 92	36,705 87
Saint Louis	3	17,215 69	5	85,684 03	102,899 72
Kansas	7	21,534 68	8	23,210 21	44,744 89
Nebraska	4	10,805 98	5	39,662 66	50,468 64
Colorado	12	70,390 95	9	119,889 14	190,280 09
Nevada	1	123 30	1	338 59	461 89
California	6	26,939 94	5	30,925 82	57,865 76
San Francisco	1	10,425 43	1	3,226 83	13,652 26
Oregon	1	21,799 20	1	22,411 26	44,210 46
Dakota	4	17,050 20	2	13,017 29	30,067 49
Montana	2	4,277 20	2	3,254 94	7,532 14
New Mexico	3	12,284 79	1	1,858 45	14,143 24
Utah	1	776 50	1	2,542 40	3,318 90
Washington			1	2,893 13	2,893 13
Wyoming	2	1,900 18	2	43 75	1,943 93
Totals for 1881	1,210	5,889,761 19	1,269	6,801,588 56	12,691,349 75
Add for 1880	1,360	7,563,886 04	1,321	7,142,519 96	14,706,406 00
Add for 1879	1,421	10,278,324 98	1,442	11,487,330 17	21,725,655 15
Add for 1878	1,304	10,903,145 04	1,430	13,563,654 85	24,466,799 89
Add for 1877	980	8,175,960 56	1,108	11,757,627 43	19,933,587 99
Aggregate losses for five years		42,771,077 81		50,752,720 97	93,523,798 78

In order to compare the losses experienced by national banks located in the different sections of the United States, the following table is given, which shows the total losses charged off in each geographical division of the country during the last five years. The number of banks reporting losses is also given:

Six months ending—	New England States.		Middle States.		Southern States.		Western States and Territories.		United States.	
	No.	Amount.	No.	Amount.	No.	Amount.	No.	Amount.	No.	Amount.
March 1, 1877	289	$2,465,328	314	$3,462,684	80	$478,252	297	$1,769,697	980	$8,175,961
September 1, 1877	312	4,825,040	353	3,945,806	86	511,841	357	2,474,940	1,108	11,757,627
Total, 1877	.....	7,290,368	.....	7,408,490	.....	990,093	.....	4,244,637	.....	19,933,588
March 1, 1878	327	3,344,012	417	4,506,813	124	672,032	436	2,380,288	1,304	10,903,145
September 1, 1878	399	4,016,814	449	5,502,770	140	1,225,602	442	2,818,469	1,430	13,563,655
Total, 1878	.....	7,360,826	.....	10,009,583	.....	1,897,634	.....	5,198,757	.....	24,466,800
March 1, 1879	379	3,612,128	459	3,592,950	125	696,646	458	2,336,600	1,421	10,238,324
September 1, 1879	384	3,388,394	463	4,360,440	139	1,235,784	456	2,502,712	1,442	11,487,330
Total, 1879	.....	7,000,522	.....	7,953,390	.....	1,932,430	.....	4,839,312	.....	21,725,654
March 1, 1880	362	2,236,928	446	3,152,317	121	530,769	431	1,643,872	1,360	7,563,886
September 1, 1880	326	1,866,658	440	2,817,870	124	787,046	431	1,670,946	1,321	7,142,520
Total, 1880	.....	4,103,586	.....	5,970,187	.....	1,317,815	.....	3,314,818	.....	14,706,406
March 1, 1881	285	1,584,675	412	2,548,203	112	384,607	401	1,372,276	1,210	5,889,761
September 1, 1881	318	1,707,338	428	2,975,110	119	797,233	404	1,321,908	1,269	6,801,589
Total, 1881	.....	3,292,013	.....	5,523,313	.....	1,181,840	.....	2,694,184	.....	12,691,350
Total for five years	.....	29,047,315	.....	36,864,963	.....	7,319,812	.....	20,291,708	.....	93,523,798

Of the losses given in the foregoing tables, a portion is on account of the depreciation in the premium on United States bonds held by the banks. The amount of premium thus charged off during the past year was $2,271,339.50; and, during the last four and a half years, it amounted to $13,107,099. The total losses, shown in the above table, extending over a period of five years, are equal to 24.5 per cent. of the entire capital of the banks, and 19.1 per cent. of their combined capital and surplus.

In order further to illustrate this subject, several of the principal cities of the United States have been selected, and the losses sustained during the past five years by the national banks located in each are given in the following table:

Cities.	1877.	1878.	1879.	1880.	1881.	Total.
New York	$4,247,941 66	$5,147,319 98	$4,135,557 37	$2,054,381 52	$2,321,002 62	$16,906,203 15
Boston	2,192,053 81	2,490,197 46	2,655,390 58	1,110,831 72	701,054 73	9,149,528 30
Philadelphia	334,248 47	561,676 30	491,558 36	399,943 74	406,249 16	2,192,676 03
Pittsburgh	289,466 59	419,036 51	333,022 99	258,128 15	258,088 09	1,557,742 33
Baltimore	200,597 74	368,915 99	294,507 00	211,329 01	90,179 76	1,174,529 50
New Orleans	286,259 47	338,496 90	272,889 87	118,080 38	74,920 25	1,090,646 87

The losses charged off by the banks during the last year are about $2,000,000 less than those experienced during the previous year. A part of the losses charged off, as shown by the preceding tables, consisted of bad debts as defined in the law—viz, debts on which interest was due and unpaid for a period of six months, and which were neither secured nor in process of collection. The bad debts so charged off consisted of other stocks and bonds on which interest had ceased, as well as of bills receivable. Since the resumption of specie payments, the value of a portion of these bad assets has been realized; and it is estimated that in this way about 25 per cent. of these losses has since been recovered.

DIVIDENDS AND EARNINGS.

From the semi-annual returns made by the banks to this Office, tables have been prepared, showing the dividends and profits, and the ratios of each to capital, and to capital and surplus combined. The following table shows the capital, surplus, dividends, and total earnings of all the national banks, for each half year, from March 1, 1869, to September 1, 1881, with the ratios, as before specified:

RATIOS.

Period of six months, ending—	No. of banks.	Capital.	Surplus.	Total dividends.	Total net earnings.	Dividends to capital.	Dividends to capital and surplus.	Earnings to capital and surplus.
						Per cent.	Per cent.	Per cent.
Sept. 1, 1869	1,481	$401,650,802	$82,105,848	$21,767,831	$29,221,184	5.42	4.50	6.04
Mar. 1, 1870	1,571	416,366,901	86,118,210	21,479,095	28,966,034	5.16	4.27	5.77
Sept. 1, 1870	1,601	425,317,104	91,630,620	21,080,343	26,813,885	4.96	4.08	5.19
Mar. 1, 1871	1,605	428,699,165	94,672,401	22,205,150	27,243,162	5.18	4.24	5.21
Sept. 1, 1871	1,693	445,999,264	98,286,591	22,125,279	27,315,311	4.96	4.07	5.02
Mar. 1, 1872	1,750	450,663,706	99,431,243	22,859,826	27,502,539	5.07	1.16	5.00
Sept. 1, 1872	1,852	465,676,023	105,181,942	23,827,289	30,572,891	5.12	4.17	5.36
Mar. 1, 1873	1,912	475,918,683	114,257,288	24,826,061	31,926,478	5.22	4.21	5.41
Sept. 1, 1873	1,955	488,100,951	118,113,848	24,823,029	33,122,000	5.09	4.09	5.46
Mar. 1, 1874	1,967	489,510,323	123,469,859	23,529,998	29,544,120	4.81	3.84	4.82
Sept. 1, 1874	1,971	489,938,284	128,364,039	24,929,307	30,636,811	5.09	4.03	4.86
Mar. 1, 1875	2,007	493,568,831	131,560,637	24,750,816	29,136,007	5.01	3.96	4.66
Sept. 1, 1875	2,047	497,864,843	134,123,649	24,317,785	28,800,217	4.88	3.85	4.56
Mar. 1, 1876	2,076	504,209,491	134,467,595	24,811,581	23,097,921	4.92	3.88	3.62
Sept. 1, 1876	2,081	500,482,271	132,251,078	22,563,829	20,540,231	4.50	3.57	3.25
Mar. 1, 1877	2,080	496,651,580	130,872,165	31,803,969	19,592,962	4.39	3.47	3.12
Sept. 1, 1877	2,072	486,324,860	124,349,254	22,117,116	15,274,028	4.54	3.62	2.50
Mar. 1, 1878	2,074	475,609,751	122,373,561	18,982,390	16,946,696	3.99	3.17	2.83
Sept. 1, 1878	2,047	470,231,896	118,687,134	17,959,223	13,658,893	3.81	3.04	2.31
Mar. 1, 1879	2,043	464,413,996	116,744,135	17,541,654	14,678,660	3.78	3.02	2.53
Sept. 1, 1879	2,045	455,132,056	115,149,351	17,401,867	16,873,200	3.82	3.05	2.96
Mar. 1, 1880	2,046	454,080,090	117,226,501	18,121,273	21,152,784	3.99	3.17	3.70
Sept. 1, 1880	2,072	454,215,062	120,145,649	18,290,200	24,639,250	4.03	3.18	4.18
Mar. 1, 1881	2,087	456,844,865	122,481,788	18,877,517	24,452,021	4.13	3.26	4.22
Sept. 1, 1881	2,100	458,934,485	127,238,394	19,499,694	20,170,816	4.25	3.33	4.98

In the following table is given, by geographical divisions, the number of national banks, with their capital, which paid no dividends to their stockholders during the two semi-annual periods of 1881, to which the totals for each semi-annual period in the four preceding years have been added:

| | Six months ending— | | | | Average for the year. | |
| Geographical divisions. | March 1, 1881. | | September 1, 1881. | | | |
	No. of banks.	Capital.	No. of banks.	Capital.	No. of banks.	Capital.
New England States	12	$1,881,000	8	$1,925,000	10	$1,903,000
Middle States	62	8,746,630	57	6,842,400	60	7,794,515
Southern States	18	2,109,900	19	1,875,150	18	1,992,525
Western States and Territories	83	7,584,000	87	7,745,000	85	7,664,500
Totals for 1881	175	20,321,530	171	18,387,550	173	19,354,510
Totals for 1880	226	30,407,200	233	26,331,150	230	28,370,675
Totals for 1879	309	53,843,700	299	41,576,300	304	49,210,000
Totals for 1878	328	58,797,900	357	58,736,950	343	53,767,425
Totals for 1877	245	40,452,000	288	41,166,200	266	40,809,100
Average for each year	257	38,764,466	269	37,840,230	263	38,302,348

The percentage to capital of dividends paid, and of dividends and earnings to combined capital and surplus, is given by similar divisions for the years 1879, 1880 and 1881, in the following table:

Geographical divisions.	1879.			1880.			1881.		
	Dividends to capital.	Dividends to capital and surplus.	Earnings to capital and surplus.	Dividends to capital.	Dividends to capital and surplus.	Earnings to capital and surplus.	Dividends to capital.	Dividends to capital and surplus.	Earnings to capital and surplus.
	Per ct.	Per ct.	Per ct.	Per ct.	Per ct.	Per ct.	Per ct.	Per ct.	Per ct.
New England States	6.4	5.2	4.2	6.8	5.5	6.4	7.2	5.8	7.3
Middle States	7.9	6.1	5.8	8.4	6.5	8.6	8.5	6.4	9.4
Southern States	7.0	6.0	5.4	7.8	6.7	7.0	8.3	6.9	11.3
Western States and Territories	9.4	7.5	7.1	9.5	7.6	9.3	10.4	8.1	11.6
United States	7.6	6.1	5.5	8.0	6.4	7.9	8.4	6.6	9.2

SURPLUS.

Under the law requiring the national banks to carry to surplus fund, before declaring dividends, a certain proportion of their earnings, the national banks of the country have accumulated a fund, in addition to their capital, which now amounts to $128,140,618. . This surplus is not infringed upon, except in case of extraordinary losses, such as cannot be paid from the current earnings of the banks, and consequently forms, with the capital, the working fund of the banks. In the following table the gradual accumulation of this fund, from the commencement of the system to the present time, is shown, as nearly as possible, by semi-annual periods. The increase or decrease for each period is also given .

Dates.	Amount.	Semi-annual increase or decrease.	Dates.	Amount.	Semi-annual increase or decrease.
		Increase.			Increase.
July 4, 1864	$1,129,910		June 13, 1873	$116,847,455	$5,437,206
January 2, 1865	8,663,311	$7,533,401	December 26, 1873	120,961,268	4,113,813
July 3, 1865	31,363,566	22,640,255	June 26, 1874	126,239,308	5,278,040
January 1, 1866	43,000,371	11,696,805	December 31, 1874	130,485,641	4,246,333
July 2, 1866	50,151,992	7,151,621	June 30, 1875	133,169,095	2,683,454
January 7, 1867	59,992,875	9,840,883			Decrease.
July 1, 1867	63,232,811	3,239,936	December 17, 1875	133,085,422	$83,673
January 6, 1868	70,586,126	7,253,315	June 30, 1876	131,897,197	1,188,225
July 6, 1868	75,840,119	5,253,993	December 22, 1876	131,390,665	506,532
January 4, 1869	81,169,937	5,329,818	June 22, 1877	124,714,073	6,676,592
June 12, 1869	82,218,576	1,048,639	December 28, 1877	121,568,455	3,145,618
January 22, 1870	90,174,281	7,955,705	June 29, 1878	118,178,531	3,389,924
June 9, 1870	91,689,834	1,515,553	January 1, 1879	116,200,864	1,977,667
December 28, 1870	94,705,740	3,015,906	June 14, 1879	114,321,376	1,879,488
June 10, 1871	98,322,204	3,616,464			Increase.
December 16, 1871	101,573,154	3,250,950	December 12, 1879	115,429,032	$1,107,656
June 10, 1872	105,181,943	3,608,789	June 11, 1880	118,102,014	2,672,982
December 27, 1872	111,410,249	6,228,306	December 31, 1880	121,824,629	3,722,615
			June 30, 1881	126,679,518	4,854,889

From December, 1875, to June, 1879 there was a constant decrease in this fund. In all other cases a gradual increase is to be noted.

UNITED STATES LEGAL-TENDER NOTES AND NATIONAL-BANK CIRCULATION.

The acts of February 25, 1862, July 11, 1862, and March 3, 1863, each authorized the issue of 150 millions of dollars of legal-tender notes, making an aggregate of 450 millions of dollars. On January 30, 1864, the amount of such notes outstanding was $449,338,902, which was the highest amount outstanding at any one time. The act of June 30, 1864, provided that the total amount of United States notes issued or to be issued should not exceed 400 millons of dollars, and such additional sum, not exceeding 50 millions, as may be temporarily required for the redemption of temporary loans. By the act of June 20, 1874, the maximum amount was fixed at $382,000,000.

Section 3 of the act of January 14, 1875, authorized an increase of the circulation of national banks in accordance with existing law, without respect to the limit previously existing, and required the Secretary of the Treasury to retire legal-tender notes to an amount equal to 80 per cent. of the national-bank notes thereafter issued, until the amount of such legal-tender notes outstanding should be 300 millions, and no more. Under the operation of this act $35,318,984 of legal-tender notes were retired, leaving the amount in circulation on May 31, 1878, the date of the repeal of the act, $346,681,016, which is the amount now outstanding.

The act of July 12, 1870, provided that no national banking association organized after that date should have circulation in excess of $500,000. As this restriction was enacted at a time when a limit existed as to the aggregate amount of circulation which could be issued to national banking associations, the necessity for it ceased after the passage of the act of January 14, 1875, which, as stated, removed all limit upon the aggregate amount of circulating notes, and a repeal of the restriction is recommended by the Comptroller. A bill was, at the last session of Congress, reported from the finance committee, authorizing all banks to receive circulation equal to the full amount of their capital, as was the case in the original bank act. The passage of this bill would give the banks the privilege of increasing their circulation up to the limit of their capital, if at certain seasons of the year such an increase should be desirable. This increase would not probably be great, for the amount of circulation outstanding is now much less than that authorized by law.

Since the passage of the act of June 20, 1874, $127,923,596 of legal-tender notes have been deposited in the Treasury by the national banks, for the purpose of reducing their circulation, and $101,034,675 of bank notes have been redeemed, destroyed, and retired. In the following table are given the amounts and kinds of the outstanding currency of the United States and of the national banks, on January 1 of each year, from 1866 to 1880, and on November 1, 1881: to which is added the amount on August 31, 1865, when the public debt reached its maximum:

Date.	United States issues.			Notes of national banks, including gold notes.	Aggregate.	Currency price of $100 gold.	Gold price of $100 currency.
	Legal-tender notes.	Old demand notes.	Fractional currency.				
Aug. 31, 1865	$432,553,912	$102,965	$26,344,742	$176,213,955	$635,515,574	$144 25	$69 32
Jan. 1, 1866	425,839,319	392,670	26,000,420	236,636,068	688,867,907	141 50	69 20
Jan. 1, 1867	380,276,160	221,632	28,732,812	298,588,419	707,819,023	133 00	75 18
Jan. 1, 1868	356,600,000	159,127	31,597,583	299,846,206	687,602,916	133 25	75 04
Jan. 1, 1869	356,000,000	128,098	34,215,715	299,747,569	690,091,382	135 00	74 07
Jan. 1, 1870	356,000,000	113,098	39,762,664	299,629,322	695,505,084	120 00	83 33
Jan. 1, 1871	356,000,000	101,086	39,995,089	306,307,672	702,403,847	110 75	90 29
Jan. 1, 1872	357,500,000	92,801	40,767,877	328,465,431	726,826,109	109 50	91 32
Jan. 1, 1873	358,557,907	81,387	45,722,061	341,582,812	745,947,167	112 00	89 28
Jan. 1, 1874	378,401,702	79,637	48,544,792	350,818,236	777,874,367	110 25	90 70
Jan. 1, 1875	382,000,000	72,317	46,390,598	354,128,250	782,591,165	112 50	88 89
Jan. 1, 1876	371,827,220	69,612	44,147,072	346,170,756	762,523,660	112 75	88 69
Jan. 1, 1877	366,055,084	65,462	26,348,206	321,595,606	714,061,358	107 00	93 46
Jan. 1, 1878	349,943,776	63,532	17,764,109	321,672,505	689,443,922	102 87	97 21
Jan. 1, 1879	346,681,016	62,035	16,108,159	323,791,674	686,612,884	100 00	100 00
Jan. 1, 1880	346,681,016	61,350	15,674,304	342,387,336	704,804,006	100 00	100 00
Jan. 1, 1881	346,681,016	60,715	15,523,461	343,792,832	706,358,057	100 00	100 00
Nov. 1, 1881	346,681,016	60,400	15,469,086	359,863,000	722,073,502	100 00	100 00

In the following table is shown by States the amount of circulation issued and retired during the year ending November 1, 1881, and the total amount issued and retired since June 20, 1874:

States and Territories.	Circulation issued.	Circulation retired.		Total.
		Act of June 20, 1874.	Liquidating banks.	
Maine	$45,000	$68,145	$23,863	$92,008
New Hampshire	10,300		5,684	5,684
Vermont	200,700	165,471	38,759	204,230
Massachusetts	3,615,840	1,586,655	8,232	1,594,887
Rhode Island	1,586,280	290,219	1,672	291,891
Connecticut	1,912,360	819,721	2,265	821,986
New York	7,198,370	4,683,765	186,681	4,870,446
New Jersey	1,186,170	310,419	110,952	421,371
Pennsylvania	5,300,690	1,511,536	93,377	1,604,913
Delaware	45,000			
Maryland	700,000	24,240	2,243	26,483
District of Columbia	500	16,655	13,013	29,668
Virginia	256,300	70,955	32,800	103,755
West Virginia		40,805	13,014	53,819
North Carolina		51,134	13,435	64,569
South Carolina	81,000	93,258		93,258
Georgia	22,480	8,541	12,354	20,895
Florida				
Alabama		34,710	8,859	43,569
Mississippi			70	70
Louisiana	338,000	55,982	12,620	68,602
Texas	121,500		6,970	6,970
Arkansas		16,442	60	16,502
Kentucky	809,950	163,376	31,238	194,614
Tennessee	201,600	9,997	23,565	33,562
Missouri	876,100	129,054	92,372	221,426
Ohio	2,549,380	460,751	116,122	576,873
Indiana	660,970	750,020	122,329	872,349
Illinois	897,560	344,914	130,434	475,348
Michigan	311,400	225,460	49,023	274,483
Wisconsin	472,500	85,784	51,457	137,241
Iowa	447,300	81,222	66,051	147,273
Minnesota	147,600	94,733	47,092	141,825
Kansas	121,480	38,301	43,429	81,730
Nebraska	198,900	40,682	2,032	42,714
Nevada			160	160
Oregon				
Colorado	149,400		10,468	10,468
Utah			3,835	3,835
Idaho				
Montana	126,000	9,934	25,483	35,417
Wyoming	27,000			
New Mexico				
Dakota	117,000			
Washington	90,000	20,365		20,365
California	135,000			
Surrendered to this office and retired				410,875
Totals	30,979,630	12,303,246	1,402,013	14,116,134
Previously retired, under act of June 20, 1874	91,748,275	71,135,348	16,194,067	87,329,415
Previously surrendered, under same act				11,794,880
Grand totals	122,727,905	83,438,594	17,596,080	113,240,429

The amount of circulation issued to national banks for the year ending November 1, 1881, was $30,979,630, including $5,233,580 issued to banks organized during the year. The amount retired during the year was $14,075,054, and the actual increase for the same period was therefore $16,904,576, making the total on November 1, $359,422,738, which is the largest amount outstanding at any one time.

During the year ending November 1, 1881, lawful money to the amount of $23,847,844 was deposited with the Treasurer to retire circulation, of which amount $1,554,790 was deposited by banks in liquidation. The amount previously deposited under the act of June 20, 1874, was $85,-684,998; by banks in liquidation, $18,390,555, to which is to be added a balance of $3,813,675, remaining from deposits made by liquidating banks prior to the passage of that act. Deducting from the total the amount of circulating notes redeemed and destroyed without reissue, $101,034,675, there remained in the hands of the Treasurer on November 1, 1881, $30,702,596 of lawful money for the redemption and retirement of bank circulation.

CIRCULATING NOTES OF THE BANK OF FRANCE AND IMPERIAL BANK OF GERMANY, BY DENOMINATIONS—NATIONAL-BANK AND LEGAL-TENDER NOTES, BY DENOMINATIONS.

The following table* exhibits by denominations the circulation of the Imperial Bank of Germany, on January 1, 1881, in thalers and marks, which are here converted into our currency:

Thalers.				Marks.			
Number of pieces.	Denominations.	Value of each piece in dollars.	Amount in dollars. (Thaler= 75 cents.)	Number of pieces.	Denominations.	Value of each piece in dollars.	Amount in dollars. (Marks= 25 cent.)
81	500 thalers.	375 00	30, 375	260, 582	1, 000 marks.	250	65, 145, 500
2, 246	100 thalers.	75 00	168, 450	217, 449	500 marks.	125	27, 181, 125
1, 690½	50 thalers.	37 50	63, 394	4, 348, 382½	100 marks.	25	108, 709, 562
8, 726	25 thalers.	18 75	163, 612				
9, 026½	10 thalers.	7 50	67, 690				
21, 770			493, 530	4, 826, 413½			201, 036, 187

The circulation of the Imperial Bank of Germany, on January 1, 1879, was $165,933,942; its circulation on January 1, 1880, was $198,201,144; showing an increase of $32,267,202 during that year.

The following table† gives the circulation of the Bank of France and its branches, with the number of pieces, and the denominations in francs and in dollars, on January 27, 1881:

Number of pieces.	Denominations.	Value of each piece in dollars.	Amount in francs.	Amount in dollars. (Franc = 20 cents.)
5	5, 000 francs.	1, 000	25, 000	5, 000
1, 370, 596	1, 000 francs.	200	1, 370, 596, 000	274, 119, 200
712, 243	500 francs.	100	356, 121, 500	71, 224, 300
2, 889	200 francs.	40	577, 800	115, 560
7, 555, 345	100 francs.	20	755, 534, 500	151, 106, 900
671, 119	50 francs.	10	33, 555, 950	6, 711, 190
25, 587	25 francs.	5	639, 675	127, 935
282, 999	20 francs.	4	5, 659, 980	1, 131, 996
189, 095	5 francs.	1	945, 475	189, 095
1, 224	Forms out of date.		425, 900	85, 180
10, 811, 102			2, 524, 081, 780	504, 816, 356

The amount of circulation of the Bank of France on January 29, 1880, was 2,321,474,365 francs, or, say, $464,294,873, showing an increase between that time and January 27, 1881, the date of the foregoing table, of 202,607,415 francs, or $40,521,483.

* London Bankers' Magazine for September, 1881, page 706. † Ibid., page 719.

5 C C

It will be seen that the Imperial Bank of Germany issues no notes of a less denomination than $7.50, and that the Bank of France issues less than two millions of dollars in notes of a less denomination than five dollars. The Bank of England issues no notes of less than twenty-five dollars, and the Banks of Ireland and Scotland none of less than five dollars.

The amount of circulation in this country in denominations of five dollars and under, on November 1, 1880, was $214,326,838. In the foreign countries named a large amount of silver and gold coin of the lower denominations enters into general circulation. It will be impossible to keep in circulation here any large amount of small gold coins or silver dollars, unless the coinage of the latter is restricted and the small notes withdrawn.

In accordance with law, no national-bank notes of denominations less than five dollars have been issued since the 1st of January, 1879. Since that date the amount of ones and twos has been reduced $5,867,465, and during the same period the amount of legal-tender notes of these denominations has been increased $7,903,621. During the last year the amount of national-bank notes of these denominations has decreased $1,648,440. The total increase, therefore, of the amount of one and two dollar bills outstanding, in national-bank and legal-tender notes, is $6,255,181.

The following table shows, by denominations, the amount of national-bank and legal-tender notes outstanding on November 1, 1881, and the aggregate amounts of both kinds of notes at the same date in 1879 and 1880:

Denominations.	1881.			1880.	1879.
	National-bank notes.	Legal-tender notes.	Aggregate.	Aggregate.	Aggregate.
Ones...........................	$1,329,112	$24,464,059	$25,793,171	$24,247,362	$22,887.502
Twos...........................	522,170	23,732,196	24,254,366	23,036,578	21,030,863
Fives	100,480,080	67,899,982	168,380,062	167,042,898	159,522,853
Tens	121,308,840	75,408,831	196,717,671	180,655,588	181,447,558
Twenties.......................	81,116,500	70,806,003	151,922,503	147,719,837	141,445,933
Fifties	23,284,200	23,157,575	46,441,775	45,777,475	46,177,945
One hundreds	29,951,000	33,239,370	63,190,370	59,958,600	58,339,780
Five hundreds..................	732,000	14,217,500	14,949.500	16,765,500	23,088,000
One thousands..................	201,000	12,065,500	12,266,500	14,640,500	23,111,500
Five thousands.................	....	2,430,000	2,430,000	565,000	3,250,000
Ten thousands..................	....	260,000	260,000	320,000	2,500,000
Add for unredeemed fragments of national-bank notes........	+16,586	....	+16,586	+15,129	+13,586
Deduct for legal-tender notes destroyed in Chicago fire....	....	−1,000,000	−1,000,000	−1,000,000	−1,000,000
Totals..................	358,941,488	346,681,016	705,622,504	688,744,467	681,815,520

The written signatures of the officers of the banks are necessary as an additional precaution against counterfeiting. It is recommended that a bill for preventing the lithographing or printing of the signatures of officers of banks, now required by law to be written on the notes, be passed by Congress, imposing a penalty of twenty dollars for a violation thereof.

REDEMPTIONS.

Section 3 of the act of June 20, 1874, provides that every national bank "shall at all times keep and have on deposit in the Treasury of the

United States, in lawful money of the United States, a sum equal to five per centum of its circulation, to be held and used for the redemption of such circulation." Since the passage of this act the banks have, as a rule, maintained their redemption fund, and their circulating notes have been promptly redeemed at the Treasury, without expense to the government.

The following table exhibits the amount of national-bank notes received for redemption monthly, by the Comptroller of the Currency, for the year ending October 31, 1881, and the amount received for the same period at the redemption agency of the Treasury, together with the total amount received since the passage of the act of June 20, 1874:

| Months. | Received by the Comptroller. | | | | | Received at redemption agency. |
	From national banks for re-issue or surrender.	From redemption agency for reissue.	Notes of national banks in liquidation.	Under act of June 20, 1874.	Total.	
1880.						
November	$11,600	$2,596,200	$78,305	$558,194	$3,244,299	$3,369,417
December	42,700	2,824,500	146,741	225,647	3,239,588	4,151,971
1881.						
January	77,624	3,218,900	203,374	656,677	4,156,575	5,550,743
February	29,905	4,005,600	139,613	751,995	4,927,113	4,498,501
March	55,230	3,251,400	125,155	858,932	4,290,717	4,804,393
April	24,400	3,071,800	143,025	2,231,988	5,471,213	6,850,425
May	3,205	4,659,300	98,006	1,540,498	6,301,069	8,035,983
June	14,900	6,220,800	310,635	2,239,566	8,785,901	7,151,961
July	50	3,149,800	57,214	647,235	3,854,299	4,988,307
August	20,850	3,467,500	99,885	1,184,073	4,772,308	4,540,053
September	58,710	2,178,700	69,233	624,066	2,930,709	3,622,833
October	67,720	3,789,600	155,472	740,834	4,753,626	4,945,668
Totals	406,894	42,434,100	1,626,718	12,259,705	56,727,417	62,510,255
Received from June 20, 1874, to October 31, 1880	12,667,195	387,314,155	16,069,075	71,345,508	487,395,933	1,038,013,014
Grand totals.	13,074,089	429,748,255	17,695,793	83,605,213	544,123,350	1,100,523,269

From the passage of the act of June 20, 1874, to October 31, 1881, there was received at the redemption agency of the Treasury $1,100,523,269 of national-bank currency. During the year ending October 31, 1881, there was received $62,510,225; of which amount $23,923,000, or about 38 per cent., was received from banks in New York City, and $5,679,000, or about 9 per cent., was received from banks in the city of Boston. The amount received from Philadelphia was $5,169,000; from Baltimore, $723,000; Pittsburgh, $624,000; Cincinnati, $1,023,000; Chicago, $2,777,000; Saint Louis, $732,000; Providence, $1,415,000. The amount of circulating notes fit for circulation returned by the redemption agency to the banks of issue during the year was $4,536,200.

The total amount received by the Comptroller of the Currency for destruction, from the redemption agency and from the national banks direct, was $56,727,417. Of this amount, $5,836,203 were issues of banks in the city of New York, $5,819,519 of Boston, $2,275,055 of Philadelphia, $912,700 of Baltimore, $971,483 of Pittsburgh, $409,300 of Cincinnati, $138,330 of Chicago, $105,800 of Saint Louis, $1,786,791 of Providence, and of each of the other principal cities less than $400,000.

The following table exhibits the number and amount of national-bank notes, of each denomination, which have been issued and redeemed since the organization of the system, and the number and amount outstanding on November 1, 1881:

Denominations.	Number.			Amount.		
	Issued.	Redeemed.	Outstanding.	Issued.	Redeemed.	Outstanding.
Ones	23, 167, 677	21, 838, 565	1, 329, 112	$23, 167, 677	$21, 838, 565	$1, 329, 112
Twos	7, 747, 519	7, 486, 434	261, 085	15, 495, 038	14, 972, 868	522, 170
Fives	73, 612, 504	53, 516, 488	20, 096, 016	368, 062, 520	267, 582, 440	100, 480, 080
Tens	29, 477, 519	17, 346, 635	12, 130, 884	294, 775, 190	173, 466, 350	121, 308, 840
Twenties	8, 940, 817	4, 884, 992	4, 055, 825	178, 816, 340	97, 699, 840	81, 116, 500
Fifties	1, 357, 574	891, 890	465, 684	67, 878, 700	44, 594, 500	23, 284, 200
One hundreds	959, 712	660, 202	299, 510	95, 971, 200	66, 020, 200	29, 951, 000
Five hundreds	21, 959	20, 495	1, 464	10, 979, 500	10, 247, 500	732, 000
One thousands	7, 144	6, 943	201	7, 144, 000	6, 943, 000	201, 000
Portions of notes lost or destroyed					−16, 586	+16, 586
Totals	145, 292, 425	106, 652, 644	38, 639, 781	1, 062, 290, 165	703, 348, 677	358, 941, 488

A table showing the numbers and denominations of national-bank notes issued and redeemed, and the number of each denomination outstanding on November 1 for the last thirteen years, will be found in the Appendix.

The following table shows the amount of national-bank notes received at this office and destroyed yearly since the establishment of the system:

Prior to November 1, 1865 .... $175, 490
During the year ending October 31, 1866 .... 1, 050, 382
During the year ending October 31, 1867 .... 3, 401, 423
During the year ending October 31, 1868 .... 4, 602, 825
During the year ending October 31, 1869 .... 8, 603, 729
During the year ending October 31, 1870 .... 14, 305, 689
During the year ending October 31, 1871 .... 24, 344, 047
During the year ending October 31, 1872 .... 30, 211, 720
During the year ending October 31, 1873 .... 36, 433, 171
During the year ending October 31, 1874 .... 49, 939, 741
During the year ending October 31, 1875 .... 137, 697, 696
During the year ending October 31, 1876 .... 98, 672, 716
During the year ending October 31, 1877 .... 76, 918, 963
During the year ending October 31, 1878 .... 57, 381. 249
During the year ending October 31, 1879 .... 41, 101, 830
During the year ending October 31, 1880 .... 35, 539, 660
During the year ending October 31, 1881 .... 54, 941, 130
Additional amount of notes of national banks in liquidation 28, 027, 215

Total 703, 348, 676

The amount of one and two dollar notes outstanding is but one-half of one per cent. of the whole circulation of the banks, the fives constitute 28 per cent., the tens 33.8 per cent., the twenties 22.6 per cent., while the fifties and over are only 15.1 per cent. of the entire circulation. While the amount of ones and twos of the national bank circulation is steadily diminishing, the legal-tender notes of these denominations are as steadily increasing. Of the entire amount of national-bank and legal-tender notes outstanding, nearly 7.1 per cent. consists of one and two dollar notes, more than 30.9 per cent of ones, twos, and fives, more than 58.8 per cent. is in notes of a less denomination than twenty dollars, while about 80.4 per cent. is in notes of a lower denomination than fifty dollars. Of the entire issue, about 19.4 per cent. is in denominations of fifties, one hundreds, five hundreds, and one thousands. There are also outstanding 486 legal-tender notes of the denomination of five thousand, and 26 notes of the denomination of ten thousand.

RESERVE.

The following table exhibits the amount of net deposits, and the reserve required thereon by the act of June 20, 1874, together with the amount and classification of reserve held by the national banks in New York City, in the other reserve cities, and by the remaining banks, at the dates of their reports in October of each year from 1875 to 1881:

NEW YORK CITY.

	Number of banks	Net deposits.	Reserve required.	Reserve held.		Classification of reserve.			
				Amount.	Ratio to deposits.	Specie.	Other lawful money.	Due from agents.	Redemption fund.
		Millions.	Millions.	Millions.	Per cent.	Millions.	Millions.	Millions.	Millions.
October 1, 1875.	48	202.3	50.6	60.5	29.9	5.0	54.4	....	1.1
October 2, 1876	47	197.9	49.5	60.7	30.7	14.6	45.3	....	0.8
October 1, 1877	47	174.9	43.7	48.1	27.5	13.0	34.3	....	0.8
October 1, 1878	47	189.8	47.4	50.9	26.8	13.3	36.5	....	1.1
October 2, 1879.	47	210.2	52.6	53.1	25.3	19.4	32.6	....	1.1
October 1, 1880.	47	268.1	67.0	70.6	26.4	58.7	11.0	....	0.9
October 1, 1881.	48	268.8	67.2	62.5	23.3	50.6	10.9	....	1.0

OTHER RESERVE CITIES.

	Number of banks	Net deposits.	Reserve required.	Reserve held.		Classification of reserve.			
				Amount.	Ratio to deposits.	Specie.	Other lawful money.	Due from agents.	Redemption fund.
October 1, 1875	188	223.9	56.0	74.5	33.3	1.5	37.1	32.3	3.6
October 2, 1876	189	217.0	54.2	76.1	35.1	4.0	37.1	32.0	3.0
October 1, 1877.	188	204.1	51.0	67.3	33.0	5.6	34.3	24.4	3.0
October 1, 1878.	184	199.9	50.0	71.1	35.6	9.4	29.4	29.1	3.2
October 2, 1879.	181	228.8	57.2	83.5	36.5	11.3	33.0	35.7	3.5
October 1, 1880.	184	289.4	72.4	105.2	36.3	28.3	25.0	48.2	3.7
October 1, 1881.	189	335.4	83.9	100.8	30.0	34.6	21.9	40.6	3.7

STATES AND TERRITORIES.

	Number of banks	Net deposits.	Reserve required.	Reserve held.		Classification of reserve.			
				Amount.	Ratio to deposits.	Specie.	Other lawful money.	Due from agents.	Redemption fund.
October 1, 1875.	1,851	307.9	46.3	100.1	32.5	1.6	33.7	53.3	11.5
October 2, 1876.	1,853	291.7	43.8	99.9	34.3	2.7	31.0	55.4	10.8
October 1, 1877	1,845	290.1	43.6	95.4	32.9	4.2	31.6	48.9	10.7
October 1, 1878	1,822	289.1	43.4	106.1	36.7	8.0	31.1	56.0	11.0
October 2, 1879	1,820	329.9	49.5	124.3	37.7	11.5	30.3	71.3	11.2
October 1, 1880	1,859	410.5	61.6	147.2	35.8	21.2	28.3	86.4	11.3
October 1, 1881.	1,895	507.2	76.1	158.3	31.2	27.5	27.1	92.4	11.4

SUMMARY.

	Number of banks	Net deposits.	Reserve required.	Reserve held.		Classification of reserve.			
				Amount.	Ratio to deposits.	Specie.	Other lawful money.	Due from agents.	Redemption fund.
October 1, 1875	2,087	734.1	152.2	235.1	32.0	8.1	125.2	85.6	16.2
October 2, 1876	2,089	706.6	147.5	236.7	33.5	21.3	113.4	87.4	14.6
October 1, 1877	2,080	669.1	138.3	210.8	31.5	22.8	100.2	73.3	14.5
October 1, 1878	2,053	678.8	140.8	228.1	33.6	30.7	97.0	85.1	15.3
October 2, 1879	2,048	768.9	159.3	260.0	33.9	42.2	95.9	107.0	15.8
October 1, 1880	2,090	968.0	201.0	325.0	33.4	108.2	64.3	134.6	15.9
October 1, 1881.	2,132	1,111.6	227.2	321.6	28.9	112.7	59.9	133.0	16.1

The following table, compiled from returns made to the clearing-house by the national banks in New York City, exhibits the movement of their reserve, weekly, during October, for the last eight years:

Week ending—	Specie.	Legal tenders.	Total.	Ratio of reserve to— Circulation and deposits.	Deposits.
				Per cent.	*Per cent.*
October 4, 1873	$9, 240, 300	$9, 251, 900	$18, 492, 200	11. 6	14. 0
October 11, 1873	10, 506, 900	8, 049, 300	18, 556, 200	11. 6	14. 1
October 18, 1873	11, 650, 100	5, 179, 800	16, 829, 900	10. 7	13. 0
October 25, 1873	11, 433, 500	7, 187, 300	18, 620, 800	12. 2	14. 8
October 3, 1874	15, 373, 400	53, 297, 600	68, 671, 000	30. 0	33. 9
October 10, 1874	14, 517, 700	52, 152, 000	66, 669, 700	29. 6	33. 3
October 17, 1874	12, 691, 400	51, 855, 100	64, 546, 500	29. 0	32. 7
October 24, 1874	11, 457, 900	49, 893, 900	61, 351, 800	28. 8	31. 7
October 31, 1874	10, 324, 900	50, 773, 000	61, 097, 900	27. 9	31. 6
October 2, 1875	5, 438, 900	56, 181, 500	61, 620, 400	28. 1	30. 6
October 9, 1875	5, 716, 200	51, 342, 300	57, 058, 500	26. 5	28. 9
October 16, 1875	5, 528, 500	48, 582, 700	54, 111, 200	25. 4	27. 7
October 23, 1875	5, 735, 000	47, 300, 900	53, 035, 900	25. 3	27. 7
October 30, 1875	8, 975, 600	45, 762, 800	54, 738, 400	26. 5	29. 0
October 7, 1876	17, 682, 600	45, 535, 600	63, 218, 200	30. 5	32. 4
October 14, 1876	16, 233, 600	43, 004, 600	59, 238, 200	28, 8	31. 1
October 21, 1876	15, 577, 500	41, 421, 700	56, 999, 200	27. 8	30. 0
October 28, 1876	14, 011, 600	41, 645, 600	55, 657, 200	28. 0	30. 3
October 6, 1877	14, 665, 600	36, 168, 300	50, 833, 900	27. 0	29. 5
October 13, 1877	14, 726, 500	35, 178, 900	49, 905, 400	26. 7	29. 2
October 20, 1877	14, 087, 400	35, 101, 700	49, 189, 100	26. 5	29 0
October 27, 1877	15, 209, 000	34, 367, 800	49, 576, 800	26. 8	29. 4
October 5, 1878	14, 995, 800	38, 304, 900	53, 300, 700	25. 7	28. 4
October 12, 1878	12, 184, 600	37, 685, 100	49, 869, 700	24. 4	27. 0
October 19, 1878	13, 531, 400	36, 576, 000	50, 107, 400	24. 7	27. 3
October 26, 1878	17, 384, 200	35, 690, 500	53, 074, 700	25. 8	28. 5
October 4, 1879	18, 979, 600	34, 368, 000	53, 347, 600	23. 3	25. 8
October 11, 1879	20, 901, 800	32, 820, 300	53, 722, 100	23. 4	25. 9
October 18, 1879	24, 686, 500	29, 305, 200	53, 991, 700	23. 5	26. 1
October 25, 1879	25, 636, 000	26, 713, 900	52, 349, 900	23. 0	25. 5
October 2, 1880	59, 823, 700	11, 129, 100	70, 952, 800	25. 4	26. 4
October 9, 1880	62, 521, 300	10, 785, 000	73, 306, 300	25. 4	27. 2
October 16, 1880	62, 760, 600	10, 939, 200	73, 699, 800	25. 5	27. 1
October 23, 1880	60, 888, 200	10, 988, 200	71. 876, 400	24. 9	26. 6
October 30, 1880	61, 471, 600	10, 925, 000	72, 396, 600	25. 0	26. 7
October 1, 1881	54, 954, 600	12, 150, 400	67, 105, 000	23. 1	24. 8
October 8, 1881	53, 287, 900	12, 153, 800	65, 441, 700	23. 1	24. 9
October 15, 1881	51, 008, 300	12, 452, 700	63, 461, 000	23. 2	25. 0
October 22, 1881	54, 016, 200	12, 496, 500	66, 512, 700	24. 6	26. 6
October 29, 1881	55, 961, 200	12, 947, 900	68, 909, 100	25. 6	27. 4

APPENDIX.

Tables will be found in the appendix, exhibiting the reserve of the national banks as shown by their reports, from October 2, 1874, to October 1, 1881; the reserve by States and principal cities for October 1, 1881; and in the States and Territories, in New York City, and in the other reserve cities, separately, at three dates in each year, from 1878 to 1881.

Special attention is called to the synopsis of judicial decisions contained in the appendix, to the numerous and carefully prepared tables in both report and appendix, and to the index of subjects and list of tables to be found at the close of the appendix. At the end of the full volume of more than seven hundred pages is an alphabetical list of the cities and villages in which the national banks are situated.

In concluding this report the Comptroller gratefully acknowledges the zeal and efficiency of the officers and clerks associated with him in the discharge of official duties.

JOHN JAY KNOX,
Comptroller of the Currency

Hon. JOSEPH WARREN KEIFER,
Speaker of the House of Representatives.

APPENDIX.

NAMES and COMPENSATION of OFFICERS and CLERKS in the OFFICE of the COMPTROLLER OF THE CURRENCY.

Name.	Grade.	Salary.
John Jay Knox	Comptroller	$5,000
John S. Langworthy	Deputy Comptroller	2,800
J. Franklin Bates	Chief of division	2,200
William B. Greene	do	2,200
John D. Patten	do	2,200
Edward Wolcott	do	2,200
John W. Griffin	Bond clerk	2,000
Edward S. Peck	Superintendent	2,000
Watson W. Eldridge	Teller	2,000
Frank A. Miller	Principal bookkeeper	2,000
Theodore O. Ebaugh	Assistant bookkeeper	2,000
James C. Brown	Fourth class	1,800
Fernando C. Cate	do	1,800
Charles H. Cherry	do	1,800
William Elder	do	1,800
Charles H. Norton	do	1,800
William Sinclair	do	1,800
George H. Wood	do	1,800
Thomas C. Folgor	Stenographer	1,600
Charles E. Brayton	Third class	1,600
David B. Brenner	do	1,600
William H. Glascott	do	1,600
John A. Hebrow	do	1,600
George T. May	do	1,600
Washington K. McCoy	do	1,600
Edmund E. Schroiner	do	1,600
Charles J. Stoddard	do	1,600
William D. Swan	do	1,600
Walter Taylor	do	1,600
Edward D. Tracy	do	1,600
J. Edward De Saules	Second class	1,400
Joseph A. Kayser	do	1,400
Edward McCauley	do	1,400
Isaac C. Miller	do	1,400
Charles McC. Taylor	do	1,400
William H. Walton	do	1,400
Arthur M. Wheeler	do	1,400
Frederick Widdows	do	1,400
Irving B. Brower	First class	1,200
Julia R. Donoho	do	1,200
Sarah F. Fitzgerald	do	1,200
Charles B. Hinckley	do	1,200
R. Le Roy Livingston	do	1,200
Mary L. McCormick	do	1,200
Morris M. Ogden	do	1,200
Margaretta L. Simpson	do	1,200
Eveline C. Bates	Clerk	1,000
Edward Myers	do	1,000
John Newman	Messenger	840
Philo Burr	Assistant messenger	720
William Griffiths	do	720

NAMES and COMPENSATION of OFFICERS and CLERKS, &c.—Continued.

Name.	Grade.	Salary.
Silas Holmes	Assistant messenger	$720
Thomas H. Austin	Watchman	720
Thomas Jackson	....do	720
L. W. Allen	Laborer	660
Lee Nance	....do	660
Eliza M. Barker	Clerk	900
Harriet M. Black	....do	900
Margaret L. Browne	....do	900
Kate R. Bruce	....do	900
Louisa Campbell	....do	900
Virginia H. Clarke	....do	900
Sarah G. Clemens	....do	900
Mary L. Conrad	....do	900
May Crosby	....do	900
Mary A. Curtis	....do	900
Margaret F. Dewar	....do	900
Jane A. Dorr	....do	900
Annabella H. Finlay	....do	900
Flora M. Fleming	....do	900
Margaret E Gooding	....do	900
Elizabeth Hutchinson	....do	900
Eliza R. Hyde	....do	900
Alice M. Kennedy	....do	900
Lucretia W. Knowlton	....do	900
Emma Lafayette	....do	900
Maggie B. Miller	....do	900
Mary F. Nessle	....do	900
Margaret F. Ogden	....do	900
Mary E. Oliver	....do	900
Carrie L. Pennock	....do	900
Eliza M. Peters	....do	900
Annie E. Ranney	....do	900
Emily H. Reed	....do	900
Marie Richardson	....do	900
Eliza A. Saunders	....do	900
Fayette C. Snead	....do	900
Amelia P. Stockdale	....do	900
Sarah A. W. Tiffey	....do	900
Julia C. Townsend	....do	900

Expenses of the office of Comptroller of the Currency for the fiscal year ending June 30, 1881.

For special dies, plates, printing, &c $112,734 86
For salaries 101,383 64

Total 214,118 50

Total expenses of the office of the Comptroller of the Currency from its organization to June 30, 1881, $5,148,649.01.

The contingent expenses of the office are not paid by the Comptroller, but from the general appropriation for contingent expenses of the Treasury Department; and as separate accounts are not kept for the different bureaus, the amount cannot be stated.

SYNOPSIS of DECISIONS of the SUPREME and CIRCUIT COURTS of the UNITED STATES and of STATE COURTS of LAST RESORT, upon questions arising under the National Bank Act, and upon cognate points of interest to banks and to parties having dealings with them. *

ABATEMENT.

I. An action brought by a creditor of a national bank is abated by a decree of a district or circuit court dissolving the corporation and forfeiting its franchises. (*First National Bank of Selma* vs. *Colby*, 21 *Wallace, p.* 609.)

II. Suit by the receiver of the *New Orleans National Banking Association* (formerly a State organization called the Bank of New Orleans) against a shareholder to enforce his personal liability. Plea in abatement that "at the date of the appointment of said receiver there was not, nor has there since been, nor is there now, any such corporation as said New Orleans National Banking Association, because said Bank of New Orleans had no power by its charter, nor authority otherwise from the State of Louisana, to change its organization to that of a national association under the laws of the United States."

On general demurrer this plea was held bad, because no authority from the State was necessary to enable the bank to make such change. The option [to do so was given by the forty-fourth section of the banking act of Congress, 13 Statutes, 112. "The power there conferred was ample, and its validity cannot be doubted." (*Casey, Receiver, &c.,* vs. *Galli,* 4 *Otto, p.* 673.)

This plea was also held bad upon the additional ground that "where a shareholder of a corporation is called upon to respond to a liability as such, and where a party has contracted with a corporation, and is sued on his contract, neither is permitted to deny the existence and legal validity of such corporation." (*Ibid.*)

"To hold otherwise," says Mr. Justice Swayne (p. 680), "would be contrary to the plainest principles of reason and good faith, and involve a mockery of justice. Parties must take the consequences of the positions they assume." "They are estopped to deny the reality of the state of things which they have made to appear to exist, and upon which others have been led to rely. Sound ethics require that the apparent, in its effects and consequences, should be as if it were real, and the law properly so regards it."

ACCOMMODATION ACCEPTANCES, INDORSEMENTS AND NOTES.

I. Where bills, indorsed by a national bank for accommodation only, had been negotiated by the bank through its usual channels of communication with its correspondents as its own bills, and the proceeds thereof have been placed to the credit of the bank, which thereupon gave the same credit to the parties for whom it had thus indorsed, and received no benefit therefrom: *Held,* that although an accommodation indorsement by a national bank, in such cases, was void in the hands of holders against whom notice of the character of the indorsement could be concluded, yet that the bank was liable for the same to holders, for value, without notice. (*Blair* vs. *First National Bank of Mansfield, Ohio. United States circuit court for Ohio, at Cleveland, November term,* 1875, *Emmons, J. Reported in Bankers' Magazine for March,* 1878, *pp.* 721–5.) Quere, whether under the provisions of section 5202 of the Revised Statutes of the United States, any indorsement by a national bank is not *ultra vires.* (*Johnston.*)

II. It is no defense to a suit against the acceptor of a draft which has been discounted, and upon which money has been advanced by plaintiff, that the draft was accepted for the accommodation of the drawer. (*Davis* vs. *Randall,* 115 *Mass., p.* 547.)

III. A national bank discounted a note made by the defendant for the benefit of the payee, and which the payee agreed to take care of at maturity : *Held,* that the bank could recover the note although it had, when it took the note, full notice of the circumstances under which it was given. (*Thatcher* vs. *West River National Bank,* 19 *Mich., p.* 196.)
(See, also, Title "EVIDENCE.")

IV. That the accommodation acceptance, indorsement, bill, or note of a corporation is *ultra vires.* (See *Bank of Genesee* vs. *Patchin Bank,* 13 *N. Y., p.* 309, and 19 *N. Y., p.* 312 ; *Bank of Auburn* vs. *Putnam, jr.,* 1 *Abb. App. Decisions, p.* 80 ; *Monfords* vs. *Farmers & Mechanics' Bank,* 26 *Barb., p.* 568 ; *Farmers & Mechanics' Bank* vs. *Troy City Bank,* 1 *Doug.* [*Mich.*], *p.* 45.)

---

* Many of the decisions cited in this synopsis will be found in "Thompson's National Bank Cases," vols. 1 and 2 ; but in most instances reference is made to the original report, thus indicating the tribunal by which the point was decided.

ACCOMMODATION ACCEPTANCES, INDORSEMENTS AND NOTES—Continued.

[NOTE.—In the United States circuit court, western district Virginia, Judge Bond has recently decided the cases of *Seligman & Co.* vs. *The Charlottesville National Bank*, and *Johnston Brothers & Co.* against the same bank. The first was an action of *covenant* upon a *letter of credit* for £5,000, issued under the seal of the bank, pursuant to a resolution of the board of directors, guaranteeing the drafts of Flannagan & Son to the amount of said letter. The latter was *assumpsit* upon five bills of exchange for $5,000 each, dated April 16, 1875, each drawn by said Charlottesville Bank upon the Citizens' National Bank of Baltimore, payable to the order of Flannagan & Son, acceptance waived, maturing upon days "fixed" within five days of each other, the first, November 20, and the last, December 10 of same year. Said bills were *not* drawn against funds due or to become due from the said Citizens' to said Charlottesville Bank, but were a mere loan of the credit of the latter bank (it being without funds) to the said Flannagan & Son, and drawn to be used by the latter, as they were used, as collateral security in part for a loan of $25,000, made by said *Johnston Brothers & Co.* to said Flannagan & Son. Said plaintiffs took said bills as such collateral security, and with full notice of all the facts aforesaid. *Held*, I. That said letter of credit and said bills of exchange were only the accommodation paper of said Charlottesville National Bank, and, as such, void in the hands of the plaintiffs, holding with full notice of their character. II. That the incidental powers conferred upon national banks are not such as are conferred upon banks generally, but only such as are necessary to carry on the specific banking business prescribed by the National-Bank Act. Hence, though such banks may borrow money for certain purposes, they have no power to loan their credit to customers. These cases were reported in the Bankers' Magazine for December, 1879.]

ACTIONS.

I. A national bank may be sued in the proper State court. (*Bank of Bethel* vs. *Pahquioque Bank*, 14 *Wall.*, *pp.* 383, 395.)

II. Such banks may sue in Federal courts. The word "by" was omitted in section 57 of act of 1864 by mistake. (*Kennedy* vs. *Gibson*, 8 *Wall.*, *pp.* 506-7.)

III. Receivers may also sue in United States courts. (*Ibid.*)

IV. When the full personal liability of shareholders is to be enforced the action *must* be at law. (*Kennedy* vs. *Gibson*, 8 *Wall.*, *p.* 505; see also *Casey, &c.*, vs. *Galli*, *supra*.)

V. But if contribution only is sought, the proceedings may be in *equity*, joining all the shareholders within the jurisdiction of the court. (*Ibid*, *pp.* 505-6.) (See, also, Title "SHAREHOLDERS, INDIVIDUAL LIABILITIES OF," VI, *post.*)

VI. But in *Bailey, Receiver, &c.*, vs. *First National Bank of Duluth, U. S. circuit court for Minnesota, Nelson, J.*—*Held*, that even where less than the par value was assessed the suit *might* be at law; and this would seem to be the true theory. (See *Bankers' Magazine, April, 1877, p.* 793.)

[NOTE.—In *Stanton, Receiver. &c.*, vs. *Wilkeson*, 8 *Ben.*, 357, the point was distinctly made before Judge Blatchford. The suit was brought to enforce an assessment of sixty per centum, and defendant insisted that plaintiff should have proceeded by bill in equity; but the court held that the action at law was the proper remedy, at the option of the receiver.]

VII. A national bank located in one State may bring action in the circuit court of the United States sitting within another State against a citizen thereof. (*Manufacturers' National Bank* vs. *Baack*, 8 *Blatch.*, *p.* 147.)

VIII. In such action it will be presumed, so far as the question of jurisdiction is concerned, that the stockholders of such bank are citizens of the State where the bank is located. (*Ibid.*) But in case of *Commercial Bank of Cleveland* vs. *Simmons*, decided in the United States circuit court northern district of Ohio, it was held that a national bank does not sue in the Federal court by virtue of any right conferred by the judiciary act of 1789, but by virtue of the right conferred by its charter, the national-bank act, and this would seem to be the true doctrine. (See *Thomp. National Bank Cases*, p. 295. Also *First National Bank of Omaha* vs. *County of Douglas*, 3 *Dillon*, *p.* 298, decided by Mr. Justice Miller of the United States Supreme Court.)

IX. National banks can be sued *only* in the courts designated in the National-Bank Act. Therefore a State court of New York has no jurisdiction of an action against a national bank located in Alabama. (*Cadle* vs. *Tracy*, 11 *Blatch.*, *p.* 101.) To the contrary of this, see *Cooke* vs. *State National Bank*, 52 *N. Y.*, *p.* 96.

X. Actions in their nature *local*, in the technical legal meaning of that word, may be brought against a national bank in the State court of the proper county. (*Casey* vs. *Adams*, 102 *U. S.*, *p.* 66.) (See, also, Title "JURISDICTION," *post.*)

ATTACHMENTS OF ASSETS.

I. When a creditor attaches the property of an insolvent national bank, he cannot hold such property against the claim of a receiver appointed after the attachment suit was commenced. Such creditor must share *pro rata* with all others. (*Bank of Selma* vs. *Colby*, 21 *Wall.*, *p.* 609; see, also, *Harvey* vs. *Allen*, 16 *Blatchf.*, *p.* 29.)

(See, also, Title "JURISDICTION," II, *post.*)

II. Section 5242 Revised Statutes United States prohibits the issuing of an attachment against a national bank by any State, county, or municipal court. before final judgment. (*Central National Bank* vs. *Richland National Bank*, 52 *Howard* [*N. Y.*], *p.* 136.)

III. In *Robinson* vs. *National Bank of New Berne*, 58 *How.*, *p.* 306, the court of appeals decides that a State court can issue attachment process against a *solvent* national bank, located in another State, upon which its funds within the jurisdiction of such court can be seized and subjected to the satisfaction of any claim established by the judgment of such tribunal. But in the supreme court of New York, in *Rhoner* vs. *First National Bank of Allentown*, 14 *Hun.*, *p.* 126, the contrary doctrine is held, in accordance with the ruling in *Central National Bank* vs. *Richland National Bank*, 52 *How.*, *p* 136, heretofore cited.

[NOTE.—It is submitted that the latter is the correct rule. The Currency Act favors the policy, on the part of country banks, of keeping a large portion of their *reserve* in certain cities. But if such banks are advised that such reserve funds are there subject, at any moment, to be seized by process of a State court, at the instance or caprice of any resident who may think himself a creditor, such deposits will be made with more or less hesitation, or not at all.]

ATTORNEYS.

I. Section 56 of Currency Act is directory only, and it cannot be objected by defense that a suit is brought by private attorney instead of United States district attorney. (*Kennedy* vs. *Gibson*, 8 *Wall.*, *p.* 504.)

BY-LAWS.

I. A national bank cannot by its by-laws create a lien on the shares of a stockholder who is a debtor of the association. (*Bullard* vs. *National Bank*, &c., 18 *Wall.*, *p.* 589.)

(See, also, case of *Bank* vs. *Lanier*, 11 *Wall.*, *p.* 369, cited under "LOANS ON SHARES," *post.*)

[NOTE.—In *Young* vs. *Vough*. 23 *N. J. Equity R.*, *p.* 325. it was held that a national bank could by its by-laws prohibit the transfer of shares by a shareholder while indebted to the bank, and that transfers in violation of such by-laws were void. As it is held by the Supreme Court of the United States that such by-laws can create no lien for indebtedness, it would seem that a regulation prohibiting such transfers can be of little practical use, even if the power exists.]

CHECKS.

I. The holder of a check on a national bank cannot sue the bank for refusing payment, in the absence of proof that it was accepted by the bank. (*National Bank of the Republic* vs. *Millard*, 10 *Wall.*, *p.* 452.)

II. The relation of banker and customer is that of debtor and creditor. Receiving deposits is an important part of the business of banking, but the moment they are received they become the moneys of the bank, may be loaned as a part of its general fund, and the check of the depositor gives no lien upon them. (*Ibid.*, *p.* 155.)

III. Perhaps, on proof that check had been charged to the drawer, and that the bank had settled with him on that basis, the holder or payee could recover on account for "*money had and received.*" (*Ibid.*, *pp.* 155–6.)

IV. The facts that the bank was a United States depositary and the check was drawn by a United States officer to a United States creditor do not vary the rule. (*Ibid.*, *pp.* 155–6.)

V. Where a bank pays a check drawn on it in favor of a party whose indorsement thereon is forged, and the same has passed through several hands, only reasonable diligence is required to be exercised in giving notice to prior holders of the forgery, after its discovery, in order to hold them liable. (*Shroeder* vs. *Harvey*, 75 *Ill.*, *p.* 638.)

VI. A clerk of plaintiffs received from their debtors checks, payable to their (plaintiffs) order, in payment of sums due. The clerk, wrongfully and without authority, indorsed the names of the plaintiffs on these checks

CHECKS—Continued.

and transferred them to other persons, appropriating the proceeds to his own use. Subsequently these checks were deposited with a bank, which in good faith collected them and paid over the proceeds to the depositors. In a suit by plaintiffs against the bank to recover the amounts so collected by it: *Held*, that the bank was liable. (*Johnson* vs. *First National Bank*, 13 *N. Y. Sup. Court.*)

VII. Bankers are presumed to know the signatures of their customers, and pay checks purporting to be drawn by them, at their peril. (*Weisser* vs. *Dennison*, 10 *N. Y.*, p. 68; *National Bank of the Commonwealth* vs. *Grocers' National Bank*, 35 *Howard* [*N. Y. Pr.*], p. 412.) This last case holds that if the bank, the drawee, pays the forged check to the holder, it cannot recover back the money so paid. The same doctrine was held in case of *First National Bank of Quincy* vs. *Ricker*, 71 *Ill.*, p. 439; but qualified by holding that it applied only where the presumed negligence was all on the side of the bank, and where the holder or payee had been guilty of no fraud or act to throw the bank off its guard.

VIII. CERTIFYING.—National banks have the power to certify checks; and this power may be exercised by the cashier without any special authorization. The directors can limit this power, but such limitation will be no defense as to parties having no notice. (*Merchants' National Bank* vs. *State National Bank*, 10 *Wall.*, p. 604.)

IX. A certificate of a bank that a check is good is equivalent to an acceptance, implying that the bank has the funds to pay it, and that they are set apart for that purpose. (*Ibid.*, p. 604.)

X. A national bank is liable on a check certified by its cashier to the holder in good faith, although the drawer has no funds in the bank when it was certified. (*Cooke* vs. *State National Bank*, 52 *N. Y.*, p. 96.)

XI. The act of Congress of March 3, 1869, making it unlawful for a national bank to certify checks unless the drawer has at the time funds on deposit to an amount equal to the amount specified in the check, does not invalidate a conditional acceptance of a check by such bank, having no funds of the drawer in its hands at the time, but engaging to pay the same when a draft left with it for collection by the drawer shall have been paid. (*First National Bank* vs. *Merchants' National Bank*, 7 *West Va.*, p. 544.)

XII. A bank is liable to pay a subsequent *bona fide* purchaser the amount of a check which it has certified, notwithstanding the check was fraudulently raised, if before certification, from a smaller amount. (*Louisiana National Bank* vs. *Citizens' Bank*, 28 *La. Annual*, p. 189.)

XIII. When a bank was chargeable with negligence in certifying a check, which was so drawn as to admit of a fraudulent alteration of the amount being easily made, and the check *was* raised: *Held*, that the bank was liable to a *bona fide* holder, for value, for the increased amount. (*Helwege* vs. *Hibernia National Bank*, 28 *La. Annual*, p. 520.)

[NOTE.—As the above case unquestionably declares the true rule of law, prudence would seem to dictate that cashiers should always insist upon such filling up of checks as to render alteration impracticable, before certifying.]

XIV. A certified check is not deemed dishonored by delay between its date and the time when it is sold to a *bona fide* purchaser, for value, so that the latter takes it as overdue, and subject to equities; because, by certifying, the bank becomes the principal debtor, and liable indefinitely, like an acceptor of a bill of exchange. Hence, one who in good faith, and after making reasonable inquiry, bought a certified check, three or four months after its date, which had been *stolen*, was held entitled to recover its amount. (*Nolan* vs. *The Bank of New York*, 67 *Barb.*, p. 24.)

XV. A check contained on its face this recital: "To hold as collateral for 1,000 P. T. Oil, pipage paid to Jan. 4, 1876"; across its face the cashier wrote "Good when properly indorsed." *Held*, that the check was not drawn in usual course of banking business, and therefore the certificate of the cashier did not bind the bank. (*Dorsey* vs. *Abrams et al., bankers*, 85 *Pa.*, p. 299. See, further, as to liability on checks, certified or otherwise, *Dodge* vs. *National Exchange Bank*, 30 *O.*, p. 1; *Security Bank* vs. *National Bank of the Republic*, 67 *N. Y.*, p. 458; *Andrews* vs. *German National Bank*, 9 *Heisk.* [*Tenn.*], p. 211.)

CITIZENSHIP.

I. National banks are *citizens* of the State in which they are organized and located, and when sued by national banks of other States have a right to demand a removal of the suit from a State to the proper Federal court. (*Chatham Na-*

CITIZENSHIP—Continued.

> *tional Bank* vs. *Merchants' National Bank*, 4 *Thompson & Cook*, *N. Y. Sup C.*, *p.* 196, *and* 1 *Hunter* [*N. Y.*], *p.* 702; *Davis* vs. *Cook*, 9 *Nevada*, *p.* 134.)
> (See also Title "ACTIONS" V and VI, *supra*.)

II. A national bank, being a citizen of the State in which it is located, may be required to give security for costs when suing in another State; and in the State of New York such security may be required, because the bank is regarded as a corporation created by a foreign State. (*National Park Bank* vs. *Gunst*, 1 *Abbott's New Cases, p.* 292.)

COLLECTIONS.

I. A bank receiving paper for collection undertakes to use due diligence in making demand at maturity, and giving the proper notices of non-payment. An unreasonable delay will charge the bank with liability for the amount; and proof that the paper would not have been paid, if presented, will constitute no defense. (*Bank of Washington* vs. *Triplett*, 1 *Peters*, *p.* 25: *Bank of New Hanover* vs. *Kenner*, 76 *N. C.*, *p.* 340; *Steele* vs. *Russell*, 5 *Nebr.*, *p.* 211; *Capital State Bank* vs. *Lane*, 52 *Miss.*, *p.* 677; *Fabens* vs. *Mercantile Bank*, 23 *Pick.* [*Mass.*], *p.* 320.)

II. And if the bank receiving paper for collection, upon a sufficient consideration, transmits it to another bank to be collected, the receiving bank will be liable for the misconduct of such other bank, unless there is some agreement to the contrary. (*Montgomery County Bank* vs. *Albany City Bank*, 7 *N. Y.*, *p.* 459; *Commercial Bank* vs. *Union Bank*, 11 *N. Y.*, *p.* 203; *Kent* vs. *Dawson*, 13 *Blatchf.*, *p.* 237; *First National Bank* vs. *First National Bank of Denver*, 4 *Dill.*, *p.* 290.)

III. A bank received a check upon itself for collection, being at the same time a large creditor of the drawer, and failed, without excuse, to notify the depositor of the non-payment of the check: *Held*, that the bank was chargeable for the negligence. (*Bank of New Hanover* vs. *Kenner*, *supra*.)

IV. A bank holding a check for collection, and accepting the certification of the bank upon which it is drawn, in lieu of payment, assumes the risk and thereby becomes liable to the owner for the amount, with interest from date of certification. (*Essex County National Bank* vs. *Bank of Montreal*, 7 *Bissell*, *p.* 193.)

V. The *Corn Exchange National Bank of Chicago* sent defendant, the *Dawson Bank*, at Wilmington, N. C., a draft drawn upon one *Wiswall*, living at Washington, N. C., for collection. Defendant by letter acknowledged the receipt of the draft, stating that it had been credited to the Corn Exchange Bank, and entered for collection. Thereupon defendant sent draft to *Burbank & Gallagher*, bankers at Washington, N. C., for collection. The latter house collected the draft, but failed and passed into bankruptcy before remitting. In a suit brought by the assignee of the Corn Exchange National Bank against the Dawson Bank to recover the proceeds of the draft: *Held*, per Wallace, J., that the latter bank was liable for the amount. (*Kent, assignee, &c*; vs. *The Dawson Bank*, 13 *Blatchf.*, *p.* 237.)

[NOTE.—The court concedes that the authorities are conflicting upon the point involved in this case. In *New York*, *Ohio*, and in *England*, the decisions sustain the conclusions of Judge Wallace, while in *Connecticut*, *Massachusetts*, *Illinois*, and *Pennsylvania* precisely the contrary rule prevails. The point was made in this case that the law of Illinois should control the rights of parties, but it was held otherwise.]

VI. In an action by G against a bank it appeared that a note was made to G's order, indorsed by him, and sent through the house of B, a banker, for collection, and by B indorsed to the defendant bank, "for collection and credit": *Held*, that B, by the indorsement, did not become the owner of the note, and had no right to pledge it, or direct its proceeds to be credited to him in payment of his indebtedness to the defendant bank. (*First National Bank* vs. *Gregg*, 79 *Pa.*, *p.* 384.)

VII. In such case, if the defendant bank had made advances, or given new credit to B on the faith of the note, it would have been entitled to retain the amount out of the proceeds. (*Ibid.*)

VIII. A bank holding a customer's demand note has a lien upon the proceeds of drafts delivered to it for collection, after the giving of the note, though collected after the filing of a petition in bankruptcy, and can apply such proceeds upon the notes. (*Re Farnsworth*, 5 *Biss.*, *p.* 223.)

IX. A collection agent who receives from his principal a bill of lading of merchandise, deliverable to order, and attaches to it a *time* draft, may, in the absence of special instructions, deliver the bill of lading to the drawee of

COLLECTIONS—Continued.

the draft, upon the latter's acceptance of the draft. It is not the duty of the agent to hold the bill after such acceptance. (*National Bank of Commerce* vs. *Merchant's National Bank,* 1 *Otto, p.* 92.)

X. *Woolen & Co.,* bankers at Indianapolis, sent to defendant, a bank at Buffalo, a draft on one Bugbee; also bills of lading for sundry car-loads of lumber. The remittance was by letter, which merely stated that the draft and bills were sent to defendant for collection and remittance of proceeds to plaintiffs, *Woolen & Co.* The draft was drawn by, and to the order of, *Coder & Co.,* indorsed by them, by Mayhew, and the plaintiffs. By the terms of the draft the drawer, indorsers, and acceptor waived presentment for payment and notice of protest and non-payment. It was payable fifteen days after its date, and it was admitted that by ordinary course of *transit* the lumber would reach its destination eight days prior to the maturity of the draft. There had been no business transactions between plaintiffs and defendants, save one collection similar to this. Defendants presented the draft to Bugbee for acceptance, and upon such acceptance delivered to him the bills of lading. Bugbee failed before the draft matured, and plaintiffs sued defendants for delivering the bills of lading to Bugbee before payment of the draft. It was conceded that the draft was drawn for the price or value of the lumber: *Held, per Wallace, J.,* that, the draft being on time, it must be presumed that it was the intent of parties that Bugbee should realize from sale of the lumber the funds to meet the draft at maturity. Therefore, upon his acceptance of the draft he was entitled to the bills of lading, and defendants were not liable for thus delivering them, but if the draft had not been upon time, a different rule might have prevailed. (*Woolen & Webb* vs. *N. Y. and Erie Bank,* 12 *Blatchf.,* p. 359.)

XI. L. transmitted to a bank a draft indorsed "for collection on his account." The bank provisionally credited the draft, when received, to L., presented it for payment, and surrendered it to the drawee on receipt of his check for the amount. Instead of demanding the money on this check the bank had it certified "good," and on the same day suspended payment. The next day the check was collected, and the money mingled with the other money in the hands of the receiver: *Held,* that the receiver held the funds in trust for L. (*Levi* vs. *Missouri Bank,* 5 *Dillon, p.* 104.)

XII. The general power of a bank to collect ceases by its suspension, as to paper previously desposited therewith. (*Jocknsch* vs. *Towsey,* 51 *Tex., p.* 129.)

COMPROMISES.

I. In adjusting and compromising contested claims against it, growing out of a legitimate banking transaction, a national bank may pay a larger sum than would have been exacted in satisfaction of them, so as to thereby obtain a transfer of stocks of railroad and other corporations, in the honest belief that, by turning them into money under more favorable circumstances than then existed, a loss which it would otherwise suffer from the transaction might be averted or diminished. (*First National Bank* vs. *National Exchange Bank,* 2 *Otto,* p. 122.)

II. So, also, it may accept stocks in satisfaction of a doubtful debt, with a view to their subsequent conversion into money, in order to make good or reduce an anticipated loss. (*Ibid.*)
(See, also, Title "ESTATE, REAL," I, *post.*)

III. A court has no power, under section 5324 of the Revised Statutes of the United States, to order the receiver of a national bank to compound debts which are not "bad or doubtful"; and a composition under such an order, of debts not bad or doubtful, is ineffectual. (*Price, Receiver, &c.,* vs. *Yates,* 2 *Thomp. Cases,* p. 204. *U. S. circuit court, western district Pa.*)

COMPTROLLER.

I. The Comptroller appoints the *receiver,* and can therefore remove him. (*Kennedy* vs. *Gibson,* 8 *Wall., p.* 498.)

II. The Comptroller's certificate, reciting the existence of the facts of which he is required to be satisfied, to justify the appointment of a receiver, under section 50 of the national-bank act, is sufficient evidence of the validity of such appointment, in an action brought by such receiver. (*Platt* vs. *Bebee,* 57 *N. Y., p.* 339.)

III. The Comptroller must authorize any increase of the capital stock of a national bank; and such increase must be certified by him as prescribed by section 13 of the act of Congress providing for the organization of national banks. (*Charleston* vs. *People's National Bank,* 5 *S. C., p.* 103,)

COMPTROLLER—Continued.

IV. The Comptroller cannot subject the United States Government to the jurisdiction of a court, though he appears and answers to the suit. (*Case* vs. *Terrill*, 11 *Wall.*, *p.* 199.)

(See, also, Title "SHAREHOLDERS, INDIVIDUAL LIABILITTY OF," *post.*)

CONVERSION.

I. The conversion of a State into a national bank works no dissolution, only a change of the original corporation; nor does the latter thereby escape any of its liabilities. (*Maynard* vs. *Bank*, 1 *Brewster, Pa.*, *p.* 483 ; *Kelsey* vs. *National Bank of Crawford County*, 69 *Pa.*, *p.* 426; *Coffey* vs. *National Bank of the State of Missouri*, 46 *Mo.*, *p.* 140.)

CREDITORS OF NATIONAL BANKS.

I. The respective rights and liabilities existing between a national bank and its creditors and debtors become fixed when its *insolvency* occurs. * * * All the property and assets of the association then become a fund legally dedicated, first, to the satisfaction of any claim of the United States, for the redemption of its circulating notes, and, second, for a ratable distribution of the balance among its general creditors, upon the principle of equality. (*Balsh* vs. *Wilson*, 2 *Thomp. Case*, *p.* 276; 25 *Minn.*, *p.* 299.)

CURRENCY.

I. The word "*currency*," in a certificate of deposit, means money, including bank notes, which, though not an absolute legal tender, are used as money by authority of law, and are in circulation generally, at the *locus in quo*, on par with coin. (*Klauber* vs. *Biggerstaff*, 47 *Wis.*, *p.* 551.)

CURRENCY ACT.

I. The purpose of the Currency Act was, in part, to provide a currency for the whole country, and, in part, *to create a market for the government loans.* (*Per Strong, J.*, in *Tiffany* vs. *National Bank of the State of Missouri*, 18 *Wall.*, *p.* 413.)

II. National banks organized under the act of Congress of June 3, 1864, are the instruments designed to be used to aid the government in the administration of an important branch of the public service; and Congress, which is the sole judge of the necessity for their creation, having brought them into existence, the States can exercise no control over them, nor in any wise affect their operation, except so far as Congress may see proper to permit. (*Per Swayne, J.*, in *Farmers and Mechanics' National Bank* vs. *Dearing*, 1 *Otto*, *p.* 29.)

III. The constitutionality of the act of June 3, 1864, is unquestioned. It rests on the same principle as the act creating the second Bank of the United States. The reasoning of Secretary Hamilton and of this court in *McCulloch* vs. *The State of Maryland*, 4 *Wheat.*, *p.* 316, and in *Osborne* vs. *Bank U. S.*, 7 *Wheat.*, *p.* 708, therefore applies.

IV. The power to create carries with it the power to preserve. The latter is a corollary of the former. (*Ibid.*, *per Swayne, J.*, *pp.* 33, 34.)

DEBTORS OF NATIONAL BANKS.

I. Debtors of an insolvent national bank, when sued by the receiver, cannot object that pleadings do not show a compliance with all the steps prescribed by statutes as preliminary to the appointment of such receiver. (*Cadle, Receiver, &c.*, vs. *Baker & Co.*, 20 *Wall.*, *p.* 650.)

II. Such ordinary debtors may be sued by receiver without previous order of the Comptroller. (*Bank* vs. *Kennedy*, 17 *Wall.*, *p.* 19.)

DEPOSITS.

I. CERTIFICATES OF.—A certificate of deposit was issued by a bank for a certain sum, subject to the order of the depositor at a certain date, payable on the return of the certificate: *Held*, in an action on said certificate against the bank, brought by an assignee, that there could be no recovery without proof of an actual demand and refusal of payment. (*Brown* vs. *McElroy*, 52 *Ind.*, *p.* 404.)

II. In a suit against the bank, upon a stolen certificate of deposit given by the defendant to the plaintiff, reciting that he had deposited in the bank a certain number of dollars, payable to his order *in current funds*, on the return of the certificate properly indorsed: *Held*, first, that the instrument should be regarded as the promissory note of the bank, assignable under the statute (of Indiana), but that it was not negotiable as an inland bill of exchange, being made payable not in money, but "in current funds"; second, that the

DEPOSITS—Continued.

payee could recover on said stolen certificate without giving a bond against a subsequent claim thereunder by another person. (*National State Bank* vs. *Ringel*, 51 Ind., p. 393.)

III. Where a bank issues a certificate of deposit, payable on its return properly indorsed, it is liable thereon to a *bona-fide* holder, to whom it was transferred *seven* years after it was issued, notwithstanding the payment thereof to the original holder. Such certificate is not dishonored until presented. (*National Bank of Fort Edward* vs. *Washington County National Bank*, 5 Hun., N. Y. Sup. Court, p. 605.)

IV. Under a statute prohibiting the circulation of bills or notes *not* payable on demand, banks have no power to issue time certificates of deposit; and such certificates, if issued, are void They are equivalent to post notes. (*Bank of Peru* vs. *Farnesworth*, 18 Ill., p. 563; *Bank of Orleans* vs. *Merrill*, 2d Hill [N. Y.], p. 295; *Leavitt* vs. *Palmer*, 3 N. Y. [Comst.], p. 19.) (See, also, "CURRENCY" *supra*.)

V. GENERAL.—The relation between a bank and its depositors is that of debtor and creditor only, and is not fiduciary. Thus, a note deposited for collection, if passed to the credit of the depositor in his general account, then overdrawn, becomes the property of the bank, which becomes indebted to him for the proceeds. Upon the bankruptcy of the bank, the proceeds are assets available to the general creditors. And the fact that the account was made good by other deposits before collection of the note makes no difference. (*In re Bank of Madison*, 5 Bissell, p. 515.)

VI. A deposit is general, unless the depositor makes it special, or deposits it expressly in some particular capacity. And in case of a general deposit of money with a banker, a previous demand by the depositor, or some other person by his order, is indispensable to the maintenance of an action for the deposit, unless circumstances are shown which amount to a legal excuse. (*Brahm* vs. *Adkins*, 77 Ill., p. 263.)

VII. A national bank having become insolvent, a depositor therein assigned his deposit to a debtor of the bank: *Held*, that the latter could not offset such deposit against his debt, in an action thereon. (*Venango National Bank* vs. *Taylor*, 56 Pa., p. 14.)

VIII. A depositor was also indebted to the bank on bond and mortgage: *Held*, that he could offset his deposit against said indebtedness, the bank being in the hands of a receiver. (*Matter of New Amsterdam Savings Bank* vs. *Gartler*, 54 How. [N. Y. Pr.], p. 385.)

IX. The claims of depositors in a suspended national bank are, when proved to the satisfaction of the Comptroller of the Currency, on the same footing as if they were reduced to judgments, and from date of such proof bear interest. (*National Bank of the Commonwealth* vs. *Michigan National Bank*, 94 U. S. [4 Otto], p. 437.)

X. SPECIAL.—The taking of special deposits to keep, merely for the accommodation of the depositor, is not within the authorized business of national banks; and the cashiers of such banks have no power to bind them on any express contract accompanying, or any implied contract arising out of, such taking. (*Wiley* vs. *First National Bank*, 47 Vt., p. 546.)

[NOTE.—To the same effect was the decision of the New York court of appeals in *First Nat. Bank of Lyons* vs. *Ocean Nat. Bank*, 60 N. Y., p. 278. But it is to be remembered that in both these cases only the act of the cashier was relied upon to bind the bank. In the latter case it was stated that there was no proof of even implied knowledge, or assent on the part of the directory. In the well-reasoned case of *Weckler* vs. *First Nat. Bank of Hagerstown*, 42 Md., p. 581, these cases are cited with decided approval: but a recent decision of the Supreme Court goes very far towards establishing a different doctrine. In *National Bank* vs. *Graham*, 100 U. S., p. 699, the Supreme Court held that section 5228 R. S. U. S. conferred upon a national bank power to receive and take charge of special deposits, such as the public securities of the government, and that such bank is liable in damages for the loss, *through gross negligence*, of such deposit, when it had been made with the knowledge and acquiescence of its officers and directors. The learned judge who delivered the opinion (Mr. Justice Swayne) cited numerous State decisions, only referring to the cases in Vermont as being in conflict with the weight of adjudications, and based the conclusion of the court upon the doctrine that "gross negligence, on the part of a gratuitous bailee, though not a fraud, was equivalent thereto in legal effect, and that the doctrine of *ultra vires* has no application in favor of a corporation, when guilty of a wrong."]

DEPOSITS, SPECIAL—Continued.

XI. A national bank receiving a special deposit for safe keeping, without reward, is liable only for gross negligence. The burden of proof is on the plaintiff, and gross negligence is not the omission of that care which every attentive and diligent person takes of his own goods, but the omission of that care which the most inattentive takes. (*First National Bank, &c.*, vs. *Rex*, 89 *Penn.*, *p.* 308.)

DIRECTORS OF NATIONAL BANKS.

I. Directors of a national bank may remove the president, both under the law of Congress and the articles of association, where the latter so provide. The power exists if the bank has adopted no by-laws. (*Taylor* vs. *Hutton*, 43 *Barb.*, *N. Y. Sup. Court*, *p.* 195; *S. C.*, 18 *Abb. Pr. R.*, *p.* 16.)

II. In all cases where an act is to be done by a corporate body, a majority of the whole number of directors is necessary to constitute a valid meeting; but at a meeting when a quorum is present the majority of those present may act. A by-law adopted when less than a majority are present is void. (*Lockwood* vs. *American National Bank*, 9 *Rhode Island*, *p.* 308.)

(See Title "OFFICERS," *post.*)

III. The power to compromise or release claims in favor of a bank is in the board of directors, and not within the scope of the cashier's authority. (*Chemical Bank* vs. *Kohner*, 8 *Daly* [*N. Y.*], *p.* 530.

EMBEZZLEMENT.

I. When the president of national bank, having charge of its funds, converts them to his own use, he embezzles and abstracts them within section 55 (R. S., sec. 5209) of the national-bank act, unless he shows authority for thus using them. (*In the matter of Van Campen*, 2 *Benedict*, *p.* 419, *per Blatchford*, *J.*)

II. Although false entries in regard to such embezzlement are made on the books of such bank by the clerk, but by the order of the president, the latter is chargeable as principal; and the intent to defraud the bank is to be inferred from the fact of such embezzlement. (*Ibid.*)

III. The cashier of a national bank was indicted under said section 55 for embezzling and willfully misapplying the moneys of the bank with intent to defraud, &c. On trial it was proved that defendant took the moneys of the bank and used them in stock speculations, carried on in his own name, by depositing the same with a stock broker as "margins" for stocks bought on his own account. *Held*, that the intent to injure or defraud was conclusively presumed upon proof of the act charged; and, therefore, evidence was not admissible to prove that the cashier used the funds with the knowledge and consent of the president and some of the directors of the bank, and on account of and for the benefit of the bank. (*United States* vs. *Taintor*, 11 *Blatchf.*, *p.* 374.)

[NOTE.—This last case was decided in the United States circuit court, southern district of New York, Woodruff, Blatchford, and Benedict, JJ., all concurring in the decision.]

IV. A State court has no jurisdiction of the crime of embezzlement by an officer of a national bank situated within the State. (*Commonwealth* vs. *Felton*, 101 *Mass.*, *p.* 204; *State* vs. *Tuller*, 34 *Conn.*, *p.* 280.) But in this latter case it was also held that while a teller of such bank could not be punished for embezzling the funds of the bank, he could be convicted, under the statute of the State, for purloining property deposited with such bank for safekeeping; and in *Commonwealth* vs. *Barry*, 116 *Mass.*, *p.* 1, it was decided that though an officer of a national bank, who has stolen its property, may be subject to punishment for embezzlement under the national law, he may also be punished for the same act, *as a larceny*, under the statute of the State.

ESTATE, REAL.

I. The want of power of a bank, or of its trustee (receiver) in insolvency, to purchase and hold real estate, does not render void an arrangement whereby land subject to a lien in favor of the bank, and to other liens, is discharged of those other liens by funds from the assets of the bank, the land being then sold, and the entire proceeds of such sale realized to the bank assets, provided the title does not pass through the bank or its trustee. (*Zantzingers* vs. *Gunton*, 19 *Wall.*, *p.* 32.)

II. In *Union National Bank et al.* vs. *Matthews*, 98 *U. S.*, *p.* 652, the court recognized the doctrine that, "where a corporation is incompetent by its charter to take a title to real estate, a conveyance to it is not void, but only voidable,

6 C C

ESTATE, REAL—Continued.

and the sovereign alone can object. It is valid unless assailed in a direct
proceeding instituted for that purpose."

[NOTE.—Thus it would seem that a mortgage executed to secure a present
loan, or any other conveyance of real estate to a national bank, must be
held valid until declared void in a direct proceeding instituted for that purpose by the United States Government.]

(See also, *Wroten's Assignee* vs. *Armat*, 31 *Grattan, p.* 238.)

III. The title to real estate taken by a national bank, on adjustment of a liability
in its favor, must be held valid until attacked by the United States, in direct
proceedings instituted for that purpose. Such title cannot be impeached
collaterally, in an ejectment suit. (*Mapes et al.* vs. *Scott et al.*, 94 *Ill., p.* 379 ;
National Bank vs. *Whitney*, 106 *U. S., p.* 99; *Graham* vs. *National Bank*, 32
N. J. Eq., p. 804; *Warner* vs. *Dewitt*, 4 *Ill. App., p.* 305.)

(See, also, Title "LOANS ON REAL ESTATE," *post.*)

ESTOPPEL.

I. A shareholder in a national bank, who has participated in its transactions as
such, and received dividends, is estopped from denying the legality of its
incorporation. The same rule applies to one accustomed to deal with a
national bank as such, as by giving his promissory note to such bank.
(*Wheelock* vs. *Kost*, 77 *Ill., p.* 296; *National Bank of Fairhaven* vs. *Phœnix
Warehousing Company*, 6 *Hun.* [*N. Y.*], *p.* 71; *Casey* vs. *Galli*, 94 *U. S., p.* 673,
and numerous cases therein cited.)

II. The *Manufacturers' National Bank of Chicago*, defendant, being the city corre-
spondent of the *People's Bank of Belleville*, plaintiff, guaranteed to the latter
bank the payment of certain notes of one Picket, pursuant to an agreement
that thus guaranteed their amount should be, *as it was, debited to the account
of the Belleville bank.* Such agreement, and the guarantee in pursuance
thereof, were made by the vice-president of the defendant bank, with the
assent of the president and cashier, but without the assent of the directors.
Held, that under the circumstances the defendant bank was estopped from
setting up, as a defense, that such guarantee was *ultra vires.* (*People's Bank*
vs. *National Bank*, 101 *U. S., p.* 181.)

[NOTE.—It will be observed that this decision stops far short of legaliz-
ing naked accommodation paper made by a national bank.]

III. A national bank which has wrongfully converted to its own use the property
of another, is estopped from denying its liability to account therefor upon
the ground that it received and held the property in carrying on the business of a warehouseman, outside the powers conferred by its charter. (*German National Bank* vs. *Meadowcroft*, 2 *Thomp. Cases, p.* 462. *Sup. Court Ill.*)

EVIDENCE.

I. Even if it be within the authority of the president of a national bank to bind
the bank by an agreement with the acceptor of a draft, which is discounted
by the bank, not to enforce the draft against him, yet *oral* evidence of such
an agreement is not competent in defense of a suit by the bank against the
acceptor. (*Davis* vs. *Randall*, 115 *Mass., p.* 547.)

II. The certificate of the Comptroller of the organization of a national bank is
conclusive evidence as to the completeness of such organization, in a suit
against one of its shareholders. (*Casey* vs. *Galli, ante ; Thatcher* vs. *West
River National Bank*, 19 *Mich., p.* 196.)

III. In ordering an assessment for the payment of the debts of an insolvent bank,
the stock certificates and stock ledger of the bank must be taken by the
Comptroller of the Currency, in the absence of fraud or mistake, as showing who the stockholders were at the time of the failure. (*Davis* vs. *Essex,
Baptist Society*, 44 *Conn., p.* 582.)

IV. The maker of a certificate of deposit cannot overcome its effect, as proof of a
deposit actually made, except by clear and satisfactory evidence. (*First
National Bank of Lacon* vs. *Meyers*, 83 *Ill., p.* 507.)

INTEREST.

I. Under section 30, act of 1864, a national bank in any State may take as high
rate of interest as by the laws of such State a natural person may stipulate
for, although State banks of issue are restricted to a less rate. (*Tiffany* vs.
National Bank of the State of Missouri, 18 *Wall., p.* 409.)

II. As the action was virtually brought to recover the penalty for *usury*, the statute (section 30) must receive a strict construction. (*Ibid., p.* 409.)

[NOTE.—In Missouri, natural persons may take ten per cent., but State

INTEREST—Continued.

> banks are restricted to eight per cent. In this case the national bank had taken nine per cent.—*Held.* legal.]

III. In a suit by a national bank upon a bill of exchange discounted by it, the acceptor cannot set up by way of counter-claim, or set-off, that the bank in discounting a series of bills of said acceptor, the proceeds of which it used to pay other bills, knowingly took, and was paid, a greater rate of interest than that allowed by law. (*Barnett* vs. *National Bank*, 98 *U. S.* [8, *Otto*], *p.* 555.)

IV. The act of June 3, 1864 (R. S.. sec. 5198), having prescribed that, as a penalty for such taking, the person paying such unlawful interest, or his legal representative, may *in an action of debt* against the bank recover back twice the amount so paid, he can resort to no other mode or form of procedure. (*Brown* vs. *Second National Bank of Erie*, 72 *Pa.*, *p.* 209; *Barnett* vs. *National Bank*, 98 *U. S.*, *p.* 555.)

> [NOTE.—The above case of *Barnett* vs. *National Bank*, 98 *U. S.*, *p.* 555, over-rules several State adjudications, and settles several points in regard to usurious interest as affecting loans by national banks. It holds that when suit is brought by such bank to recover a loan made at usurious rate, stipulated for, but not paid, the entire interest thus agreed upon, but no part of the principal, is forfeited, and the latter may be recovered in full; that when the usurious interest has been paid, twice its sum may be recovered back by the borrower, but this can only be done by a suit directly brought for that purpose, which suit must be in the nature of an action of *debt*, commenced, of course, within the two years specified. Suppose, then, A borrows $1,000 from a national bank on 90 days' time, and for the loan actually pays usurious interest in advance. Suppose his paper is protested and suit is brought upon it. It follows that while A cannot offset twice the usurious interest he has paid, nor any part thereof, in reduction of the face of his paper, the bank can recover from him not only the principal of the loan, but legal interest thereon from the date of maturity of the note or bill.]

> (See, also, *Natl. Bank* vs. *Dearing*, 91 *U. S.*, *p.* 29, and Title "USURY," *post.*)

V. ON CLAIMS OF CREDITORS.—Where a national bank is put in charge of a receiver, under section 50 of the original Currency Act (R. S., sec. 5234), and a sufficient sum is realized from its assets to pay all claims against it and leave a surplus, the Comptroller ought to allow interest on the claims during the period of administration, before appropriating the surplus to the stockholders of the bank. An action of assumpsit by the holder of such a claim will not lie against the Comptroller, nor against the receiver, but will lie against the bank. (*Chemical National Bank* vs. *Bailey*, 12 *Blatchf.. p.* 480.)

VI. In such action interest is recoverable on all demands originating in contract, conditioned for the payment of interest, and on all demands for money due and unpaid, by way of damages for non-payment after such demands became due. And interest is recoverable on a balance due a depositor in such bank, although he has made no formal demand of payment. (*Ibid.*) But, as to this last point, see the ruling of the Supreme Court.

VII. In the case of *National Bank of the Commonwealth* vs. *Mechanics' National Bank*, 4 *Otto*, *p.* 437, the United States Supreme Court decided that a depositor in a national bank, when it suspends payment and a receiver is appointed, is entitled from the date of his demand to interest on the deposit; that the claims of depositors in such bank at date of suspension, for the amount of their deposits, are, when proved to the satisfaction of the Comptroller of the Currency, placed upon the same footing as if reduced to judgments; that is to say, they draw interest from the time of such proof and allowance. It was also decided that, such interest being a liquidated sum at the time of the payment of the deposit, an action lies to recover it, *and interest thereon.*

VIII. When the Comptroller assesses shareholders to pay the debts of an insolvent national bank, such assessment bears interest from the date of the Comptroller's order. (*Casey* vs. *Galli*, *ante.*)

JUDGMENTS.

I. A judgment against a national bank in the hands of a receiver, upon a claim, only establishes the validity of such claim; the plaintiff can have no execution on such judgment, but must await *pro rata* distribution. (*Bank of Bethel* vs. *Pahquioque Bank*, 14 *Wall.*, *p.* 383, and *Clifford, J.*, *p.* 402.)

JURISDICTION.

I. A United States district court has jurisdiction to authorize a receiver of an insolvent national bank to compromise a debt. (*Matter of Platt*, 1 *Ben.*, *p.* 534.)

JURISDICTION—Continued.

II. A resident (citizen) of Kentucky was a creditor of a national bank located in
Alabama, and commenced a suit on his claim against said bank in the supreme court of the State of New York, at the same time attaching certain
moneys belonging to said bank, in the hands of the National Park Bank, in
New York. Subsequently the receiver of the Alabama bank (which had
failed) was, on his own motion, made party defendant to the action pending
in the New York supreme court, and pleaded "*want of jurisdiction*," and
other defenses. The supreme court overruled his plea to the jurisdiction,
rendered judgment against the receiver on the merits, and ordered satisfaction to be made from the moneys attached. Thereupon the receiver filed
his bill in chancery in the *United States circuit court* for the proper circuit,
praying an injunction to restrain the collection of the judgment rendered by
said supreme court, and that the moneys attached be paid to him as receiver.
Held, that, by the provisions of the Currency Act, the State court was de-
prived of jurisdiction of the attachment proceedings; that the receiver was
not estopped by the proceedings in said State court from asserting his
rights in said circuit court, and that he was entitled to the relief prayed
for in his bill. (*Cadle, Receiver, &c.*, vs. *Tracy*, 11 *Blatchf.*, *p.* 101.)
(See, also, Title "RECEIVERS," VII, *post.*)

III. State courts have no jurisdiction of actions to recover penalties imposed by
the National-Bank Act. (*Newell* vs. *National Bank of Somerset*, 12 *Bush.* [*Ky.*].
p. 57.)
(See, also, Title "EMBEZZLEMENT." IV, *ante.*)

IV. The United States circuit court has no jurisdiction of a suit by a private person to restrain or interfere with the Treasurer of the United States or the
Comptroller of the Currency in the discharge of their duties in respect to
bonds deposited to secure the redemption of circulating notes of a national
bank. (*Van Antwerp* vs. *Hulburd.* 7 *Blatchf.*, *p.* 426.)

V. An action will not lie against the Comptroller nor the receiver, upon a claim
against an insolvent national bank, but will lie against such bank. (*Chemical National Bank* vs. *Bailey*, *ante.* See, also, *Bank of Bethel* vs. *Pahquioque
Bank. ante.*)

VI. A national bank cannot be sued in the United States district courts outside
of the district where it is located. (*Main* vs. *Second Nat. Bank of Chicago.*
6 *Bissell*, *p.* 26.)

VII. Nor can such action be brought against a national bank in a State court, save
in the county or city where it is located. (*Crocker* vs. *Marine National Bank*,
101 *Mass.*, *p.* 240.)
(See, also, Title "ACTION," VII, *ante;* also "EMBEZZLEMENT." IV, *ante.*)

VIII. The provision of Section 5198, U. S. Rev. Stats., requiring that suits, actions,
and proceedings against a national bank in any State, county, or municipal
court must be brought in the county in which such bank is located, are held
to apply to transitory actions only, and not to such actions as are by law
local in their character. (*Casey, Receiver, &c.*, vs. *Adams*, 2 *Thomp. Cases, p.*
102. *U. S. Supreme Court.*)
[NOTE.—The jurisdiction of the local court was sustained in this cause,
although it seemed clear that a complete remedy might have been had in
the U. S. circuit court at New Orleans, where the bank was situated.]

IX. National banks are not entitled, by force of the National-Bank Act, to have
any suit in a State court, wherein they are parties defendant, removed to a
Federal court. (*Wilder* vs. *Union National Bank*, 2 *Thomp. Cases*, *p.* 124.)

LOANS IN EXCESS.

I. A loan by a national bank in excess of the restriction of section 29 of the act
of 1864 (Revised Statutes, section 5200), which provides that the total liabilities of any person (borrower) shall not exceed ten per centum of the
capital stock, &c., is not void on that account. The loan may be enforced,
though the bank may be liable to proceedings for forfeiture of its privileges,
&c., for making it. (*Stewart* vs. *National Union Bank of Maryland*, 2 *Abb..
United States, p.* 424. See, also, *O'Hare* vs. *Second National Bank*, 77 *Pa.*, *p.*
96.)

II. In *Samuel M. Shoemaker* vs. *The National Mechanics' Bank*, and *The same* vs.
The National Union Bank, application for injunction, &c., United States circuit court, Baltimore, Md.. Judge Giles held, " * * * "As to the first
charge in this bill against the defendant, in reference to the amount loaned
to Bayne & Co., in violation of the twenty-ninth section of the act of June
3, 1864, I would only say that the loan made under such circumstances is

LOANS IN EXCESS—Continued.

not void ; it can be enforced as any other loan made by the bank." (*Vide* 31 *Md.*, *p.* 306.)

III. The validity of a loan in excess of the above-named statutory restriction was established and set at rest by the decision of the United States Supreme Court, in the case of *Gold Mining Company* vs. *Rocky Mountain National Bank*, 96 *U. S.* [6 *Otto*]. *p.* 640.

LOANS ON REAL ESTATE.

I. A executed a note to B, and, to secure payment thereof, also executed a deed of trust on lands, which was in effect a mortgage, with a power of sale thereto annexed. A national bank, on the security of the note *and deed*, loaned money to B, who thereupon assigned them to the bank. The note not being paid at maturity, the trustee was proceeding to sell the lands pursuant to the power, when A filed a bill in chancery to enjoin the sale upon the ground that by sections 5136–'37, Revised Statutes, the deed did not inure as a security for a loan made by the bank at the time of the assignment of said note and deed : *Held*, that the bank was entitled to enforce collection of the note by a sale of the lands pursuant to the power in the deed of trust. (*Union National Bank of St. Louis* vs. *Matthews*, 98 *U. S.* [3 *Otto*], *p.* 621.) Mr. Justice Miller dissented, holding the note valid, but that the deed was inoperative as security to the bank.

[NOTE.—It is now well settled that a mortgage given to secure a loan from a national bank, executed directly to the bank when the loan is made, is valid, unless set aside by proceedings instituted for that purpose by the government. *National Bank* vs. *Whitney*, 103 *U. S.*, *p.* 99. *Graham* vs. *National Bank*, 32 *N. J. Eq.*, *p.* 804. *Warner* vs. *Dewitt*, 4 *Ill. App.*, *p.* 305.]

LOANS ON SHARES.

I. National banks are governed by the act of 1864, which repealed the act of 1863, and cannot, therefore, make loans on the security of their own shares, unless to secure a pre-existing debt, contracted in good faith. (*Bank, &c.*, vs. *Lanier*, 11 *Wall.*, *p.* 369.)

II. The placing of funds by one bank on permanent deposit with another bank is a loan within the spirit of section 35 of act of 1864. (*Ibid*, *p.* 369.)

III. Loans by such banks to their shareholders do not create a lien on the shares of such borrowers. (*Ibid*, *p.* 369.)

(See, also, *Bullard* vs. *Bank*, 18 *Wall.*, *p.* 580 ; and "BY-LAWS," *supra*.)

IV. But a national bank has the right to make loans on negotiable notes secured by the stock of another corporation, of marketable values. (*Shoemaker* vs. *National Mechanics' Bank*, 1 *Hugh.*, *p.* 101.) The same doctrine was also held in case of *Germania National Bank et al.* vs. *F. F. Case, receiver, &c.*, decided by the United States Supreme Court at its last term. It will be reported in 99 U. S.

LOCATION.

I. Under sections 6, 8, 10, 15, 18, and 44 of the original Currency Act (13 Stat. at Large, 101), respecting the location of banking associations, a national bank is to be regarded as located at the place specified in its organization certificate. If such a place is in a State, the association is located in that State. (*Manufacturers' National Bank* vs. *Baack, & Blatchf.*, *p.* 137.)

OFFICERS.

I. CASHIER. The cashier is the general executive officer of a bank, having charge of its funds, notes, bills, and other choses in action. Either directly or through his subordinates he receives all moneys and notes of the bank, delivers up discounted paper when paid, draws checks to withdraw funds of the bank when deposited, and generally, as such executive officer, transacts most of the bank business. (*United States* vs. *City Bank of Columbus*, 21 *How.*, *p.* 356, and numerous later decisions.)

II. But the cashier can make no declaration binding the bank not within the scope of his general powers. (*Bank of Metropolis* vs. *Jones, & Pet.*, *p.* 12; *S. P.*, 3 *Watts & S.*, *Pa.*, *p.* 317; 3 *Gill* [*Md.*], *p.* 96.)

III. A cashier who has made sale of corporate property, and holds a balance in his hands, is the agent of the board of directors, and not of the respective stockholders, and cannot be charged by an individual stockholder as holding such balance for his benefit. (*Brown* vs. *Adams*, 5 *Biss.*, *p.* 131.)

IV. A cashier, without special authority, cannot bind his bank by an official indorsement of his individual note, and the *onus* is on the payee to show such

OFFICERS, CASHIER.—Continued.

authority. (*West Saint Louis Savings Bank* vs. *Shawnee Co. Bank*. 3 *Dill*, *p.* 403.)

V. Although the cashier of a bank may, in the ordinary course of business, without the action of the directors, dispose of the negotiable securities of the bank, he has not the power to pledge its assets for the payment of an antecedent debt. (*State of Tennessee* vs. *Davis*, 50 *How*. [*N. Y.*], *p.* 447.)

VI. A cashier has not the authority to compromise or release a claim of the bank. (*Chemical Bank* vs. *Kohner, & Daley* [*N. Y.*], *p.* 530.)

VII. DIRECTORS. It is the duty of directors of a bank to to use ordinary diligence in acquiring knowledge of its business. They cannot be heard, when sued, to say that they were not apprised of facts the existence of which is shown by the books, accounts, and correspondence of the bank. They should control the subordinate officers of the bank in all important transactions. Therefore, under the circumstances proved in this particular case, they were held liable for the abstraction and sale of special deposits by the latter. (*United Society, &c.*, vs. *Underwood*, 9 *Bush* [*Ky.*], *p.* 609; *German Bank* vs. *Wulfekuhler*, 19 *Kansas*, *p.* 60.)

VIII. The cashier of a national bank, who had executed no bond, embezzled its funds, discovery whereof might have been effected by use of slight diligence on the part of the directory. They, however, published, according to law, a statement of the condition of the bank, which showed that its affairs were being prudently and honestly administered, and from which the public had a right to believe that he was trustworthy. Afterward, persons who had seen this report became sureties on the official bond of the cashier, and for his subsequent embezzlements were sought to be held liable thereon: *Held*, that such sureties, being mislead by the statement, were released. They had a right to believe that the directors, before publishing it, investigated the condition of the bank. (*Graves* vs. *Lebanon National Bank*, 10 *Bush* [*Ky.*], *p.* 23.)

IX. The mere fact that directors of a bank knew of and sanctioned overdrafts will not release from liability the sureties of a teller who causes a loss to the bank by permitting overdrafts; for the directors of a bank have no power to sanction overdrafts. (*Market Street Bank* vs. *Stumpe*, 2 *Mo.*, *app.*, 545.)

X. PRESIDENT. A guarantee against loss for signing as sureties, given by a bank president without authority from the directors, to those whom he had solicited thus to sign a note, given to the bank to retire a prior note held by it against their principal, is held to be the individual contract of the president, and not binding upon the bank. (*First National Bank* vs. *Bennett*, 33 *Mich.*, *p.* 520.)

XI. A president of a bank bought the stock of A. for $1,000, and in payment gave up to A. his note for that amount, which the bank held against A.: *Held*, that the President exceeded his powers, and that the bank could recover from A. the amount of the note thus surrendered. (*Rhoads* vs. *Webb*, 24 *Minn.*, *p.* 292.)

XII. A president of a bank, who, with the cashier, had the general charge of its business, permitted and directed the drawing of moneys from the bank by one irresponsible, without security, and for a business in which the president was interested with the party drawing the funds. He requested the cashier not to say anything of it to the directors: *Held*, that the president was personally responsible for the moneys thus drawn. (*First National Bank of Sturgis* vs *Reed*, 36 *Mich.*, *p.* 263.) *Quere:* Would not an indictment for embezzlement lie under the National-Bank Act?

XIII. The president of a bank, as such, has no authority to release the claims of the bank against any one. Such authority must come from the directors, by vote or implication. (*Olney* vs. *Chadsey*, 7 *R. I.*, *p.* 224.)

POST-NOTES.

I. Certificates of deposit, payable at a fixed future day, held to be equivalent to post-notes, and therefore void, as prohibited by a State law. (See *ante*, Title "DEPOSITS, CERTIFICATES OF," IV, and cases there cited.)

RECEIVERS.

I. The receiver of a national bank is the instrument of the Comptroller, and may be removed by him. (*Kennedy* vs. *Gibson, & Wall.*, *p.* 505.)

II. Such receiver is the statutory assignee of the assets of the bank, and may sue to collect the same in his own name, or in the name of the bank for his use, (*Ibid.*, *p.* 506.)

RECEIVERS—Continued.

III. In such suit it is not necessary to make the bank or creditors parties. (*Ibid.*, p. 506.)

IV. The receiver of a national bank represents such bank and its creditors, but he in no sense represents the United States Government, and cannot subject the government to the jurisdiction of any court. (*Case vs. Terrill*, 11 *Wall.*, p. 199.)

V. The decision of a receiver, rejecting a claim against his bank, is not final. Claimant may still sue. (*Bank of Bethel vs. Pahquioque Bank*, 14 *Wall.*, p. 383.)

VI. The clause of section 50, act of 1864, which prescribes that the receiver shall be "under the direction of the Comptroller," means only that he shall be *subject* to his direction, not that he shall not act without orders. He may and must collect the assets. That is what he is appointed for. (*Bradley, J.,* in *Bank vs. Kennedy,* 17 *Wall.,* pp. 22–3.)

VII. Receivers of national banks are officers of the United States, within the meaning of the act of Congress of March 3, 1815, giving United States courts jurisdiction of actions by United States officers, and may sue in such courts. (*Platt, receiver, &c.,* vs. *Beach,* 2 *Ben.,* p. 303.)

[NOTE.—The judge places stress upon the provision of section 31 of the act of 1864, which requires (in that particular instance) that the Secretary of the Treasury shall concur in the appointment of the receiver.]

VIII. Receiver not liable to be sued on a claim against the bank. (See Title "JURISDICTION," V, *ante.*)

SET-OFF.

I. In an action brought to enforce the individual liability of a shareholder of an insolvent bank, such shareholder cannot set off against such liability the amount due to him as a creditor of the bank. (*Garrison vs. Howe,* 17 *N. Y.,* p. 458; *In re Empire City Bank,* 18 *N. Y.,* p. 199.)

[NOTE.—Though these cases were decided by a State tribunal (New York court of appeals), and the rulings were based upon provisions of a State constitution and a State statute, yet the principle they enunciate is recognized and fully affirmed in *Sawyer* vs. *Hoag,* 17 *Wall.,* p. 610, and *Scammon* vs. *Kimball,* 2 *Otto,* p. 342. See, also, *Venango National Bank* vs. *Taylor,* 56 *Pa.,* p. 14.]

II. A creditor of an insolvent national bank, being such at date of its suspension, may set-off the amount of his claim against any claim held by the bank against him at the same date; as, for example, his note, even though such note had not then matured. (*Berry vs. Brett,* 6 *Bos.* [N. Y.], p. 627; *New Amsterdam Savings Bank* vs. *Gartter,* 54 *How.* [*P. R.*], p. 385; *Platt, receiver,* vs. *Bentley,* 11 *Am. Law Register,* p. 171; *Hade, receiver,* vs. *McVay,* 31 *O. St.,* p. 231; same case, *Brown's National Bankrupt Cases,* p. 353; and see the cases cited on p. 357, viz, 56 *Maine,* 167; 1 *Paige* [*N. Y.*], p. 444; 12 *Gray* [*Mass.*], p. 233.)

III. Usurious interest *paid* cannot be set-off. (*Hade* vs. *McVay,* 31, *O. St.,* p. 231; *Barnet* vs. *National Bank,* 98 *U. S.,* p. 555.

SHAREHOLDERS.

I. GENERAL RULES. A person is presumed to be the owner of stock when his name appears on the books of a company as a stockholder; and when he is sued as such, the burden of disproving such presumption is cast upon him. (*Turnbull* vs. *Payson,* 95 *U. S.* [5 *Otto*], p. 418.)

II. Shareholders have no standing in court to interfere for the protection of their company, until the board of directors has neglected, or refused on application, to take the proper steps to protect the interests of the company. (*Fifth National Bank, &c.,* vs. *Railroad Co.,* 2 *Thomp. Cases,* p. 190.)

III. Shares of stock in a national bank are salable and transferable like other personal property; and the statute recognizes this transferability by authorizing each association to prescribe the manner of their transfer. (*Johnston* vs. *Laflin,* 103 *U. S., per Field, J.,* on p. 803.)

IV. This power can only go to the extent of prescribing conditions essential to the protection of the association against fraudulent transfers, or such as are designed to evade just responsibility. It must be exercised reasonably. Transfers cannot be clogged with useless restrictions, nor be made dependent on the consent of directors or stockholders. (*Ibid.*)

V. As between the parties to a sale, it is enough that the certificate of stock is delivered, with authority to the purchaser, or any one he may name, to transfer it on the books of the association, and payment of the price. (*Ibid.*, p. 804.)

SHAREHOLDERS—Continued.

VI. The entry of the transaction on the books of the association is required, not for the translation of title, but for the protection of parties and others dealing with the bank, to enable the bank to know who are its stockholders, entitled to vote and receive dividends. *It is necessary to protect the seller against subsequent liability as stockholder,* and, perhaps also, to protect the purchaser against proceedings by creditors of the seller. (*Ibid., Field J., p. 804.*)

VII. When a national bank reduces its capital, each shareholder is entitled to a return of his proportional amount, and the bank cannot retain the funds as surplus, or for any other purpose; and having refused to permit shares thus retired to be transferred on its books, the bank is liable for the value of the shares to the holders. (*Seeley vs. New York National Exchange Bank,* 4 *Abb. New Cases, p.* 61.)

VIII. INDIVIDUAL LIABILITY OF. The Comptroller must decide when and for what amount the personal liability of the shareholders of an insolvent national bank shall be enforced. (*Kennedy vs. Gibson,* × *Wall., p.* 505.)

IX. His decision as to this is conclusive. Shareholders cannot controvert it. (*Ibid., p.* 505; *Casey vs. Galli,* 94 *U. S.* [*4 Otto*], *p.* 673; *Germania National Bank et al. vs. Case, Receiver, U. S. Supreme Court,* not yet reported.)

[NOTE.—These cases are decisive against the ruling in *Bowden vs. Morris,* 1 *Hugh., p.* 378.]

X. In any suit brought to enforce such personal liability, such decision of the Comptroller must be averred by the plaintiff, and, if put in issue, must be proved. (*Kennedy vs. Gibson, supra.*)

XI. The liability of shareholders is several, and not joint. (*Ibid., p.* 505.)

XII. The limit of such liabilities is the par value of the stock held by each one. (*Ibid., p.* 505.)

XIII. Where the whole amount is sought to be recovered, the proceeding must be at law; where less is required, the proceeding may be in equity, and in such case an interlocutory decree may be taken for contribution, and the case may stand over for the further action of the court, if such action should subsequently prove to be necessary, until the full amount of the liability is exhausted. (*Ibid., p.* 505.)

XIV. In such equity suit, all shareholders within the jurisdiction of the court should be made parties defendant; but it is no defense that those not within the jurisdiction are not joined. (*Kennedy vs. Gibson, supra.*)

XV. Suits to enforce personal liability of shareholders may properly be brought before other assets are exhausted. (*Ibid., pp.* 505–6.)

XVI. One Stevens bought shares in a national bank, and caused them to be transferred to one Elston, a porter in the office of his New York broker, and irresponsible. At the time of the transfer, there was no suspicion of the insolvency of the bank, and it remained in good credit for more than a year afterward: *Held,* that Stevens was liable as stockholder upon the failure of the bank. (*Davis, Receiver, vs. Stevens,* 2 *Thomp. Cases, p.* 158. *U. S. circuit court southern district N. Y., per Waite, C. J.*)

XVII. Where, before the failure of a bank, stock was transferred on its books to the name of an irresponsible person, for the purpose of escaping liability, and so stood at the time of the appointment of a receiver: *Held,* that the receiver could show who the real owner was, and that the latter was liable for the assessment. (*Ibid.*)

XVIII. RATABLE LIABILITY OF. Mr. Morse, in his Treatise on Banks, &c., second edition, p. 503, states the law in substance as follows: "The liability of each stockholder is precisely for his ratable proportion of that indebtedness of the bank which is to be borne by the shareholders. It is for his share of such total indebtedness, not for his proportion of each item thereof. Neither are the solvent shareholders, or those who can be come at for collection, liable to assessment beyond the proportional amount as above stated, by reason of the insolvency or inaccessibility of others of the shareholders. Those who are solvent and accessible have not the burden of paying off the sum which is due from all together; only their own proportionate share." This theory was fully sustained by the United States Supreme Court, in the case of *United States* vs. *Knox,* 102 *U. S., p.* 422. See also the cases there cited.

XIX. LIABILITY OF EXECUTOR, ADMINISTRATOR, AND HEIRS OF. Where stockholder died before failure of bank, stock not having been transferred to name of administrator: *Held,* that the stock is not to be regarded as having been at the time of the failure the property of the administrator, in such a sense as to constitute him a shareholder within the meaning of sec. 5152, U. S. Rev. Stat., so as to limit liability of the estate to funds actually in the hands of administrator. *Held,* also, that the provision of the act exempting execu-

SHAREHOLDERS, LIABILITY OF EXECUTOR OF, &C.—Continued.

tors, administrators and trustees from personal liability was not intended to affect the liability to assessment of estates in process of settlement, but only to prevent a personal liability from running against persons acting in a trust capacity, who had received the stock for the benefit of trust estates. (*Davis* vs. *Weed*, 44 *Conn.*, *p.* 569.)

XX. The liability of a stockholder is in the nature of a *contract*, and as such was a personal liability, for which his estate was holden at his death. (*Davis* vs. *Weed*, *supra*, citing *Hawthorne* vs. *Calef*, 2 *Wall.*, *p.* 22; *Lowry* vs. *Jamen*, 46 *N. Y.*, *p.* 119: *Bailey* vs. *Hollister*, 26 *N. Y.*, *p.* 112.)

XXI. LIABILITY OF TRUSTEE OF. To protect trustee of stock from personal liability it must appear upon the books that he held as such trustee. (*Davis* vs. *Essex Baptist Society*, 44 *Conn.*, *p.* 582.)

XXII. Creditors have a right to know who have pledged their personal liability. (*Ibid.*)

XXIII. If a trustee wishes to disclose his trusteeship, there is no difficulty in giving notice upon the books of the bank. If he does not do so he is guilty of laches, for which others should not suffer. (*Ibid.*)

XXIV. The settlement of the affairs of an insolvent bank would be rendered a matter of great labor, expense, and delay if persons who appeared upon the books of the bank as individual stockholders were permitted to relieve themselves by proof *aliunde* that they held the stock as executors, guardians, or trustees. (*Ibid.*)

[NOTE.]—The last-cited case, and *Davis* vs. *Weed*, *supra*, although reported in the Connecticut Reports, were decided by the United States district court.]

XXV. LIABILITY OF TRANSFEREE OF. The transferee of shares, when such transfer is absolute on the books of the bank, is liable to creditors to the amount of such shares, although in fact he holds them as collateral security for a loan to the shareholder who transferred them. (*Hale* vs. *Walker*, 31 *Iowa*, *p.* 614; *Adderley* vs. *Storm*, 6 *Hill*, *p.* 624; *Van Riker's case*, 20 *Wend.*, *p.* 614; *Bowden, Receiver*, vs. *Santos et al.*, 1 *Hugh.*, *p.* 158; *Marcy* vs. *Clark*, 17 *Mass*, *p.* 330.)

[NOTE.—In the *Bankers' Magazine* for January, 1875, is a notice of the case of *Mann, Receiver*, vs. *Dr. Cheeseman*, decided by Blatchford, J., in the United States circuit court, in New York, in which the judge held that until there was a transfer of shares *on the books of the bank*, the shareholder whose name there appeared was liable for the debts of the bank; that an actual sale and the signing of the ordinary power of attorney on the back of the certificate will not relieve the seller. To the foregoing rulings of State and other subordinate tribunals may now be added the decision of the Supreme Court of the United States, in *Germania Bank et al.* vs. *Case, Receiver*, already cited. The Germania National Bank of New Orleans discounted a note for the firm of Phelps, McCullough & Co. for $14,000, at ninety days, taking as part security therefor the pledge of 100 shares of the Crescent City National Bank stock, with power of attorney to the Germania cashier to transfer, sell, &c., on default in payment of the note. Phelps, McCullough & Co. failed, and the note was protested at maturity. Prior to the maturity of the note, the Crescent City Bank sustained such heavy losses that it was notoriously in bad repute in New Orleans; and yet, when the note fell due, the cashier of the Germania immediately transferred to his own bank, upon the books of the Crescent City Bank, the 100 shares so pledged. Afterwards, on the same day, he transferred 76 of these shares to one Waldo, a clerk of the Germania Bank; and on the day following transferred the remainder to said Waldo. It was proved that Waldo paid nothing, was the mere agent of the Germania Bank, which still owned the 100 shares as security for the payment of said note, and that one of the principal reasons for the transfers to Waldo was the possible liability of the shareholders of the Crescent City Bank for its debts in case of insolvency. Soon after the Crescent City Bank failed. *Held, per* Strong, J., that the transfers to said Waldo were void as against said receiver, and that although the Germania Bank only held said shares as collateral security for the payment of said discount, it was still liable as owner for the assessment in this case ordered by the Comptroller. The opinion is able and fortified by numerous authorities. In this same case, at a former term, upon a motion to dismiss the appeals of certain of the appellants, the Supreme Court recognized the right of the Comptroller to make an additional assessment, if deemed necessary; and for this reason sustained the appeals, holding that the matter in dispute was, or might be, over $5,000, although the decrees appealed from were severally less than that amount. The assessment was for 70 per cent.]

(See, also, *Pullman* vs. *Upton*, 96 *U. S.* [6 *Otto*], *p.* 328, as to liability of transferee.)

SHARES OF STOCK.

I. A national bank whose certificates of stock specify that the shares are transferable on the books of the bank on surrender of the certificates, *and not
otherwise*, and which suffers a shareholder to transfer without such surrender, is liable to a *bona fide* transferee, for value of same stock, who produces
such certificate with usual power of attorney to transfer; and this is so
though no notice had been given to the bank of the transfer. (*Bank* vs.
Lanier, 11 *Wall.*, *p.* 369.)

II. Shares are *quasi* negotiable. (*Ibid.*, *p.* 369.)

SURPLUS FUND.

I. Where the shares of a national bank are assessed for taxation at their par
value, the surplus fund of such bank, in excess of the amount required by
law to be kept on hand, is taxable. (*First National Bank* vs. *Peterborough*, 56
N. H., *p.* 38.) But when such shares are assessed at their *market* value, and
the amount of such surplus is taken into account in estimating such market
value, it is not taxable. (*State* vs. *City of Newark*, 10 *Vroom* [*N. J.*], *p.* 380.)

II. Neither a dividend which has been declared, nor a portion of capital of a national bank remaining after a reduction has been made, can be retained by
the directors to constitute a surplus fund. (*Seeley* vs. *New York National
Exchange Bank*, 4 *Abb.* [*N. Y.*], *p.* 61.)

III. The surplus fund which a national bank is required, by section 5199, U. S. Revised Statutes, to reserve from its net profits, is not excluded, in the valuation of its shares for taxation. (*Strafford National Bank* vs. *Dover*, 2 *Thomp.
Cases*, *p.* 296, *Sup. Court N. H.*, following *National Bank* vs. *Commonwealth*,
9 *Wall.*, *p.* 353; *People* vs. *Commissioners*, 94 *U. S.*, *p.* 415.)

TAXATION.

I. BY LICENSE. The District of Columbia imposed a *license tax* on all the national
banks in the District, the rate being 50 cents annually on each $1,000 of the
capital invested. The *Citizens' National Bank* refused to pay this assessment, and a test case was made in the District criminal court, Mr. Justice
MacArthur presiding. This court, after full argument, held the tax illegal
and void, as being contrary to the mode of taxation prescribed by Congress,
which mode was held to be exclusive.

II. OF INSOLVENT BANKS. A tax levied upon the property of a national bank,
subsequent to its insolvency is subordinate to the rights of a receiver, even
though he be appointed after such levy. (*Woodward* vs. *Ellsworth*, 4 *Colo.*,
p. 580.)
(See Title "SURPLUS FUND," *supra*.)

III. OF INTEREST AND DIVIDENDS. Under the internal-revenue act of July, 1870,
interest paid and dividends declared during the last five months of 1870 are
taxable, as well as those declared during the year 1871. (*Blake* vs. *National
Banks*, 23 *Wall.*, *p.* 307.)

IV. OF SHARES OF STOCK. The act of 1864, rightly construed, subjects the shares
of the association in the hands of shareholders to taxation by the States,
under certain limitations set forth in section 41, without regard to the fact
that part or the whole of the capital of such association is invested in national securities, which are declared by law exempt from State taxation.
(*Van Allen* vs. *Assessors*, 3 *Wall.*, 573. Chase, C. J., and other judges dissented.)

V. Act thus construed is constitutional. (*Ibid*, *p.* 573.)

VI. A certain statute of New York, which taxed *shares* of national-bank stock,
declared void, because *shares* of State banks were not taxed, although their
capital was; the act of Congress prescribing that shares of national banks
shall be taxed only as *shares* of State banks are. (*Ibid.* *p.* 573. The ruling
as to taxing shares of stock reaffirmed in *Bradley* vs. *People*, 4 *Wall.*, *p.* 459;
National Bank vs. *Commonwealth*, 9 *Wall.*, *p.* 353.)

VII. In last case, *held*, that a State law requiring the cashier to pay the tax was
valid. *Held*, also, that a certain State tax law virtually taxed "*shares* of
moneyed corporations," &c. (*Ibid*, *p.* 353.)

VIII. Section 5219 of United States Revised Statutes applies to and includes as well
the *valuation* of shares for taxation as the *rate* of tax to be imposed, and
prohibits a State from discriminating, detrimentally to a national bank, as
to either valuation or rate. Therefore, a statute of the State of New York
which permitted a party, when being assessed, to deduct his just debts from
the value of all his personal property, save such as was invested in shares
of national-bank stock, was held void as to taxation of such shares. (*People* vs. *Weaver*, 100 *U. S.*, *p.* 539, overruling the judgment of New York court
of appeals in same cause.)

TAXATION OF SHARES OF STOCK—Continued.

IX. So in another case, where local assessors valued all other property below its cash worth, but assessed shares of national-bank stock at par, or their full value : *Held*, that the tax upon shares thus assessed was invalid, and that, upon payment of the amount justly assessable, a court of equity would enjoin collection of the residue. (*Pelton vs. Commercial National Bank of Cleveland*, 101 *U. S.*, *p.* 143.)

X. Where it appeared that throughout a portion of Ohio, including Lucas County, and perhaps all over the State, a settled rule with the equalizing officers was to value real estate and ordinary personal property at one-third of their worth, while moneyed capital was fixed at three-fifths, and the State board of equalization, without changing the valuation thus made of real estate and ordinary personalty, assessed national-bank shares at par : *Held*, that such unequal valuation was in violation of the constitutional rights of such shareholders : and, on payment of the tax justly due, equity would enjoin collection of the residue. (*Cummings vs. Merchants' National Bank of Toledo*, 101 *U. S.*, *p.* 153.)

XI. Shares of stock in national banks are personal property, and though in one sense incorporeal, the law which created them could separate them from the person of their owner, for taxation, and give them a *situs* of their own. (*Tappan, Collector, vs. Bank*, 19 *Wall.*, *p.* 490.)

XII. Section 41 did thus separate them and give them a *situs* of their own. (*Ibid*, *p.* 490.)

XIII. This provision of the National Currency Act became a law of the property (in shares), and every State in which a bank was located acquired jurisdiction, for taxation, of all the shares, whether owned by residents or non-residents, and power to legislate accordingly. (*Ibid*, *p.* 490.)

XIV. Under the act of Congress of February 10, 1868, enacting that each State legislature may direct the manner of taxing all shares of stock of national banks located within the State, subject to the restriction that the taxation shall not be greater than the rate assessed *upon other moneyed capital* in the hands of individual citizens of such State, and of a certain act of the legislature of Pennsylvania which provided that such shares shall be assessed for school, municipal and local purposes at the same rate as is now or may hereafter be assessed and imposed upon other moneyed capital in the hands of individual citizens of the State : *Held*, that shares of national-bank stock may be valued for taxation for county, school, municipal, and local purposes, *at an amount above their par value*. (*Hepburn vs. School Directors of the borough of Carlisle*, 23 *Wall.*, *p.* 480.)

[NOTE.—In this case it appeared that Hepburn owned several thousand dollars of national-bank stock, the par value of which was $100 per share, and that it was valued for taxation, for a school tax, at $150 per share. This assessment was held valid, notwithstanding that by a certain act of the State legislature, applicable to the county of Cumberland, in which the borough of Carlisle was situated, certain specified kinds of moneyed obligations were exempt from taxation except for State purposes.]

XV. The rate of taxation of shares of a national bank by a State should be the same as, or not greater than, that upon the moneyed capital of the individual citizen which is liable to taxation ; that is, no greater in proportion or percentage of tax on the valuation of shares should be levied than upon other moneyed taxable capital in the hands of the citizen. (*People vs. The Commissioners, &c.*, 4 *Wall.*, *p.* 256.)

XVI. The act of Congress approved June 3, 1864 (R. S., sec. 5219), was not intended to curtail the power of the States on the subject of taxation, or to prohibit the exemption of particular kinds of property, but to protect the corporations formed under its authority from unfriendly discrimination by the States in the exercise of their taxing power. (*Adams vs. Nashville*, 95 *U. S.* [5 *Otto*], *p.* 19. See, also, *Saint Louis National Bank, National Bank of the State of Missouri, Third National Bank, Valley National Bank*, and *Merchants' National Bank of Saint Louis*, vs. *Papin*, in United States circuit court, eastern district of Missouri, September term, 1876. Also, *Gallatin National Bank of New York* vs. *Commissioners of Taxes*, supreme court of New York, first department, general term, November, 1876. These latter cases are published in the *Bankers' Magazine* for December, 1876.)

XVII. OF TOWN AND CITY NOTES, ETC. Section 3413, U. S. Revised Statutes, which enacts that every national bank, State bank, or banker, or association, shall pay a tax of ten per centum on the amount of notes of any town, city, or municipal corporation paid out by them, imposes the tax thus laid, *not on the notes, but on their use as a circulating medium*, and is therefore constitutional. (*National Bank vs. United States*, 101 *U. S.*, *p.* 1.)

TRANSFERS OF ASSETS.

I. A preference of one creditor to another, within the meaning of section 5242, Revised Statutes. is a preference given by the bank to secure or pay a pre-existing debt. Where a person, knowing that a national bank is embarrassed, makes to it a loan, taking as security therefor a pledge of part of the assets of the bank, this transfer does not give him the preference prohibited by the statute. (*Casey* vs. *Le Société de Crédit Mobilier*, 2 *Woods*, p. 77.)

II. WHEN NOT BINDING. Under said section 5242, which declares void transfers of its property by a national bank, made in contemplation of insolvency, and with a view to give a preference to one creditor over another, or with a view to prevent the application of the assets of the bank in the manner prescribed by law, such a transfer is void if the insolvency is in the contemplation of the bank making the transfer, although the party to whom it is made does not know or contemplate the insolvency of the bank. (*Case, Receiver*, vs. *Citizens' Bank*, 2 *Woods*, p. 23.)

III. As to when a *pledge* of assets, even when intended as security for a loan to a national bank, will be held invalid, as against general creditors, see the cases of *Casey, Receiver*, vs. *Le Société de Crédit Mobilier*; *Same* vs. *National Park Bank*; and *Same* vs. *Schuchardt*, 96 *U. S.*, [6 *Otto*], pp. 467, 492, 494.

ULTRA VIRES.

I. WHAT IS.—National banks cannot sell railroad bonds for third parties on commission, or engage in business of that character. (*Susan Weckler* vs. *First National Bank of Hagerstown*, court of appeals of Maryland, 42 Md., p. 581.)

II. In an action of deceit against a national bank, for alleged false representations of its teller in the sale to plaintiff of certain railroad bonds: *Held*, that the selling of such bonds on commission was not within the authorized business of a national bank, and being thus beyond the scope of its corporate powers, the defense of *ultra vires* was open to it, and it was not responsible for the deceit of its teller. (*Ibid.*)

III. A national bank has no inherent power to act as agent in the purchase of bonds or stocks for third persons, and its president cannot bind it by an agreement so to act without special authority. (*First National Bank of Allentown* vs. *Hoch*, 89 *Penn.*, p. 324.)   *Quere*: If the bank has no such inherent power, how can it confer "special authority" on the president?

[NOTE.—Whether the *purchase* of promissory notes by a bank empowered to discount them is *ultra vires*, is a question upon which the adjudications are in conflict. That such purchase is valid, see *Pape* vs. *Capitol Bank of Topeka*, 20 *Kans.*, p. 440; *Smith* vs. *Exchange Bank* 26 *O.*, p. 141, &c. Per contra, see *Farmers and Mechanics' Bank* vs. *Baldwin*, 23 *Minn.*, p. 198; *First National Bank of Rochester* vs. *Peirson*, 1 *Thomp. Cases*, p. 673. There is much in the point that if a national bank can *purchase* promissory notes, it can do so for such price as the seller may be willing to take; and thus the prohibitions as to usury may be practically nullified. But further, why should not the rule "*expressio unius est exclusio alterius*" control?]

IV. WHAT IS NOT.—A national bank took a lien upon real estate to secure a pre-existing debt. Afterward the bank paid $500 to discharge a prior lien upon the land, taking a note and mortgage on land in Kansas to secure this advance. Lien and mortgage held valid and warranted by law. (*Orm* vs. *Merchants' National Bank*, 16 *Kans.*, p. 341.)

V. A *chattel mortgage* taken by a national bank to secure a pre-existing debt is valid, and will be enforced. (*Spofford* vs. *First National Bank*, 37 *Iowa*, p. 181.)

VI. A bank organized under the National-Bank Act has power to sell any immovable it may own, and may reserve a mortgage and vendor's privilege (lien) thereon. (*New Orleans National Bank* vs. *Raymond*, 29 *La Annual*, p. 355.)

VII. It would seem that where a national bank had realized the consideration agreed upon for its guarantee of the paper of another, the doctrine of *estoppel in pais* precludes such bank from asserting that such guarantee is *ultra vires*. (*People's Bank* vs. *National Bank*, 101 *U. S.*, p. 181.)

VIII. A national bank has corporate power to enter into an agreement with a customer to exchange for him non-registered for registered United States bonds; and it is bound by an agreement to that effect, made for a sufficient consideration by its cashier. (*Yerkes* vs. *National Bank*, 69 *N. Y.*, p. 382.)

(See, also, Title "DEPOSITS, SPECIAL," ante.)

IX. A township in Vermont issued its bonds with interest coupons attached. Each coupon contained an express promise to pay, &c. A national bank bought of these bonds, and sued the township in assumpsit, *on unpaid cou-*

ULTRA VIRES, WHAT IS NOT—Continued.

> pons: *Held*, that the action was in due form, and that a national bank could legally buy, hold, and sue upon such bonds and upon the coupons. (*North Bennington Bank* vs. *Bennington*, 16 *Blatchf., p.* 53.)

USURY.

I. State laws relative to usury do not apply to national banks. (*Farmers and Mechanics' National Bank* vs. *Dearing*, 1 *Otto, p.* 29.)

II. The only forfeiture declared by the 30th section of the act of June 3, 1864, (Revised Statutes, section 5198), is of the *entire interest* which the note or bill carries with it, or which has been agreed to be paid thereon, when the rate knowingly reserved or charged by a national bank is in excess of that allowed by that section; and no loss of the entire debt is incurred by such bank as a penalty or otherwise, by reason of the provision of the usury law of a State. (*Farmers and Mechanics' National Bank* vs. *Dearing*, above cited; *National Exchange Bank* vs. *Moore*, 2 *Bond, p.* 170; *Barnett* vs. *National Bank*, 98 *U. S.* [8 *Otto*], *p.* 555.)

III. If usurious interest has been *paid* to a national bank, twice the amount of interest thus paid may be recovered from such bank by the person paying the same, or his legal representative; but as this provision of the statute is penal and the same statute prescribes how such recovery may be had, no other remedy can be resorted to. It must be recovered, if at all, in a suit in the nature of an action of debt. That the borrower from a national bank has paid usurious interest can avail him nothing, as a defense, or by way of a set off, when sued for the amount of the loan, by the bank. (*Barnett* vs. *National Bank*, above cited.)
(See Title " INTEREST." *ante.*)

IV. While the National-Bank Act prescribes penalties for usury, it does not make the contract (*e. g.* contract of indorser) void: and for the court so to decide would be to add a penalty not imposed by the statute. This the court will not do. (*Oates* vs. *First National Bank of Montgomery*, 100 *U. S., p.* 239.)

V. The assignee in bankruptcy of a borrower from a national bank may sue for and recover the penalty for having received usurious interest. (*Wright* vs. *First National Bank of Greensburg*, 2 *Thomp. Cases, p.* 138, *U. S. Cir. Court, Indiana.*)

VI. The exacting of usurious interest by a national bank, upon the discount of a note, works a forfeiture of interest accruing *after* as well as before the maturity of the note. (*National Bank of Uniontown* vs. *Stauffer*, 2 *Thomp. Cases, p.* 178, *U. S. Cir. Court, western district Penn.*)

VISITORIAL POWERS.

I. Section 5241 U. S. Rev. Stats. prohibits a State court from compelling officers of a national bank to produce the bank books, for the purpose of ascertaining facts upon which to impose a State tax upon the deposits of depositors. (*National Bank of Youngstown* vs. *Hughes, Auditor, &c.*, 2 *Thomp. Cases, p.* 176, *U. S. Circuit Court N. Dist. Ohio.*).

Table showing the amounts of gold coin, silver coin, paper currency, and checks and drafts received by the national banks in New York City, in the other reserve cities, and in the States and Territories on June 30, 1881.

Cities, States, and Territories.	No. of banks.	Gold coin.	Silver coin.	Paper currency.	Checks, drafts, &c.	Total.
New York City	48	$460,094	$15,997	$1,796,604	$165,254,164	$167,437,759
Boston	54	292,363	8,711	848,004	31,939,002	33,088,080
Albany	7	19,345	982	67,591	1,329,786	1,417,704
Philadelphia	32	42,505	42,922	631,180	17,344,958	18,061,565
Pittsburgh	22	15,741	8,324	183,083	1,941,918	2,149,066
Baltimore	16	4,566	10,931	260,246	3,599,512	3,875,255
Washington	5	7,113	2,789	72,786	123,913	206,601
New Orleans	7	1,798	7,717	113,052	1,084,192	1,206,759
Louisville	8	6,772	3,317	43,442	688,799	742,330
Cincinnati	8	20,471	7,049	327,704	2,610,131	2,965,355
Cleveland	6	4,246	4,052	96,906	1,645,833	1,731,037
Chicago	9	130,980	8,887	512,082	7,489,240	8,141,189
Detroit	4	2,641	3,604	94,442	705,524	806,211
Milwaukee	3	2,402	702	45,529	368,611	417,244
Saint Louis	5	4,904	3,356	334,659	1,597,134	1,940,053
San Francisco	1	25,223	1,142	1,004	304,897	332,266
Totals for cities	187	581,070	114,485	3,631,710	72,773,450	77,100,715
Maine	67	8,455	4,524	194,169	960,136	1,167,284
New Hampshire	45	4,928	1,906	119,058	383,702	509,594
Vermont	41	2,991	3,825	77,473	320,967	405,256
Massachusetts	182	44,584	17,070	640,203	3,545,111	4,246,968
Rhode Island	58	3,866	2,957	142,689	1,086,374	1,235,886
Connecticut	79	12,661	8,518	298,290	2,213,639	2,533,108
New York	226	76,548	37,826	739,286	4,205,574	5,059,234
New Jersey	62	23,056	16,769	273,718	3,593,928	3,907,471
Pennsylvania	179	44,617	46,814	506,691	3,336,314	3,934,436
Delaware	14	2,515	2,853	37,590	270,670	313,628
Maryland	20	876	1,893	42,553	232,776	278,008
District of Columbia	1	478	484	9,100	17,921	27,983
Virginia	18	9,205	8,006	142,133	1,359,136	1,518,480
West Virginia	16	747	1,019	37,577	73,072	112,415
North Carolina	12	8,886	3,065	39,788	292,981	344,720
South Carolina	9	14,013	3,750	37,883	339,795	395,441
Georgia	11	34,269	6,020	45,651	196,355	281,995
Florida	2	188	661	16,711	5,456	23,026
Alabama	8	2,776	1,719	23,569	72,113	100,177
Texas	14	1,996	7,292	84,951	198,547	292,786
Arkansas	2	1,175	972	15,828	35,245	53,220
Kentucky	37	1,350	5,798	96,577	342,550	446,275
Tennessee	21	32,710	7,668	213,203	448,797	702,408
Ohio	112	49,053	24,528	490,044	2,261,441	2,825,066
Indiana	80	37,496	23,417	274,364	986,522	1,321,819
Illinois	120	26,062	17,094	371,482	997,269	1,411,907
Michigan	70	9,488	8,464	244,415	726,523	988,890
Wisconsin	30	9,956	3,539	91,101	439,339	543,935
Iowa	68	45,126	10,787	254,913	665,130	975,956
Minnesota	25	16,968	3,661	215,547	991,594	1,227,770
Missouri	13	276	4,264	48,916	110,025	163,481
Kansas	10	11,423	3,101	77,879	329,341	421,744
Nebraska	11	45,073	4,250	73,424	388,976	511,723
Colorado	13	40,840	4,421	178,267	961,859	1,185,387
Nevada	1	3,020	68	....	3,455	6,543
California	8	107,214	6,196	8,220	113,454	235,384
Oregon	1	42,879	1,119	2,587	118,835	165,420
Dakota	5	1,472	863	12,904	33,235	48,474
Idaho	..	....	....	....	....	....
Montana	2	120	88	2,025	17,429	19,662
New Mexico	4	559	1,176	18,435	96,835	117,305
Utah	1	31,826	506	14,309	46,328	92,969
Washington	1	6,865	977	1,870	5,814	15,526
Wyoming	2	3,435	78	990	2,270	6,782
Totals for States	1,731	822,041	310,516	6,216,433	32,826,552	40,175,542
Totals for United States	1,966	1,864,105	440,998	11,554,747	270,854,166	284,714,016

Table showing the amounts of gold coin, silver coin, paper currency, and checks and drafts received by the national banks in New York City, in the other reserve cities, and in the States and Territories on September 17, 1881.

Cities, States, and Territories.	No. of banks.	Gold coin.	Silver coin.	Paper currency.	Checks, drafts. &c.	Total.
New York City	48	$905,588	$7,857	$1,071.316	$163,208,586	$165,193,347
Boston	54	275,737	26,337	1,227,407	22,564,580	24,094,061
Albany	7	3,261	1,478	48,017	1,433,559	1,486,315
Philadelphia	32	53,771	32,787	561,657	17,182,433	17,830,648
Pittsburgh	22	33,587	10,922	388,680	2,693,560	3,126,749
Baltimore	16	29,355	9,824	229,110	4,156,824	4,425,113
Washington	5	6,404	1,988	114,437	103,864	226,783
New Orleans	7	105,260	4,000	211,823	1,299,088	1,620,771
Louisville	8	39,784	4,319	84,817	646,384	775,304
Cincinnati	10	14,374	10,623	362,742	3,489,046	3,876,785
Cleveland	6	5,911	2,203	119,719	2,490,231	2,618,064
Chicago	9	788,421	23,324	457,964	11,757,126	13,026,835
Detroit	4	3,208	2,259	74,174	1,139,840	1,219,481
Milwaukee	3	14,848	639	18,908	635,777	670,172
Saint Louis	5	12,010	3,863	469,764	2,141,408	2,627,045
San Francisco	1	62,395	3,082	1,826	230,818	298,121
Totals for cities	189	1,448,416	138,248	4,371,045	71,964,538	77,922,247
Maine	69	7,914	3,712	183,368	821,084	1,016,018
New Hampshire	47	13,500	2,155	104,987	379,586	500,318
Vermont	47	15,925	4,684	84,309	392,505	407,423
Massachusetts	190	103,942	21,409	631,346	3,290,991	4,047,688
Rhode Island	62	11,766	3,607	162,123	1,308,648	1,486,144
Connecticut	85	26,089	6,547	302,370	3,201,100	3,536,106
New York	243	116,869	37,946	785,128	4,694,641	5,634,586
New Jersey	67	39,371	19,380	336,841	4,017,028	4,412,620
Pennsylvania	191	181,799	70,440	568,169	4,897,680	5,718,088
Delaware	14	4,070	5,561	32,293	339,153	381,077
Maryland	22	4,178	2,195	49,770	196,327	252,470
District of Columbia	1	741	212	9,612	34,134	44,699
Virginia	18	68,573	3,730	112,461	1,254,807	1,439,571
West Virginia	17	685	1,305	47,908	130,729	180,627
North Carolina	15	7,675	2,969	74,308	307,013	391,965
South Carolina	13	30,165	3,972	108,507	585,660	728,573
Georgia	12	32,067	7,764	128,104	570,991	738,926
Florida	2	332	751	7,981	31,675	40,739
Alabama	9	5,904	1,290	34,354	251,168	293,226
Texas	15	4,342	14,040	175,070	639,471	832,923
Arkansas	2	177	881	10,856	39,269	51,183
Kentucky	42	4,788	4,960	79,398	509,053	688,199
Tennessee	25	46,900	7,702	186,660	651,796	893,058
Ohio	161	43,620	23,925	686,231	2,397,011	3,150,787
Indiana	93	77,486	24,478	138,597	1,551,970	2,092,531
Illinois	31	70,411	22,321	577,033	2,662,682	3,332,447
Michigan	76	40,813	9,452	275,446	1,097,560	1,423,241
Wisconsin	130	61,687	4,591	128,553	350,388	545,019
Iowa	76	95,645	13,612	334,793	1,108,431	1,552,481
Minnesota	27	181,961	5,475	203,424	1,393,286	1,784,146
Missouri	17	32,126	4,398	63,663	466,674	566,861
Kansas	13	44,294	5,684	86,225	259,682	395,885
Nebraska	12	58,360	1,831	102,070	653,220	815,481
Colorado	17	61,087	2,804	161,275	1,307,738	1,533,501
Nevada	1	2,935	325	3,675	624	7,559
California	10	114,068	3,558	5,135	136,956	260,637
Oregon	1	43,591	958	3,243	126,734	174,526
Dakota	8	8,177	1,261	82,541	165,163	257,412
Idaho	1	5,274	......	3,476	9,171	17,921
Montana	3	340	102	31,272	44,002	75,716
New Mexico	4	1,445	764	22,616	95,147	119,972
Utah	1	11,984	463	9,594	90,723	112,764
Washington	2	24,849	545	1,380	11,478	38,242
Wyoming	3	14,505	736	2,475	127,080	144,796
Totals for States	1,895	1,724,040	354,197	7,439,210	42,600,738	52,118,185
Totals for United States	2,132	4,078,044	500,302	12,881,571	277,773,862	295,233,779

Table showing the ratios of gold coin, silver coin, paper currency, and checks and drafts received by the national banks in New York City, in the other reserve cities, and in the States and Territories on June 30 and September 17, 1881.

Cities, States, and Territories.	June 30, 1881.					September 17, 1881.				
	No. of banks.	Gold coin.	Silver coin.	Paper currency.	Checks, drafts, &c.	No. of banks.	Gold coin.	Silver coin.	Paper currency.	Checks, drafts, &c.
		Per ct.	*Per ct.*	*Per ct.*	*Per ct.*		*Per ct.*	*Per ct.*	*Per ct.*	*Per ct.*
New York City	48	0.27	0.01	1.02	98.70	48	0.54	0.01	0.65	98.80
Boston	54	0.88	0.03	2.56	96.53	54	1.14	0.11	5.10	93.65
Albany	7	1.36	0.07	4.77	93.80	7	0.22	0.10	3.23	96.45
Philadelphia	32	0.24	0.24	3.49	96.03	32	0.30	0.18	3.15	96.37
Pittsburgh	22	0.73	0.39	8.52	90.36	22	1.07	0.35	12.43	86.15
Baltimore	16	0.12	0.28	6.72	92.88	16	0.66	0.22	5.18	93.94
Washington	5	3.44	13.50	35.23	59.98	5	2.86	0.88	50.46	45.80
New Orleans	7	0.15	0.64	9.37	89.84	7	6.50	0.28	13.07	80.15
Louisville	8	0.91	0.45	5.85	92.79	8	5.13	0.56	10.94	83.37
Cincinnati.........	8	0.69	0.24	11.05	88.02	10	0.37	0.27	9.36	90.00
Cleveland	6	0.25	0.23	5.53	93.99	6	0.23	0.08	4.57	95.12
Chicago	9	1.61	0.11	6.29	91.99	9	6.05	0.18	3.52	90.25
Detroit	4	0.33	0.45	11.71	87.51	4	0.26	0.19	6.08	93.47
Milwaukee..........	3	0.58	0.17	10.91	88.34	3	2.22	0.09	2.82	94.87
Saint Louis	5	0.25	0.17	17.25	82.33	5	0.46	0.15	17.88	81.51
San Francisco	1	7.59	0.35	0.30	91.76	1	20.95	1.03	0.61	77.43
Totals for cities	187	0.76	0.15	4.71	94.38	189	1.86	0.18	5.61	92.35
Maine	67	0.72	0.39	16.63	82.26	69	0.78	0.37	18.04	80.81
New Hampshire....	45	0.97	0.37	23.36	75.30	47	2.72	0.43	20.98	75.87
Vermont	41	0.74	0.94	19.12	79.20	47	3.91	1.14	20.70	74.25
Massachusetts	182	1.05	0.40	15.07	83.48	190	2.57	0.53	15.60	81.30
Rhode Island.......	58	0.31	0.24	11.54	87.91	62	0.80	0.24	10.90	88.06
Connecticut	79	0.50	0.24	11.78	87.38	85	0.74	0.18	8.55	90.53
New York..........	226	1.51	0.75	14.61	83.13	243	2.07	0.67	13.94	83.32
New Jersey	62	0.59	0.44	7.00	91.97	67	0.89	0.44	7.63	91.04
Pennsylvania	179	1.13	1.19	12.88	84.80	191	3.18	1.23	9.94	85.65
Delaware...........	14	0.80	0.91	11.98	86.31	14	1.07	1.46	8.47	89.00
Maryland	20	0.32	0.65	15.31	83.72	22	1.66	0.87	19.71	77.76
District of Columbia	1	1.71	1.73	32.52	64.04	1	1.60	0.48	21.50	76.36
Virginia............	18	0.61	0.53	9.36	89.50	18	4.76	0.26	7.81	87.17
West Virginia......	16	0.60	0.92	33.43	65.05	17	0.38	0.72	26.52	72.38
North Carolina.....	12	2.58	0.89	11.54	84.99	15	1.96	0.76	18.96	78.32
South Carolina	9	3.54	0.95	9.58	85.93	13	4.14	0.55	14.90	80.41
Georgia............	11	12.15	2.14	16.19	69.52	12	4.34	1.05	17.34	77.27
Florida............	2	0.82	2.87	72.57	23.74	2	0.82	1.84	19.59	77.75
Alabama	8	2.77	1.71	23.53	71.99	9	2.01	0.41	11.92	85.66
Texas	14	0.68	2.49	29.01	67.82	15	0.52	1.69	21.02	76.77
Arkansas	2	2.21	1.83	29.74	66.22	2	0.35	1.72	21.21	76.72
Kentucky	37	0.30	1.30	21.64	76.76	42	0.70	0.72	11.54	87.04
Tennessee..........	21	4.66	1.09	30.36	63.89	25	5.25	0.86	20.90	72.99
Ohio	142	1.74	0.87	17.34	80.05	161	1.38	0.76	21.78	76.08
Indiana	80	2.84	1.77	20.76	74.63	93	3.70	1.17	20.96	74.17
Illinois	120	1.84	1.21	26.31	70.64	130	2.11	0.07	17.32	79.90
Michigan...........	70	0.96	0.86	24.72	73.46	76	2.87	0.06	19.95	77.12
Wisconsin..........	30	1.83	0.65	16.74	80.78	31	11.32	0.80	23.59	64.29
Iowa	68	4.61	1.11	26.12	68.16	76	6.16	0.88	21.56	71.40
Minnesota..........	25	1.38	0.30	17.56	80.76	27	10.20	0.31	11.40	78.09
Missouri...........	13	0.17	2.61	29.92	67.30	17	5.67	0.78	11.23	82.32
Kansas	10	2.71	0.37	18.47	78.49	13	11.19	1.43	21.78	65.60
Nebraska	11	8.81	0.83	14.34	76.02	12	7.15	0.22	12.53	80.10
Colorado	13	3.44	0.37	15.04	81.15	17	4.02	0.18	10.52	85.28
Nevada	1	46.16	1.04	.....	52.80	1	38.83	4.30	48.42	8.25
California	8	45.54	2.76	3.49	48.21	10	44.12	1.37	1.97	52.54
Oregon	1	25.82	0.68	1.56	71.84	1	24.96	0.55	1.86	72.61
Dakota.............	5	3.04	1.78	26.62	68.56	8	3.18	0.49	32.06	64.27
Idaho	....	.....	.....	.....	.....	1	29.43	.....	19.40	51.17
Montana	2	0.61	0.45	10.30	88.64	3	0.44	0.14	41.30	58.12
New Mexico........	4	0.48	1.26	15.73	82.53	4	1.20	0.46	18.85	79.31
Utah	1	34.23	0.54	15.40	49.83	1	10.63	0.41	8.51	80.45
Washington........	1	44.22	6.29	12.04	37.45	2	64.98	1.40	3.61	30.01
Wyoming	2	50.64	1.15	14.60	33.61	3	10.02	0.51	1.71	87.76
Totals for States	1,731	2.04	0.77	15.47	81.72	1,805	3.31	0.68	14.27	81.74
United States ..	1,966	0.65	0.16	4.06	95.13	2,132	1.38	0.17	4.36	94.09

Classification of the loans and discounts of the banks in New York City, in Boston, Philadelphia and Baltimore, in the other reserve cities, and in the States and Territories, on October 1, 1881.

Cities, States, and Territories.	No. of banks.	On single-name paper.	On U. S. bonds.	On other stocks.	All other loans.	Total.
New York City	48	$20,935,878	$2,539,928	$97,249,162	$120,032,691	$246,757,659
Boston	54	15,230,358	123,974	18,706,619	89,523,632	123,644,583
Philadelphia	32	13,443,834	266,290	17,051,743	31,513,529	62,275,396
Baltimore	16	5,731,469	24,900	3,493,164	16,645,141	25,894,674
Totals	102	34,465,661	415,164	39,251,526	137,682,302	211,814,653
Albany	7	333,348	9,000	2,818,200	5,131,492	8,292,040
Pittsburgh	22	1,045,120	7,500	939,422	20,308,236	22,300,278
Washington	5	19,524	17,184	498,083	1,247,885	1,782,676
New Orleans	7	60,981	33,200	1,854,577	6,701,231	8,649,989
Louisville	8	175		679,743	6,405,893	7,085,811
Cincinnati	10	3,871,703	177,276	3,094,891	11,745,861	18,889,731
Cleveland	6	627,551	8,000	1,396,940	7,879,054	9,911,545
Chicago	9	4,573,291	161,350	8,783,702	20,202,997	33,721,340
Detroit	4	510,681		1,071,026	5,876,039	7,457,746
Milwaukee	3	417,121	54,986	808,320	2,601,364	3,881,791
Saint Louis	5	140,757		2,252,193	7,817,597	10,210,547
San Francisco	1	1,304,086		30,061	888,857	2,223,004
Totals	87	12,904,338	468,496	24,227,158	96,806,506	134,406,498
Maine	69	1,017,133	3,150	634,951	15,650,674	17,305,908
New Hampshire	47	539,984	7,045	865,398	6,105,590	7,518,017
Vermont	47	636,762	29,028	522,558	9,710,924	10,899,272
Massachusetts	190	12,939,909	155,090	5,005,119	63,503,779	81,603,897
Rhode Island	62	4,608,722	11,643	429,867	23,386,650	28,496,882
Connecticut	85	19,152,269	131,930	2,796,634	30,394,479	43,475,312
New York	243	5,063,982	1,525,858	5,922,226	62,695,791	75,207,857
New Jersey	67	5,090,124	272,008	4,881,091	18,990,167	29,233,480
Pennsylvania	191	3,350,946	281,845	1,714,547	48,946,374	54,293,712
Delaware	14	113,920		89,960	3,292,023	3,495,903
Maryland	22	441,930		100,560	3,768,519	4,311,009
District of Columbia	1			119,046	185,153	304,199
Virginia	18	302,124		758,644	8,121,021	9,181,789
West Virginia	17	90,913		10,599	3,058,120	3,159,632
North Carolina	15	141,776	1,500	97,644	4,526,269	4,767,189
South Carolina	13	38,708	1,500	479,714	3,871,346	4,391,268
Georgia	12	198,907		1,063,799	3,138,666	4,401,372
Florida	2	8,413		75,000	200,157	283,570
Alabama	9	262,766		313,934	1,644,036	2,220,736
Texas	15	518,930		299,205	2,372,538	3,190,673
Arkansas	2	8,996	5,300	117,204	248,701	380,201
Kentucky	42	570,558		434,550	9,683,972	10,689,080
Tennessee	25	983,980	46,068	1,562,918	5,269,363	7,862,329
Ohio	161	3,238,713	31,300	2,193,480	32,253,839	37,717,332
Indiana	93	2,266,700	29,794	714,552	21,887,977	24,899,023
Illinois	130	4,113,016	45,052	1,064,392	22,611,905	27,834,365
Michigan	76	2,423,476	1,000	498,968	13,947,816	16,871,254
Wisconsin	31	1,081,757	2,500	150,158	5,620,630	6,855,045
Iowa	76	2,016,959	20,000	476,979	10,942,127	13,456,065
Minnesota	27	5,526,924	130	191,416	9,230,929	14,949,399
Missouri	17	492,675	200	109,698	3,052,001	3,654,574
Kansas	13	425,491		57,637	1,971,698	2,454,826
Nebraska	12	559,989	59,225	425,967	3,117,190	4,162,371
Colorado	17	1,732,488		440,954	4,211,619	6,385,061
Nevada	1	72,466		13,463	90,386	176,315
California	10	707,886		622,627	2,825,385	4,155,898
Oregon	1	431,676			573,865	1,005,541
Dakota	8	223,893		84,860	848,883	1,157,636
Idaho	1	34,405			62,734	97,139
Montana	3	346,167		997	929,554	1,276,718
New Mexico	4	87,227			624,281	711,508
Utah	1	46,073			290,896	336,969
Washington	2	6,482			500,424	506,906
Wyoming	3	138,196		82,580	485,486	706,262
Totals	1,895	73,114,405	2,661,256	35,423,896	464,843,937	576,043,494
United States	2,132	117,420,282	6,084,814	196,151,742	819,365,436	1,169,022,304

Table showing the increase in loans, United States bonds on hand, capital, surplus, net deposits, specie, and legal-tender notes, in various States, at corresponding dates for three years.

MASSACHUSETTS.

Items of resources and liabilities.	October 1, 1881. 244 banks.	October 1, 1880. 242 banks.	October 2, 1879. 241 banks.
Loans and discounts	$205, 353, 470	$186, 489, 818	$152, 353, 248
U. S. bonds on hand	1, 733, 200	2, 119, 950	9, 315, 900
Capital	96, 177, 500	95, 605, 000	94, 957, 000
Surplus	24, 579, 919	23, 229, 611	22, 385, 889
Net deposits	142, 625, 424	129, 977, 085	97, 148, 583
Specie	10, 219, 504	10, 475, 697	4, 414, 233
Legal tenders and U. S. certificates	5, 079, 824	4, 386, 888	6, 437, 750

CONNECTICUT.

	85 banks.	84 banks.	84 banks.
Loans and discounts	$43, 623, 195	$39, 852, 932	$34, 011, 863
U. S. bonds on hand	786, 950	778, 900	2, 061, 800
Capital	25, 539, 620	25, 464, 620	25, 564, 620
Surplus	6, 701, 095	6, 608, 169	6, 260, 728
Net deposits	25, 734, 382	21, 347, 206	17, 423, 522
Specie	1, 227, 371	1, 044, 280	620, 749
Legal tenders and U. S. certificates	949, 922	970, 451	1, 082, 544

NEW YORK.*

	250 banks.	249 banks.	238 banks.
Loans and discounts	$83, 995, 959	$74, 598, 339	$64, 300, 480
U. S. bonds on hand	6, 237, 000	3, 935, 750	7, 079, 200
Capital	34, 630, 160	34, 697, 160	34, 452, 160
Surplus	9, 415, 698	9, 104, 250	8, 776, 899
Net deposits	80, 597, 774	69, 257, 511	60, 600, 913
Specie	3, 123, 330	2, 661, 340	1, 530, 069
Legal tenders and U. S. certificates	3, 745, 414	3, 964, 106	4, 312, 708

NEW YORK CITY.

	48 banks.	47 banks.	47 banks.
Loans and discounts	$246, 901, 392	$238, 495, 325	$195, 976, 976
U. S. bonds on hand	7, 854, 050	7, 011, 450	10, 140, 900
Capital	51, 150, 000	50, 650, 000	50. 750, 000
Surplus	19, 947, 316	18, 185, 383	16, 006, 435
Net deposits	268, 779, 373	268, 087, 386	210, 159, 157
Specie	50, 627, 368	58, 693, 315	19, 349, 868
Legal tenders and U. S. certificates	10, 898, 371	11, 136, 363	32, 638, 584

NEW JERSEY.

	67 banks.	66 banks.	68 banks.
Loans and discounts	$29, 266, 739	$26, 496, 481	$23, 732, 094
U. S. bonds on hand	1, 648, 950	983, 050	2, 139, 050
Capital	12, 960, 000	12, 905, 350	13, 445, 350
Surplus	3, 814, 181	3, 713, 672	3, 680, 327
Net deposits	28, 733, 695	25, 422, 804	20, 613, 438
Specie	977, 443	970, 308	597, 670
Legal tenders and U. S. certificates	1, 497, 897	1, 632, 083	1, 659, 810

Exclusive of New York City.

Tables showing the increase in loans, United States bonds on hand, capital, surplus, &c.—Cont'd.

PENNSYLVANIA.

Items of resources and liabilities.	October 1, 1881. 245 banks.	October 1, 1880. 240 banks.	October 2, 1879. 235 banks.
Loans and discounts	$139, 295, 507	$121, 813, 994	$106, 560, 450
U. S. bonds on hand	6, 569, 700	3, 834, 450	6, 732, 050
Capital	56, 518, 340	56, 153, 340	55, 116, 640
Surplus	19, 060, 835	17, 799, 555	17, 628, 614
Net deposits	144, 867, 670	125, 179, 909	101, 653, 014
Specie	12, 484, 445	12, 836, 828	5, 039, 520
Legal tenders and U. S. certificates	9, 173, 970	11, 085, 019	15, 521, 761

OHIO.

	177 banks.	170 banks.	162 banks.
Loans and discounts	$166, 980, 017	$54, 401, 634	$46, 821, 293
U. S. bonds on hand	2, 764, 550	1, 678, 500	2, 590, 050
Capital	29, 389, 000	26, 561, 900	26, 221, 900
Surplus	5, 420, 723	5, 166, 761	4, 946, 295
Net deposits	67, 138, 506	52, 098, 488	44, 748, 187
Specie	3, 487, 590	2, 490, 962	1, 505, 776
Legal tenders and U. S. certificates	6, 876, 566	6, 498, 393	6, 984, 789

INDIANA.

	93 banks.	92 banks.	91 banks.
Loans and discounts	$25, 162, 246	$23, 193, 224	$19, 873, 322
U. S. bonds on hand	1, 525, 950	698, 100	1, 038, 550
Capital	13, 093, 500	13, 202, 500	13, 277, 500
Surplus	3, 854, 159	3, 976, 906	3, 912, 896
Net deposits	23, 715, 274	20, 193, 522	17, 656, 800
Specie	1, 602, 772	1, 329, 925	639, 328
Legal tenders and U. S. certificates	1, 856, 791	2, 048, 185	2, 454, 354

ILLINOIS.

	139 banks.	136 banks.	136 banks.
Loans and discounts	$62, 061, 411	$45, 662, 490	$38, 402, 857
U. S. bonds on hand	4, 448, 000	2, 729, 800	3, 182, 600
Capital	15, 199, 600	14, 964, 600	14, 834, 600
Surplus	6, 359, 571	5, 823, 483	5, 539, 108
Net deposits	85, 607, 445	63, 460, 698	45, 898, 799
Specie	11, 790, 647	6, 758, 687	1, 818, 408
Legal tenders and U. S. certificates	4, 289, 117	5, 912, 295	7, 022, 769

MICHIGAN.

	80 banks.	79 banks.	79 banks.
Loans and discounts	$24, 520, 929	$19, 937, 971	$16, 902, 324
U. S. bonds on hand	232, 650	400, 700	564, 850
Capital	9, 435, 000	9, 335, 000	9, 337, 200
Surplus	2, 786, 545	2, 591, 122	2, 585, 603
Net deposits	24, 179, 357	18, 641, 039	14, 988, 340
Specie	1, 839, 086	970, 110	414, 525
Legal tenders and U. S. certificates	1, 445, 294	1, 706, 479	1, 774, 646

Table showing the increase in loans, United States bonds on hand, capital, surplus, &c.—Cont'd.

IOWA.

Items of resources and liabilities.	October 1, 1881. 76 banks.	October 1, 1880. 75 banks.	October 2, 1879. 73 banks.
Loans and discounts	$13,725,450	$11,373,097	$9,603,900
U. S. bonds on hand	699,450	399,500	443,400
Capital	5,950,000	5,867,000	5,707,000
Surplus	1,542,083	1,419,101	1,380,170
Net deposits	15,892,754	11,715,956	8,834,461
Specie	1,161,487	795,002	429,058
Legal tenders and U. S. certificates	1,261,344	1,174,973	1,233,677

MINNESOTA.

	27 banks.	30 banks.	30 banks.
Loans and discounts	$15,037,774	$12,201,168	$10,005,489
U. S. bonds on hand	51,900	5,150	107,950
Capital	4,900,000	5,150,000	4,660,000
Surplus	981,726	937,004	786,459
Net deposits	14,212,887	9,578,154	7,712,842
Specie	607,544	259,003	135,461
Legal tenders and U. S. certificates	849,160	899,983	706,238

KANSAS.

	13 banks.	12 banks.	12 banks.
Loans and discounts	$2,508,754	$1,794,360	$1,562,482
U. S. bonds on hand	40,350	11,700	108,750
Capital	925,000	875,000	838,450
Surplus	225,210	193,050	184,839
Net deposits	3,585,502	2,884,852	2,453,250
Specie	203,633	185,526	45,704
Legal tenders and U. S. certificates	326,411	303,911	326,475

NEBRASKA.

	12 banks.	10 banks.	10 banks.
Loans and discounts	$4,271,798	$3,193,158	$2,896,872
U. S. bonds on hand	375,650	3,300	160,700
Capital	910,000	850,000	925,000
Surplus	294,000	229,700	210,300
Net deposits	6,221,485	4,085,685	3,842,017
Specie	306,722	292,297	179,213
Legal tenders and U. S. certificates	261,401	273,738	200,976

COLORADO.

	17 banks.	14 banks.	14 banks.
Loans and discounts	$6,510,663	$5,050,713	$3,804,641
U. S. bonds on hand	52,400	177,650	445,950
Capital	1,276,800	1,070,000	1,070,000
Surplus	468,000	298,500	206,500
Net deposits	10,488,622	8,561,805	6,319,042
Specie	655,826	248,590	121,839
Legal tenders and U. S. certificates	626,903	748,009	704,836

Number of banks organized and in operation, with their capital, bonds on deposit, and circulation issued, redeemed, and outstanding on November 1, 1881.

States and Territories.	Banks.			Capital stock paid in.	U. S. bonds on deposit.	Circulation.		
	Organized.	In liquidation.	In operation.			Issued.	Redeemed.	Outstanding.
Maine	74	5	69	$10,285,000	$9,222,800	$23,257,800	$14,623,096	$8,634,704
New Hampshire	49	2	47	5,830,000	5,993,500	14,048,165	8,801,544	5,246,621
Vermont	54	7	47	7,801,000	7,075,900	21,825,840	14,573,660	7,252,180
Massachusetts	250	5	245	96,477,500	81,638,350	204,083,165	130,351,546	73,731,619
Rhode Island	63	1	62	20,065,050	16,324,200	43,460,205	28,084,848	15,375,357
Connecticut	89	4	85	25,539,620	20,638,650	57,104,430	37,596,393	19,508,037
Eastern States	579	24	555	165,998,170	140,893,400	363,779,605	234,031,087	129,748,518
New York	366	68	298	86,390,160	55,320,550	201,404,395	145,316,836	56,087,559
New Jersey	74	7	67	12,950,000	12,419,850	35,209,120	23,259,570	11,949,550
Pennsylvania	276	28	248	56,824,540	48,883,100	132,683,595	83,448,341	49,235,254
Delaware	14		14	1,743,985	1,804,200	4,139,745	2,559,245	1,580,500
Maryland	40	2	38	13,603,030	9,224,100	26,517,150	17,505,625	9,011,525
Middle States	770	105	665	171,511,715	127,651,800	399,954,005	272,089,617	127,864,388
Dist. Columbia	11	5	6	1,377,000	1,110,000	3,827,800	2,855,941	971,859
Virginia	30	12	18	2,966,000	3,002,200	8,578,170	5,825,943	2,752,227
West Virginia	22	5	17	1,836,000	1,429,600	5,500,480	3,917,065	1,583,415
North Carolina	16	1	15	2,501,000	1,853,000	4,905,410	3,008,289	1,897,121
South Carolina	13		13	1,886,200	1,380,000	4,079,185	2,727,842	1,351,343
Georgia	18	6	12	2,281,000	2,080,000	5,612,170	3,567,898	2,044,272
Florida	3	1	2	100,000	80,000	101,700	31,700	70,000
Alabama	11	2	9	1,508,000	1,437,000	3,362,580	1,962,584	1,399,996
Mississippi	2	2				66,000	65,724	276
Louisiana	11	4	7	2,875,000	2,515,000	7,592,930	5,221,831	2,371,099
Texas	17	2	15	1,475,000	1,030,000	2,259,120	1,367,300	891,820
Arkansas	3	1	2	205,000	205,000	593,400	387,582	205,548
Kentucky	60	8	52	10,630,900	9,836,700	22,093,255	12,891,495	9,801,760
Tennessee	35	9	26	3,472,800	3,338,500	7,534,700	4,678,474	2,856,226
Missouri	46	24	22	4,710,000	2,330,000	12,756,025	9,790,592	2,965,433
Southern States	298	82	216	37,823,900	31,633,000	89,462,925	58,300,260	31,162,395
Ohio	219	40	179	20,560,000	25,596,800	66,886,200	42,614,145	24,272,055
Indiana	121	28	93	13,203,500	10,209,800	38,937,575	27,183,986	11,753,589
Illinois	173	33	140	15,095,100	10,461,500	38,191,495	27,570,123	10,621,372
Michigan	95	15	80	9,321,300	6,292,800	19,894,500	12,765,418	7,129,082
Wisconsin	59	23	36	3,190,000	2,614,500	8,915,080	5,953,131	2,961,949
Iowa	109	30	79	6,052,500	5,243,500	14,887,170	9,814,820	5,072,350
Minnesota	42	12	30	4,983,700	2,276,400	8,261,920	5,567,330	2,694,590
Kansas	29	16	13	925,000	815,000	3,299,440	2,343,299	956,141
Nebraska	14	2	12	960,000	769,000	2,269,520	1,393,264	876,256
Western States	861	199	662	83,300,100	64,309,300	201,542,900	135,205,516	66,337,384
Nevada	2	1	1	75,000	40,000	167,700	129,717	37,983
Oregon	1		1	250,000	250,000	560,000	332,800	227,200
Colorado	22	5	17	1,276,800	1,185,000	2,359,240	1,304,099	1,055,141
Utah	4	3	1	200,000	200,000	815,730	604,521	211,209
Idaho	1		1	100,000	100,000	234,340	156,539	77,801
Montana	8	4	4	325,000	353,000	802,720	426,706	376,014
Wyoming	3		3	225,000	94,000	180,300	96,390	83,910
New Mexico	4		4	400,000	400,000	802,450	452,210	350,240
Dakota	12		12	750,000	545,000	443,630	116,880	326,750
Washington	2		2	200,000	100,000	276,940	29,155	247,785
California	8		8	1,300,000	1,004,000	907,680	72,910	834,770
Pacific States and Territories	67	13	54	5,101,800	4,271,000	7,550,730	3,721,927	3,828,803
Add for mutilated notes retired								481,250
Total currency banks	2,575	423	2,152	463,735,685	368,758,500	1,062,290,165	703,348,677	359,422,738
Add gold banks	6	3	3	2,000,000	850,000	3,117,510	2,195,998	921,512
United States	2,581	426	2,155	465,735,685	369,608,500	1,065,407,675	705,544,675	360,344,250

Number of State banks and trust companies, private bankers, and savings banks, with the aver·
months ending

States and Territories.	State banks and trust companies.				Private		
	Banks.	Capital.	Deposits.	Invested in U.S. bonds.	Banks.	Capital.	Deposits.
1 Maine..................	1	....	$2, 340	$8, 313	5	$47, 319	$120, 155
2 New Hampshire......	1	$50, 000	36, 003	5, 202	5	1, 000	61, 240
3 Vermont.............	5	350, 000	1, 607, 553	36, 984	1	3, 700	16, 025
4 Massachusetts	3	260, 000	1, 323, 634	185, 063	4	250, 000	434, 415
5 Boston	3	644, 349	6, 120, 670	568, 043	42	4, 483, 750	1, 636, 216
6 Rhode Island........	15	3, 074, 385	3, 611, 242	630, 543	7	234, 119	334, 718
7 Connecticut..........	12	2, 476, 896	3, 767, 165	254, 312	10	140, 000	1, 140, 936
New England States	40	6, 855, 630	16, 468, 616	1, 688, 460	74	5, 159, 888	3, 743, 705
8 New York	49	7, 001, 542	19, 581, 388	1, 941, 768	163	1, 524, 103	11, 402, 788
9 New York City	31	18, 148, 114	86, 794, 593	7, 624, 691	452	31, 187, 192	30, 552, 744
10 Albany.............	2	550, 000	1, 390, 139	354, 521	3	91, 000	71, 649
11 New Jersey	11	1, 255, 373	2, 973, 119	268, 883	6	20, 180	920
12 Pennsylvania	85	4, 411, 404	10, 072, 689	478, 606	185	4, 378, 527	18, 727, 365
13 Philadelphia	15	762, 175	25, 234, 689	81, 876	42	1, 346, 729	4, 104, 001
14 Pittsburgh	21	3, 270, 897	5, 215, 545	653, 938	6	324, 382	1, 474, 866
15 Delaware............	5	673, 689	917, 742	20, 000	1	2, 000	1, 824
16 Maryland	4	455, 841	441, 056	251, 189	3	98, 508	143, 185
17 Baltimore	11	2, 447, 511	2, 274, 006	106, 863	18	667, 256	2, 072, 366
18 Washington.........	...	....	....	....	6	357, 000	2, 988, 231
Middle States	234	38, 976, 546	154, 894, 971	11, 782, 335	885	40, 005, 937	71, 540, 139
19 Virginia	54	2, 321, 590	5, 137, 220	270, 208	20	374, 472	2, 061, 637
20 West Virginia	17	1, 177, 128	3, 089, 199	87, 488	3	70, 000	945, 544
21 North Carolina.......	9	747, 894	1, 477, 416	....	4	42, 427	119, 216
22 South Carolina	4	295, 000	611, 067	52, 333	9	216, 499	47, 745
23 Georgia	27	3, 634, 625	4, 341, 983	....	29	433, 654	683, 840
24 Florida..............	...	....	....	....	8	81, 830	272, 706
25 Alabama............	6	615, 000	1, 012, 426	....	20	425, 241	1, 257, 221
26 Mississippi...........	17	644, 205	1, 441, 669	123, 758	16	439, 485	1, 193, 246
27 Louisiana	...	....	....	....	3	126, 265	87, 343
28 New Orleans	3	2, 723, 698	4, 632, 122	643, 013	8	53, 333	....
29 Texas	18	1, 939, 276	2, 280, 131	3, 000	87	1, 761, 804	4, 052, 620
30 Arkansas	2	133, 000	412, 310	74, 017	13	112, 110	165, 318
31 Kentucky	49	5, 705, 038	5, 902, 969	218, 553	22	394, 628	1, 795, 145
32 Louisville	12	5, 060, 444	5, 116, 149	471, 197	3	206, 584	687, 524
33 Tennessee............	23	1, 697, 764	3, 050, 686	112, 388	7	71, 464	172, 054
Southern States	241	26, 694, 662	38, 505, 356	2, 055, 955	252	4, 809, 796	13, 541, 159
34 Ohio	31	1, 278, 058	3, 132, 931	163, 656	213	4, 361, 082	17, 004, 516
35 Cincinnati.........	4	626, 760	1, 350, 032	20, 882	8	775, 472	3, 042, 679
36 Cleveland	3	940, 924	4, 198, 909	623, 837	5	105, 000	826, 114
37 Indiana	27	1, 201, 244	2, 169, 517	88, 268	103	3, 164, 190	9, 590, 096
38 Illinois	25	987, 033	3, 228, 683	117, 717	286	3, 042, 881	13, 282, 590
39 Chicago	10	3, 681, 114	8, 846, 734	2, 398, 878	23	586, 381	3, 726, 779
40 Michigan	31	1, 337, 700	3, 378, 821	88, 973	124	1, 009, 099	3, 727, 131
41 Detroit...........	5	710, 000	4, 849, 999	329, 692	8	206, 041	826, 455
42 Wisconsin	28	785, 614	2, 654, 682	112, 477	81	793, 229	3, 309, 346
43 Milwaukee.........	5	478, 231	6, 252, 293	13, 489	4	161, 500	1, 536, 607
44 Iowa	60	2, 521, 985	6, 100, 367	222, 112	245	2, 583, 754	7, 017, 806
45 Minnesota..........	22	971, 307	1, 911, 978	51, 924	70	935, 068	2, 814, 325
46 Missouri	95	3, 167, 050	10, 360, 654	325, 025	75	1, 083, 125	4, 966, 562
47 Saint Louis	18	5, 250, 582	18, 074, 610	849, 920	10	454, 973	614, 080
48 Kansas	31	767, 707	1, 810, 416	47, 883	117	796, 437	3, 066, 734
49 Nebraska	12	192, 032	480, 354	....	71	461, 458	1, 539, 460
Western States.....	407	24, 892, 350	78, 800, 979	5, 454, 733	1, 443	20, 520, 090	76, 871, 288
50 Oregon	...	....	....	....	14	1, 203, 466	974, 571
51 California	58	8, 283, 006	11, 269, 822	197, 341	20	466, 913	818, 052
52 San Francisco......	5	7, 901, 233	18, 199, 412	3, 319, 780	12	2, 681, 517	7, 912, 530
53 Colorado	7	259, 250	515, 512	....	31	325, 667	2, 934, 365
54 Nevada	4	108, 000	98, 560	....	9	256, 457	735, 988
55 Utah	...	....	....	....	11	206, 000	1, 233, 952
56 New Mexico	...	....	....	....	5	6, 667	181, 925
57 Wyoming	...	....	....	....	4	128, 034	271, 201
58 Idaho	...	....	....	....	2	5, 358	18, 368
59 Dakota	...	....	....	....	18	127, 511	396, 279
60 Montana	...	....	....	....	13	446, 708	724, 031
61 Washington.........	...	....	....	....	4	257, 000	525, 109
62 Arizona............	...	....	....	....	5	112, 932	243, 673
Pacific States, &c ..	74	16, 551, 489	30, 113, 306	3, 517, 121	148	5, 626, 250	16, 970, 944
United States	996	113, 970, 677	318, 783, 228	24, 498, 604	2, 802	76, 121, 961	182, 667, 235

age amount of their capital, deposits, and investments in United States bonds, for the six May 31, 1880.

bankers.				Savings banks.	Total.				
Invested in U.S. bonds.	Banks.	Capital.	Deposits.	Invested in U.S. bonds.	Banks.	Capital.	Deposits.	Invested in U.S. bonds.	
	58		$21,599,469	$3,284,637	64	$47,319	$21,721,964	$3,292,950	1
	65		28,204,306	919,297	71	51,000	28,301,549	924,499	2
	16		6,907,562	653,862	22	353,700	8,531,140	690,846	3
$38,550	154		142,510,224	13,633,993	161	510,000	144,268,273	13,857,606	4
1,984,618	12		56,796,871	6,499,110	57	5,128,099	64,553,766	9,051,771	5
7,045	34		39,188,748	4,570,369	56	3,308,504	43,134,708	5,207,957	6
18,420	83		73,549,860	8,131,932	105	2,616,896	78,457,961	8,404,864	7
2,048,633	422		368,757,040	37,693,200	536	12,015,518	388,969,361	41,430,293	
358,430	91		131,291,297	45,993,290	303	8,525,645	162,275,473	48,293,488	8
7,528,342	23		174,566,730	73,737,079	506	49,335,306	291,914,072	88,890,112	9
3,000	7		12,289,861	2,552,905	12	641,000	13,751,649	2,910,426	10
800	34	$40,000	17,417,079	5,871,992	51	1,324,553	20,391,118	6,141,075	11
274,180	1		270,878	70,000	271	8,789,931	29,071,132	822,786	12
117,527	4		22,157,080	6,472,097	61	2,108,904	51,496,370	6,671,500	13
7,425	4	458,300	7,961,178	1,679,366	31	4,053,579	14,651,589	2,340,729	14
	2		1,207,860		8	675,689	2,127,426	20,000	15
	5	10,085	235,703	13,538	12	564,434	819,944	264,727	16
203,037	9	20,075	21,467,947	9,890,353	38	3,134,842	25,814,319	10,200,253	17
280,758	1		317,644	20,535	7	357,060	3,305,875	310,293	18
8,782,400	181	528,460	389,183,857	146,301,155	1,300	79,510,943	615,618,967	166,865,989	
24,000	2	340,912	558,336		76	3,036,974	7,757,202	294,208	19
50,000					20	1,247,128	4,034,743	137,488	20
					13	790,321	1,596,632		21
					13	511,499	658,812	52,333	22
18,050	2		885,004	1,000	58	4,068,279	5,910,827	19,050	23
	1	2,000	14,583		9	83,830	287,280		24
742					26	1,040,241	2,269,647	742	25
85,600					33	1,083,690	2,634,915	209,358	26
45,000					3	126,265	87,343	45,000	27
					11	2,777,031	4,632,122	643,013	28
160,133					105	3,701,080	1,332,751	163,133	29
1,085					15	245,110	577,628	75,102	30
88,426					71	6,099,666	7,698,114	306,979	31
					15	5,267,028	5,803,673	471,197	32
13,000					30	1,769,228	3,222,740	125,388	33
486,036	5	342,912	1,457,923	1,000	498	31,847,370	53,504,438	2,542,991	
704,819	4	65,000	697,202	86,959	248	5,704,140	20,834,648	954,434	34
254,780					12	1,402,241	4,392,711	275,671	35
54,542	1		8,940,548	2,151,270	9	1,045,924	13,965,571	2,829,649	36
419,685	14		1,413,171	42,061	144	4,365,434	13,172,783	550,014	37
557,880	5	62,400	550,515	60,000	316	4,092,314	17,061,788	735,606	38
160,945	1	5,000	10,570		34	4,272,495	12,584,083	2,559,823	39
65,921					155	2,346,799	7,105,952	154,804	40
16,050	1	150,000	1,867,594	134,267	14	1,086,041	7,544,048	480,009	41
72,284					109	1,578,843	5,964,028	184,761	42
2,425					9	634,731	7,788,900	15,914	43
97,764	4	48,167	208,018		309	5,153,906	13,326,191	319,876	44
68,044	3		273,847		95	1,906,375	5,000,150	119,968	45
103,183					170	4,250,175	15,307,216	428,208	46
23,475					28	5,705,555	18,688,699	873,395	47
42,514					148	1,564,144	4,877,150	90,397	48
39,492					83	653,890	2,019,814	39,492	49
2,682,821	33	330,567	13,961,465	2,474,557	1,883	45,743,007	169,633,732	10,612,111	
112,423	1	41,742	58,532	6,300	15	1,245,208	1,033,103	118,723	50
	7	680,710	2,839,944		85	9,430,629	14,928,710	197,341	51
129,272	9	2,110,796	41,385,352	2,711,604	26	12,104,546	67,497,204	6,160,656	52
					38	584,917	3,479,877		53
100,000					13	364,457	834,548	100,000	54
					11	206,000	1,233,952		55
					5	6,667	181,925		56
					4	128,054	271,201		57
					2	5,358	18,368		58
					18	127,511	396,279		59
					13	446,708	724,031		60
					4	257,000	525,109		61
25,000					5	112,932	243,673	25,000	62
366,695	17	2,842,248	44,283,828	2,717,904	239	25,019,987	91,368,078	6,691,720	
14,366,684	658	4,014,187	817,644,113	189,187,816	4,456	194,136,825	1,319,094,576	228,053,104	

Number of State banks and trust companies, private bankers, and savings banks, with the months ending

	States and Territories.	State banks and trust companies.				Private		
		Banks.	Capital.	Deposits.	Invested in U.S. bonds.	Banks.	Capital.	Deposits.
1	Maine	2	....	$77,409	....	7	$53,200	$169,764
2	New Hampshire	1	$50,000	25,658	$1,375	4	1,000	45,234
3	Vermont..............	6	350,000	2,057,666	113,748	1	2,804	17,267
4	Massachusetts........	3	260,000	1,977,822	167,614	3	50,000	539,028
5	Boston..............	3	790,633	8,153,354	592,798	47	4,065,097	2,570,068
6	Rhode Island	15	3,361,608	4,212,867	909,584	7	358,181	462,268
7	Connecticut	11	2,451,600	4,463,846	132,725	12	168,500	1,359,079
	New England States	41	7,263,841	20,968,622	1,917,844	80	4,698,782	5,162,708
8	New York	48	7,211,333	25,277,222	1,832,351	163	1,551,347	12,609,067
9	New York City......	31	20,527,888	105,898,639	6,987,938	508	45,482,515	45,414,376
10	Albany..............	2	66,000	182,579	....	3	550,000	1,611,470
11	New Jersey...........	10	1,167,683	3,487,561	323,675	5	26,231	1,560
12	Pennsylvania	73	3,718,015	11,590,119	388,685	172	4,140,679	19,978,585
13	Philadelphia........	18	768,280	33,648,619	48,033	52	1,800,614	6,174,785
14	Pittsburgh	18	2,922,125	5,943,543	623,348	7	563,910	2,025,477
15	Delaware	4	604,561	844,743	10,000	1	5,000	19,183
16	Maryland............	4	447,812	548,605	256,675	2	49,177	43,742
17	Baltimore............	10	1,846,816	2,346,610	36,189	19	773,657	2,389,032
18	Washington	....	....	....	....	6	364,000	3,747,703
	Middle States......	218	39,280,513	189,777,240	10,506,894	938	55,397,130	94,104,980
19	Virginia	53	2,280,452	6,371,435	208,136	18	369,792	2,102,077
20	West Virginia	16	1,158,983	3,313,510	66,790	3	70,000	992,892
21	North Carolina	9	463,807	1,063,523	50	4	40,833	102,240
22	South Carolina	4	305,000	1,553,145	45,000	8	229,956	53,921
23	Georgia...............	22	2,959,758	3,961,950	....	30	478,910	1,308,131
24	Florida..............	....	....	....	....	6	99,079	521,699
25	Alabama	6	615,000	1,109,300	....	21	564,085	1,372,342
26	Mississippi...........	17	675,293	1,311,167	122,693	11	314,579	833,326
27	Louisiana............	....	....	....	....	3	146,329	35,812
28	New Orleans	7	2,237,803	5,147,188	395,161	5	32,000	....
29	Texas	13	1,487,013	1,777,780	....	107	2,560,951	7,033,240
30	Arkansas............	3	130,236	495,204	65,230	11	87,066	184,305
31	Kentucky	52	5,683,563	7,065,484	91,177	23	368,731	1,936,815
32	Louisville	12	4,967,554	5,903,221	249,922	3	178,000	728,464
33	Tennessee	26	1,748,019	3,356,247	199,763	5	48,517	118,240
	Southern States	240	24,712,481	42,429,163	1,443,922	258	5,588,828	17,323,504
34	Ohio.................	28	1,225,363	3,390,421	162,308	213	4,119,220	19,931,774
35	Cincinnati...........	4	562,150	1,558,046	60,094	8	812,167	3,863,817
36	Cleveland............	3	1,004,667	4,876,490	491,161	4	55,000	963,938
37	Indiana..............	24	1,303,220	2,291,526	40,190	106	3,130,268	11,870,104
38	Illinois	14	320,682	1,301,320	26,333	310	4,183,346	21,656,149
39	Chicago.............	7	1,951,000	8,793,445	1,001,700	24	2,004,197	10,455,063
40	Michigan............	22	1,156,704	3,404,975	42,227	137	1,213,796	5,218,413
41	Detroit	6	732,772	5,887,273	300,367	7	161,256	945,669
42	Wisconsin...........	29	982,117	5,204,860	95,236	79	848,746	4,901,883
43	Milwaukee	4	373,231	6,954,542	1,717	4	64,667	530,047
44	Iowa	58	2,655,731	7,975,671	291,564	276	2,975,737	10,388,843
45	Minnesota...........	20	2,196,744	4,475,337	23,774	89	679,227	2,772,567
46	Missouri.............	101	3,245,859	14,816,825	339,742	81	1,120,244	6,843,267
47	Saint Louis	19	5,501,723	24,807,700	339,419	11	261,302	304,976
48	Kansas	40	920,399	2,342,089	30,937	135	1,001,172	4,076,393
49	Nebraska............	12	209,072	607,705	....	86	675,300	2,053,586
	Western States	391	24,401,434	98,688,243	3,246,769	1,570	23,305,645	106,776,549
50	Oregon	4	456,344	461,049	6,300	12	436,500	973,519
51	California............	57	7,778,073	12,105,968	254,290	22	287,709	1,022,592
52	San Francisco	7	8,726,011	18,816,574	4,219,649	9	1,275,918	8,271,660
53	Colorado.............	8	355,613	1,159,507	5,000	51	547,827	2,705,441
54	Nevada	6	89,000	617,119	....	9	292,851	637,530
55	Utah	2	51,000	97,808	....	10	157,225	1,484,711
56	New Mexico..........	....	....	....	....	8	13,333	459,518
57	Wyoming............	....	....	....	....	4	135,208	421,310
58	Idaho...............	....	....	....	....	2	6,561	19,097
59	Dakota	....	....	....	....	37	216,263	484,335
60	Montana	....	....	....	....	13	512,706	904,498
61	Washington	....	....	....	....	9	284,050	657,015
62	Arizona.............	4	80,000	198,669	50,000	5	67,319	436,587
	Pacific States, &c...	88	17,526,041	33,756,694	4,535,239	192	4,333,470	18,477,813
	United States........	978	113,194,310	385,619,962	21,650,668	3,038	93,323,855	241,845,554

average amount of their capital, deposits, and investments in United States bonds for the six May 31, 1881.

	bankers.			Savings banks.			Total.			
Invested in U.S. bonds.	Banks.	Capital.	Deposits.	Invested in U.S. bonds.	Banks.	Capital.	Deposits.	Invested in U.S. bonds.	
$6,966	57	....	$24,116,117	$4,049,652	66	$53,200	$24,363,290	$4,956,618	1
....	67	$25,000	32,092,232	738,716	72	76,000	32,163,124	740,091	2
....	16	....	7,971,977	508,777	22	352,804	10,046,910	622,525	3
16,667	157	....	162,120,982	14,485,728	163	310,000	164,637,832	14,670,009	4
1,003,343	12	....	59,921,155	5,720,483	62	4,855,730	70,644,577	7,316,624	5
32,613	33	....	38,364,066	4,228,338	55	3,719,789	43,039,201	5,170,535	6
8,063	83	....	78,466,347	6,909,101	106	2,620,100	84,289,272	7,049,889	7
1,067,652	425	25,000	403,052,876	36,640,795	546	11,987,623	429,184,206	39,626,291	
364,268	89	....	145,650,176	54,898,091	300	8,762,680	183,626,465	57,094,710	8
9,670,751	24	....	192,517,560	83,257,940	563	66,010,403	343,830,575	99,916,629	9
351,000	7	....	13,981,392	2,964,825	12	616,000	15,775,441	3,315,825	10
333	33	45,000	20,388,409	7,729,081	48	1,238,914	23,877,530	8,053,089	11
288,461	1	....	369,457	67,850	246	7,858,694	31,947,161	744,996	12
224,208	4	....	25,007,693	6,534,649	74	2,658,894	64,831,097	6,806,850	13
20,374	5	533,300	9,918,603	2,372,208	30	4,019,335	17,887,623	3,015,950	14
....	2	....	1,435,466	....	7	609,561	2,299,392	10,000	15
....	5	10,085	295,395	10,976	11	507,074	887,742	267,651	16
195,384	10	20,225	23,123,778	10,749,845	39	2,640,698	27,859,420	10,981,418	17
287,029	1	....	397,172	31,585	7	364,000	4,144,875	318,614	18
11,401,808	181	608,610	433,085,101	168,617,050	1,337	95,286,253	716,967,321	190,525,752	
35,000	3	418,741	813,449	21,689	74	3,068,985	9,286,961	264,825	19
35,617	....	....	....	....	19	1,228,983	4,306,402	102,407	20
....	....	....	....	....	13	504,640	1,165,763	50	21
....	2	15,000	307,201	....	14	549,956	1,914,267	45,000	22
7,000	2	....	929,082	....	54	3,438,668	6,199,163	7,000	23
....	1	2,000	17,750	....	7	101,079	539,449	....	24
800	....	....	....	....	27	1,179,085	2,481,642	800	25
48,280	....	....	....	....	28	989,872	2,144,493	170,973	26
30,000	....	....	....	....	3	146,329	35,812	30,000	27
....	1	2,129	2,397	....	13	2,271,932	5,149,585	395,161	28
14,000	....	....	....	....	120	4,047,964	8,811,029	14,000	29
1,250	....	....	....	....	14	217,302	679,509	66,480	30
80,000	....	....	....	....	75	6,052,294	9,002,299	171,177	31
....	....	....	....	....	15	5,145,554	6,631,685	249,922	32
11,833	....	....	....	....	31	1,796,536	3,474,487	211,596	33
263,780	9	437,870	2,069,879	21,689	507	30,739,179	61,822,546	1,729,391	
656,222	5	165,000	1,173,782	118,369	246	5,509,583	24,495,977	936,899	34
280,205	....	....	....	....	12	1,374,317	5,421,863	340,290	35
8,967	1	....	10,021,320	2,133,583	8	1,059,667	15,861,757	2,033,711	36
571,999	15	....	1,716,516	122,645	145	4,433,488	15,878,206	734,834	37
1,245,738	6	75,350	946,035	85,234	330	4,579,378	23,903,504	1,357,305	38
172,589	2	10,000	67,515	24,648	33	3,915,197	19,316,023	1,198,937	39
74,464	2	75,000	393,671	550	161	2,445,500	9,017,059	117,241	40
7,333	1	150,000	2,586,087	202,292	14	1,044,028	9,419,029	509,992	41
111,960	....	....	....	....	108	1,830,863	10,106,752	207,196	42
350	....	....	....	....	8	437,898	7,484,589	2,067	43
67,287	3	40,000	228,281	2,125	337	5,671,468	18,592,795	360,976	44
45,848	3	....	506,510	....	112	2,875,971	7,754,414	69,622	45
131,142	....	....	....	....	182	4,366,103	21,660,092	473,884	46
44,406	....	....	....	....	30	5,763,025	25,112,676	383,825	47
32,600	....	....	....	....	175	1,921,571	6,418,482	63,537	48
14,070	....	....	....	....	98	944,372	2,661,291	14,070	49
3,468,180	38	515,350	17,639,717	2,689,446	1,999	48,222,429	223,104,509	9,404,395	
250,000	....	....	....	....	16	892,844	1,434,568	256,300	50
....	4	681,965	2,233,524	....	83	8,847,747	15,662,084	254,290	51
104,074	8	1,951,243	41,892,395	6,911,198	24	11,953,172	68,980,629	11,234,921	52
15,000	....	....	....	....	59	903,440	3,864,948	20,000	53
100,000	....	....	....	....	15	381,851	1,254,649	100,000	54
....	....	....	....	....	12	208,225	1,582,519	....	55
....	....	....	....	....	8	13,333	459,518	....	56
....	....	....	....	....	4	135,208	421,310	....	57
....	....	....	....	....	2	6,561	19,097	....	58
....	....	....	....	....	37	216,263	484,335	....	59
....	....	....	....	....	14	512,706	904,498	....	60
....	....	....	....	....	9	284,050	657,015	....	61
....	....	....	....	....	9	147,319	635,256	50,000	62
489,074	12	2,633,208	44,125,919	6,911,198	292	24,502,719	96,360,426	11,915,511	
16,670,494	665	4,220,038	899,973,492	214,880,178	4,681	210,738,203	1,527,439,008	253,201,340	

Lawful-money reserve of the national banks, as shown by the reports

STATES AND

		Number of banks.	Deposits.	Reserve required.
1	Maine	69	$9, 558, 878	$1, 433, 832
2	New Hampshire	47	4, 867, 637	730, 146
3	Vermont	47	5, 239, 644	785, 947
4	Massachusetts	190	46, 849, 038	7, 027, 356
5	Rhode Island	62	13, 006, 588	1, 950, 988
6	Connecticut	85	25, 734, 382	3, 860, 157
7	New York	243	70, 500, 180	10, 575, 027
8	New Jersey	67	28, 733, 695	4, 310, 054
9	Pennsylvania	191	57, 603, 203	8, 640, 480
10	Delaware	14	3, 818, 586	572, 788
11	Maryland	22	5, 349, 990	802, 499
12	District of Columbia	1	589, 060	88, 359
13	Virginia	18	9, 569, 105	1, 435, 366
14	West Virginia	17	2, 373, 936	356, 090
15	North Carolina	15	3, 287, 102	493, 065
16	South Carolina	13	3, 189, 944	478, 492
17	Georgia	12	3, 321, 577	498, 237
18	Florida	2	318, 545	47, 782
19	Alabama	9	1, 773, 415	266, 012
20	Texas	15	4, 022, 055	603, 308
21	Arkansas	2	487, 793	73, 169
22	Kentucky	42	7, 974, 654	1, 196, 198
23	Tennessee	25	8, 663, 170	1, 299, 476
24	Ohio	161	38, 782, 485	5, 817, 373
25	Indiana	93	23, 715, 274	3, 557, 291
26	Illinois	130	34, 657, 785	5, 198, 668
27	Michigan	76	16, 058, 341	2, 408, 751
28	Wisconsin	31	8, 325, 581	1, 248, 837
29	Iowa	76	15, 892, 754	2, 383, 913
30	Minnesota	27	14, 212, 887	2, 131, 933
31	Missouri	17	4, 468, 367	670, 255
32	Kansas	13	3, 585, 562	537, 834
33	Nebraska	12	6, 221, 485	933, 223
34	Colorado	17	10, 488, 622	1, 573, 293
35	Nevada	1	161, 568	24, 235
36	California	10	*4, 703, 498	725, 354
37	Oregon	1	2, 095, 498	314, 325
38	Dakota	8	1, 792, 374	268, 856
39	Idaho	1	320, 169	48, 025
40	Montana	3	1, 482, 594	222, 389
41	New Mexico	4	1, 125, 640	168, 846
42	Utah	1	1, 012, 435	151, 865
43	Washington	2	456, 042	68, 406
44	Wyoming	3	856, 065	128, 401
	Totals	1, 895	507, 247, 143	76, 106, 901

NOTE.—Prior to June 20, 1874, the required reserve in States and Territories was 15 per

RESERVE

1	Boston	54	$95, 776, 386	$23, 944, 096
2	Albany	7	10, 097, 594	2, 524, 399
3	Philadelphia	32	66, 145, 400	16, 536, 350
4	Pittsburgh	22	21, 176, 058	5, 294, 015
5	Baltimore	16	19, 952, 679	4, 988, 170
6	Washington	5	1, 977, 830	494, 458
7	New Orleans	7	8, 871, 346	2, 217, 837
8	Louisville	8	5, 953, 453	1, 488, 363
9	Cincinnati	10	19, 640, 318	4, 910, 079
10	Cleveland	6	8, 715, 703	2, 178, 926
11	Chicago	9	50, 949, 660	12, 737, 415
12	Detroit	4	8, 121, 016	2, 030, 254
13	Milwaukee	3	5, 332, 201	1, 333, 050
14	Saint Louis	5	10, 631, 992	2, 657, 998
15	San Francisco	1	*2, 327, 590	581, 897
	Totals	189	335, 669, 226	83, 917, 307
	New York	48	268, 769, 373	67, 192, 343

* Includes National

NOTE.—Prior to June 20, 1874, the required reserve in reserve cities was 25 per *of their condition at the close of business on October* 1, 1881.

TERRITORIES.

Reserve held.	Ratio of reserve.	Classification of reserve held.					
		Specie.	Legal tenders.	United States certificates of deposit.	Due from reserve agents.	Redemption fund with Treasurer.	
	Per cent.						
$3, 581, 746	37. 47	$450, 583	$143, 907	....	$2, 573, 543	$413, 713	1
1, 803, 954	37. 04	198, 676	98, 655	....	1, 245, 973	250, 750	2
1, 893, 828	36. 26	224, 575	227, 000	....	1, 123, 437	324, 807	3
12, 734, 514	27. 18	*1, 933, 322	1, 362, 445	$185, 000	7, 306, 973	1, 946, 774	4
4, 259, 023	32. 74	394, 457	390, 066	....	2, 733, 838	740, 662	5
6, 647, 980	25. 83	1, 227, 371	939, 922	10, 000	3, 565, 027	905, 660	6
20, 225, 908	28. 69	2, 621, 275	2, 760, 944	285, 000	13, 235, 249	1, 323, 440	7
9, 982, 879	34. 74	977, 443	1, 487, 897	10, 000	6, 984, 533	522, 986	8
19, 663, 638	34. 14	3, 663, 992	2, 770, 438	60, 000	11, 933, 427	1, 235, 781	9
1, 315, 605	34. 45	181, 894	141, 262	30, 000	886, 910	75, 539	10
1, 925, 966	36. 00	260, 690	421, 391	....	1, 143, 417	100, 468	11
262. 730	44. 60	54, 186	75, 000	....	122, 294	11, 250	12
2, 192. 435	22. 91	342, 888	452, 872	....	1, 273, 375	123, 300	13
814, 652	34. 32	197. 047	240, 593	....	306, 769	70, 243	14
683, 180	20. 78	172, 547	262, 707	....	169, 485	78, 441	15
674, 648	21. 14	211, 989	254, 406	....	149, 227	59, 026	16
719, 267	21. 65	301, 198	225, 473	....	95, 351	97. 245	17
71, 080	22. 31	19, 602	36, 474	....	11, 344	3, 600	18
696, 800	39. 30	133, 648	220, 077	....	278, 059	65, 115	19
1, 617, 884	40. 23	306, 240	516, 100	....	749, 194	46, 350	20
123, 137	25. 24	17, 688	35, 515	....	60, 509	9, 225	21
2, 648, 468	33. 21	302, 042	397, 893	....	1, 638, 039	310, 494	22
2, 433, 661	28. 09	506, 411	731, 391	....	1, 066, 681	129, 178	23
13, 154, 256	33. 92	2, 407, 952	3, 036, 591	....	6, 935, 259	774, 454	24
8, 090. 178	34. 11	1, 602, 772	1, 856, 794	....	4, 191, 416	439, 196	25
11, 744, 324	33. 80	2, 305, 607	2, 050, 597	10, 000	6, 968, 671	379, 449	26
5, 144, 154	32. 03	1, 123, 894	895, 883	....	2, 903, 705	220, 672	27
2, 439, 357	29. 30	579, 117	397, 094	....	1, 374, 736	88, 410	28
5, 548, 461	34. 91	1, 161, 487	1, 231, 344	30, 000	2, 903, 306	222, 324	29
3, 425, 191	24. 10	607, 544	849, 160	....	1, 876, 299	92, 188	30
1, 409, 655	31. 54	188, 173	294, 756	....	869, 726	57, 000	31
1, 125, 301	31. 38	203, 633	326, 411	....	562, 293	32, 964	32
1, 626, 257	26. 14	306, 722	261, 401	....	1, 024, 879	33, 255	33
4, 021, 501	38. 34	655, 826	626, 903	....	2, 689, 833	48, 939	34
46, 286	28. 64	39, 658	2, 519	....	2, 309	1, 800	35
1, 326, 677	28. 21	800, 399	15, 782	....	469. 466	41, 030	36
558, 060	26. 66	347, 143	2, 200	....	198, 067	11, 250	37
430, 854	24. 04	90, 684	148, 223	....	176, 422	15, 525	38
45, 923	14 34	18, 173	23, 250	....	....	4, 500	39
195, 744	15. 20	43, 398	81, 150	....	63, 096	8, 100	40
425, 244	37. 78	83, 030	81, 147	....	243, 067	18, 000	41
263, 640	26. 04	141. 530	24, 470	....	88, 640	9, 000	42
81, 100	17. 78	32, 006	19, 940	....	23, 304	5, 850	43
218, 117	25. 48	71, 049	54, 950	....	87, 888	4. 230	44
158, 299, 042	31. 21	27, 509, 821	26, 473, 002	620, 000	92, 335, 036	11, 361, 183	

centum of circulation and deposits; since that date, 15 per centum of deposits only.

CITIES.

Reserve held.	Ratio of reserve.	Specie.	Legal tenders.	United States certificates of deposit.	Due from reserve agents.	Redemption fund with Treasurer.	
$25, 157, 688	26. 27	$8, 286, 182	$3, 457, 379	$75, 000	$11, 735, 499	$1, 603, 628	1
3, 134, 090	31. 04	502. 055	154, 470	545, 000	1, 856, 968	75, 597	2
18, 713, 629	24. 29	7, 156, 059	2, 529, 521	1, 820, 000	6, 607, 950	690, 099	3
7, 256, 730	31. 27	1, 664, 394	1, 994, 011	....	3, 257, 058	341, 267	4
6, 085, 183	30. 50	2, 020, 682	947, 170	255, 000	2, 522, 644	339, 687	5
582, 877	29. 47	128, 806	222, 126	....	200, 445	31, 500	6
2, 746, 692	30. 61	1, 143, 325	1, 141, 612	....	350, 880	110, 875	7
1, 246, 251	20. 93	149, 907	411, 257	....	551, 420	133, 667	8
6, 416, 802	32. 67	674, 484	1, 919, 975	835, 000	2, 778, 616	208, 727	9
2, 595, 157	29. 78	405, 151	1, 070, 000	15, 000	1, 003, 223	101, 780	10
18, 301, 194	35. 92	9, 485, 040	1, 508, 520	660, 000	6, 547, 134	40, 500	11
2, 933, 645	36. 12	715, 192	549, 411	....	1, 606, 192	62, 250	12
1, 419, 672	26. 62	327, 916	376, 779	....	695, 697	29, 250	13
3, 632, 767	28. 52	702, 411	1, 352, 000	....	919, 421	58, 935	14
1, 183, 730	50. 86	1, 183, 730	....	....	....	....	15
100, 895, 507	30. 03	34, 535, 367	17, 694, 231	4, 205, 000	40, 633, 147	3, 737, 762	
62, 512, 546	23. 27	50, 627, 368	8, 983, 371	1, 915, 000	....	1, 016, 807	

Gold Bank circulation.
centum of circulation and deposits; since that date, 25 per centum of deposits only.

Table of the state of the lawful-money reserve of the national banks

STATES AND

	Dates.	Number of banks.	Net deposits.	Reserve required.
1	Oct. 1, 1875	1,851	$307,920,794	$46,304,791
2	Dec. 17, 1875	1,850	297,071,465	44,647,965
3	Mar. 10, 1876	1,853	303,046,873	45,535,811
4	May 12, 1876	1,853	299,442,980	44,990,757
5	June 30, 1876	1,855	299,479,094	44,996,205
6	Oct. 2, 1876	1,853	291,744,349	43,862,907
7	Dec. 22, 1876	1,848	288,950,818	43,416,361
8	Jan. 20, 1877	1,849	299,364,605	44,978,935
9	Apr. 14, 1877	1,839	294,192,806	44,203,308
10	June 22, 1877	1,844	291,600,630	43,814,051
11	Oct. 1, 1877	1,845	290,136,048	43,594,978
12	Dec. 28, 1877	1,834	287,728,891	43,616,668
13	Mar. 15, 1878	1,831	286,105,648	42,990,070
14	May 1, 1878	1,827	282,678,523	42,476,500
15	June 29, 1878	1,824	283,101,236	42,539,987
16	Oct. 1, 1878	1,822	289,071,448	43,437,474
17	Dec. 6, 1878	1,825	283,181,956	42,555,776
18	Jan. 1, 1879	1,821	290,504,788	43,654,032
19	Apr. 4, 1879	1,819	293,817,962	44,126,773
20	June 14, 1879	1,819	300,097,942	45,068,973
21	Oct. 2, 1879	1,820	329,874,452	49,535,540
22	Dec. 12, 1879	1,824	348,834,775	52,379,535
23	Feb. 21, 1880	1,831	375,281,538	56,346,847
24	Apr. 23, 1880	1,844	384,765,183	57,766,633
25	June 11, 1880	1,845	385,168,252	57,801,806
26	Oct. 1, 1880	1,859	410,522,448	61,598,298
27	Dec. 31, 1880	1,863	439,354,304	65,922,995
28	Mar. 11, 1881	1,860	447,410,923	67,131,602
29	May 6, 1881	1,868	460,478,466	69,091,733
30	June 30, 1881	1,880	484,089,521	72,633,329
31	Oct. 1, 1881	1,895	507,247,143	76,196,945

RESERVE

	Oct.			
1	Oct. 1, 1875	236	$426,168,021	$106,542,005
2	Dec. 17, 1875	236	383,453,858	95,863,466
3	Mar. 10, 1876	238	418,141,702	104,535,425
4	May 12, 1876	236	395,106,986	98,776,747
5	June 30, 1876	236	415,443,362	103,860,841
6	Oct. 2, 1876	236	414,887,769	103,721,942
7	Dec. 22, 1876	234	396,950,934	99,237,733
8	Jan. 20, 1877	234	421,845,188	105,461,297
9	Apr. 14, 1877	234	402,090,332	100,522,583
10	June 22, 1877	234	420,184,865	105,046,216
11	Oct. 1, 1877	235	378,992,700	94,748,175
12	Dec. 28, 1877	233	372,696,990	93,174,248
13	Mar. 15, 1878	232	384,942,505	96,235,626
14	May 1, 1878	233	373,875,154	93,468,789
15	June 29, 1878	232	395,473,477	98,868,369
16	Oct. 1, 1878	231	389,031,686	97,257,896
17	Dec. 6, 1878	230	381,431,393	95,357,848
18	Jan. 1, 1879	230	384,519,202	96,130,280
19	Apr. 4, 1879	229	366,814,853	91,703,715
20	June 14, 1879	229	414,518,542	103,629,635
21	Oct. 2, 1879	228	439,009,954	109,752,489
22	Dec. 12, 1879	228	458,944,779	114,736,195
23	Feb. 21, 1880	230	498,980,548	124,745,137
24	Apr. 23, 1880	231	482,230,794	120,557,698
25	June 11, 1880	231	516,491,857	129,122,964
26	Oct. 1, 1880	231	557,508,975	139,377,244
27	Dec. 31, 1880	232	544,501,717	136,125,429
28	Mar. 11, 1881	234	536,112,658	134,028,165
29	May 6, 1881	234	588,714,401	147,178,600
30	June 30, 1881	235	655,815,066	163,953,766
31	Oct. 1, 1881	237	604,438,599	151,109,650

as shown by their reports from October 1, 1875, to October 1, 1881.

TERRITORIES.

Amount.	Ratio to liabilities.	Specie.	Legal tenders.	United States certificates of deposit.	Due from reserve agents.	Redemption fund with Treasurer.	
	Per cent.						
$100,128,907	32.5	$1,555,034	$32,783,502	$900,000	$53,322,15?	$11,568,219	1
97,855,940	32.9	1,452,639	32,073,246	805,000	52,073,208	11,451,847	2
108,547,092	35.8	1,800,017	32,141,468	1,180,000	62,102,613	11,322,994	3
104,514,789	34.9	1,912,171	33,630,711	1,285,000	56,654,668	11,032,230	4
103,832,286	34.7	2,469,391	31,920,120	1,280,000	57,268,334	10,894,411	5
99,985,627	34.3	2,763,198	29,723,138	1,280,000	56,362,468	10,856,823	6
101,429,533	35.1	3,427,133	30,714,772	1,280,000	55,244,747	10,762,881	7
108,706,493	36.3	3,941,458	32,707,525	1,245,000	60,110,762	10,701,848	8
103,945,584	35.3	4,166,989	31,948,207	1,180,000	55,904,422	10,745,584	9
101,962,783	35.0	4,208,317	30,879,163	1,250,000	55,012,171	10,613,132	10
95,379,331	32.9	4,155,631	30,316,538	1,315,000	48,885,195	10,706,607	11
101,860,983	35.1	4,486,185	32,730,224	1,225,000	52,587,886	10,837,688	12
108,782,223	38.0	6,305,680	31,528,169	1,115,000	58,950,369	10,883,005	13
99,320,989	35.1	7,007,260	32,024,586	1,035,000	48,325,035	10,929,108	14
102,308,371	36.1	7,049,274	29,390,198	1,040,000	54,033,882	10,795,017	15
106,045,159	36.7	7,988,990	30,064,665	995,000	56,023,564	10,972,940	16
106,004,028	37.4	9,048,396	30,579,974	1,140,000	54,268,698	10,965,960	17
110,164,553	37.9	11,578,143	32,374,428	1,035,000	54,197,445	10,979,537	18
105,684,344	36.0	11,872,699	29,074,259	895,000	52,916,702	10,925,684	19
112,463,409	37.5	12,135,564	26,433,762	695,000	62,257,734	10,941,349	20
124,315,513	37.7	11,474,961	29,528,096	735,000	71,302,887	11,184,569	21
124,606,178	35.7	13,257,825	29,357,057	670,000	70,017,269	11,304,027	22
139,480,054	37.2	15,931,208	28,471,133	670,000	83,134,259	11,282,454	23
133,960,543	34.8	18,523,230	30,138,708	645,000	73,296,236	11,363,369	24
138,632,303	36.0	18,988,001	28,650,254	605,000	79,126,763	11,262,285	25
147,105,244	35.8	21,145,738	27,613,370	640,000	86,371,229	11,334,907	26
155,406,393	35.4	25,108,888	29,063,892	630,000	89,258,930	11,344,683	27
150,919,045	33.7	26,660,882	26,783,131	585,000	86,060,705	10,829,697	28
155,258,612	33.7	27,842,501	28,672,789	585,000	87,109,924	11,048,428	29
170,055,750	35.1	27,635,215	27,416,230	575,000	103,297,184	11,132,121	30
158,299,042	31.2	27,509,821	26,473,002	620,000	92,335,036	11,361,183	31

CITIES.

Amount.	Ratio to liabilities.	Specie.	Legal tenders.	United States certificates of deposit.	Due from reserve agents.	Redemption fund with Treasurer.	
$134,976,509	31.7	$6,495,294	$43,585,429	$47,910,000	$32,322,812	$4,664,974	1
118,291,125	30.8	15,618,267	38,563,571	30,200,000	29,389,472	4,519,815	2
142,753,190	34.1	27,277,329	44,603,718	20,605,000	36,965,578	4,301,565	3
126,179,248	31.9	19,802,423	46,171,398	26,095,000	36,114,214	3,996,213	4
142,906,797	34.4	22,749,078	58,852,046	26,675,000	30,719,768	3,910,905	5
136,821,941	34.2	18,598,456	54,488,415	27,890,000	31,981,995	3,863,045	6
122,279,996	30.8	29,572,511	35,466,510	24,815,000	28,544,429	3,881,546	7
142,409,114	33.8	45,767,909	39,908,797	24,225,000	28,587,547	3,919,861	8
127,205,252	29.0	22,903,049	40,330,831	30,920,000	29,038,296	4,013,076	9
138,499,197	33.0	17,127,679	47,072,388	43,180,000	27,119,929	3,999,201	10
115,320,428	30.5	18,503,188	36,544,645	32,095,000	24,398,938	3,787,666	11
119,011,844	31.9	28,421,566	37,767,420	25,290,000	23,372,201	4,190,652	12
131,007,266	34.2	48,416,378	32,422,675	19,490,000	27,066,622	4,211,591	13
121,342,350	32.5	39,016,496	35,163,963	19,060,000	23,606,184	4,195,707	14
120,369,019	32.7	22,202,196	42,209,969	35,865,000	24,841,174	4,250,740	15
121,993,977	31.3	22,699,646	34,306,906	31,695,000	29,059,854	4,232,601	16
122,549,392	32.1	25,306,854	34,074,142	31,380,000	27,464,439	4,328,807	17
124,982,261	32.3	29,921,614	38,162,935	27,880,000	23,727,624	4,290,088	18
111,075,311	30.3	29,275,864	35,373,905	20,990,000	21,105,059	4,330,483	19
130,843,837	31.6	30,197,723	40,611,933	24,465,000	31,185,730	4,383,451	20
136,610,443	31.1	30,698,771	39,557,866	26,035,000	35,720,660	4,502,146	21
138,638,047	30.2	65,527,137	25,362,067	16,180,000	32,725,183	4,843,660	22
149,451,113	30.6	73,215,503	26,749,506	10,090,000	34,759,986	4,738,976	23
140,898,106	29.2	67,110,642	30,889,350	7,225,000	30,667,994	4,705,120	24
169,206,207	32.8	80,023,104	35,821,472	11,895,000	36,808,905	4,657,726	25
175,852,592	31.5	87,035,651	29,023,558	7,015,000	48,191,549	4,586,834	26
157,724,336	29.0	80,609,813	30,150,982	5,520,000	36,806,084	4,544,457	27
117,304,032	27.5	77,490,354	25,371,178	5,525,000	34,759,986	4,161,544	28
180,221,803	30.6	93,525,721	33,842,177	7,460,000	40,862,229	4,531,676	29
197,889,047	30.2	100,058,123	31,308,173	8,965,000	52,961,453	4,596,298	30
163,348,053	27.0	85,162,735	26,677,602	6,120,000	40,633,147	4,754,569	31

110   REPORT OF THE COMPTROLLER OF THE CURRENCY.

Table of the liabilities of the national banks, and of the reserve required and held at three dates in each year from 1878 to 1881.

STATES AND TERRITORIES, EXCLUSIVE OF RESERVE CITIES.

Dates.	Number of banks.	Net deposits.	Res've req'red.	Reserve held. Amo'nt	Ratio to dep'sits	Classification of reserve. Specie.	Other lawful money.	Due from agents.	Redemption fund.
		Mill'ns.	*Mill'ns.*	*Mill'ns.*	*Per cent*	*Mill'ns.*	*Mill'ns.*	*Mill'ns.*	*Millions.*
May 1, 1878	1,827	282.7	42.5	99.3	35.1	7.0	33.1	48.3	10.9
June 29, 1878	1,824	283.1	42.5	102.3	36.1	7.1	30.4	54.0	10.8
October 1, 1878	1,822	289.1	43.4	106.1	36.7	8.0	31.1	56.0	11.0
April 4, 1879	1,819	293.8	44.1	105.7	36.0	11.9	30.0	52.9	10.9
June 14, 1879	1,819	300.1	45.1	112.4	37.5	12.1	27.1	62.3	10.9
October 2, 1879	1,820	329.9	49.5	124.3	37.7	11.5	30.3	71.3	11.2
April 23, 1880	1,844	384.8	57.8	134.0	34.8	18.5	30.8	73.3	11.4
June 11, 1880	1,845	385.2	57.8	138.6	36.0	19.0	29.2	79.1	11.3
October 1, 1880	1,859	410.5	61.6	147.2	35.8	21.2	28.3	86.4	11.3
May 6, 1881	1,868	460.5	69.1	155.3	33.7	27.8	29.3	87.1	11.0
June 30, 1881	1,880	484.1	72.6	170.1	35.1	27.6	28.0	103.3	11.1
October 1, 1881	1,895	507.2	76.1	158.3	31.2	27.5	27.1	92.4	11.4

NEW YORK CITY.

Dates.	Number of banks.	Net deposits.	Res've req'red.	Reserve held. Amo'nt	Ratio to dep'sits	Classification of reserve. Specie.	Other lawful money.	Due from agents.	Redemption fund.
		Mill'ns.	*Mill'ns.*	*Mill'ns.*	*Per cent*	*Mill'ns.*	*Mill'ns.*	*Mill ns.*	*Millions.*
May 1, 1878	47	182.0	45.5	56.9	31.3	28.1	27.7	....	1.1
June 29, 1878	47	196.6	49.1	60.1	30.6	13.9	45.1	....	1.1
October 1, 1878	47	189.8	47.4	50.9	26.8	13.3	36.5	....	1.1
April 4, 1879	47	172.2	43.1	46.6	27.0	17.5	28.0	....	1.1
June 14, 1879	47	203.5	50.9	56.6	27.8	18.3	37.2	....	1.1
October 2, 1879	47	210.2	52.6	53.1	25.3	19.4	32.6	....	1.1
April 23, 1880	47	224.1	56.0	58.4	26.0	44.6	12.8	....	1.0
June 11, 1880	47	247.7	61.9	76.4	30.8	57.4	18.0	....	1.0
October 1, 1880	47	268.1	67.0	70.6	26.4	58.7	11.0	....	0.9
May 1, 1881	48	277.3	69.3	79.9	28.8	64.1	14.9	....	1.0
June 30, 1881	48	312.1	78.0	81.9	26.2	66.5	14.4	....	1.0
October 1, 1881	48	268.8	67.2	62.5	23.3	50.6	10.9	....	1.0

OTHER RESERVE CITIES.

Dates.	Number of banks.	Net deposits.	Res've req'red.	Reserve held. Amo'nt	Ratio to dep'sits	Classification of reserve. Specie.	Other lawful money.	Due from agents.	Redemption fund.
		Mill'ns.	*Mill'ns.*	*Mill'ns.*	*Per cent*	*Mill'ns.*	*Mill'ns.*	*Mill'ns.*	*Millions.*
May 1, 1878	185	191.9	48.0	64.4	33.6	10.9	27.4	23.0	3.1
June 29, 1878	185	198.9	49.7	69.2	34.8	8.3	32.9	24.8	3.2
October 1, 1878	184	199.9	50.0	71.1	35.6	9.4	29.4	29.1	3.2
April 4, 1879	182	194.6	48.6	64.5	33.1	11.7	28.4	21.1	3.3
June 14, 1879	182	211.0	52.7	74.3	35.2	11.9	27.9	31.2	3.3
October 2, 1879	181	228.8	57.2	83.5	36.5	11.3	33.0	35.7	3.5
April 23, 1880	184	258.1	64.5	82.5	32.0	22.8	25.3	30.7	3.7
June 11, 1880	184	268.8	67.2	92.8	34.5	22.6	29.8	36.8	3.6
October 1, 1880	184	289.4	72.4	100.5	36.3	28.3	25.0	48.2	3.7
May 1, 1881	186	311.4	77.9	100.3	32.2	29.5	26.4	40.9	3.6
June 30, 1881	187	343.7	86.0	116.0	33.7	33.6	25.9	53.0	3.6
October 1, 1881	189	335.6	83.9	109.8	30.0	34.6	21.9	40.6	3.7

SUMMARY.

Dates.	Number of banks.	Net deposits.	Res've req'red.	Reserve held. Amo'nt	Ratio to dep'sits	Classification of reserve. Specie.	Other lawful money.	Due from agents.	Redemption fund.
		Mill'ns.	*Mill'ns.*	*Mill'ns.*	*Per cent*	*Mill'ns.*	*Mill'ns.*	*Mill'ns.*	*Millions.*
May 1, 1878	2,059	656.6	136.0	220.6	33.6	46.0	88.2	71.3	15.1
June 29, 1878	2,056	678.6	141.3	231.6	34.1	29.3	108.4	78.8	15.1
October 1, 1878	2,053	678.8	140.8	228.1	33.6	30.7	97.0	85.1	15.3
April 4, 1879	2,048	660.6	135.8	216.8	32.8	41.1	86.4	74.0	15.3
June 14, 1879	2,048	714.6	148.7	243.3	34.0	42.3	92.2	93.5	15.3
October 2, 1879	2,048	768.9	159.3	260.9	33.9	42.2	95.9	107.6	15.8
April 23, 1880	2,075	867.0	178.3	274.9	31.7	85.9	68.9	104.0	16.1
June 11, 1880	2,076	901.7	186.9	307.8	34.1	99.0	77.0	115.9	15.9
October 1, 1880	2,090	968.0	201.0	323.0	33.4	108.2	64.3	134.6	15.9
May 1, 1881	2,102	1,019.2	216.3	335.5	32.0	121.4	70.6	128.0	15.6
June 30, 1881	2,115	1,139.9	246.6	368.0	32.3	127.7	68.3	156.3	15.7
October 1, 1881	2,132	1,111.6	227.2	321.6	28.9	112.7	59.9	133.0	16.1

Average weekly deposits, circulation, and reserve of the national banks in New York City, as reported to the New York Clearing House, for the months of September and October in each year from 1874 to 1881.

Week ending—	Liabilities.			Reserve.			
	Circulation.	Net deposits.	Total.	Specie.	Legal tenders.	Total.	Ratio to liabilities.
	Dollars.	Dollars.	Dollars.	Dollars.	Dollars.	Dollars.	Per ct.
Sept. 5, 1874..	25,630,500	202,018,100	228,548,600	16,807,500	54,878,100	71,785,600	31.41
Sept. 12, 1874..	27,701,700	205,166,500	232,808,200	17,589,200	54,715,700	72,304,900	31.05
Sept. 19, 1874..	25,595,700	204,285,600	229,881,300	17,453,200	55,017,300	72,470,500	31.52
Sept. 26, 1874..	25,593,900	187,139,700	212,733,600	16,799,500	53,977,900	70,777,400	33.27
Oct. 3, 1874..	25,387,700	202,605,300	227,993,000	15,373,400	53,297,600	68,671,000	30.01
Oct. 10, 1874..	25,083,900	200,054,500	225,138,400	11,517,700	52,152,000	66,669,700	29.61
Oct. 17, 1874..	25,028,600	197,261,900	222,290,500	12,691,400	51,855,100	64,546,500	29.04
Oct. 24, 1874..	24,981,600	193,514,600	218,496,200	11,457,900	49,893,900	61,351,800	28.82
Oct. 31, 1874..	25,025,100	193,611,700	218,636,800	10,324,900	50,773,000	61,097,900	27.94
Sept. 4, 1875..	18,093,700	210,397,200	228,490,900	9,155,700	58,810,600	67,966,300	29.75
Sept. 11, 1875..	17,725,000	209,802,100	227,527,100	8,494,500	57,828,300	66,322,800	29.15
Sept. 18, 1875..	17,223,200	206,916,800	224,640,000	6,538,200	57,856,600	64,394,800	28.67
Sept. 25, 1875..	17,902,600	205,483,200	223,385,800	6,432,400	56,348,400	62,780,800	28.10
Oct. 2, 1875..	17,894,100	201,409,700	219,303,800	5,438,900	56,181,500	61,620,400	28.10
Oct. 9, 1875..	17,820,700	197,555,800	215,376,500	5,716,200	51,342,300	57,058,500	26.49
Oct. 16, 1875..	17,781,200	195,192,400	212,973,600	5,528,500	48,582,700	54,111,200	25.41
Oct. 23, 1875..	17,844,600	191,468,500	209,313,100	5,735,000	47,300,900	53,035,900	25.34
Oct. 30, 1875..	17,900,100	189,068,800	206,968,900	8,975,600	45,762,800	54,738,400	26.45
Sept. 2, 1876..	14,577,300	197,992,400	212,569,700	19,617,600	48,238,000	67,855,600	31.92
Sept. 9, 1876..	14,339,700	200,754,700	215,094,400	20,202,700	48,699,700	68,902,400	32.03
Sept. 16, 1876..	14,403,500	202,734,500	217,138,000	20,068,900	49,338,200	69,407,100	31.96
Sept. 23, 1876..	14,400,800	200,794,800	215,195,600	16,907,800	48,625,500	65,533,300	30.45
Sept. 30, 1876..	14,615,700	196,590,400	211,206,100	14,751,200	47,538,900	62,290,100	29.40
Oct. 7, 1876..	11,897,000	195,145,700	207,042,700	17,682,600	45,535,600	63,218,200	30.53
Oct. 14, 1876..	14,693,300	190,699,600	205,392,900	16,233,600	43,004,600	59,238,200	28.84
Oct. 21, 1876..	14,809,200	190,019,900	204,829,100	15,577,500	41,421,700	56,999,200	27.83
Oct. 28, 1876..	15,059,600	183,810,200	198,869,800	14,011,600	41,645,600	55,657,200	27.99
Sept. 1, 1877..	15,357,900	181,741,500	197,099,400	13,993,800	41,460,400	55,454,200	28.14
Sept. 8, 1877..	15,543,000	182,949,400	198,492,400	17,811,000	39,019,800	56,830,800	28.63
Sept. 15, 1877..	15,551,700	181,584,100	197,135,800	17,451,000	38,429,900	55,880,900	28.35
Sept. 22, 1877..	15,570,700	180,633,700	196,204,400	16,945,100	37,113,200	54,058,300	27.55
Sept. 29, 1877..	15,699,000	175,036,800	190,735,800	14,682,100	36,978,900	51,661,000	27.09
Oct. 6, 1877..	15,964,900	172,106,000	188,070,900	14,665,600	36,168,300	50,833,900	27.03
Oct. 13, 1877..	16,055,600	171,058,500	187,114,100	14,726,500	35,178,900	49,905,400	26.67
Oct. 20, 1877..	16,205,000	169,670,500	185,875,500	14,087,400	35,101,700	49,189,100	26.46
Oct. 27, 1877..	16,600,700	168,373,800	184,974,500	15,209,000	34,367,800	49,576,800	26.80
Sept. 7, 1878..	19,037,000	191,650,200	210,687,200	14,583,200	43,260,300	57,843,500	27.45
Sept. 14, 1878..	19,453,000	191,090,500	210,543,500	15,929,300	41,673,400	57,602,700	27.36
Sept. 21, 1878..	19,591,000	190,268,100	209,859,100	15,590,400	41,894,700	57,485,100	27.40
Sept. 28, 1878..	19,592,500	189,832,700	209,425,200	15,373,300	39,762,000	55,135,300	26.33
Oct. 5, 1878..	19,552,200	187,568,400	207,120,600	14,995,800	38,304,100	53,300,700	25.73
Oct. 12, 1878..	19,567,800	184,825,400	204,393,200	12,181,600	37,685,100	49,869,700	24.40
Oct. 19, 1878..	19,575,900	183,627,600	203,203,500	13,531,400	36,576,000	50,107,400	24.66
Oct. 26, 1878..	19,864,400	186,082,100	205,946,500	17,384,200	35,690,500	53,074,700	25.77
Sept. 6, 1879..	21,354,100	201,608,400	222,962,500	18,502,900	36,275,800	54,778,700	24.57
Sept. 13, 1879..	21,585,300	201,071,200	222,656,500	18,538,000	36,181,600	54,719,600	24.58
Sept. 20, 1879..	21,366,700	203,326,900	224,693,600	18,670,400	37,781,100	56,451,500	25.12
Sept. 27, 1879..	21,513,700	204,964,400	226,478,100	18,731,600	35,901,900	54,633,500	24.12
Oct. 4, 1879..	21,914,200	206,866,800	228,781,000	18,979,600	34,368,000	53,347,600	23.32
Oct. 11, 1879..	22,061,900	207,684,500	229,746,400	20,101,800	33,620,900	53,722,100	23.38
Oct. 18, 1879..	22,268,600	207,200,200	229,468,800	24,686,500	29,305,200	53,991,700	23.53
Oct. 25, 1879 .	22,430,500	205,496,800	227,927,300	25,636,000	26,713,900	52,349,900	22.97
Sept. 4, 1880..	19,324,200	267,791,300	287,115,500	61,269,200	12,545,900	73,815,100	25.71
Sept. 11, 1880..	19,335,500	267,792,600	287,128,100	60,716,000	11,952,000	72,668,000	25.31
Sept. 18, 1880..	19,326,400	268,244,300	287,570,700	61,522,200	11,407,100	72,929,300	25.36
Sept. 25, 1880..	18,864,400	264,358,200	283,222,600	60,026,600	11,090,500	71,116,100	25.11
Oct. 2, 1880..	18,618,600	263,755,000	282,373,600	50,823,700	11,129,100	70,952,800	25.37
Oct. 9, 1880..	18,555,600	269,993,400	288,549,000	62,521,300	10,785,000	73,306,300	25.42
Oct. 16, 1880..	17,611,000	271,907,700	289,518,700	62,760,600	10,939,200	73,699,800	25.46
Oct. 23, 1880..	18,082,500	270,708,600	288,391,100	60,888,200	10,988,200	71,876,400	24.92
Oct. 30, 1880..	18,628,400	271,230,700	289,859,100	61,471,600	10,925,000	72,396,600	24.98
Sept. 3, 1881..	19,669,400	278,211,700	297,911,100	57,816,100	13,226,600	71,042,700	23.85
Sept. 10, 1881..	19,764,500	277,011,700	296,776,200	59,991,600	12,591,300	72,582,900	24.46
Sept. 17, 1881..	19,768,100	279,404,900	299,173,000	61,224,100	11,979,000	73,203,100	24.47
Sept. 24, 1881..	19,747,500	277,258,600	297,016,100	60,476,000	12,451,300	72,927,300	24.55
Oct. 1, 1881..	19,841,400	270,727,400	290,568,800	54,954,600	12,150,400	67,105,000	23.09
Oct. 8, 1881..	19,849,400	263,081,600	282,931,000	53,287,900	12,153,800	65,441,700	23.13
Oct. 15, 1881..	19,878,400	254,224,700	274,103,100	51,008,300	12,452,700	63,461,000	23.15
Oct. 22, 1881..	19,901,400	250,299,000	270,200,400	54,016,200	12,496,500	66,512,700	24.61
Oct. 29, 1881..	19,930,400	251,480,300	271,410,700	55,961,200	12,947,900	68,909,100	25.61

Amount and rate of taxation (United States and State) of the national banks for the year 1867.

States and Territories.	Capital stock.	Amount of taxes.			Ratio of taxation to capital.		
		United States.	State.	Total.	United States.	State.	Total.
					Per ct.	*Pr. ct.*	*Pr. ct.*
Maine	$9,085,000	$180,119	$141,226	$321,345	2.0	1.5	3.5
New Hampshire	4,735,000	88,773	93,179	181,952	1.9	1.9	3.8
Vermont	6,510,912	122,214	144,164	266,377	1.9	2.2	4.1
Massachusetts	79,932,000	1,616,825	1,562,128	3,178,953	2.0	2.0	4.0
Rhode Island	20,364,800	324,844	195,355	520,200	1.5	1.0	2.5
Connecticut	24,584,220	434,440	387,146	821,587	1.7	1.6	3.3
New York	116,494,941	3,022,662	4,058,706	7,081,368	2.6	3.5	6.1
New Jersey	11,333,350	253,359	223,106	476,465	2.2	2.0	4.2
Pennsylvania	50,277,795	1,242,037	278,268	1,520,305	2.5	0.5	3.0
Delaware	1,428,185	32,621	1,261	33,881	2.3	0.1	2.4
Maryland	12,590,203	260,261	166,054	426,315	2.1	1.3	3.4
District of Columbia	1,350,000	15,330	3,286	18,615	1.3	0.3	1.6
Virginia	2,500,000	48,345	13,926	62,270	1.9	0.6	2.5
West Virginia	2,216,400	46,966	51,457	98,424	2.1	2.3	4.4
North Carolina	583,300	9,049	5,144	14,193	1.5	0.9	2.4
Georgia	1,700,000	40,845	6,050	46,895	2.5	0.4	2.9
Alabama	500,000	8,763	3,830	12,592	1.7	1.0	2.7
Louisiana	1,300,000	35,894	20,042	55,936	2.8	1.5	4.3
Texas	576,450	6,865	2,149	9,015	1.2	0.4	1.6
Arkansas	200,000	5,745	1,351	7,096	2.9	0.7	3.6
Kentucky	2,885,000	59,816	17,467	77,283	2.1	0.6	2.7
Tennessee	2,100,000	52,460	27,975	80,435	2.7	1.4	4.1
Ohio	22,404,700	514,681	520,951	1,035,633	2.3	2.3	4.6
Indiana	12,867,000	278,798	200,372	479,170	2.2	1.5	3.7
Illinois	11,620,000	321,406	231,917	553,323	2.8	2.0	4.8
Michigan	5,070,010	111,790	68,061	179,851	2.2	1.3	3.5
Wisconsin	2,935,000	76,583	62,012	138,595	2.6	2.1	4.7
Iowa	3,992,000	106,349	88,281	194,631	2.7	2.2	4.9
Minnesota	1,660,000	39,132	29,522	68,655	2.0	1.3	3.3
Missouri	7,559,300	133,142	189,248	322,389	1.4	2.0	3.4
Kansas	400,000	10,229	7,801	18,030	2.5	2.0	4.5
Nebraska	250,000	10,735	7,014	17,749	4.3	2.8	7.1
Oregon	100,000	1,624	....	1,624	2.4	.....	2.4
Colorado	350,000	9,702	1,615	11,317	2.8	0.4	3.2
Utah	150,000	1,887	1,097	2,984	1.3	0.7	2.0
Idaho	100,000	479	1,405	1,884	0.5	1.4	1.9
Montana	100,000	837	560	1,397	0.8	0.6	1.4
Totals	422,804,666	9,525,607	8,813,126	18,338,734	2.2	2.1	4.3

Amount and rate of taxation (United States and State) of the national banks for the year 1869.

States and Territories.	Capital stock.	Amount of taxes.			Ratio of tax to capital.		
		United States.	State.	Total.	United States.	State.	Total.
					Per. ct.	*Pr.ct.*	*Pr. ct.*
Maine	$9,185,000	$191,779	$164,150	$355,929	2.1	1.8	3.9
New Hampshire	4,835,000	97,245	102,812	200,057	2.0	2.1	4.1
Vermont	6,385,012	129,059	117,107	246,166	2.0	1.8	3.8
Massachusetts	81,282,000	1,691.620	1,329,018	3,020,638	2.1	1.6	3.7
Rhode Island	20,164,800	344,687	175,466	520,153	1.7	0.9	2.6
Connecticut	24,606,820	476,244	366,457	842,701	1.9	1.5	3.4
New York	112,267,841	2,958,089	2,980,104	5,938,193	2.6	2.7	5.3
New Jersey	11,465,350	279,410	200,121	479,531	2.4	1.8	4.2
Pennsylvania	49,560,390	1,312,419	266,186	1,578,605	2.7	0.5	3.2
Delaware	1,428,185	30,907	3,265	34,172	2.2	0.2	2.4
Maryland	12,790,203	277,590	147,854	425,444	2.2	1.1	3.3
District of Columbia	1,050,000	23,814	1,850	25,664	2.2	0.2	2.4
Virginia	2,221,860	59,281	8,882	68,163	2.7	0.4	3.1
West Virginia	2,116,400	51,979	37,053	89,032	2.3	1.7	4.0
North Carolina	683,400	15,712	2,455	18,167	2.3	0.4	2.7
South Carolina	823,500	19,763	7,952	27,715	2.4	1.0	3.4
Georgia	1,500,000	45,824	8,254	54,078	3.0	0.6	3.6
Alabama	400,000	5,926	490	6,416	1.5	0.1	1.6
Louisiana	1,300,000	27,455	7,107	34,562	2.1	0.6	2.7
Texas	525,000	11,184	4,375	15,559	2.2	0.8	3.0
Arkansas	200,000	4,284	6,998	11,282	2.1	3.5	5.6
Kentucky	2,835,000	62,836	10,236	73,072	2.2	0.4	2.6
Tennessee	1,987,400	47,164	6,570	53,734	2.4	0.3	2.7
Ohio	21,917,399	635,935	573,576	1,209,511	2.9	2.6	5.5
Indiana	12,752,000	298,336	218,888	517,224	2.4	1.7	4.1
Illinois	12,370,000	369,742	217,652	587,304	3.0	1.8	4.8
Michigan	5,510,000	143,649	34,384	178,033	2.6	0.6	3.2
Wisconsin	2,710,000	80,963	50,663	131,626	3.0	1.9	4.9
Iowa	3,717,000	122,162	53,621	175,783	3.3	1.4	4.7
Minnesota	1,770,000	45,223	29,873	75,096	2.5	1.7	4.2
Missouri	7,810,300	171,198	120,720	291,918	2.2	1.5	3.7
Kansas	400,000	17,443	16,009	33,452	4.4	4.0	8.4
Nebraska	400,000	14,593	10,838	25,431	3.7	2.7	6.4
Oregon	100,000	2,917		2,917	2.9		2.9
Colorado	350,000	11,902	11,286	23,188	3.4	3.2	6.6
Idaho	100,000	1,179	2,541	3,720	1.2	2.5	3.7
Montana	100,000	1,731	2,283	4,014	1.7	2.3	4.0
Totals	419,619,860	10,081,244	7,297,096	17,378,340	2.4	1.7	4.1

S C C

Amount and rate of taxation (United States and State) of the national banks for the year 1874.

States and Territories.	Capital stock.	Amount of taxes.			Ratio of tax to capital.		
		United States.	State.	Total.	United States.	State.	Total.
					Per. ct.	Pr. ct.	Pr. ct.
Maine	$9, 654, 019	$111, 403	$192, 290	$303, 693	1.2	2.0	3.2
New Hampshire	5, 317, 637	60, 002	106, 587	166, 589	1.1	2.1	3.2
Vermont	7, 862, 712	88, 152	139, 297	227, 449	1.1	1.8	2.9
Massachusetts	91, 754, 078	1, 163, 858	1, 878, 368	3, 042, 226	1.3	2.1	3.4
Rhode Island	20, 504, 800	201, 317	224, 540	425, 857	1.0	1.1	2.1
Connecticut	25, 424, 620	271, 801	439, 402	711, 203	1.1	1.8	2.9
New York	106, 599, 708	2, 026, 960	3, 044, 565	5, 071, 525	1.9	2.9	4.8
New Jersey	13, 830, 466	205, 451	282, 645	488, 096	1.5	2.1	3.6
Pennsylvania	53, 178, 261	871, 220	377, 546	1, 248, 766	1.6	0.7	2.3
Delaware	1, 523, 185	20, 798	6, 630	27, 428	1.4	0.4	1.8
Maryland	13, 720, 997	181, 249	194, 697	375, 946	1.3	1.5	2.8
District of Columbia	1, 309, 512	19, 747	5, 288	25, 035	1.5	0.4	1.9
Virginia	3, 580, 913	54, 957	52, 207	107, 164	1.5	1.6	3.1
West Virginia	2, 375, 216	33, 484	34, 507	67, 991	1.4	1.8	3.2
North Carolina	2, 173, 338	30, 837	38, 601	69, 438	1.4	1.9	3.3
South Carolina	3, 156, 250	34, 421	111, 654	146, 075	1.1	3.6	4.7
Georgia	2, 843, 962	31, 656	53, 872	85, 528	1.1	1.9	3.0
Alabama	1, 634, 883	18, 746	25, 289	44, 035	1.2	1.7	2.9
Louisiana	4, 000, 000	61, 642	52, 270	113, 912	1.5	1.4	2.9
Texas	1, 054, 897	14, 384	22, 863	37, 247	1.4	2.3	3.7
Arkansas	205, 000	2, 488	8, 030	10, 518	1.2	3.9	5.1
Kentucky	9, 076, 127	103, 635	47, 655	151, 290	1.1	0.5	1.6
Tennessee	3, 457, 897	50, 290	70, 844	121, 134	1.5	2.2	3.7
Ohio	29, 112, 642	403, 697	642, 054	1, 045, 751	1.4	2.2	3.6
Indiana	17, 936, 404	214, 977	429, 585	644, 562	1.2	2.6	3.8
Illinois	20, 507, 963	367, 718	420, 461	788, 179	1.8	2.2	4.0
Michigan	10, 098, 162	134, 052	149, 720	283, 772	1.3	1.5	2.8
Wisconsin	3, 704, 032	67, 485	76, 330	143, 815	1 8	2.3	4.1
Iowa	6, 048, 562	98, 421	117, 115	215, 536	1.6	2.1	3.7
Minnesota	4, 268, 026	63, 224	76, 876	140, 100	1.5	2.0	3.5
Missouri	9, 308, 198	112, 525	190, 140	302, 665	1.2	2.1	3.3
Kansas	1, 783, 235	26, 182	41, 867	68, 049	1.5	3.3	4.8
Nebraska	1, 025, 000	20, 883	34, 282	55, 165	2.0	3.3	5.3
Oregon	250, 000	5, 808	3, 488	9, 296	2.3	1.4	3.7
California	3, 358, 594	46, 044		46, 044	1.4		1.4
Colorado	748, 581	16, 983	10, 750	27, 733	2.3	2.1	4.4
Utah	439, 402	5, 387	4, 137	9, 524	1.2	1.4	2.6
New Mexico	300, 000	3, 718	3, 150	6, 868	1.2	1.1	2.3
Wyoming	125, 000	1, 697	1, 180	2, 877	1.4	2.5	3.9
Idaho	100, 000	1, 393	129	1, 522	1.4	0.1	1.5
Dakota	50, 000	614	1, 225	1, 839	1.2	2.5	3.7
Montana	350, 000	6, 777	8, 190	14, 967	1.9	2.3	4.2
Totals	*493, 751, 679	7, 256, 083	9, 620, 326	16, 876, 409	1.5	2.0	3.5

* Including capital of banks from which returns of the amount of State taxation were not received.

Amount and rate of taxation (United States and State) of the national banks for the year 1875

States and Territories.	Capital stock	Amount of taxes. United States.	State.	Total.	Ratio of tax to capital. United States.	State.	Total.
					Per ct.	Per ct.	Per ct.
Maine	$9,790,104	$112,652	$215,981	$328,633	1.2	2.2	3.4
New Hampshire	5,482,514	61,006	103,949	164,955	1.1	1.9	3.0
Vermont	8,216,467	89,360	169,044	258,404	1.1	2.2	3.3
Massachusetts	43,063,374	491,157	865,198	1,356,355	1.1	2.0	3.1
Boston	51,362,454	703,218	957,283	1,660,501	1.4	1.9	3.3
Rhode Island	20,548,433	201,639	269,402	471,041	1.0	1.3	2.3
Connecticut	25,852,987	277,984	435,680	713,664	1.1	1.7	2.8
New York	35,471,333	529,804	962,982	1,492,786	1.5	2.7	4.2
New York City	68,466,576	1,376,541	2,093,143	3,469,684	2.0	3.1	5.1
Albany	2,088,462	62,215	71,740	133,955	3.0	3.6	6.6
New Jersey	14,072,520	208,559	300,894	509,453	1.5	2.1	3.6
Pennsylvania	29,655,994	410,928	175,059	585,987	1.4	0.6	2.0
Philadelphia	17,019,239	346,950	128,996	475,946	2.0	0.8	2.8
Pittsburgh	10,059,041	141,545	56,246	197,791	1.4	0.5	1.9
Delaware	1,523,185	22,025	7,952	29,977	1.5	0.5	2.0
Maryland	2,268,238	30,468	31,355	61,823	1.3	1.4	2.7
Baltimore	11,469,355	150,003	230,368	380,371	1.3	2.0	3.3
District of Columbia	252,000	4,555	262	4,817	1.8	0.1	1.9
Washington	1,239,564	16,905	3,462	20,367	1.4	0.3	1.7
Virginia	3,535,719	54,132	70,710	124,842	1.5	2.0	3.5
West Virginia	1,971,000	25,775	30,102	55,877	1.3	1.7	3.0
North Carolina	2,232,150	31,406	34,584	65,990	1.4	1.6	3.0
South Carolina	3,135,000	34,747	106,760	141,507	1.1	3.4	4.5
Georgia	2,716,974	29,023	45,790	74,813	1.1	1.6	2.7
Florida	50,000	854	1,056	1,910	1.7	2.1	3.8
Alabama	1,638,866	18,865	22,204	41,069	1.2	1.4	2.6
New Orleans	3,766,667	59,314	9,870	69,184	1.6	0.3	1.9
Texas	1,205,350	15,819	20,844	36,663	1.3	1.7	3.0
Arkansas	205,000	1,983	3,288	5,271	1.0	1.6	2.6
Tennessee	3,468,992	47,341	78,427	125,768	1.4	2.3	3.7
Kentucky	7,201,765	80,777	36,311	117,088	1.1	0.5	1.6
Louisville	3,358,000	45,012	16,290	61,302	1.3	0.5	1.8
Ohio	21,110,393	292,900	507,231	800,131	1.4	2.4	3.8
Cincinnati	4,000,000	80,198	105,199	185,397	2.0	2.6	4.6
Cleveland	4,550,000	51,011	104,872	155,883	1.1	2.3	3.4
Indiana	18,588,189	229,606	470,836	700,442	1.2	2.6	3.8
Illinois	11,873,363	186,188	271,636	457,824	1.6	2.3	3.9
Chicago	7,673,757	173,506	188,524	362,030	2.3	2.5	4.8
Michigan	8,568,270	105,676	146,993	252,669	1.2	1.7	2.9
Detroit	1,900,000	33,331	24,744	58,075	1.8	1.3	3.1
Wisconsin	2,974,651	47,584	55,156	102,740	1.6	1.9	3.5
Milwaukee	700,000	16,263	19,229	35,492	2.3	3.0	5.3
Minnesota	4,391,068	60,781	93,736	154,517	1.4	2.3	3.7
Iowa	6,416,607	104,667	126,088	230,755	1.6	2.0	3.6
Missouri	2,742,199	36,361	93,467	129,828	1.3	3.5	4.8
Saint Louis	6,360,300	75,135	177,464	252,599	1.2	2.8	4.0
Kansas	1,588,821	22,901	45,548	68,449	1.4	3.2	4.6
Nebraska	994,758	22,277	21,689	43,966	2.2	2.3	4.5
Oregon	250,000	5,654	3,037	8,691	2.3	1.2	3.5
California	1,552,622	17,180		17,186	1.1	0.0	1.1
San Francisco	2,917,112	35,780		35,780	1.2	0.0	1.2
New Mexico	300,000	4,228	3,250	7,478	1.4	1.1	2.5
Colorado	923,478	18,997	25,714	44,711	2.1	3.3	5.4
Utah	300,000	3,472	2,550	6,022	1.2	1.3	2.5
Idaho	100,000	1,429	2,367	3,796	1.4	2.4	3.6
Montana	350,000	7,047	9,137	16,184	2.0	2.6	4.8
Wyoming	125,000	2,049	3,523	5,572	1.6	2.8	4.4
Dakota	50,000	742	900	1,642	1.5	1.8	3.3
Totals	503,687,911	7,317,531	10,058,122	17,375,653	1.5	2.0	3.5

Amount and rate of taxation (United States and State) of the national banks for the year 1876.

States and Territories.	Capital stock.	Amount of taxes.			Ratio of tax to capital.		
		United States.	State.	Total.	United States.	State.	Total.
					Per ct.	*Per ct.*	*Per ct.*
Maine	$10,635,819	$115,272	$237,792	$353,064	1.1	2.2	3.3
New Hampshire	5,615,000	62,627	97,255	159,882	1.1	1.7	2.8
Vermont	8,722,369	91,777	179,876	271,653	1.1	2.1	3.2
Massachusetts	44,299,557	497,228	825,685	1,322,913	1.1	1.9	3.0
Boston	52,200,000	704,655	855,446	1,560,101	1.4	1.6	3.0
Rhode Island	20,579,800	200,420	279,765	480,185	1.0	1.3	2.3
Connecticut	26,015,834	275,991	438,989	714,980	1.0	1.7	2.7
New York	35,326,077	512,233	826,929	1,339,162	1.5	2.4	3.9
New York City	66,607,325	1,278,956	2,197,681	3,476,637	1.9	3.5	5.4
Albany	2,000,000	63,650	67,972	131,622	3.2	3.4	6.6
New Jersey	14,238,634	204,512	292,024	496,536	1.4	2.1	3.5
Pennsylvania	29,354,981	417,324	182,003	599,327	1.4	0.6	2.0
Philadelphia	17,189,489	356,204	119,655	475,859	2.1	0.7	2.8
Pittsburgh	10,531,592	142,232	56,620	198,852	1.4	0.5	1.9
Delaware	1,571,730	22,030	6,900	28,930	1.4	0.4	1.8
Maryland	2,299,960	31,280	28,046	59,326	1.4	1.3	2.7
Baltimore	11,491,985	142,102	229,484	371,586	1.2	2.0	3.2
District of Columbia	252,000	4,478	3,906	8,384	1.8	1.2	3.0
Washington	1,300,000	15,246	14,096	29,342	1.2	1.1	2.3
Virginia	3,339,307	51,297	71,827	123,124	1.5	2.1	3.6
West Virginia	1,746,000	21,783	28,878	50,661	1.2	1.7	2.9
North Carolina	2,499,499	31,021	39,933	70,954	1.2	1.6	2.8
South Carolina	3,172,500	31,793	84,863	116,656	1.0	2.7	3.7
Georgia	2,504,317	26,265	41,764	68,029	1.0	2.0	3.0
Florida	50,000	941	948	1,889	1.9	1.9	3.8
Alabama	1,690,412	19,184	16,888	36,072	1.1	1.0	2.1
New Orleans	3,436,786	53,388	6,534	59,922	1.6	0.2	1.8
Texas	1,038,782	14,518	19,057	33,575	1.4	1.9	3.3
Arkansas	205,000	2,055	2,830	4,885*	1.0	1.4	2.4
Kentucky	7,259,641	79,609	32,587	112,196	1.1	0.5	1.6
Louisville	3,095,500	42,676	14,576	57,252	1.4	0.5	1.9
Tennessee	3,401,449	49,251	70,479	119,730	1.4	2.1	3.5
Ohio	20,757,903	274,814	560,408	834,312	1.3	2.8	4.1
Cincinnati	4,373,680	74,720	128,087	202,807	1.7	2.9	4.6
Cleveland	4,550,000	49,454	114,072	163,526	1.1	2.5	3.6
Indiana	17,781,910	210,769	424,904	635,673	1.2	2.5	3.7
Illinois	11,728,823	173,495	231,693	405,188	1.5	2.0	3.5
Chicago	6,950,123	154,246	200,866	355,112	2.2	3.0	5.2
Michigan	8,238,899	100,414	128,446	228,860	1.2	1.6	2.8
Detroit	1,900,000	31,078	28,633	59,711	1.6	1.5	3.1
Wisconsin	2,827,322	43,783	53,499	97,282	1.5	1.9	3.4
Milwaukee	650,000	14,207	18,606	32,813	2.2	2.9	5.1
Iowa	6,430,308	91,667	122,519	214,186	1.4	2.0	3.4
Minnesota	4,455,478	60,336	86,923	147,259	1.4	2.0	3.4
Missouri	2,574,000	35,824	53,580	89,404	1.4	2.2	3.6
Saint Louis	5,742,596	73,344	76,071	149,415	1.3	2.6	3.9
Kansas	1,369,167	20,722	34,518	55,240	1.5	3.0	4.5
Nebraska	975,000	21,839	23,274	45,113	2.2	2.5	4.7
Oregon	237,500	6,319	2,550	8,869	2.7	1.0	3.7
California*	1,700,000	17,484	3,463	20,947	1.0	0.2	1.2
San Francisco*	2,875,000	23,526	705	24,231	0.8	0.0	0.8
New Mexico	300,000	3,976	3,513	7,489	1.3	1.2	2.5
Colorado	824,025	18,276	16,465	34,741	2.2	2.2	4.4
Utah	250,000	2,840	2,625	5,465	1.1	1.3	2.4
Idaho	100,000	1,278	2,370	3,648	1.3	2.4	3.7
Montana	350,000	6,811	9,561	16,372	1.9	2.7	4.6
Wyoming	125,000	1,976	3,367	5,343	1.6	2.7	4.3
Dakota	50,000	891	636	1,527	1.8	1.3	3.1
Totals	†501,788,079	7,076,087	9,701,732	16,777,819	1.4	2.0	3.4

*California banks pay no State taxes on capital, except on such as is invested in real estate.
†The capital of the banks that paid State, county, and municipal taxes on stock and real estate is $488,272,782.

Amount and rate of taxation (United States and State) of the national banks for the year 1877.

States and Territories.	Capital stock.	Amount of taxes. United States.	State.	Total.	Ratio of tax to capital. United States.	State.	Total.
					Per ct.	*Per ct.*	*Per ct.*
Maine	$10,689,837	$113,855	$240,442	$354,297	1.1	2.2	3.3
New Hampshire	5,683,750	63,252	100,700	163,952	1.1	1.8	2.9
Vermont	8,568,700	88,659	168,551	257,210	1.0	2.0	3.0
Massachusetts	44,413,464	493,489	828,064	1,321,553	1.1	1.9	3.0
Boston	52,329,080	684,562	830,847	1,515,409	1.3	1.6	2.9
Rhode Island	20,271,650	193,088	273,227	466,315	1.0	1.4	2.4
Connecticut	25,831,994	270,871	422,288	693,159	1.0	1.6	2.6
New England States	167,788,475	1,907,776	2,864,119	4,771,895	1.1	1.7	2.8
New York	34,118,002	498,204	754,951	1,253,155	1.5	2.3	3.8
New York City	60,057,247	1,250,636	1,822,196	3,072,832	2.1	2.9	5.0
Albany	2,000,000	59,870	64,281	124,151	3.0	3.2	6.2
New Jersey	14,278,350	202,678	276,680	479,358	1.4	1.9	3.3
Pennsylvania	28,417,582	409,062	200,841	609,903	1.4	0.7	2.1
Philadelphia	16,985,667	357,311	120,471	477,782	2.1	0.7	2.8
Pittsburgh	10,347,500	139,751	54,335	194,086	1.4	0.5	1.9
Delaware	1,663,985	23,398	6,842	30,240	1.4	0.4	1.8
Maryland	2,302,459	31,818	30,395	62,213	1.4	1.3	2.7
Baltimore	11,233,651	137,075	205,830	342,905	1.2	1.9	3.1
District of Columbia	252,000	4,317	312	4,629	1.8	0.8	2.6
Washington	1,229,119	15,870	7,728	23,598	1.3	0.7	2.0
Middle States	182,885,562	3,129,990	3,544,862	6,674,852	1.7	1.9	3.6
Virginia	3,285,229	49,796	64,684	114,480	1.5	2.0	3.5
West Virginia	1,746,000	21,461	27,737	49,198	1.2	1.6	2.8
North Carolina	2,586,096	30,792	33,945	64,737	1.2	1.4	2.6
South Carolina	2,927,643	28,918	74,027	102,945	1.0	2.6	3.6
Georgia	2,146,305	25,547	42,632	68,179	1.2	2.1	3.3
Florida	50,000	818	1,023	1,841	1.6	2.0	3.6
Alabama	1,668,060	18,653	19,372	38,025	1.1	1.2	2.3
New Orleans	3,300,000	50,099	26,387	76,486	1.5	0.9	2.4
Texas	1,081,782	14,597	20,655	35,252	1.4	2.2	3.6
Arkansas	205,000	2,760	3,601	6,361	1.3	1.8	3.1
Kentucky	7,008,500	77,141	30,636	107,777	1.1	0.4	1.5
Louisville	3,095,500	42,265	15,936	58,201	1.4	0.5	1.9
Tennessee	3,112,233	48,639	68,514	117,153	1.6	2.2	3.8
Southern States	32,212,288	411,486	429,149	840,635	1.3	1.4	2.7
Ohio	19,944,625	269,544	428,902	698,446	1.4	2.3	3.7
Cincinnati	4,400,000	73,817	128,159	201,076	1.7	2.9	4.6
Cleveland	4,416,667	48,139	97,591	145,730	1.1	2.2	3.3
Indiana	16,559,568	202,594	347,744	550,338	1.2	2.3	3.5
Illinois	11,489,927	163,585	223,996	387,581	1.4	2.0	3.4
Chicago	6,472,418	145,367	131,744	277,111	2.2	2.9	5.1
Michigan	7,871,463	94,201	120,716	214,917	1.2	1.7	2.9
Detroit	2,000,000	31,105	34,885	65,990	1.6	1.7	3.3
Wisconsin	2,814,808	43,360	50,969	94,329	1.5	1.9	3.4
Milwaukee	650,000	15,395	16,610	32,005	2.4	2.6	5.0
Iowa	6,090,538	85,085	121,291	206,376	1.4	2.1	3.5
Minnesota	4,519,779	61,429	93,923	155,352	1.4	2.2	3.6
Missouri	2,391,167	34,718	41,243	75,961	1.5	2.6	4.1
Saint Louis	4,015,639	56,812	65,722	122,534	1.4	2.5	3.9
Kansas	1,108,333	18,993	18,855	37,848	1.7	2.6	4.3
Nebraska	938,398	21,485	19,922	41,407	2.3	2.3	4.6
Colorado	976,872	20,544	23,951	44,495	2.1	3.0	5.1
Oregon	250,000	7,224	2,650	9,874	2.9	1.1	4.0
California*	1,579,167	18,416	3,910	22,326	1.2	0.2	1.4
San Francisco*	2,750,000	23,292	535	23,827	0.8	0.0	0.8
New Mexico	500,000	4,192	3,168	7,360	1.4	1.1	2.5
Utah	200,000	2,779	2,750	5,529	1.4	1.4	2.8
Idaho	100,000	1,367	3,184	4,551	1.4	3.2	4.6
Montana	350,000	6,795	6,432	13,227	1.9	3.2	5.1
Wyoming	125,000	1,973	1,599	3,572	1.6	2.1	3.7
Dakota	50,000	1,110	693	1,803	2.2	1.4	3.6
Western States and Territories	102,364,369	1,453,321	1,991,174	3,414,495	1.4	2.1	3.5
Totals	485,250,694	6,962,573	8,829,304	15,731,877	1.4	1.9	3.3

* California banks pay no State taxes on capital, except on such as is invested in real estate.
† The capital of the banks that paid State, county, and municipal taxes on stock and real estate is $471,667,771.

Amount and rate of taxation (United States and State) of the national banks for the year 1878.

States and Territories.	Capital stock.	Amount of taxes.			Ratio of tax to capital.		
		United States.	State.	Total.	United States.	State.	Total.
					Per ct.	Per ct.	Per ct.
Maine	$10,760,000	$114,880	$231,655	$346,535	1.1	2.2	3.3
New Hampshire	5,740,000	64,849	101,484	166,333	1.1	1.8	2.9
Vermont	8,544,285	88,157	158,588	246,745	1.0	1.9	2.9
Massachusetts	44,260,128	499,959	760,115	1,260,074	1.1	1.7	2.9
Boston	51,927,865	672,766	702,834	1,375,600	1.3	1.3	2.6
Rhode Island	20,031,112	191,410	257,654	449,064	0.9	1.3	2.2
Connecticut	25,474,204	268,714	380,713	649,427	1.0	1.5	2.5
New England States	166,737,594	1,900,735	2,593,043	4,493,778	1.1	1.6	2.7
New York	33,541,481	499,197	700,786	1,199,983	1.5	2.1	3.6
New York City	55,150,348	1,226,933	1,606,049	2,832,982	2.2	2.9	5.1
Albany	2,000,000	55,609	56,440	112,049	2.8	2.8	5.6
New Jersey	14,101,926	203,567	257,276	460,843	1.4	1.8	3.2
Pennsylvania	28,549,169	395,089	187,709	582,798	1.4	0.7	2.1
Philadelphia	16,843,000	333,161	114,235	447,396	2.0	0.7	2.7
Pittsburgh	10,350,000	134,072	54,068	188,140	1.3	0.5	1.8
Delaware	1,738,294	24,451	6,980	31,431	1.4	0.4	1.8
Maryland	2,264,510	31,847	29,903	61,750	1.4	1.3	2.7
Baltimore	10,762,648	129,571	197,716	327,287	1.2	1.8	3.0
District of Columbia	252,000	4,392	255	4,647	1.7	0.1	1.8
Washington	1,215,023	16,687	6,068	22,755	1.4	0.6	2.0
Middle States	176,768,399	3,054,576	3,217,485	6,272,061	1.7	1.8	3.5
Virginia	3,221,202	48,789	66,607	115,396	1.5	2.2	3.7
West Virginia	1,714,179	21,411	27,196	48,607	1.2	1.6	2.8
North Carolina	2,553,083	30,495	31,982	62,477	1.2	1.3	2.5
South Carolina	2,853,154	29,515	59,010	88,525	1.0	2.1	3.1
Georgia	2,083,322	25,769	37,667	63,436	1.2	1.8	3.0
Florida	50,000	779	851	1,630	1.6	1.7	3.3
Alabama	1,668,000	19,826	22,404	42,230	1.2	1.3	2.5
New Orleans	3,040,538	46,068	28,332	74,400	1.5	1.0	2.5
Texas	1,072,099	14,803	15,104	29,967	1.4	1.7	3.1
Arkansas	205,000	3,243	2,705	5,948	1.6	1.3	2.9
Kentucky	7,030,396	78,046	39,830	117,876	1.1	0.6	1.7
Louisville	3,012,075	40,741	16,469	57,210	1.4	0.5	1.9
Tennessee	3,080,300	50,204	57,919	108,213	1.6	2.1	3.7
Southern States	31,583,348	409,839	406,076	815,915	1.3	1.3	2.6
Ohio	18,903,630	254,030	390,062	644,092	1.3	2.1	3.4
Cincinnati	4,333,333	65,684	120,832	186,516	1.5	2.7	4.2
Cleveland	4,289,130	46,252	86,779	133,031	1.1	2.0	3.1
Indiana	15,381,544	194,104	316,918	511,022	1.3	2.1	3.4
Illinois	11,319,200	157,543	210,986	368,529	1.4	2.0	3.4
Chicago	4,770,166	118,637	106,157	224,794	2.5	2.6	5.1
Michigan	7,561,740	90,915	113,231	204,146	1.2	1.5	2.7
Detroit	2,100,000	35,165	31,099	66,264	1.7	1.5	3.2
Wisconsin	2,690,000	40,748	49,903	90,651	1.5	2.0	3.5
Milwaukee	650,000	15,556	17,144	32,700	2.4	2.6	5.0
Iowa	6,048,704	81,949	115,594	197,543	1.4	2.1	3.5
Minnesota	4,793,131	62,850	92,720	155,570	1.3	2.0	3.3
Missouri	1,725,817	24,512	31,987	56,499	1.4	2.5	3.9
Saint Louis	2,653,750	44,014	62,748	106,762	1.6	2.4	4.0
Kansas	952,320	15,238	21,131	36,369	1.6	2.6	4.2
Nebraska	950,000	21,690	23,706	45,396	2.3	2.6	4.9
Colorado	1,003,750	24,002	23,106	47,108	2.4	2.4	4.8
Oregon	250,000	7,710	2,925	10,635	3.1	1.2	4.3
California*	1,550,000	18,547	3,696	22,243	1.2	0.3	1.5
San Francisco*	2,750,000	22,570	169	22,739	0.8	0.0	0.8
New Mexico	300,000	4,280	5,243	9,523	1.4	1.8	3.2
Utah	200,000	2,803	2,750	5,553	1.4	1.4	2.8
Idaho	100,000	1,396	3,147	4,543	1.4	3.2	4.6
Montana	332,880	6,637	4,588	11,225	2.0	3.1	5.1
Wyoming	125,000	2,188	2,636	4,824	1.8	2.1	3.9
Dakota	129,124	2,363	672	3,035	1.8	1.3	3.1
Washington	111,671	699		699	0.6	0.0	0.6
Western States and Territories	95,974,897	1,362,082	1,839,929	3,202,011	1.4	2.0	3.4
Totals	†471,064,238	6,727,232	8,056,533	14,783,765	1.4	1.7	3.1

*California banks pay no State taxes on capital, except on such as is invested in real estate.
†The capital of the banks that reported State, county, and municipal taxes on stock and real estate is $463,983,724.

Amount and rate of taxation (United States and State) of the national banks for the year 1879.

States and Territories.	Capital stock.	Amount of taxes.			Ratio of tax to capital.		
		United States.	State.	Total.	United States.	State.	Total.
					Per ct.	*Per ct.*	*Per ct.*
Maine	$10,507,115	$114,855	$228,030	$342,885	1.1	2.2	3.3
New Hampshire	5,666,257	65,138	97,950	163,088	1.2	1.7	2.9
Vermont	8,528,353	80,863	169,699	250,562	1.0	2.1	3.1
Massachusetts	44,302,447	517,410	719,629	1,237,039	1.2	1.6	2.8
Boston	50,445,725	678,371	675,691	1,354,062	1.3	1.3	2.6
Rhode Island	20,009,800	195,509	251,079	446,588	1.0	1.2	2.2
Connecticut	25,572,815	281,063	389,926	670,989	1.1	1.5	2.6
New England States.	165,032,512	1,942,209	2,532,004	4,474,213	1.2	1.5	2.7
New York	32,973,066	511,243	637,489	1,148,732	1.5	2.0	3.5
New York City	50,813,657	1,299,166	1,466,570	2,765,736	2.6	2.9	5.5
Albany	1,920,229	56,177	50,532	106,709	2.9	2.5	5.4
New Jersey	13,553,308	205,856	241,379	447,235	1.5	1.8	3.3
Pennsylvania	28,513,098	408,310	191,626	599,936	1.4	0.7	2.1
Philadelphia	16,818,000	358,023	109,508	467,531	2.1	0.7	2.8
Pittsburgh	9,897,977	143,056	59,834	202,890	1.4	0.6	2.0
Delaware	1,763,085	25,527	6,215	31,742	1.4	0.4	1.8
Maryland	2,265,125	32,841	30,522	63,363	1.5	1.3	2.8
Baltimore	10,535,760	129,781	138,415	268,196	1.2	1.3	2.5
District of Columbia	252,000	4,509	130	4,639	1.8	0.1	1.9
Washington	1,125,000	15,624	4,049	19,673	1.4	0.4	1.8
Middle States	170,431,205	3,190,113	2,936,269	6,126,382	1.9	1.7	3.6
Virginia	2,947,560	49,380	53,710	103,090	1.7	1.9	3.6
West Virginia	1,656,000	21,523	26,915	48,438	1.3	1.6	2.9
North Carolina	2,500,884	31,586	38,356	69,942	1.3	1.6	2.9
South Carolina	2,450,000	28,709	49,787	78,496	1.2	2.0	3.2
Georgia	2,119,216	27,807	36,037	63,844	1.3	1.7	3.0
Florida	50,000	794	815	1,609	1.6	1.6	3.2
Alabama	1,662,000	20,267	31,530	51,797	1.2	2.0	3.2
New Orleans	2,875,000	50,212	13,144	63,356	1.7	0.5	2.2
Texas	1,050,000	15,439	19,596	35,035	1.5	1.9	3.4
Arkansas	205,000	3,217	2,870	6,087	1.6	1.4	3.0
Kentucky	7,037,974	82,347	39,814	122,161	1.2	0.6	1.8
Louisville	2,995,500	44,606	19,285	63,891	1.5	0.6	2.1
Tennessee	3,005,884	50,110	52,068	102,178	1.7	1.8	3.5
Southern States	30,555,018	425,997	383,927	809,924	1.4	1.3	2.7
Ohio	18,451,403	264,013	368,946	632,959	1.4	2.0	3.4
Cincinnati	4,108,333	79,722	99,415	179,137	1.9	2.4	4.3
Cleveland	3,887,500	50,530	78,862	129,392	1.3	2.0	3.3
Indiana	13,828,674	196,213	289,943	486,156	1.4	2.1	3.5
Illinois	11,068,214	169,594	194,416	364,010	1.5	1.8	3.3
Chicago	4,020,054	137,681	94,288	231,969	3.4	2.4	5.8
Michigan	7,263,673	96,743	118,018	214,761	1.3	1.6	2.9
Detroit	2,100,000	38,391	46,687	85,078	1.8	2.2	4.0
Wisconsin	2,530,093	41,295	44,425	85,720	1.6	1.8	3.4
Milwaukee	650,000	18,190	16,236	34,426	2.8	2.5	5.3
Iowa	5,809,832	86,537	118,056	204,593	1.5	2.1	3.6
Minnesota	4,662,307	65,598	85,475	151,073	1.4	1.8	3.2
Missouri	1,282,065	18,740	28,637	47,377	1.5	2.4	3.9
Saint Louis	2,650,000	47,910	55,642	103,552	1.8	2.1	3.9
Kansas	816,394	17,066	21,763	38,829	2.1	2.7	4.8
Nebraska	927,141	24,321	23,814	48,135	2.6	2.6	5.2
Colorado	1,050,000	34,545	35,412	69,957	3.3	3.4	6.7
Oregon	250,000	6,836	2,900	9,736	2.7	1.2	3.9
California*	1,550,045	19,645	4,229	23,874	1.3	0.3	1.6
San Francisco*	2,750,000	21,543	122	21,665	0.8	0.0	0.8
New Mexico	325,000	4,598	4,264	8,862	1.4	1.4	2.8
Utah	200,000	3,098	3,350	6,448	1.5	1.7	3.2
Idaho	100,000	1,434	3,478	4,912	1.4	3.5	4.9
Montana	200,000	5,416	4,477	9,893	2.7	3.0	5.7
Wyoming	125,000	2,403	2,731	5,134	1.9	2.2	4.1
Dakota	185,041	4,206	3,509	7,715	2.3	2.0	4.3
Washington	150,000	1,544	1,937	3,481	1.0	1.3	2.3
Western States and Territories	90,949,769	1,457,812	1,751,032	3,208,844	1.6	2.0	3.6
Totals	456,968,504	7,016,131	7,603,232	14,619,363	1.5	1.7	3.2

California banks pay no State taxes on capital except on such as is invested in real estate.
† The capital of the banks that reported State, county, and municipal taxes on stock and real estate is $452,869,712.

Dividends and earnings of the national banks, arranged by geographical divisions, for semi-annual periods from September 1, 1872, to September 1, 1881.

Geographical divisions.	No. of b'nks.	Capital.	Surplus.	Dividends.	Net earnings.	Dividends to capital.	Dividends to capital and surplus.	Earnings to capital and surplus.
						Pr. ct.	*Pr. ct.*	*Pr. ct.*
Sept., 1872, to March, 1873:								
New England States...	495	$155,659,232	$36,858,324	$7,938,341	$10,324,340	5.1	4.1	5.4
Middle States..........	594	192,845,660	53,303,503	9,766,087	11,642,716	5.1	4.0	4.7
Southern States.......	147	31,328,787	3,207,788	1,612,680	2,170,179	5.1	4.7	6.3
Western States........	676	100,684,995	20,887,673	5,508,953	7,789,243	5.5	4.5	6.4
Totals..............	1,912	480,518,683	114,257,288	24,826,061	31,926,478	5.2	4.2	5.4
March, 1873, to Sept., 1873:								
New England States...	496	157,014,832	38,303,887	7,941,687	10,103,736	5.1	4.1	5.2
Middle States..........	591	192,234,009	53,431,089	9,575,193	12,565,331	5.0	3.9	5.1
Southern States.......	161	33,259,530	3,600,607	1,544,046	2,246,024	4.6	4.2	6.1
Western States........	707	195,592,580	22,778,265	5,762,103	8,206,909	5.5	4.5	6.4
Totals	1,955	488,100,951	118,113,848	24,823,029	33,122,000	5.1	4.1	5.5
Sept., 1873, to March, 1874:								
New England States ..	503	159,041,832	39,714,859	7,627,811	9,682,704	4.8	3.8	4.9
Middle States..........	588	190,368,660	55,931,654	9,164,682	10,983,048	4.8	3.7	4.5
Southern States	159	32,605,522	3,865,491	1,415,933	1,750,914	4.3	3.9	4.8
Western States........	717	107,494,300	23,957,855	5,321,571	7,127,454	4.9	4.0	5.4
Totals..............	1,967	489,510,323	123,469,859	23,529,997	29,544,120	4.8	3.8	4.8
March, 1874, to Sept., 1874:								
New England States...	506	159,531,832	41,978,153	7,838,007	9,603,512	4.9	3.9	4.8
Middle States	586	189,365,019	57,176,298	9,163,707	11,214,753	5.0	3.8	4.5
Southern States	159	33,138,800	4,121,405	1,594,208	1,871,562	4.8	4.3	5.0
Western States	720	107,882,633	25,088,183	6,033,384	7,346,084	5.6	4.5	5.5
Totals	1,971	489,938,284	128,364,039	24,929,306	30,036,811	5.1	4.0	4.9
Sept., 1874, to March, 1875:								
New England States...	510	160,461,832	43,020,505	7,785,166	9,031,409	4.8	3.8	4.4
Middle States..........	589	189,639,519	57,749,497	9,537,118	10,361,652	5.0	3.9	4.2
Southern States.......	160	33,681,310	4,646,468	1,463,170	1,861,758	4.3	3.8	4.9
Western States........	739	109,786,170	26,144,167	5,965,362	7,881,188	5.4	4.4	5.8
Totals..............	2,007	493,568,831	131,560,637	24,750,816	29,136,007	5.0	4.0	4.7
March, 1875, to Sept., 1875:								
New England States ..	512	161,928,732	43,563,385	7,758,460	8,767,978	4.8	3.8	4.3
Middle States..........	603	190,775,569	57,826,444	9,151,653	9,985,736	4.8	3.7	4.0
Southern States.......	175	34,640,100	4,965,170	1,530,234	1,956,203	4.4	3.9	4.9
Western States	757	110,520,432	27,768,650	5,868,438	8,090,300	5.3	4.2	5.8
Totals..............	2,047	497,864,833	134,123,649	24,317,785	28,800,217	4.9	3.8	4.6
Sept., 1875, to March, 1876:								
New England States...	531	166,393,620	43,739,079	7,371,060	7,548,855	4.4	3.5	3.6
Middle States..........	625	190,272,820	56,379,205	10,171,655	5,770,198	5.2	4.1	2.3
Southern States........	174	33,399,100	5,348,175	1,509,125	2,211,357	4.5	3.9	5.7
Western States........	746	110,588,500	29,061,135	5,756,741	7,507,511	5.2	4.1	5.4
Totals..............	2,076	504,209,491	134,467,594	24,811,581	23,097,921	4.9	3.9	3.6
March, 1876, to Sept., 1876:								
New England States...	539	167,902,820	43,319,060	6,770,149	6,098,661	4.0	3.2	2.9
Middle States...... ...	626	190,928,351	54,527,758	8,818,572	6,751,345	4.6	3.6	3.2
Southern States........	179	33,392,600	5,486,630	1,432,101	1,498,873	4.3	3.7	3.9
Western States	737	108,258,500	28,917,630	5,542,914	6,191,353	5.1	4.0	4.5
Totals..............	2,081	500,482,271	132,251,078	22,563,829	20,540,232	4.5	3.6	3.3
Sept., 1876, to March, 1877:								
New England States...	542	168,178,520	43,109,865	6,501,179	6,128,206	3.9	3.1	2.9
Middle States..........	631	190,272,820	53,430,368	8,328,761	6,787,978	4.4	3.4	2.8
Southern States........	175	32,120,440	5,678,226	1,387,478	1,470,475	4.3	3.7	3.9
Western States	732	106,079,800	28,653,706	5,586,551	5,206,303	5.3	4.1	3.9
Totals..............	2,080	496,651,580	130,872,165	21,803,969	19,592,962	4.4	3.5	3.1

Dividends and earnings of the national banks, &c.—Continued.

Geographical divisions.	No. of b'nks.	Capital.	Surplus.	Dividends.	Net earnings.	Dividends to capital.	Dividends to capital and surplus.	Earnings to capital and surplus.
						Pr. ct.	*Pr. ct.*	*Pr. ct.*
March, 1877, to Sept., 1877:								
New England States	541	$167,237,820	$41,370,408	$6,147,573	$3,744,799	3.7	2.9	1.8
Middle States	631	185,468,951	51,871,038	7,686,267	6,185,157	4.1	3.2	2.6
Southern States	175	32,599,989	5,571,362	1,299,476	1,207,343	4.0	3.4	3.2
Western States	725	101,018,100	25,536,446	6,983,800	4,136,729	6.9	5.5	3.3
Totals	2,072	486,324,860	124,349,264	22,117,116	15,274,028	4.5	3.6	2.5
Sept., 1877, to March, 1878:								
New England States	544	166,546,320	40,560,405	5,903,213	4,985,926	3.5	2.9	2.4
Middle States	631	178,149,931	51,551,601	7,261,608	6,283,445	4.1	3.2	2.7
Southern States	176	32,166,800	5,482,012	1,217,880	1,174,220	3.8	3.2	3.1
Western States	722	98,746,700	24,770,543	4,599,689	4,503,105	4.7	3.7	3.7
Totals	2,074	475,609,751	122,373,561	18,982,390	16,946,696	4.0	3.2	2.8
March, 1878, to Sept., 1878:								
New England States	543	166,587,820	38,956,871	5,459,786	3,846,183	3.3	2.7	1.9
Middle States	629	176,694,576	50,182,622	6,674,618	4,999,505	3.8	2.9	2.2
Southern States	176	31,491,800	5,684,035	1,115,865	951,995	3.5	3.0	2.6
Western States	699	95,457,700	23,863,663	4,708,954	3,861,210	4.9	4.0	3.2
Totals	2,047	470,231,896	118,687,134	17,959,223	13,658,893	3.8	3.0	2.3
Sept., 1878, to March, 1879:								
New England States	544	165,645,820	38,037,115	5,295,347	3,658,080	3.2	2.6	1.8
Middle States	630	173,979,676	50,084,782	6,876,398	5,826,662	4.0	3.1	2.6
Southern States	175	30,882,800	5,240,054	1,077,333	961,734	3.5	3.0	2.7
Western States	694	93,905,700	23,382,183	4,201,976	4,231,275	4.6	3.6	3.6
Totals	2,043	464,413,996	116,744,134	17,541,054	14,678,660	3.8	3.0	2.5
March, 1879, to Sept., 1879:								
New England States	542	164,450,120	37,441,984	5,257,526	4,761,422	3.2	2.6	2.4
Middle States	640	169,645,936	49,779,783	6,690,394	7,128,979	3.9	3.0	3.2
Southern States	175	30,281,800	5,198,481	1,056,594	979,496	3.5	3.0	2.7
Western States	688	90,754,200	22,720,103	4,397,353	4,003,303	4.8	3.9	3.5
Totals	2,045	455,132,056	115,140,351	17,401,867	16,873,200	3.8	3.1	3.0
Sept., 1879, to March, 1880:								
New England States	546	164,820,020	37,860,312	5,409,351	5,610,287	3.3	2.7	2.8
Middle States	640	166,399,170	51,306,583	7,151,166	9,220,826	4.2	3.2	4.2
Southern States	175	30,432,700	5,210,198	1,246,470	1,278,605	4.1	3.5	3.6
Western States	685	89,428,200	22,840,408	4,314,286	5,042,976	4.8	3.8	4.5
Totals	2,046	454,080,090	117,226,501	18,121,273	21,152,784	4.0	3.2	3.7
March, 1880, to Sept., 1880:								
New England States	548	165,380,212	38,450,297	5,858,434	7,413,622	3.5	2.9	3.6
Middle States	654	169,313,870	52,762,674	7,120,204	9,805,148	4.2	3.2	1.1
Southern States	176	30,423,700	5,516,335	1,139,203	1,431,102	3.7	3.2	4.0
Western States	694	89,067,250	23,446,343	4,172,359	5,380,078	4.7	3.7	4.8
Totals	2,072	454,215,062	120,145,649	18,290,200	24,033,250	4.0	3.2	4.2
Sept., 1880, to March, 1881:								
New England States	550	165,623,120	38,941,841	5,900,861	6,757,787	3.6	2.9	3.3
Middle States	657	170,739,045	53,536,248	6,974,934	9,162,771	4.1	3.1	4.1
Southern States	178	30,448,700	5,898,107	1,264,398	1,905,090	4.2	3.5	5.2
Western States	702	90,034,000	24,102,592	4,737,324	6,625,773	5.3	4.2	5.8
Totals	2,087	456,844,865	122,481,788	18,877,517	24,452,021	4.1	3.3	4.2
March, 1881, to Sept., 1881:								
New England States	550	165,373,120	39,878,448	6,005,608	8,166,022	3.6	2.9	4.0
Middle States	660	171,560,315	55,747,501	7,558,407	11,925,784	4.1	3.3	5.3
Southern States	181	30,973,950	6,530,694	1,282,120	2,300,624	4.1	3.4	6.1
Western States	709	91,027,100	25,081,751	4,653,833	6,778,112	5.1	3.9	5.8
Totals	2,100	458,934,485	127,238,394	19,499,968	29,170,542	4.3	3.3	5.0
General averages	2,038	478,701,795	123,993,107	21,397,554	23,446,490	4.5	3.6	3.9

Abstract of reports of dividends and earnings of national banks in the United States from September 1, 1880, to March 1, 1881.

States and Territories.	No. of banks.	Capital stock.	Surplus.	Dividends.	Net earnings.	Dividends to capital.	Dividends to capital and surplus.	Earnings to capital and surplus.
						Pr ct.	*Pr ct.*	*Pr ct.*
Maine	69	$10,435,000	$2,448,881 84	$459,025 00	$529,569 30	4.40	3.56	4.11
New Hampshire	47	5,830,000	1,093,403 55	229,500 00	230,275 10	3.94	3.31	3.33
Vermont	47	8,301,000	1,905,832 72	338,480 00	332,142 88	4.08	3.32	3.25
Massachusetts	188	45,105,000	12,654,809 02	1,771,500 94	2,038,197 84	3.93	3.07	3.53
Boston	54	50,500,000	10,632,385 60	1,457,262 00	1,813,822 84	2.89	2.38	2.97
Rhode Island	61	20,009,800	3,625,392 88	668,334 00	484,587 40	3.34	2.83	2.05
Connecticut	84	25,442,320	6,584,135 41	976,759 45	1,329,191 71	3.84	3.05	4.15
New England States	550	165,623,120	38,944,841 02	5,900,861 43	6,757,787 07	3.56	2.88	3.30
New York	242	32,846,660	7,861,556 36	1,206,809 83	1,644,364 27	3.67	2.96	4.04
New York City	47	50,650,000	18,494,884 02	2,271,000 00	3,132,405 52	4.49	3.20	4.54
Albany	7	1,800,000	1,400,000 00	111,085 00	130,158 33	6.17	3.47	4.07
New Jersey	66	12,995,350	3,728,668 72	549,890 50	646,011 83	4.23	3.20	3.86
Pennsylvania	186	28,904,570	7,222,398 10	1,097,278 70	1,392,244 68	3.79	3.04	3.85
Philadelphia	32	17,358,000	7,740,849 11	760,800 00	929,961 01	4.38	3.03	3.71
Pittsburgh	22	9,850,000	3,145,251 75	339,500 00	479,821 45	3.44	2.61	3.69
Delaware	14	1,743,985	487,990 93	76,683 35	94,396 20	4.40	3.44	4.23
Maryland	20	2,331,700	712,076 31	108,384 50	126,875 88	4.65	3.56	4.17
Baltimore	15	10,881,780	2,449,015 51	411,296 75	569,996 34	3.78	3.09	4.28
Dist. of Columbia	1	252,000	58,000 00	10,080 00	12,628 23	4.00	3.25	4.07
Washington	5	1,125,000	235,557 14	29,125 00	3,876 73	2.59	2.14	.28
Middle States	657	170,739,045	53,536,247 95	6,974,933 64	9,162,770 47	4.08	3.11	4.09
Virginia	17	2,866,000	854,100 00	121,980 00	178,787 52	4.26	3.28	4.31
West Virginia	17	1,761,000	439,828 04	83,027 50	92,997 24	4.71	3.77	4.22
North Carolina	15	2,501,000	340,826 02	92,580 00	134,521 95	3.70	3.26	4.73
South Carolina	12	1,949,900	396,849 58	99,500 00	219,994 47	5.10	4.24	9.37
Georgia	13	2,221,000	467,491 02	84,300 00	143,432 51	3.80	3.14	5.33
Florida	1	50,000	3,000 00	2,500 00	4,328 49	5.00	4.72	8.17
Alabama	9	1,518,000	236,500 00	53,400 00	97,030 36	3.52	3.04	5.58
New Orleans	7	2,875,000	637,500 00	122,250 00	215,133 49	4.25	3.48	6.12
Texas	13	1,300,000	293,732 17	50,000 00	83,259 20	3.84	3.14	5.22
Arkansas	2	205,000	41,000 00	13,000 00	13,757 17	6.34	5.28	5.59
Kentucky	41	7,201,000	1,199,932 96	265,110 00	355,488 06	3.68	3.16	4.23
Louisville	8	2,995,500	407,084 23	106,820 00	146,186 15	3.57	3.14	4.30
Tennessee	23	3,005,300	580,263 10	169,930 00	219,873 83	5.65	4.74	6.13
Southern States	178	30,448,700	5,898,107 12	1,264,397 50	1,905,690 44	4.15	3.48	5.24
Ohio	157	18,821,900	3,787,737 35	802,973 75	1,050,225 37	4.26	3.55	4.64
Cincinnati	6	4,100,000	723,000 00	186,000 00	264,746 77	4.54	3.86	5.49
Cleveland	6	3,700,000	795,000 00	152,000 00	190,282 74	4.11	3.38	4.23
Indiana	92	13,202,500	4,001,640 51	614,977 21	749,167 04	4.66	3.57	4.44
Illinois	127	10,714,600	3,608,022 08	689,412 04	786,762 84	6.44	4.81	5.49
Chicago	9	4,250,000	2,470,000 00	403,000 00	591,713 46	9.48	6.00	8.81
Michigan	75	7,235,000	1,944,806 34	374,700 00	508,213 91	5.18	4.08	5.54
Detroit	4	2,100,000	715,000 00	102,000 00	128,133 93	4.86	3.62	4.55
Wisconsin	32	2,400,000	698,460 80	155,165 98	188,700 18	6.46	5.01	6.09
Milwaukee	3	650,000	225,000 00	26,000 00	96,889 93	4.00	2.97	11.07
Iowa	74	5,790,000	1,491,876 99	305,995 00	412,051 19	5.28	4.20	5.66
Minnesota	30	5,150,000	951,811 11	238,100 00	426,673 82	4.62	3.90	6.99
Missouri	16	1,400,000	330,526 00	109,250 00	94,078 69	7.80	3.31	5.47
Saint Louis	5	2,650,000	770,557 94	99,000 00	176,133 81	3.74	2.89	5.03
Kansas	12	875,000	200,550 00	29,750 00	72,901 47	3.40	2.77	6.78
Nebraska	10	850,000	250,100 00	65,000 00	148,415 82	7.65	5.91	13.49
Western States	658	83,889,000	22,964,091 76	4,353,323 98	5,885,690 97	5.19	4.07	5.51
Colorado	11	1,070,000	331,000 00	115,000 00	219,566 95	10.75	8.21	15.67
Nevada	1	50,000	2,036 04	2,500 00	4,536 04	5.00	4.80	8.72
California	9	1,650,000	205,043 11	75,500 00	123,589 39	4.58	4.07	6.66
San Francisco	1	1,500,000	171,004 33	60,000 00	93,285 97	4.00	3.59	5.58
Oregon	1	250,000	50,000 00	30,600 00	41,363 20	12.00	10.00	13.79
Dakota	6	425,000	76,500 00	15,500 00	85,938 52	3.65	3.09	17.14
Idaho	1	100,000	20,000 00	18,000 00	17,525 51	18.00	15.00	14.60
Montana	3	200,000	40,000 00	0 00	27,146 94	0	0	11.31
New Mexico	4	400,000	87,916 96	25,500 00	60,852 32	6.38	5.23	12.47
Utah	2	200,000	75,000 00	12,000 00	29,618 26	6.00	4.36	7.50
Washington	1	150,000	30,000 00	0 00	20,000 00	0	0	11.11
Wyoming	2	150,000	50,000 00	30,000 00	25,658 80	20.00	15.00	12.83
Pacific States and Territories	44	6,145,000	1,138,500 44	384,000 00	749,081 90	6.25	5.27	10.16
Grand totals	2,087	456,844,865	122,481,788 29	18,877,516 54	24,452,020 85	4.13	3.26	4.22

Abstract of reports of dividends and earnings of national banks in the United States from March 1, 1881, to September 1, 1881.

States and Territories.	No. of banks.	Capital stock.	Surplus.	Dividends.	Net earnings.	Dividends to capital.	Dividends to capital and surplus.	Earnings to capital and surplus.
						Pr. ct.	Pr. ct.	Pr. ct.
Maine	69	$10,385,000	$2,585,948 40	$452,550 00	$659,102 04	4.36	3.49	5.08
New Hampshire	47	5,830,000	1,109,897 59	218,725 00	265,521 56	3.75	3.15	3.83
Vermont	46	8,101,000	1,766,369 55	432,480 00	351,332 83	5.34	4.38	3.56
Massachusetts	188	45,105,000	13,175,678 06	1,767,911 22	2,563,626 16	3.92	3.03	4.40
Boston	54	50,500,000	10,815,466 22	1,405,450 00	2,057,577 86	2.78	2.29	3.36
Rhode Island	61	19,909,800	3,715,156 00	674,214 00	951,027 52	3.39	2.85	4.03
Connecticut	85	25,542,320	6,709,931 89	1,054,277 95	1,317,834 34	4.13	3.27	4.09
New England States	550	165,373,120	39,878,447 71	6,005,608 17	8,166,022 31	3.63	2.93	3.98
New York	242	32,892,160	7,960,014 83	1,361,878 67	1,821,961 57	4.14	3.33	4.46
New York City	48	51,150,000	19,890,006 84	2,568,000 00	5,037,656 19	5.02	3.61	7.09
Albany	7	1,800,000	1,400,000 00	76,500 00	125,494 50	4.25	2.39	3.92
New Jersey	65	12,875,350	3,826,378 78	535,977 25	751,039 09	4.16	3.21	4.50
Pennsylvania	187	29,030,340	7,402,670 69	1,190,479 70	1,590,948 45	4.10	3.27	4.37
Philadelphia	32	17,358,000	7,993,098 97	764,388 00	1,091,878 25	4.40	3.02	4.31
Pittsburgh	22	9,850,000	3,263,545 97	366,500 00	598,024 79	3.72	2.80	4.56
Delaware	14	1,743,985	501,304 31	76,683 35	131,866 98	4.40	3.42	5.88
Maryland	21	2,381,700	706,068 00	133,751 00	139,729 82	5.62	4.33	4.53
Baltimore	16	11,101,780	2,495,312 23	446,769 99	598,093 70	4.02	3.29	4.40
Dist. of Columbia	1	252,000	59,000 00	10,680 00	11,192 41	4.00	3.24	3.60
Washington	5	1,125,000	250,100 00	27,125 00	28,171 69	2.41	1.97	2.03
Middle States	660	171,560,315	55,747,500 62	7,358,132 96	11,926,057 44	4.41	3.33	5.25
Virginia	18	2,966,000	900,100 00	121,980 00	213,338 53	4.11	3.16	5.52
West Virginia	7	1,761,000	452,810 22	80,590 00	101,060 97	4.58	3.64	4.57
North Carolina	15	2,501,000	347,828 22	91,750 00	137,715 53	3.67	3.22	4.83
South Carolina	13	1,884,150	416,457 96	67,500 00	164,667 77	3.58	2.93	7.16
Georgia	12	2,186,000	485,359 43	84,750 00	146,989 05	3.88	3.17	5.50
Florida	2	100,000	4,000 00	2,500 00	10,856 30	2.50	2.40	10.44
Alabama	9	1,518,000	250,350 00	56,480 00	90,639 66	3.72	3.19	5.13
New Orleans	7	2,875,000	815,000 00	118,000 00	280,588 91	4.10	3.20	7.60
Texas	13	1,320,000	312,200 00	76,500 00	163,410 52	5.80	4.69	10.01
Arkansas	2	205,000	42,000 00	7,500 00	16,254 23	3.66	3.04	6.58
Kentucky	41	7,201,000	1,350 118 21	275,100 00	448,381 07	3.82	3.22	5.24
Louisville	8	3,151,500	525,542 46	130,940 00	201,271 08	4.16	3.56	7.92
Tennessee	24	3,305,300	628,927 40	168,530 00	235,449 22	5.11	4.28	5.98
Southern States	181	30,973,950	6,530,693 90	1,282,120 00	2,300,623 74	4.14	3.42	6.13
Ohio	160	18,889,000	3,895,321 84	835,673 95	1,111,198 50	4.42	3.67	4.88
Cincinnati	7	5,100,000	727,000 00	194,000 00	208,181 97	3.80	3.33	5.11
Cleveland	6	3,700,000	820,000 00	152,000 00	225,796 18	4.11	3.36	5.00
Indiana	92	12,918,500	4,026,639 58	659,422 79	807,118 27	5.11	3.89	4.76
Illinois	129	10,764,600	3,732,338 60	613,831 25	910,092 59	5.70	4.23	6.28
Chicago	9	4,250,000	2,605,000 00	208,000 00	677,310 08	4.89	3.03	9.84
Michigan	75	7,285,000	1,995,345 31	360,450 00	575,111 67	4.95	3.88	6.20
Detroit	4	2,100,000	800,000 00	107,000 00	187,456 88	5.10	3.69	6.46
Wisconsin	31	2,375,000	702,419 31	129,150 00	187,114 78	5.43	4.20	6.08
Milwaukee	3	650,000	235,000 00	26,000 00	49,279 49	4.00	2.94	5.57
Iowa	76	5,940,000	1,566,961 38	308,921 85	214,191 22	5.20	4.12	3.25
Minnesota	28	4,925,000	990,225 88	395,100 00	411,753 54	8.02	6.68	6.96
Missouri	16	1,400,000	317,178 70	60,500 00	96,234 16	4.32	3.46	5.51
Saint Louis	5	2,650,000	753,181 29	99,000 00	126,502 09	3.74	2.91	3.72
Kansas	12	875,000	225,210 18	31,750 00	80,975 49	3.63	2.89	7.36
Nebraska	10	850,000	271,500 00	63,000 00	75,229 62	7.41	5.62	6.72
Western States	663	84,682,100	23,713,321 90	4,243,799 84	6,063,576 49	5.01	3.92	5.59
Colorado	14	1,070,000	411,800 00	103,500 00	175,347 16	9.67	6.99	11.83
Nevada	1	50,000	5,814 02	2,500 00	6,277 98	5.00	4.48	11.25
California	10	1,770,000	214,612 35	71,033 32	102,115 78	4.18	3.73	5.15
San Francisco	1	1,500,000	179,603 36	60,000 00	85,990 29	4.00	3.57	5.12
Oregon	1	250,000	50,000 00	80,000 00	50,037 67	32.00	26.67	16.68
Dakota	7	505,000	83,100 00	30,500 00	85,585 13	6.04	5.19	14.55
Idaho	1	100,000	20,000 00	28,000 00	27,753 88	28.00	23.33	23.13
Montana	3	200,000	40,000 00	0 00	39,791 26	0	0	16.58
New Mexico	4	400,000	183,500 00	19,500 00	40,761 22	4.87	3.34	6.99
Utah	2	200,000	100,000 00	12,000 00	59,795 49	6.00	1.00	19.93
Washington	1	150,000	30,000 00	0 00	31,000 00	0	0	17.22
Wyoming	2	150,000	50,000 00	0 00	10,046 90	0	0	5.02
Pacific States and Territories	46	6,345,000	1,368,429 73	410,033 32	714,535 76	6.46	5.32	9.26
Grand totals	2,100	158,934,485	127,238,393 86	19,499,691 29	29,170,815 74	4.25	3.33	4.98

Table, by States and reserve cities, of the ratios to capital, and to capital and surplus, of

States, Territories, and reserve cities.	Ratio of dividends to capital for six months ending—										Ratio of	
	1877.		1878.		1879.		1880.		1881.		1877.	
	Mar. 1.	Sept. 1.	Mar. 1.	Sept. 1.	Mar. 1.	Sept. 1.	Mar. 1.	Sept. 1.	Mar. 1.	Sept. 1.	Mar. 1.	Sept. 1.
	Pr. ct.	Pr. ct.	Pr. ct.	Pr. ct.	Pr. ct.	Pr. ct.	Pr. ct.	Pr. ct.	Pr. ct.	Pr. ct.	Pr. ct.	Pr. ct.
1 Maine	4.8	5.1	4.5	4.4	4.7	4.2	4.1	4.4	4.4	4.4	3.9	4.1
2 New Hampshire	4.3	4.1	3.9	3.8	3.9	3.9	3.7	3.7	3.9	3.7	3.7	3.5
3 Vermont	4.0	4.0	4.0	3.6	3.4	3.7	3.7	4.5	4.1	5.3	3.2	3.2
4 Massachusetts	4.1	4.0	3.9	3.4	3.4	3.7	3.4	3.6	3.9	3.9	3.2	3.1
5 Boston	3.1	3.0	2.9	2.3	2.2	2.2	2.5	2.9	2.9	2.8	2.5	2.4
6 Rhode Island	3.5	3.3	3.3	3.4	3.3	3.0	3.3	3.4	3.3	3.4	2.9	2.7
7 Connecticut	4.7	4.0	3.9	4.2	4.0	3.7	4.0	4.1	3.8	4.1	3.7	3.2
8 New York	4.4	4.3	4.2	3.8	3.9	4.2	3.5	3.8	3.7	4.1	3.5	3.5
9 New York City	4.1	3.7	3.7	3.6	4.2	3.8	5.1	4.4	4.5	5.0	3.2	2.9
10 Albany	5.4	5.0	5.2	4.7	4.9	4.5	4.6	4.3	6.2	4.2	3.1	2.9
11 New Jersey	4.4	4.3	4.7	4.0	4.0	4.0	4.1	4.2	4.2	4.2	3.5	3.4
12 Pennsylvania	4.4	4.1	3.9	3.6	3.5	3.5	3.8	4.4	3.8	4.1	3.4	3.2
13 Philadelphia	5.4	5.0	5.1	4.6	4.7	4.4	4.5	4.5	4.4	4.4	3.7	3.5
14 Pittsburgh	4.0	4.0	3.8	3.6	3.3	3.5	3.6	3.7	3.4	3.7	3.1	3.1
15 Delaware	4.9	4.9	4.7	4.7	4.4	4.1	4.4	4.4	4.4	4.4	3.9	3.9
16 Maryland	5.4	4.8	5.1	4.8	4.5	4.4	4.6	4.5	4.6	5.6	4.2	3.7
17 Baltimore	4.4	4.1	3.9	3.3	3.5	4.3	3.9	4.2	3.8	4.0	3.7	3.4
18 District of Columbia	4.0	4.0	4.0	4.0	4.0	4.0	4.0	4.0	4.0	4.0	3.4	3.3
19 Washington	4.1	8.0	2.3	2.6	1.8	2.7	2.4	2.3	2.6	2.4	3.4	6.3
20 Virginia	3.9	3.6	3.2	3.5	4.2	4.2	4.0	4.2	4.3	4.1	3.1	2.9
21 West Virginia	4.4	4.6	4.1	4.2	4.0	4.0	4.0	4.2	4.7	4.6	3.5	3.6
22 North Carolina	4.3	2.7	2.5	2.3	3.1	3.3	3.7	2.5	3.7	3.7	3.9	2.4
23 South Carolina	4.0	3.8	3.5	2.3	1.6	1.9	1.9	1.4	5.1	3.6	3.3	3.3
24 Georgia	3.2	4.8	3.4	3.5	3.8	3.0	3.3	3.7	3.8	3.9	2.7	4.1
25 Florida	5.0	4.0	3.0	3.0					5.0	2.5	4.8	3.9
26 Alabama	3.4	2.9	2.3	2.7	2.6	2.8	4.8	3.5	3.5	3.7	3.1	2.7
27 New Orleans	3.5	4.6	4.3	6.2	4.2	4.2	4.1	4.3	4.2	4.1	3.1	3.0
28 Texas	9.0	3.2	8.4	4.5	4.0	3.6	5.4	4.5	3.8	5.8	7.2	2.5
29 Arkansas		1.3		1.6	5.3	3.7	6.3	3.7	6.3	3.7		1.2
30 Kentucky	4.3	4.1	3.9	3.7	3.7	3.2	3.5	3.8	3.7	3.8	3.7	3.5
31 Louisville	4.5	3.8	3.5	1.6	2.5	3.2	3.6	3.8	3.6	4.2	4.1	3.4
32 Tennessee	5.5	5.2	4.8	4.6	4.2	4.8	7.9	5.4	5.6	5.1	4.7	4.4
33 Ohio	4.9	5.5	4.6	4.4	4.9	4.1	4.9	4.4	4.3	4.4	4.0	4.6
34 Cincinnati	4.5	5.9	4.4	4.5	2.8	5.2	5.6	4.7	4.5	3.8	3.7	4.9
35 Cleveland	4.0	5.3	3.4	4.1	3.0	3.5	3.7	3.9	4.1	4.1	3.4	4.5
36 Indiana	5.5	4.9	4.5	5.0	4.2	4.0	4.3	4.5	4.7	5.1	4.3	3.9
37 Illinois	5.7	5.8	5.5	4.8	5.1	6.1	5.2	5.3	6.4	5.7	4.3	4.3
38 Chicago	9.4	31.0	1.8	6.6	3.8	6.8	4.9	4.8	9.5	4.9	5.5	21.8
39 Michigan	5.4	4.5	5.7	4.5	6.0	5.9	4.7	4.4	5.2	4.9	4.3	3.5
40 Detroit	5.5	5.5	5.3	17.2	5.1	4.9	5.1	5.1	4.9	5.1	3.7	3.7
41 Wisconsin	6.9	5.1	5.5	5.0	5.9	5.8	7.2	5.0	6.5	5.4	5.4	4.1
42 Milwaukee	5.6	5.6	4.7	2.9	2.9	2.9	3.1	4.0	4.0	4.0	4.1	4.1
43 Iowa	5.1	5.2	5.5	4.7	4.5	4.4	4.8	4.4	5.3	5.2	4.1	4.2
44 Minnesota	5.2	4.6	5.5	5.3	4.9	6.0	5.1	5.6	4.6	8.0	4.3	3.9
45 Missouri	4.5	4.0	3.8	5.3	4.6	3.3	4.7	6.5	7.8	4.3	3.8	3.3
46 Saint Louis	1.1	3.9	3.6	2.0	1.3	2.8	3.2	3.2	3.7	3.7	1.0	3.3
47 Kansas	5.3	4.4	3.8	4.9	2.5	3.1	5.3	3.6	3.4	3.6	4.4	3.5
48 Nebraska	6.2	7.6	6.8	5.4	6.7	10.8	7.7	7.5	7.6	7.4	5.2	6.3
49 Colorado	4.8	3.8	2.1	2.4	2.7	2.8	4.1	4.5	10.7	9.6	2.6	3.3
50 Nevada								5.0	5.0			
51 California	5.6	5.1	0.0	3.7	7.5	4.2	3.7	1.4	4.6	4.2	5.3	4.7
52 San Francisco	3.6	3.6	2.9	4.1	3.7	3.5	3.1	4.0	4.0	4.0	3.5	3.5
53 Oregon	12.0	37.0	12.0	12.0	17.0	22.0	12.0	12.0	12.0	32.0	10.0	30.8
54 Dakota	5.0	5.0	5.0	4.0	2.0	9.4	0.9	10.0	3.6	5.0	4.2	4.2
55 Idaho	25.0	15.0	18.0	10.0	20.0	15.0	15.0	15.0	18.0	28.0	20.7	12.4
56 Montana	4.1	5.7	5.5	1.5	8.6	1.8	3.3				3.4	4.6
57 New Mexico	6.5	6.5	4.0	2.5	4.5	4.5	3.5	2.6	6.4	4.9	5.7	5.9
58 Utah	6.0	6.0	6.0	6.0	6.0	6.0	6.0	6.0	6.0	6.0	5.0	5.0
59 Washington												
60 Wyoming							18.0	38.0		20.0		
Averages	4.9	4.5	4.4	4.5	3.9	3.8	4.0	4.0	4.1	4.2	3.5	3.6

NOTE.—Figures printed in bold-faced type in column

the dividends and earnings of national banks, from March 1, 1877, to September 1, 1881.

| Dividends to capital and surplus for six months ending— | | | | | | | | Ratio of earnings to capital and surplus for six months ending— | | | | | | | | | | No. |
| 1878 | | 1879 | | 1880 | | 1881 | | 1877 | | 1878 | | 1879 | | 1880 | | 1881 | | |
Mar. 1.	Sept. 1.	Mar. 1.	Sept. 1.	Mar. 1.	Sept. 1.	Mar. 1.	Sept. 1.	Mar. 1.	Sept. 1.	Mar. 1.	Sept. 1.	Mar. 1.	Sept. 1.	Mar. 1.	Sept. 1.	Mar. 1.	Sept. 1.	
3.7	3.6	3.8	3.5	3.3	3.6	3.6	3.5	4.0	3.1	4.2	3.2	3.2	3.5	3.6	4.3	4.1	5.1	1
3.3	3.2	3.3	3.3	3.1	3.3	3.1	4.7	3.7	3.9	2.0	3.4	2.9	4.0	3.4	3.3	3.8		2
3.2	2.9	2.8	3.0	2.9	3.7	3.3	4.4	4.6	4.3	2.9	2.2	2.5	2.7	3.3	3.2	3.2	3.6	3
3.0	2.6	2.6	2.9	2.7	2.9	3.1	3.0	3.1	2.9	2.6	1.9	1.4	2.5	3.5	3.6	3.5	4.4	4
2.4	1.9	1.8	1.8	2.1	2.4	2.4	2.3	1.9	1.4	1.2	0.9	0.8	1.4	2.3	3.4	3.0	3.4	5
2.8	2.9	2.8	2.6	2.8	2.8	2.8	2.8	2.8	0.3	1.9	2.0	2.4	2.9	2.4	3.9	2.0	4.0	6
3.1	3.3	3.2	3.0	3.2	3.2	3.0	3.3	3.2	0.1	3.7	2.7	2.9	2.8	3.8	3.9	4.1	4.1	7
3.4	3.1	3.1	3.4	2.8	3.1	3.0	3.3	3.5	2.9	2.8	2.7	2.8	2.7	4.0	3.7	4.0	4.5	8
2.8	2.8	3.2	2.9	3.8	3.2	3.3	3.6	1.4	1.5	2.0	2.0	2.5	3.6	5.8	6.2	4.5	7.1	9
3.0	2.7	2.8	2.6	2.5	2.4	3.5	2.4	3.9	2.5	1.1	0.7	1.2	1.4	3.1	1.9	4.1	3.9	10
3.7	3.2	3.2	3.1	3.2	3.0	3.3	3.2	3.2	3.6	3.4	1.9	2.5	3.1	3.3	3.8	3.9	4.5	11
3.1	2.8	2.8	2.8	3.0	3.5	3.0	3.3	3.8	2.8	3.1	2.5	2.3	2.8	3.3	3.4	3.8	4.4	12
3.5	3.2	3.3	3.1	3.1	3.0	3.0	3.0	3.2	3.8	2.3	3.4	3.4	3.4	3.4	3.9	3.7	4.3	13
2.9	2.8	2.6	2.7	2.8	2.6	2.6	2.8	3.0	3.2	3.4	1.2	2.4	3.1	3.0	3.6	3.7	4.6	14
3.7	3.7	3.5	3.2	3.5	3.4	3.4	3.4	4.3	4.0	3.9	3.4	4.0	3.6	4.3	4.5	4.2	5.9	15
4.0	3.7	3.4	3.4	3.5	3.5	3.6	4.3	4.4	4.4	3.5	4.1	3.2	3.4	3.9	3.9	4.2	4.5	16
3.3	2.7	2.9	3.5	3.2	3.4	3.1	3.3	3.2	4.2	2.8	2.2	1.9	4.8	3.3	4.0	4.3	4.4	17
3.3	3.3	3.3	3.3	3.3	3.3	3.2	3.2	4.7	4.8	4.5	3.9	4.6	4.3	4.2	3.2	4.1	3.6	18
2.0	2.1	1.5	2.2	2.0	1.9	2.1	2.0	1.9	4.5	3.0	1.2	1.4	1.5	1.5	1.7	0.3	2.0	19
2.6	2.8	3.3	3.3	3.3	3.3	3.2	3.3	3.2	1.6	1.6	3.4	3.0	4.2	4.3	4.8	5.5		20
2.3	3.4	3.2	3.2	3.2	3.4	3.8	3.6	3.7	2.3	3.4	3.2	2.2	3.5	3.7	4.1	4.2	4.6	21
2.2	2.1	2.7	2.9	3.3	2.2	3.3	3.2	4.2	4.0	2.3	0.1	4.2	2.5	4.0	1.0	4.7	4.8	22
3.0	2.0	1.4	1.7	1.6	1.2	4.2	2.9	5.2	2.9	2.4	2.2	1.1	1.4	3.0	**2.0**	9.4	7.2	23
2.9	2.6	3.2	2.6	2.8	3.1	3.1	3.2	3.2	1.8	2.8	3.1	3.2	2.6	2.5	4.6	5.3	5.5	24
2.8	2.9			4.7	2.4	4.0	3.2	3.8	4.0	1.1	2.8	**5.2**	1.7	8.2	10.4			25
2.1	2.5	2.4	2.5	4.2	3.0	3.0	3.2	3.5	3.4	2.5	0.9	3.5	4.7	3.6	7.2	5.6	5.1	26
3.7	5.1	3.7	3.7	3.6	3.6	3.5	3.2	2.2	3.8	4.5	9.8	**1.0**	2.4	4.0	6.3	6.1	7.6	27
6.6	3.5	3.1	2.8	4.2	3.6	3.1	4.7	5.5	3.7	4.7	2.7	5.7	0.1	5.0	1.6	5.2	10.0	28
	1.4	4.5	3.1	5.3	3.1	5.3	3.0	3.6	1.0	3.5	0.5	2.1	3.5	7.2	4.4	5.6	6.6	29
3.3	3.2	3.2	2.8	3.1	3.3	3.2	3.2	4.0	3.9	3.4	2.2	2.1	2.7	2.8	3.6	4.2	5.2	30
3.1	1.5	2.3	2.9	3.3	3.4	3.1	3.6	4.6	3.8	2.7	**0.2**	3.0	1.9	2.9	5.0	4.3	7.9	31
4.1	4.0	3.6	4.1	6.8	4.6	4.7	4.3	4.3	3.5	4.2	2.5	4.8	4.7	5.4	6.8	6.1	6.0	32
3.8	3.7	4.0	3.4	4.1	3.7	3.5	3.7	4.2	2.1	4.0	3.1	3.4	2.0	3.8	3.9	4.6	4.9	33
3.7	3.7	2.4	4.4	4.6	3.9	3.9	3.3	3.6	1.0	3.8	3.8	3.5	4.0	5.7	5.1	5.5	5.1	34
2.9	3.5	2.6	3.0	3.1	3.3	3.4	3.4	4.6	3.9	3.5	0.4	3.2	2.1	4.6	5.1	4.2	5.0	35
3.5	3.9	3.3	3.1	3.3	3.5	3.6	3.9	4.0	3.5	3.7	2.6	3.3	2.9	3.1	3.3	4.4	4.8	36
4.1	3.6	3.9	4.6	3.9	4.0	4.8	4.2	5.2	4.0	4.1	3.1	2.0	3.7	4.3	4.4	5.5	6.3	37
1.3	4.5	2.5	4.5	3.1	3.1	6.0	3.0	1.5	2.2	**1.6**	4.8	5.0	6.8	7.7	8.8	8.8	9.8	38
4.5	3.5	4.7	4.7	3.7	3.5	4.1	3.9	3.2	3.9	4.3	3.9	4.1	3.7	4.0	4.6	5.5	6.2	39
3.7	12.8	3.8	3.6	3.8	3.6	3.7	4.7	5.4	5.1	4.5	2.0	5.0	5.2	6.0	4.5	6.5		40
1.3	3.9	4.6	4.5	5.6	3.9	5.0	4.2	5.3	5.3	4.2	4.2	4.9	4.4	5.3	5.7	6.1	6.1	41
3.5	2.2	2.2	2.2	2.3	3.0	3.0	2.9	2.8	4.2	1.0	1.1	3.3	3.6	5.2	4.1	11.1	5.6	42
4.4	3.7	3.6	3.5	3.9	3.5	4.2	4.1	5.5	3.7	3.4	3.1	3.4	3.6	4.5	4.2	5.7	3.2	43
4.0	4.5	4.2	5.1	4.4	4.8	3.9	6.7	5.1	2.9	4.5	4.2	5.0	4.1	4.7	5.7	7.0	7.0	44
3.2	4.3	3.7	2.6	3.8	5.3	3.3	3.5	3.5	4.4	2.6	4.4	3.0	2.5	6.7	5.3	5.5	5.5	45
3.0	1.6	1.0	2.2	2.6	2.5	2.9	2.9	0.5	1.0	2.0	1.6	2.8	1.4	2.7	3.8	5.0	3.7	46
3.1	4.1	2.0	2.5	4.3	2.9	2.8	2.9	3.9	4.5	3.9	**6.3**	5.2	0.9	5.7	4.3	6.8	7.4	47
5.8	4.3	5.5	8.0	6.2	5.9	5.9	5.6	7.4	5.7	6.7	7.3	6.0	5.4	7.2	6.3	13.5	6.7	48
2.0	2.6	2.3	2.4	3.3	3.5	8.2	7.0	1.2	0.9	3.5	0.6	4.1	3.7	10.7	8.3	15.7	11.8	49
				4.8	4.5										8.7	11.2		50
6.8	3.4	6.9	3.8	3.9	4.1	3.7	7.1	5.9	6.4	5.6	6.0	4.5	3.6	4.9	6.7	5.1		51
2.8	3.9	3.5	3.3	2.9	3.6	3.6	3.6	1.8	3.9	3.6	3.8	3.6	2.8	3.1	4.4	5.6	5.1	52
10.0	10.0	14.2	18.3	10.0	10.0	26.7	11.0	11.1	12.6	14.9	17.4	16.6	18.9	19.6	13.8	10.7		53
4.2	3.3	1.8	8.4	0.8	9.2	3.1	5.2	3.4	6.8	6.1	**1.6**	14.9	11.4	9.2	12.6	17.1	14.5	54
15.0	8.3	16.7	12.5	12.5	15.0	23.3	18.3	13.1	12.9	7.7	16.9	12.5	13.2	12.1	14.6	23.1		55
4.4	1.2	6.1	1.3	2.8			7.3	4.0	10.8	4.8	11.8	4.8	8.4	13.3	11.3	16.6		56
3.6	2.2	4.0	4.0	3.1	2.3	6.4	3.3	6.3		4.8	4.4	4.5	3.7	**2.9**	7.6	12.5	7.0	57
5.0	5.0	4.8	4.8	4.8	3.3	1.4	4.0	6.9	5.5	7.3	3.6	5.7	7.2	5.7	6.1	7.5	19.9	58
										6.0	6.2	8.1	8.9	11.1	17.2			59
		12.9	27.1		15.0		17.2	10.1	11.3	11.0	13.0	**7.8**	16.7	4.5	12.8	5.0		60
3.2	3.0	3.0	3.1	3.2	3.2	3.3	3.3	3.1	2.5	2.8	2.3	2.5	3.0	3.7	4.2	4.2	5.0	

for 1878, 1879, and 1880, signify percentage of loss.

Number and denominations of national-bank notes issued and redeemed, and the number of each denomination outstanding, on November 1 in each year, from 1869 to 1881.

	Ones.	Twos.	Fives.	Tens.	Twenties.	Fifties.	One hundreds.	Five hundreds.	One thousands.
1869.									
Issued	9,589,160	3,209,388	23,676,760	8,094,645	2,269,764	363,523	274,790	13,668	4,769
Redeemed	904,013	232,224	985,940	272,495	71,655	22,859	25,968	2,585	2,415
Outstanding	8,685,147	2,977,164	22,690,820	7,821,150	2,198,109	334,664	248,831	11,083	2,354
1870.									
Issued	10,729,327	3,590,157	24,636,720	8,413,244	2,370,056	378,482	284,460	13,926	4,779
Redeemed	2,568,703	667,733	1,737,983	484,135	129,185	47,845	43,599	3,952	3,263
Outstanding	8,160,624	2,922,424	22,898,737	7,929,109	2,240,871	330,637	240,861	9,974	1,516
1871.									
Issued	12,537,657	4,195,791	28,174,940	9,728,375	2,779,302	433,426	321,103	14,642	4,843
Redeemed	5,276,057	1,493,326	3,276,374	933,445	245,361	82,972	76,287	6,017	4,005
Outstanding	7,261,600	2,702,465	24,898,566	8,794,930	2,534,031	350,454	244,876	8,625	838
1872.									
Issued	14,297,360	4,782,628	31,933,348	11,253,452	3,225,688	407,199	367,797	15,621	4,933
Redeemed	7,919,389	2,408,389	5,960,667	1,699,702	438,852	126,180	110,989	7,867	4,315
Outstanding	6,377,971	2,374,239	25,972,681	9,553,750	2,786,836	371,019	256,808	7,754	618
1873.									
Issued	15,524,189	5,195,111	34,894,456	12,560,399	3,608,219	559,722	416,590	16,496	5,148
Redeemed	9,891,606	3,120,723	9,141,963	2,573,070	653,071	168,976	144,057	9,658	4,530
Outstanding	5,632,583	2,074,388	25,752,493	9,987,329	2,955,148	390,746	272,533	6,838	618
1874.									
Issued	16,548,259	5,539,113	39,243,136	13,337,076	3,962,109	666,950	492,482	17,344	5,240
Redeemed	11,143,606	3,755,019	13,041,605	3,912,707	971,608	231,556	196,572	11,676	4,683
Outstanding	5,404,653	1,784,094	26,201,531	9,424,369	2,990,501	435,394	295,910	5,668	557
1875.									
Issued	18,046,176	6,039,752	47,055,184	17,410,507	5,296,064	884,165	645,838	18,476	5,530
Redeemed	14,092,126	4,816,623	24,926,771	7,608,532	2,004,464	381,037	299,428	14,471	5,048
Outstanding	3,954,050	1,223,129	22,128,413	9,801,975	3,291,600	503,128	346,418	4,005	482
1876.									
Issued	18,849,264	6,307,448	51,783,528	20,008,652	6,086,492	985,615	710,900	18,721	5,539
Redeemed	15,556,708	5,324,546	32,382,056	10,369,214	2,852,246	515,784	395,785	16,217	5,272
Outstanding	3,292,556	982,902	19,401,472	9,639,438	3,234,246	469,831	315,115	2,504	267
1877.									
Issued	20,616,024	6,896,968	56,816,848	22,266,064	6,776,253	1,079,781	767,317	20,022	5,668
Redeemed	16,815,568	5,755,526	38,115,868	12,434,779	3,503,528	634,679	479,317	17,615	5,411
Outstanding	3,800,456	1,141,442	18,700,980	9,831,285	3,272,725	445,102	288,000	2,407	257
1878.									
Issued	22,478,415	7,517,765	61,191,288	24,157,203	7,344,167	1,147,578	812,903	20,210	6,204
Redeemed	18,194,196	6,226,692	42,683,433	13,859,149	3,933,178	728,222	541,859	18,895	5,900
Outstanding	4,284,219	1,291,073	18,507,855	10,298,144	3,410,989	419,356	271,044	1,315	304
1879.									
Issued	23,167,677	7,747,519	65,578,440	25,904,223	7,869,95?	1,211,761	850,720	20,570	6,340
Redeemed	19,600,477	6,701,270	45,996,076	14,930,599	4,237,343	785,263	581,604	19,287	6,057
Outstanding	3,567,200	1,046,249	19,582,364	10,973,624	3,632,608	426,498	269,116	1,283	283
1880.									
Issued	23,167,677	7,747,519	69,131,076	27,203,168	8,266,398	1,253,865	879,490	20,763	6,303
Redeemed	20,875,215	7,143,889	49,149,824	15,821,110	4,484,820	825,499	610,601	19,484	6,124
Outstanding	2,292,462	603,630	19,982,152	11,382,058	3,781,578	428,366	268,889	1,279	239
1881.									
Issued	23,167,677	7,747,519	73,612,504	29,477,519	8,940,817	1,357,574	959,712	21,959	7,144
Redeemed	21,838,565	7,486,434	53,516,488	17,346,635	4,884,992	891,800	660,202	20,493	6,943
Outstanding	1,329,112	261,085	20,096,016	12,130,884	4,055,825	465,684	299,510	1,464	201

Table showing by States the amount of national-bank circulation issued, the amount of legal-tender notes deposited in the United States Treasury to retire national-bank circulation, from June 20, 1874, to November 1, 1881, and amount remaining on deposit at latter date.

States and Territories.	National-bank notes issued since June 20, 1874.	Legal-tender notes deposited to retire national-bank circulation since June 20, 1874.			Legal-tender notes on deposit with the U.S. Treasurer on Nov. 1, 1881.
		For redemption of notes of liquidating banks.	To retire circulation under act of June 20, 1874.	Total deposits.	
Maine	$1, 506, 180	$317, 000	$764, 700	$1, 081, 700	$263, 624
New Hampshire	643, 165	72, 997	55, 800	128, 797	25, 686
Vermont	2, 000, 360	351, 097	1, 753, 040	2, 104, 137	746, 936
Massachusetts	24, 510, 990	234, 800	9, 680, 700	9, 915, 500	1, 506, 080
Rhode Island	3, 396, 600	32, 350	1, 409, 885	1, 442, 235	354, 908
Connecticut	4, 412, 970	65, 350	3, 731, 030	3, 796, 380	1, 420, 476
New York	28, 141, 215	2, 651, 693	30, 520, 580	33, 172, 273	7, 170, 820
New Jersey	2, 899, 335	467, 603	2, 563, 137	3, 030, 740	1, 097, 827
Pennsylvania	16, 383, 230	1, 311, 226	12, 145, 871	13, 457, 097	5, 108, 018
Delaware	277, 275				
Maryland	2, 002, 310	166, 600	1, 718, 380	1, 884, 980	75, 174
District of Columbia	457, 000	432, 664	530, 060	962, 724	97, 366
Virginia	1, 101, 800	919, 360	1, 036, 010	1, 955, 379	265, 166
West Virginia	226, 810	731, 060	386, 685	1, 117, 745	140, 455
North Carolina	1, 235, 660	128, 200	1, 147, 585	1, 275, 785	209, 991
South Carolina	180, 700		1, 187, 380	1, 187, 380	161, 443
Georgia	542, 830	330, 925	437, 675	768, 600	98, 032
Florida	72, 000				
Alabama	207, 000	90, 000	179, 100	269, 100	86, 826
Mississippi					221
Louisiana	1, 623, 110	656, 413	2, 099, 250	2, 755, 663	59, 799
Texas	489, 600	61, 290	229, 340	290, 630	42, 240
Arkansas	171, 000		171, 000	171, 000	8, 998
Kentucky	4, 621, 380	629, 867	2, 175, 833	2, 805, 700	832, 637
Tennessee	848, 770	370, 401	551, 859	922, 260	146, 057
Missouri	1, 643, 360	1, 043, 450	3, 862, 135	4, 905, 585	647, 353
Ohio	5, 683, 560	1, 704, 597	4, 651, 034	6, 355, 631	1, 979, 636
Indiana	3, 900, 850	1, 414, 597	7, 859, 083	9, 273, 680	2, 757, 933
Illinois	3, 460, 925	1, 884, 334	7, 706, 046	9, 590, 380	1, 711, 005
Michigan	2, 454, 310	536, 800	3, 237, 475	3, 774, 275	1, 297, 792
Wisconsin	1, 253, 030	680, 860	1, 259, 580	1, 940, 449	527, 790
Iowa	1, 980, 700	858, 669	1, 760, 615	2, 619, 284	468, 543
Minnesota	1, 165, 400	554, 495	1, 883, 445	2, 437, 940	762, 740
Kansas	269, 080	781, 721	316, 550	1, 098, 271	257, 496
Nebraska	266, 400	45, 000	449, 980	494, 980	216, 506
Nevada	36, 000				1, 718
Colorado	721, 800	147, 225	149, 400	296, 625	16, 916
Utah	134, 900	161, 191	196, 800	357, 991	12, 608
Montana	255, 600	111, 700	81, 000	192, 700	56, 145
Wyoming	30, 600				
New Mexico	90, 000				
Washington	225, 000		90, 000	90, 000	69, 635
Dakota	202, 500				
California	912, 600				
Legal-tender notes deposited prior to June 20, 1874, and remaining on deposit at that date				3, 813, 675	
Totals	122, 727, 905	19, 945, 544	107, 978, 052	131, 737, 271	30, 702, 596

Statement of the monthly increase and decrease of national-bank circulation, from November 1, 1878, to October 31, 1881, to which is added the preceding yearly increase since January 14, 1875.

Months.	National-bank circulation.		Increase.	Decrease.
	Issued.	Retired.		
1878.				
November	$1,219,720	$189,219	$1,030,501	
December	801,830	270,633	531,197	
1879.				
January	1,075,510	287,475	788,035	
February	2,078,190	424,428	1,653,762	
March	2,003,460	919,814	1,083,646	
April	2,957,650	478,746	2,478,904	
May	1,290,920	893,239	397,681	
June	1,428,480	1,147,294	281,186	
July	955,430	674,991	280,439	
August	1,628,130	732,819	895,311	
September	3,912,120	427,017	3,485,103	
October	3,582,050	594,722	2,987,328	
November	3,109,350	194,920	2,914,430	
December	2,576,580	229,322	2,347,258	
1880.				
January	1,603,875	249,887	1,353,988	
February	703,490	540,569	162,921	
March	1,143,450	365,210	778,240	
April	1,316,886	649,987	666,893	
May	626,100	343,017	283,083	
June	463,610	1,134,326		$670,716
July	658,950	950,055		291,105
August	506,590	567,844		61,254
September	196,040	412,645		216,605
October	497,300	555,271		57,971
November	412,500	359,406	53,094	
December	1,195,650	635,483	560,167	
1881.				
January	626,630	366,645	259,985	
February	577,640	1,023,785		446,145
March	4,820,620	1,174,376	3,646,244	
April	7,292,630	2,228,435	5,064,195	
May	3,342,070	1,724,319	1,617,751	
June	3,199,520	2,264,377	935,143	
July	3,027,820	745,882	2,281,938	
August	2,036,660	1,319,587	717,073	
September	1,554,700	673,821	880,879	
October	2,893,190	1,189,143	1,704,047	
Totals	67,315,335	26,938,709	42,120,422	1,743,796
From January 14, 1875, to October 31, 1875	10,986,675	14,570,305		3,583,630
From November 1, 1875, to October 31, 1876	7,093,680	27,506,981		20,413,301
From November 1, 1876, to October 31, 1877	16,306,630	18,265,331		1,959,301
From November 1, 1877, to October 31, 1878	16,291,685	10,986,116	5,305,569	
	117,993,405	98,267,442	47,425,991	27,700,028
Circulation surrendered to this office and retired		12,205,755		
Grand totals	117,993,405	110,473,197	47,425,991	27,700,028

Clearings and balances of the banks of New York City for the weeks ending at the dates given.

Week ending—	Clearings.	Balances.
Sept. 6, 1873	$553,727,902 28	$22,328,640 26
Sept. 13, 1873	548,295,978 73	22,855,801 28
Sept. 20, 1873	654,392,916 42	23,131,846 63
Sept. 27, 1873	302,201,999 44	22,883,461 74
Oct. 4, 1873	318,257,024 83	18,008,688 12
Oct. 11, 1873	329,152,694 92	15,642,330 07
Oct. 18, 1873	352,555,457 62	17,780,057 56
Oct. 25, 1873	307,267,809 59	13,374,437 98
Nov. 1, 1873	316,235,255 26	15,957,165 33
Nov. 8, 1873	330,422,376 35	14,831,208 01
Nov. 15, 1873	329,556,276 45	13,361,572 96
Nov. 22, 1873	357,181,656 40	12,424,216 40
Nov. 29, 1873	326,834,705 78	13,831,781 11
Sept. 1, 1877	400,793,928 37	17,195,538 34
Sept. 8, 1877	397,270,385 61	21,276,952 69
Sept. 15, 1877	379,235,603 05	16,226,864 42
Sept. 22, 1877	405,632,278 32	18,062,064 62
Sept. 29, 1877	419,336,185,05	17,638,612 67
Oct. 6, 1877	428,838,637 02	17,969,027 54
Oct. 13, 1877	485,782,249 45	19,466,542 22
Oct. 20, 1877	478,165,840 10	21,282,891 22
Oct. 27, 1877	437,387,453 60	16,555,158 76
Nov. 3, 1877	458,025,653 36	23,219,535 73
Nov. 10, 1877	358,005,167 11	16,400,805 41
Nov. 17, 1877	401,980,936 84	20,952,083 11
Nov. 24, 1877	417,104,418 66	17,367,124 75
Sept. 7, 1878	348,022,456 02	17,551,602 23
Sept. 14, 1878	330,877,791 01	17,037,659 82
Sept. 21, 1878	333,606,506 02	17,080,319 34
Sept. 28, 1878	370,111,767 49	17,596,844 29
Oct. 5, 1878	453,971,364 93	18,225,691 56
Oct. 12, 1878	424,149,900 70	22,636,490 39
Oct. 19, 1878	482,291,920 94	21,414,267 79
Oct. 26, 1878	392,878,293 23	16,507,373 90
Nov. 2, 1878	488,571,553 53	24,886,588 26
Nov. 9, 1878	408,903,425 00	19,531,868 14
Nov. 16, 1878	460,572,737 80	20,918,299 11
Nov. 23, 1878	404,637,742 00	17,061,847 48
Nov. 30, 1878	368,238,659 90	16,450,900 37
Sept. 6, 1879	452,345,265 71	23,606,921 32
Sept. 13, 1879	507,109,348 67	23,279,390 27
Sept. 20, 1879	530,921,306 52	24,859,791 40
Sept. 27, 1879	591,859,560 99	26,691,095 46
Oct. 4, 1879	747,278,535 78	28,371,132 68
Oct. 11, 1879	741,448,440 55	29,463,295 51
Oct. 18, 1879	798,960,746 51	26,950,734 21
Oct. 25, 1879	761,277,728 00	28,333,087 73
Nov. 1, 1879	805,862,857 05	32,796,457 88
Nov. 8, 1879	772,150,134 18	30,021,579 21
Nov. 15, 1879	870,092,059 78	39,899,377 29
Nov. 22, 1879	912,922,768 23	30,443,292 71
Nov. 29, 1879	779,955,847 24	28,364,989 12
Sept. 4, 1880	603,877,203 02	33,414,325 94
Sept. 11, 1880	625,650,183 37	26,812,778 80
Sept. 18, 1880	623,375,655 48	30,733,842 94
Sept. 25, 1880	573,355,801 73	30,070,332 13
Oct. 2, 1880	705,508,706 46	32,827,400 90
Oct. 9, 1880	651,160,020 35	28,586,849 16
Oct. 16, 1880	693,917,360 86	27,875,042 64
Oct. 23, 1880	872,895,695 57	32,910,082 09
Oct. 30, 1880	785,361,621 85	31,018,354 80
Nov. 6, 1880	866,393,048 37	33,236,599 77
Nov. 13, 1880	896,540,451 66	34,579,373 05
Nov. 20, 1880	868,076,513 35	34,404,639 13
Nov. 27, 1880	1,072,680,747 81	32,472,796 33
Sept. 3, 1881	857,413,263 85	37,132,230 86
Sept. 10, 1881	630,907,979 97	28,808,004 38
Sept. 17, 1881	925,116,460 37	36,408,897 13
Sept. 24, 1881	773,491,695 57	29,389,049 08
Oct. 1, 1881	758,155,052 10	26,349,314 58
Oct. 8, 1881	1,154,052,466 33	35,187,686 23
Oct. 15, 1881	975,722,717 38	31,673,440 10
Oct. 22, 1881	953,850,125 23	35,159,491 42
Oct. 29, 1881	881,124,243 74	32,450,957 70
Nov. 5, 1881	1,021,882,159 85	37,173,439 72
Nov. 12, 1881	796,664,256 97	27,635,753 35
Nov. 19, 1881	892,319,707 29	31,043,351 43
Nov. 26, 1881	892,475,563 06	23,882,023 31

Number of State banks, savings banks, trust companies, and private bankers, with their average capital and deposits, and the tax thereon, for the six months ending November 30, 1876.

States and Territories.	No. of banks.	Capital.	Deposits.	Tax. On capital	On deposits	Total.
Maine	66	$177,658	$27,017,950	$403	$5,837	$6,240
New Hampshire	78	151,000	30,937,358	314	12,757	13,071
Vermont	21	302,500	8,123,983	650	4,348	4,998
Massachusetts	168	855,000	163,436,726	1,569	6,546	8,115
Boston	67	3,108,788	84,686,258	4,442	18,732	23,174
Rhode Island	58	3,923,222	52,888,125	8,482	45,724	54,206
Connecticut	112	3,027,892	82,818,889	5,815	50,228	56,043
New England States	570	11,546,060	449,909,289	21,675	144,172	165,847
New York	340	10,850,325	151,986,519	23,044	111,326	134,370
New York City	472	48,518,475	278,634,125	78,635	271,833	350,468
Albany	15	579,500	12,754,543	452	10,177	10,629
New Jersey	67	2,418,120	36,110,777	5,243	28,120	33,363
Pennsylvania	344	12,475,573	41,393,026	29,125	102,767	131,892
Philadelphia	66	2,502,021	47,415,908	5,845	78,369	84,214
Pittsburgh	43	5,137,193	13,937,144	11,863	24,939	36,802
Delaware	10	708,596	1,684,846	1,687	2,000	3,687
Maryland	17	631,885	543,171	1,293	875	2,168
Baltimore	40	4,066,837	24,876,590	8,591	18,217	26,808
District of Columbia	1	20,000	28,452	50	71	121
Washington	11	595,102	3,618,467	412	7,973	8,385
Middle States	1,426	88,503,627	612,983,558	166,240	656,667	822,907
Virginia	77	3,563,878	7,188,428	8,723	16,925	25,648
West Virginia	25	1,426,858	3,939,744	3,553	9,849	13,402
North Carolina	15	576,662	885,795	1,442	2,214	3,656
South Carolina	18	1,006,452	1,008,034	2,516	2,341	4,857
Georgia	69	4,823,597	3,383,964	12,059	8,264	20,323
Florida	3	39,000	240,821	97	602	699
Alabama	18	1,095,900	1,501,305	2,650	3,753	6,403
Mississippi	29	1,251,577	1,196,752	2,423	2,992	5,415
Louisiana	2	54,000	40,508	135	101	236
New Orleans	24	3,611,584	6,290,194	9,029	11,796	20,825
Texas	98	3,400,041	4,302,285	7,559	10,756	18,315
Arkansas	13	225,167	264,300	561	661	1,222
Kentucky	72	7,488,271	6,086,657	18,132	15,216	33,348
Louisville	18	5,592,382	5,976,005	13,838	14,940	28,778
Tennessee	31	1,723,291	2,775,023	4,172	6,938	11,110
Southern States	512	35,878,660	45,079,815	86,889	107,348	194,237
Ohio	262	6,327,007	16,069,106	14,181	38,794	52,975
Cincinnati	21	1,963,150	8,955,100	3,454	20,312	23,766
Cleveland	10	802,819	11,859,737	1,863	16,446	18,309
Indiana	149	6,033,563	10,533,776	12,847	22,287	35,134
Illinois	315	5,452,244	17,518,220	12,205	41,832	54,037
Chicago	41	4,918,350	14,913,591	9,538	20,172	29,710
Michigan	140	2,597,657	4,935,755	6,391	12,339	18,730
Detroit	14	1,172,902	6,148,749	2,292	15,372	17,664
Wisconsin	87	1,328,035	3,645,026	2,927	9,112	12,039
Milwaukee	12	677,522	6,236,008	1,415	15,590	17,005
Iowa	266	4,832,196	8,738,362	11,691	21,846	33,537
Minnesota	68	1,158,438	2,539,637	2,732	6,306	9,038
Missouri	165	3,467,093	9,921,900	7,597	24,805	32,402
Saint Louis	54	7,928,799	24,723,031	18,496	60,801	79,297
Kansas	109	1,638,143	2,800,868	3,887	7,002	10,889
Nebraska	35	407,354	1,250,342	1,011	3,126	4,137
Western States	1,748	50,705,272	150,780,217	112,527	336,142	448,669
Oregon	7	546,985	1,209,830	1,266	3,024	4,290
California	84	9,917,377	16,928,318	24,739	35,258	59,997
San Francisco	49	23,728,485	96,733,616	57,129	166,926	224,055
Colorado	29	549,540	1,007,576	1,374	2,519	3,893
Nevada	17	290,438	1,690,357	749	4,226	4,975
Utah	6	151,000	588,283	377	1,471	1,848
New Mexico	3	2,000	33,743	5	84	89
Wyoming	3	38,372	54,368	96	136	232
Idaho	3	57,417	25,990	143	65	208
Dakota	7	24,000	137,911	65	345	405
Montana	6	97,431	69,863	244	175	419
Washington	4	222,947	272,450	557	681	1,238
Arizona	1	8,333	4,167	21	10	31
Pacific States and Territories	219	35,643,325	118,756,472	86,760	214,920	301,680
Grand totals	4,475	222,276,944	1,377,518,351	474,091	1,459,249	1,933,340

Number of State banks, savings banks, trust companies, and private bankers, with their average capital and deposits, and the tax thereon, for the six months ending May 31, 1877.

State and Territories.	No. of banks.	Capital.	Deposits.	Tax. On capital.	Tax. On deposits.	Tax. Total.
Maine	66	$173,905	$26,499,218	$393	$4,412	$4,805
New Hampshire	72	52,333	30,896,234	124	6,900	7,024
Vermont	21	335,0?0	8,107,445	714	4,198	4,912
Massachusetts	167	819,333	162,477,183	1,473	6,514	7,987
Boston	64	3,127,387	88,716,005	3,516	18,490	22,006
Rhode Island	58	3,894,673	53,631,370	8,340	45,213	53,553
Connecticut	109	2,809,642	82,893,262	5,593	47,952	53,545
New England States	**557**	**11,272,273**	**452,620,717**	**20,153**	**133,679**	**153,832**
New York	336	11,061,720	148,889,703	22,840	106,653	129,493
New York City	466	45,785,796	271,948,412	69,121	258,215	327,336
Albany	14	637,000	12,529,737	713	9,362	10,075
New Jersey	65	2,170,838	35,457,184	4,482	26,330	30,812
Pennsylvania	346	12,216,780	39,203,675	28,753	97,282	126,035
Philadelphia	60	2,091,742	31,884,459	4,798	68,671	73,469
Pittsburgh	41	5,018,826	14,616,683	11,405	24,481	35,886
Delaware	10	717,411	1,780,850	1,709	2,116	3,825
Maryland	15	623,378	566,984	1,196	899	2,095
Baltimore	40	4,104,003	25,023,652	8,709	18,051	26,760
District of Columbia	1	5,917	7,008	15	18	33
Washington	10	595,350	3,657,830	362	8,144	8,506
Middle States	**1,404**	**85,028,770**	**585,568,186**	**154,103**	**620,222**	**774,325**
Virginia	78	3,407,110	6,809,858	8,182	16,138	24,320
West Virginia	24	1,455,900	3,917,534	3,632	9,794	13,426
North Carolina	14	574,451	872,287	1,436	2,181	3,617
South Carolina	19	1,003,105	1,095,859	2,508	2,597	5,105
Georgia	66	4,392,147	4,363,519	10,980	10,718	21,698
Florida	5	47,000	271,057	92	678	770
Alabama	20	1,034,733	1,747,031	2,458	4,368	6,826
Mississippi	28	1,264,396	1,413,033	2,274	3,532	5,806
Louisiana	2	54,000	49,915	135	125	260
New Orleans	29	3,558,192	7,310,099	8,640	14,303	22,943
Texas	107	3,494,002	4,891,428	8,235	12,228	20,463
Arkansas	15	258,333	376,619	558	942	1,500
Kentucky	73	7,279,957	6,626,535	17,478	16,566	34,044
Louisville	17	5,404,361	6,041,033	13,373	15,103	28,476
Tennessee	33	1,768,147	3,019,790	3,983	7,549	11,532
Southern States	**524**	**34,995,834**	**48,805,597**	**83,964**	**116,822**	**200,786**
Ohio	257	6,334,477	16,640,560	14,051	40,293	54,344
Cincinnati	23	2,008,549	9,016,478	3,436	20,231	23,667
Cleveland	9	836,290	12,767,959	1,653	17,940	19,593
Indiana	146	5,626,955	11,128,830	13,051	23,336	36,387
Illinois	319	5,483,644	17,299,602	12,270	41,303	53,573
Chicago	42	4,836,153	15,136,791	9,568	23,426	32,994
Michigan	145	2,605,763	4,914,596	6,367	12,286	18,653
Detroit	18	1,240,932	5,870,285	2,250	14,676	16,926
Wisconsin	90	1,389,348	3,765,813	3,190	9,414	12,604
Milwaukee	12	672,065	6,328,969	1,406	15,822	17,228
Iowa	279	5,178,643	8,730,477	12,545	21,661	34,206
Minnesota	71	1,168,965	2,508,685	2,757	6,135	8,892
Missouri	180	3,806,220	11,223,423	8,418	28,058	36,506
Saint Louis	46	7,530,583	22,691,281	16,947	56,281	73,228
Kansas	114	1,725,224	3,116,289	4,039	7,791	11,830
Nebraska	39	465,664	1,184,932	1,114	2,962	4,076
Western States	**1,790**	**50,909,484**	**152,325,060**	**113,092**	**341,615**	**454,707**
Oregon	8	610,724	1,319,112	1,418	3,373	4,791
California	91	12,110,922	41,522,335	30,113	68,587	98,700
San Francisco	38	26,902,567	65,865,076	61,308	123,034	184,342
Colorado	30	588,858	971,936	1,472	2,430	3,902
Nevada	19	417,039	1,545,409	1,043	3,864	4,907
Utah	8	179,521	587,894	449	1,470	1,919
New Mexico	4	5,667	36,342	14	91	105
Wyoming	4	55,489	98,987	139	247	386
Idaho	3	56,507	16,182	141	40	181
Dakota	8	34,167	140,321	85	351	436
Montana	8	103,637	93,800	258	234	492
Washington	4	222,312	317,696	556	794	1,350
Arizona	1	10,000	5,000	25	13	38
Pacific States and Territories	**226**	**41,296,810**	**112,550,090**	**97,021**	**204,528**	**301,549**
Grand totals	**4,501**	**223,503,171**	**1,351,867,650**	**468,333**	**1,416,866**	**1,885,199**

Number of State banks, savings banks, trust companies, and private bankers, with their average capital and deposits, and the tax thereon, for the six months ending May 31, 1878.

States and Territories.	No. of banks.	Capital.	Deposits.	Tax. On capital.	On deposits.	Total.
Maine	69	$92,108	$28,957,428	$188 98	$1,253 21	$1,442 19
New Hampshire	71	61,000	28,309,624	152 50	4,270 50	4,423 00
Vermont	21	344,167	8,140,383	829 33	4,096 57	4,925 90
Massachusetts	170	834,666	157,816,812	1,429 33	5,085 19	6,514 52
Boston	59	3,061,397	70,746,941	3,826 47	17,694 04	21,520 51
Rhode Island	58	3,883,267	50,028,328	8,188 16	39,301 63	47,489 79
Connecticut	107	2,840,000	78,858,210	5,604 82	31,271 53	36,876 35
New England States	555	11,116,605	422,857,726	20,219 59	102,972 67	123,192 26
New York	328	10,427,448	148,258,669	20,290 36	100,972 62	121,262 98
New York City	443	40,700,289	247,964,314	56,276 58	214,356 85	270,633 43
Albany	14	642,000	12,153,189	706 47	4,039 36	4,745 83
New Jersey	59	1,741,071	19,326,498	3,536 29	14,587 16	18,123 45
Pennsylvania	313	10,807,358	29,979,015	25,172 82	74,851 74	100,024 56
Philadelphia	59	2,113,756	42,552,729	4,648 68	61,604 26	66,252 94
Pittsburgh	37	4,657,547	13,727,252	10,284 93	22,599 96	32,884 89
Delaware	9	712,578	1,798,521	1,667 97	2,031 54	3,699 51
Maryland	13	627,513	559,703	962 01	913 51	1,875 52
Baltimore	41	4,162,516	24,604,030	8,795 49	15,740 49	24,535 98
Washington	10	496,742	3,151,613	513 18	6,469 94	6,983 12
Middle States	1,326	77,088,818	544,075,533	132,854 78	518,167 43	651,022 21
Virginia	77	3,281,667	6,499,580	7,753 69	15,421 29	23,174 98
West Virginia	22	1,496,792	3,927,737	3,668 37	9,819 28	13,487 65
North Carolina	13	588,290	978,018	1,470 72	2,445 03	3,915 75
South Carolina	18	911,523	1,004,808	2,278 77	2,428 28	4,707 05
Georgia	67	4,317,817	3,948,488	10,711 40	9,190 49	19,901 89
Florida	6	89,483	233,405	223 70	583 48	807 18
Alabama	22	993,276	1,813,605	2,420 69	4,533 93	6,954 62
Mississippi	32	1,289,573	1,732,597	2,535 64	4,331 42	6,867 06
Louisiana	3	116,000	48,110	177 50	120 28	297 78
New Orleans	21	4,473,905	7,994,123	10,726 42	15,184 95	25,911 37
Texas	102	3,707,057	4,626,420	8,744 54	11,565 63	20,310 17
Arkansas	15	225,576	298,605	514 24	746 48	1,260 72
Kentucky	74	7,010,103	6,287,262	16,656 29	15,718 26	32,374 55
Louisville	17	5,288,296	5,650,057	12,971 68	14,125 04	27,096 72
Tennessee	31	1,769,671	2,731,199	4,233 85	6,828 00	11,061 85
Southern States	520	35,559,029	47,774,074	85,087 50	113,041 84	198,129 34
Ohio	255	6,042,364	15,952,238	12,959 68	38,776 39	51,736 07
Cincinnati	21	2,622,369	7,361,629	3,388 23	17,295 38	20,683 61
Cleveland	9	898,623	12,244,967	1,590 98	17,403 31	18,994 20
Indiana	150	5,081,175	10,224,039	11,724 36	21,838 78	33,563 14
Illinois	319	4,509,738	12,472,557	10,153 55	29,981 71	40,135 26
Chicago	31	3,612,908	6,892,759	4,892 45	17,043 45	21,935 90
Michigan	153	2,636,767	4,737,722	6,454 25	11,844 11	18,298 36
Detroit	15	1,108,368	5,179,609	1,800 91	11,038 32	12,839 23
Wisconsin	89	1,386,425	3,714,069	3,026 20	9,284 96	12,311 16
Milwaukee	11	729,853	5,747,509	1,669 66	14,368 72	16,038 38
Iowa	287	5,255,013	8,224,785	12,711 94	20,377 82	33,089 76
Minnesota	77	1,510,502	3,233,693	3,662 47	7,950 50	11,612 97
Missouri	176	4,124,269	10,184,792	9,811 03	25,461 50	35,272 53
Saint Louis	32	6,576,033	16,387,002	14,540 48	40,967 45	55,507 93
Kansas	109	1,472,344	2,598,746	3,441 85	6,496 55	9,938 40
Nebraska	48	503,595	1,189,250	1,203 76	2,972 96	4,176 72
Western States	1,782	47,470,286	126,284,766	103,031 80	293,101 91	396,133 71
Oregon	10	643,225	1,489,547	1,499 49	3,602 45	5,101 94
California	84	9,943,129	17,422,175	24,733 99	37,946 00	62,679 49
San Francisco	33	21,787,036	78,070,620	46,256 46	132,601 59	178,858 05
Colorado	28	526,190	934,915	1,315 46	2,336 38	3,651 84
Nevada	18	412,268	1,914,583	1,030 66	4,786 37	5,817 03
Utah	8	190,000	714,555	475 00	1,786 37	2,261 37
New Mexico	4	5,000	61,180	12 50	152 95	165 45
Wyoming	3	82,794	148,682	198 69	371 70	570 39
Idaho	2	54,000	16,358	135 00	40 88	175 88
Dakota	12	78,039	277,927	195 10	604 80	889 90
Montana	8	133,413	188,918	333 53	472 28	805 81
Washington	3	208,000	537,450	520 00	1,343 62	1,863 62
Arizona	4	85,000	25,885	212 50	64 70	277 20
Pacific States and Territories	217	34,148,094	101,802,804	76,918 38	186,200 09	263,118 47
Grand totals	4,400	205,382,832	1,242,794,903	418,112 05	1,213,483 94	1,631,595 99

Number of State banks, savings banks, trust companies, and private bankers, with their average capital and deposits, and the tax thereon, for the six months ending May 31, 1879.

States and Territories.	No. of banks.	Capital.	Deposits.	On capital.	On deposits.	Total.
				Tax.		
Maine	66	$41,209	$22,801,402	$65 52	$645 16	$710 68
New Hampshire	71	61,000	26,766,055	152 50	2,041 34	2,193 84
Vermont	22	351,200	7,890,150	819 20	3,436 90	4,256 10
Massachusetts	164	810,000	148,785,115	1,358 70	5,149 48	6,508 18
Boston	57	3,357,412	61,086,908	3,573 93	17,432 42	21,006 35
Rhode Island	53	3,565,961	42,614,408	7,059 33	23,961 69	31,021 02
Connecticut	103	2,640,000	74,227,500	4,862 83	19,758 50	24,621 33
New England States	536	10,826,782	384,171,538	17,892 01	72,425 49	90,317 50
New York	317	9,339,629	142,418,399	16,790 91	75,556 01	92,346 92
New York City	489	43,027,777	250,534,151	59,323 50	222,203 75	281,527 25
Albany	12	641,000	12,744,636	706 62	3,619 02	4,325 64
New Jersey	55	1,554,540	18,073,791	2,725 00	9,078 48	11,803 48
Pennsylvania	280	9,328,171	23,888,582	21,540 22	59,110 99	80,651 21
Philadelphia	59	1,952,718	43,417,806	4,075 69	60,591 74	64,667 43
Pittsburgh	33	4,166,965	12,614,729	9,407 67	17,249 02	26,656 69
Delaware	8	640,412	1,745,570	1,545 05	1,691 70	3,236 75
Maryland	12	570,723	630,081	718 99	1,119 07	1,838 06
Baltimore	38	3,871,880	23,801,161	8,051 40	11,617 84	19,669 24
Washington	7	377,550	2,571,645	137 50	5,730 27	5,867 77
Middle States	1,280	75,771,374	532,560,551	125,022 55	467,567 80	592,590 44
Virginia	75	3,226,654	6,769,857	7,258 98	16,098 18	23,357 16
West Virginia	21	1,478,645	3,797,525	3,201 90	9,493 76	12,785 66
North Carolina	12	442,377	833,385	1,105 95	2,083 43	3,189 38
South Carolina	14	720,633	806,592	1,497 83	2,016 43	3,514 26
Georgia	60	3,957,486	4,545,928	9,644 67	10,315 17	19,959 84
Florida	6	81,783	215,970	204 45	539 92	744 37
Alabama	24	1,060,999	1,908,807	2,586 65	4,771 92	7,358 57
Mississippi	29	1,226,268	1,682,166	2,375 15	4,205 25	6,580 40
Louisiana	3	111,450	59,575	166 12	148 93	315 05
New Orleans	10	3,988,198	6,316,557	8,037 57	13,602 94	21,640 51
Texas	103	3,620,868	5,503,345	8,215 82	13,758 32	21,974 14
Arkansas	14	207,903	336,328	352 60	840 82	1,193 42
Kentucky	68	6,454,156	6,134,643	15,010 92	15,336 37	30,847 29
Louisville	16	5,585,957	5,271,471	12,706 05	13,178 64	25,884 69
Tennessee	30	1,758,029	2,837,835	3,365 55	7,094 48	10,460 03
Southern States	494	33,921,406	47,019,984	75,820 21	113,484 56	189,304 77
Ohio	239	5,968,718	15,602,726	12,562 33	37,890 15	50,452 48
Cincinnati	16	1,707,174	4,591,510	2,777 02	11,478 76	14,255 78
Cleveland	10	962,317	12,663,332	1,439 88	15,102 54	16,542 42
Indiana	149	1,836,292	10,541,861	10,777 33	23,132 38	33,909 71
Illinois	317	4,634,349	12,394,243	8,655 23	29,216 94	37,872 17
Chicago	33	3,984,828	7,836,766	4,045 84	19,574 49	23,620 33
Michigan	146	2,327,238	5,183,535	5,511 93	12,958 57	18,470 50
Detroit	16	1,116,775	5,848,086	1,869 26	12,808 17	14,677 43
Wisconsin	92	1,105,619	3,649,814	3,152 14	9,124 45	12,276 59
Milwaukee	10	743,541	5,765,170	1,772 20	14,412 91	16,185 11
Iowa	290	5,081,219	9,291,284	11,920 27	23,055 51	34,975 78
Minnesota	82	1,670,319	3,526,000	4,077 73	8,237 51	12,315 24
Missouri	171	4,653,300	10,637,055	8,988 61	26,594 39	35,583 00
Saint Louis	28	6,335,969	16,543,846	12,324 13	41,359 89	53,684 02
Kansas	126	1,369,532	3,175,805	3,183 11	7,939 29	11,122 40
Nebraska	46	444,319	1,250,437	1,053 30	3,125 92	4,179 22
Western States	1,771	46,638,539	128,502,460	94,110 31	296,011 87	390,122 18
Oregon	12	1,078,739	1,353,172	2,573 01	3,254 83	5,827 84
California	87	10,337,967	16,707,656	25,482 40	36,277 48	61,759 88
San Francisco	28	21,369,142	64,312,295	40,606 29	110,794 98	151,401 27
Colorado	32	635,180	1,724,854	1,587 84	4,312 04	5,899 88
Nevada	19	368,737	1,688,318	921 83	4,220 76	5,142 59
Utah	10	230,000	857,933	575 00	2,144 79	2,719 79
New Mexico	5	5,000	86,251	12 50	215 62	228 12
Wyoming	4	106,411	191,290	266 03	478 22	744 25
Idaho	3	6,083	45,304	15 20	113 25	128 45
Dakota	12	103,093	200,995	254 81	502 46	757 27
Montana	8	151,204	284,136	385 51	710 31	1,095 82
Washington	4	207,000	339,991	517 50	849 96	1,367 46
Arizona	7	81,827	76,107	201 56	190 24	391 80
Pacific States and Territories	231	34,683,383	87,868,302	73,402 48	164,064 04	237,467 42
Grand totals	4,312	201,241,484	1,180,122,835	386,247 56	1,113,554 75	1,499,802 31

Number of State banks, savings banks, trust companies, and private bankers, with their average capital and deposits, and the tax thereon, for the six months ending May 31, 1880.

States and Territories.	No. of banks.	Capital.	Deposits.	Tax.		
				On capital.	On deposits.	Total.
Maine	64	$47,319	$21,721,964	$97 52	$472 44	$569 96
New Hampshire	71	51,000	28,301,549	114 49	1,082 04	1,196 53
Vermont	22	353,700	8,531,140	791 79	4,088 58	4,880 37
Massachusetts	161	510,000	144,268,273	715 96	4,664 95	5,380 91
Boston	57	5,126,099	64,553,706	6,438 60	19,426 34	25,864 94
Rhode Island	56	3,308,504	43,134,708	6,677 32	16,977 36	23,654 68
Connecticut	105	2,616,896	78,457,961	5,860 40	14,951 09	20,811 49
New England States	536	12,015,518	388,969,361	20,696 08	61,662 80	82,358 88
New York	303	8,525,645	162,275,473	15,563 57	78,945 75	94,509 32
New York City	506	49,335,306	291,914,072	85,455 58	293,743 04	379,198 62
Albany	12	641,000	13,751,649	708 69	3,654 47	4,363 16
New Jersey	51	1,324,553	20,391,118	2,537 17	7,719 79	10,256 96
Pennsylvania	271	8,789,931	29,071,132	20,093 39	72,000 44	92,093 83
Philadelphia	61	2,108,904	51,496,370	4,773 76	73,346 71	78,120 47
Pittsburgh	31	4,053,579	14,651,589	8,353 69	18,319 50	26,673 19
Delaware	8	675,689	2,127,426	1,639 18	2,320 03	3,959 21
Maryland	12	564,434	819,944	783 09	1,525 23	2,308 32
Baltimore	38	3,134,842	25,814,319	7,062 34	10,983 21	18,045 55
Washington	7	357,060	3,305,875	168 25	7,470 56	7,638 81
Middle States	1,300	79,510,943	615,618,967	147,138 71	570,028 73	717,167 44
Virginia	76	3,036,974	7,757,202	6,856 90	18,257 23	25,114 13
West Virginia	20	1,247,128	4,034,743	2,774 11	10,086 80	12,860 91
North Carolina	13	790,321	1,596,632	1,975 80	3,991 55	5,967 35
South Carolina	13	511,499	658,812	1,147 91	1,647 01	2,794 92
Georgia	58	4,068,279	5,910,827	10,125 53	13,615 93	23,741 46
Florida	9	83,830	287,289	209 56	681 76	891 32
Alabama	26	1,040,241	2,269,647	2,598 71	5,674 02	8,272 73
Mississippi	33	1,083,000	2,634,915	2,185 86	6,587 20	8,773 06
Louisiana	3	126,265	87,343	203 16	218 35	421 51
New Orleans	11	2,777,031	4,632,122	5,335 03	11,580 30	16,915 33
Texas	105	3,701,080	6,332,751	8,844 86	15,832 10	24,676 96
Arkansas	15	245,110	577,628	425 02	1,444 01	1,869 03
Kentucky	71	6,099,666	7,698,114	14,481 65	19,245 06	33,726 71
Louisville	15	5,267,028	5,803,673	11,989 56	14,509 16	26,498 72
Tennessee	30	1,769,228	3,222,740	4,109 60	8,056 73	12,166 33
Southern States	498	31,847,370	53,504,438	73,263 26	131,427 21	204,690 47
Ohio	248	5,704,140	20,834,648	11,993 31	50,407 23	62,400 54
Cincinnati	12	1,402,241	4,392,711	2,816 43	10,981 78	13,798 21
Cleveland	9	1,045,924	13,965,571	918 87	12,562 56	13,481 43
Indiana	144	4,365,434	13,172,783	9,643 63	29,581 35	39,224 98
Illinois	316	4,092,314	17,061,788	8,541 52	41,336 76	49,878 28
Chicago	34	4,272,495	12,584,083	4,281 60	31,433 74	35,715 43
Michigan	155	2,346,799	7,105,952	5,479 68	17,764 58	23,244 26
Detroit	14	1,066,941	7,544,048	1,800 75	14,693 74	16,494 49
Wisconsin	109	1,378,843	5,964,028	3,485 19	14,909 89	18,395 08
Milwaukee	9	634,731	7,788,000	1,547 05	19,472 26	21,019 31
Iowa	309	5,153,906	13,326,191	12,084 91	32,879 70	44,964 61
Minnesota	95	1,906,375	5,000,150	4,466 02	11,878 55	16,344 57
Missouri	170	4,250,175	15,307,216	9,564 76	38,267 88	47,832 64
Saint Louis	28	5,705,555	18,688,699	12,080 40	46,721 75	58,802 15
Kansas	148	1,564,144	4,877,150	3,684 19	12,192 78	15,876 97
Nebraska	83	653,890	2,019,814	1,535 90	5,049 38	6,585 28
Western States	1,883	45,743,007	169,633,732	93,914 30	390,133 93	484,048 23
Oregon	15	1,245,208	1,033,103	2,816 21	2,446 89	5,263 10
California	85	9,430,629	11,928,718	23,083 17	32,355 28	55,438 45
San Francisco	26	12,104,546	67,497,294	20,528 20	98,276 22	118,804 42
Colorado	38	584,917	3,479,877	1,462 30	8,699 65	10,161 95
Nevada	13	364,457	834,548	661 12	2,086 31	2,747 43
Utah	11	206,000	1,233,952	515 00	3,084 82	3,599 82
New Mexico	5	6,667	181,025	16 66	454 81	471 47
Wyoming	4	128,054	271,201	320 14	678 00	998 14
Idaho	2	5,358	18,368	13 39	45 92	59 31
Dakota	18	127,544	396,279	318 78	890 67	1,209 45
Montana	13	446,708	724,631	1,116 75	1,810 04	2,926 79
Washington	4	257,000	525,109	642 50	1,312 77	1,955 27
Arizona	5	112,932	243,673	219 83	609 17	829 00
Pacific States and Territories	239	25,019,987	91,368,078	51,714 05	152,850 55	204,564 60
Grand totals	4,456	194,136,825	1,319,094,576	386,726 40	1,306,103 22	1,692,820 62

Number of State banks, savings banks, trust companies, and private bankers, with their average capital and deposits, and the tax thereon, for the six months ending May 31, 1881.

States and Territories.	No. of banks.	Capital.	Deposits.	Tax. On capital.	Tax. On deposits.	Total.
Maine	66	$53,200	$24,363,290	$115 59	$795 15	$910 74
New Hampshire	72	76,000	32,163,124	186 56	1,216 24	1,402 80
Vermont	22	352,804	10,046,910	597 64	5,210 14	5,807 78
Massachusetts	163	310,000	164,637,832	314 31	6,525 74	6,840 05
Boston	62	4,855,730	70,644,577	8,148 93	26,810 53	34,959 46
Rhode Island	55	3,719,789	43,039,201	6,943 98	17,985 83	24,920 81
Connecticut	106	2,620,100	84,280,272	6,198 28	18,487 29	24,685 57
New England States	546	11,987,623	429,184,206	22,505 29	77,030 92	99,536 21
New York	300	8,762,680	183,626,465	16,415 12	96,467 79	112,882 91
New York City	563	66,010,403	343,830,575	123,379 20	378,521 80	501,901 00
Albany	12	616,000	15,775,441	662 50	4,485 12	5,147 62
New Jersey	48	1,248,914	23,877,530	2,174 76	9,076 64	11,251 40
Pennsylvania	246	7,858,694	31,947,161	17,953 87	78,943 90	96,807 77
Philadelphia	74	2,658,894	64,831,097	5,966 64	99,558 49	105,525 13
Pittsburgh	30	4,019,335	17,887,623	8,350 90	22,109 80	30,460 79
Delaware	7	609,561	2,299,392	1,498 89	2,179 13	3,678 02
Maryland	11	507,074	887,742	625 98	1,565 32	2,191 30
Baltimore	39	2,640,698	27,859,420	6,022 80	12,073 38	18,096 18
Washington	7	364,000	4,144,875	192 43	9,369 25	9,561 68
Middle States	1,337	95,286,253	716,967,321	183,243 09	714,350 71	897,593 80
Virginia	74	3,068,985	9,286,961	7,010 47	21,558 82	28,569 29
West Virginia	19	1,228,984	4,306,402	2,816 42	10,765 99	13,582 41
North Carolina	13	504,640	1,165,763	1,261 46	2,914 43	4,175 89
South Carolina	14	549,956	1,914,267	1,262 39	4,238 05	5,500 44
Georgia	54	3,438,668	6,199,163	8,579 16	11,061 09	22,640 25
Florida	7	101,079	539,449	252 69	1,304 20	1,556 89
Alabama	27	1,179,085	2,481,642	2,945 74	6,204 03	9,149 77
Mississippi	28	980,872	2,144,493	2,047 25	5,361 18	7,408 43
Louisiana	3	146,329	35,812	200 82	89 52	380 34
New Orleans	13	2,271,932	5,149,585	4,691 92	12,867 95	17,559 87
Texas	120	4,047,964	8,811,029	10,084 92	22,027 48	32,112 40
Arkansas	14	217,302	679,509	377 05	1,698 75	2,075 80
Kentucky	75	6,052,294	9,002,209	14,702 80	22,505 60	37,208 40
Louisville	15	5,145,554	6,631,685	12,239 07	16,579 17	28,818 24
Tennessee	31	1,796,536	3,474,487	3,962 35	8,686 11	12,648 46
Southern States	507	30,739,179	61,822,546	72,524 51	150,862 37	223,386 88
Ohio	246	5,509,583	24,495,977	11,629 60	58,439 37	70,059 97
Cincinnati	12	1,374,317	5,421,863	2,585 05	13,554 66	16,139 71
Cleveland	8	1,059,667	15,861,757	1,398 85	14,601 10	15,999 05
Indiana	145	4,433,488	15,878,206	9,553 25	35,556 69	45,109 94
Illinois	330	4,579,378	23,903,504	8,257 80	57,507 25	65,765 05
Chicago	33	2,965,197	10,316,023	6,971 51	48,122 96	55,094 47
Michigan	161	2,445,500	9,017,059	5,821 95	21,666 56	27,488 51
Detroit	14	1,044,028	9,419,029	1,840 83	18,081 01	19,921 84
Wisconsin	108	1,830,863	10,106,752	4,059 21	25,266 77	29,325 98
Milwaukee	8	437,866	7,484,580	1,080 54	18,711 45	19,800 99
Iowa	337	5,671,468	18,592,795	13,276 07	45,943 62	59,219 69
Minnesota	112	2,875,971	7,754,414	7,015 81	18,273 96	25,289 77
Missouri	182	4,366,103	21,660,092	9,730 42	54,149 87	63,880 29
Saint Louis	30	5,763,025	25,112,676	13,448 00	62,781 65	76,229 65
Kansas	175	1,921,571	6,418,482	4,644 97	16,046 02	20,690 99
Nebraska	98	944,372	2,661,291	2,325 66	6,652 75	8,978 41
Western States	1,999	48,222,420	223,104,509	103,639 52	515,355 69	618,995 21
Oregon	16	892,844	1,434,568	1,591 36	3,586 36	5,177 72
California	83	8,847,747	15,662,084	21,483 57	35,389 80	56,873 37
San Francisco	24	11,953,172	68,080,629	16,908 58	91,580 19	108,488 77
Colorado	59	903,440	3,864,948	2,208 61	9,662 32	11,870 93
Nevada	15	381,851	1,254,649	704 63	3,136 62	3,841 25
Utah	12	208,225	1,582,519	520 56	3,956 27	4,476 83
New Mexico	8	13,333	459,518	33 34	1,148 80	1,182 14
Wyoming	4	135,208	421,310	338 02	1,053 27	1,391 29
Idaho	2	6,561	19,097	16 40	47 74	64 14
Dakota	37	216,263	484,335	540 66	1,210 78	1,751 44
Montana	14	512,706	904,408	1,281 74	2,261 19	3,542 93
Washington	9	284,050	657,015	710 11	1,642 52	2,352 63
Arizona	9	147,319	635,256	243 30	1,583 06	1,831 36
Pacific States and Territories	292	24,502,719	96,360,426	46,580 88	156,263 92	202,814 80
Grand totals	4,681	210,738,203	1,527,439,008	428,493 29	1,613,863 61	2,042,356 90

Table, by geographical divisions, of the number, and average capital and deposits, of State banks, private bankers, and trust and loan companies, and of savings banks with and without capital, for the six months ending November 30, 1875.

Geographical divisions.	State banks, private bankers, and trust companies.			Savings banks with capital.			Savings banks without capital.		Total.		
	No.	Capital.	Deposits.	No.	Capital.	Deposits.	No.	Deposits.	No.	Capital.	Deposits.
		Mill'ns.	*Mill'ns.*		*Mill'ns.*	*Mill'ns.*		*Mill'ns.*		*Mill'ns.*	*Mill'ns.*
New England States	126	11.6	24.0	2	0.3	5.2	436	413.9	564	11.9	443.1
Middle States	1,270	90.8	232.4	3	0.2	0.8	218	382.8	1,491	91.0	616.0
Southern States	517	36.0	42.6	3	0.4	0.5	3	1.9	523	36.4	45.0
Western States and Territories	1,853	70.9	188.0	19	4.1	32.6	38	47.0	1,910	75.0	267.6
United States	3,766	209.3	487.0	27	5.0	39.1	695	845.6	4,488	214.3	1,371.7

Table, by geographical divisions, of the number, and average capital and deposits, of State banks, private bankers, and trust and loan companies, and of savings banks with and without capital, for the six months ending May 31, 1876.

Geographical divisions.	State banks, private bankers, and trust companies.			Savings banks with capital.			Savings banks without capital.		Total.		
	No.	Capital.	Deposits.	No.	Capital.	Deposits.	No.	Deposits.	No.	Capital.	Deposits.
		Mill'ns.	*Mill'ns.*		*Mill'ns.*	*Mill'ns.*		*Mill'ns.*		*Mill'ns.*	*Mill'ns.*
New England States	135	11.7	23.6	1	0.2	4.4	436	415.1	572	11.9	443.1
Middle States	1,256	89.2	223.4	3	0.3	1.2	212	382.5	1,471	89.5	607.1
Southern States	516	35.7	44.9	3	0.4	0.6	4	2.0	523	36.1	47.5
Western States and Territories	1,896	77.4	188.1	19	4.1	31.0	39	45.0	1,954	81.5	264.1
United States	3,803	214.0	480.0	26	5.0	37.2	691	844.6	4,520	219.0	1,361.8

Table, by geographical divisions, of the number, and average capital and deposits, of State banks, private bankers, and trust and loan companies, and of savings banks with and without capital, for the six months ending November 30, 1876.

Geographical divisions.	State banks, private bankers, and trust companies.			Savings banks with capital.			Savings banks without capital.		Total.		
	No.	Capital.	Deposits.	No.	Capital.	Deposits.	No.	Deposits.	No.	Capital.	Deposits.
		Mill'ns.	*Mill'ns.*		*Mill'ns.*	*Mill'ns.*		*Mill'ns.*		*Mill'ns.*	*Mill'ns.*
New England States	131	11.34	22.76	1	0.20	4.15	438	422.90	570	11.54	449.90
Middle States	1,213	88.34	226.40	2	0.16	0.77	211	385.82	1,426	88.50	612.99
Southern States	505	35.40	42.40	4	0.48	0.64	3	2.04	512	35.88	45.08
Western States and Territories	1,915	82.14	192.49	17	4.21	32.38	35	41.68	1,967	86.35	269.53
United States	3,764	217.22	484.05	24	5.05	37.94	687	855.53	4,475	222.27	1,377.52

Table, by geographical divisions, of the number, and average capital and deposits, of State banks, private bankers, and trust and loan companies, and of savings banks with and without capital, for the six months ending May 31, 1877.

Geographical divisions.	State banks, private bankers, and trust companies.			Savings banks with capital.			Savings banks without capital.		Total.		
	No.	Capital.	Depos. its.	No.	Capital.	Depos. its.	No.	Depos. its.	No.	Capital.	Depos. its.
		Mill'ns.	*Mill'ns.*		*Mill'ns.*	*Mill'ns.*		*Mill'ns.*		*Mill'ns.*	*Mill'ns.*
New England States	117	11.07	19.99	1	0.20	3.94	439	428.69	557	11.27	452.62
Middle States	1,202	84.87	215.87	2	0.16	0.88	200	368.81	1,404	85.03	585.56
Southern States	517	34.58	46.17	3	0.42	0.52	4	2.12	524	35.00	48.81
Western States and Territories	1,963	88.11	188.51	20	4.09	32.83	33	43.54	2,016	92.20	264.88
United States	3,799	218.63	470.54	26	4.87	38.17	676	843.16	4,501	223.50	1,351.87

Table, by geographical divisions, of the number, and average capital and deposits, of State banks, private bankers, and trust and loan companies, and of savings banks with and without capital, for the six months ending May 31, 1878.

Geographical divisions.	State banks, private bankers, and trust companies.			Savings banks with capital.			Savings banks without capital.		Total.		
	No.	Capital.	Depos. its.	No.	Capital.	Depos. its.	No.	Depos. its.	No.	Capital.	Depos. its.
		Mill'ns.	*Mill'ns.*		*Mill'ns.*	*Mill'ns.*		*Mill'ns.*		*Mill'ns.*	*Mill'ns.*
New England States	113	11.05	18.29	1	0.07	1.14	441	403.43	555	11.12	422.86
Middle States	1,133	76.93	184.02	3	0.16	1.37	190	358.68	1,326	77.09	544.07
Southern States	513	34.68	44.35	4	0.88	1.28	3	2.14	520	35.56	47.77
Western States and Territories	1,950	79.49	166.65	15	2.13	22.39	34	39.05	1,999	81.62	228.09
United States	3,709	202.15	413.31	23	3.24	26.18	668	803.30	4,400	205.39	1,242.79

Table, by geographical divisions, of the number, and average capital and deposits, of State banks and trust companies, private bankers, and savings banks with and without capital, for the six months ending May 31, 1878, the private bankers being given separately.

Geographical divisions.	State banks and trust companies.			Private bankers.			Savings banks with capital.			Savings banks without capital.	
	No.	Capital.	Depos. its.	No.	Capital.	Depos. its.	No.	Capital.	Depos. its.	No.	Depos. its.
		Mill'ns.	*Mill'ns.*		*Mill'ns.*	*Mill'ns.*		*Mill'ns.*	*Mill'ns.*		*Mill'ns.*
New England States	42	8.19	15.06	71	2.86	3.23	1	0.07	1.14	441	403.43
Middle States	217	42.45	122.10	916	34.48	61.92	3	0.16	1.37	190	358.68
Southern States	233	27.38	30.67	280	7.30	13.68	4	0.88	1.28	3	2.14
Western States and Territories	361	46.33	61.65	1,589	33.16	105.00	15	2.13	22.39	34	39.05
United States	853	124.35	229.18	2,856	77.80	183.83	23	3.24	26.18	668	803.30

Table, by geographical divisions, of the number, and average capital and deposits, of State banks, private bankers, savings banks, and trust and loan companies, for the six months ending May 31, 1878, and of the number, capital, and deposits of the national banks on June 29, 1878.

Geographical divisions.	State banks, savings banks, private bankers, and trust companies.			National banks.			Total.		
	No.	Capital.	Deposits.	No.	Capital.	Deposits.	No.	Capital.	Deposits.
		Millions.	*Millions.*		*Millions.*	*Millions.*		*Millions.*	*Millions.*
New England States.	555	11.12	422.86	542	166.52	128.83	1,097	177.64	551.69
Middle States	1,326	77.09	544.07	634	177.18	374.89	1,960	254.27	918.96
Southern States	520	35.55	47.77	176	31.49	35.94	696	67.04	83.71
Western States and Territories	1,999	81.62	228.09	704	95.20	137.50	2,703	176.82	365.59
United States..	4,400	205.38	1,242.79	2,056	470.39	677.16	6,456	675.77	1,919.95

Table, by geographical divisions, of the number, and average capital and deposits, of State banks and trust companies, private bankers, and savings banks with and without capital, for the six months ending May 31, 1879, the private bankers being given separately.

Geographical divisions.	State banks and trust companies.			Private bankers.			Savings banks with capital.			Savings banks without capital.	
	No.	Capital.	Deposits.	No.	Capital.	Deposits.	No.	Capital.	Deposits.	No.	Deposits.
		Mill'ns.	*Mill'ns.*		*Mill'ns.*	*Mill'ns.*		*Mill'ns.*	*Mill'ns.*		*Mill'ns.*
New England States..	40	7.10	14.39	70	3.72	3.32	.....	.....	.....	426	366.46
Middle States	239	40.72	124.64	853	34.54	54.53	6	0.51	2.44	182	350.95
Southern States	251	27.43	32.60	237	5.64	11.89	3	0.86	0.83	3	1.69
Western States and Territories	475	52.02	85.44	1,474	25.85	70.18	20	2.85	32.80	33	27.96
United States ..	1,005	127.27	257.07	2,634	69.75	139.92	29	4.22	36.07	644	747.06

Table, by geographical divisions, of the number, and average capital and deposits, of State banks, private bankers, savings banks, and trust and loan companies, for the six months ending May 31, 1879, and of the number, capital, and deposits of the national banks on June 14, 1879.

Geographical divisions.	State banks, savings banks, private bankers, &c.			National banks.			Total.		
	No.	Capital.	Deposits.	No.	Capital.	Deposits.	No.	Capital.	Deposits.
		Millions.	*Millions.*		*Millions.*	*Millions.*		*Millions.*	*Millions.*
New England States.	536	10.83	384.17	544	164.43	126.72	1,080	175.26	510.89
Middle States	1,280	75.77	532.56	640	170.21	393.12	1,920	245.98	925.68
Southern States	494	33.92	47.02	176	30.40	37.93	670	64.32	84.95
Western States and Territories	2,002	80.72	216.37	688	90.20	155.63	2,690	170.92	372.00
United States .	4,312	201.24	1,180.12	2,048	455.24	713.40	6,360	656.48	1,893.52

Table, by geographical divisions, of the number and average capital and deposits of State banks and trust companies, private bankers, and savings banks with and without capital, for the six months ending May 31, 1880, the private bankers being given separately.

Geographical divisions.	State banks and trust companies.		Private bankers.			Savings banks with capital.		Savings banks without capital.	
	No.	Capital.	Depos- its.	No.	Capital.	Depos- its.	No.	Capital.	Depos- its.	No.	Depos- its.
		Mill'ns.	Mill'ns.		Mill'ns.	Mill'ns.		Mill'ns.	Mill'ns.		Mill'ns.
New England States....	40	6.86	16.47	74	5.16	3.74	....	......	......	422	368.76
Middle States	234	38.98	154.89	885	40.01	71.54	6	0.53	3.19	175	386.00
Southern States	241	26.69	38.51	252	4.81	13.54	3	0.34	0.57	2	0.88
Western States and Territories..............	481	41.44	108.91	1,591	26.14	93.85	20	3.17	30.85	30	27.39
United States	996	113.97	318.78	2,802	76.12	182.67	29	4.04	34.61	629	783.03

Table, by geographical divisions, of the number and average capital and deposits of State banks, private bankers, savings banks, and trust and loan companies, for the six months ending May 31, 1880, and of the number, capital, and deposits of the national banks on June 11, 1880.

Geographical divisions.	State banks, savings banks, private bankers, &c.			National banks.			Total.		
	No.	Capital.	Deposits.	No.	Capital.	Net de- posits.	No.	Capital.	Deposits.
		Millions.	Millions.		Millions.	Millions.		Millions.	Millions.
New England States	536	12.02	388.97	548	165.60	161.96	1,084	177.62	550.93
Middle States	1,300	79.51	615.62	654	170.44	480.06	1,954	249.95	1,095.68
Southern States	498	31.85	53.50	177	30.79	45.90	675	62.64	99.40
Western States and Territories	2,122	70.76	261.00	697	89.08	212.87	2,819	159.84	473.87
United States...	4,456	194.14	1,319.09	2,076	455.91	900.79	6,532	650.05	2,219.88

Table of the resources and liabilities of State banks at various dates.

RESOURCES.	New Hampshire, Mar., 1881.	Vermont, July 1, 1881.	Rhode Island, Dec. 1, 1880.	Connecticut, Oct. 1, 1880.	New York, Sept. 24, 1881.
	1 bank.	6 banks.	14 banks.	4 banks.	49 banks.
Loans and discounts	$78,098	$1,537,951	$3,215,520	$2,239,786	$30,034,011
Overdrafts				3,524	58,494
United States bonds		137,420	125,018	111,831	
Other stocks, bonds, &c	7,275	638,660	184,774	125,203	3,178,199
Due from banks		136,722	256,327	740,202	5,521,882
Real estate	6,654	26,266	132,926	128,812	799,619
Other assets		79,174	13,401	8,124	196,363
Expenses			3,013	5,376	175,685
Cash items					362,780
Specie			35,056		306,418
Legal tenders, bank notes, &c	1,416	20,353	162,397	170,510	1,170,460
Totals	93,443	2,576,546	4,129,032	3,533,368	41,803,911
LIABILITIES.					
Capital stock	50,000	450,000	2,568,885	1,350,000	7,603,000
Circulation	1,130		11,620	19,494	16,009
Surplus fund	16,838	62,771		68,000	1,733,586
Undivided profits			212,538	137,135	1,424,651
Dividends unpaid			17,255	3,122	
Deposits	14,872	2,052,878	1,225,816	1,520,191	27,003,064
Due to banks	10,603		81,181	435,426	2,285,567
Other liabilities		10,897	11,737		1,718,034
Totals	93,443	2,576,546	4,129,032	3,533,368	41,803,911

Resources and liabilities of State banks at various dates—Continued.

RESOURCES.	New York City, Sept. 24, 1881.	New Jersey, Jan., 1881.	Pennsylvania, Nov., 1880.	Maryland, Sept., 1881.	South Carolina, Sept. 20, 1880.
	21 banks.	7 banks.	82 banks.	8 banks.	2 banks.
Loans and discounts	$47,658,739	$2,682,535	$16,224,428	$3,766,469	$457,633
Overdrafts	46,503	337			
United States bonds		334,425	651,874	95,000	50,000
Other stocks, bonds, &c	1,140,944	15,700	2,739,755	346,574	402,145
Due from banks	3,035,266	390,334	3,920,191	440,388	8,986
Real estate	1,235,514	226,623	2,219,645	433,780	42,468
Other assets	80,818	31,662	832,764	7,607	2,813
Expenses	168,133	3,928	181,237	12,590	5,240
Cash items	9,718,855			46,463	
Specie	4,985,820	2,598	254,236	40,886	
Legal tenders, bank notes, &c	3,444,409	145,143	2,074,865	355,682	35,517
Totals	71,524,001	3,833,285	29,098,995	5,354,439	1,004,802
LIABILITIES.					
Capital stock	11,387,700	999,607	7,458,579	1,808,340	140,000
Circulation	17,611			471	
Surplus fund	3,341,461	76,348	1,018,030	171,000	15,000
Undivided profits	2,403,066	57,936	537,122	149,443	19,660
Dividends unpaid		1,207		15,356	
Deposits	48,627,155	2,588,921	18,524,039	3,243,688	811,951
Due to banks	5,300,654	66,266	1,354,321	130,953	18,191
Other liabilities	446,054	43,000	206,904	35,188	
Totals	71,524,001	3,833,285	29,098,995	5,354,439	1,004,802

Resources and liabilities of State banks at various dates—Continued.

RESOURCES.	Georgia, June 30, 1881.	Louisiana, Dec., 1879.	Texas, June, 1881.	Kentucky, July 1, 1881.	Missouri, Aug. 31, 1881.	Ohio, April 4, 1881.
	21 banks.	10 banks.	5 banks.	61 banks.	120 banks.	29 banks.
Loans and discounts	$5,790,539	$6,108,587	$943,882	$10,456,987	$32,543,689	$5,110,487
Overdrafts	98,762	301	11,488	44,487	527,658	30,250
United States bonds		600,000		268,750	2,845,229	222,938
Other stocks, bonds, &c	3,709,888	2,053,140	13,857	1,725,303	4,048,282	238,231
Due from banks	1,021,687	1,435,795	308,072	3,435,950	9,443,298	733,452
Real estate	366,751	745,141	131,160	930,748	1,320,440	274,329
Other assets	1,076,794	343,631	18,395	395,331	298,905	80,026
Expenses	60,598	52,393	18,929	16,624		41,102
Cash items		569,858			5,751,629	86,909
Specie		503,297			1,470,561	73,701
Legal tenders, bank notes, &c	1,224,323	1,584,515	319,020	2,295,268	5,440,756	596,684
Totals	13,359,342	13,996,658	1,764,803	28,575,457	63,690,447	7,488,118
LIABILITIES.						
Capital stock	2,534,775	4,458,198	625,000	10,943,027	8,868,870	1,731,800
Circulation		8,712		199,671		
Surplus fund	85,200		13,153	873,438	3,394,026	193,910
Undivided profits	576,633	161,208	79,110	922,561		111,766
Dividends unpaid	28,373	56,241	56	245,883	57,225	1,403
Deposits	4,634,538	7,086,841	1,021,175	14,448,066	46,081,170	5,088,136
Due to banks	869,460	1,697,403	25,963	815,670	5,338,566	94,805
Other liabilities	4,630,363	528,055	346	127,141	40,590	266,298
Totals	13,359,342	13,996,658	1,764,803	28,575,457	63,690,447	7,488,118

Resources and liabilities of State banks at various dates—Continued.

RESOURCES.	Indiana, Nov., 1880.	Michigan, July 4, 1881.	Wisconsin, July 4, 1881.	Iowa, Sept. 30, 1881.	Minnesota, Oct. 3, 1881.	California, July 1, 1881.
	19 banks.	29 banks.	31 banks.	53 banks.	24 banks.	56 banks.
Loans and discounts	$2,019,029	$10,560,405	$11,715,628	$8,643,970	$7,515,923	$32,515,124
Overdrafts	40,303	44,986	128,167	231,954	68,087	
United States bonds	37,265			299,482	22,200	6,247,020
Other stocks, bonds, &c	40,481	1,869,481	1,236,101	303,243	193,357	595,307
Due from banks	515,354	1,740,991	3,047,722	1,693,719	1,002,593	7,819,368
Real estate	152,487	461,146	183,126	385,000	200,723	3,504,880
Other assets	50,057		223	75,694	51,717	6,898,767
Expenses	17,144	27,945	30,659	103,286	41,745	
Cash items	14,427		255,511	51,462	42,431	
Specie	44,749		205,113	217,102	61,089	8,870,809
Legal tenders, bank notes, &c	267,747	1,513,712	912,902	744,060	891,297	416,010
Totals	3,199,046	16,217,766	17,715,152	12,838,972	10,091,172	66,867,305
LIABILITIES.						
Capital stock	1,068,940	2,179,285	1,524,431	2,456,755	2,263,650	20,451,683
Circulation			223			
Surplus fund	112,263	345,389	250,558		125,010	9,141,186
Undivided profits	66,062	267,778		520,394	296,403	
Dividends unpaid	943			138,907	1,200	
Deposits	1,947,030	13,229,168	12,486,840	9,667,216	7,239,855	32,819,393
Due to banks	3,808	146,149		55,700	139,690	
Other liabilities		49,997	3,414,100		25,364	4,455,043
Totals	3,199,046	16,217,766	17,715,152	12,838,972	10,091,172	66,867,305

Aggregate resources and liabilities of State banks from 1877 to 1881.

RESOURCES.	1876-'77.	1877-'78.	1878-'79.	1879-'80.	1880-'81.
	592 banks.	475 banks.	616 banks.	620 banks.	652 banks.
Loans and discounts	$266,585,314	$169,391,427	$191,444,093	$206,821,194	$250,819,420
Overdrafts	516,565	319,959	447,302	528,543	1,335,310
United States bonds	929,260	2,150,880	7,739,203	7,142,532	12,048,452
Other stocks, bonds, &c	23,209,670	19,398,287	21,916,024	17,117,117	24,904,903
Due from banks	25,201,782	25,107,149	22,169,065	36,180,435	46,657,328
Real estate	12,609,160	11,092,118	14,264,835	14,227,927	13,914,238
Other assets	6,442,710	10,694,390	9,221,760	5,801,796	10,542,266
Expenses	1,211,416	914,726	801,005	878,696	965,327
Cash items	9,816,456	7,320,845	8,767,391	11,176,374	16,900,325
Specie	2,319,659	3,041,676	1,979,701	6,201,617	17,071,445
Legal tenders, bank notes, &c.	34,415,712	28,480,374	37,088,961	48,828,255	23,797,046
Totals	383,257,704	277,911,831	315,839,340	354,904,486	418,956,060
LIABILITIES.					
Capital stock	110,949,515	95,193,292	104,124,871	90,816,575	92,922,525
Circulation	387,661	388,298	389,542	283,308	274,941
Surplus fund	5,665,854	7,983,996	16,667,574	18,816,496	20,976,167
Undivided profits	18,283,567	11,693,064	5,666,221	6,721,615	7,943,466
Dividends unpaid	335,904	324,176	501,831	474,567	567,171
Deposits	226,654,538	142,764,491	166,958,229	208,751,611	261,362,303
Due to banks	9,412,876	10,348,911	13,093,069	18,462,707	18,870,466
Other liabilities	11,567,789	9,215,603	8,438,003	10,577,607	16,039,021
Totals	383,257,704	277,911,831	315,839,340	354,904,486	418,956,060

Resources and liabilities of trust and loan companies at various dates.

RESOURCES.	Massachusetts, Oct., 1880.	Rhode Island. Dec. 1, 1880.	Connecticut, Oct. 1, 1880.	New York, Jan. 1, 1881.	Pennsylvania, Oct., 1881.
	5 banks.	1 bank.	10 banks.	8 banks.	7 banks.
Loans and discounts	$7,265,933	$3,410,089	$5,136,672	$61,650,926	$24,442,946
Overdrafts			12,568	457	59,360
United States bonds	1,529,307	1,000,000	23,043	11,561,297	1,517,926
Other stocks, bonds, &c	723,724	1,832,600	207,110	2,933,918	11,728,702
Due from banks	2,166,161		574,446	2,653,134	2,611,760
Real estate	33,000		2,415,972	1,445,680	3,587,882
Other assets	106,103	236,809	351,709	597,673	107,181
Expenses	46,354		13,338		111,408
Cash items					437
Specie					854,183
Legal tenders, bank notes, &c.	542,036	763,131	127,428	64,074	2,097,602
Totals	12,412,618	7,242,629	8,862,286	80,907,159	47,119,387
LIABILITIES.					
Capital stock	1,387,200	800,000	2,676,600	7,000,000	7,325,000
Circulation					
Surplus fund	185,000		89,306	4,219,765	2,387,738
Undivided profits	219,505	32,684	325,288	2,094,007	1,022,170
Dividends unpaid	1,077		3,955	124	4,086
Deposits	10,002,103	3,265,398	2,792,682	64,074,890	31,535,256
Due to banks			142,148		93,050
Other liabilities	617,733	3,144,347	2,832,307	2,918,373	4,752,087
Totals	12,412,618	7,242,629	8,862,286	80,907,159	47,119,387

Aggregate resources and liabilities of trust and loan companies from 1877 to 1881.

RESOURCES.	1876-'77.	1877-'78.	1878-'79.	1879-'80.	1880-'81.
	39 banks.	35 banks.	32 banks.	30 banks.	31 banks.
Loans and discounts	$67,946,390	$59,303,327	$61,171,877	$74,675,537	$101,906,566
Overdrafts	13,948	11,565	26,291	69,156	72,385
United States bonds	19,805,685	19,445,460	17,948,856	19,109,650	15,631,573
Other stocks, bonds, &c	17,960,260	17,296,237	16,892,230	18,544,675	17,426,054
Due from banks	8,028,415	5,536,854	6,011,039	4,159,910	8,005,501
Real estate	3,544,221	3,700,375	4,044,285	5,261,159	7,482,534
Other assets	3,410,232	2,412,519	2,874,164	1,572,241	1,399,475
Expenses	105,157	274,911	124,563	100,796	171,100
Cash items	59,393	43,215	54,879	218	437
Specie	22,952	360,831	377,272	704,360	854,183
Legal tenders, bank notes, &c.	2,715,846	2,449,309	2,284,480	2,671,971	3,594,271
Totals	123,612,499	110,843,603	111,809,936	126,869,673	156,544,079
LIABILITIES.					
Capital stock	22,347,440	22,086,611	21,101,876	18,501,876	19,188,800
Circulation					
Surplus fund	7,164,673	7,925,303	7,714,316	6,191,935	6,881,809
Undivided profits	1,239,539	691,651	1,480,254	4,053,116	4,293,854
Dividends unpaid	387,764	11,261	24,637	11,527	9,242
Deposits	84,215,849	73,136,578	75,873,219	90,008,008	111,670,329
Due to banks		521,426	140,443	150,629	235,198
Other liabilities	7,924,045	6,470,773	5,475,191	7,952,582	14,204,847
Totals	123,612,499	110,843,603	111,809,936	126,869,673	156,544,079

Table, by geographical divisions, of the resources and liabilities of the State banks and trust companies, 1880-'81.

RESOURCES.	New England States.	Middle States.	Southern States.	Western States.	Pacific States.	Aggregate.
	41 banks.	182 banks.	99 banks.	305 banks.	56 banks.	683 banks.
Loans and discounts	$22,884,049	$186,460,054	$32,757,628	$78,109,131	$32,515,124	$352,725,986
Overdrafts	16,092	165,151	155,038	1,071,414		1,407,695
United States bonds	2,926,619	14,160,522	918,750	3,427,114	6,247,020	27,680,025
Other stocks, bonds, &c	3,719,346	22,092,792	7,904,363	8,019,179	595,307	42,330,957
Due from banks	3,873,858	18,581,955	6,210,499	18,177,129	7,819,388	54,662,829
Real estate	2,743,630	9,948,743	2,222,268	2,977,251	3,504,880	21,396,772
Other assets	795,320	1,854,068	1,836,964	556,622	6,898,767	11,941,741
Expenses	68,681	652,981	153,781	260,981		1,136,427
Cash items		10,128,535	569,858	6,202,369		16,900,762
Specie	35,056	6,444,141	503,207	2,072,325	8,870,809	17,925,628
Legal tenders, bank notes, &c	1,787,271	9,352,235	5,468,643	10,367,158	416,010	27,391,317
Totals	38,849,922	279,841,177	58,701,062	131,240,673	66,867,305	575,500,139
LIABILITIES.						
Capital stock	9,282,685	43,582,226	18,701,000	20,093,731	20,451,683	112,111,325
Circulation	32,244	34,091	208,383	223		274,941
Surplus fund	421,915	12,987,928	986,791	4,340,156	9,141,186	27,857,976
Undivided profits	927,350	8,288,395	1,759,172	1,262,403		12,237,320
Dividends unpaid	25,409	20,773	330,553	199,678		576,413
Deposits	20,873,940	195,597,343	28,002,571	95,739,415	32,819,393	373,032,632
Due to banks	669,358	9,230,811	3,426,687	5,778,808		19,105,664
Other liabilities	6,617,021	10,119,640	5,285,905	3,826,259	4,455,043	30,303,808
Totals	38,849,922	279,841,177	58,701,062	131,240,673	66,867,305	575,500,139

Resources and liabilities of savings banks organized under State laws at various dates.

RESOURCES.	Maine, Nov. 1, 1880.	New Hampshire, March, 1881.	Vermont, July 1, 1881.	Massachusetts, Oct. 30, 1880.	Rhode Island. Dec. 1. 1880.
	55 banks.	64 banks.	16 banks.	164 banks.	39 banks.
Loans on real estate	$5,239,463	$10,841,203	$4,360,702	$52,431,984	$20,083,898
Loans on personal and collateral security	2,065,087	6,665,389	1,266,807	43,041,658	7.154,467
United States bonds	4,185,911	709,900	529,600	20,502,530	4,368,557
State, municipal, and other bonds and stocks	7,213,900	6,370,077	1,512,591	17,362,528	5,060,882
Railroad bonds and stocks	2,367,089	5,515,415	....	7,011,551	2,501,750
Bank stock	1,114,474	1,436,870	131,827	24,078,449	2,062,973
Real estate	1,124,144	1,001,113	221,307	11,806,368	3,238,868
Other assets	774,896	868,246	246,447	1,066,852	126,755
Expenses	....	....	....	....	....
Due from banks	....	....	502,870	16,154,777	....
Cash	1,261,024	921,220	122,194	1,664,492	1,601,785
Totals	25,345,988	34,329,433	8,894,285	225,823,189	46,796,935
LIABILITIES.					
Deposits	23,277,676	32,097,734	8,606,607	218,047,922	44,755,625
Surplus fund	1,346,969	938,548	271,158	2,670,153	....
Undivided profits	666,631	1,293,151	....	4,758,195	1,944,256
Other liabilities	54,712	....	16,520	346,919	97,054
Totals	25,345,988	34,329,433	8,894,285	225,823,189	46,796,935

Resources and liabilities of savings banks organized under State laws—Continued.

RESOURCES.	Connecticut, Oct. 1, 1880.	New York, Jan. 1, 1881.	New Jersey, Jan. 1, 1881.	Pennsylvania Oct. 1, 1881.	Maryland. July 1, 1881.
	85 banks.	128 banks.	31 banks.	4 banks.	13 banks.
Loans on real estate	$42,791,160	$87,622,376	$7,610,194	$4,665,505	$3,129,644
Loans on personal and collateral security	4,300,209	13,268,077	1,538,182	4,292,086	8,078,674
United States bonds	7,245,223	137,375,190	7,097,945	7,661,305	10,048,727
State, municipal, and other bonds and stocks	9,614,629	98,765,988	2,026,091	5,111,176	969,650
Railroad bonds and stocks	2,806,304	....	....	5,867,489	999,450
Bank stock	4,260,985	....	....	....	163,625
Real estate	5,397,281	10,412,881	936,849	590,146	439,044
Other assets	290,938	31,586,603	815,000	....	....
Expenses	....	....	....	97,244	....
Due from banks	2,873,689	17,887,264	875,191	....	....
Cash	363,240	4,026,001	184,509	1,150,446	....
Totals	79,943,658	400,944,380	21,083,961	29,435,687	23,828,814
LIABILITIES.					
Deposits	76,518,571	353,629,657	19,863,638	26,895,295	23,824,354
Surplus fund	3,254,566	47,099,094	1,036,008	1,633,813	....
Undivided profits	....	....	....	906,579	....
Other liabilities	170,521	215,629	184,255	....	4,460
Totals	79,943,658	400,944,380	21,083,961	29,435,687	23,828,814

Resources and liabilities of savings-banks organized under State laws—Continued.

RESOURCES.	District of Columbia, October 1, 1881.	Louisiana, February 28, 1879.	Ohio, April 4, 1881.	Indiana, November 1, 1880.	California, July 1, 1881.
	1 bank.	1 bank.	4 banks.	6 banks.	18 banks.
Loans on real estate	$105,158	$534,536	$3,301,590	$536,218	$33,845,437
Loans on personal and collateral security		425,523	709,952	432,535	2,578,995
United States bonds	30,000	154,710	2,204,900	103,504	8,627,312
State, municipal, and other bonds and stocks	208,033	134,849	3,942,271	82,362	844,975
Railroad bonds and stocks					
Bank stock					
Real estate	97,792	511,693	174,964	54,270	5,983,954
Other assets	2,381	425	69,599	34,312	925,709
Expenses	1,094	12,065	22,895	2,274	
Due from banks	284		981,016		1,226,550
Cash	23,012	60,975	192,900	207,037	1,979,191
Totals	467,754	1,834,776	11,597,167	1,452,512	56,012,123
LIABILITIES.					
Deposits	462,636	1,794,086	10,902,052	1,330,956	49,954,333
Surplus fund				93,975	1,945,561
Undivided profits	5,118	32,174	692,115	27,581	
Other liabilities		8,516	3,000		*4,112,229
Totals	467,754	1,834,776	11,597,167	1,452,512	56,012,123

* Includes $3,704,507 capital stock.

Aggregate resources and liabilities of savings-banks from 1877 to 1881.

RESOURCES.	1876-'77.	1877-'78.	1878-'79.	1879-'80.	1880-'81.
	675 banks.	663 banks.	639 banks.	629 banks.	629 banks.
Loans on real estate	$369,770,878	$408,921,601	$352,695,026	$315,273,232	$307,096,158
Loans on personal and collateral security	114,474,163	88,192,337	65,694,465	70,175,090	95,817,641
United States bonds	115,389,880	129,362,890	156,415,159	187,413,220	210,845,514
State, municipal, and other bonds and stocks	184,116,602	170,155,076	154,804,318	150,440,359	159,819,942
Railroad bonds and stocks	24,586,503	24,752,650	18,737,917	20,705,378	27,069,048
Bank stock	34,571,531	34,793,256	32,452,020	32,225,923	33,249,203
Real estate	21,037,426	29,952,494	33,573,091	39,638,502	41,987,674
Other assets	18,135,673	18,169,863	16,643,100	27,053,152	37,408,463
Expenses	1,029,238	216,690	194,113	216,423	135,572
Due from banks	23,522,572	22,551,208	22,880,849	22,063,091	40,603,641
Cash	16,160,096	17,469,085	14,056,894	17,072,680	13,758,106
Totals	922,794,562	941,447,150	865,146,952	881,677,350	967,790,662
LIABILITIES.					
Deposits	866,498,452	879,897,425	802,490,298	819,106,973	891,961,142
Surplus fund	43,835,885	43,892,563	50,195,200	51,226,472	60,289,905
Undivided profits	9,200,778	6,964,177	4,019,569	4,710,861	10,625,800
Other liabilities	3,259,447	10,693,015	8,141,885	6,603,044	5,213,815
Totals	922,794,562	941,447,150	865,146,952	884,677,350	967,790,662

Table, by States, of the aggregate deposits of savings banks, with the number of their depositors and the average amount due to each, in 1880 and 1881.

States.	1879-'80.			1880-'81.		
	Number of depositors.	Amount of deposits.	Average to each depositor.	Number of depositors.	Amount of deposits.	Average to each depositor.
Maine	75,443	$20,978,140	$278 07	80,947	$23,277,676	$287 57
New Hampshire	89,934	28,204,791	313 62	96,881	32,097,734	331 31
Vermont	29,143	7,348,812	252 16	32,081	8,606,667	268 28
Massachusetts	675,555	206,378,709	305 49	706,395	218,047,922	308 68
Rhode Island	93,193	43,095,534	463 51	97,682	44,755,625	458 18
Connecticut	202,385	72,842,443	359 92	213,913	76,518,571	357 71
New York	864,470	319,258,501	369 31	953,707	353,629,657	370 79
New Jersey	68,457	17,470,014	255 20	74,965	19,863,638	264 97
Pennsylvania	88,680	23,956,285	270 14	99,416	26,895,295	270 53
Maryland	°54,500	19,981,366	366 63	64,911	23,824,354	367 00
District of Columbia	4,077	367,692	90 19	4,492	462,636	102 99
Louisiana	6,178	1,794,086	290 40	6,178	1,794,086	290 40
Ohio	°24,570	9,710,771	395 23	28,587	10,902,052	381 36
Indiana				°3,502	1,330,956	380 00
California	*58,997	47,719,829	808 85	65,092	49,954,333	• 767 44
Totals	2,335,582	819,106,973	350 71	2,528,749	891,961,142	352 73

Estimated.

Statement showing the amount of national-bank and legal-tender notes outstanding on June 20, 1874, January 14, 1875, May 31, 1878. and November 1, 1881, and the increase or decrease in each.

NATIONAL-BANK NOTES.

Amount outstanding June 20, 1874	$349,894,182
Amount outstanding January 14, 1875	351,861,450
Amount outstanding May 31, 1878	322,555,905
Amount outstanding November 1, 1881*	339,422,738
Increase during the last month	1,652,248
Increase since November 1, 1880	16,904,576

LEGAL-TENDER NOTES.

Amount outstanding June 20, 1874	382,000,000
Amount outstanding January 14, 1875	382,000,000
Amount retired under act of January 14, 1875, to May 31, 1878	35,318,984
Amount outstanding on and since May 31, 1878	346,681,016
Amount on deposit with the Treasurer United States to redeem notes of insolvent and liquidating banks, and banks retiring circulation under act of June 20, 1874	30,702,596
Decrease in deposit during the last month	1,134,328
Increase in deposit since November 1, 1880	10,142,584

* The notes of three national gold banks located in the State of California, which have an aggregate capital of $2,000,000 and a circulation of $921,512, not included.

National banks that have gone into voluntary liquidation under the provisions of Sections 5220 and 5221 of the Revised Statutes of the United States, with the dates of liquidation, the amount of their capital, circulation issued and retired, and circulation outstanding November 1, 1881.

Name and location of bank.	Date of liquidation.	Capital.	Circulation. Issued.	Retired.	Outstanding.
First National Bank, Penn Yan, N. Y*..	Apr. 6, 1864				
First National Bank, Norwich, Conn' ..	May 2, 1864				
Second National Bank, Ottumwa, Iowat..	May 2, 1864				
Second National Bank, Canton, Ohiot....	Oct. 3, 1864				
First National Bank, Lansing, Mich†...	Dec. 5, 1864				
First National Bank. Columbia, Mo.....	Sept. 19, 1864	$100,000	$90,000	$89,825	$175
First National Bank. Carondelet, Mo ...	Mar. 15, 1865	30,000	25,500	25,359	141
First National Bank, Utica, N. Y*.......	June 9, 1865				
Pittston National Bank, Pittston, Pa....	Sept. 16, 1865	200,000			
Fourth National Bank, Indianapolis, Ind.	Nov. 30, 1865	100,000	100,000	98,720	1,280
Berkshire National Bank, Adams, Mass*	Dec. 8, 1865	100,000			
National Union Bank, Rochester, N. Y..	Apr. 26, 1866	400,000	192,500	189,873	2,627
First National Bank, Leonardsville, N. Y	July 11, 1866	50,000	45,000	44,100	900
Farmers' National Bank, Richmond, Va	Oct. 22, 1866	100,000	85,000	82,363	2,637
Farmers' National Bank, Waukesha, Wis	Nov. 25, 1866	100,000	90,000	89,330	670
National Bank of Metropolis, Washington, D.C	Nov. 28, 1866	200,000	180,000	175,219	4,781
First National Bank, Providence, Pa ...	Mar. 1, 1867	100,000	90,000	87,070	2,930
First National Bank of Newton, Newtonville, Mass	Mar. 11, 1867	150,000	130,000	127,257	2,743
National State Bank, Dubuque, Iowa ...	Mar. 9, 1867	150,000	127,000	124,936	2,064
First National Bank, New Ulm, Minn ..	Apr. 18, 1867	60,000	54,000	52,795	1,205
National Bank Crawford County, Meadville, Pa......	Apr. 19, 1867	300,000			
Kittanning National Bank, Kittanning, Pa	Apr. 29, 1867	200,000			
City National Bank, Savannah, Ga.....	May 28, 1867	100,000			
Ohio National Bank, Cincinnati, Ohio...	July 3, 1867	500,000	450,000	440,180	9,820
First National Bank, Kingston, N. Y....	Sept. 26, 1867	200,000	180,000	175,284	4,716
First National Bank, Bluffton, Ind ...	Dec. 5, 1867	50,000	45,000	44,306	694
National Exchange Bank, Richmond, Va.	Dec. 5, 1867	200,000	180,000	177,770	2,230
First National Bank, Skaneateles, N. Y..	Dec. 21, 1867	150,000	135,000	132,955	2,045
First National Bank. Jackson, Miss....	Dec. 26, 1867	100,000	40,500	39,995	505
First National Bank, Downingtown, Pa	Jan. 14, 1868	100,000	90,000	88,070	1,930
First National Bank, Titusville, Pa......	Jan. 15, 1868	100,000	86,750	84,857	1,893
Appleton National Bank, Appleton, Wis.	Jan. 21, 1868	50,000	45,000	44,208	792
National Bank, Whitestown, N. Y.......	Feb. 14, 1868	120,000	44,500	43,943	557
First National Bank, New Brunswick, N. J	Feb. 26, 1868	100,000	90,000	87,519	2,481
First National Bank, Cuyahoga Falls, Ohio	Mar. 4, 1868	50,000	45,000	44,246	754
First National Bank, Cedarburg, Wis...	Mar. 23, 1868	100,000	90,000	88,937	1,063
Commercial National Bank, Cincinnati, Ohio	Apr. 28, 1868	500,000	345,950	310,470	5,480
Second National Bank, Watertown, N.Y.	July 21, 1868	100,000	90,000	86,000	4,000
First National Bank, South Worcester, N. Y	Aug. 4, 1868	175,500	157,100	155,026	2,374
National Mechanics and Farmers' Bank, Albany, N. Y	Aug. 4, 1868	350,000	314,950	310,535	4,415
Second National Bank, Des Moines, Iowa.	Aug. 5, 1868	50,000	42,500	41,927	573
First National Bank, Steubenville, Ohio.	Aug. 8, 1868	150,000	135,000	129,192	5,808
First National Bank, Plumer, Pa	Aug. 25, 1868	100,000	87,500	84,287	3,213
First National Bank, Danville, Va	Sept. 30, 1868	50,000	45,000	44,260	740
First National Bank, Dorchester, Mass..	Nov. 23, 1868	150,000	132,500	128,564	3,936
First National Bank, Oskaloosa, Iowa...	Dec. 17, 1868	75,000	67,500	66,726	774
Merchants' and Mechanics' National Bank, Troy, N. Y......	Dec. 31, 1868	300,000	181,750	182,232	2,518
National Savings Bank, Wheeling, W. Va.	Jan. 7, 1869	100,000	90,000	88,680	1,320
First National Bank. Marion, Ohio.....	Jan. 12, 1869	125,000	109,850	108,214	1,636
National Insurance Bank, Detroit, Mich.	Feb. 26, 1869	200,010	85,000	84,069	931
National Bank of Lansingburg, N. Y.....	Mar. 6, 1869	150,000	135,000	132,942	2,058
National Bank of North America, New York, N. Y	Apr. 15, 1869	1,000,000	333,000	328,560	4,410
First National Bank, Hallowell, Me.....	Apr. 19, 1869	60,000	53,350	52,662	688
First National Bank, Clyde, N. Y	Apr. 23, 1869	50,000	44,000	42,780	1,220
Pacific National Bank, New York, N. Y.	May 10, 1869	422,700	134,990	133,137	1,853
Grocers' National Bank, New York, N. Y.	June 7, 1869	200,000	85,250	84,656	594
Savannah National Bank, Savannah, Ga	June 22, 1869	100,000	85,000	83,790	1,210
First National Bank, Frostburg, Md.....	July 30, 1869	50,000	45,000	44,523	477
First National Bank, La Salle, Ill	Aug. 30, 1869	50,000	45,000	44,305	695
National Bank Commerce, Georgetown, D.C ...	Oct. 28, 1869	100,000	90,000	88,435	1,565
Miners' National Bank, Salt Lake City, Utah......	Dec. 2, 1869	150,000	135,000	133,094	1,906

* New bank with same title.   † Never completed organization.   ‡ Consolidated with another bank.

National banks that have gone into liquidation, &c.—Continued.

Name and location of bank.	Date of liqui-dation.	Capital.	Circulation. Issued.	Circulation. Retired.	Circulation. Outstand-ing.
First National Bank, Vinton, Iowa	Dec. 13, 1869	$50,000	$42,500	$42,148	$352
National Exchange Bank, Philadelphia, Pa	Jan. 8, 1870	300,000	175,750	171,180	4,570
First National Bank, Decatur, Ill	Jan. 10, 1870	100,000	85,250	83,954	1,296
National Union Bank, Owego, N. Y	Jan. 11, 1870	100,000	88,250	85,214	3,036
First National Bank, Berlin, Wis	Jan. 25, 1870	50,000	44,000	43,657	343
Central National Bank, Cincinnati, Ohio	Mar. 31, 1870	500,000	425,000	417,385	7,615
First National Bank, Dayton, Ohio	Apr. 9, 1870	150,000	135,000	132,851	2,149
National Bank of Chemung, Elmira, N. Y	June 10, 1870	100,000	90,000	89,137	863
Merchants' National Bank, Milwaukee, Wis	June 14, 1870	100,000	90,000	88,445	1,555
First National Bank, Saint Louis, Mo	July 16, 1870	200,000	179,990	177,132	2,858
Chemung Canal National Bank, Elmira, N. Y	Aug. 3, 1870	100,000	90,000	88,712	1,288
Central National Bank, Omaha, Nebr	Sept. 23, 1870	100,000			
First National Bank, Clarksville, Va	Oct. 13, 1870	50,000	27,000	26,605	395
First National Bank, Burlington, Vt	Oct. 15, 1870	300,000	270,000	261,143	8,857
First National Bank, Lebanon, Ohio	Oct. 24, 1870	100,000	85,000	83,759	1,241
National Exchange Bank, Lansingburg, N. Y	Dec. 27, 1870	100,000	90,000	88,746	1,254
Muskingum National Bank, Zanesville, Ohio	Jan. 7, 1871	100,000	90,000	88,285	1,715
United National Bank, Winona, Minn	Feb. 15, 1871	50,000	45,000	44,280	720
First National Bank, Des Moines, Iowa	Mar. 25, 1871	100,000	90,000	88,514	1,486
State National Bank, Saint Joseph, Mo	Mar. 31, 1871	100,000	90,000	89,202	798
Saratoga County National Bank, Waterford, N. Y	Mar. 28, 1871	150,000	135,000	133,075	1,925
First National Bank, Fenton, Mich	May 2, 1871	100,000	49,500	48,813	687
First National Bank, Wellsburg, W. Va	June 24, 1871	100,000	90,000	88,508	1,492
Clarke National Bank, Rochester, N. Y	Aug. 11, 1871	200,000	180,000	177,284	2,716
Commercial National Bank, Oshkosh, Wis	Nov. 22, 1871	100,000	90,000	88,437	1,563
Fort Madison National Bank, Fort Madison, Iowa	Dec. 26, 1871	75,000	67,500	66,250	1,250
National Bank of Maysville, Ky	Jan. 6, 1872	300,000	270,000	265,491	4,509
Fourth National Bank, Syracuse, N. Y	Jan. 9, 1872	105,500	91,700	90,094	1,606
American National Bank, New York, N. Y	May 10, 1872	500,000	450,000	436,905	13,095
Carroll County National Bank, Sandwich, N. H	May 24, 1872	50,000	45,000	43,167	1,833
Second National Bank, Portland, Me	June 24, 1872	100,000	81,000	78,213	2,787
Atlantic National Bank, Brooklyn, N. Y	July 15, 1872	200,000	165,000	161,990	3,010
Merchants and Farmers' National Bank, Quincy, Ill	Aug. 8, 1872	150,000	135,000	132,215	2,785
First National Bank, Rochester, N. Y	Aug. 9, 1872	400,000	206,100	201,663	4,437
Lawrenceburg National Bank, Ind	Sept. 10, 1872	200,000	180,000	175,433	4,567
Jewett City National Bank, Conn	Oct. 4, 1872	60,000	48,750	47,267	1,483
First National Bank, Knoxville, Tenn	Oct. 22, 1872	100,000	80,910	78,704	2,206
First National Bank, Goshen, Ind	Nov. 7, 1872	115,000	103,500	100,971	2,529
Kidder National Gold Bank, Boston, Mass	Nov. 8, 1872	300,000	120,000	120,000	
Second National Bank, Zanesville, Ohio	Nov. 16, 1872	154,700	138,140	134,283	3,857
Orange County National Bank, Chelsea, Vt	Jan. 14, 1873	200,000	180,000	172,281	7,719
Second National Bank, Syracuse, N. Y	Feb. 18, 1873	100,000	90,000	87,790	2,210
Richmond National Bank, Richmond, Ind	Feb. 28, 1873	230,000	207,000	207,000	
First National Bank, Adams, N. Y	Mar. 7, 1873	75,000	66,900	64,893	2,007
Mechanics' National Bank, Syracuse, N. Y	Mar. 11, 1873	140,000	93,800	91,570	2,230
Farmers and Mechanics' National Bank, Rochester, N. Y	Apr. 15, 1873	100,000	83,250	81,005	2,245
Montana National Bank, Helena, Mont	Apr. 15, 1873	100,000	31,500	30,965	535
First National Bank, Havana, N. Y	June 3, 1873	50,000	45,000	42,905	2,095
Merchants and Farmers' National Bank, Ithaca, N. Y	June 30, 1873	50,000	45,000	43,466	1,534
National Bank of Cazenovia, N. Y	July 18, 1873	150,000	116,770	113,356	3,414
Merchants' National Bank, Memphis, Tenn	Aug. 30, 1873	250,000	225,000	217,508	7,492
Second National Bank, Chicago, Ill	Sept. 25, 1873	100,000	97,500	93,076	4,424
Merchants' National Bank, Dubuque, Iowa	Sept. 30, 1873	200,000	180,000	169,098	10,902
Beloit National Bank, Beloit, Wis	Oct. 2, 1873	50,000	45,000	43,338	1,662
Union National Bank, Saint Louis, Mo	Oct. 22, 1873	500,000	150,300	142,343	7,957
City National Bank, Green Bay, Wis	Nov. 29, 1873	50,000	45,000	41,794	3,206
First National Bank, Shelbina, Mo	Jan. 1, 1874	100,000	90,000	85,159	4,841
Second National Bank, Nashville, Tenn	Jan. 8, 1874	125,000	92,920	88,600	4,320
First National Bank, Oneida, N. Y	Jan. 13, 1874	125,000	110,500	104,539	5,961
Merchants' National Bank, Hastings, Minn	Feb. 7, 1874	100,000	90,000	84,267	5,733

* Never completed organization.   † New bank organized with same title.

National banks that have gone into voluntary liquidation, &c.—Continued.

Name and location of bank.	Date of liqui-dation.	Capital.	Circulation.		
			Issued.	Retired.	Outstand-ing.
National Bank of Tecumseh, Mich	Mar. 3, 1874	$50,000	$45,000	$42,795	$2,205
Gallatin National Bank, Shawneetown, Ill	Mar. 7, 1874	250,000	225,000	212,268	12,732
First National Bank, Brookville, Pa	Mar. 26, 1874	100,000	90,000	85,060	4,940
Citizens' National Bank, Sioux City, Iowa	Apr. 14, 1874	50,000	45,000	43,485	1,515
Farmers' National Bank, Warren, Ill	Apr. 28, 1874	50,000	45,000	42,312	2,688
First National Bank. Medina, Ohio	May 6, 1874	75,000	45,000	43,057	1,943
Croton River National Bank, South East, N. Y	May 25, 1874	200,000	166,550	160,048	6,502
Merchants' National Bank of West Virginia, Wheeling, W. Va	July 7, 1874	500,000	450,000	426,788	23,212
Central National Bank, Baltimore, Md.	July 15, 1874	200,000	180,090	170,583	9,417
Second National Bank, Leavenworth, Kans	July 22, 1874	100,000	90,000	83,121	6,879
Teutonia National Bank, New Orleans, La	Sept. 2, 1874	300,000	270,000	249,875	20,125
City National Bank, Chattanooga, Tenn	Sept. 10, 1874	170,000	153,000	142,652	10,348
First National Bank, Cairo, Ill	Oct. 10, 1874	100,000	90,000	83,985	6,015
First National Bank, Olathe, Kans	Nov. 9, 1874	50,000	45,000	43,152	1,848
First National Bank, Beverly, Ohio	Nov. 10, 1874	102,000	90,000	83,237	6,763
Union National Bank, La Fayette, Ind.	Dec. 4, 1874	250,000	224,095	211,859	12,236
Ambler National Bank, Jacksonville, Fla	Dec. 7, 1874	42,500			
Mechanics' National Bank, Chicago, Ill.	Dec. 30, 1874	250,000	144,900	133,850	11,050
First National Bank, Evansville, Wis	Jan. 9, 1875	55,000	45,000	42,603	2,397
First National Bank, Baxter Springs, Kans	Jan. 12, 1875	50,000	36,000	34,082	1,918
People's National Bank, Pueblo, Col	Jan. 12, 1875	50,000	27,000	25,810	1,190
National Bank of Commerce, Green Bay, Wis	Jan. 12, 1875	100,000	90,000	84,940	5,060
First National Bank, Millersburg, Ohio	Jan. 12, 1875	100,000	72,000	68,385	3,615
First National Bank, Staunton, Va	Jan. 23, 1875	100,000	90,000	83,102	6,898
National City Bank, Milwaukee, Wis	Feb. 24, 1875	100,000	76,500	71,590	4,910
Irasburg National Bank of Orleans, Irasburg, Vt.	Mar. 17, 1875	75,000	67,500	62,922	4,578
First National Bank, Pekin, Ill	Mar. 25, 1875	100,000	90,000	81,062	8,938
Merchants and Planters' National Bank, Augusta, Ga	Mar. 30, 1875	200,000	180,000	164,235	15,765
Monticello National Bank, Monticello, Iowa	Mar. 30, 1875	100,000	45,000	39,319	5,681
Iowa City National Bank, Iowa City, Iowa	Apr. 14, 1875	125,000	112,500	105,024	7,476
First National Bank, Wheeling, W. Va.	Apr. 22, 1875	250,000	225,000	202,338	22,662
First National Bank, Mount Clemens, Mich	May 20, 1875	50,000	27,000	24,745	2,255
First National Bank, Knob Noster, Mo.	May 29, 1875	50,000	45,000	42,602	2,398
First National Bank, Brodhead, Wis	June 24, 1875	50,000	45,000	41,548	3,452
Auburn City National Bank, Auburn, N.Y	June 26, 1875	200,000	141,300	128,621	12,679
First National Bank, El Dorado, Kans	June 30, 1875	50,000	45,000	41,472	3,528
First National Bank, Junction City, Kans	July 1, 1875	50,000	45,000	41,205	3,795
First National Bank, Chetopa, Kans	July 19, 1875	50,000	36,000	32,888	3,112
First National Bank, Golden, Col	Aug. 25, 1875	50,200	27,000	25,405	1,595
National Bank of Jefferson, Wis	Aug. 26, 1875	50,000	54,000	47,552	6,448
Green Lane National Bank, Green Lane, Pa	Sept. 9, 1875	100,000	90,000	84,074	5,926
State National Bank, Topeka, Kans	Sept. 15, 1875	60,500	30,600	28,487	2,113
Farmers' National Bank, Marshalltown, Iowa	Sept. 18, 1875	50,000	27,000	24,295	2,705
Richland National Bank, Mansfield, Ohio	Sept. 25, 1875	150,000	135,000	114,927	20,073
Planters' National Bank, Louisville, Ky.	Sept. 30, 1875	350,000	315,000	261,218	53,782
First National Bank, Gallatin, Tenn	Oct. 1, 1875	75,000	45,000	41,195	3,805
First National Bank, Charleston, W. Va.	Oct. 2, 1875	100,000	90,000	83,501	6,499
People's National Bank, Winchester, Ill.	Oct. 4, 1875	75,000	67,500	58,820	8,680
First National Bank, New Lexington, Ohio	Oct. 12, 1875	50,000	45,000	41,632	3,368
First National Bank, Ishpeming, Mich	Oct. 20, 1875	50,000	45,000	40,555	4,445
Fayette County National Bank, Washington, Ohio	Oct. 26, 1875	100,000	90,000	82,090	7,910
Merchants' National Bank, Fort Wayne, Ind	Nov. 8, 1875	100,000	90,000	85,540	4,460
Kansas City National Bank, Kansas City, Mo	Nov. 13, 1875	100,000	90,000	81,914	8,086
First National Bank, Schoolcraft, Mich	Nov. 17, 1875	50,000	45,000	40,447	4,553
First National Bank, Curwensville, Pa	Dec. 17, 1875	100,000	90,000	75,773	14,227
National Marine Bank, St. Paul, Minn	Dec. 28, 1875	100,000	90,000	81,010	8,990
First National Bank, Rochester, Ind	Jan. 11, 1876	50,000	45,000	38,836	6,164
First National Bank, Lodi, Ohio	Jan. 11, 1876	100,000	90,000	73,193	16,807
Lion National Bank, Portsmouth, Ohio	Jan. 19, 1876	100,000	90,000	81,597	8,403
First National Bank, Ashland, Nebr	Jan. 26, 1876	50,000	45,000	40,078	4,922

* No circulation.

National banks that have gone into voluntary liquidation, &c.—Continued.

Name and location of bank.	Date of liquidation.	Capital.	Circulation. Issued.	Retired.	Outstanding.
First National Bank, Paxton, Ill	Jan. 28, 1876	$50,000	$45,000	$38,894	$6,106
First National Bank, Bloomfield, Iowa ..	Feb. 5, 1876	55,000	49,500	42,090	7,410
Marietta National Bank, Marietta, Ohio.	Feb. 16, 1876	150,000	135,000	121,806	13,194
Salt Lake City National Bank of Utah, at Salt Lake City, Utah	Feb. 21, 1876	100,000	90,000	84,948	5,052
First National Bank, La Grange, Mo....	Feb. 24, 1876	50,000	45,000	37,397	7,603
First National Bank, Atlantic, Iowa	Mar. 7, 1876	50,000	45,000	37,680	7,320
First National Bank, Spencer, Ind	Mar. 11, 1876	70,000	63,000	54,001	8,999
National Currency Bank, New York, N. Y	Mar. 23, 1876	100,000	90,000	85,265	4,735
Caverna National Bank, Caverna, Ky ...	May 13, 1876	50,000	45,000	39,085	5,915
City National Bank, Pittsburgh, Pa ...	May 25, 1876	200,000	90,000	73,893	16,107
National State Bank, Des Moines, Iowa	June 21, 1876	100,000	90,000	80,240	9,760
First National Bank, Trenton, Mo	June 22, 1876	50,000	45,000	37,426	7,574
First National Bank, Bristol, Tenn......	July 10, 1876	50,000	45,000	38,999	6,001
First National Bank, Leon, Iowa	July 11, 1876	60,000	45,000	38,962	6,038
Anderson County National Bank, Lawrenceburg, Ky	July 29, 1876	100,000	45,000	39,100	5,900
First National Bank, Newport, Ind......	Aug. 7, 1876	60,000	45,000	33,428	11,572
First National Bank, De Pere, Wis.....	Aug. 17, 1876	50,000	31,500	28,214	3,286
Second National Bank, Lawrence, Kans.	Aug. 23, 1876	100,000	90,000	78,895	11,105
Commercial National Bank, Versailles, Ky	Aug. 26, 1876	170,000	153,000	126,391	26,609
State National Bank, Atlanta, Ga	Aug. 31, 1876	200,000	135,000	119,490	15,510
Syracuse National Bank, Syracuse, N. Y.	Sept. 25, 1876	200,000	180,000	155,820	24,180
First National Bank, Northumberland, Pa	Oct. 6, 1876	100,000	90,000	80,042	9,958
First National Bank, Lancaster, Mo ...	Nov. 14, 1876	50,000	27,000	22,652	4,348
First National Bank, Council Grove, Kans ..	Nov. 28, 1876	50,000	26,500	21,522	4,978
National Bank of Commerce, Chicago, Ill	Dec. 2, 1876	250,000	166,500	152,088	14,412
First National Bank, Palmyra, Mo	Dec. 12, 1876	100,000	90,000	80,821	9,179
First National Bank, Newton, Iowa....	Dec. 16, 1876	50,000	45,000	27,683	17,317
National Southern Kentucky Bank, Bowling Green, Ky	Dec. 23, 1876	50,000	27,000	22,239	4,761
First National Bank, Monroe, Iowa	Jan. 1, 1877	60,000	45,000	36,256	8,744
First National Bank, New London, Conn	Jan. 9, 1877	100,000	91,000	81,337	9,663
Winona Deposit National Bank, Winona, Minn	Jan. 28, 1877	100,000	90,000	70,852	19,148
First National Bank, South Charleston, Ohio	Feb. 24, 1877	100,000	90,000	67,980	22,020
Lake Ontario National Bank, Oswego, N. Y.	Feb. 24, 1877	275,000	238,150	226,002	12,148
First National Bank, Sidney, Ohio	Feb. 26, 1877	52,000	46,200	33,092	13,108
Chillicothe National Bank, Chillicothe, Ohio	Apr. 9, 1877	100,000	89,990	74,820	15,170
First National Bank, Manhattan, Kans .	Apr. 13, 1877	50,000	44,200	32,516	11,684
National Bank of Monticello, Ky	Apr. 23, 1877	60,000	49,500	27,855	21,645
First National Bank, Rockville, Ind.....	Apr. 25, 1877	200,000	173,090	112,405	60,685
Georgia National Bank, Atlanta, Ga ...	May 31, 1877	100,000	90,000	79,604	10,396
First National Bank, Adrian, Mich......	June 11, 1877	100,000	88,500	73,587	14,913
First National Bank, Napoleon, Ohio ..	June 30, 1877	50,000	90,000	77,071	12,929
First National Bank, Lancaster, Ohio ..	Aug. 1, 1877	60,000	54,000	36,791	17,209
First National Bank, Minerva, Ohio....	Aug. 24, 1877	50,000	45,000	31,607	13,393
Kinney National Bank, Portsmouth, Ohio	Aug. 28, 1877	100,000	90,000	61,235	28,765
First National Bank, Green Bay, Wis...	Oct. 19, 1877	50,000	45,000	28,223	16,777
National Exchange Bank, Wakefield, R. I	Oct. 27, 1877	70,000	34,650	23,001	11,649
First National Bank, Union City, Ind...	Nov. 10, 1877	50,000	15,000	28,875	16,125
First National Bank, Negaunee, Mich...	Nov. 13, 1877	50,000	45,000	27,714	17,256
Tenth National Bank, New York, N. Y	Nov. 23, 1877	500,000	411,000	294,629	116,371
First National Bank, Paola, Kans	Dec. 1, 1877	50,000	44,350	25,637	18,713
National Exchange Bank, Troy, N. Y ..	Dec. 6, 1877	100,000	90,000	63,147	26,853
Second National Bank, La Fayette, Ind	Dec. 20, 1877	200,000	52,167	33,567	18,600
State National Bank, Minneapolis, Minn	Dec. 31, 1877	100,000	82,500	43,387	39,113
Second National Bank, Saint Louis, Mo	Jan. 8, 1878	200,000	53,055	31,314	21,711
First National Bank, Sullivan, Ind	Jan. 8, 1878	50,000	45,000	28,460	16,540
Rockland County National Bank, Nyack, N. Y.	Jan. 10, 1878	100,000	89,000	58,456	30,544
First National Bank, Wyandott, Kans .	Jan. 19, 1878	50,000	45,000	28,209	16,791
First National Bank, Boone, Iowa......	Jan. 22, 1878	50,000	32,400	20,275	12,125
First National Bank, Pleasant Hill, Mo.	Feb. 7, 1878	50,000	45,000	26,300	18,700
National Bank of Gloversville, N. Y	Feb. 28, 1878	100,000	64,750	41,437	23,293
First National Bank, Independence, Mo	Mar. 1, 1878	50,000	27,000	13,773	13,227
National State Bank, Lima, Ind	Mar. 2, 1878	100,000	33,471	15,867	17,604
First National Bank, Tell City, Ind	Mar. 4, 1878	50,000	44,500	30,524	13,976

*National banks that have gone into voluntary liquidation, &c.—*Continued.

Name and location of bank.	Date of liqui- dation.	Capital.	Circulation.		
			Issued.	Retired.	Outstand- ing.
First National Bank, Pomeroy, Ohio....	Mar. 5, 1878	$200,000	$75,713	$50,580	$25,124
Eleventh Ward National Bank, Boston, Mass	Mar. 14, 1878	200,000	89,400	64,665	24,735
First National Bank, Prophetstown, Ill	Mar. 19, 1878	50,000	45,000	34,689	10,311
First National Bank, Jackson, Mich	Mar. 26, 1878	100,000	88,400	50,215	38,185
First National Bank, Eau Claire, Wis...	Mar. 30, 1878	60,000	38,461	20,499	17,962
First National Bank, Washington, Ohio.	Apr. 5, 1878	200,000	69,750	38,113	31,637
First National Bank, Middleport, Ohio..	Apr. 20, 1878	80,000	31,500	20,525	10,975
First National Bank, Streator, Ill	Apr. 24, 1878	50,000	40,500	24,795	15,705
First National Bank, Muir. Mich........	Apr. 25, 1878	50,000	44,200	24,471	19,729
Kane County National Bank, Saint Charles, Ill............	May 31, 1878	50,000	26,300	13,758	12,542
First National Bank, Carthage, Mo	June 1, 1878	50,000	44,500	22,561	21,939
Security National Bank, Worcester, Mass	June 5, 1878	100,000	49,000	31,895	17,105
First National Bank, Lake City, Colo ...	June 15, 1878	50,000	25,300	14,654	10,646
People's National Bank, Norfolk, Va....	July 31, 1878	100,000	85,705	36,480	49,225
Topeka National Bank, Topeka, Kans...	Aug. 7, 1878	100,000	89,300	34,812	54,488
First National Bank, Saint Joseph, Mo..	Aug. 13, 1878	100,000	67,110	25,015	42,095
First National Bank, Winchester, Ind...	Aug. 24, 1878	60,000	52,700	22,849	29,851
Muscatine National Bank, Muscatine, Iowa	Sept. 2, 1878	100,000	44,200	15,436	28,764
Traders' National Bank, Chicago, Ill....	Sept. 4, 1878	200,000	43,700	16,107	27,593
Union National Bank, Rahway, N. J	Sept. 10, 1878	100,000	89,200	45,252	43,948
First National Bank, Sparta, Wis........	Sept. 14, 1878	50,000	45,000	20,149	24,851
Herkimer County National Bank, Little Falls, N. Y	Oct. 11, 1878	200,000	178,300	85,466	92,834
Farmers' National Bank, Bangor, Me....	Nov. 22, 1878	100,000	89,100	42,377	46,723
Pacific National Bank, Council Bluffs, Iowa	Nov. 30, 1878	100,000	45,000	24,457	20,543
First National Bank, Anamosa, Iowa ...	Dec. 14, 1878	50,000	44,500	14,959	29,541
Smithfield National Bank, Pittsburgh, Pa	Dec. 16, 1878	200,000	90,000	40,400	49,600
First National Bank, Buchanan, Mich...	Dec. 21, 1878	50,000	27,000	13,238	13,762
First National Bank, Prairie City, Ill...	Dec. 24, 1878	50,000	27,000	6,160	20,840
Corn Exchange National Bank, Chicago, Ill............	Jan. 4, 1879	500,000	450,000	421,784	28,216
Franklin National Bank, Columbus, Ohio	Jan. 4, 1879	100,000	180,000	130,273	49,727
Traders' National Bank, Bangor, Me....	Jan. 14, 1879	100,000	76,400	29,498	46,902
First National Bank, Conic, N. H........	Jan. 14, 1879	60,000	45,597	20,488	25,109
First National Bank, Salem, N. C........	Jan. 14, 1879	150,000	128,200	42,525	85,675
First National Bank, Granville, Ohio ...	Jan. 14, 1879	50,000	45,000	23,249	21,751
Commercial National Bank, Petersburg, Va	Jan. 14, 1879	120,000	99,800	31,598	68,202
First National Gold Bank, Stockton, Cal.	Jan. 14, 1879	300,000	238,600	83,983	154,617
First National Bank, Sheboygan, Wis...	Jan. 14, 1879	50,000	45,000	17,817	27,183
First National Bank, Boscobel, Wis	Jan. 21, 1879	50,000	43,900	16,648	27,252
National Marine Bank, Oswego, N. Y ...	Jan. 25, 1879	120,000	44,300	22,175	22,125
Central National Bank, Hightstown, N. J	Feb. 15, 1879	100,000	32,400	15,405	16,995
Brookville National Bank, Brookville, Ind	Feb. 18, 1879	100,000	89,000	24,915	64,085
Farmers' National Bank, Centreville, Iowa	Feb. 27, 1879	50,000	41,500	13,727	27,773
First National Bank, Clarinda, Iowa....	Mar. 1, 1879	50,000	45,000	21,275	23,725
Waterville National Bank, Waterville, Me	Mar. 3, 1879	125,000	110,300	50,491	59,809
First National Bank, Tremont, Pa	Mar. 4, 1879	75,000	64,600	18,965	45,635
First National Bank, Atlanta, Ill........	Apr. 15, 1879	50,000	26,500	5,900	20,600
Union National Bank, Aurora, Ill........	Apr. 22, 1879	125,000	82,000	19,549	62,451
National Bank of Menasha. Wis	Apr. 26, 1879	50,000	44,500	16,860	27,640
National Exchange Bank, Jefferson City, Mo	May 8, 1879	50,000	45,000	15,270	29,730
First National Bank, Hannibal, Mo	May 15, 1879	100,000	88,200	22,726	65,474
Merchants' National Bank, Winona, Minn	June 16, 1879	100,000	35,000	12,731	22,269
Farmers' National Bank, Keithsburg, Ill.	July 3, 1879	50,000	27,000	7,545	19,455
First National Bank, Franklin, Ky......	July 5, 1879	100,000	54,000	15,545	38,455
National Bank of Salem, Ind...........	July 8, 1879	50,000	44,400	17,938	26,462
Fourth National Bank, Memphis, Tenn..	July 19, 1779	125,000	45,000	10,630	34,370
Bedford National Bank, Bedford, Ind....	July 21, 1879	100,000	87,200	34,513	52,687
First National Bank, Afton, Iowa	Aug. 15, 1879	50,000	26,500	6,400	20,100
First National Bank, Deer Lodge, Mont.	Aug. 16, 1879	50,000	45,000	16,980	28,020
First National Bank, Batavia, Ill........	Aug. 30, 1879	50,000	44,300	14,796	29,504
National Gold Bank and Trust Company, San Francisco, Cal	Sept. 1, 1879	750,000	40,000	14,215	25,785
Gainesville National Bank, Gainesville, Ala............	Nov. 25, 1789	100,000	90,000	16,532	73,468
First National Bank, Hackensack, N. J..	Dec. 6, 1879	100,000	90,000	23,802	66,198
National Bank of Delavan, Wis.........	Jan. 7, 1880	50,000	27,000	5,690	21,310
Mechanics' National Bank, Nashville, Tenn	Jan. 13, 1880	100,000	90,000	21,250	68,750
Manchester National Bank, Manchester, Ohio	Jan. 13, 1880	50,000	48,303	10,955	37,348
First National Bank, Meyersdale, Pa....	Mar. 5, 1880	50,000	30,600	9,575	21,025

National banks that have gone into liquidation, &c.—Continued.

Name and location of bank.	Date of liqui-dation.	Capital.	Circulation.		
			Issued.	Retired.	Outstand-ing.
First National Bank, Mifflinburg, Pa....	Mar. 8, 1880	$100, 000	$90, 000	$15, 030	$74, 970
National Bank of Michigan, Marshall, Mich.............................	May 14, 1880	120, 000	100, 800	15, 547	85, 253
First National Bank, Rondout, N. Y*...	Oct. 11, 1880	300, 000	270, 000	37, 067	232, 933
Ascutney National Bank, Windsor, Vt..	Oct. 19, 1880	100, 000	90, 000	11, 955	78, 045
National Exchange Bank, Houston, Tex	Sept. 10, 1880	100, 000	31, 500	3, 405	28, 095
First National Bank, Seneca Falls, N. Y.	Nov. 23, 1880	60, 000	54, 000	36, 285	17, 715
First National Bank, Baraboo, Wis	Nov. 27, 1880	50, 000	27, 000	2, 983	24, 017
Bundy National Bank, New Castle, Ind..	Dec. 6, 1880	50, 000	45, 000	7, 865	37, 135
Vineland National Bank, Vineland, N. J.	Jan. 11, 1881	50, 000	45, 000	6, 225	38, 775
Ocean County National Bank, Toms River, N. J...........................	Jan. 11, 1881	100, 000	119, 405	12, 380	107, 025
Hungerford National Bank, Adams, N. Y	Jan. 27, 1881	50, 000	45, 000	4, 483	40, 517
Merchants' National Bank, Minneapolis, Minn................................	Jan. 31, 1881	150, 000	98, 268	15, 348	82, 920
First National Bank, Huntington, Ind*..	Jan. 31, 1881	100, 000	90, 000	10, 983	79, 017
Farmers' National Bank, Mechanicsburg, Ohio................................	Feb. 18, 1881	100, 000	30, 140	3, 155	26, 985
First National Bank, Green Spring, Ohio.	Feb. 18, 1881	50, 000	45, 000	5, 116	39, 884
First National Bank, Cannon Falls, Minn	Feb. 21, 1881	50, 000	45, 000	4, 220	40, 780
First National Bank, Coshocton, Ohio...	Feb. 21, 1881	50, 000	53, 058	6, 996	46, 062
Manufacturers' National Bank, Three Rivers, Mich	Feb. 25, 1881	50, 000	45, 000	4, 085	40, 915
First National Bank, Lansing, Iowa......	Feb. 25, 1881	50, 000	45, 000	4, 605	40, 395
First National Bank, Watertown, N. Y...	May 26, 1881	100, 000	90, 000	14, 490	75, 510
First National Bank, Americus, Ga	June 17, 1881	60, 000	45, 000	3, 720	41, 280
First National Bank, Saint Joseph, Mich	June 30, 1881	50, 000	27, 000	650	26, 350
First National Bank, Indianapolis, Ind*	July 5, 1881	300, 000	234, 248	....	234, 248
First National Bank, Logan, Ohio	July 8, 1881	50, 000	45, 000	1, 500	43, 500
First National Bank, Shakopee, Minn ...	Aug. 10, 1881	50, 000	45, 000	....	45, 000
First National Bank, Rochelle, Ill	Aug. 9, 1881	50, 000	45, 000	600	44, 400
National State Bank, Oskaloosa, Iowa...	Aug. 13, 1881	50, 000	36, 685	....	36, 685
Attica National Bank, Attica, N. Y. ...	Aug. 30, 1881	50, 000	45, 000	2, 600	42, 400
First National Bank, Hobart, N. Y	Aug. 27, 1881	100, 000	90, 000	1, 900	88, 100
Totals.....................................		40, 860, 610	30, 020, 481	23, 947, 960	6, 072, 521

* New bank organized with same title.

*National banks that have been placed in the hands of receivers, together with their capital,
circulation issued, lawful money deposited with the Treasurer to redeem circulation, the
amount redeemed, and the amount outstanding on November 1, 1881.*

Name and location of bank.	Capital stock.	Lawful money de-posited.	Circulation.		
			Issued.	Redeemed.	Outstand-ing.
First National Bank, Attica, N. Y	$50, 000	$44, 000	$44, 000	$43, 686	$314
Venango National Bank, Franklin, Pa...	390, 000	85, 000	85, 000	84, 648	352
Merchants' National Bank, Washington, D. C...............................	200, 000	180, 000	180, 000	178, 869	1, 131
First National Bank, Medina, N. Y.....	50, 000	40, 000	40, 000	39, 707	293
Tennessee National Bank, Memphis, Tenn	100, 000	90, 000	90, 000	89, 498	502
First National Bank, Selma, Ala........	100, 000	85, 000	85, 000	84, 437	563
First National Bank, New Orleans, La..	500, 000	180, 000	180, 000	178, 220	1, 780
National Unadilla Bank, Unadilla, N. Y.	120, 000	100, 000	100, 000	99, 644	356
Farmers and Citizens' National Bank, Brooklyn, N. Y.......................	300, 000	253, 900	253, 900	252, 124	1, 776
Croton National Bank, New York, N. Y..	200, 000	180, 000	180, 000	179, 369	631
First National Bank, Bethel, Conn......	60, 000	26, 300	26, 300	26, 054	246
First National Bank, Keokuk, Iowa.....	100, 000	90, 000	90, 000	89, 449	551
National Bank of Vicksburg, Miss......	50, 000	25, 500	25, 500	25, 354	146
First National Bank, Rockford, Ill	50, 000	45, 000	45, 000	44, 533	467
First National Bank of Nevada, Austin, Nev.............................	250, 000	129, 700	129, 700	127, 981	1, 719
Ocean National Bank, New York, N. Y.	1, 000, 000	800, 000	800, 000	784, 792	15, 208
Union Square National Bank, New York, N. Y..............................	200, 000	50, 000	50, 000	49, 357	643
Eighth National Bank, New York, N. Y.	250, 000	243, 393	243, 393	238, 963	4, 430
Fourth National Bank, Philadelphia, Pa.	200, 000	179, 000	179, 000	175, 580	3, 420
Waverly National Bank, Waverly, N. Y.	100, 100	71, 000	71, 000	69, 285	1, 715
First National Bank, Fort Smith, Ark...	50, 000	45, 000	45, 000	44, 200	800

National banks that have been placed in the hands of receivers, &c.—Continued.

Name and location of bank.	Capital stock.	Lawful money deposited.	Circulation. Issued.	Circulation. Redeemed.	Circulation. Outstanding.
Scandinavian National Bank, Chicago, Ill	$250,000	$135,000	$135,000	$133,188	$1,812
Wallkill National Bank, Middletown, N. Y	175,000	118,900	118,900	115,725	3,175
Crescent City National Bank, New Orleans, La	500,000	450,000	450,000	437,545	12,455
Atlantic National Bank, New York, N. Y.	300,000	100,000	100,000	97,523	2,477
First National Bank, Washington, D. C.	500,000	450,000	450,000	428,694	21,306
National Bank of Commonwealth, New York, N. Y	750,000	234,000	234,000	224,419	9,581
Merchants' National Bank, Petersburg, Va	400,000	360,000	360,000	337,075	22,925
First National Bank, Petersburg, Va	200,000	179,200	179,200	167,740	11,460
First National Bank, Mahsfield, Ohio	100,000	90,000	90,000	85,585	4,415
New Orleans National Banking Association, New Orleans, La	600,000	350,000	360,000	346,500	13,500
First National Bank, Carlisle, Pa	50,000	45,000	45,000	42,790	2,210
First National Bank, Anderson, Ind	50,000	45,000	45,000	42,794	2,206
First National Bank, Topeka, Kans	100,000	90,000	90,000	85,022	4,978
First National Bank, Norfolk, Va	100,000	95,000	95,000	89,135	5,865
Gibson County National Bank, Princeton, Ind	50,000	43,800	43,800	40,670	3,130
First National Bank of Utah, Salt Lake City, Utah	150,000	134,991	134,991	129,340	5,651
Cook County National Bank, Chicago, Ill	500,000	298,400	315,900	297,823	18,077
First National Bank, Tiffin, Ohio	100,000	68,850	68,850	63,993	4,857
Charlottesville National Bank, Charlottesville, Va	200,000	128,585	146,585	128,410	18,175
Miners' National Bank, Georgetown, Col.	150,000	40,000	45,000	38,140	6,860
Fourth National Bank, Chicago, Ill	200,000	180,000	180,000	167,535	12,465
First National Bank, Bedford, Iowa	30,000	18,512	27,000	17,920	9,080
First National Bank, Osceola, Iowa	50,000	45,000	45,000	38,539	6,461
First National Bank, Duluth, Minn	100,000	90,000	90,000	86,084	3,916
First National Bank, La Crosse, Wis	50,000	45,000	45,000	38,753	6,247
City National Bank, Chicago, Ill	250,000	225,000	225,000	205,716	19,284
Watkins National Bank, Watkins, N. Y.	75,000	67,500	67,500	55,656	11,844
First National Bank, Wichita, Kans	60,000	52,200	52,200	45,671	6,529
First National Bank, Greenfield, Ohio	50,000	50,000	50,000	44,862	5,138
National Bank of Fishkill, N. Y	200,000	140,200	177,200	140,882	36,318
First National Bank, Franklin, Ind	132,000	130,992	130,992	101,227	29,765
Northumberland County National Bank, Shamokin, Pa	67,000	46,300	60,300	45,575	14,725
First National Bank, Winchester, Ill	50,000	45,000	45,000	31,773	13,227
National Exchange Bank, Minneapolis, Minn	100,000	90,000	90,000	54,630	35,370
National Bank of the State of Missouri, Saint Louis, Mo	2,500,000	1,648,800	1,693,660	1,599,402	94,258
First National Bank, Delphi, Ind	50,000	35,000	45,000	34,695	10,305
First National Bank, Georgetown, Col.	75,000	31,000	45,000	29,370	15,630
Lock Haven National Bank, Lock Haven, Pa	120,000	45,000	71,200	43,458	27,742
Third National Bank, Chicago, Ill	750,000	325,500	597,810	321,347	276,493
Central National Bank, Chicago, Ill	200,000	28,500	45,000	28,778	16,222
First National Bank, Kansas City, Mo	500,000	44,940	44,940	25,590	19,350
Commercial National Bank, Kansas City, Mo	100,000	44,500	44,500	26,794	17,706
First National Bank, Ashland, Pa	112,500	88,000	88,000	52,870	35,130
First National Bank, Tarrytown, N. Y.	100,000	55,000	89,200	54,586	34,614
First National Bank, Allentown, Pa	250,000	78,644	78,644	46,365	32,276
First National Bank, Waynesburg, Pa.	100,000	69,345	69,345	66,185	3,160
Washington County National Bank, Greenwich, N. Y	200,000	114,220	114,220	68,804	45,416
First National Bank, Dallas, Tex	50,000	29,800	29,800	15,645	14,155
People's National Bank, Helena, Mont	100,000	42,300	89,300	42,065	47,235
First National Bank, Bozeman, Mont	50,000	24,400	44,400	23,075	21,325
Citizens' National Bank, Charlottesville, Va	100,000	90,000	90,000	84,694	5,306
Merchants' National Bank, Fort Scott, Kans	50,000	15,000	15,000	26,502	18,498
Farmers' National Bank, Platte City, Mo.	50,000	27,000	27,000	9,970	17,030
First National Bank, Warrensburg, Mo	100,000	15,000	45,000	24,117	20,883
German-American National Bank, Washington, D. C	130,000	39,500	62,500	40,389	22,111
German National Bank, Chicago, Ill	500,000	367,000	450,000	426,050	23,950
Commercial National Bank, Saratoga Springs, N. Y	100,000	86,900	86,900	51,620	35,280
Second National Bank, Scranton, Pa	200,000	91,465	91,165	35,530	55,635
National Bank, Poultney, Vt	100,000	90,000	90,000	41,037	48,963

National banks that have been placed in the hands of receivers, &c.—Continued.

Name and location of bank.	Capital stock.	Lawful money deposited.	Circulation.		
			Issued.	Redeemed.	Outstanding.
First National Bank, Monticello, Ind ...	$50,000	$12,000	$27,000	$10,618	$16,382
First National Bank, Butler, Pa	50,000	31,165	71,165	19,720	51,445
Manufacturers' National Bank, Chicago, Ill......................................	500,000	438,750	450,000	431,344	18,656
First National Bank, Meadville, Pa	100,000	20,000	89,500	17,037	72,463
First National Bank, Newark, N. J	300,000	91,643	327,653	85,839	241,814
First National Bank, Brattleboro', Vt...	300,000	20,000	90,000	16,750	73,250
Totals...........................	18,762,600	11,825,592	12,968,440	11,112,930	1,855,510

Insolvent national banks, with date of appointment of receivers, amount of capital stock and claims proved, and rate of dividends paid to creditors.

Name and location of bank.	Receiver appointed—	Capital stock.	Proved claims.	Dividends paid.	Remarks.
				Pr.cent.	
First National Bank of Attica, N. Y.	Apr. 14, 1865	$50,000	$122,089	58	Finally closed.
Venango National Bank of Franklin, Pa.	May 1, 1866	300,000	434,186	15	
Merchants' National Bank of Washington, D. C.	May 8, 1866	200,000	669,513	24 7/10	Finally closed.
First National Bank of Medina, N. Y.	Mar. 13, 1867	50,000	82,338	39 2/3	Do.
Tennessee National Bank of Memphis, Tenn.	Mar. 21, 1867	100,000	376,932	17½	Do.
First National Bank of Selma, Ala.	Apr. 30, 1867	100,000	289,467	42	
First National Bank of New Orleans, La.	May 20, 1867	500,000	1,119,213	70	
National Unadilla Bank of Unadilla, N. Y.	Aug. 29, 1867	120,000	127,801	45 2/10	Finally closed.
Farmers and Citizens' National Bank of Brooklyn, N. Y.	Sept. 6, 1867	300,000	1,191,500	96	Do.
Croton National Bank of New York, N. Y.	Oct. 1, 1867	200,000	170,752	88½	Do.
First National Bank of Bethel, Conn.	Feb. 28, 1868	60,000	68,986	100	Do.
First National Bank of Keokuk, Iowa.	Mar. 3, 1868	100,000	205,256	68½	Do.
National Bank of Vicksburg, Miss.	Apr. 24, 1868	50,000	33,562	35	
First National Bank of Rockford, Ill.	Mar. 15, 1869	50,000	69,874	41 8/10	Finally closed.
First National Bank of Nevada, Austin, Nev.	Oct. 13, 1869	250,000	170,012	90	
Ocean National Bank of New York, N. Y.	Dec. 13, 1871	1,000,000	1,282,254	100	30 per cent. interest dividend.
Union Square National Bank of New York, N. Y.	Dec. 15, 1871	200,000	157,120	100	10 per cent. paid to stockholders, and finally closed.
Eighth National Bank of New York, N. Y.	Dec. 15, 1871	250,000	378.772	100	Finally closed.
Fourth National Bank of Philadelphia, Pa.	Dec. 20, 1871	200,000	645,558	100	Do.
Waverly National Bank of Waverly, N. Y.	Apr. 23, 1872	106,100	79,864	100	32½ per cent. paid to stockholders, and finally closed.
First National Bank of Fort Smith, Ark.	May 2, 1872	50,000	15,142	100	13 per cent. paid to stockholders, and finally closed.
Scandinavian National Bank of Chicago, Ill.	Dec. 12, 1872	250,000	249,174	40	
Wallkill National Bank of Middletown, N. Y.	Dec. 31, 1872	175,000	171,468	100	30 per cent. interest dividend, and finally closed.
Crescent City National Bank of New Orleans, La.	Mar. 18, 1873	500,000	657,020	84 83/100	Finally closed.
Atlantic National Bank of New York, N. Y.	Apr. 28, 1873	300,000	574,513	95	
First National Bank of Washington, D. C	Sept. 19, 1873	500,000	1,619,965	100	Finally closed.
National Bank of the Commonwealth, New York, N. Y.	Sept. 22, 1873	750,000	796,995	100	35 per cent. paid to stockholders and finally closed.

Insolvent national banks, with date of appointment of receivers, &c.—Continued.

Name and location of bank.	Receiver appointed.	Capital stock.	Proved claims.	Dividends paid.	Remarks.
				Pr. cent.	
Mechanics' National Bank of Petersburg, Va.	Sept. 25, 1873	$400,000	$992,636	34	Finally closed.
First National Bank of Petersburg, Va.	Sept. 25, 1873	200,000	167,285	76	Do.
First National Bank of Mansfield, Ohio.	Oct. 18, 1873	100,000	175,068	45	
New Orleans National Banking Association of New Orleans, La.	Oct. 23, 1873	600,000	1,426,858	55	
First National Bank of Carlisle, Pa.	Oct. 24, 1873	50,000	65,729	72	
First National Bank of Anderson, Ind.	Nov. 23, 1873	50,000	143,534	25	
First National Bank of Topeka, Kans.	Dec. 16, 1873	100,000	55,372	58⁷⁄₁₀	Finally closed.
First National Bank of Norfolk, Va.	June 3, 1874	100,000	176,330	49	4 per cent. since last report.
Gibson County National Bank of Princeton, Ind.	Nov. 28, 1874	50,000	62,646	100	Finally closed.
First National Bank of Utah, Salt Lake City, Utah.	Dec. 10, 1874	150,000	93,021	24³ˣ¹⁄₁₀₀₀	Do.
Cook County National Bank of Chicago, Ill.	Feb. 1, 1875	500,000	988,878	8	
First National Bank of Tiffin, Ohio.	Oct. 22, 1875	100,000	237,824	66	Finally closed.
Charlottesville National Bank of Charlottesville, Va.	Oct. 28, 1875	200,000	342,794	55	5 per cent. since last report.
Miners' National Bank of Georgetown, Colo.	Jan 24, 1876	150,000	92,624	65	30 per cent. since last report.
Fourth National Bank of Chicago, Ill.	Feb. 1, 1876	200,000	35,801	50	
First National Bank of Bedford, Iowa.	Feb. 1, 1876	30,000	50,781	12½	
First National Bank of Osceola, Iowa.	Feb. 25, 1876	50,000	34,535	100	Finally closed.
First National Bank of Duluth, Minn.	Mar. 13, 1876	100,000	87,786	100	Finally closed.
First National Bank of La Crosse, Wis.	Apr. 11, 1876	50,000	135,952	45	
City National Bank of Chicago, Ill.	May 17, 1876	250,000	703,658	77	7 per cent. since last report.
Watkins National Bank of Watkins, N. Y.	July 12, 1876	75,000	59,114	100	Finally closed.
First National Bank of Wichita, Kans.	Sept. 23, 1876	60,000	97,464	70	
First National Bank of Greenfield, Ohio.*	Dec. 12, 1876	50,000	....	....	
National Bank of Fishkill, Fishkill, N. Y.	Jan. 27, 1877	200,000	345,320	100	15 per cent. since last report.
First National Bank of Franklin, Ind.	Feb. 13, 1877	132,000	184,457	100	Finally closed.
Northumberland County National Bank, Shamokin, Pa.	Mar. 12, 1877	67,000	165,435	75	
First National Bank of Winchester, Ill.	Mar. 16, 1877	50,000	143,300	63¹⁰⁄₁₀₀	Finally closed.
National Exchange Bank of Minneapolis, Minn.	May 24, 1877	100,000	223,942	88⁸⁄₁₀₀	Finally closed.
National Bank of the State of Missouri, Saint Louis, Mo.	June 23, 1877	2,500,000	1,847,584	95	5 per cent. since last report.
First National Bank of Delphi, Ind.	July 20, 1877	50,000	133,112	100	
First National Bank of Georgetown, Colo.	Aug. 18, 1877	75,000	168,760	22½	Finally closed.
Lock Haven National Bank of Lock Haven, Pa.	Aug. 20, 1877	120,000	243,736	90	10 per cent. since last report.
Third National Bank of Chicago, Ill.	Nov. 24, 1877	750,000	988,641	100	10 per cent. since last report.
Central National Bank of Chicago, Ill.	Dec. 1, 1877	200,000	298,321	60	
First National Bank of Kansas City, Mo.	Feb. 11, 1878	500,000	392,391	10	
Commercial National Bank of Kansas City, Mo.	Feb. 11, 1878	100,000	75,175	100	31 per cent. paid to stockholders.
First National Bank of Ashland, Pa.*	Feb. 28, 1878	112,500	33,105	100	Finally closed.
First National Bank of Tarrytown, N. Y.	Mar. 23, 1878	100,000	118,371	85	
First National Bank of Allentown, Pa.*	Apr. 15, 1878	250,000	50,486	50	
First National Bank of Waynesburg, Pa.	May 15, 1878	100,000	22,146	40	
Washington County National Bank of Greenwich, N. Y.	June 8, 1878	200,000	262,812	100	Finally closed.

* Formerly in voluntary liquidation.

Insolvent national banks, with date of appointment of receivers, &c.—Continued.

Name and location of bank.	Receiver appointed.	Capital stock.	Proved claims.	Dividends paid.	Remarks.
				Pr.cent.	
First National Bank of Dallas, Tex.	June 8, 1878	$50,000	$73,804	37	
People's National Bank of Helena, Mont.	Sept. 13, 1878	100,000	168,048	30	15 per cent. since last report.
First National Bank of Bozeman, Mont.	Sept. 14, 1878	50,000	69,631	85	15 per cent. since last report.
Citizens' National Bank of Charlottesville, Va.*	Sept. 14, 1878	100,000	....	....	
Merchants' National Bank of Fort Scott, Kans.*	Sept. 25, 1878	50,000	27,801	60	Finally closed.
Farmers' National Bank of Platte City, Mo.	Oct. 1, 1878	50,000	12,449	100	18 per cent. paid to stockholders and finally closed.
First National Bank of Warrensburg, Mo.	Nov. 1, 1878	100,000	156,260	100	25 per cent. since last report, and finally closed.
German-American National Bank of Washington, D. C.	Nov. 1, 1878	130,000	270,205	40	20 per cent. since last report.
German National Bank of Chicago, Ill.*	Dec 20, 1878	500,000	141,484	80	25 per cent. since last report.
Commercial National Bank of Saratoga Springs, N. Y.	Feb. 11, 1879	100,000	128,832	100	15 per cent. since last report, and finally closed.
Second National Bank of Scranton, Pa.*	Mar. 15, 1879	200,000	118,638	25	25 per cent. since last report.
National Bank of Poultney, Vt....	Apr. 7, 1879	100,000	81,801	100	40 per cent. since last report, and finally closed.
First National Bank of Monticello, Ind.	July 18, 1879	50,000	14,206	30	
First National Bank of Butler, Pa.	July 23, 1879	50,000	108,385	40	10 per cent. since last report.
Manufacturers' National Bank of Chicago, Ill.*	Feb. 10, 1880	500,000	....		
First National Bank of Meadville, Pa.	June 9, 1880	100,000	93,625	100	35 per cent. since last report.
First National Bank of Newark, N. J.	June 14, 1880	300,000	552,177	90	10 per cent. since last report.
First National Bank of Brattleboro', Vt.	June 19, 1880	300,000	86,669	100	10 per cent. since last report.
Total......................	....	18,762,600	25,786,261		

*Formerly in voluntary liquidation.

AGGREGATE RESOURCES AND LIABILITIES

OF

THE NATIONAL BANKS

FROM

OCTOBER, 1863, TO OCTOBER, 1881.

Aggregate resources and liabilities of the National

1 8 6 3.

Resources.	JANUARY.	APRIL.	JULY.	OCTOBER 5.
				66 banks.
Loans and discounts.........				$5,466,088 23
U. S. bonds and securities....				5,662,600 00
Other items...............				106,009 12
Due from nat'l and other b'ks.				2,625,597 05
Real estate, furniture, &c				177,565 69
Current expenses				53,808 92
Premiums paid				2,503 69
Checks and other cash items..				492,138 58
Bills of nat'l and other banks.				764,725 00
Specie and other lawful mon'y.				1,446,607 62
Total				16,797,644 00

1 8 6 4.

	JANUARY 4.	APRIL 4.	JULY 4.	OCTOBER 3.
	139 banks.	307 banks.	467 banks.	508 banks.
Loans and discounts..........	$10,666,095 60	$31,593,943 43	$70,746,513 33	$93,238,637 92
U. S. bonds and securities....	15,112,250 00	41,175,150 00	92,530,500 00	108,064,400 00
Other items.................	74,571 48	432,059 95	842,017 73	1,434,739 76
Due from national banks		4,699,479 56	15,935,730 13	19,965,720 47
Due from other b'ks and b'k'rs	*4,786,124 58	8,537,908 94	17,337,558 66	14,051,396 31
Real estate, furniture, &c....	381,144 00	755,696 41	1,694,049 46	2,202,318 29
Current expenses	118,854 43	352,720 77	502,341 31	1,021,569 02
Checks and other cash items..	577,507 92	2,651,916 96	5,057,122 90	7,640,169 14
Bills of nat'l and other banks.	895,521 00	1,660,000 00	5,344,172 00	4,687,727 00
Specie and other lawful mon'y.	5,018,622 57	22,961,411 64	42,283,798 23	44,801,497 48
Total	37,630,691 58	114,820,287 66	252,273,803 75	297,108,195 30

1 8 6 5.

	JANUARY 2.	APRIL 3.	JULY 3.	OCTOBER 2.
	638 banks.	907 banks.	1,294 banks.	1,513 banks.
Loans and discounts..........	$166,448,718 00	$252,404,208 07	$362,442,743 08	$487,170,136 29
U. S. bonds and securities....	176,578,750 00	277,619,900 00	391,744,850 00	427,731,300 00
Other items.................	3,294,883 27	4,275,769 51	12,569,120 38	19,048,513 15
Due from national banks	30,820,175 44	40,963,243 47	76,977,539 59	89,978,980 55
Due from other b'ks and b'k'rs	19,836,072 83	22,554,636 57	26,078,028 01	17,393,232 25
Real estate, furniture, &c....	4,083,226 12	6,525,118 80	11,231,257 28	14,703,281 77
Current expenses	1,053,725 34	2,298,025 65	2,338,775 56	4,539,525 11
Premiums paid	1,323,623 56	1,823,291 81	2,243,210 31	2,585,501 06
Checks and other cash items..	17,837,496 77	29,681,394 13	41,314,904 50	72,309,854 44
Bills of nat'l and other banks.	14,275,153 00	13,710,370 00	21,651,826 00	16,247,241 00
Specie	4,481,937 68	6,659,660 47	9,437,060 40	18,072,012 59
Legal tenders and fract'l cur'y	72,535,504 67	112,999,320 59	168,426,166 55	189,988,496 28
Total	512,568,666 68	771,514,039 10	1,126,455,481 66	1,359,768,074 49

* Including amount due from national banks.

Banks from October, 1863, *to October,* 1881.

1863.

Liabilities.	JANUARY.	APRIL.	JULY.	OCTOBER 5. 66 banks.
Capital stock				$7,188,393 00
Undivided profits				128,030 06
Individual and other deposits				8,497,681 84
Due to nat'l and other banks*				981,178 59
Other items				2,360 51
Total				16,797,644 00

1864.

	JANUARY 4. 139 banks.	APRIL 4. 307 banks.	JULY 4. 407 banks.	OCTOBER 3. 508 banks.
Capital stock	$14,740,522 00	$42,204,474 00	$75,213,945 00	$86,782,802 00
Surplus fund			1,129,910 22	2,010,286 10
Undivided profits	432,827 81	1,625,656 87	3,094,330 11	5,982,392 22
National b'k notes outstanding	30,155 00	9,797,975 00	25,825,665 00	45,260,504 00
Individual and other deposits	19,450,492 53	51,274,914 01	119,414,239 03	122,166,536 43
Due to nat'l and other banks*	2,153,779 38	6,814,930 40	27,382,006 37	34,862,384 81
Other items	822,914 86	3,102,337 38	213,708 02	43,289 77
Total	37,630,691 58	114,820,287 66	252,273,803 75	297,108,195 30

1865.

	JANUARY 2. 638 banks.	APRIL 3. 907 banks.	JULY 3. 1,294 banks.	OCTOBER 2. 1,513 banks.
Capital stock	$135,618,674 00	$215,326,023 00	$325,634,558 00	$393,157,206 00
Surplus fund	8,663,311 22	17,318,942 65	31,303,565 64	38,713,380 72
Undivided profits	12,283,812 65	17,869,307 14	23,159,408 17	32,350,278 19
National b'k notes outstanding	66,709,375 00	98,896,488 00	131,452,158 00	171,321,903 00
Individual and other deposits	183,479,636 98	262,961,473 13	398,357,559 59	500,910,873 22
United States deposits	37,764,729 77	57,630,141 01	58,632,720 67	48,170,381 31
Due to national banks	30,619,175 57	41,301,031 16	78,261,045 64	90,044,837 08
Due to other b'ks and bankers*	37,104,130 62	59,602,581 64	79,591,594 93	84,155,161 27
Other items	265,620 87	578,951 37	462,871 02	944,053 70
Total	512,568,666 68	771,514,939 10	1,126,455,481 66	1,359,768,074 49

* Including State bank circulation outstanding.

Aggregate resources and liabilities of the National

1866.

Resources.	JANUARY 1. 1,582 banks.	APRIL 2. 1,612 banks.	JULY 2. 1,634 banks.	OCTOBER 1. 1,644 banks.
Loans and discounts	$500,650,109 19	$528,080,526 70	$550,253,094 17	$603,314,704 83
U. S. b'ds dep'd to secure circ'n	298,376,850 00	315,850,300 00	326,483,350 00	331,843,200 00
Other U. S. b'ds and securities	142,003,500 00	125,625,750 00	121,152,950 00	91,974,650 00
Oth'r stocks, b'ds, and mortg's	17,483,753 18	17,379,738 92	17,565,911 46	15,887,490 06
Due from national banks	93,254,551 02	87,564,329 71	96,696,482 66	107,650,174 18
Due from other b'ks and b'k'rs	14,658,229 87	13,682,345 12	13,982,613 23	15,211,117 16
Real estate, furniture, &c....	15,436,296 16	15,895,564 46	16,730,923 62	17,154,002 58
Current expenses............	3,193,717 78	4,927,599 79	3,032,716 27	5,311,253 35
Premiums paid	2,423,918 02	2,233,516 31	2,398,872 26	2,403,773 47
Checks and other cash items.	89,837,684 50	105,490,619 36	96,077,134 53	103,684,249 21
Bills of national and other b'ks	20,406,442 00	18,279,816 00	17,866,742 00	17,437,779 00
Specie................	19,205,018 75	17,529,778 42	12,629,376 30	9,226,831 82
Legal tenders and tract'l cur'y	187,846,548 82	189,867,852 52	201,425,041 63	205,793,578 76
Total................	1,404,776,619 29	1,442,407,737 31	1,476,395,208 13	1,526,962,804 42

1867.

	JANUARY 7. 1,648 banks.	APRIL 1. 1,642 banks.	JULY 1. 1,636 banks.	OCTOBER 7. 1,642 banks.
Loans and discounts	$608,771,799 61	$597,648,286 53	$588,450,396 12	$609,675,214 61
U. S. b'ds dep'd to secure circ'n	339,570,700 00	328,863,650 00	337,684,250 00	338,640,150 00
U. S. b'ds dep'd to sec're dep'ts	36,185,950 00	38,465,800 00	38,368,950 00	37,862,100 00
U. S. b'ds and sec'ties on hand.	52,949,300 00	46,639,400 00	45,633,700 00	42,460,800 00
Oth'r stocks, b'ds, and mortg's	15,073,737 45	20,194,875 21	21,452,615 43	21,507,881 42
Due from national banks.....	92,552,206 29	94,121,186 21	92,308,911 87	95,217,610 14
Due from other b'ks and b'k'rs	12,996,157 49	10,737,392 90	9,663,322 82	8,389,226 47
Real estate, furniture, &c....	18,925,315 51	19,625,893 81	19,800,905 86	20,639,708 23
Current expenses............	2,822,675 18	5,693,784 17	3,249,153 31	5,297,494 13
Premiums paid	2,860,398 85	3,411,325 56	3,338,600 37	2,764,186 35
Checks and other cash items.	101,430,220 18	87,951,405 13	128,312,177 79	134,603,231 51
Bills of national banks	19,263,718 00	12,873,785 00	16,138,709 00	11,841,104 00
Bills of other banks	1,176,142 00	825,748 00	531,267 00	333,209 00
Specie.....................	19,726,043 20	11,444,529 15	11,128,672 98	12,798,044 40
Legal tenders and fract'l cur'y	104,872,371 64	92,861,254 17	102,534,613 46	100,550,849 91
Compound interest notes.....	82,047,250 00	84,065,790 00	75,488,290 00	56,888,250 00
Total..................	1,511,222,985 40	1,465,451,105 84	1,494,084,526 01	1,490,469,060 17

1868.

	JANUARY 6. 1,642 banks.	APRIL 6. 1,643 banks.	JULY 6. 1,640 banks.	OCTOBER 5. 1,643 banks.
Loans and discounts.	$616,603,479 89	$628,029,347 65	$655,729,546 42	$657,668,847 83
U. S. b'ds dep'd to secure circ'n	339,064,200 00	339,686,650 00	339,569,100 00	340,487,050 00
U. S. b'ds dep'd to sec're dep'ts	37,315,750 00	37,446,000 00	37,853,150 00	37,360,150 00
U. S. b'ds and sec'ties on hand.	44,104,500 00	45,938,550 00	43,068,350 00	36,817,600 00
Oth'r stocks, b'ds, and mortg's	19,365,864 77	19,874,384 33	20,007,327 42	20,693,406 40
Due from national banks.....	99,131,446 60	95,900,606 35	114,434,097 93	102,278,547 77
Due from other b'ks and b'k'rs	8,480,199 74	7,074,297 44	8,642,456 72	7,848,822 24
Real estate, furniture, &c....	21,125,665 68	22,082,570 25	22,699,829 70	22,747,875 18
Current expenses............	2,986,893 86	5,428,460 25	2,938,519 04	5,278,101 22
Premiums paid	2,464,536 96	2,660,106 09	2,432,074 37	1,819,815 50
Checks and other cash items.	109,390,266 37	114,993,036 23	124,076,007 71	143,241,394 99
Bills of national banks	16,655,572 00	12,573,340 00	13,210,179 00	11,842,974 00
Bills of other banks	261,269 00	196,106 00	342,550 00	222,668 00
Fractional currency..........	1,927,876 78	1,825,640 16	1,863,358 91	2,262,791 97
Specie	20,981,601 45	18,373,943 22	20,755,919 04	13,003,713 39
Legal-tender notes..........	114,306,491 00	84,390,219 00	100,166,100 00	92,453,475 00
Compound interest notes.....	39,097,030 00	38,917,490 00	19,473,420 00	4,513,730 00
Three per cent. certificates ..	8,245,000 00	24,255,000 00	44,905,000 00	59,080,000 00
Total..................	1,502,647,644 10	1,499,668,920 97	1,572,167,076 26	1,559,621,773 49

Banks from October, 1863, *to October*, 1881 —Continued.

1 8 6 6.

Liabilities.	JANUARY 1. 1,582 banks.	APRIL 2. 1,612 banks.	JULY 2. 1,634 banks.	OCTOBER 1. 1,644 banks.
Capital stock	$403, 357, 346 00	$409, 273, 534 00	$414, 270, 493 00	$415, 472, 369 00
Surplus fund	43, 000, 370 78	44, 687, 810 54	50, 151, 991 77	53, 359, 277 64
Undivided profits	28, 972, 493 70	30, 964, 422 73	29, 286, 175 45	32, 593, 486 69
National b'k notes outstanding	213, 239, 530 00	248, 886, 282 00	267, 798, 678 00	280, 253, 818 00
State bank notes outstanding.	45, 449, 155 00	33, 800, 863 00	19, 996, 163 00	9, 748, 025 00
Individual deposits	522, 507, 829 27	534, 734, 950 33	533, 338, 174 25	564, 616, 777 64
U. S. deposits	29, 747, 236 15	29, 150, 729 82	36, 038, 185 03	30, 420, 819 80
Dep'ts of U. S. disb'sing officers			3, 066, 892 22	2, 979, 955 77
Due to national banks	94, 709, 074 15	89, 067, 501 51	96, 496, 726 42	110, 531, 957 31
Due to other b'ks and bankers	23, 793, 584 24	21, 841, 641 35	25, 951, 728 99	26, 986, 317 57
Total	1, 404, 776, 619 29	1, 442, 407, 737 31	1, 476, 395, 208 13	1, 526, 962, 804 42

1 8 6 7.

	JANUARY 7. 1,648 banks.	APRIL 1. 1,642 banks.	JULY 1. 1,636 banks.	OCTOBER 7. 1,642 banks.
Capital stock	$420, 229, 739 00	$419, 399, 484 00	$418, 558, 148 00	$420, 073, 415 00
Surplus fund	59, 992, 874 57	60, 206, 013 58	63, 232, 811 12	66, 695, 587 01
Undivided profits	26, 961, 382 60	31, 131, 034 39	30, 656, 222 84	33, 751, 446 21
National b'k notes outstanding	291, 436, 749 00	292, 788, 572 00	291, 769, 553 00	293, 887, 941 00
State bank notes outstanding	6, 961, 499 00	5, 460, 312 00	4, 484, 112 00	4, 092, 153 00
Individual deposits	558, 699, 768 06	512, 046, 182 47	539, 599, 076 10	540, 797, 837 51
U. S. deposits	27, 284, 876 93	27, 473, 005 66	29, 838, 391 53	23, 062, 119 92
Dep'ts of U. S. disb'sing officers	2, 477, 500 48	2, 650, 981 39	3, 474, 192 74	4, 352, 379 43
Due to national banks	92, 761, 998 43	91, 156, 890 89	89, 821, 751 60	93, 111, 240 89
Due to other b'ks and bankers	24, 416, 588 33	23, 138, 629 46	22, 659, 267 08	19, 644, 940 20
Total	1, 511, 222, 985 40	1, 465, 451, 105 84	1, 494, 084, 526 01	1, 499, 469, 060 17

1 8 6 8.

	JANUARY 6. 1,642 banks.	APRIL 6. 1,643 banks.	JULY 6. 1,640 banks.	OCTOBER 5. 1,643 banks.
Capital stock	$420, 260, 790 00	$420, 676, 210 00	$420, 105, 011 00	$420, 634, 511 00
Surplus fund	70, 586, 125 70	72, 349, 119 60	75, 840, 118 04	77, 995, 761 40
Undivided profits	31, 399, 877 57	32, 861, 597 08	33, 543, 223 35	36, 095, 883 98
National b'k notes outstanding	294, 377, 390 00	295, 336, 044 00	294, 908, 264 00	295, 760, 489 00
State bank notes outstanding.	3, 792, 013 00	3, 310, 177 00	3, 163, 771 00	2, 900, 352 00
Individual deposits	534, 704, 709 00	532, 011, 480 36	575, 842, 070 12	580, 940, 820 85
U. S. deposits	24, 305, 638 02	22, 750, 342 77	24, 603, 676 96	17, 573, 250 64
Dep'ts of U. S. disb'sing officers	3, 208, 783 03	4, 076, 682 31	3, 499, 389 99	4, 570, 478 16
Due to national banks	98, 144, 669 61	94, 073, 631 25	113, 306, 346 34	99, 414, 397 28
Due to other b'ks and bankers	21, 867, 648 17	21, 323, 036 60	27, 355, 204 56	23, 720, 829 18
Total	1, 502, 647, 644 10	1, 499, 668, 920 97	1, 572, 167, 076 26	1, 559, 621, 773 49

Aggregate resources and liabilities of the National

1869.

Resources.	JANUARY 4. 1,628 banks.	APRIL 17. 1,620 banks.	JUNE 12. 1,619 banks.	OCTOBER 9. 1,617 banks.
Loans and discounts	$644,945,039 53	$662,084,813 47	$680,347,755 81	$682,883,106 97
U. S. bonds to secure circ'lat'n	338,539,950 00	338,379,250 00	338,699,750 00	339,480,100 00
U. S. bonds to secure deposits	34,538,350 00	29,721,350 00	27,625,350 00	18,704,000 00
U. S. b'ds and sec'ties on hand	35,010,600 00	30,226,550 00	27,476,650 00	25,903,950 00
Oth'r stocks, b'ds, and mortg's	20,127,732 96	20,074,435 69	20,777,560 53	22,250,697 14
Due from redeeming agents	65,727,070 80	57,554,382 55	62,912,636 82	56,669,562 84
Due from other national banks	36,067,316 84	30,520,527 89	35,556,504 53	35,393,563 47
Due from State b'ks and b'k'rs	7,715,719 34	8,075,595 60	9,149,919 24	8,790,418 57
Real estate, furniture, &c	23,289,838 28	23,798,188 13	23,850,271 17	25,169,188 95
Current expenses	3,265,990 81	5,641,195 01	5,820,577 87	5,646,382 96
Premiums paid	1,654,352 70	1,716,210 13	1,809,070 01	2,092,364 85
Checks and other cash items	142,605,984 92	154,137,191 23	161,614,852 66	108,809,817 37
Bills of other national banks	14,684,799 00	11,725,239 00	11,554,447 00	10,776,023 00
Fractional currency	2,280,471 06	2,088,545 18	1,804,855 53	2,090,727 38
Specie	29,626,750 26	9,944,532 15	18,455,090 48	23,002,405 83
Legal-tender notes	88,239,300 00	80,875,161 00	80,934,119 00	83,719,295 00
Three per cent. certificates	52,075,000 00	51,190,000 00	49,815,000 00	45,845,000 00
Total	1,540,394,266 50	1,517,753,167 03	1,564,174,410 65	1,497,226,604 33

1870.

	JANUARY 22. 1,615 banks.	MARCH 24. 1,615 banks.	JUNE 9. 1,612 banks.	OCTOBER 8. 1,615 banks.	DECEMBER 28. 1,648 banks.
Loans and discounts	$688,875,203 70	$710,848,609 39	$719,341,186 06	$715,928,079 81	$725,515,538 49
Bonds for circulation	339,350,750 00	339,251,350 00	338,845,200 00	340,857,450 00	344,104,200 00
Bonds for deposits	17,592,000 00	16,102,000 00	15,790,000 00	15,381,500 00	15,189,500 00
U. S. bonds on hand	24,677,100 00	27,292,150 00	28,276,600 00	22,323,800 00	23,893,300 00
Other stocks and b'ds	21,082,412 00	20,524,294 55	23,300,681 87	23,614,721 25	22,686,358 59
Due from red'g agents	71,641,486 05	73,435,117 98	74,635,405 61	66,275,668 92	64,805,002 88
Due from nat'l banks	31,994,609 26	29,510,688 11	36,128,750 66	33,948,805 65	37,478,166 49
Due from State banks	9,319,560 54	10,238,219 85	10,430,781 32	9,202,496 71	9,824,144 18
Real estate, &c	26,002,713 01	26,330,701 24	26,593,357 00	27,470,746 97	28,021,637 44
Current expenses	3,469,588 00	6,683,189 54	6,324,955 47	5,871,750 02	6,905,073 32
Premiums paid	2,439,591 41	2,680,882 39	3,076,456 74	2,491,222 11	3,251,648 72
Cash items	111,624,822 00	11,267,703 12	11,497,534 13	12,536,613 57	13,229,403 34
Clear'g-house exch'gs		75,317,992 22	83,936,515 64	79,089,688 39	76,208,707 00
National bank notes	15,840,669 00	14,226,817 00	16,342,582 00	12,512,927 00	17,001,846 00
Fractional currency	2,476,966 75	2,285,499 02	2,184,714 39	2,078,178 05	2,150,522 89
Specie	48,345,383 72	37,096,543 44	31,099,437 78	18,460,011 47	26,307,251 59
Legal-tender notes	87,708,502 00	82,485,978 00	94,573,751 00	79,324,577 00	80,580,745 00
Three per cent. cert'fs	43,820,000 00	43,570,000 00	43,465,000 00	43,345,000 00	41,845,000 00
Total	1,546,261,357 44	1,529,147,735 85	1,565,756,909 67	1,510,713,236 92	1,538,998,105 93

1871.

	MARCH 18. 1,688 banks.	APRIL 29. 1,707 banks.	JUNE 10. 1,723 banks.	OCTOBER 2. 1,767 banks.	DECEMBER 16. 1,790 banks.
Loans and discounts	$767,858,490 59	$779,321,828 11	$789,416,568 13	$831,552,210 00	$818,996,311 74
Bonds for circulation	351,556,700 00	354,427,200 00	357,388,950 00	364,475,800 00	366,840,200 00
Bonds for deposits	15,231,500 00	15,236,500 00	15,250,500 00	28,087,500 00	23,155,150 00
U. S. bonds on hand	23,911,350 00	22,487,950 00	24,200,300 00	17,753,650 00	17,675,500 00
Other stocks and b'ds	22,763,869 20	22,414,659 05	23,132,871 05	24,517,059 35	23,061,184 20
Due from red'g agents	83,809,188 92	85,061,016 31	92,360,246 71	86,878,608 84	77,985,600 53
Due from nat'l banks	30,201,119 99	38,332,679 74	39,636,579 35	43,525,362 05	43,313,344 78
Due from State banks	10,271,605 34	11,478,174 71	11,853,308 60	12,772,669 83	13,060,301 44
Real estate, &c	28,805,814 79	29,242,762 79	29,637,999 30	30,089,783 85	30,070,330 57
Current expenses	6,694,014 17	6,764,159 73	6,295,099 46	6,153,370 29	7,330,424 12
Premiums paid	3,939,995 20	4,414,755 40	5,026,385 97	5,500,890 17	6,950,073 74
Cash items	11,642,644 74	12,749,289 84	13,101,497 95	14,058,268 86	13,784,424 76
Clear'g-house exch'gs	100,693,917 54	130,855,698 15	102,091,311 75	101,165,854 52	114,538,539 93
National bank notes	13,137,006 00	16,632,323 00	19,101,389 00	14,197,653 00	13,085,904 00
Fractional currency	2,103,298 16	2,135,763 09	2,160,713 22	2,095,485 79	2,061,600 89
Specie	25,769,166 64	22,732,027 02	19,992,955 16	13,252,998 17	29,555,299 56
Legal-tender notes	91,072,349 00	106,219,126 00	122,137,660 00	109,414,735 00	93,942,707 00
Three per cent. cert'fs	37,570,000 00	33,935,000 00	30,690,000 00	25,075,000 00	21,400,000 00
Total	1,627,032,030 28	1,694,440,912 94	1,703,415,335 65	1,730,566,899 72	1,715,861,897 22

Banks from October, 1863, *to October,* 1881—Continued.

1 8 6 9.

Liabilities.	JANUARY 4. 1,628 banks.	APRIL 17. 1,620 banks.	JUNE 12. 1,619 banks.	OCTOBER 9. 1,617 banks.
Capital stock	$419,040,931 00	$420,818,721 00	$422,659,260 00	$426,399,151 00
Surplus fund	81,169,936 52	82,653,989 19	82,218,576 47	86,165,334 32
Undivided profits	35,318,273 71	87,489,314 82	43,812,898 70	40,687,300 92
Nat'l banknotes outstanding	294,476,702 00	292,457,008 00	292,753,286 00	293,503,645 00
State bank notes outstanding	2,734,669 00	2,615,387 00	2,558,874 00	2,454,697 00
Individual deposits	568,530,934,11	547,922,174 91	574,307,382 77	511,400,196 63
U. S. deposits	13,211,850 19	10,114,328 32	10,301,907 71	7,112,646 67
Dep'ts U.S. disbursing officers.	3,472,884 90	3,665,131 61	2,454,048 99	4,516,648 12
Due to national banks	95,453,139 33	92,662,648 49	100,933,910 03	95,067,892 83
Due to State banks and b'k'rs	26,984,945 74	23,018,610 62	28,046,771 30	23,849,371 62
Notes and bills re-discounted		2,464,849 81	2,392,205 61	3,839,357 10
Bills payable		1,870,913 26	1,735,289 07	2,140,363 12
Total	1,540,394,266 50	1,517,753,167 03	1,564,174,410 65	1,497,226,604 33

1 8 7 0.

	JANUARY 22. 1,615 banks.	MARCH 24. 1,615 banks.	JUNE 9. 1,612 banks.	OCTOBER 8. 1,615 banks.	DECEMBER 28. 1,648 banks.
Capital stock	$426,074,954 00	$427,504,247 00	$427,235,701 00	$430,399,301 00	$435,356,004 00
Surplus fund	90,174,281 14	90,229,954 59	91,689,834 12	94,061,438 95	94,705,740 34
Undivided profits	34,300,430 80	43,109,471 62	42,861,712 59	38,608,618 91	46,056,428 55
Nat'l bank circulation	292,838,935 00	292,509,149 00	291,183,614 00	291,798,640 00	296,205,446 00
State bank circulation	2,351,993 00	2,279,469 00	2,222,793 00	2,138,548 00	2,091,799 00
Dividends unpaid	2,299,296 27	1,483,416 15	1,517,595 18	2,462,591 31	2,242,556 49
Individual deposits	546,236,881 57	516,058,085 26	542,261,503 18	501,407,586 90	507,368,618 07
U. S. deposits	6,750,139 19	6,424,421 25	10,677,873 92	6,807,978 49	6,074,407 90
Dep'ts U. S. dis. offi'rs	2,592,001 21	4,778,225 93	2,592,967 54	4,550,142 68	4,155,304 25
Due to national banks	108,351,300 33	109,667,715 95	115,456,491 84	100,348,292 45	106,090,414 53
Due to State banks	28,904,849 14	29,767,575 21	33,012,162 78	29,603,910 80	29,200,587 29
Notes re-discounted	3,842,542 30	2,462,647 49	2,741,843 53	3,843,577 67	4,612,131 08
Bills payable	1,543,753 40	2,873,357 40	2,302,756 99	4,592,609 76	4,838,667 83
Total	1,546,261,357 44	1,529,147,735 85	1,565,756,000 67	1,510,713,236 92	1,538,008,105 93

1 8 7 1.

	MARCH 18. 1,688 banks.	APRIL 29. 1,707 banks.	JUNE 10. 1,723 banks.	OCTOBER 2. 1,767 banks.	DECEMBER 16. 1,790 banks.
Capital stock	$444,232,771 00	$446,925,493 00	$450,330,841 00	$458,255,696 00	$460,225,866 00
Surplus fund	96,862,081 66	97,620,099 28	98,322,203 80	101,112,671 91	101,573,153 62
Undivided profits	43,883,357 64	44,776,030 71	45,535,227 79	42,008,714 38	48,630,925 81
Nat'l bank circulation	301,713,460 00	306,131,393 00	307,793,880 00	315,519,117 00	318,265,481 00
State bank circulation	2,635,800 00	1,982,580 00	1,968,058 00	1,921,056 00	1,886,538 00
Dividends unpaid	1,263,767 70	2,235,248 46	1,408,628 25	4,540,194 61	1,393,427 98
Individual deposits	561,190,830 41	611,025,174 10	602,110,758 16	600,868,486 55	596,586,487 54
U. S. deposits	6,314,057 81	6,521,572 92	6,265,167 04	20,511,935 98	14,829,525 65
Dep'ts U. S. dis. offi'rs	4,813,016 66	3,757,873 84	4,893,907 25	5,393,598 89	5,399,108 34
Due to national banks	118,904,865 84	128,037,469 17	135,167,847 69	131,730,713,04	118,657,614 16
Due to State banks	37,311,519 13	36,113,290 67	41,219,802 96	40,211,971 67	38,116,950 67
Notes re-discounted	5,256,896 42	3,573,723 02	3,120,039 09	3,964,552 57	4,922,455 78
Bills payable	5,248,206,01	5,740,964 77	5,278,973 72	4,528,191 12	5,374,362 67
Total	1,627,032,030 28	1,694,440,912 94	1,703,415,335 65	1,730,566,899 72	1,715,861,897 22

Aggregate resources and liabilities of the National

1872.

Resources.	FEBRUARY 27.	APRIL 19.	JUNE 10.	OCTOBER 3.	DECEMBER 27.
	1,814 banks.	1,843 banks.	1,853 banks.	1,919 banks.	1,940 banks.
Loans and discounts	$839, 665, 077 91	$844, 902, 253 49	$871, 531, 448 67	$877, 197, 923 47	$885, 653, 449 62
Bonds for circulation	370, 924, 700 00	374, 428, 450 00	377, 029, 700 00	382, 046, 400 00	384, 458, 500 00
Bonds for deposits...	15, 870, 000 00	13, 169, 000 00	15, 409, 950 00	15, 479, 750 00	16, 304, 750 00
U. S. bonds on hand.	21, 323, 150 00	19, 292, 100 00	16, 458, 250 00	12, 142, 550 00	10, 306, 100 00
Other stocks and b'ds	22, 838, 338 80	21, 538, 914 06	22, 270, 610 47	23, 533, 151 73	23, 160, 557 29
Due from red'g agents	80, 548, 329 93	82, 120, 017 24	91, 564, 269 53	80, 717, 071 30	86, 401, 459 44
Due from nat'l banks.	38, 282, 905 86	36, 697, 592 81	39, 468, 323 39	34, 486, 593 87	42, 707, 613 54
Due from State banks	12, 269, 822 08	12, 299, 716 94	13, 014, 265 26	12, 976, 878 01	12, 008, 843 54
Real estate, &c......	30, 637, 676 75	30, 809, 274 98	31, 123, 843 21	32, 276, 498 17	33, 014, 796 83
Current expenses....	6, 265, 655 13	7, 026, 041 23	6, 719, 794 90	6, 310, 428 79	8, 454, 803 97
Premiums paid......	6, 308, 821 86	6, 544, 279 29	6, 616, 174 75	6, 546, 848 52	7, 097, 847 86
Cash items	12, 143, 403 12	12, 461, 171 40	13, 458, 753 80	14, 916, 784 34	13, 696, 723 85
Clear'g-house exch'gs	93, 154, 319 74	114, 195, 966 36	88, 592, 800 16	110, 086, 315 37	90, 145, 482 72
National bank notes.	15, 552, 087 00	18, 492, 832 00	16, 253, 560 00	15, 787, 296 00	19, 070, 322 00
Fractional currency .	2, 278, 143 24	2, 143, 249 29	2, 060, 464 12	2, 151, 747 88	2, 270, 576 32
Specie	25, 507, 825 32	24, 433, 899 46	24, 256, 644 14	10, 229, 756 79	19, 047, 336 45
Legal-tender notes...	97, 865, 400 00	105, 732, 455 00	122, 994, 417 00	105, 121, 104 00	102, 922, 369 00
U. S. cert'fs of deposit	....	....	....	6, 710, 000 00	12, 650, 000 00
Three per cent. cert's	18, 980, 000 00	15, 365, 000 00	12, 005, 000 00	7, 140, 000 00	4, 185, 000 00
Total..........	1,719,415,657 34	1,743,652,213 55	1,770,837,269 40	1,755,857,098 24	1,773,556,592 43

1873.

	FEBRUARY 28.	APRIL 25.	JUNE 13.	SEPTEMBER 12.	DECEMBER 26.
	1,947 banks.	1,962 banks.	1,968 banks.	1,976 banks.	1,976 banks.
Loans and discounts	$913, 265, 189 67	$912, 064, 267 31	$925, 557, 682 42	$944, 220, 116 34	$856, 816, 555 05
Bonds for circulation.	384, 675, 050 00	386, 703, 800 00	388, 080, 300 00	388, 330, 400 00	389, 394, 400 00
Bonds for deposits...	15, 035, 000 00	16, 235, 000 00	15, 935, 000 00	14, 805, 000 00	14, 815, 200 00
U. S. bonds on hand.	10, 436, 950 00	9, 613, 550 00	9, 789, 400 00	8, 824, 850 00	8, 630, 650 00
Other stocks and b'ds	22, 063, 306 20	22, 449, 146 04	22, 912, 415 63	23, 709, 034 53	24, 358, 125 06
Due from red'g agents	95, 773, 077 10	88, 815, 537 80	97, 143, 326 94	96, 134, 120 66	73, 032, 046 87
Due from nat'l banks.	39, 483, 700 00	38, 671, 088 63	43, 328, 792 29	41, 413, 680 06	40, 404, 757 97
Due from State banks	13, 595, 679 17	12, 883, 353 37	14, 073, 287 77	12, 022, 873 41	11, 185, 253 08
Real estate, &c	34, 023, 057 77	34, 216, 678 07	34, 820, 562 77	34, 661, 823 21	35, 556, 746 48
Current expenses....	6, 977, 831 35	7, 410, 045 87	7, 154, 211 69	6, 985, 436 99	8, 678, 170 39
Premiums paid......	7, 205, 259 67	7, 559, 967 67	7, 890, 902 14	7, 732, 843 87	7, 987, 707 14
Cash items	11, 761, 711 50	11, 425, 209 00	13, 036, 482 58	11, 433, 913 22	12, 321, 972 80
Clear'g-house exch'gs	131, 383, 860 95	94, 132, 125 24	91, 918, 526 59	88, 926, 003 53	62, 881, 342 16
National bank notes.	15, 998, 779 00	19, 310, 202 00	20, 394, 772 00	16, 103, 842 00	21, 403, 179 00
Fractional currency .	2, 289, 680 21	2, 198, 973 37	2, 197, 559 84	2, 302, 775 26	2, 287, 454 03
Specie	17, 777, 673 53	16, 808, 808 74	27, 950, 086 72	19, 868, 469 45	26, 907, 037 58
Legal-tender notes...	97, 141, 909 00	100, 605, 287 00	106, 381, 491 00	92, 522, 663 00	108, 719, 506 00
U. S. cert'fs of deposit	18, 460, 000 00	18, 370, 000 00	22, 365, 000 00	20, 610, 000 00	24, 010, 000 00
Three per cent. cert's	1, 805, 000 00	710, 000 00	305, 000 00	....	....
Total..........	1,839,152,715 21	1,800,303,280 11	1,851,234,860 38	1,830,627,845 53	1,729,380,303 61

1874.

	FEBRUARY 27.	MAY 1.	JUNE 26.	OCTOBER 2.	DECEMBER 31.
	1,975 banks.	1,978 banks.	1,983 banks.	2,004 banks.	2,027 banks.
Loans and discounts.	$897, 859, 600 46	$923, 347, 030 79	$926, 195, 671 70	$954, 394, 791 59	$955, 862, 580 51
Bonds for circulation.	389, 614, 700 00	389, 249, 100 00	390, 281, 700 00	383, 254, 800 00	382, 976, 200 00
Bonds for deposits. .	14, 600, 200 00	14, 890, 200 00	14, 890, 200 00	14, 691, 700 00	14, 714, 000 00
U. S. bonds on hand.	11, 043, 400 00	10, 152, 000 00	10, 456, 900 00	13, 313, 550 00	15, 290, 300 00
Other stocks and b'ds	25, 305, 736 24	25, 460, 460 20	27, 010, 727 48	27, 807, 826 92	28, 313, 473 12
Due from res've ag'ts	101, 502, 861 58	94, 017, 603 31	97, 871, 517 06	83, 885, 126 04	80, 488, 831 45
Due from nat'l banks.	36, 624, 001 39	41, 291, 015 24	45, 770, 715 59	39, 695, 309 47	48, 100, 842 02
Due from State banks	11, 496, 711 47	12, 374, 391 28	12, 469, 592 33	11, 196, 611 73	11, 655, 573 07
Real estate, &c......	36, 043, 741 50	36, 708, 066 39	37, 270, 876 51	38, 112, 026 52	39, 196, 683 04
Current expenses....	6, 998, 875 75	7, 547, 203 05	7, 550, 125 20	7, 658, 738 82	5, 510, 566 47
Premiums paid......	8, 741, 028 77	8, 680, 370 84	8, 563, 262 27	8, 376, 650 07	8, 626, 112 16
Cash items	10, 269, 955 50	11, 949, 020 71	10, 496, 257 00	12, 296, 416 77	14, 005, 517 33
Clear'g-house exch'gs	62, 768, 119 19	94, 877, 796 52	63, 896, 271 31	97, 383, 687 11	112, 995, 317 55
National bank notes.	20, 003, 251 00	20, 673, 452 00	23, 527, 991 00	18, 450, 013 00	22, 532, 336 00
Fractional currency	2, 309, 019 73	2, 187, 186 69	2, 283, 898 92	2, 224, 043 12	2, 392, 668 74
Specie	33, 365, 868 58	32, 560, 069 26	22, 326, 207 27	21, 240, 945 23	22, 486, 761 04
Legal-tender notes...	102, 717, 563 00	101, 692, 930 00	103, 108, 350 00	80, 021, 946 00	82, 604, 791 00
U. S. cert'fs of deposit	37, 235, 000 00	40, 135, 000 00	47, 780, 000 00	42, 825, 000 00	33, 670, 000 00
Dep. with U. S. Treas	....	....	91, 250 00	20, 349, 950 15	21, 043, 084 36
Total..........	1,808,500,529 16	1,867,802,796 28	1,851,840,913 64	1,877,180,942 44	1,902,409,638 46

Banks from October, 1863, to October, 1881—Continued.

1872.

Liabilities.	FEBRUARY 27.	APRIL 10.	JUNE 10.	OCTOBER 3.	DECEMBER 27.
	1,814 banks.	1,843 banks.	1,853 banks.	1,919 banks.	1,940 banks.
Capital stock	$464,081,744 00	$467,924,318 00	$470,543,301 00	$479,629,174 00	$482,606,252 00
Surplus fund.........	103,787,082 62	104,312,525 81	105,181,943 28	110,257,516 45	111,410,248 98
Undivided profits....	43,310,344 46	46,428,590 90	50,234,298 32	46,623,784 50	56,762,411 89
Nat'l bank circulation	321,634,675 00	325,305,752 00	327,002,752 00	333,495,027 00	336,280,285 00
State bank circulation	1,830,563 00	1,763,885 00	1,700,935 00	1,567,143 00	1,511,396 00
Dividends unpaid....	1,451,746 20	1,561,914 45	1,454,044 06	3,149,749 61	1,356,934 48
Individual deposits ..	593,645,666 16	620,775,265 78	618,801,619 49	613,290,671 45	598,114,079 26
U. S. deposits........	7,114,893 47	6,353,722 95	6,993,014 77	7,853,772 41	7,863,894 93
Dep'ts U.S.dis.officers	5,024,699 44	3,416,371 16	5,463,953 48	4,563,853 79	5,136,597 74
Due to national banks	128,627,494 44	120,755,565 86	132,804,924 02	110,047,347 67	124,218,392 83
Due to State banks ..	39,025,165 44	35,005,127 84	39,878,826 42	33,789,083 82	31,794,963 37
Notes re-discounted..	3,818,686 91	4,225,622 04	4,745,178 22	5,549,431 88	6,545,059 78
Bills payable........	6,062,896 11	5,821,551 76	5,942,479 34	6,040,562 66	6,946,416 17
Total..........	1,719,415,657 34	1,743,652,213 55	1,770,837,269 40	1,755,857,098 24	1,773,556,532 43

1873.

	FEBRUARY 28.	APRIL 25.	JUNE 13.	SEPTEMBER 12.	DECEMBER 26.
	1,947 banks.	1,962 banks.	1,968 banks.	1,976 banks.	1,976 banks.
Capital stock	$484,551,811 00	$487,891,251 00	$490,109,801 00	$491,072,616 00	$490,266,611 00
Surplus fund.........	114,681,048 73	115,805,574 57	116,847,454 62	120,314,499 20	120,961,267 91
Undivided profits....	48,578,045 28	52,415,348 46	55,306,154 69	54,515,131 76	58,375,160 43
Nat'l bank circulation	336,292,459 00	338,163,864 00	338,788,504 00	339,081,799 00	341,320,256 00
State bank circulation	1,368,271 00	1,280,208 00	1,224,470 00	1,188,853 00	1,130,585 00
Dividends unpaid....	1,465,993 60	1,462,336 77	1,400,491 90	1,402,547 89	1,269,474 74
Individual deposits ..	656,187,551 61	616,848,358 25	641,121,775 27	622,685,563 20	540,510,602 78
U. S. deposits........	7,044,848 34	7,880,057 73	8,601,001 95	7,829,327 73	7,680,375 26
Dep'ts U.S.dis.officers	5,835,696 60	4,425,750 14	6,416,275 10	8,008,560 13	4,705,593 36
Due to national banks	134,231,842 95	126,631,926 24	137,856,085 67	133,672,732 94	114,996,666 54
Due to State banks ..	38,124,803 85	35,036,433 18	40,741,788 47	39,298,148 14	36,598,076 29
Notes re-discounted..	5,117,810 50	5,403,043 38	5,515,900 67	5,987,512 36	3,811,487 89
Bills payable........	5,672,532 75	7,059,128 39	7,215,157 04	5,480,554 09	7,754,137 41
Total..........	1,839,152,715 21	1,800,303,280 11	1,851,234,860 38	1,830,627,845 53	1,729,380,303 61

1874.

	FEBRUARY 27.	MAY 1.	JUNE 26.	OCTOBER 2.	DECEMBER 31.
	1,975 banks.	1,978 banks.	1,983 banks.	2,004 banks.	2,027 banks.
Capital stock	$490,859,101 00	$490,077,001 00	$491,003,711 00	$493,765,121 00	$495,802,481 00
Surplus fund.........	123,497,347 20	125,561,081 23	126,239,308 41	128,958,106 84	130,485,641 37
Undivided profits....	50,236,919 68	54,331,713 13	58,332,965 71	51,484,437 32	51,477,629 33
Nat'l bank circulation	339,602,955 00	340,267,649 00	338,538,743 00	333,225,298 00	331,193,159 00
State bank circulation	1,078,988 00	1,049,286 00	1,000,021 00	964,567 00	800,417 00
Dividends unpaid....	1,201,055 63	2,259,129 91	1,242,474 81	3,516,276 99	6,088,845 01
Individual deposits ..	595,350,334 90	649,280,298 95	622,863,154 44	609,068,995 88	682,840,607 45
U. S. deposits........	7,276,959 87	7,994,422 27	7,322,830 85	7,302,153 58	7,492,307 78
Dep'ts U.S.dis.officers	5,034,624 46	3,297,680 24	3,238,639 20	3,927,828 27	3,579,722 94
Due to national banks	138,435,388 39	135,640,418 24	143,033,822 25	125,102,049 93	129,188,671 42
Due to State banks ..	48,112,223 40	48,683,924 34	50,227,426 18	50,718,007 87	51,629,602 36
Notes re-discounted.	3,448,828 92	4,581,420 38	4,436,256 22	4,197,372 25	6,365,652 97
Bills payable........	4,275,002 51	4,772,662 50	4,352,560 57	4,950,727 51	5,398,900 83
Total..........	1,808,500,529 16	1,867,802,796 28	1,851,840,913 64	1,877,180,942 44	1,902,409,638 46

Aggregate resources and liabilities of the National

1875.

Resources.	MARCH 1. 2,029 banks.	MAY 1. 2,046 banks.	JUNE 30. 2,076 banks.	OCTOBER 1. 2,088 banks.	DECEMBER 17. 2,086 banks.
Loans and discounts	$956,485,039 35	$971,835,298 74	$972,926,532 14	$984,691,434 40	$962,571,807 70
Bonds for circulation	380,682,650 00	378,026,900 00	375,127,900 00	370,321,700 00	363,618,100 00
Bonds for deposits ..	14,492,200 00	14,372,200 00	14,147,200 00	14,097,200 00	13,981,500 00
U. S. bonds on hand	18,062,150 00	14,297,650 00	12,753,000 00	13,989,950 00	16,009,550 00
Other stocks and b'ds	28,268,841 60	29,102,197 10	32,010,316 18	33,505,045 15	31,657,960 52
Due from res've ag'ts	80,991,175 34	80,620,878 75	89,788,903 73	85,701,259 82	81,462,682 27
Due from nat'l banks	44,720,304 11	46,039,597 57	48,513,388 86	47,028,769 18	44,831,891 48
Due from State banks	12,724,243 97	12,094,086 39	11,625,647 15	11,963,768 90	11,895,551 08
Real estate, &c	39,430,952 12	40,312,285 99	40,960,020 49	42,366,647 65	41,583,311 94
Current expenses....	7,790,581 86	7,766,700 42	4,992,044 34	7,841,213 05	9,218,455 47
Premiums paid	9,006,880 92	8,434,453 14	8,742,393 83	8,670,091 18	9,442,801 54
Cash items	11,734,762 42	13,122,145 88	12,433,100 43	12,758,872 03	11,238,720 72
Clear'g-house exch'gs	81,127,796 39	116,970,819 05	88,924,025 93	75,142,863 45	67,886,967 04
Bills of other banks..	18,909,397 00	19,504,640 00	24,261,961 00	18,528,837 00	17,166,190 00
Fractional currency..	3,008,592 12	2,702,326 44	2,620,504 26	2,505,631 78	2,901,023 10
Specie	16,667,106 17	10,620,361 64	18,959,582 30	8,050,329 73	17,070,903 90
Legal-tender notes. ..	78,508,170 00	84,015,028 00	87,492,895 00	76,458,734 00	70,725,077 00
U. S. cert'fs of deposit	37,200,000 00	38,615,000 00	47,310,000 00	48,810,000 00	31,005,000 00
Due from U. S. Treas.	21,007,919 76	21,454,422 29	19,640,785 52	19,686,960 30	19,202,256 68
Total	1,869,819,753 22	1,909,847,891 40	1,913,239,201 16	1,882,209,307 62	1,823,460,752 44

1876.

	MARCH 10. 2,091 banks.	MAY 12. 2,089 banks.	JUNE 30. 2,091 banks.	OCTOBER 2. 2,089 banks.	DECEMBER 22. 2,082 banks.
Loans and discounts	$950,205,555 02	$939,895,085 34	$933,686,530 43	$931,304,714 06	$929,066,408 42
Bonds for circulation.	354,547,750 00	344,537,350 00	339,141,750 00	337,170,400 00	336,705,300 00
Bonds for deposits...	14,216,500 00	14,128,000 00	14,328,000 00	14,698,000 00	14,757,000 00
U. S. bonds on hand..	25,910,650 00	26,577,000 00	30,842,300 00	33,142,150 00	31,937,950 00
Other stocks and b'ds	30,425,430 43	30,905,195 82	32,482,805 75	34,445,157 16	31,565,914 50
Due from res've ag'ts	99,068,360 35	86,769,083 37	87,989,900 90	87,326,950 48	83,789,174 65
Due from nat'l banks.	42,341,542 67	44,328,609 46	47,417,029 03	47,525,080 98	44,011,664 97
Due from State banks	11,180,562 15	11,262,193 96	10,989,507 95	12,061,283 08	12,415,841 97
Real estate, &c	41,937,617 25	42,183,958 78	42,722,415 27	43,121,942 01	43,408,445 49
Current expenses....	8,296,207 85	6,820,573 35	5,025,549 38	6,987,644 46	9,818,422 88
Premiums paid	10,946,713 15	10,414,347 28	10,621,634 03	10,715,251 16	10,811,300 66
Cash items	9,517,868 86	9,693,186 37	11,724,592 67	12,043,139 68	10,658,709 26
Clear'g-house exch'gs	58,863,182 43	56,806,632 63	75,328,878 84	87,870,817 06	68,027,016 40
Bills of other banks..	18,536,502 00	20,347,964 00	20,398,422 00	15,910,315 00	17,521,663 00
Fractional currency .	3,215,594 30	2,771,886 26	1,987,897 44	1,417,203 06	1,146,741 94
Specie	29,077,345 85	21,714,594 36	25,218,469 92	21,360,767 42	32,999,647 89
Legal-tender notes..	76,768,446 00	79,858,661 00	90,836,876 00	84,250,847 00	66,221,400 00
U. S. cert'fs of deposit	30,805,000 00	27,380,000 00	27,955,000 00	29,170,000 00	26,005,000 00
Due from U. S. Treas.	18,479,112 79	16,911,680 20	17,063,407 65	16,743,605 40	16,350,491 73
Total	1,834,369,941 70	1,793,306,002 78	1,825,760,967 28	1,827,263,367 61	1,787,407,093 76

1877.

	JANUARY 20. 2,083 banks.	APRIL 14. 2,073 banks.	JUNE 22. 2,078 banks.	OCTOBER 1. 2,080 banks.	DECEMBER 28. 2,074 banks.
Loans and discounts	$920,561,018 65	$911,946,833 88	$901,731,416 03	$891,920,593 54	$881,856,744 87
Bonds for circulation	337,590,700 00	339,658,100 00	337,754,100 00	336,810,950 00	343,869,550 00
Bonds for deposits ..	14,782,000 00	15,084,000 00	14,971,000 00	14,903,000 00	13,538,000 00
U. S. bonds on hand.	31,988,650 00	32,964,250 00	32,344,650 00	30,088,700 00	28,470,800 00
Other stocks and b'ds	31,819,930 20	32,554,591 44	35,653,755 29	34,435,995 21	32,169,491 03
Due from res've ag'ts.	88,608,308 85	84,942,718 41	82,132,099 96	73,284,133 12	75,900,087 27
Due from nat'l banks.	44,844,616 68	42,027,778 81	44,567,303 63	45,217,246 82	44,123,924 97
Due from State banks	13,680,990 81	11,911,437 36	11,246,349 79	11,415,761 60	11,479,045 65
Real estate, &c	43,704,335 47	44,736,549 09	44,818,722 07	45,229,983 25	45,511,932 23
Current expenses....	4,131,516 48	7,842,296 86	7,910,864 84	6,915,792 50	8,958,903 60
Premiums paid	10,991,714 50	10,494,505 12	10,320,674 84	9,319,174 62	8,841,989 00
Cash items	10,295,404 19	10,410,623 87	10,009,988 46	11,674,587 50	10,205,059 49
Clear'g-house exch'gs	81,117,889 04	65,159,422 74	57,861,481 13	74,525,215 89	64,664,415 01
Bills of other banks..	18,418,727 00	17,942,603 00	15,533,467 00	15,531,407 00	20,312,692 00
Fractional currency..	1,238,228 08	1,114,820 09	1,055,123 61	900,805 47	778,084 78
Specie	49,709,267 55	27,076,037 78	21,335,996 06	22,658,820 31	32,907,750 70
Legal-tender notes. ..	72,689,710 00	72,351,573 00	78,004,386 00	66,920,684 00	70,568,248 00
U. S. cert'fs of deposit	25,470,000 00	32,100,000 00	33,410,000 00	33,410,000 00	26,515,000 00
Due from U. S. Treas.	16,441,509 98	16,291,040 84	17,932,574 60	16,021,753 01	16,493,577 08
Total	1,818,174,517 68	1,796,603,275 29	1,774,352,833 81	1,741,084,663 84	1,737,293,145 79

Banks from October, 1863, *to October*, 1881—Continued.

1875.

Liabilities.	MARCH 1.	MAY 1.	JUNE 30.	OCTOBER 1.	DE JEMBER 17.
	2,029 banks.	2,046 banks.	2,076 banks.	2,088 banks.	2,086 banks.
Capital stock	$496,272,901 00	$498,717,143 00	$501,568,563 50	$504,829,769 00	$505,485,865 00
Surplus fund.........	131,249,079 47	131,604,608 66	133,169,094 79	134,356,076 41	133,085,422 30
Undivided profits	51,650,243 62	55,007,619 95	52,160,104 68	52,964,953 50	50,204,957 81
Nat'l bank circulation	324,525,349 00	323,321,230 00	318,148,406 00	318,350,379 00	314,979,451 00
State bank circulation	824,876 00	815,229 00	786,844 00	772,348 00	752,722 00
Dividends unpaid	1,601,255 48	2,501,742 39	6,195,519 34	4,003,534 90	1,353,396 80
Individual deposits ..	647,735,879 69	695,347,677 70	686,478,630 48	664,579,619 39	618,517,245 74
U. S. deposits........	7,971,932 75	6,797,972 00	6,714,328 70	6,507,531 59	6,652,556 67
Dep'ts U.S.dis.officers	5,330,414 16	2,766,387 41	3,459,061 80	4,271,195 19	4,232,550 87
Due to national banks	137,735,121 44	127,280,034 02	138,914,828 39	129,810,681 60	119,843,665 44
Due to State banks...	53,294,663 84	53,037,582 89	55,714,055 18	49,918,530 95	47,048,174 56
Notes re-discounted..	4,841,600 20	5,671,031 44	4,261,464 45	5,254,453 66	5,257,160 61
Bills payable........	4,786,436 57	6,079,632 94	5,758,299 85	6,590,234 43	7,050,583 64
Total	1,869,819,753 22	1,909,847,891 40	1,913,239,201 16	1,882,209,307 62	1,823,469,752 44

1876.

	MARCH 10.	MAY 12.	JUNE 30.	OCTOBER 2.	DECEMBER 22.
	2,091 banks.	2,089 banks.	2,091 banks.	2,089 banks.	2,082 banks.
Capital stock	$504,818,666 00	$500,982,006 00	$500,393,796 00	$499,802,232 00	$497,482,016 00
Surplus fund.........	133,091,739 50	131,795,199 94	131,897,197 21	132,202,282 00	131,390,064 67
Undivided profits	51,177,031 26	49,039,278 75	46,609,341 51	46,445,215 59	52,327,715 08
Nat'l bank circulation	307,476,155 00	300,252,085 00	294,444,678 00	291,544,020 00	292,011,575 00
State bank circulation	714,539 00	667,060 00	658,938 00	628,847 00	608,548 00
Dividends unpaid	1,405,829 06	2,325,523 51	6,116,679 30	3,848,705 64	1,286,540 28
Individual deposits ..	620,674,211 05	612,355,096 50	641,432,886 08	651,385,210 19	619,350,223 06
U. S. deposits........	6,606,394 90	8,493,878 18	7,667,722 97	7,256,801 42	6,727,155 14
Dep'ts U.S.dis.officers	4,313,915 45	2,505,273 30	3,392,939 48	3,746,781 58	4,749,615 39
Due to national banks	139,407,880 06	127,880,045 04	131,702,164 87	131,535,969 04	122,351,818 09
Due to State banks...	54,002,131 54	46,706,969 52	51,403,095 59	48,250,111 63	48,685,392 14
Notes re-discounted..	4,631,882 57	4,653,460 08	3,867,622 24	4,464,407 31	4,553,158 76
Bills payable........	6,049,566 31	5,650,126 87	6,173,006 03	6,151,784 21	5,882,672 15
Total	1,834,369,941 70	1,793,306,002 78	1,825,760,907 28	1,827,265,367 61	1,787,407,093 76

1877.

	JANUARY 20.	APRIL 14.	JUNE 22.	OCTOBER 1.	DECEMBER 28.
	2,083 banks.	2,073 banks.	2,078 banks.	2,080 banks.	2,074 banks.
Capital stock	$493,634,611 00	$489,684,645 00	$481,044,771 00	$479,467,771 00	$477,128,771 00
Surplus fund.........	130,224,169 02	127,793,320 52	124,714,072 93	122,776,121 24	121,618,455 32
Undivided profits....	37,436,530 32	45,609,418 27	50,508,351 70	44,572,678 72	51,530,910 18
Nat'l bank circulation	292,851,351 00	294,710,313 00	290,002,057 00	291,874,236 00	299,240,475 00
State bank circulation	581,242 00	535,963 00	521,611 00	481,738 00	470,540 00
Dividends unpaid....	2,448,909 70	1,853,974 79	1,398,101 52	3,623,703 43	1,404,178 34
Individual deposits ..	659,891,969 76	641,772,528 08	636,267,529 20	616,403,987 12	604,512,514 52
U. S. deposits........	7,234,696 96	7,584,267 72	7,187,431 67	7,972,714 75	6,520,031 09
Dep'ts U.S.dis.officers	3,108,316 55	3,076,878 70	3,710,167 20	2,376,983 02	3,780,759 43
Due to national banks	130,293,566 36	125,422,444 43	121,443,601 23	115,026,954 38	115,773,660 58
Due to State banks...	49,965,770 27	48,604,820 09	48,352,583 90	46,577,439 88	44,807,958 79
Notes re-discounted..	4,000,063 82	3,985,459 75	2,953,128 58	3,791,219 47	4,654,784 51
Bills payable........	6,483,320 92	5,969,241 94	6,249,426 88	6,137,116 83	5,843,107 03
Total	1,818,174,517 68	1,796,603,275 29	1,774,352,833 81	1,741,084,663 84	1,737,295,145 79

Aggregate resources and liabilities of the National

1878.

Resources.	MARCH 15.	MAY 1.	JUNE 29.	OCTOBER 1.	DECEMBER 6.
	2,063 banks.	2,059 banks.	2,056 banks.	2.053 banks.	2,055 banks.
Loans and discounts	$854,750,708 87	$847,620,392 49	$835,078,133 13	$833,988,450 55	$826,017,455 87
Bonds for circulation	343,871,350 00	345,256,350 00	347,332,100 00	347,556,650 00	347,812,300 00
Bonds for deposits...	13,329,000 00	19,536,000 00	28,371,000 00	47,936,850 00	49,110,800 00
U. S. bonds on hand..	34,881,600 00	33,615,700 00	40,479,900 00	46,785,600 00	44,255,850 00
Other stocks and b'ds	34,674,307 21	34,607,320 53	36,694,996 24	36,850,534 82	35,816,810 47
Due from res've ag'ts	86,016,990 78	71,331,219 27	78,875,055 92	85,083,418 51	81,733,137 00
Due from nat'l banks	39,692,105 87	40,545,522 72	41,897,858 89	41,492,918 75	43,144,220 68
Due from State banks	11,683,050 17	12,413,579 10	12,232,316 30	12,314,698 11	12,259,856 09
Real estate, &c	45,792,363 73	45,001,536 93	46,153,409 35	46,702,476 26	46,728,147 36
Current expenses....	7,786,572 42	7,239,365 78	4,718,618 66	6,272,566 73	7,608,128 83
Premiums paid	7,806,252 00	7,574,285 95	7,335,454 49	7,134,735 68	6,978,768 71
Cash items	10,107,583 76	10,989,440 78	11,525,376 07	10,982,432 89	9,985,004 21
Clear'g-house exch'gs	66,498,965 23	95,525,134 28	87,498,287 82	82,372,537 88	61,908,286 11
Bills of other banks..	16,250,560 00	18,363,335 00	17,063,576 00	16,929,721 00	19,392,281 00
Fractional currency .	697,398 86	661,044 69	610,084 25	515,661 04	496,864 34
Specie...............	54,729,558 02	46,023,756 06	29,251,460 77	30,688,606 59	34,355,250 36
Legal-tender notes...	64,034,972 00	67,245,975 00	71,643,402 00	64,428,600 00	64,072,762 00
U. S. cert'fs of deposit	20,605,000 00	20,995,000 00	36,905,000 00	32,600,000 00	32,520,000 00
Due from U. S. Treas.	16,257,608 98	16,364,030 47	16,798,667 62	16,343,674 36	17,940,918 34
Total..........	1,729,465,956 90	1,741,898,959 05	1,750,464,706 51	1,767,279,133 21	1,742,826,837 37

1879.

	JANUARY 1.	APRIL 4.	JUNE 14.	OCTOBER 2.	DECEMBER 12.
	2,051 banks.	2,048 banks.	2,048 banks.	2,048 banks.	2,052 banks.
Loans and discounts.	$823,906,765 68	$814,653,422 69	$835,875,012 36	$878,503,097 45	$933,543,661 93
Bonds for circulation	347,118,300 00	348,487,700 00	352,208,000 00	357,313,300 00	364,272,700 00
Bonds for deposits...	66,507,350 00	309,348,450 00	257,038,200 00	18,204,650 00	14,788,800 00
U. S. bonds on hand .	44,257,250 00	54,601,750 00	62,180,300 00	52,942,100 00	40,677,500 00
Other stocks and b'ds	35,569,400 93	36,747,129 40	37,617,015 13	39,671,916 50	38,836,369 80
Due from res've ag't's	77,925,068 68	74,003,830 40	93,443,463 95	107,023,546 81	102,742,452 54
Due from nat'l banks.	44,161,948 46	39,143,386 90	48,192,531 93	46,692,994 78	55,352,459 82
Due from State banks	11,892,540 26	10,535,252 99	11,258,520 43	13,630,772 63	14,425,072 00
Real estate, &c	47,001,964 70	47,461,614 54	47,796,108 26	47,817,169 36	47,992,332 99
Current expenses.....	4,033,024 67	6,693,668 43	6,913,430 46	6,111,256 56	7,474,082 10
Premiums paid	6,366,048 85	6,609,390 80	5,674,497 80	4,332,419 63	4,150,836 17
Cash items	13,564,550 25	10,011,204 64	10,209,982 43	11,306,132 48	10,377,272 77
Clear'g-house exch'gs	100,035,237 82	63,712,445 55	83,152,359 49	112,964,964 25	112,172,677 95
Bills of other banks..	19,535,588 00	17,068,505 00	16,685,484 00	16,707,550 00	16,406,218 00
Fractional currency .	475,538 50	407,177 47	446,217 26	396,065 06	374,227 02
Specie...............	41,490,757 32	41,148,563 41	42,333,287 44	42,173,731 23	79,013,041 59
Legal-tender notes...	70,561,233 00	64,461,231 00	67,059,152 00	69,196,696 00	54,715,096 00
U. S. cert'fs of deposit	28,915,000 00	21,885,000 00	25,180,000 00	26,770,000 00	10,800,000 00
Due from U. S. Treas	17,175,435 13	17,029,121 31	16,620,986 20	17,029,065 45	17,054,816 40
Total..........	1,800,592,002 25	1,984,068,936 53	2,019,884,549 10	1,868,787,428 19	1,925,229,617 08

1880.

	FEBRUARY 21.	APRIL 23.	JUNE 11.	OCTOBER 1.	DECEMBER 31.
	2,061 banks.	2,075 banks.	2,076 banks.	2,090 banks.	2,095 banks.
Loans and discounts	$974,295,360 70	$992,970,823 10	$994,712,646 41	$1,040,977,267 53	$1,071,356,141 79
Bonds for circulation	361,901,700 00	361,274,650 00	359,512,050 00	357,789,350 00	358,042,550 00
Bonds for deposits ..	14,917,000 00	14,722,000 00	14,727,000 00	14,827,000 00	14,726,500 00
U. S. bonds on hand	36,798,600 00	29,503,600 00	28,605,800 00	28,793,400 00	25,016,400 00
Other stocks and b'ds	41,223,583 33	42,494,927 73	44,947,345 75	48,863,150 22	48,628,372 77
Due from res've ag'ts	117,791,356 81	103,964,229 84	115,935,668 27	134,562,778 76	126,155,014 40
Due from nat'l banks	53,230,034 03	54,493,465 09	56,578,444 69	63,023,796 84	69,079,326 15
Due from State banks	14,561,152 51	13,293,775 94	13,861,582 77	15,881,197 74	17,111,241 03
Real estate, &c	47,845,915 77	47,808,207 09	47,979,241 53	48,045,832 54	47,784,461 47
Current expenses ..	6,404,743 54	7,007,404 19	6,778,829 19	6,386,182 01	4,442,440 02
Premiums paid	3,908,059 27	3,791,703 33	3,702,354 00	3,488,470 11	3,298,602 63
Cash items	10,320,274 51	9,857,645 34	9,980,179 32	12,729,002 19	14,713,920 02
Clear'g-house exch'gs	166,736,402 44	86,429,732 21	122,390,409 45	121,005,240 72	239,733,904 59
Bills of other banks..	15,309,257 00	21,061,504 00	21,908,193 00	18,210,943 00	21,549,367 00
Fractional currency .	397,187 23	395,747 67	387,226 13	367,171 73	389,921 75
Specie...............	89,442,051 75	86,429,732 21	99,506,035 24	109,346,502 49	107,172,900 02
Legal tender notes ..	55,229,408 00	61,048,911 00	64,470,717 00	56,640,458 00	59,216,934 00
U. S. cert'fs of deposit	10,760,000 00	7,890,000 00	12,510,000 00	7,655,000 00	6,150,000 00
Due from U. S. Treas	16,994,381 37	17,226,060 01	16,999,083 78	17,103,866 00	17,125,822 37
Total..........	2,038,066,498 46	1,974,600,472 95	2,035,493,280 15	2,105,786,625 82	2,241,683,829 91

Banks from October, 1863, to October, 1881—Continued.

1878.

Liabilities.	MARCH 15. 2,063 banks.	MAY 1. 2,059 banks.	JUNE 29. 2,056 banks.	OCTOBER 1. 2,053 banks.	DECEMBER 6. 2,055 banks.
Capital stock	$473,952,541 00	$471,971,627 00	$470,393,366 00	$466,147,436 00	$464,874,996 00
Surplus fund	120,870,290 10	119,231,126 13	118,178,530 75	116,897,779 98	116,402,118 84
Undivided profits	45,040,851 85	43,938,961 98	40,482,522 64	40,936,213 58	44,040,171 84
Nat'l bank circulation	300,926,284 00	301,884,704 00	299,621,059 00	301,888,092 00	303,324,733 00
State bank circulation	439,339 00	426,504 00	417,808 00	413,913 00	400,715 00
Dividends unpaid	1,207,472 68	1,930,669 58	5,466,350 52	3,118,380 91	1,473,784 86
Individual deposits	602,882,585 17	625,479,771 12	621,632,160 06	620,236,176 82	598,805,775 56
U. S. deposits	7,243,253 29	13,811,474 14	22,686,619 67	41,654,812 08	40,260,825 72
Dep'ts U.S. dis. officers	3,004,064 90	2,392,281 61	2,903,531 99	3,342,794 73	3,451,436 56
Due to national banks	123,239,448 50	109,720,396 70	117,845,495 88	122,496,513 92	120,261,774 54
Due to State banks	43,979,239 39	44,006,551 05	43,360,527 86	42,636,703 42	41,767,755 07
Notes re-discounted	2,465,390 79	2,834,012 00	2,453,839 77	3,007,324 85	3,228,132 93
Bills payable	4,215,196 23	4,270,879 74	5,022,894 37	4,502,982 92	4,525,617 45
Total	1,729,465,956 90	1,741,898,959 05	1,750,464,706 51	1,767,279,133 21	1,742,826,837 37

1879.

	JANUARY 1. 2,051 banks.	APRIL 4. 2,048 banks.	JUNE 14. 2,048 banks.	OCTOBER 2. 2,048 banks.	DECEMBER 12. 2,052 banks.
Capital stock	$462,031,396 00	$455,611,362 00	$455,244,415 00	$454,067,365 00	$454,498,515 00
Surplus fund	116,200,863 52	114,823,316 49	114,321,375 87	114,786,528 10	115,429,031 93
Undivided profits	36,836,269 21	40,812,777 50	45,802,845 82	41,390,941 40	47,573,820 75
Nat'l bank circulation	303,506,470 00	304,467,130 00	307,328,695 00	313,786,342 00	321,949,154 00
State bank circulation	388,368 00	352,452 00	339,927 00	325,954 00	322,502 00
Dividends unpaid	5,816,348 82	2,158,516 79	1,309,059 13	2,658,337 46	1,305,480 45
Individual deposits	643,337,745 26	598,822,604 02	648,934,141 42	719,737,568 89	755,450,966 01
U. S. deposits	59,701,222 90	303,463,505 69	248,421,340 25	11,018,862 74	6,923,323 97
Dep'ts U.S. dis. officers	3,556,801 25	2,689,189 44	3,682,320 67	3,469,600 02	3,893,217 43
Due to national banks	118,311,635 60	110,481,176 98	137,360,091 60	149,200,257 16	152,484,079 44
Due to State banks	44,035,787 56	43,709,770 14	50,403,064 54	52,022,453 99	59,232,391 93
Notes re-discounted	2,926,434 95	2,224,491 91	2,226,396 39	2,205,015 54	2,116,484 47
Bills payable	3,942,659 18	4,452,544 48	4,510,876 47	4,208,291 89	4,041,649 70
Total	1,800,592,002 25	1,684,068,936 53	2,019,884,549 16	1,868,787,428 19	1,925,229,617 08

1880.

	FEBRUARY 21. 2,061 banks.	APRIL 23. 2,075 banks.	JUNE 11. 2,076 banks.	OCTOBER 1. 2,090 banks.	DECEMBER 31. 2,095 banks.
Capital stock	$454,548,585 00	$456,097,935 00	$455,909,565 00	$457,553,985 00	$458,540,085 00
Surplus fund	117,044,043 03	117,299,350 09	118,102,014 11	120,518,583 43	121,824,629 03
Undivided profits	42,863,804 95	48,226,087 61	50,443,635 45	46,139,692 24	47,946,741 64
Nat'l bank circulation	320,303,874 00	320,759,472 00	318,088,562 00	317,350,036 00	317,484,496 00
State bank circulation	303,452 00	299,790 00	290,738 00	271,045 00	258,499 00
Dividends unpaid	1,365,001 91	1,542,447 98	1,330,179 85	3,452,504 17	6,198,238 38
Individual deposits	848,926,599 86	791,555,059 63	833,701,034 20	873,537,637 07	1,006,452,852 82
U. S. deposits	7,856,791 97	7,925,988 37	7,680,905 17	7,548,538 67	7,898,100 94
Dep'ts U.S. dis. officers	3,069,880 74	3,220,606 64	3,026,757 34	3,344,386 62	3,489,501 01
Due to national banks	170,245,061 08	157,209,759 14	171,462,131 23	192,124,705 10	192,413,205 78
Due to State banks	65,439,334 51	63,317,107 96	67,938,795 35	75,735,677 06	71,185,817 08
Notes re-discounted	1,918,788 88	2,616,900 55	2,258,544 72	3,178,232 50	3,354,697 18
Bills payable	4,181,280 53	4,529,967 98	5,260,417 43	5,031,604 96	4,636,876 05
Total	2,038,066,498 46	1,974,600,472 95	2,035,493,280 15	2,105,786,625 82	2,241,683,829 91

1881.

Resources.	MARCH 11. 2,094 banks.	MAY 6. 2,102 banks.	JUNE 30. 2.115 banks.	OCTOBER 1. 2.132 banks.
Loans and discounts	$1,073,786,749 70	$1,093,649,362 18	$1,144,988,949 45	$1,173,796,083 09
Bonds for circulation	339,811,950 00	352,653,500 00	358,287,500 00	363,335,500 00
Bonds for deposits	14,851,500 00	15,240,000 00	15,265,000 00	15,540,000 00
U. S. bonds on hand	46,626,150 00	44,116,500 00	48,584,950 00	40,972,450 00
Other stocks and bonds	49,545,154 92	52,908,123 98	58,049,292 63	61,806,702 95
Due from reserve agents	120,820,691 09	128,017,627 03	156,258,637 05	132,968,183 12
Due from national banks	62,295,517 34	63,176,225 67	75,703,599 78	78,505,446 17
Due from State banks	17,032,261 64	16,938,734 56	18,850,775 34	19,306,826 62
Real estate, &c	47,525,790 02	47,791,348 36	47,834,060 20	47,329,111 16
Current expenses	7,810,930 83	6,096,109 78	4,235,911 19	6,731,936 48
Premiums paid	3,530,516 71	4,024,763 60	4,115,980 01	4,138,585 71
Cash items	10,144,682 87	11,826,603 16	13,534,227 31	14,841,879 30
Clearing-house exchanges	147,761,543 96	196,633,558 01	143,960,236 84	189,222,255 95
Bills of other banks	17,733,032 00	25,120,933 00	21,631,932 00	17,732,712 00
Fractional currency	386,569 63	386,950 21	372,140 23	373,945 96
Specie	105,156,195 24	122,628,562 08	128,638,927 50	114,334,736 12
Legal-tender notes	52,156,439 00	62,516,296 00	58,728,713 00	53,158,441 00
U. S. certificates of deposits	6,120,000 00	8,045,000 00	9,540,000 00	6,740,000 00
Due from U. S. Treasurer	17,015,269 83	18,456,600 14	17,251,868 22	17,472,595 96
Total	2,140,110,944 78	2,270,226,817 76	2,325,832,700 75	2,358,387,391 59

Banks from October, 1863, to October, 1881—Continued.

1 8 8 1 .

Liabilities.	MARCH 11. 2,004 banks.	MAY 6. 2,102 banks.	JUNE 30. 2,115 banks.	OCTOBER 1. 2,132 banks.
Capital stock	$458,254,935 00	$459,039,205 00	$460,227,835 00	$463,821,985 00
Surplus fund	122,470,996 73	124,405,926 91	126,679,517 97	128,140,617 75
Undivided profits	54,072,225 49	54,906,090 47	54,684,137 16	56,372,190 92
National bank circulation	298,590,802 00	309,737,193 00	312,223,352 00	320,200,069 00
State bank circulation	252,765 00	252,647 00	242,967 00	244,309 00
Dividends unpaid	1,402,118 43	2,617,134 37	5,871,595 59	3,836,445 84
Individual deposits	933,392,430 75	1,027,040,514 10	1,031,731,043 42	1,070,997,531 71
U. S. deposits	7,381,149 25	9,504,081 25	8,971,826 73	8,476,689 74
Deposits U. S. disburs'g officers	3,839,324 77	3,371,512 48	3,272,610 45	3,631,803 41
Due to national banks	181,677,285 37	191,250,091 90	223,503,034 19	205,862,945 80
Due to State banks	71,579,477 47	80,700,506 06	91,035,599 65	89,047,471 00
Notes re-discounted	2,616,203 05	2,908,370 45	2,220,053 02	3,091,165 30
Bills payable	4,581,231 47	4,493,544 77	5,169,128 57	4,664,077 12
Total	2,140,110,944 78	2,270,226,817 76	2,325,832,700 75	2,358,387,391 59

ABSTRACT

OF

REPORTS OF THE CONDITION

OF

THE NATIONAL BANKS

ON

DECEMBER 31, 1880, MARCH 11, MAY 6, JUNE 30, AND OCTOBER 1, 1881.

Arranged by States, Territories, and Reserve Cities

NOTE.—The abstract of each State is exclusive of any reserve city therein.

173

Abstract of reports since October 1, 1880,

MAINE.

Resources.	DECEMBER 31. 69 banks.	MARCH 11. 69 banks.	MAY 6. 69 banks.	JUNE 30. 69 banks.	OCTOBER 1. 69 banks.
Loans and discounts	$15,602,673 95	$15,633,411 49	$16,060,093 84	$16,181,220 48	$17,323,678 03
Bonds for circulation	9,277,300 00	9,194,300 00	9,194,300 00	9,224,300 00	9,244,300 00
Bonds for deposits ..	175,000 00	170,000 00	170,000 00	170,000 00	170,000 00
U. S. bonds on hand..	264,200 00	280,150 00	275,350 00	221,100 00	179,400 00
Other stocks and b'ds	460,422 26	557,301 51	490,132 38	506,183 10	519,845 89
Due from res've ag'ts	3,430,008 14	2,848,206 70	2,449,202 88	3,136,309 32	2,573,542 53
Due from nat'l banks	444,194 53	361,935 80	343,177 10	536,691 60	534,015 91
Due from State banks	11,025 89	10,884 05	7,890 11	7,972 80	10,965 49
Real estate, &c......	353,416 98	333,830 82	325,914 13	320,215 92	320,485 02
Current expenses....	17,870 33	47,572 87	54,316 40	18,553 94	50,396 02
Premiums paid......	21,873 09	16,743 71	15,948 04	16,071 11	19,256 15
Cash items..........	357,106 70	315,876 66	351,663 51	399,445 06	418,357 86
Clear'g-house exch'gs					
Bills of other banks..	491,462 00	279,820 00	426,181 00	368,390 00	228,406 00
Fractional currency.	3,927 19	3,198 49	3,682 56	3,503 26	3,515 49
Specie	435,746 76	430,109 65	436,870 09	434,540 02	452,463 21
Legal-tender notes ..	215,849 00	191,578 00	221,541 00	204,209 00	143,907 00
U. S. cert's of deposits					
Due from U.S. Treas.	429,887 15	420,481 40	428,036 55	426,341 60	425,413 50
Total..........	31,971,363 97	31,095,101 15	31,254,299 59	32,175,027 21	32,617,948 10

NEW HAMPSHIRE.

	47 banks.	47 banks.	47 banks.	47 banks.	47 banks.
Loans and discounts	$7,336,048 54	$7,409,050 28	$7,198,777 29	$7,107,672 38	$7,547,354 28
Bonds for circulation	5,778,000 00	5,777,000 00	5,777,000 00	5,777,000 00	5,777,000 00
Bonds for deposits ..	347,000 00	347,000 00	347,000 00	372,000 00	372,000 00
U. S. bonds on hand..	70,050 00	127,550 00	160,450 00	196,850 00	208,850 00
Other stocks and b'ds	923,334 08	1,004,620 63	1,039,322 25	1,109,626 74	1,218,186 70
Due from res've ag'ts	1,360,885 68	1,096,375 98	1,008,722 90	1,565,673 38	1,245,972 82
Due from nat'l banks	53,653 00	59,647 55	55,909 44	78,645 83	89,436 49
Due from State banks	66,674 18	45,692 58	48,148 44	39,940 46	47,198 77
Real estate, &c......	294,411 49	257,043 79	253,504 03	246,914 03	241,626 23
Current expenses....	43,600 85	47,735 56	37,570 12	45,013 67	53,550 13
Premiums paid......	37,064 45	26,655 73	30,218 10	22,378 28	27,082 75
Cash items..........	175,224 05	190,515 45	163,884 43	235,813 83	144,223 12
Clear'g-house exch'gs					
Bills of other banks..	206,751 00	205,556 00	208,777 00	200,127 00	184,107 00
Fractional currency.	4,335 82	4,659 37	3,378 18	3,758 48	3,523 53
Specie	227,152 86	205,277 04	198,470 84	200,538 58	198,705 81
Legal-tender notes ..	99,481 00	81,030 00	91,788 60	94,011 00	98,655 00
U. S. cert's of deposits					
Due from U.S. Treas	260,917 84	266,899 67	266,299 67	265,440 07	261,357 77
Total..........	17,344,674 84	17,152,309 63	16,889,220 69	17,571,312 73	17,719,740 40

VERMONT.

	46 banks.	46 banks.	46 banks.	46 banks.	47 banks.
Loans and discounts	$10,481,193 11	$10,525,618 38	$10,419,803 87	$10,284,593 60	$11,012,260 97
Bonds for circulation	7,719,000 00	7,154,000 00	7,154,000 00	7,061,000 00	7,219,000 00
Bonds for deposits ..	50,000 00	50,000 00	50,000 00	50,000 00	50,000 00
U. S. bonds on hand..	589,450 00	677,250 00	526,850 00	561,500 00	524,400 00
Other stocks and b'ds	729,579 62	764,980 89	761,832 11	836,979 79	803,684 49
Due from res've ag'ts	1,080,656 01	914,176 02	983,305 01	1,273,523 05	1,123,436 78
Due from nat'l banks	245,453 63	160,183 32	178,357 81	261,342 15	141,497 35
Due from State banks	13,820 96	26,282 87	25,403 66	25,321 13	32,644 50
Real estate, &c......	464,562 72	431,380 08	419,951 71	413,656 94	395,870 36
Current expenses....	45,054 99	25,803 66	38,541 63	44,927 83	37,093 88
Premiums paid......	27,708 99	14,372 03	17,471 15	28,304 68	10,423 00
Cash items..........	86,192 69	75,013 95	93,584 70	97,382 02	104,088 75
Clear'g-house exch'gs					
Bills of other banks..	188,208 00	108,443 00	155,321 00	155,765 00	126,310 00
Fractional currency.	3,141 73	2,498 64	3,415 58	2,478 13	2,723 94
Specie	208,318 67	200,216 66	201,147 59	201,623 49	224,604 79
Legal-tender notes ..	242,686 00	181,779 00	212,194 00	211,412 00	227,009 00
U. S. cert's of deposits					
Due from U.S. Treas	353,099 90	318,703 00	322,817 00	320,467 00	327,049 00
Total..........	22,528,177 02	21,640,290 90	21,563,996 85	21,833,278 72	22,364,493 21

arranged by States and reserve cities.

MAINE.

Liabilities.	DECEMBER 31. 69 banks.	MARCH 11. 69 banks.	MAY 6. 69 banks.	JUNE 30. 69 banks.	OCTOBER 1. 69 banks.
Capital stock	$10,435,000 00	$10,435,000 00	$10,385,000 00	$10,385,000 00	$10,385,000 00
Surplus fund	2,443,877 80	2,548,881 84	2,553,814 46	2,564,971 32	2,586,507 56
Undivided profits	1,144,649 91	1,262,466 88	1,380,479 21	1,269,075 10	1,346,138 76
Nat'l bank circulation	8,228,303 00	8,071,240 00	8,181,334 00	8,152,008 00	8,211,247 00
State bank circulation	1,432 00	1,432 00	1,432 00	1,432 00	1,432 00
Dividends unpaid	297,552 52	56,443 77	85,631 59	256,259 82	100,141 81
Individual deposits	8,308,008 81	8,030,207 19	7,986,982 06	8,491,968 74	9,325,082 88
U. S. deposits	77,340 16	72,959 14	64,546 37	64,520 27	79,314 17
Dep'ts U.S.dis.officers	36,400 92	37,793 21	56,306 56	44,343 70	54,339 07
Due to national banks	932,541 20	503,583 03	476,691 71	851,226 46	359,445 25
Due to State banks	66,258 65	75,094 09	66,867 97	55,676 41	96,364 90
Notes re-discounted			15,213 66	37,174 66	72,844 70
Bills payable				1,370 73	
Total	31,971,363 97	31,095,101 15	31,254,299 59	32,175,027 21	32,617,948 10

NEW HAMPSHIRE.

	47 banks.	47 banks.	47 banks.	47 banks.	47 banks.
Capital stock	$5,830,000 00	$5,830,000 00	$5,830,000 00	$5,830,000 00	$5,830,000 00
Surplus fund	1,093,673 25	1,093,764 33	1,090,904 34	1,095,552 13	1,110,297 50
Undivided profits	544,861 14	540,744 61	528,532 89	559,781 29	559,335 45
Nat'l bank circulation	5,166,960 00	5,139,348 00	5,140,869 00	5,112,765 00	5,158,159 00
State bank circulation	7,676 00	7,676 00	7,676 00	7,676 00	7,676 00
Dividends unpaid	79,205 48	21,845 20	37,987 60	79,068 09	30,179 01
Individual deposits	3,924,967 93	3,940,928 59	3,601,207 65	4,068,405 72	4,292,686 85
U. S. deposits	114,800 37	151,585 42	144,570 09	133,627 29	146,724 30
Dep'ts U.S.dis.officers	119,775 17	107,574 71	113,344 97	127,617 19	103,179 07
Due to national banks	321,349 06	191,729 19	239,046 99	292,781 95	345,949 57
Due to State banks	141,316 14	127,113 58	116,831 16	182,438 07	85,552 66
Notes re-discounted			5,250 00		
Bills payable			33,000 00	61,000 00	50,000 00
Total	17,344,674 84	17,152,309 63	16,889,220 69	17,571,312 73	17,719,740 40

VERMONT.

	46 banks.	46 banks.	46 banks.	46 banks.	47 banks.
Capital stock	$8,201,000 00	$8,201,000 00	$8,101,000 00	$8,101,000 00	$8,151,000 00
Surplus fund	1,843,052 40	1,750,274 56	1,730,980 10	1,717,944 15	1,778,953 86
Undivided profits	592,329 30	547,224 90	684,921 17	674,987 06	608,646 91
Nat'l bank circulation	6,887,183 00	6,349,917 00	6,380,915 00	6,275,103 00	6,442,899 00
State bank circulation	4,000 00	4,000 00	4,000 00	4,000 00	4,000 00
Dividends unpaid	173,655 87	11,920 98	10,010 38	91,099 48	13,151 98
Individual deposits	4,594,697 86	4,340,461 22	4,328,334 74	4,780,060 45	5,191,351 89
U. S. deposits	23,543 66	28,989 84	32,175 75	37,657 17	24,976 48
Dep'ts U.S.dis.officers	8,702 85	5,683 00	4,190 58	8,336 23	10,163 43
Due to national banks	114,689 36	118,740 75	101,160 12	100,489 97	101,310 44
Due to State banks	4,790 47	799 37	17,137 93	25,100 62	12,989 22
Notes re-discounted	68,352 25	196,149 28	128,521 08	66,850 59	
Bills payable	12,200 00	54,900 00	40,650 00	50,650 00	25,650 00
Total	22,528,177 02	21,610,290 90	21,563,996 85	21,933,278 72	22,361,493 21

MASSACHUSETTS.

Resources.	DECEMBER 31. 188 banks.	MARCH 11. 189 banks.	MAY 6. 190 banks.	JUNE 30. 190 banks.	OCTOBER 1. 190 banks.
Loans and discounts.	$74,825,769 39	$76,279,794 31	$76,292,413 55	$76,963,633 12	$81,675,506 56
Bonds for circulation.	42,648,600 00	42,643,600 00	42,658,100 00	43,178,100 00	43,453,100 00
Bonds for deposits...	430,000 00	430,000 00	430,000 00	430,000 00	430,000 00
U. S. bonds on hand..	1,379,700 00	1,365,350 00	1,567,050 00	1,544,500 00	1,376,450 00
Other stocks and b'ds	3,931,923 23	3,996,774 81	4,221,617 51	4,223,302 66	4,300,126 68
Due from res'veag'ts.	6,526,964 01	6,291,900 61	8,100,019 59	8,898,577 84	7,306,973 31
Due from nat'l banks.	942,847 30	835,794 81	660,207 50	1,063,804 63	1,116,772 19
Due from State banks	206,939 36	129,271 77	182,467 33	268,310 70	144,827 57
Real estate, &c......	2,199,156 29	2,143,677 08	2,155,220 22	2,187,372 60	2,159,864 10
Current expenses....	363,237 55	587,401 57	178,858 51	220,108 22	232,586 46
Premiums paid......	228,877 60	219,120 61	215,642 37	235,526 89	203,188 09
Cash items.........	855,483 86	583,665 49	670,327 79	959,152 65	853,298 06
Clear'g-hous 'exch'gs	19,476 30	14,474 19	25,244 11	19,869,38	47,894 63
Bills of other banks..	1,311,164 00	1,053,432 00	1,289,587 00	1,563,697 00	1,161,409 00
Fractional currency .	31,459 35	31,174 50	29,450 77	29,403 74	31,223 76
Specie..............	1,760,271 56	1,772,228 07	1,908,702 71	1,903,471 41	1,934,421 50
Legal-tender notes ..	1,379,693 00	1,126,152 00	1,269,027 00	1,405,489 00	1,362,445 00
U. S. cert's of deposit.	165,000 00	185,000 00	185,000 00	185,000 00	185,000 00
Due from U. S. Treas.	1,944,603 79	1,953,494 07	1,961,281 60	1,970,473 70	1,986,311 30
Total..........	141,151,076 61	141,642,215 89	144,003,208 56	147,249,193 84	149,961,399 11

CITY OF BOSTON.

	54 banks.	54 banks.	54 banks.	54 banks.	54 banks.
Loans and discounts	$115,869,046 97	$113,819,996 94	$114,734,198 62	$126,152,471 26	$123,677,965 84
Bonds for circulation	35,554,500 00	34,611,500 00	35,719,500 00	36,289,500 00	36,289,500 00
Bonds for deposits ..	100,000 00	100,000 00	100,000 00	100,000 00	175,000 00
U. S. bonds on hand..	461,650 00	1,347,300 00	2,789,500 00	1,513,150 00	356,750 00
Other stocks and b'ds	1,258,558 68	1,103,545 66	1,465,562 73	2,987,691 06	3,094,823 53
Due from res'veag'ts	10,202,987 60	9,901,169 21	14,209,817 15	10,225,327 29	11,735,498 91
Due from nat'l banks	8,750,549 23	7,775,519 07	9,104,757 60	11,147,665 70	9,108,037 13
Due from State banks	118,910 53	600,906 15	390,298 97	386,076 97	426,744 21
Real estate, &c......	3,526,135 07	3,543,167 66	3,501,005 42	3,505,349 66	3,494,552 11
Current expenses....	720,298 72	1,382,716 51	194,067 50	359,595 02	18,836 03
Premiums paid......	175,247 59	161,097 13	219,411 29	133,783 99	111,582 88
Cash items.........	527,976 15	215,462 30	417,690 27	680,490 45	621,290 35
Clear'g-house exch'gs	11,770,050 55	8,076,367 00	9,142,122 00	12,814,518 00	14,784,242 06
Bills of other banks..	2,113,177 00	1,167,647 00	1,304,139 00	1,662,795 00	897,638 00
Fractional currency .	7,696 64	8,411 42	6,608 80	7,201 81	7,484 58
Specie..............	7,131,656 24	5,911,354 33	7,251,417 43	9,426,188 64	8,291,541 76
Legal-tender notes ..	3,867,883 00	2,397,070 00	3,008,860 00	3,462,601 00	3,457,379 00
U. S. cert's of deposit	290,000 00	185,000 00	180,000 00	165,000 00	75,000 00
Due from U. S. Treas	1,591,276 89	1,592,419 68	1,637,792 95	1,721,942 10	1,690,587 85
Total..........	204,037,000 86	193,900,680 66	205,396,749 75	231,941,347 95	218,323,252 24

RHODE ISLAND.

	61 banks.	61 banks.	61 banks.	61 banks.	62 banks.
Loans and discounts	$26,969,183 23	$26,830,328 17	$26,850,320 35	$27,320,681 57	$28,518,758 24
Bonds for circulation.	15,616,300 00	15,123,300 00	15,819,300 00	16,314,300 00	16,503,300 00
Bonds for deposits...	150,000 00	150,000 00	150,000 00	150,000 00	150,000 00
U. S. bonds on hand..	456,300 00	736,650 00	305,450 00	438,600 00	561,750 00
Other stocks and b'ds	602,644 91	596,742 32	677,472 19	687,302 73	690,268 49
Due from res'veag'ts	1,841,528 96	1,505,214 62	2,187,495 53	2,621,627 44	2,733,834 28
Due from nat'l banks	661,165 64	548,119 89	620,081 00	551,792 16	601,716 33
Due from State banks	86,003 17	85,088 61	61,704 88	78,514 70	35,858 37
Real estate, &c......	863,663 65	861,711 39	815,697 26	829,803 19	842,039 92
Current expenses....	96,470 25	152,242 34	138,741 64	89,368 01	122,891 68
Premiums paid......	269,234 51	238,440 73	173,088 98	208,034 21	193,432 96
Cash items.........	733,131 19	464,673 61	497,568 11	386,398 34	550,581 08
Clear'g-house exch'gs					
Bills of other banks .	387,328 00	313,016 00	347,332 00	383,616 00	353,766 00
Fractional currency .	11,139 95	11,178 54	8,594 61	10,427 06	11,243 43
Specie..............	396,936 07	365,221 62	387,987 58	387,826 39	394,476 95
Legal-tender notes ..	516,553 00	375,495 00	432,976 00	410,679 00	390,066 00
U. S. cert's of deposit.					
Due from U. S. Treas	720,326 28	683,443 98	705,544 86	762,427 23	776,792 98
Total..........	50,377,908 81	49,050,866 82	50,100,354 99	51,661,418 03	53,520,780 71

*by States and reserve cities—*Continued.

MASSACHUSETTS.

Liabilities.	DECEMBER 31. 188 banks.	MARCH 11. 189 banks.	MAY 6. 190 banks.	JUNE 30. 190 banks.	OCTOBER 1. 190 banks.
Capital stock	$45,105,000 00	$45,205,000 00	$45,152,500 00	$45,327,500 00	$45,327,500 00
Surplus fund	12,656,809 14	12,689,439 18	13,116,777 51	13,244,137 13	13,335,416 93
Undivided profits	3,989,172 31	4,981,841 76	3,858,138 11	4,457,122 43	3,567,231 62
Nat'l bank circulation	38,077,852 00	37,980,214 00	38,025,835 00	37,905,345 00	38,710,362 00
State bank circulation	10,557 00	10,557 00	10,557 00	10,557 00	10,557 00
Dividends unpaid	315,917 54	100,784 08	240,907 60	342,100 90	918,559 93
Individual deposits	37,088,177 95	37,540,248 32	40,600,718 65	42,041,983 86	44,506,149 62
U. S. deposits	245,556 49	265,456 02	313,432 76	267,601 04	260,984 47
Dep'ts U.S.dis.officers	39,185 98	22,696 81	17,785 49	20,375 08	32,312 93
Due to national banks	2,762,327 78	1,947,868 43	1,942,349 26	2,465,177 13	2,208,116 83
Due to State banks	198,762 44	253,514 14	271,549 57	320,929 14	133,378 67
Notes re-discounted	193,058 12	121,685 02	133,252 14	156,653 19	277,494 52
Bills payable	468,690 86	507,911 13	319,345 47	689,713 94	565,304 59
Total	141,151,076 61	141,642,215 89	144,003,208 56	147,249,193 84	149,961,309 11

CITY OF BOSTON.

	54 banks.	54 banks.	54 banks.	54 banks.	54 banks.
Capital stock	$50,500,000 00	$50,500,000 00	$50,800,000 00	$50,850,000 00	$50,850,000 00
Surplus fund	10,632,385 60	10,552,385 60	10,756,226 74	10,770,466 22	11,244,202 05
Undivided profits	3,741,816 72	5,190,599 89	3,191,550 50	4,597,989 88	2,821,775 62
Nat'l bank circulation	31,441,683 00	30,652,794 00	31,632,193 00	31,791,635 00	32,547,727 00
State bank circulation					
Dividends unpaid	79,424 96	42,495 46	115,969 46	73,701 46	1,242,985 76
Individual deposits	74,345,219 56	65,567,150 85	69,589,681 59	89,477,550 06	80,602,174 11
U. S. deposits	54,689 17	29,419 35	34,941 81	67,510 56	43,508 27
Dep'ts U.S.officers		8,727 05	8,164 39	10,601 48	107,140 34
Due to national banks	24,437,201 55	22,553,498 52	25,692,289 65	30,228,386 50	27,956,075 66
Due to State banks	6,941,060 98	6,920,497 50	11,791,072 27	11,875,182 52	10,143,725 06
Notes re-discounted	382,313 84	528,672 17	521,476 19	475,936 18	
Bills payable	1,481,205 48	1,354,440 27	1,263,280 06	1,722,298 00	764,138 37
Total	204,037,000 86	193,900,680 66	205,396,749 75	231,941,347 95	218,323,252 24

RHODE ISLAND.

	61 banks.	61 banks.	61 banks.	61 banks.	62 banks.
Capital stock	$20,009,800 00	$19,909,800 00	$19,909,800 00	$19,909,800 00	$20,065,050 00
Surplus fund	3,622,208 85	3,594,578 51	3,659,367 87	3,701,826 87	3,762,776 36
Undivided profits	1,091,187 28	1,215,356 35	1,276,918 12	1,287,782 77	1,211,420 18
Nat'l bank circulation	13,931,956 00	13,508,340 00	13,918,757 00	14,460,051 00	14,718,956 00
State bank circulation	7,114 00	7,114 00	7,103 00	7,103 00	9,000 00
Dividends unpaid	249,698 64	93,593 91	134,973 45	248,522 60	175,010 70
Individual deposits	8,928,074 73	8,724,591 17	9,157,194 40	10,031,663 73	11,317,338 41
U. S. deposits	72,190 22	55,811 39	85,686 67	76,743 04	47,778 71
Dep'ts U.S.dis.officers	13,249 63	47,592 24	33,750 16	20,335 31	46,294 27
Due to national banks	1,654,333 84	1,202,440 79	1,224,088 69	1,143,503 20	1,234,074 80
Due to State banks	797,801 62	641,639 46	666,672 91	700,086 51	913,660 24
Notes re-discounted					
Bills payable		50,000 00	125,042 72	65,000 00	19,415 64
Total	50,377,908 81	49,050,866 82	50,199,354 99	51,661,418 03	53,520,780 71

12 C C

Abstract of reports since October 1, 1880, *arranged*

CONNECTICUT.

Resources.	DECEMBER 31.	MARCH 11.	MAY 6.	JUNE 30.	OCTOBER 1.
	85 banks.	85 banks.	85 banks.	85 banks.	85 banks.
Loans and discounts.	$41,451,428 70	$41,850,367 54	$41,143,154 95	$41,732,657 56	$43,623,195 10
Bonds for circulation.	19,911,000 00	19,087,000 00	19,664,500 00	20,319,500 00	20,169,500 00
Bonds for deposits...	320,000 00	320,000 00	370,000 00	370,000 00	370,000 00
U. S. bonds on hand..	687,350 00	1,346 700 00	1,203,700 00	861,500 00	786,950 00
Other stocks and b'ds	1,065,167 20	1,833,198 47	1,849,961 60	2,262,475 04	2,304,735 56
Due from res've ag'ts	5,873,298 43	5,471,726 21	5,825,268 83	6,252,469 51	3,565,027 47
Due from nat'l banks.	2,888,940 48	2,418,382 31	1,998,049 47	3,041,083 05	2,597,725 10
Due from State banks	278,893 50	239,125 50	205,535 06	286,741 32	190,564 29
Real estate, &c	1,696,625 31	1,696,432 24	1,673,540 12	1,669,259 46	1,641,101 97
Current expenses....	96,181 38	200,876 89	263,990 25	85,353 83	243,955 06
Premiums paid......	109,275 27	182,046 43	206,596 75	196,686 10	195,912 11
Cash items	652,799 06	386,423 65	464,442 83	491,396 39	383,703 20
Clear'g-house exch'gs	196,487 72	103,079 51	139,183 82	265,302 04	365,747 41
Bills of other banks..	725,058 00	529,250 00	870,312 00	814,136 00	548,508 00
Fractional currency .	14,643 75	15,873 50	16,504 16	14,270 98	15,478 67
Specie	1,091,579 96	1,150,255 96	1,230,638 20	1,209,742 70	1,227,470 85
Legal-tender notes ..	991,589 00	939,794 00	1,007,003 00	975,540 00	939,922 00
U. S. cert's of deposit.	10,000 00	10,000 00	10,000 00	10,000 00	10,000 00
Due from U. S. Treas	919,888 21	865,473 94	919 230 24	944,807 28	935,369 98
Total..........	79,580,205 97	78,646,106 15	79,061,611 28	81,602,981 26	80,112,866 77

NEW YORK.

	241 banks.	240 banks.	242 banks.	242 banks.	243 banks.
Loans and discounts.	$71,281,253 32	$71,294,309 97	$72,783,752 28	$73,125,639 91	$75,697,528 14
Bonds for circulation.	29,754,750 00	28,250,600 00	28,841,600 00	29,225,800 00	29,701,900 00
Bonds for deposits...	845,000 00	895,000 00	895,000 00	895,000 00	895,000 00
U. S. bonds on hand..	3,932,850 00	5,734,950 00	5,064,600 00	5,308,500 00	5,205,250 00
Other stocks and b'ds	4,996,136 28	4,708,472 29	4,795,899 06	4,814,748 57	5,124,054 87
Due from res've ag'ts	13,282,194 42	12,946,552 80	12,564,720 18	16,023,693 84	13,235,248 70
Due from nat'l banks	2,956,642 94	2,573,699 14	2,280,156 45	2,969,492 87	2,810,205 12
Due from State banks	793,600 78	749,177 98	870,259 83	999,453 12	998,407 75
Real estate, &c	3,264,480 49	3,278,483 24	3,247,075 46	3,179,681 09	3,017,575 14
Current expenses....	386,720 55	466,099 17	540,987 87	374,146 18	449,935 21
Premiums paid......	279,034 77	294,781 84	328,118 73	365,998 10	442,394 23
Cash items	1,910,514 94	1,098,043 09	1,314,462 10	1,524,208 42	1,638,094 99
Clear'g-house exch'gs	61,514 39	17,390 26	25,197 78	36,211 32	48,321 72
Bills of other banks..	960,456 00	935,704 00	1,163,163 00	1,144,101 00	832,953 00
Fractional currency .	24,088 76	25,736 33	25,716 21	22,986 68	22,543 50
Specie	2,492,000 03	2,553,506 25	2,731,620 68	2,675,685 10	2,648,064 61
Legal-tender notes ..	2,995,894 00	2,901,567 00	2,912,885 90	2,927,133 00	2,760,944 00
U. S. cert's of deposit	330,000 00	310,000 00	290,000 00	295,000 00	285,000 00
Due from U. S. Treas	1,392,888 95	1,306,133 89	1,333,584 16	1,348,818 32	1,391,126 64
Total..........	141,940,020 62	140,340,207 25	142,008,798 79	147,156,297 52	147,204,547 72

CITY OF NEW YORK.

	47 banks.	48 banks.	48 banks.	48 banks.	48 banks.
Loans and discounts	$235,039,174 06	$226,541,684 45	$232,774,381 26	$262,820,875 67	$246,901,391 62
Bonds for circulation	21,020,500 00	18,274,500 00	21,271,500 00	22,352,500 00	22,991,500 00
Bonds for deposits...	820,000 00	820,000 00	820,000 00	820,000 00	820,000 00
U. S. bonds on hand..	2,540,250 00	10,370,950 00	10,521 900 00	15,657,800 00	7,854,050 00
Other stocks and b'ds	9,882,611 56	10,076,216 20	11,863,045 24	11,537,551 15	13,413,566 67
Due from res've ag'ts					
Due from nat'l banks	17,414,792 82	13,758,767 96	14,723,643 27	15,691,553 53	19,917,055 29
Due from State banks	2,834,190 99	3,151,115 75	2,837,866 49	2,079,233 16	3,278,155 53
Real estate, &c	10,141,322 47	10,195,819 24	10,659,141 00	10,730,409 62	10,760,837 91
Current expenses....	176,626 47	914,451 50	1,074,024 49	171,715 44	1,089,101 58
Premiums paid......	437,894 91	681,814 24	1,089,474 87	1,217,065 01	1,061,796 60
Cash items	2,641,634 67	1,835,685 40	2,190,570 06	2,307,926 45	2,513,143 81
Clear'g-house exch'gs	193,851,069 71	124,274,902 62	170,855,737 62	113,212,382 92	146,597,213 41
Bills of other banks..	1,787,709 00	1,720,700 00	3,956,162 00	2,562,098 00	1,580,588 00
Fractional currency .	46,344 36	41,003 15	42,846 72	43,115 08	37,963 55
Specie	54,720,759 01	51,558,983 90	65,044,008 60	67,194,190 87	51,524,768 04
Legal-tender notes ..	8,842,320 00	8,783,463 00	11,788,084 00	11,518,256 00	8,983,371 00
U. S. cert's of deposit.	990,000 00	1,010,000 00	3,005,000 00	2,850,000 00	1,915,000 00
Due from U. S. Treas.	1,295,995 39	1,981,535 79	2,872,958 39	1,498,429 73	1,411,986 93
Total..........	564,492,195 42	485,991,593 20	567,480,339 61	544,268,102 63	542,651,489 94

by States and reserve cities—Continued.

CONNECTICUT.

Liabilities.	DECEMBER 31. 85 banks.	MARCH 11. 85 banks.	MAY 6. 85 banks.	JUNE 30. 85 banks.	OCTOBER 1. 85 banks.
Capital stock	$25,539,620 00	$25,539,620 00	$25,539,620 00	$25,539,620 00	$25,539,620 00
Surplus fund	6,572,176 78	6,594,488 62	6,610,482 53	6,695,154 15	6,701,094 54
Undivided profits	1,247,289 30	1,674,162 08	2,002,438 04	1,368,235 29	1,746,904 49
Nat'l bank circulation	17,737,176 00	16,787,176 00	17,388,359 00	17,782,769 00	17,966,332 00
State bank circulation	41,781 00	41,766 00	41,763 00	41,698 00	41,660 00
Dividends unpaid	654,717 49	100,275 68	101,368 26	655,024 73	116,706 42
Individual deposits	23,232,610 53	24,757,870 91	24,371,367 02	24,989,842 33	25,761,230 83
U. S. deposits	105,740 15	194,238 16	230,299 60	219,267 02	195,753 47
Dep'ts U.S.dis.officers	28,123 24	14,013 14	17,374 66	22,020 44	26,438 17
Due to national banks	3,723,803 77	2,508,874 70	2,204,438 25	3,716,359 25	1,694,771 90
Due to State banks	587,167 71	334,620 86	363,522 80	572,991 05	322,264 95
Notes re-discounted	20,000 00		6,000 00		
Bills payable			183,578 12		
Total	79,580,205 97	78,646,106 15	79,061,611 28	81,602,981 26	80,112,866 77

NEW YORK.

	241 banks.	240 banks.	242 banks.	242 banks.	243 banks.
Capital stock	$32,837,160 00	$32,787,160 00	$32,892,160 00	$32,792,160 00	$32,830,160 00
Surplus fund	7,749,473 04	7,877,930 27	7,880,239 81	7,944,066 65	8,015,608 13
Undivided profits	4,692,431 80	4,454,941 66	5,169,721 28	4,953,409 56	4,889,321 32
Nat'l bank circulation	26,543,902 00	24,991,500 00	25,470,578 00	25,717,885 00	26,328,096 00
State bank circulation	46,129 00	41,129 00	41,119 00	41,119 00	41,119 00
Dividends unpaid	357,295 23	78,269 98	81,496 46	336,630 28	81,941 68
Individual deposits	63,407,366 99	64,541,570 23	64,741,332 02	68,366,217 90	69,771,208 83
U. S. deposits	522,560 87	457,854 54	694,728 65	673,427 20	507,416 70
Dep'ts U.S.officers	100,641 01	91,556 55	68,000 23	69,675 15	115,405 12
Due to national banks	3,612,539 20	3,131,851 87	2,882,579 30	4,157,070 51	2,600,682 38
Due to State banks	1,354,907 53	1,051,231 12	1,215,881 37	1,289,135 70	1,280,459 84
Notes re-discounted	274,935 22	261,164 39	283,925 40	277,714 80	315,078 09
Bills payable	440,678 64	574,047 64	587,037 27	537,785 77	428,050 63
Total	141,940,020 62	140,340,207 25	142,008,798 79	147,156,297 52	147,204,547 72

CITY OF NEW YORK.

	47 banks.	48 banks.	48 banks.	48 banks.	48 banks.
Capital stock	$50,650,000 00	$50,900,000 00	$51,150,000 00	$51,150,000 00	$51,150,000 00
Surplus fund	18,528,757 35	18,534,884 02	19,076,605 36	19,882,931 70	19,947,315 89
Undivided profits	9,215,593 81	11,544,539 38	12,431,941 87	10,768,757 01	12,832,314 51
Nat'l bank circulation	18,521,915 00	15,549,250 00	19,098,445 00	19,359,190 00	20,112,590 00
State bank circulation	47,482 00	47,480 00	47,480 00	47,472 00	47,472 00
Dividends unpaid	1,511,561 99	175,848 79	305,733 89	1,429,052 90	246,228 22
Individual deposits	337,561,625 61	266,649,881 92	332,797,995 18	284,242,159 78	295,692,012 40
U. S. deposits	495,642 03	361,529 83	427,874 43	568,039 25	437,422 35
Dep'ts U.S.dis.officers	103,121 01	178,958 90	193,277 51	108,091 64	89,934 21
Due to national banks	96,851,137 60	92,103,283 68	98,573,226 30	117,651,167 17	104,089,161 13
Due to State banks	31,005,959 02	29,945,936 59	33,377,760 07	30,060,641 18	38,007,039 23
Notes re-discounted					
Bills payable					
Total	564,492,195 42	485,991,593 20	567,480,339 61	544,268,102 63	542,651,489 94

Abstract of reports since October 1, 1880, arranged

CITY OF ALBANY.

Resources.	DECEMBER 31. 7 banks.	MARCH 11. 7 banks.	MAY 6. 7 banks.	JUNE 30. 7 banks.	OCTOBER 1. 7 banks.
Loans and discounts	$6,825,642 08	$7,671,083 71	$7,504,228 95	$7,166,344 91	$8,298,430 89
Bonds for circulation	1,710,000 00	1,390,000 00	1,640,000 00	1,680,000 00	1,680,000 00
Bonds for deposits	100,000 00	100,000 00	100,000 00	100,000 00	100,000 00
U. S. bonds on hand	176,550 00	662,500 00	500,500 00	1,336,950 00	1,031,750 00
Other stocks and b'ds	178,378 44	162,978 44	162,459 33	119,704 33	119,632 08
Due from res'veag'ts	1,769,688 57	1,391,843 66	2,929,979 14	2,507,720 28	1,856,967 80
Due from nat'l banks	865,779 13	678,082 15	877,254 29	936,516 67	961,273 89
Due from State banks	96,466 56	178,489 62	111,721 03	103,038 75	175,202 38
Real estate, &c	347,520 99	347,580 99	347,461 49	347,614 25	364,675 75
Current expenses		2,703 11	5,971 16	8,861 87	3,634 22
Premiums paid	63,545 38	63,545 38	63,545 38	58,551 63	58,551 63
Cash items	135,649 11	89,165 50	116,995 69	127,585 96	158,197 99
Clear'g-house exch'gs	206,570 06	112,533 77	119,131 42	164,892 98	223,125 45
Bills of other banks	133,881 00	88,294 00	129,686 00	119,613 00	64,407 00
Fractional currency	1,560 57	2,834 43	3,258 52	2,324 97	3,398 11
Specie	446,847 91	501,320 64	478,355 66	543,193 38	502,054 84
Legal-tender notes	424,450 00	405,906 00	468,341 00	203,933 00	154,470 00
U. S. cert's of deposit	215,000 00	265,000 00	225,000 00	545,000 00	545,000 00
Due from U. S. Treas	84,170 95	59,787 00	91,707 50	79,797 50	89,097 50
Total	13,781,700 75	14,173,648 40	15,875,596 56	16,151,643 48	16,389,869 53

NEW JERSEY.

	66 banks.	65 banks.	65 banks.	66 banks.	67 banks.
Loans and discounts	$26,604,615 75	$27,428,500 68	$27,623,072 38	$27,441,349 55	$29,266,738 80
Bonds for circulation	11,968,350 00	10,911,350 00	11,711,350 00	11,741,350 00	11,671,350 00
Bonds for deposits	300,000 00	300,000 00	300,000 00	300,000 00	300,000 00
U. S. bonds on hand	842,100 00	1,327,800 00	1,357,550 00	1,495,850 00	1,648,950 00
Other stocks and b'ds	1,052,016 59	1,188,526 47	1,171,159 15	1,447,091 64	1,518,299 79
Due from res'veag'ts	7,385,414 09	6,670,872 94	6,990,592 78	8,211,192 72	6,984,533 47
Due from nat'l banks	1,502,726 48	1,296,218 91	1,466,117 62	1,835,379 07	1,588,037 57
Due from State banks	257,335 09	190,516 03	254,029 22	338,874 32	278,954 48
Real estate, &c	1,784,481 87	1,687,941 17	1,662,587 95	1,691,146 20	1,695,038 14
Current expenses	131,001 14	177,984 57	200,757 80	134,890 86	195,847 00
Premiums paid	51,294 32	65,629 75	82,617 25	76,827 00	107,162 24
Cash items	978,535 08	499,599 24	549,071 77	747,839 64	838,302 08
Clear'g-house exch'gs					
Bills of other banks	378,884 00	390,440 00	496,718 00	557,239 00	374,006 00
Fractional currency	13,379 97	12,595 56	11,011 74	12,838 94	12,987 77
Specie	945,425 45	972,410 82	967,755 02	971,576 10	980,832 61
Legal-tender notes	1,465,812 00	1,618,796 00	1,753,328 00	1,789,088 00	1,487,807 00
U. S. cert's of deposit	10,000 00	10,000 00	10,000 00	10,000 00	10,000 00
Due from U. S. Treas	603,290 22	510,844 47	506,147 17	548,696 07	544,696 67
Total	56,274,662 05	55,260,026 61	57,194,445 78	59,351,229 11	59,503,634 58

PENNSYLVANIA.

	186 banks.	187 banks.	188 banks.	190 banks.	191 banks.
Loans and discounts	$49,550,124 78	$50,614,986 51	$52,728,137 55	$51,614,727 06	$54,025,127 70
Bonds for circulation	27,280,400 00	26,392,400 00	27,278,400 00	27,499,400 00	27,817,100 00
Bonds for deposits	580,000 00	580,000 00	580,000 00	580,000 00	580,000 00
U. S. bonds on hand	2,193,000 00	3,424,550 00	3,384,850 00	4,001,200 00	4,339,350 00
Other stocks and b'ds	4,380,977 09	4,445,929 81	4,751,159 15	5,309,384 36	5,644,554 76
Due from res'veag'ts	10,235,274 74	12,332,071 96	12,238,056 87	13,041,539 97	11,933,427 09
Due from nat'l banks	3,350,185 46	3,341,967 86	3,487,253 63	4,273,659 47	3,956,880 24
Due from State banks	1,233,075 55	1,304,164 33	1,432,991 33	1,634,298 74	1,334,383 13
Real estate, &c	3,347,548 03	3,363,317 72	3,356,261 44	3,380,037 16	3,373,379 18
Current expenses	302,849 22	487,724 87	392,748 35	339,258 08	554,780 14
Premiums paid	220,206 40	191,169 99	229,083 48	255,305 08	251,569 31
Cash items	801,496 06	648,707 89	723,988 08	734,852 57	884,642 27
Clear'g-house exch'gs					
Bills of other banks	1,090,002 00	826,562 00	1,245,031 00	1,261,294 00	990,160 00
Fractional currency	35,112 80	38,215 39	37,066 10	36,209 65	36,512 40
Specie	3,459,456 07	3,475,500 66	3,941,679 85	3,862,236 46	3,726,222 09
Legal-tender notes	3,098,411 00	2,687,347 00	3,286,603 00	2,990,361 00	2,770,438 00
U. S. cert's of deposit	30,000 00	20,000 00	30,000 00	15,000 00	60,000 00
Due from U. S. Treas	1,272,709 40	1,235,649 53	1,268,186 28	1,284,681 29	1,278,868 27
Total	112,460,831 60	115,413,256 52	120,391,506 11	122,113,534 89	124,177,403 58

by States and reserve cities—Continued.

CITY OF ALBANY.

Liabilities.	DECEMBER 31. 7 banks.	MARCH 11. 7 banks.	MAY 6. 7 banks.	JUNE 30. 7 banks.	OCTOBER 1. 7 banks.
Capital stock	$1,800,000 00	$1,800,000 00	$1,800,000 00	$1,800,000 00	$1,800,000 00
Surplus fund	1,400,000 00	1,400,000 00	1,400,000 00	1,400,000 00	1,400,000 00
Undivided profits	236,370 34	213,948 36	237,954 03	233,542 65	226,533 67
Nat'l bank circulation	1,438,990 00	1,101,390 00	1,337,190 00	1,472,740 00	1,506,140 00
State bank circulation					
Dividends unpaid	36,892 00	7,051 96	7,237 23	25,723 94	19,374 94
Individual deposits	5,471,222 78	6,530,397 58	7,302,901 36	6,832,654 70	7,390,558 40
U. S. deposits	59,107 40	65,883 41	94,441 40	72,157 52	54,915 58
Dep'ts U.S.dis.officers	12,694 09	3,879 24	1,861 21	22,448 80	16,107 99
Due to national banks	2,870,432 12	2,631,024 11	3,055,188 49	3,461,358 13	3,325,313 24
Due to State banks	455,992 02	420,073 74	638,822 84	831,017 74	650,925 71
Notes re-discounted					
Bills payable					
Total	13,781,700 75	14,173,648 40	15,875,596 56	16,151,643 48	16,389,869 53

NEW JERSEY.

	66 banks.	65 banks.	65 banks.	66 banks.	67 banks.
Capital stock	$12,995,350 00	$12,855,350 00	$12,875,350 00	$12,910,350 00	$12,960,000 00
Surplus fund	3,705,209 60	3,702,919 29	3,735,919 29	3,808,025 57	3,844,180 88
Undivided profits	1,409,379 71	1,486,629 07	1,632,515 84	1,496,664 30	1,651,164 90
Nat'l bank circulation	10,683,802 00	9,684,889 00	10,226,009 00	10,370,569 00	10,386,784 00
State bank circulation	16,970 00	16,970 00	16,965 00	9,120 00	9,118 00
Dividends unpaid	291,377 07	57,694 03	52,034 44	272,604 23	96,985 68
Individual deposits	24,914,656 81	24,981,422 95	25,576,509 06	27,907,776 29	28,250,617 84
U. S. deposits	169,441 25	202,701 92	244,556 64	207,918 32	206,844 58
Dep'ts U.S.dis.officers	10,737 93	11,136 05	12,287 23	15,727 48	12,267 85
Due to national banks	1,602,592 51	1,912,152 80	2,330,277 48	1,991,389 06	1,798,106 13
Due to State banks	184,365 74	237,898 00	310,037 50	158,797 14	235,864 72
Notes re-discounted	154,079 43	95,563 50	127,284 30	47,587 72	7,000 00
Bills payable	76,700 00	14,700 00	54,700 00	64,700 00	44,700 00
Total	56,274,662 05	55,260,026 61	57,194,445 78	59,351,229 11	59,503,634 58

PENNSYLVANIA.

	186 banks.	187 banks.	188 banks.	190 banks.	191 banks.
Capital stock	$28,945,340 00	$29,030,340 00	$29,105,340 00	$29,220,340 00	$29,310,340 00
Surplus fund	7,117,646 40	7,255,707 96	7,334,356 14	7,469,888 84	7,635,415 97
Undivided profits	2,462,599 48	2,544,241 09	2,560,745 28	2,714,683 84	3,003,168 00
Nat'l bank circulation	21,182,405 09	23,130,324 00	23,795,788 00	23,970,598 00	24,405,793 00
State bank circulation	30,153 00	30,140 00	30,110 00	28,384 00	27,959 00
Dividends unpaid	217,565 16	164,693 05	428,208 45	284,319 10	146,712 14
Individual deposits	46,380,949 71	50,011,930 04	54,064,347 39	54,511,240 83	57,084,597 57
U. S. deposits	343,730 85	314,579 88	437,204 54	401,589 56	360,639 97
Dep'ts U.S.dis.officers	11,171 71	11,239 44	11,859 34	12,225 36	11,253 55
Due to national banks	2,244,374 40	2,253,572 10	2,252,613 39	2,888,553 07	1,793,262 97
Due to State banks	336,639 07	576,188 21	303,820 08	434,726 22	317,388 90
Notes re-discounted	181,766 54	115,810 47	51,593 22	94,344 03	50,382 23
Bills payable	6,490 28	171,490 28	15,490 28	82,642 04	490 28
Total	112,460,831 60	115,413,256 52	120,391,566 11	122,113,534 89	121,177,403 58

CITY OF PHILADELPHIA.

R sources.	DECEMBER 31. 32 banks.	MARCH 11. 32 banks.	MAY 6. 32 banks.	JUNE 30. 32 banks.	OCTOBER 1. 32 banks.
Loans and discounts	$53,355,881 51	$54,401,000 76	$58,471,790 14	$61,836,884 27	$62,286,150 23
Bonds for circulation	14,285,700 00	11,823,700 00	12,645,700 00	13,288,700 00	13,430,200 00
Bonds for deposits ..	250,000 00	250,000 00	250,000 00	250,000 00	250,000 00
U. S. bonds on hand..	2,101,300 00	3,903,500 00	3,484,500 00	1,934,000 00	1,751,300 00
Other stocks and b'ds	2,603,514 19	2,896,926 79	2,805,853 88	4,213,137 13	4,203,375 17
Due from res'veag'ts.	7,237,144 74	6,259,340 26	6,512,317 10	6,250,739 99	6,607,949 64
Due from nat'l banks	3,802,816 02	3,472,870 36	3,895,621 97	4,338,158 52	4,079,247 03
Due from State banks	814,259 45	617,167 16	767,503 31	887,958 14	899,412 16
Real estate, &c	2,740,619 03	2,743,945 11	2,723,019 31	2,720,710 94	2,591,521 96
Current expenses....	244,942 27	507,134 68	95,277 88	247,866 66	609,873 09
Premiums paid	199,376 68	131,426 64	120,615 41	79,273 03	78,493 26
Cash items	887,457 49	398,342 02	513,400 06	601,177 18	620,838 07
Clear'g-house exch'gs	15,170,128 04	7,498,398 67	7,989,916 41	9,322,939 41	8,852,901 95
Bills of other banks..	645,649 00	606,212 00	792,713 00	710,716 00	627,729 00
Fractional currency	22,201 17	23,842 32	22,017 71	21,729 62	20,879 43
Specie	7,004,909 45	6,760,281 79	8,104,618 93	9,753,900 45	7,233,819 45
Legal-tender notes ..	4,752,424 00	2,824,020 00	3,537,674 00	3,477,974 00	2,529,521 00
U. S. cert's of deposit	2,150,000 00	2,125,000 00	1,795,000 00	2,580,000 00	1,820,000 00
Due from U. S. Treas	671,248 62	585,637 43	647,640 43	640,070 93	690,324 93
Total	120,939,661 66	107,888,745 99	115,175,469 54	123,165,836 27	119,201,545 37

CITY OF PITTSBURGH.

	22 banks.	22 banks.	22 banks.	22 banks.	22 banks.
Loans and discounts	$20,364,869 05	$20,076,836 44	$20,757,613 56	$20,921,312 41	$22,384,220 25
Bonds for circulation	7,209,000 00	6,217,000 00	7,317,000 00	7,317,000 00	7,592,000 00
Bonds for deposits ..	250,000 00	250,000 00	250,000 00	250,000 00	250,000 00
U. S. bonds on hand..	433,150 00	1,028,400 00	453,450 00	485,350 00	479,050 00
Other stocks and b'ds	779,664 12	758,283 24	789,372 97	1,089,268 66	1,076,684 67
Due from res'veag'ts.	2,941,587 12	3,368,362 44	3,207,566 69	3,946,913 79	3,257,058 33
Due from nat'l banks	880,545 74	1,202,953 87	1,158,347 50	1,512,122 50	919,217 52
Due from State banks	239,723 37	397,014 32	374,468 62	500,858 66	342,742 40
Real estate, &c	1,841,684 00	1,860,877 45	1,799,976 10	1,804,127 94	1,790,594 52
Current expenses....	71,061 74	155,281 15	117,349 82	120,123 14	190,568 61
Premiums paid	41,532 34	39,139 91	44,940 07	31,953 13	38,840 11
Cash items	188,333 04	133,958 63	171,184 88	228,179 87	306,391 80
Clear'g-house exch'gs	1,136,811 23	1,008,207 09	1,048,796 84	963,662 02	1,194,210 21
Bills of other banks..	291,518 00	308,154 00	963,040 00	255,876 00	303,575 00
Fractional currency	9,468 42	10,855 99	12,642 93	9,518 00	12,738 45
Specie	1,378,486 35	1,332,997 88	1,804,188 33	1,807,687 18	1,664,394 05
Legal-tender notes ..	1,703,372 00	1,582,197 00	2,460,635 00	2,098,256 00	1,994,011 00
U. S. cert's of deposit	...	...	...	...	...
Due from U. S. Treas	360,019 24	301,050 07	345,757 46	367,857 36	396,660 86
Total	40,100,828 76	40,631,569 48	43,076,260 77	43,712,064 66	44,201,957 78

DELAWARE.

	14 banks.	14 banks.	14 banks.	14 banks.	14 banks.
Loans and discounts	$3,196,522 78	$3,174,387 91	$3,207,495 75	$3,264,748 53	$3,497,474 68
Bonds for circulation	1,695,200 00	1,693,200 00	1,662,200 00	1,743,200 00	1,693,200 00
Bonds for deposits ..	60,000 00	60,000 00	60,000 00	60,000 00	60,000 00
U. S. bonds on hand..	268,550 00	237,550 00	287,550 00	127,550 00	352,550 00
Other stocks and b'ds	192,091 79	196,079 70	256,579 70	251,079 70	297,077 70
Due from res'veag'ts	674,713 01	838,053 18	1,080,642 91	1,100,618 27	886,910 07
Due from nat'l banks	204,980 03	169,841 19	213,475 78	341,981 76	282,046 12
Due from State banks	68,058 56	46,626 48	72,189 95	55,923 36	65,892 06
Real estate, &c	223,235 33	223,270 53	223,275 10	223,214 76	213,297 20
Current expenses....	22,268 07	15,979 73	20,580 23	19,799 05	19,910 56
Premiums paid	7,357 00	7,357 00	7,357 00	6,977 00	7,988 25
Cash items	76,154 16	56,002 69	62,508 37	67,037 89	108,635 49
Clear'g-house exch'gs	...	...	...	...	...
Bills of other banks..	76,789 00	63,386 00	48,515 00	73,481 00	77,621 00
Fractional currency	1,587 23	1,973 50	2,258 67	1,461 20	1,881 58
Specie	170,573 02	185,217 95	174,097 51	150,000 41	181,894 21
Legal-tender notes ..	117,831 00	149,835 00	131,659 00	147,888 00	141,262 00
U. S. cert's of deposit	30,000 00	30,000 00	30,000 00	30,000 00	30,000 00
Due from U. S. Treas	80,812 51	76,838 75	88,818 75	77,738 75	81,038 75
Total	7,286,756 49	7,226,199 61	7,663,203 72	7,742,699 08	7,998,079 70

by States and reserve cities—Continued.

CITY OF PHILADELPHIA.

Liabilities.	DECEMBER 31. 32 banks.	MARCH 11. 32 banks.	MAY 6. 32 banks.	JUNE 30. 32 banks.	OCTOBER 1. 32 banks.
Capital stock	$17,358,000 00	$17,358,000 00	$17,358,000 00	$17,358,000 00	$17,358,000 00
Surplus fund	7,733,732 99	7,757,894 90	7,969,732 07	8,135,053 08	8,157,053 08
Undivided profits	1,439,989 40	1,703,356 91	1,143,454 02	1,742,650 28	2,262,370 70
Nat'l bank circulation	12,533,474 00	10,359,404 00	10,782,953 00	10,823,457 00	11,446,341 00
State bank circulation	1,519 00	819 00	819 00	819 00	819 00
Dividends unpaid	46,475 41	35,874 21	323,342 01	53,905 46	40 548 21
Individual deposits	65,723,663 43	54,338,613 37	60,363,490 59	65,269,582 97	61,966,671 56
U. S. deposits	225,976 24	201,476 03	206,373 14	235,251 25	211,081 55
Dep'ts U.S.dis.officers					
Due to national banks	12,891,738 25	12,793,489 67	13,364,398 73	15,731,116 27	14,448,898 20
Due to State banks	2,925,092 94	3,279,617 90	3,602,906 98	3,756,001 01	3,309,762 07
Notes re-discounted					
Bills payable	60,000 00	60,000 00	60,000 00	60,000 00	
Total	120,939,661 66	107,888,745 99	115,175,409 54	123,165,836 27	119,201,545 37

CITY OF PITTSBURGH.

	22 banks.	22 banks.	22 banks.	22 banks.	22 banks.
Capital stock	$9,850,000 00	$9,850,000 00	$9,850,000 00	$9,850,000 00	$9,850,000 00
Surplus fund	3,178,748 23	3,201,589 35	3,216,259 38	3,241,350 65	3,268,366 11
Undivided profits	601,963 11	727,712 54	706,664 00	762,806 95	863,618 71
Nat'l bank circulation	6,301,758 00	5,340,758 00	6,351,418 00	6,280,618 00	6,577,113 00
State bank circulation					
Dividends unpaid	73,091 75	39,104 75	126,583 25	92,236 75	54,710 25
Individual deposits	16,358,640 68	17,492,416 32	18,600,076 61	19,143,578 25	18,994,882 94
U. S. deposits	137,844 43	95,790 51	102,485 88	142,006 29	149,133 92
Dep'ts U.S.dis.officers	50,588 02	128,032 98	53,120 19	43,983 28	79,712 87
Due to national banks	2,259,132 09	2,335,314 84	2,744,643 81	2,812,228 41	2,783,258 16
Due to State banks	1,289,061 85	1,320,850 19	1,265,109 65	1,340,256 08	1,570,529 95
Notes re-discounted					10,631 87
Bills payable		100,000 00			
Total	40,100,828 76	40,631,569 48	43,076,360 77	43,712,064 66	44,201,957 78

DELAWARE.

	14 banks.	14 banks.	14 banks.	14 banks.	14 banks.
Capital stock	$1,743,985 00	$1,743,985 00	$1,743,985 00	$1,743,985 00	$1,743,985 00
Surplus fund	483,451 99	491,781 31	491,990 79	492,509 79	509,038 81
Undivided profits	170,861 79	131,790 34	171,279 16	211,538 42	143,145 83
Nat'l bank circulation	1,476,069 00	1,463,989 00	1,456,104 00	1,441,149 00	1,438,099 00
State bank circulation	855 00	855 00	855 00	855 00	855 00
Dividends unpaid	9,101 00	13,935 80	14,959 05	10,066 50	13,979 90
Individual deposits	2,901,029 49	3,008,064 48	3,364,340 95	3,461,450 83	3,754,299 04
U. S. deposits	40,512 46	31,971 71	38,783 46	39,832 99	45,845 08
Dep'ts U.S.dis.officers	7,823 37	1,086 33	2,164 21	2,645 23	4,461 82
Due to national banks	403,686 21	309,786 26	357,120 91	332,377 68	322,032 28
Due to State banks	19,384 15	28,954 41	21,621 19	6,289 24	22,358 00
Notes re-discounted					
Bills payable					
Total	7,246,756 49	7,226,199 64	7,663,203 72	7,742,699 68	7,908,079 76

Abstract of reports since October 1, 1880, arranged

MARYLAND.

Resources.	DECEMBER 31.	MARCH 11.	MAY 6.	JUNE 30.	OCTOBER 1.
	21 banks.	21 banks.	21 banks.	21 banks.	22 banks.
Loans and discounts.	$3,972,961 53	$4,011,217 17	$4,108,753 18	$4,132,798 60	$4,348,551 31
Bonds for circulation.	2,156,550 00	2,096,550 00	2,216,550 00	2,216,550 00	2,246,550 00
Bonds for deposits ..	100,000 00	100,000 00	100,000 00	100,000 00	100,000 00
U. S. bonds on hand..	570,600 00	695,200 00	503,050 00	540,900 00	659,400 00
Other stocks and b'ds	355,723 81	346,503 81	452,925 20	370,980 20	361,620 20
Due from res've ag'ts.	888,941 98	947,956 75	967,023 34	981,896 52	1,143,417 21
Due from nat'l banks	362,285 55	379,660 67	354,294 25	461,347 12	607,886 86
Due from State banks	23,495 96	26,003 55	42,814 79	38,865 64	68,490 95
Real estate, &c	208,580 46	210,192 48	234,113 23	233,495 33	238,524 15
Current expenses....	21,316 02	46,657 85	53,335 51	27,414 51	51,325 86
Premiums paid	21,912 39	24,142 68	28,794 18	28,347 81	44,781 73
Cash items	39,777 79	48,920 52	35,563 50	69,184 57	68,631 35
Clear'g-house exch'gs					
Bills of other banks..	63,494 00	50,073 00	89,625 00	103,780 00	93,874 00
Fractional currency .	3,105 06	2,901 79	2,987 99	2,835 09	3,689 18
Specie	227,185 58	230,265 98	260,146 62	252,372 11	262,669 97
Legal-tender notes ..	378,997 00	347,345 00	412,945 00	392,582 00	421,391 00
U. S. cert's of deposit					
Due from U. S. Treas.	98,395 19	96,226 68	103,596 38	100,517 25	103,567 50
Total	9,493,322 32	9,659,877 93	9,906,428 17	10,053,866 75	10,824,371 27

CITY OF BALTIMORE.

	15 banks.	16 banks.	16 banks.	16 banks.	16 banks.
Loans and discounts	$22,412,814 18	$25,099,055 81	$24,980,654 01	$25,633,944 05	$25,906,037 07
Bonds for circulation	7,052,100 00	7,102,100 00	7,532,100 00	7,532,100 00	7,562,100 00
Bonds for deposits ..	200,000 00	200,000 00	200,000 00	200,000 00	200,000 00
U. S. bonds on hand..	500,000 00	530,000 00	530,000 00	630,000 00	410,000 00
Other stocks and b'ds	167,892 52	124,305 02	115,555 02	86,488 87	88,072 47
Due from res've ag'ts.	2,731,242 44	1,990,049 17	2,097,504 06	2,113,118 31	2,522,644 58
Due from nat'l banks.	1,052,783 77	933,141 38	690,802 89	939,711 79	955,906 89
Due from State banks	209,125 21	190,893 36	182,189 85	271,961 32	169,880 30
Real estate, &c	647,841 13	650,458 37	650,780 57	648,001 64	653,286 64
Current expenses....	36,748 01	116,879 28	164,745 08	148,846 77	163,373 80
Premiums paid	61,134 04	62,009 04	80,284 03	101,599 99	57,087 49
Cash items	59,530 60	46,723 79	49,418 08	54,107 26	95,526 56
Clear'g-house exch'gs	1,742,104 21	1,654,162 19	1,690,494 51	1,630,374 89	3,561,277 85
Bills of other banks..	294,127 00	264,352 00	506,843 00	502,128 00	277,411 00
Fractional currency .	2,753 58	2,848 33	3,068 96	3,316 30	3,062 13
Specie	1,362,992 97	1,740,508 00	1,478,933 41	1,591,544 53	2,058,981 66
Legal-tender notes ..	1,491,123 00	1,218,211 00	1,519,254 00	1,735,518 00	947,170 00
U. S. cert's of deposit	675,000 00	875,000 00	690,000 00	765,000 00	255,000 00
Due from U. S. Treas	342,637 00	341,487 00	354,252 00	352,437 00	371,987 00
Total	41,041,949 66	43,142,174 74	43,516,879 47	44,940,198 72	46,258,805 44

DISTRICT OF COLUMBIA.

	1 bank.	1 bank.	1 bank.	1 bank.	1 bank.
Loans and discounts	$279,211 25	$245,298 67	$242,332 19	$257,635 88	$304,434 42
Bonds for circulation	250,000 00	250,000 00	250,000 00	250,000 00	250,000 00
Bonds for deposits....					
U. S. bonds on hand..	250,000 00	275,000 00	276,000 00	276,000 00	276,000 00
Other stocks and b'ds	15,930 00	15,930 00	15,930 00	15,930 00	930 00
Due from res've ag'ts	85,808 77	89,135 22	111,226 67	133,083 75	122,293 60
Due from nat'l banks	11,949 24	7,614 76	6,144 58	21,248 09	13,683 19
Due from State banks	2,476 98	2,793 99	4,099 29	4,665 55	269 77
Real estate, &c	17,950 00	17,950 00	17,950 00	17,950 00	17,950 00
Current expenses....	131 88	2,267 29	4,124 90	72 75	2,770 37
Premiums paid......		2,200 00	2,200 00	2,200 00	2,200 00
Cash items	4,130 46	5,420 00	8,654 19	8,709 05	9,104 01
Clear'g-house exch'gs					
Bills of other banks..	12,743 00	17,832 00	10,943 00	20,001 00	10,003 00
Fractional currency .	25 00	9 10	14 00	16 00	12 00
Specie	50,416 00	69,466 00	65,816 00	63,198 00	57,286 00
Legal-tender notes ..	81,500 00	85,000 00	74,000 00	80,500 00	75,000 00
U. S. cert's of deposit					
Due from U. S. Treas	11,250 00	11,250 00	11,250 00	11,250 00	11,250 00
Total	1,082,522 58	1,097,167 03	1,100,684 82	1,162,460 07	1,153,186 36

by States and reserve cities—Continued.

MARYLAND.

Liabilities.	DECEMBER 31. 21 banks.	MARCH 11. 21 banks.	MAY 6. 21 banks.	JUNE 30. 21 banks.	OCTOBER 1. 22 banks.
Capital stock........	$2,366,700 00	$2,381,700 00	$2,381,700 00	$2,381,700 00	$2,412,700 00
Surplus fund.........	710,615 89	712,576 31	714,576 31	705,259 70	706,868 00
Undivided profits....	175,340 52	236,116 85	278,833 22	209,221 77	235,816 20
Nat'l bank circulation	1,888,607 00	1,820,522 00	1,928,617 00	1,926,187 00	1,967,472 00
State bank circulation	35 00	35 00	35 00	34 00	34 00
Dividends unpaid....	62,565 30	16,727 47	18,674 86	64,941 97	33,667 85
Individual deposits...	3,942,630 08	4,161,681 87	4,487,143 42	4,521,457 82	5,253,859 18
U. S. deposits........	21,347 90	25,624 59	29,747 18	28,798 97	9,233 96
Dep'ts U.S.dis.officers	36,729 88	17,599 77	20,041 55	33,206 38	53,209 45
Due to national banks	106,606 69	119,138 92	88,065 04	154,340 50	129,750 42
Due to State banks...	25,482 29	17,992 27	18,994 59	28,718 64	21,740 21
Notes re-discounted..	20,000 00				
Bills payable........	136,661 77	150,162 88			
Total	9,493,322 32	9,659,877 93	9,966,428 17	10,053,866 75	10,824,371 27

CITY OF BALTIMORE.

	15 banks.	16 banks.	16 banks.	16 banks.	16 banks.
Capital stock........	$10,890,330 00	$11,110,330 00	$11,110,330 00	$11,110,330 00	$11,190,330 00
Surplus fund.........	2,463,304 32	2,480,390 07	2,484,013 83	2,497,847 01	2,552,847 01
Undivided profits....	673,809 58	946,460 71	1,214,824 71	1,008,716 33	1,203,128 02
Nat'l bank circulation	6,156,501 00	6,174,901 00	6,509,601 00	6,495,711 00	6,637,961 00
State bank circulation	34,800 00	34,800 00	34,800 00	34,795 00	34,795 00
Dividends unpaid....	368,228 89	71,089 29	64,130 95	248,670 19	73,167 95
Individual deposits...	17,646,877 61	18,159,562 77	18,803,709 31	20,168,350 21	20,863,490 71
U. S. deposits........	109,888 24	105,335 25	110,453 80	112,562 70	111,652 59
Dep'ts U.S.dis.officers					
Due to national banks	2,286,496 01	3,599,117 87	2,750,769 50	2,742,626 23	3,118,248 23
Due to State banks...	411,714 01	460,187 78	434,246 37	520,584 05	473,184 93
Notes re-discounted..					
Bills payable........					
Total	41,011,949 66	43,142,174 74	43,516,879 47	44,940,198 72	46,258,805 44

DISTRICT OF COLUMBIA.

	1 bank.	1 bank.	1 bank.	1 bank.	1 bank.
Capital stock........	$252,000 00	$252,000 00	$252,000 00	$252,000 00	$252,000 00
Surplus fund.........	58,000 00	58,000 00	58,000 00	59,000 00	59,000 00
Undivided profits....	29,713 53	34,906 50	42,328 70	27,713 96	39,458 79
Nat'l bank circulation	222,300 00	215,000 00	219,700 00	213,300 00	207,600 00
State bank circulation					
Dividends unpaid....	11,896 00	1,884 00	1,668 00	11,672 00	1,908 00
Individual deposits...	503,572 06	528,780 26	521,069 49	596,284 81	587,152 45
U. S. deposits........					
Dep'ts U.S.dis.officers					
Due to national banks	5,022 09	6,522 48	5,374 80	2,407 30	2,300 88
Due to State banks...	18 90	73 79	543 83	82 00	3,766 24
Notes re-discounted..					
Bills payable........					
Total	1,082,522 58	1,097,167 03	1,100,684 82	1,162,460 07	1,153,186 36

Abstract of reports since October 1, 1880, arranged

CITY OF WASHINGTON.

Resources.	DECEMBER 31. 5 banks.	MARCH 11. 5 banks.	MAY 6. 5 banks.	JUNE 30. 5 banks.	OCTOBER 1. 5 banks.
Loans and discounts	$1,596,843 12	$1,646,832 76	$1,761,023 67	$1,753,970 33	$1,786,185 27
Bonds for circulation	780,000 00	730,000 00	730,000 00	730,000 00	730,000 00
Bonds for deposits	100,000 00	100,000 00	100,000 00	100,000 00	100,000 00
U. S. bonds on hand	63,400 00	154,150 00	122,750 00	191,500 00	150,300 00
Other stocks and b'ds	121,915 70	131,657 32	127,089 35	143,929 35	138,605 66
Due from res'v ag'ts	222,271 41	305,270 00	305,026 77	340,830 56	200,444 90
Due from nat'l banks	126,647 01	88,635 19	171,709 04	171,651 41	153,430 89
Due from State banks	3,133 44	5,853 13	4,960 13	10,187 19	9,008 63
Real estate, &c	420,997 38	421,065 67	421,065 67	420,865 67	418,865 67
Current expenses	15,289 52	18,350 30	30,789 72	10,867 66	24,127 52
Premiums paid	5,119 46	8,846 30	3,858 30	5,604 26	6,091 83
Cash items	65,748 78	68,248 97	79,486 36	64,905 00	67,400 70
Clear'g-house exch'gs					
Bills of other banks	25,581 00	40,151 00	38,895 00	11,447 00	22,786 00
Fractional currency	6,293 98	6,714 96	6,340 35	5,025 85	5,536 12
Specie	196,625 76	225,996 25	197,578 00	150,696 25	143,806 00
Legal-tender notes	229,702 00	159,540 00	143,832 00	142,458 00	222,126 00
U. S. cert's of deposit			50,000 00		
Due from U. S. Treas	35,100 00	31,500 00	31,500 00	31,500 00	31,500 00
Total	4,014,668 56	4,142,811 85	4,325,904 36	4,293,918 53	4,219,215 19

VIRGINIA.

	17 banks.	18 banks.	18 banks.	18 banks.	18 banks.
Loans and discounts	$7,585,302 17	$7,900,601 39	$8,161,746 37	$8,384,036 38	$9,226,776 15
Bonds for circulation	2,643,350 00	2,578,350 00	2,673,350 00	2,673,350 00	2,753,350 00
Bonds for deposits	575,000 00	575,000 00	575,000 00	575,000 00	575,000 00
U. S. bonds on hand	114,700 00	262,100 00	293,250 00	293,900 00	369,400 00
Other stocks and b'ds	171,428 54	341,622 66	336,900 93	561,799 51	456,127 88
Due from res'v ag'ts	1,653,857 94	1,162,427 26	1,065,087 12	1,424,785 85	1,273,375 01
Due from nat'l banks	329,972 14	411,930 48	558,045 86	599,986 41	607,627 00
Due from State banks	282,024 12	253,715 40	510,396 96	324,915 90	326,281 66
Real estate, &c	372,182 41	328,432 20	332,666 46	349,688 08	353,496 93
Current expenses	12,739 07	51,395 00	84,330 55	31,519 46	68,308 52
Premiums paid	14,775 00	22,985 93	32,884 37	30,796 87	27,632 81
Cash items	242,127 93	191,141 83	210,267 88	391,592 48	287,149 05
Clear'g-house exch'gs					
Bills of other banks	210,839 00	238,358 00	220,863 00	179,589 00	158,026 00
Fractional currency	1,708 24	1,805 25	2,102 99	1,885 00	2,102 51
Specie	431,052 06	538,264 26	576,631 76	588,207 45	343,387 80
Legal-tender notes	735,964 00	748,529 00	622,565 00	699,233 00	452,872 00
U. S. cert's of deposit					
Due from U. S. Treas	143,271 34	130,806 69	135,027 24	142,062 54	132,535 64
Total	15,480,293 96	15,737,465 35	16,391,136 49	17,252,348 02	17,413,449 56

WEST VIRGINIA.

	17 banks.	17 banks.	17 banks.	17 banks.	17 banks.
Loans and discounts	$2,854,126 82	$2,882,915 34	$3,061,391 18	$3,177,403 15	$3,170,422 77
Bonds for circulation	1,595,950 00	1,595,950 00	1,595,950 00	1,585,950 00	1,561,950 00
Bonds for deposits					
U. S. bonds on hand	35,000 00	36,400 00	36,200 00	36,900 00	41,200 00
Other stocks and b'ds	86,899 11	60,456 61	69,559 11	42,252 11	54,152 11
Due from res'v ag'ts	373,481 82	343,168 62	219,942 16	243,458 08	306,769 26
Due from nat'l banks	186,520 23	177,538 85	167,463 04	156,452 46	210,408 02
Due from State banks	98,215 87	117,602 86	61,649 16	70,580 20	97,906 32
Real estate, &c	186,431 33	186,329 33	186,531 93	185,856 93	185,214 20
Current expenses	30,066 99	21,997 89	29,136 43	26,168 04	23,952 28
Premiums paid	17,705 57	17,858 02	16,251 84	14,730 76	14,383 28
Cash items	14,310 88	17,281 44	10,816 62	9,062 94	14,657 05
Clear'g-house exch'gs					
Bills of other banks	69,344 00	41,875 00	55,510 00	52,239 00	84,379 00
Fractional currency	1,595 16	1,638 10	1,852 77	1,453 25	2,593 92
Specie	151,897 28	155,979 30	157,975 67	112,812 57	197,047 17
Legal-tender notes	281,980 00	252,694 00	255,366 00	237,582 00	240,593 00
U. S. cert's of deposit					
Due from U. S. Treas	75,100 62	72,892 75	74,292 75	81,493 00	75,217 25
Total	6,058,625 68	5,882,578 11	5,999,828 66	6,064,394 49	6,280,845 63

by States and reserve cities—Continued.

CITY OF WASHINGTON.

Liabilities.	DECEMBER 31. 5 banks.	MARCH 11. 5 banks.	MAY 6. 5 banks.	JUNE 30. 5 banks.	OCTOBER 1. 5 banks.
Cap al stock	$1,125,000 00	$1,125,000 00	$1,125,000 00	$1,125,000 00	$1,125,000 00
Surplus fund	235,257 14	235,557 14	235,557 14	249,800 00	250,100 00
Undivided profits	70,012 45	70,121 20	102,740 25	62,389 01	78,145 41
Nat'l bank circulation	698,200 00	615,700 00	619,600 00	613,300 00	625,700 00
State bank circulation					
Dividends unpaid	17,733 50	1,877 50	1,719 00	17,424 00	1,891 00
Individual deposits	1,623,597 05	1,862,400 47	1,978,629 13	2,080,622 99	1,940,125 30
U. S. deposits	27,707 23	61,595 68	86,368 57	28,934 60	25,631 48
Dep'ts U.S.dis.officers					
Due to national banks	200,201 42	158,463 72	160,797 11	104,761 59	154,412 34
Due to State banks	16,959 77	12,096 14	15,493 16	11,685 44	18,209 66
Notes re-discounted					
Bills payable					
Total	4,014,668 56	4,142,811 85	4,325,904 36	4,293,918 53	4,219,215 19

VIRGINIA.

	17 banks.	18 banks.	18 banks.	18 banks.	18 banks.
Capital stock	$2,866,000 00	$2,964,750 00	$2,966,000 00	$2,966,000 00	$2,966,000 00
Surplus fund	853,650 00	864,100 00	864,100 00	896,100 00	943,100 00
Undivided profits	252,716 57	307,562 67	432,408 67	305,775 82	415,192 25
Nat'l bank circulation	2,358,850 00	2,257,350 00	2,337,100 00	2,304,800 00	2,444,700 00
State bank circulation					
Dividends unpaid	108,842 00	3,464 00	2,434 00	97,634 00	2,718 50
Individual deposits	7,804,476 05	8,051,097 31	8,524,291 66	9,408,383 10	9,088,959 44
U. S. deposits	317,643 63	348,852 33	421,406 85	397,884 44	406,458 50
Dep'ts U.S.officers	111,747 63	89,597 68	70,115 60	77,327 70	70,968 47
Due to national banks	340,286 26	417,729 28	378,459 47	317,916 50	434,609 63
Due to State banks	336,748 07	352,962 08	294,820 24	325,496 46	376,593 11
Notes re-discounted	73,333 75	30,000 00	20,000 00	15,000 00	199,149 66
Bills payable	50,000 00	50,000 00	80,000 00	140,000 00	65,000 00
Total	15,489,293 96	15,737,165 35	16,391,136 49	17,252,348 02	17,413,449 56

WEST VIRGINIA.

	17 banks.	17 banks.	17 banks.	17 banks.	17 banks.
Capital stock	$1,761,000 00	$1,761,000 00	$1,761,000 00	$1,761,000 00	$1,736,000 00
Surplus fund	435,919 22	411,826 88	441,826 88	448,132 25	454,225 80
Undivided profits	128,316 35	103,549 23	146,855 19	134,755 96	118,231 68
Nat'l bank circulation	1,122,925 00	1,422,800 00	1,118,665 00	1,411,210 00	1,387,310 00
State bank circulation					
Dividends unpaid	35,737 25	19,755 07	18,593 00	37,505 00	25,273 00
Individual deposits	2,115,487 20	2,082,023 32	2,038,918 54	2,103,519 66	2,348,663 27
U. S. deposits					
Dep'ts U.S.officers					
Due to national banks	102,095 51	101,449 28	110,542 41	98,723 44	131,641 69
Due to State banks	17,115 15	39,171 33	52,427 64	50,263 18	49,612 19
Notes re-discounted		3,000 00	11,000 00	19,285 00	29,885 00
Bills payable	10,000 00	5,000 00			
Total	6,058,625 68	5,982,578 11	5,999,828 66	6,061,391 49	6,280,845 63

NORTH CAROLINA.

Resources.	DECEMBER 31.	MARCH 11.	MAY 6.	JUNE 30.	OCTOBER 1.
	15 banks.	15 banks.	15 banks.	15 banks.	15 banks.
Loans and discounts	$3,899,195 93	$4,201,766 04	$4,207,481 84	$4,417,659 57	$4,877,098 59
Bonds for circulation	2,018,000 00	1,868,000 00	1,868,000 00	1,868,000 00	1,868,000 00
Bonds for deposits	200,000 00	200,000 00	200,000 00	200,000 00	200,000 00
U. S. bonds on hand	161,100 00	311,200 00	266,200 00	81,200 00	81,200 00
Other stocks and b'ds	304,637 25	214,921 37	221,486 78	226,625 28	219,016 36
Due from res've ag'ts	550,281 36	392,152 26	368,772 96	262,185 51	169,484 91
Due from nat'l banks	450,622 88	318,611 45	272,700 80	174,665 12	224,773 27
Due from State banks	74,872 06	103,768 78	52,256 05	67,491 49	56,015 20
Real estate, &c	349,064 37	323,393 32	352,609 73	348,869 63	348,833 18
Current expenses	51,536 17	51,284 74	69,747 43	59,472 96	46,005 00
Premiums paid	72,367 37	77,154 37	67,729 37	45,604 37	42,979 37
Cash items	50,599 42	53,018 26	55,497 15	33,791 60	59,463 90
Clear'g-house exch'gs					
Bills of other banks	133,579 00	130,992 00	125,770 00	116,458 00	112,707 00
Fractional currency	6,286 78	3,440 87	3,370 41	3,971 47	2,532 78
Specie	209,513 74	246,159 25	228,396 10	244,294 57	183,917 49
Legal-tender notes	379,915 00	276,229 00	262,226 00	300,918 00	262,707 00
U. S. cert's of deposit					
Due from U. S. Treas	103,970 30	84,895 27	86,290 67	83,871 05	83,651 25
Total	9,016,141 63	8,856,986 98	8,708,535 29	8,535,078 62	8,838,385 30

SOUTH CAROLINA.

	12 banks.	12 banks.	13 banks.	13 banks.	13 banks.
Loans and discounts	$2,920,684 90	$2,735,045 97	$3,234,649 21	$3,671,267 89	$4,482,622 25
Bonds for circulation	1,285,000 00	1,285,000 00	1,315,000 00	1,325,000 00	1,325,000 00
Bonds for deposits	150,000 00	150,000 00	150,000 00	150,000 00	150,000 00
U. S. bonds on hand	416,100 00	410,100 00	330,100 00	240,100 00	210,100 00
Other stocks and b'ds	518,309 87	474,725 94	456,029 99	447,510 48	438,185 38
Due from res've ag'ts	1,234,786 26	1,357,667 50	648,811 09	332,522 98	149,227 10
Due from nat'l banks	476,612 37	619,847 07	461,001 83	362,229 38	237,880 37
Due from State banks	76,855 62	81,467 11	146,616 71	116,880 49	29,029 81
Real estate, &c	217,713 12	209,538 95	225,824 49	225,602 51	225,527 51
Current expenses	80,891 57	35,039 82	63,575 72	78,164 47	44,486 92
Premiums paid	15,718 75	6,931 25	10,308 75	10,293 75	10,293 75
Cash items	14,242 92	18,508 39	20,166 79	10,710 25	26,312 78
Clear'g-house exch'gs					
Bills of other banks	330,051 00	306,886 00	147,918 00	102,479 00	115,078 00
Fractional currency	3,002 14	2,617 32	3,046 85	2,464 43	1,990 01
Specie	306,553 58	441,480 65	403,707 19	471,624 36	216,099 18
Legal-tender notes	455,706 00	421,432 00	347,899 00	257,710 00	254,406 00
U. S. cert's of deposit					
Due from U. S. Treas	60,751 28	62,647 93	56,071 08	57,316 95	62,226 70
Total	8,562,979 38	8,618,935 90	8,020,786 70	7,861,876 94	7,978,465 76

GEORGIA.

	13 banks.	13 banks.	13 banks.	12 banks.	12 banks.
Loans and discounts	$3,381,707 40	$3,240,801 53	$3,571,957 97	$3,728,541 89	$4,468,430 86
Bonds for circulation	2,211,000 00	2,211,000 00	2,211,000 00	2,161,000 00	2,161,000 00
Bonds for deposits	110,000 00	110,000 00	110,000 00	110,000 00	110,000 00
U. S. bonds on hand	1,600 00	46,600 00	101,600 00	1,600 00	1,600 00
Other stocks and b'ds	313,771 86	316,519 36	279,083 61	283,103 61	284,654 61
Due from res've ag'ts	466,696 33	298,584 43	182,504 67	167,464 23	95,350 52
Due from nat'l banks	193,655 27	227,481 46	153,903 94	150,247 73	208,760 63
Due from State banks	100,512 86	117,514 39	266,950 76	67,114 76	96,569 79
Real estate, &c	222,543 24	221,844 54	214,867 79	210,624 89	213,619 65
Current expenses	61,614 66	36,310 26	51,094 74	64,449 77	53,183 66
Premiums paid	24,599 32	22,136 82	20,621 10	18,774 32	18,261 82
Cash items	112,242 71	111,791 68	176,000 46	100,786 20	192,274 35
Clear'g-house exch'gs					
Bills of other banks	283,065 00	333,628 00	282,044 00	237,762 00	159,183 00
Fractional currency	2,240 83	2,375 88	2,662 16	4,872 77	2,394 49
Specie	399,512 36	447,666 73	380,579 53	427,444 12	421,758 22
Legal-tender notes	252,211 00	234,431 00	292,563 00	239,404 00	225,473 00
U. S. cert's of deposit					
Due from U. S. Treas	111,812 25	111,900 34	145,317 13	115,990 33	105,697 00
Total	8,251,185 09	8,090,619 39	8,442,750 86	8,098,180 71	8,818,211 60

*by States and reserve cities—*Continued.

NORTH CAROLINA.

Liabilities.	DECEMBER 31. 15 banks.	MARCH 11. 15 banks.	MAY 6. 15 banks.	JUNE 30. 15 banks.	OCTOBER 1. 15 banks.
Capital stock	$2,501,000 00	$2,501,000 00	$2,501,000 00	$2,501,000 00	$2,501,000 00
Surplus fund	321,337 91	340,826 02	300,826 02	308,076 02	347,828 22
Undivided profits	295,517 02	260,937 67	328,259 15	349,888 32	273,793 80
Nat'l bank circulation	1,804,990 00	1,670,675 00	1,660,765 00	1,643,765 00	1,676,930 00
State bank circulation					
Dividends unpaid	38,560 00	6,078 00	4,998 00	26,525 00	8,525 00
Individual deposits	3,495,392 81	3,522,064 81	3,268,106 06	3,077,872 09	3,041,067 44
U. S. deposits	143,103 61	135,307 04	190,851 60	163,057 83	184,460 54
Dep'ts U.S.dis.officers	23,995 15	46,868 23	73,731 24	23,520 97	19,143 94
Due to national banks	158,217 57	219,028 63	142,855 11	194,418 46	262,803 33
Due to State banks	29,463 86	25,931 86	46,095 65	23,559 89	51,890 22
Notes re-discounted	129,565 70	62,669 69	181,047 46	213,395 04	325,942 81
Bills payable	75,000 00	65,000 00	100,000 00	10,000 00	145,000 00
Total	9,016,141 63	8,856,986 98	8,708,535 29	8,535,078 62	8,838,385 30

SOUTH CAROLINA.

	12 banks.	12 banks.	13 banks.	13 banks.	13 banks.
Capital stock	$1,949,900 00	$1,835,000 00	$1,865,520 00	$1,884,150 00	1,885,000 00
Surplus fund	382,059 42	399,249 58	400,189 58	400,707 54	417,707 96
Undivided profits	396,732 85	309,583 98	402,886 93	422,371 74	395,299 23
Nat'l bank circulation	1,125,395 00	1,140,500 00	1,137,225 00	1,148,895 00	1,187,190 00
State bank circulation					
Dividends unpaid	6,883 00	9,844 50	7,123 50	22,090 50	8,456 50
Individual deposits	4,133,139 43	4,196,412 94	3,775,235 01	3,543,916 01	2,970,402 68
U. S. deposits	54,528 87	25,152 83	45,841 31	41,627 90	81,803 74
Dep'ts U.S.dis.officers	79,044 24	117,173 42	120,994 34	78,431 30	65,614 64
Due to national banks	304,010 68	428,614 19	182,977 30	160,092 48	215,527 24
Due to State banks	111,285 89	147,404 16	82,793 73	65,814 85	115,014 05
Notes re-discounted	10,000 00	10,000 00		93,779 62	419,414 72
Bills payable	10,000 00				217,000 00
Total	8,562,979 38	8,618,935 90	8,020,786 70	7,861,876 94	7,978,465 76

GEORGIA.

	13 banks.	13 banks.	13 banks.	12 banks.	12 banks.
Capital stock	$2,221,000 00	$2,221,000 00	$2,246,000 00	$2,186,000 00	$2,281,000 00
Surplus fund	440,803 27	457,809 14	463,809 14	463,491 02	483,959 43
Undivided profits	282,637 53	188,706 61	256,854 89	296,585 47	252,256 58
Nat'l bank circulation	1,972,800 00	1,917,165 00	1,953,804 00	1,888,780 00	1,896,860 00
State bank circulation					
Dividends unpaid	6,735 00	6,713 50	7 727 00	11,235 00	4,601 00
Individual deposits	2,651,881 81	2,787,713 69	2,929,350 78	2,778,925 18	2,766,497 56
U. S. deposits	58,608 63	52,422 82	115,891 30	85,519 18	80,971 64
Dep'ts U.S.dis.officers	38,931 12	25,787 12	30,365 59	9,506 57	16,676 74
Due to national banks	237,440 20	183,624 64	285,803 76	128,357 66	504,904 49
Due to State banks	319,199 53	182,196 87	123,575 40	222,408 13	253,255 73
Notes re-discounted			13,500 00	11,372 50	195,228 43
Bills payable	21,055 00	37,480 00	16,000 00	16,000 00	82,000 00
Total	8,251,185 09	8,090,619 39	8,442,750 86	8,098,180 71	8,818,211 60

Abstract of reports since October 1, 1880, arranged

FLORIDA.

Resources.	DECEMBER 31.	MARCH 11.	MAY 6.	JUNE 30.	OCTOBER 1.
	2 banks.	2 banks.	2 banks.	2 banks.	2 banks.
Loans and discounts	$161,799 62	$170,783 41	$225,953 61	$239,361 51	$289,798 63
Bonds for circulation	80,000 00	80,000 00	80,000 00	80,000 00	80,000 00
Bonds for deposits					
U. S. bonds on hand	550 00	5,650 00	5,650 00	5,650 00	650 00
Other stocks and b'ds	1,833 89	22,473 52	1,813 13	1,189 43	1,402 95
Due from res've ag'ts	68,656 81	123,962 04	37,274 35	52,067 92	11,343 55
Due from nat'l banks	11,783 25	70,200 07	67,435 36	53,549 34	21,197 59
Due from State banks	16,694 88	24,423 58	28,757 56	22,314 03	2,070 68
Real estate, &c	20,230 93	19,946 88	21,304 16	21,023 36	21,000 76
Current expenses	3,956 56	3,476 19	6,389 22	8,301 61	2,343 19
Premiums paid	1,052 50	1,063 50	1,063 50	1,063 50	2,630 74
Cash items	2,503 15	8,065 21	4,471 01	2,580 87	3,377 84
Clear'g-house exch'gs					
Bills of other banks	16,091 00	20,056 00	16,523 00	4,491 00	5,753 00
Fractional currency	9 60	17 82	2 42	4 05	4 40
Specie	7,911 25	5,203 65	9,726 70	22,612 33	19,662 43
Legal-tender notes	28,602 00	61,943 00	81,040 00	50,323 00	36,474 00
U. S. cert's of deposit					
Due from U. S. Treas.	4,086 95	3,386 35	2,990 95	4,490 95	4,290 35
Total	425,762 39	620,651 22	590,394 97	569,022 90	502,000 11

ALABAMA.

	9 banks.	9 banks.	9 banks.	9 banks.	9 banks.
Loans and discounts	$1,713,828 82	$1,769,616 65	$1,978,175 19	$2,067,223 23	$2,244,275 16
Bonds for circulation	1,481,000 00	1,447,000 00	1,447,000 00	1,447,000 00	1,447,000 00
Bonds for deposits	50,000 00	50,000 00	50,000 00	50,000 00	50,000 00
U. S. bonds on hand	300 00	6,000 00		800 00	
Other stocks and b'ds	250,861 11	204,316 38	212,665 99	239,753 49	246,376 34
Due from res've ag'ts	386,126 86	421,098 01	236,584 18	131,888 87	278,058 79
Due from nat'l banks	196,599 40	266,090 70	151,002 99	135,409 41	230,412 92
Due from State banks	112,426 27	106,788 02	95,652 17	54,806 38	130,614 62
Real estate, &c	127,180 24	126,600 30	126,601 15	126,652 73	126,452 77
Current expenses	41,859 16	29,160 89	45,791 50	48,559 72	30,618 94
Premiums paid	30,227 42	30,227 42	30,227 42	15,727 42	16,217 42
Cash items	7,820 45	8,345 79	9,822 78	13,737 79	10,631 11
Clear'g-house exch'gs					
Bills of other banks	112,526 00	61,383 00	55,389 00	68,533 00	92,594 00
Fractional currency	708 09	1,119 79	924 06	1,090 06	1,151 24
Specie	162,373 28	173,485 35	172,302 40	133,972 35	134,358 05
Legal-tender notes	211,961 00	204,598 00	177,677 00	184,041 00	220,077 00
U. S. cert's of deposit					
Due from U. S. Treas	65,341 60	67,573 60	64,311 10	64,000 40	67,643 25
Total	4,951,199 70	4,973,403 90	4,854,126 93	4,783,195 85	5,326,481 61

CITY OF NEW ORLEANS.

	7 banks.	7 banks.	7 banks.	7 banks.	7 banks.
Loans and discounts	$7,223,383 98	$7,415,345 85	$7,858,709 50	$7,502,090 93	$8,676,180 65
Bonds for circulation	2,100,000 00	2,100,000 00	2,475,000 00	2,475,000 00	2,475,000 00
Bonds for deposits					
U. S. bonds on hand	38,400 00	262,550 00	236,800 00	68,050 00	43,200 00
Other stocks and b'ds	532,880 30	575,193 60	564,092 70	459,468 95	367,163 17
Due from res've ag'ts	860,611 46	617,048 53	858,393 88	1,879,820 58	350,879 91
Due from nat'l banks	247,432 24	224,572 26	187,348 74	239,527 92	81,943 40
Due from State banks	762,712 59	541,910 79	656,079 12	378,428 36	132,398 48
Real estate, &c	372,167 69	318,330 59	319,024 26	318,873 61	311,705 95
Current expenses	38,613 66	76,497 90	128,113 48	41,278 48	98,011 46
Premiums paid	4,500 00	30,500 00	30,500 00	4,000 00	4,000 00
Cash items	89,348 62	9,585 25	5,129 00	6,406 47	49,144 75
Clear'g-house exch'gs	1,536,933 59	1,517,555 92	840,634 43	685,056 21	995,305 07
Bills of other banks	93,126 00	308,303 00	269,055 00	207,677 00	136,855 00
Fractional currency	3,842 55	4,490 03	4,969 36	4,211 11	3,880 81
Specie	888,619 40	773,332 65	849,320 65	709,649 45	1,283,325 25
Legal-tender notes	955,011 00	1,384,201 00	1,308,252 00	1,412,236 00	1,141,612 00
U. S. cert's of deposit					
Due from U. S. Treas	99,100 00	99,100 00	98,710 00	111,775 00	113,075 00
Total	15,846,683 08	16,258,517 37	16,750,132 12	16,504,450 10	16,263,770 90

by States and reserve cities—Continued.

FLORIDA.

Liabilities.	DECEMBER 31. 2 banks.	MARCH 11. 2 banks.	MAY 6. 2 banks.	JUNE 30. 2 banks.	OCTOBER 1. 2 banks.
Capital stock	$100,000 00	$100,000 00	$100,000 00	$100,000 00	$100,000 00
Surplus fund.........	2,000 00	3,000 00	3,000 00	3,000 00	7,073 51
Undivided profits....	10,688 12	9,713 21	15,828 27	20,706 46	7,931 33
Nat'l bank circulation	69,480 00	68,280 00	65,280 00	63,800 00	66,700 00
State bank circulation					
Dividends unpaid....					
Individual deposits...	242,996 50	439,658 01	405,991 31	381,516 44	318,545 13
U. S. deposits					
Dep'ts U.S.dis.officers					
Due to national banks	593 21		239 70		
Due to State banks...	4 56		55 69		1,150 14
Notes re-discounted ..					
Bills payable.........					
Total	425,762 39	620,651 22	590,394 97	569,022 90	502,000 11

ALABAMA.

	9 banks.	9 banks.	9 banks.	9 banks.	9 banks.
Capital stock	$1,518,000 00	$1,518,000 00	$1,518,000 00	$1,518,000 00	$1,518,000 00
Surplus fund	223,995 74	236,500 00	236,500 00	236,850 00	250,350 00
Undivided profits....	225,832 53	181,364 73	236,908 87	291,387 45	197,416 20
Nat'l bank circulation	1,324,367 00	1,287,367 00	1,280,367 00	1,276,367 00	1,280,067 00
State bank circulation					
Dividends unpaid....	1,113 00	2,342 00	1,368 00	1,253 00	5,345 03
Individual deposits..	1,499,641 66	1,626,036 72	1,465,161 37	1,312,368 54	1,719,064 91
U. S. deposits.......	27,887 15	26,762 87	44,171 59	40,053 41	47,913 65
Dep'ts U.S.dis.officers	1,560 05	680 46	8,981 87	1,785 72	1,091 82
Due to national banks	46,664 77	35,195 98	29,579 44	51,718 76	84,859 05
Due to State banks...	54,552 43	28,334 02	32,989 72	12,285 90	21,868 40
Notes re-discounted..	27,585 37	30,820 12	9,099 07	41,096 07	200,505 58
Bills payable........					
Total	4,951,199 70	4,973,403 90	4,854,126 93	4,783,195 85	5,326,481 61

CITY OF NEW ORLEANS.

	7 banks.	7 banks.	7 banks.	7 banks.	7 banks.
Capital stock	$2,875,000 00	$2,875,000 00	$2,875,000 00	$2,875,000 00	$2,875,000 00
Surplus fund.........	627,500 00	637,500 00	637,500 00	800,000 00	815,000 00
Undivided profits....	296,750 47	307,329 75	478,367 75	289,504 20	345,677 68
Nat'l bank circulation	1,870,800 00	1,861,520 00	1,953,500 00	2,171,350 00	2,157,100 00
State bank circulation					
Dividends unpaid....	83,496 11	20,891 02	18,661 02	79,233 02	23,893 47
Individual deposits ..	8,691,649 21	9,534,660 50	9,541,582 25	9,038,514 64	8,478,486 66
U. S. deposits.......					
Dep'ts U.S.dis.officers					
Due to national banks	600,657 11	345,683 05	547,065 41	430,500 33	796,243 18
Due to State banks...	800,830 18	675,933 05	698,455 09	811,347 91	782,369 91
Notes re-discounted..					
Bills payable........					
Total	15,846,683 08	16,258,517,37	16,750,132 12	16,504,450 10	16,263,770 90

TEXAS.

Resources.	DECEMBER 31. 14 banks.	MARCH 11. 13 banks.	MAY 6. 14 banks.	JUNE 30. 15 banks.	OCTOBER 1. 15 banks.
Loans and discounts	$2,345,496 56	$2,284,104 12	$2,491,835 56	$2,692,941 11	$3,256,578 61
Bonds for circulation	930,000 00	895,000 00	975,000 00	1,025,000 00	1,030,000 00
Bonds for deposits ...	200,000 00	200,000 00	200,000 00	200,000 00	200,000 00
U. S. bonds on hand ..	....	....	400 00	2,450 00	5,700 00
Other stocks and b'ds	181,916 26	204,020 47	235,247 44	136,384 09	128,328 21
Due from res'veag'ts	320,935 53	305,984 58	501,696 49	616,102 13	749,194 46
Due from nat'l banks	215,803 97	227,297 54	292,829 67	429,903 13	351,260 35
Due from State banks	208,632 09	263,800 13	210,966 83	344,517 05	395,446 49
Real estate, &c ......'	177,733 19	172,377 34	170,877 86	163,467 31	161,582 37
Current expenses....	39,630 79	29,456 53	41,135 73	34,318 65	38,603 87
Premiums paid	11,843 44	4,705 59	6,547 52	6,527 52	8,085 02
Cash items	101,125 72	31,372 70	25,028 22	35,775 78	85,052 09
Clear'g-house exch'gs	....	....	....	....	....
Bills of other banks..	165,801 00	361,703 00	257,709 00	132,633 00	184,830 00
Fractional currency .	1,730 04	2,534 18	1,907 52	1,152 73	1,778 94
Specie	243,359 46	248,443 19	267,595 35	311,278 80	321,100 08
Legal-tender notes ..	552,595 00	624,766 00	639,231 00	546,048 00	516,100 00
U. S. cert's of deposit	....	....	....	....	....
Due from U. S. Treas	45,003 12	44,310 72	47,653 32	51,944 62	50,017 87
Total..........	5,741,606 17	5,899,906 09	6,365,661 51	6,730,443 92	7,483,658 36

ARKANSAS.

	2 banks.	2 banks.	2 banks.	2 banks.	2 banks.
Loans and discounts	$205,026 58	$272,024 90	$329,663 52	$366,532 85	$381,042 19
Bonds for circulation	205,000 00	205,000 00	205,000 00	205,000 00	205,000 00
Bonds for deposits...	100,000 00	100,000 00	100,000 00	100,000 00	100,000 00
U. S. bonds on hand..	450 00	450 00	350 00	20,350 00	20,350 00
Other stocks and b'ds	39,466 70	41,421 73	36,390 27	40,948 56	42,272 79
Due from res'veag'ts	101,416 13	126,788 70	389,571 00	221,391 52	60,509 44
Due from nat'l banks	70,171 59	189,953 66	22,152 28	37,414 58	48,690 51
Due from State banks	2,140 63	4,646 71	4,089 10	2,726 71	20,030 33
Real estate, &c	4,500 00	....	....	....	....
Current expenses......	....	117 17	11 00	....	1 75
Premiums paid	....	....	....	....	....
Cash items	....	3,369 58	1,002 40	8,126 70	1,681 97
Clear'g-house exch'gs	....	....	....	....	....
Bills of other banks..	56,866 00	2,632 00	9,317 00	6,205 00	9,307 00
Fractional currency.	91 61	36 54	494 06	33 57	40 51
Specie	42,363 15	46,797 75	71,107 25	21,436 45	17,918 05
Legal-tender notes ..	109,219 00	25,565 00	34,385 00	31,156 00	35,515 00
U. S. cert's of deposit	....	....	....	....	....
Due from U. S. Treas	9,225 00	9,225 00	9,225 00	9,725 00	9,825 00
Total..........	945,936 39	1,028,026 74	1,212,757 88	1,071,046 94	952,184 56

KENTUCKY.

	41 banks.	41 banks.	41 banks.	42 banks.	42 banks.
Loans and discounts.	$10,245,236 18	$10,510,005 35	$10,601,465 98	$10,727,974 51	$10,821,944 33
Bonds for circulation	6,901,000 00	6,601,000 00	6,876,000 00	6,956,000 00	7,011,000 00
Bonds for deposits...	270,000 00	300,000 00	300,060 00	300,000 00	300,000 00
U. S. bonds on hand..	162,100 00	328,250 00	156,450 00	185,600 00	356,700 00
Other stocks and b'ds	806,281 62	808,149 55	794,042 97	799,198 07	645,765 18
Due from res'veag'ts.	1,418,165 48	1,112,698 76	1,145,449 38	1,172,087 74	1,638,039 06
Due from nat'l banks.	890,370 31	766,654 62	627,716 01	778,658 37	865,491 61
Due from State banks	336,089 88	289,385 73	194,177 70	256,374 59	313,447 35
Real estate, &c	542,978 66	544,994 17	544,838 72	533,454 04	527,734 16
Current expenses....	38,397 72	67,105 74	80,326 28	34,830 02	85,300 69
Premiums paid	92,555 25	108,628 86	106,888 43	106,375 38	120,957 35
Cash items	38,557 87	29,100 22	74,852 76	60,553 59	50,188 28
Clear'g-house exch'gs	....	....	....	....	....
Bills of other banks..	285,570 00	214,452 00	223,619 00	258,356 00	156,322 00
Fractional currency .	2,199 36	1,870 04	1,980 16	2,137 30	1,512 38
Specie	307,034 18	296,595 94	296,151 81	303,234 30	303,832 08
Legal-tender notes ..	446,409 00	464,936 00	432,930 00	469,274 00	397,893 00
U. S. cert's of deposit	....	....	....	....	....
Due from U. S. Treas	314,929 08	296,235 58	297,488 75	296,476 98	316,449 68
Total..........	23,097,874 59	22,740,062 56	22,754,377 95	23,240,584 89	23,912,577 15

by States and reserve cities—Continued.

TEXAS.

Liabilities.	DECEMBER 31. 14 banks.	MARCH 11. 13 banks.	MAY 6. 14 banks.	JUNE 30. 15 banks.	OCTOBER 1. 15 banks.
Capital stock	$1,420,000 00	$1,320,000 00	$1,375,000 00	$1,425,000 00	$1,475,000 00
Surplus fund	280,048 40	279,581 89	280,281 89	283,281 89	315,700 00
Undivided profits	177,561 56	134,607 51	183,886 16	230,945 29	228,150 92
Nat'l bank circulation	820,490 00	784,589 00	818,359 00	856,359 00	905,439 00
State bank circulation					
Dividends unpaid	6,056 00	999 00	238 00	14,238 00	3,458 20
Individual deposits	2,338,823 17	2,883,730 72	3,077,474 00	3,379,874 09	3,691,490 37
U. S. deposits	117,425 46	84,268 96	187,596 26	67,563 62	106,722 91
Dep'ts U.S.dis.officers	139,009 82	132,225 37	197,602 55	141,291 10	220,383 94
Due to national banks	146,546 64	53,851 26	54,097 65	69,614 53	173,099 63
Due to State banks	163,542 21	195,993 60	169,126 00	170,276 40	157,819 77
Notes re-discounted	122,102 91	25,058 78		5,000 00	106,393 62
Bills payable	10,000 00		20,000 00	85,000 00	100,000 00
Total	5,741,606 17	5,899,906 09	6,365,661 51	6,730,443 92	7,483,658 36

ARKANSAS.

	2 banks.	2 banks.	2 banks.	2 banks.	2 banks.
Capital stock	$205,000 00	$205,000 00	$205,000 00	$205,000 00	$205,000 00
Surplus fund	40,000 00	41,000 00	41,000 00	42,000 00	42,000 00
Undivided profits	23,059 83	11,008 95	16,743 77	12,174 11	21,464 32
Nat'l bank circulation	184,500 00	184,000 00	183,400 00	184,500 00	183,800 00
State bank circulation					
Dividends unpaid	400 00	930 00	230 00	7,615 00	100 00
Individual deposits	405,366 09	403,418 55	684,866 40	546,090 23	412,344 55
U. S. deposits	47,977 31	36,888 35	35,120 88	40,900 44	63,954 63
Dep'ts U.S.dis.officers	24,118 90	24,047 85	40,282 36	27,857 73	11,394 08
Due to national banks	10,022 95	26,672 39		2,700 49	5,005 87
Due to State banks	4,891 31	5,060 65	6,114 47	2,199 94	7,121 11
Notes re-discounted					
Bills payable					
Total	945,936 39	1,028,026 74	1,212,757 88	1,071,046 94	952,184 56

KENTUCKY.

	41 banks.	41 banks.	41 banks.	42 banks.	42 banks.
Capital stock	$7,201,000 00	$7,201,000 00	$7,201,000 00	$7,261,000 00	$7,283,600 00
Surplus fund	1,195,687 20	1,260,932 96	1,211,851 63	1,302,918 21	1,316,595 29
Undivided profits	326,811 82	425,005 82	543,156 09	373,974 30	422,939 05
Nat'l bank circulation	6,177,848 00	5,840,653 00	5,924,378 00	6,107,163 00	6,212,088 00
State bank circulation					
Dividends unpaid	113,504 00	27,664 50	18,912 50	107,994 00	47,514 00
Individual deposits	7,184,316 34	7,149,181 42	7,055,892 03	7,234,403 86	7,742,059 07
U. S. deposits	166,858 80	180,358 80	180,142 12	180,000 00	180,000 00
Dep'ts U.S.dis.officers	3,930 82	2,947 11	5,211 90	554 00	5,081 23
Due to national banks	320,045 52	340,850 00	260,980 77	355,443 32	314,053 32
Due to State banks	390,882 09	319,768 95	285,892 91	298,551 70	348,247 19
Notes re-discounted	16,000 00	50,700 00	35,960 00	17,582 50	25,000 00
Bills payable	1,000 00	1,000 00	1,000 00	1,000 00	14,500 00
Total	23,097,874 59	22,740,062 56	22,754,377 95	23,240,584 89	23,912,577 15

13 C C

Abstract of reports since October 1, 1880, arranged

CITY OF LOUISVILLE.

Resources.	DECEMBER 31.	MARCH 11.	MAY 6.	JUNE 30.	OCTOBER 1.
	8 banks.	8 banks.	8 banks.	8 banks.	8 banks.
Loans and discounts	$6,622,815 46	$6,302,757 41	$6,688,885 51	$6,831,808 35	$7,164,117 81
Bonds for circulation	3,083,700 00	2,733,700 00	2,733,700 00	2,883,700 00	2,983,700 00
Bonds for deposits ..	600,000 00	600,000 00	600,000 00	600,000 00	600,000 00
U.S. bonds on hand..	15,500 00	6,350 00	6,250 00	6,650 00	107,250 00
Other stocks and b'ds	13,900 00	152,757 91	149,819 99	145,401 41	130,292 64
Due from res'veng'ts	407,697 87	683,982 50	565,148 22	848,324 88	551,419 62
Due from nat'l banks.	266,128 79	269,711 13	263,211 00	332,275 80	315,289 30
Due from State banks	153,113 42	208,028 85	112,305 84	161,138 04	125,547 28
Real estate, &c	166,472 10	121,416 52	120,672 21	118,641 16	119,492 29
Current expenses....	16,323 79	59,776 56	26,597 32	15,124 80	82,619 82
Premiums paid	135,283 24	135,283 24	48,272 07	72,829 11	88,672 61
Cash items	27,283 33	39,724 92	31,040 25	61,681 55	32,899 16
Clear'g-house exch'gs	19,837 13	45,099 22	24,225 77	88,503 00	40,868 42
Bills of other banks..	94,109 00	62,185 00	89,158 00	71,158 00	51,994 00
Fractional currency .	153 49	212 34	206 73	183 76	180 50
Specie	235,395 07	285,863 92	297,133 91	215,661 29	172,697 16
Legal-tender notes ..	514,413 00	366,250 00	356,097 00	306,910 00	411,257 00
U.S. cert's of deposit					
Due from U.S. Treas	144,436 50	130,213 93	127,134 50	127,166 50	137,969 05
Total...........	12,516,542 28	12,203,313 45	12,239,859 22	12,887,213 65	13,116,266 66

TENNESSEE.

	23 banks.	23 banks.	24 banks.	24 banks.	25 banks.
Loans and discounts.	$6,680,098 64	$6,321,779 81	$6,558,372 61	$6,715,446 64	$7,936,508 15
Bonds for circulation	2,786,000 00	2,776,000 00	2,876,000 00	2,950,000 00	2,988,000 00
Bonds for deposits ..	350,000 00	350,000 00	350,000 00	350,000 00	350,000 00
U.S. bonds on hand..	60,300 00	230,250 00	151,750 00	116,000 00	25,100 00
Other stocks and b'ds	236,749 21	283,556 91	305,143 35	324,315 27	398,190 90
Due from res'veng'ts.	905,791 48	1,061,173 03	1,225,889 30	1,996,675 44	1,066,681 89
Due from nat'l banks.	548,315 05	590,123 77	590,995 63	665,429 66	707,085 34
Due from State banks	133,768 73	217,666 11	148,932 49	107,727 56	106,363 96
Real estate, &c	350,171 55	343,545 10	332,450 72	330,301 43	330,531 39
Current expenses....	41,084 56	69,691 85	70,365 49	49,355 10	58,431 25
Premiums paid	69,352 19	91,383 87	91,258 24	91,186 32	72,996 12
Cash items	263,597 26	175,219 36	170,757 54	192,082 89	264,259 54
Clear'g-house exch'gs					
Bills of other banks..	448,733 00	526,424 00	721,059 00	545,971 00	434,012 00
Fractional currency	5,470 76	5,473 84	6,396 23	5,033 77	7,545 63
Specie	472,956 05	487,706 85	630,419 53	640,086 82	520,410 71
Legal-tender notes ..	723,487 00	882,224 00	971,318 00	436,519 00	731,891 00
U.S. cert's of deposit					
Due from U.S. Treas	126,932 12	145,359 04	170,520 04	167,618 74	134,415 29
Total...........	14,202,807 62	14,557,577 54	15,371,628 17	16,183,740 64	16,131,952 67

OHIO.

	161 banks.	159 banks.	160 banks.	160 banks.	161 banks.
Loans and discounts	$34,905,258 88	$35,412,331 05	$35,499,924 79	$36,559,678 08	$38,140,891 61
Bonds for circulation	17,953,500 00	16,863,800 00	17,138,800 00	17,176,600 00	17,461,300 00
Bonds for deposits ..	350,000 00	350,000 00	350,000 00	350,000 00	450,000 00
U.S. bonds on hand..	1,183,550 00	2,206,700 00	1,603,550 00	1,735,250 00	1,956,200 00
Other stocks and b'ds	1,901,552 48	1,929,881 54	1,949,090 25	2,041,660 74	2,337,649 81
Due from res'veng'ts.	5,886,252 81	5,079,592 32	5,043,482 88	6,587,814 74	6,935,238 74
Due from nat'l banks	2,253,166 95	2,047,698 80	1,879,489 73	2,481,035 32	2,500,651 61
Due from State banks	777,035 56	542,450 69	657,810 93	693,574 80	800,233 13
Real estate, &c	1,835,319 33	1,815,283 71	1,788,470 80	1,822,641 89	1,832,666 73
Current expenses....	212,333 07	395,273 15	193,451 46	187,357 55	414,290 03
Premiums paid	140,509 08	139,350 71	122,232 91	132,316 67	170,498 43
Cash items	409,283 29	426,874 44	400,447 66	435,829 50	542,828 22
Clear'g-house exch'gs	80,420 55	59,687 66	60,939 33	45,647 88	77,795 11
Bills of other banks..	1,098,472 00	1,128,615 00	1,382,711 00	1,112,662 00	1,464,167 00
Fractional currency	22,042 79	24,869 59	24,377 91	23,644 02	21,266 25
Specie	2,107,026 55	2,297,284 46	2,430,593 80	2,244,347 70	2,418,512 08
Legal-tender notes ..	2,863,622 00	2,882,147 00	3,399,716 00	2,886,140 00	3,036,591 00
U.S. cert's of deposit	25,000 00				
Due from U.S. Treas	843,574 48	795,782 45	810,102 42	783,683 53	837,481 30
Total	74,907,988 85	74,397,566 57	74,735,189 93	77,299,885 48	31,418,281 05

by States and reserve cities—Continued.

CITY OF LOUISVILLE.

Liabilities.	DECEMBER 31. 8 banks.	MARCH 11. 8 banks.	MAY 6. 8 banks.	JUNE 30. 8 banks.	OCTOBER 1. 8 banks.
Capital stock	$3,151,500 00	$3,151,500 00	$3,151,500 00	$3,151,500 00	$3,151,500 00
Surplus fund	408,566 13	408,566 13	511,194 03	525,512 46	525,542 46
Undivided profits	149,746 82	261,096 27	184,312 57	167,005 34	264,565 45
Nat'l bank circulation	2,710,543 00	2,455,173 00	2,451,673 00	2,584,423 00	2,672,123 00
State bank circulation					
Dividends unpaid	27,362 00	5,942 50	25,273 50	34,859 00	5,803 50
Individual deposits	2,315,458 98	2,565,658 83	2,613,501 87	2,929,336 64	2,932,750 83
U. S. deposits	395,031 10	363,606 84	444,093 05	456,022 56	426,757 31
Dep'ts U.S.dis.officers	137,934 04	176,781 54	120,678 05	98,897 60	116,291 86
Due to national banks	1,594 252 62	1,471,495 02	1,568,950 66	1,625,984 50	1,548,728 14
Due to State banks	1,249,621 55	1,247,790 77	1,159,449 40	1,308 652 55	1,404,825 04
Notes re-discounted	276,526 07	95,702 55	9,233 09	4,900 00	68,378 17
Bills payable	100,000 00				
Total	12,516,542 28	12,203,313 45	12,239,859 22	12,887,213 65	13,116,266 66

TENNESSEE.

	23 banks.	23 banks.	24 banks.	24 banks.	25 banks.
Capital stock	$3,005,300 00	$3,005,300 00	$3,305,300 00	$3,305,300 00	$3,430,300 00
Surplus fund	566,239 80	581 263 10	587,114 82	597,114 82	615,267 12
Undivided profits	317,972 53	257,208 30	302,840 29	360,506 97	295,333 51
Nat'l bank circulation	2,485,300 00	2,468,540 00	2,550,020 00	2,590,350 00	2,627,495 00
State bank circulation					
Dividends unpaid	18,828 00	7,968 00	7,062 00	18,328 00	14,186 00
Individual deposits	7,045,064 67	7,570,346 03	7,907,952 34	8,666,082 85	8,322,110 64
U. S. deposits	165,687 47	141,164 38	192,533 50	138,669 37	179,445 64
Dep'ts U.S.officers	105,235 23	106,598 22	113,097 44	150,726 88	147,427 25
Due to national banks	241,444 55	335,812 73	218,636 97	254,708 72	262,069 95
Due to State banks	199,126 72	72,376 78	87,551 72	85,072 03	196,317 56
Notes re-discounted	47,608 65	12,000 00	9,600 00	16,800 00	12,000 00
Bills payable	5,000 00				
Total	14,202,897 62	14,557,577 54	15,371,628 17	16,183,740 64	16,131,952 67

OHIO.

	161 banks.	159 banks.	160 banks.	160 banks.	161 banks.
Capital stock	$19,009,000 00	$18,824,000 00	$18,799,000 00	$18,824,000 00	$19,239,000 00
Surplus fund	3,758,935 13	3,766,896 60	3,818,745 85	3,884,525 03	3,874,723 46
Undivided profits	1,485,500 41	1,732,164 98	1,492,811 84	1,584,801 35	1,987,425 17
Nat'l bank circulation	15,887,996 00	14,737,279 00	15,026,880 00	15,120,000 00	15,443,800 00
State bank circulation	7,996 00	7,992 00	7,903 00	7,903 00	7,903 00
Dividends unpaid	72,125 10	25,464 04	109,673 60	91,242 63	37,539 14
Individual deposits	32,474,897 54	33,214,686 23	33,440,644 15	35,417,311 65	38,487,881 53
U. S. deposits	193,815 94	217,428 18	287,735 51	267,364 63	311,611 23
Dep'ts U.S.dis.officers	50,830 78	20,343 82	36,479 95	37,679 92	23,217 70
Due to national banks	947,375 94	910,571 84	817,142 26	966,380 93	929,138 84
Due to State banks	800,481 07	732,603 97	727,808 56	948,417 60	779,149 96
Notes re-discounted	92,000 00	24,996 99	59,491 87	18,409 60	18,000 00
Bills payable	118,634 94	187,049 91	110,894 34	122,233 34	209,891 02
Total	74,907,984 85	74,397,566 57	74,735,189 93	77,299,885 48	81,118,281 05

Abstract of reports since October 1, 1880, arranged

CITY OF CINCINNATI.

Resources.	DECEMBER 31.	MARCH 11.	MAY 6.	JUNE 30.	OCTOBER 1.
	7 banks.	7 banks.	7 banks.	8 banks.	10 banks.
Loans and discounts	$15,739,170 17	$16,163,673 23	$15,141,929 67	$15,405,696 84	$18,907,396 79
Bonds for circulation	4,087,200 00	4,086,000 00	4,086,000 00	4,186,000 00	4,726,000 00
Bonds for deposits	834,500 00	834,500 00	823,000 00	823,000 00	823,000 00
U. S. bonds on hand	642,000 00	366,200 00	549,550 00	815,250 00	687,550 00
Other stocks and b'ds	482,547 54	416,522 74	577,402 74	707,030 45	676,656 41
Due from res'v eag'ts	2,403,350 71	1,524,487 48	1,725,401 55	3,429,394 58	2,778,616 27
Due from nat'l banks	747,937 64	735,128 97	614,497 51	1,115,420 85	1,341,287 45
Due from State banks	785,993 84	554,199 10	469,271 09	1,489,352 84	814,474 97
Real estate, &c	265,565 62	260,485 78	260,699 81	276,067 23	280,819 56
Current expenses	50,850 09	119,124 06	112,258 26	72,472 03	130,549 31
Premiums paid	61,018 03	50,904 78	67,460 11	84,164 38	98,239 17
Cash items	102,810 50	108,796 52	129,156 49	133,674 00	186,921 41
Clear'g-house exch'gs	263,169 40	253,588 58	255,438 32	334,289 63	357,244 71
Bills of other banks	283,356 00	164,498 00	272,536 00	536,888 00	319,856 00
Fractional currency	3,612 95	2,027 28	2,132 24	4,824 86	3,066 42
Specie	412,931 11	443,531 63	512,230 36	641,922 55	677,984 42
Legal-tender notes	1,263,458 00	1,210,263 00	1,267,362 00	1,153,761 00	1,919,975 00
U. S. cert's of deposit	820,000 00	565,000 00	930,000 00	1,365,000 00	835,000 00
Due from U. S. Treas	178,890 64	193,283 64	200,278 64	200,628 64	213,281 14
Total	29,428,362 24	28,052,214 79	27,996,604 79	32,794,837 88	35,777,919 03

CITY OF CLEVELAND.

Resources.	6 banks.	6 banks.	6 banks.	6 banks.	6 banks.
Loans and discounts	$7,989,597 28	$8,392,017 45	$8,351,810 27	$8,507,428 99	$9,931,728 44
Bonds for circulation	2,367,000 00	1,958,000 00	2,098,000 00	2,298,000 00	2,367,000 00
Bonds for deposits	325,000 00	325,000 00	575,000 00	575,000 00	575,000 00
U. S. bonds on hand	107,500 00	516,500 00	350,800 00	158,300 00	120,800 00
Other stocks and b'ds	76,740 77	76,740 77	232,772 27	87,122 27	188,702 93
Due from res'v eag'ts	1,439,528 99	1,346,072 38	755,783 17	1,434,594 03	1,003,223 06
Due from nat'l banks	766,835 85	951,610 77	522,361 62	908,060 11	981,469 77
Due from State banks	711,400 73	685,991 04	169,106 13	616,521 20	503,061 56
Real estate, &c	254,433 43	255,590 24	245,692 78	245,100 85	236,312 58
Current expenses	48,709 38	101,892 20	4,233 78	24,331 27	120,511 27
Premiums paid	468 75	468 75	468 75	468 75	468 75
Cash items	116,995 40	117,494 22	157,642 29	190,924 46	90,476 36
Clear'g-house exch'gs	109,502 55	125,295 21	99,585 50	150,687 15	241,316 67
Bills of other banks	287,625 00	176,882 00	454,284 00	197,819 00	257,339 00
Fractional currency	10,127 73	8,979 76	10,529 68	8,764 29	7,753 73
Specie	341,986 35	440,214 90	613,610 21	533,572 48	405,153 50
Legal-tender notes	1,050,000 00	847,000 00	1,160,000 00	885,000 00	1,070,000 00
U. S. cert's of deposit	15,000 00	15,000 00	15,000 00	15,000 00	15,000 00
Due from U. S. Treas	105,015 03	82,820 68	82,409 68	85,690 50	108,640 90
Total	16,123,467 24	16,423,570 37	15,949,090 13	16,931,385 35	18,223,958 52

INDIANA.

Resources.	91 banks.	92 banks.	92 banks.	93 banks.	93 banks.
Loans and discounts	$24,386,654 94	$24,736,195 72	$25,206,808 08	$25,113,266 89	$25,162,245 70
Bonds for circulation	11,083,800 00	9,529,800 00	9,679,800 00	9,744,800 00	9,999,800 00
Bonds for deposits	600,000 00	600,000 00	700,000 00	700,000 00	700,000 00
U. S. bonds on hand	814,250 00	1,625,550 00	1,380,350 00	1,631,000 00	1,535,950 00
Other stocks and b'ds	1,498,944 97	1,199,381 80	1,195,251 91	1,136,298 33	990,014 17
Due from res'v eag'ts	4,074,480 96	3,852,050 56	3,848,010 31	3,599,282 17	4,191,415 97
Due from nat'l banks	3,640,782 53	3,246,653 77	2,955,209 16	3,407,589 94	3,727,066 48
Due from State banks	698,577 72	753,572 40	772,729 42	594,595 94	710,831 63
Real estate, &c	1,750,846 84	1,626,250 91	1,621,062 71	1,591,618 01	1,527,166 64
Current expenses	148,815 79	167,624 90	252,316 97	164,641 57	191,899 67
Premiums paid	60,421 85	66,835 94	64,883 85	65,530 41	82,560 67
Cash items	292,049 59	243,874 72	285,315 97	284,808 99	366,673 93
Clear'g-house exch'gs	158,810 95	162,564 72	262,322 97	220,637 76	87,387 43
Bills of other banks	1,197,515 00	757,143 00	1,052,103 00	857,112 00	944,836 00
Fractional currency	15,562 59	13,181 73	12,327 53	12,565 49	10,441 25
Specie	1,766,384 45	1,619,799 09	1,711,145 35	1,608,192 26	1,608,192 26
Legal-tender notes	2,052,595 00	1,869,385 00	1,986,872 00	1,819,439 00	1,856,794 00
U. S. cert's of deposit					
Due from U. S. Treas	533,726 41	432,816 74	445,048 89	454,581 30	475,962 21
Total	54,771,360 59	52,502,681 00	53,432,452 24	53,053,205 13	54,169,238 01

by States and reserve cities—Continued.

CITY OF CINCINNATI.

Liabilities.	DECEMBER 31. 7 banks.	MARCH 11. 7 banks.	MAY 6. 7 banks.	JUNE 30. 8 banks.	OCTOBER 1. 10 banks.
Capital stock	$5,100,000 00	$5,100,000 00	$5,100,000 00	$5,350,000 00	$6,450,000 00
Surplus fund	720,000 00	723,000 00	723,000 00	723,000 00	727,000 00
Undivided profits	728,329 11	792,105 25	855,356 01	915,036 79	915,054 13
Nat'l bank circulation	3,663,770 00	3,643,090 00	3,640,290 00	3,643,090 00	3,961,640 00
State bank circulation					
Dividends unpaid	91,093 00	4,428 00	3,469 00	14,714 00	8,704 90
Individual deposits	10,134,292 65	9,942,127 99	10,464,236 22	14,607,318 39	14,403,351 32
U. S. deposits	750,000 00	750,000 00	757,500 00	765,000 00	765,000 00
Dep'ts U.S.dis.officers					
Due to national banks	5,564,304 73	4,678,178 00	4,284,184 72	4,493,663 41	5,540,819 73
Due to State banks	1,914,082 75	1,756,385 55	1,507,608 84	1,662,115 20	2,435,449 85
Notes re-discounted					
Bills payable	759,400 00	662,900 00	660,900 00	620,900 00	570,960 00
Total	29,428,362 24	28,052,214 79	27,996,604 79	32,794,837 88	35,777,919 03

CITY OF CLEVELAND.

	6 banks.	6 banks.	6 banks.	6 banks.	6 banks.
Capital stock	$3,700,000 00	$3,700,000 00	$3,700,000 00	$3,700,000 00	$3,700,000 00
Surplus fund	795,000 00	795,000 00	820,000 00	820,000 00	820,000 00
Undivided profits	150,154 02	306,891 61	89,057 96	268,841 21	445,648 44
Nat'l bank circulation	2,096,450 00	1,744,720 00	1,860,030 00	1,883,900 00	2,063,040 00
State bank circulation					
Dividends unpaid	834 00	884 00	55,692 00	941 00	288 50
Individual deposits	6,951,418 91	7,579,338 98	6,663,012 30	7,353,485 87	8,069,440 89
U. S. deposits	165,189 13	136,671 48	280,831 89	231,646 25	281,575 76
Dep'ts U.S.dis.officers	40,663 89	135,552 79	45,805 63	52,488 62	131,070 03
Due to national banks	1,060,702 79	863,089 40	804,729 55	921,328 24	1,051,434 60
Due to State banks	764,048 28	727,902 86	937,336 05	1,007,659 91	904,741 05
Notes re-discounted					
Bills payable	398,976 22	433,510 25	692,594 25	691,094 25	753,719 25
Total	16,123,467 24	16,423,570 37	15,949,090 13	16,931,385 35	18,223,058 52

INDIANA.

	91 banks.	92 banks.	92 banks.	93 banks.	93 banks.
Capital stock	$13,152,500 00	$12,918,500 00	$12,818,500 00	$12,913,500 00	$13,093,500 00
Surplus fund	3,971,706 43	4,001,732 28	4,006,535 20	4,046,216 61	3,854,159 38
Undivided profits	1,451,670 43	1,384,718 57	1,583,346 20	1,390,752 15	1,400,954 72
Nat'l bank circulation	9,881,890 00	8,337,102 00	8,561,500 00	8,499,000 00	8,767,700 00
State bank circulation					
Dividends unpaid	125,635 48	23,813 19	31,773 69	117,447 03	12,839 68
Individual deposits	21,931,180 59	21,715,648 61	22,353,369 77	22,218,578 15	23,206,436 48
U. S. deposits	384,848 72	316,754 87	349,619 74	476,446 31	416,190 77
Dep'ts U.S.dis.officers	92,266 23	196,039 70	186,391 02	128,305 95	167,194 96
Due to national banks	2,529,320 79	2,419,788 89	2,253,327 16	2,130,696 22	2,083,984 73
Due to State banks	1,220,341 92	1,139,840 03	1,240,067 62	1,055,931 99	1,158,277 29
Notes re-discounted		10,742 56	30,021 84	9,830 72	
Bills payable	33,000 00	38,000 00	18,000 00	66,500 00	8,000 00
Total	54,774,369 59	52,502,681 00	53,432,452 24	53,053,205 13	54,169,238 01

Abstract of reports since October 1, 1880, arranged

ILLINOIS.

Resources.	DECEMBER 31. 127 banks.	MARCH 11. 129 banks.	MAY 6. 129 banks.	JUNE 30. 129 banks.	OCTOBER 1. 130 banks.
Loans and discounts	$24,588,425 02	$25,980,936 20	$26,983,782 16	$26,771,201 72	$28,309,671 81
Bonds for circulation	8,461,000 00	8,174,500 00	8,376,500 00	8,401,500 00	8,587,000 00
Bonds for deposits	875,000 00	875,000 00	875,000 00	875,000 00	875,000 00
U. S. bonds on hand	651,200 00	1,100,400 00	1,143,100 00	1,212,950 00	1,249,750 00
Other stocks and b'ds	1,294,605 43	1,469,950 93	1,422,035 39	1,563,109 42	1,887,753 71
Due from res'veag'ts	6,443,225 40	6,878,231 04	6,154,994 61	6,944,549 44	6,908,671 04
Due from nat'l banks	2,166,995 51	2,292,396 05	1,859,843 86	2,151,779 93	2,593,095 58
Due from State banks	424,579 27	445,700 38	368,364 63	405,719 55	599,177 31
Real estate, &c	1,445,925 01	1,431,182 03	1,437,607 90	1,436,293 67	1,433,302 99
Current expenses	182,985 83	231,376 85	272,068 77	209,770 61	212,087 99
Premiums paid	80,486 36	71,922 17	87,030 95	87,478 49	120,041 14
Cash items	382,539 70	337,680 81	398,448 14	430,440 46	555,692 01
Clear'g-house exch'gs					
Bills of other banks	989,875 00	1,019,671 00	909,515 00	913,041 00	831,678 00
Fractional currency	13,013 19	14,951 18	13,708 81	12,074 87	10,381 98
Specie	1,854,802 98	2,060,843 54	2,135,242 76	2,183,160 97	2,307,857 04
Legal-tender notes	2,316,463 00	2,270,440 00	2,058,662 00	1,935,322 00	2,050,597 00
U. S. cert's of deposit					10,000 00
Due from U. S. Treas	427,004 19	411,222 95	430,159 16	431,737 82	442,020 77
Total	52,592,125 89	55,086,414 13	54,926,067 54	55,965,129 95	59,073,778 37

CITY OF CHICAGO.

	9 banks.	9 banks.	9 banks.	9 banks.	9 banks.
Loans and discounts	$28,637,077 30	$29,167,012 71	$29,522,360 19	$31,856,908 16	$33,751,739 32
Bonds for circulation	1,250,000 00	1,150,000 00	1,250,000 00	1,350,000 00	1,350,000 00
Bonds for deposits	100,000 00	100,000 00	100,000 00	100,000 00	100,000 00
U. S. bonds on hand	1,781,250 00	2,647,450 00	2,227,700 00	2,498,100 00	3,198,250 00
Other stocks and b'ds	638,967 24	834,340 21	1,066,005 60	1,343,911 10	1,016,302 14
Due from res'veag'ts	4,504,305 68	4,805,951 74	4,429,213 24	6,906,416 17	6,547,134 35
Due from nat'l banks	2,306,312 39	1,997,124 28	2,463,896 80	3,275,155 03	4,413,546 51
Due from State banks	998,678 83	1,026,720 98	965,425 64	1,090,575 00	1,020,717 70
Real estate, &c	595,377 02	649,909 29	678,460 57	677,568 22	602,334 47
Current expenses		32,529 35	45,963 34	7,058 82	37,750 02
Premiums paid	8,812 50	13,087 75	31,156 02	17,490 11	41,094 23
Cash items	21,999 75	115,588 18	80,201 46	100,025 47	52,058 57
Clear'g-house exch'gs	2,491,221 74	1,704,764 00	2,651,418 85	2,706,861 12	9,852,424 33
Bills of other banks	820,876 00	526,780 00	1,690,306 00	898,553 00	534,674 00
Fractional currency	3,724 63	3,198 56	3,287 43	2,728 98	4,722 81
Specie	5,252,858 24	5,964,722 93	5,466,588 80	5,626,145 93	9,486,540 00
Legal-tender notes	2,373,000 00	1,692,960 00	3,071,800 00	2,441,350 00	1,568,520 00
U. S. cert's of deposit	365,000 00	335,000 00	450,000 00	680,000 00	660,000 00
Due from U. S. Treas	67,750 00	48,200 00	66,500 00	69,516 10	72,500 00
Total	52,217,211 32	52,815,349 87	56,260,284 03	61,648,363 21	74,310,308 54

MICHIGAN.

	76 banks.	75 banks.	75 banks.	75 banks.	76 banks.
Loans and discounts	$14,944,416 74	$15,853,774 04	$16,917,329 64	$16,970,554 84	$17,058,011 93
Bonds for circulation	5,307,900 00	5,357,900 00	5,387,900 00	4,967,900 00	4,991,900 00
Bonds for deposits	50,000 00	50,000 00	50,000 00	50,000 00	50,000 00
U. S. bonds on hand	142,750 00	199,850 00	204,200 00	218,800 00	197,650 00
Other stocks and b'ds	573,544 85	535,965 99	549,181 13	575,205 12	628,568 02
Due from res'veag'ts	2,674,794 40	2,038,690 78	1,589,491 80	2,056,250 66	2,903,705 04
Due from nat'l banks	988,737 65	737,383 47	516,223 46	576,676 00	937,822 52
Due from State banks	183,296 70	121,668 44	83,194 01	137,840 11	183,532 04
Real estate, &c	919,900 84	915,077 71	898,864 84	881,678 94	884,244 12
Current expenses	78,706 48	115,864 27	159,090 91	67,411 98	157,139 21
Premiums paid	40,605 16	37,243 01	40,502 59	41,406 85	42,884 29
Cash items	171,145 54	128,934 88	136,680 52	154,370 90	230,379 10
Clear'g-house exch'gs					
Bills of other banks	534,193 00	364,905 00	451,711 00	441,154 00	588,780 00
Fractional currency	7,838 56	7,551 50	8,608 29	7,570 23	7,442 12
Specie	915,732 04	1,010,059 56	1,031,868 93	1,007,982 35	1,130,113 71
Legal-tender notes	1,159,426 00	795,051 00	916,872 00	885,111 00	895,883 00
U. S. cert's of deposit					
Due from U. S. Treas	266,277 64	260,485 44	261,063 06	240,925 56	240,467 16
Total	28,989,635 54	28,530,405 09	29,202,782 18	29,280,937 54	31,148,582 26

by States and reserve cities—Continued.

ILLINOIS.

Liabilities.	DECEMBER 31.	MARCH 11.	MAY 6.	JUNE 30.	OCTOBER 1.
	127 banks.	129 banks.	129 banks.	129 banks.	130 banks.
Capital stock	$10,714,600 00	$10,864,600 00	$10,764,600 00	$10,764,600 00	$10,949,600 00
Surplus fund	3,592,504 09	3,607,572 29	3,662,997 06	3,686,030 28	3,724,571 05
Undivided profits	1,277,415 05	1,133,456 22	1,313,711 75	1,447,587 28	1,370,873 70
Nat'l bank circulation	7,514,060 00	7,193,255 00	7,381,836 00	7,451,448 00	7,536,992 00
State bank circulation					
Dividends unpaid	93,878 50	25,321 44	38,866 67	72,003 42	37,795 50
Individual deposits	28,051,785 48	30,824,134 27	30,265,765 14	31,157,699 06	33,913,950 48
U. S. deposits	662,348 93	647,364 44	717,280 61	603,838 13	666,902 68
Dep'ts U.S.dis.officers	37,824 26	22,563 08	22,277 60	71,225 46	39,136 78
Due to national banks	123,076 07	125,941 74	117,658 02	140,680 87	178,499 60
Due to State banks	500,666 84	618,067 18	586,308 02	558,516 55	613,473 48
Notes re-discounted	13,200 00	13,371 80	39,000 00		22,483 10
Bills payable	10,766 67	10,766 67	15,766 67	11,500 00	19,500 00
Total	52,592,125 89	53,086,414 13	54,926,067 54	55,965,129 95	59,073,778 37

CITY OF CHICAGO.

	9 banks.	9 banks.	9 banks.	9 banks.	9 banks.
Capital stock	$4,250,000 00	$4,250,000 00	$4,250,000 00	$4,250,000 00	$4,250,000 00
Surplus fund	2,470,000 00	2,470,000 00	2,470,000 00	2,475,000 00	2,635,000 00
Undivided profits	970,004 02	1,129,066 84	1,326,672 28	1,469,152 44	1,560,762 97
Nat'l bank circulation	941,497 00	466,597 00	539,697 00	571,097 00	628,197 00
State bank circulation					
Dividends unpaid	102,675 00	4,017 25	2,793 50	76,483 25	29,430 75
Individual deposits	23,704,816 58	23,245,565 50	26,686,593 48	28,081,401 81	39,058,451 83
U. S. deposits	60,453 74	49,967 67	42,787 59	16,037 76	41,916 49
Dep'ts U.S.dis.officers					
Due to national banks	11,970,550 76	12,054,274 56	12,203,508 93	13,651,235 09	14,795,546 27
Due to State banks	7,747,214 22	9,145,861 05	8,738,231 25	11,057,895 86	11,310,994 23
Notes re-discounted					
Bills payable					
Total	52,217,211 32	52,815,349 87	56,260,284 03	61,648,363 21	74,310,308 54

MICHIGAN.

	76 banks.	75 banks.	75 banks.	75 banks.	76 banks.
Capital stock	$7,335,000 00	$7,285,000 00	$7,285,000 00	$7,285,000 00	$7,335,000 00
Surplus fund	1,916,818 19	1,932,306 34	1,933,806 34	2,000,264 09	1,986,545 34
Undivided profits	944,858 17	940,147 35	1,195,547 25	1,003,263 81	1,167,263 09
Nat'l bank circulation	4,690,485 00	4,689,365 00	4,756,985 00	4,393,460 00	4,387,830 00
State bank circulation					
Dividends unpaid	133,853 79	12,607 78	9,920 61	160,286 27	18,707 12
Individual deposits	13,689,262 75	13,214,076 68	13,091,692 61	13,791,214 67	16,006,195 22
U. S. deposits	23,482 34	26,715 88	40,279 08	25,062 63	26,261 57
Dep'ts U.S.dis.officers	9,530 30	12,363 30	10,175 22	6,908 61	7,176 77
Due to national banks	81,296 68	69,030 23	101,258 71	92,215 41	61,470 55
Due to State banks	98,951 61	102,166 73	103,852 58	110,658 65	85,222 04
Notes re-discounted	59,616 71	241,625 80	609,264 78	401,703 40	66,410 56
Bills payable	6,500 00	5,000 00	5,000 00	10,000 00	500 00
Total	28,989,655 54	28,530,405 09	29,202,782 18	29,280,937 54	31,148,582 26

Abstract of reports since October 1, 1880, arranged

CITY OF DETROIT.

Resources.	DECEMBER 31. 4 banks.	MARCH 11. 4 banks.	MAY 6. 4 banks.	JUNE 30. 4 banks.	OCTOBER 1. 4 banks.
Loans and discounts	$6,594,752 10	$6,911,505 35	$7,162,291 24	$6,564,000 66	$7,471,917 51
Bonds for circulation	1,403,400 00	1,403,400 00	1,403,400 00	1,403,400 00	1,383,400 00
Bonds for deposits...	500,000 00	500,000 00	500,000 00	500,000 00	500,000 00
U. S. bonds on hand..	36,700 00	36,700 00	35,500 00	35,000 00	35,000 00
Other stocks and b'ds	71,506 05	70,574 75	69,074 75	71,202 25	89,531 25
Due from res've ag'ts	909,872 66	1,309,179 20	1,025,363 55	1,459,392 52	1,606,191 93
Due from nat'l banks	441,545 68	803,394 59	534,647 87	676,735 80	658,822 29
Due from State banks	104,068 81	40,160 30	103,425 35	82,263 56	142,439 62
Real estate, &c......	104,311 60	104,640 33	102,146 89	96,708 89	98,161 78
Current expenses....	25,169 76	44,333 16	19,908 28	6,957 27	8,964 47
Premiums paid......	1,937 50	1,937 50	....	....	....
Cash items.........	26,953 58	64,734 38	22,013 24	66,912 73	36,129 46
Clear'g-house exch'gs	178,494 83	150,055 62	143,952 35	166,053 46	188,724 67
Bills of other banks..	270,430 00	75,990 00	221,475 00	133,492 00	155,425 00
Fractional currency .	10,490 94	6,227 22	8,760 04	12,131 73	7,963 38
Specie	628,674 75	706,490 46	645,811 87	657,081 36	716,582 31
Legal-tender notes ..	620,861 00	395,615 00	594,810 00	389,041 00	549,411 00
U. S. cert's of deposit	....	....	....	....	....
Due from U. S. Treas.	78,658 16	79,521 16	87,482 26	76,329 96	73,603 33
Total..........	12,007,827 42	12,704,459 02	12,680,662 69	12,396,763 19	13,722,268 00

WISCONSIN.

	31 banks.	31 banks.	31 banks.	31 banks.	31 banks.
Loans and discounts.	$6,134,307 27	$6,333,629 89	$6,405,616 20	$6,731,488 25	$6,933,776 98
Bonds for circulation	1,778,000 00	1,778,000 00	1,854,500 00	1,979,500 00	1,979,500 00
Bonds for deposits...	100,000 00	100,000 00	100,000 00	100,000 00	100,000 00
U. S. bonds on hand..	84,850 00	75,650 00	91,100 00	140,500 00	152,750 00
Other stocks and b'ds	276,470 21	249,916 41	259,250 37	347,833 84	475,394 28
Due from res've ag'ts	1,479,355 02	1,578,774 81	1,459,940 81	1,323,864 21	1,374,736 13
Due from nat'l banks	837,931 32	760,443 23	732,866 33	663,319 34	775,490 73
Due from State banks	115,779 43	100,193 63	113,167 45	143,904 50	137,659 77
Real estate, &c......	272,850 26	276,618 10	275,794 10	277,920 00	275,967 45
Current expenses....	45,461 68	49,343 35	54,557 63	33,465 23	59,857 02
Premiums paid......	6,421 06	9,066 22	10,433 05	17,908 05	18,817 38
Cash items.........	49,076 70	43,378 38	99,656 11	69,615 82	74,799 67
Clear'g-house exch'gs	....	....	....	....	....
Bills of other banks..	241,409 00	163,446 00	164,112 00	193,199 00	213,446 00
Fractional currency .	5,169 70	4,186 82	4,492 11	3,827 37	2,952 63
Specie	563,819 43	604,076 97	615,631 44	601,828 73	579,116 67
Legal-tender notes ..	456,540 00	399,033 00	361,813 00	381,042 00	397,094 00
U. S. cert's of deposit	....	....	....	....	....
Due from U. S. Treas	89,109 21	87,557 30	94,344 90	90,071 60	93,443 90
Total..........	12,536,640 29	12,613,314 11	12,697,275 50	13,099,287 94	13,644,802 61

CITY OF MILWAUKEE.

	3 banks.	3 banks.	3 banks.	3 banks.	3 banks.
Loans and discounts	$3,900,619 51	$3,831,869 97	$3,817,219 03	$3,656,471 01	$3,888,585 77
Bonds for circulation	615,000 00	450,000 00	450,000 00	650,000 00	650,000 00
Bonds for deposits...	450,000 00	450,000 00	450,000 00	450,000 00	550,000 00
U. S. bonds on hand..	1,750 00	40,200 00	3,800 00	112,400 00	....
Other stocks and b'ds	252,375 16	248,501 50	261,501 50	297,842 34	360,722 50
Due from res've ag'ts.	642,744 01	607,336 99	677,104 80	660,433 47	695,697 42
Due from nat'l banks	107,295 08	132,726 38	341,366 70	332,929 00	171,571 47
Due from State banks	59,148 91	63,036 51	60,605 67	55,833 92	84,414 75
Real estate, &c......	121,308 33	121,337 32	120,519 45	120,401 49	119,666 98
Current expenses....	10,725 10	12,352 38	10,017 37	13,423 48	8,047 63
Premiums paid......	148 88	....	....	....	....
Cash items.........	3,887 39	4,827 02	3,652 70	6,885 48	3,896 64
Clear'g-house exch'gs	155,693 42	135,219 76	192,842 90	131,463 25	275,997 35
Bills of other banks..	17,150 00	12,979 00	22,388 00	14,807 00	21,726 00
Fractional currency .	3,317 31	2,296 59	4,654 29	2,438 18	2,465 00
Specie	427,276 95	349,926 00	370,358 00	272,918 00	317,946 00
Legal-tender notes ..	489,465 00	394,482 00	589,976 00	440,873 00	376,779 00
U. S. cert's of deposit	....	....	....	....	....
Due from U. S. Treas	34,303 63	25,250 00	27,250 00	28,300 00	35,250 00
Total..........	7,292,208 98	6,882,341 42	7,403,256 41	7,247,409 62	7,562,766 71

by States and reserve cities—Continued.

CITY OF DETROIT.

Liabilities.	DECEMBER 31. 4 banks.	MARCH 11. 4 banks.	MAY 6. 4 banks.	JUNE 30. 4 banks.	OCTOBER 1. 4 banks.
Capital stock.........	$2,100,000 00	$2,100,000 00	$2,100,000 00	$2,100,000 00	$2,100,000 00
Surplus fund.........	715,000 00	715,000 00	715,000 00	800,000 00	800,000 00
Undivided profits....	552,187 55	622,199 26	606,726 63	504,796 35	484,118 38
Nat'l bank circulation	1,239,777 00	1,225,177 00	1,214,847 00	1,207,947 00	1,227,147 00
State bank circulation					
Dividends unpaid....	33,527 00	1,165 00	2,835 00	56,590 00	14,232 50
Individual deposits ..	5,723,851 28	6,436,724 55	6,414,962 36	6,064,482 88	7,120,988 58
U. S. deposits........	216,147 25	117,959 55	229,529 81	289,036 23	228,960 58
Dep'ts U.S.dis.officers	142,695 17	327,510 69	185,656 10	172,969 34	237,583 82
Due to national banks	702,418 46	580,304 31	568,674 91	623,345 72	816,705 12
Due to State banks..	582,223 71	578,418 66	611,830 88	577,595 67	692,532 02
Notes re-discounted..					
Bills payable........					
Total..........	12,007,827 42	12,704,459 02	12,680,062 69	12,396,763 19	13,722,268 00

WISCONSIN.

	31 banks.	31 banks.	31 banks.	31 banks.	31 banks.
Capital stock	$2,350,000 00	$2,375,000 00	$2,375,000 00	$2,375,000 00	$2,375,000 00
Surplus fund........	684,452 28	699,260 34	699,260 34	700,260 34	696,000 33
Undivided profits....	376,341 23	347,387 66	385,787 44	423,043 86	438,931 17
Nat'l bank circulation	1,569,206 00	1,560,126 00	1,626,163 00	1,663,863 00	1,745,563 00
State bank circulation					
Dividends unpaid....	14,855 00	240 00	200 00	13,935 00	1,264 00
Individual deposits .	7,302,088 01	7,425,812 97	7,441,375 97	7,822,627 87	8,259,950 89
U. S. deposits........	63,227 48	38,547 21	111,542 30	62,056 26	56,651 14
Dep'ts U.S.dis.officers	12,745 86	9,585 33	9,109 43	8,348 25	7,714 56
Due to national banks	22,620 42	22,604 22	17,592 32	11,182 54	21,018 53
Due to State banks ..	130,983 17	124,542 54	7,394 98	18,774 73	22,551 55
Notes re-discounted..			23,653 63		20,000 00
Bills payable........	10,120 84	10,120 84	196 09	196 09	157 44
Total	12,536,640 29	12,613,314 11	12,697,275 50	13,099,287 94	13,644,802 61

CITY OF MILWAUKEE.

	3 banks.	3 banks.	3 banks.	3 banks.	3 banks.
Capital stock	$650,000 00	$650,000 00	$650,000 00	$650,000 00	$650,000 00
Surplus fund	220,000 00	225,000 00	225,000 00	225,000 00	235,000 00
Undivided profits ...	198,819 15	187,295 29	210,161 00	213,770 84	228,582 11
Nat'l bank circulation	553,500 00	405,000 00	405,000 00	530,000 00	585,000 00
State bank circulation					
Dividends unpaid....	786 00			2,820 00	
Individual deposits ..	3,497,346 61	3,699,661 07	3,715,020 33	3,874,262 37	4,075,474 81
U. S. deposits........	157,730 66	173,654 39	228,663 45	178,987 21	173,048 43
Dep'ts U.S.officers	230,781 35	202,151 85	191,304 54	231,527 76	264,046 04
Due to national banks	1,055,122 43	832,578 64	1,156,509 96	880,951 15	870,487 09
Due to State banks...	587,053 05	482,000 18	575,597 13	460,090 29	481,128 23
Notes re-discounted..	141,069 73	25,000 00	46,000 00		
Bills payable					
Total	7,292,208 98	6,882,341 42	7,403,256 41	7,247,409 62	7,562,766 71

IOWA.

Resources.	DECEMBER 31. 75 banks.	MARCH 11. 74 banks.	MAY 6. 74 banks.	JUNE 30. 76 banks.	OCTOBER 1. 76 banks.
Loans and discounts.	$12,254,130 76	$12,819,732 95	$12,897,009 37	$12,814,795 04	$13,725,449 82
Bonds for circulation.	4,757,000 00	4,635,000 00	4,700,000 00	4,901,000 00	5,049,500 00
Bonds for deposits...	75,000 00	75,000 00	75,000 00	75,000 00	75,000 00
U. S. bonds on hand..	339,800 00	472,450 00	577,100 00	526,050 00	600,450 00
Other stocks and b'ds	603,027 21	896,604 98	850,006 59	879,442 37	1,027,707 09
Due from res've ag'ts.	2,131,012 95	2,493,641 83	2,833,620 96	3,393,831 71	2,903,305 50
Due from nat'l banks.	1,095,284 25	1,510,863 71	1,439,141 09	1,546,094 52	1,669,516 94
Due from State banks	199,271 65	203,049 49	300,261 84	639,126 02	349,366 16
Real estate, &c	908,908 86	883,442 58	871,271 49	893,169 42	898,372 07
Current expenses....	120,289 49	185,768 36	201,587 08	160,181 51	161,723 92
Premiums paid......	44,629 08	50,267 80	51,020 77	62,211 91	65,394 62
Cash items	179,079 42	150,826 53	173,188 88	169,389 11	198,371 62
Clear'g-house exch'gs	....	....	....	....	....
Bills of other banks..	629,003 00	567,194 00	569,747 00	553,518 00	492,158 00
Fractional currency..	7,638 20	8,960 64	8,352 38	7,070 34	8,210 96
Specie	981,700 92	1,119,933 14	1,216,792 26	1,157,491 97	1,161,716 57
Legal-tender notes ..	1,308,213 00	1,195,037 00	1,268,600 00	1,181,334 00	1,231,344 00
U. S. cert's of deposit.	30,000 00	30,000 00	30,000 00	30,000 00	30,000 00
Due from U. S. Treas.	242,214 32	248,121 73	236,265 44	244,735 47	250,658 79
Total..........	25,996,204 01	27,545,894 74	28,298,965 15	29,234,441 39	29,997,246 06

MINNESOTA.

	30 banks.	28 banks.	28 banks.	28 banks.	27 banks.
Loans and discounts.	$12,320,870 94	$13,068,193 64	$13,454,467 52	$13,693,946 03	$15,037,773 72
Bonds for circulation.	2,299,500 00	2,049,500 00	2,099,500 00	2,123,500 00	2,073,500 00
Bonds for deposits ..	450,000 00	500,000 00	500,000 00	500,000 00	500,000 00
U. S. bonds on hand..	2,600 00	105,050 00	51,600 00	59,050 00	51,900 00
Other stocks and b'ds	367,675 55	221,106 03	235,136 59	293,012 08	480,416 89
Due from res've ag'ts	1,434,091 89	1,210,263 77	1,187,316 61	2,904,413 17	1,876,298 66
Due from nat'l banks	624,945 04	497,052 51	542,123 68	789,635 05	1,020,233 59
Due from State banks	143,686 23	159,341 06	179,894 80	240,185 30	332,744 90
Real estate, &c	422,070 75	484,419 62	486,292 62	477,352 13	394,185 43
Current expenses....	64,368 29	66,771 02	111,638 07	68,438 08	64,167 47
Premiums paid......	10,780 12	7,230 00	7,230 00	3,962 25	2,946 25
Cash items	82,780 28	50,218 05	98,085 42	91,630 54	106,293 20
Clear'g-house exch'gs	67,170 34	46,755 87	71,846 16	57,613 60	143,649 14
Bills of other banks..	476,025 00	143,404 00	236,845 00	206,932 00	279,455 00
Fractional currency.	3,258 31	2,913 58	2,560 40	2,635 95	2,968 84
Specie	534,563 67	454,441 51	443,092 24	491,256 79	767,544 31
Legal-tender notes ..	916,530 00	638,251 00	681,678 00	698,001 00	849,160 00
U. S. cert's of deposit.					
Due from U. S. Treas.	107,935 15	92,158 48	96,905 88	97,539 73	106,435 18
Total..........	20,328,851 56	19,797,071 04	20,486,212 99	22,799,103 79	24,089,672 58

MISSOURI.

	16 banks.	16 banks.	16 banks.	16 banks.	17 banks.
Loans and discounts.	$2,765,278 61	$2,759,643 93	$2,927,344 78	$2,925,613 24	$3,681,292 90
Bonds for circulation	1,080,000 00	1,046,950 00	1,280,000 00	1,280,000 00	1,310,000 00
Bonds for deposits ...	....	....	....	....	....
U. S. bonds on hand..	70,800 00	142,350 00	225,200 00	222,300 00	245,000 00
Other stocks and b'ds	787,811 14	789,026 91	793,951 12	806,103 90	915,222 64
Due from res've ag'ts.	764,984 55	1,049,680 45	716,767 89	940,478 86	869,725 79
Due from nat'l banks.	81,061 68	95,654 83	129,047 46	119,740 17	161,702 62
Due from State banks	127,390 03	186,897 92	132,808 41	99,086 72	180,217 94
Real estate, &c	228,802 35	223,399 00	220,122 14	211,139 20	183,246 88
Current expenses....	30,446 26	48,336 31	51,766 22	41,862 21	37,038 87
Premiums paid......	2,774 18	5,217 68	5,738 18	5,539 02	4,301 93
Cash items	51,554 16	35,192 30	37,605 26	35,850 25	36,854 65
Clear'g-house exch'gs	9,448 49	7,315 93	13,768 41	9,889 19	63,217 77
Bills of other banks..	174,149 00	171,429 00	183,785 00	179,181 00	188,508 00
Fractional currency.	1,260 57	1,090 56	751 14	680 73	1,217 55
Specie	146,069 80	141,736 27	142,488 02	151,883 97	190,173 24
Legal-tender notes ..	310,046 00	257,131 00	334,346 00	343,848 00	294,756 00
U. S. cert's of deposit.					
Due from U. S. Treas.	55,787 42	47,579 60	61,424 60	59,431 90	60,912 95
Total..........	6,687,664 24	7,011,631 69	7,256,914 63	7,432,637 36	8,423,389 13

by States and reserve cities—Continued.

IOWA.

Liabilities.	DECEMBER 31. 75 banks.	MARCH 11. 74 banks.	MAY 6. 74 banks.	JUNE 30. 76 banks.	OCTOBER 1. 76 banks.
Capital stock	$5,800,000 00	$5,750,000 00	$5,750,000 00	$5,950,000 00	$5,950,000 00
Surplus fund	1,435,432 28	1,401,076 93	1,483,691 18	1,508,939 80	1,542,083 00
Undivided profits	763,127 70	633,664 09	736,226 60	802,044 78	747,712 76
Nat'l bank circulation	4,199,758 00	4,071,378 00	4,086,518 00	4,243,973 00	4,414,103 00
State bank circulation					
Dividends unpaid	63,114 50	55,074 66	57,137 66	75,008 16	50,758 50
Individual deposits	12,505,061 05	14,171,525 44	11,714,420 73	15,249,050 91	15,770,131 05
U. S. deposits	37,603 47	35,084 35	61,822 69	36,229 48	37,125 28
Dep'ts U.S.dis.officers	10,336 88	15,982 07	7,850 62	21,328 19	34,736 28
Due to national banks	494,207 48	453,153 34	520,611 64	485,609 72	475,318 32
Due to State banks	556,533 52	770,510 14	838,012 72	833,298 96	894,116 54
Notes re-discounted	130,939 13	119,410 72	31,673 31	25,959 39	81,158 33
Bills payable			11,000 00		
Total	25,996,204 01	2',34',8.54 74	28,298,965 15	29,234,441 39	29,997,246 06

MINNESOTA.

	30 banks.	28 banks.	28 banks.	28 banks.	27 banks.
Capital stock	$5,150,000 00	$4,925,000 00	$4,925,000 00	$4,925,000 00	$4,900,000 00
Surplus fund	949,003 67	903,511 11	903,511 11	965,011 11	981,725 88
Undivided profits	580,220 98	462,821 93	629,298 95	595,452 54	588,197 65
Nat'l bank circulation	2,050,998 00	1,824,037 00	1,874,337 00	1,860,642 00	1,845,234 00
State bank circulation					
Dividends unpaid	8,370 00	6,896 00	5,161 00	29,040 00	5,236 00
Individual deposits	9,756,730 77	9,925,206 83	10,115,361 04	11,820,571 20	12,650,432 88
U. S. deposits	82,989 47	77,687 60	153,537 73	103,457 74	78,017 67
Dep'ts U.S.officers	366,437 23	382,038 98	204,772 63	302,931 99	272,976 92
Due to national banks	712,873 01	538,079 59	676,267 28	872,519 69	1,528,781 00
Due to State banks	481,995 61	612,173 48	649,304 72	1,161,059 50	1,165,070 15
Notes re-discounted	169,232 82	133,718 52	249,661 48	161,418 02	65,000 43
Bills payable	20,000 00		10,000 00		
Total	20,328,851 56	19,797,071 04	20,486,212 99	22,799,103 70	24,089,672 58

MISSOURI.

	16 banks.	16 banks.	16 banks.	16 banks.	17 banks.
Capital stock	$1,400,000 00	$1,400,000 00	$1,400,000 00	$1,400,000 00	$1,705,000 00
Surplus fund	323,904 75	334,404 75	339,404 75	341,554 75	367,554 75
Undivided profits	254,196 13	226,960 85	253,682 00	237,980 56	280,216 04
Nat'l bank circulation	962,853 00	930,172 00	1,108,177 00	1,121,253 00	1,141,953 00
State bank circulation					
Dividends unpaid	16,562 50	629 50	501 50	1,591 50	12,972 50
Individual deposits	3,397,383 46	3,794,188 12	3,846,084 64	3,991,611 67	4,300,178 11
U. S. deposits					
Dep'ts U.S.dis.officers					
Due to national banks	73,785 41	73,088 49	53,609 89	65,682 92	229,490 47
Due to State banks	225,092 64	224,414 48	235,324 35	248,222 46	339,863 46
Notes re-discounted	20,000 00				30,000 00
Bills payable	13,886 35	27,743 50	20,070 50	24,740 50	25,160 50
Total	6,687,664 24	7,011,631 69	7,256,914 63	7,432,637 36	8,123,380 13

CITY OF ST. LOUIS.

Resources.	DECEMBER 31. 5 banks.	MARCH 11. 5 banks.	MAY 6. 5 banks.	JUNE 30. 5 banks.	OCTOBER 1. 5 banks.
Loans and discounts	$9,898,865 72	$9,487,791 55	$8,284,138 24	$8,614,576 14	$10,251,480 74
Bonds for circulation	860,000 00	860,000 00	860,000 00	860,000 00	1,310,000 00
Bonds for deposits...	250,000 00	250,000 00	250,000 00	250,000 00	250,000 00
U. S. bonds on hand..	195,500 00	278,000 00	462,100 00	535,450 00	439,850 00
Other stocks and b'ds	432,801 88	411,279 11	411,339 11	447,499 11	450,162 10
Due from res've ag'ts.	623,050 57	649,802 39	1,563,609 49	1,947,426 45	919,420 74
Due from nat'l banks	558,548 03	481,829 48	736,146 63	1,188,735 92	312,231 00
Due from State banks	207,424 01	241,733 62	190,186 40	253,269 59	241,555 76
Real estate, &c	253,381 40	250,618 10	249,965 06	236,587 61	240,109 87
Current expenses....	9,569 50	76,569 07	83,181 19	49,047 27	130,735 78
Premiums paid	8,949 64	20,830 89	49,066 89	20,936 39	14,537 14
Cash items	49,782 29	56,185 34	31,713 66	58,372 79	64,756 92
Clear'g-house exch'gs	508,135 43	753,715 71	882,477 27	853,957 28	1,097,886 67
Bills of other banks..	236,412 00	239,168 00	337,932 00	147,333 00	145,559 00
Fractional currency	3,613 94	3,929 88	4,260 09	3,246 26	3,256 27
Specie	568,863 35	682,048 40	897,356 75	675,230 40	702,411 05
Legal-tender notes	1,573,500 00	1,710,000 00	2,427,000 00	1,440,000 00	1,352,000 00
U. S. cert's of deposit	....	150,000 00	30,000 00	....	....
Due from U. S. Treas	50,684 50	56,604 50	49,684 50	47,474 50	58,934 50
Total	16,289,082 26	16,660,196 04	17,710,157 28	17,629,142 71	17,984,896 54

KANSAS.

	12 banks.	12 banks.	12 banks.	12 banks.	13 banks.
Loans and discounts	$1,965,981 15	$1,821,655 64	$1,862,598 93	$2,038,687 67	$2,508,754 34
Bonds for circulation	710,000 00	620,000 00	670,000 00	670,000 00	755,000 00
Bonds for deposits ..	375,000 00	375,000 00	375,000 00	375,000 00	375,000 00
U. S. bonds on hand..	62,400 00	139,000 00	50,500 00	30,300 00	40,350 00
Other stocks and b'ds	40,074 61	24,073 36	47,915 51	46,979 15	50,094 35
Due from res've ag'ts..	397,900 63	410,811 18	667,366 57	651,914 10	562,293 37
Due from nat'l banks.	199,686 89	235,774 58	244,447 75	277,937 55	270,112 92
Due from State banks	107,875 69	100,483 01	147,217 99	148,037 28	328,252 11
Real estate, &c	166,567 76	159,351 45	161,425 73	155,730 74	155,776 25
Current expenses....	22,349 54	20,358 49	31,014 84	22,568 24	28,007 85
Premiums paid	10,028 15	9,338 33	7,188 33	8,188 33	10,782 08
Cash items	77,735 30	50,018 90	22,659 11	36,418 92	45,126 97
Clear'g-house exch'gs	....	....	....	....	....
Bills of other banks..	190,036 00	149,254 00	100,820 00	119,938 00	165,974 00
Fractional currency .	2,663 19	2,322 32	2,176 33	1,689 44	1,577 88
Specie	161,745 06	161,489 33	169,979 01	179,024 14	205,633 41
Legal-tender notes...	320,765 00	338,105 00	287,682 00	261,904 00	326,411 00
U. S. cert's of deposit	....	....	....	....	....
Due from U. S. Treas	38,566 02	40,699 05	37,945 10	39,613 30	42,563 65
Total	4,849,374 99	4,657,734 64	4,885,937 20	5,063,930 86	5,871,800 18

NEBRASKA.

	10 banks.	10 banks.	10 banks.	11 banks.	12 banks.
Loans and discounts.	$3,677,274 46	$3,563,714 90	$3,544,757 34	$3,490,916 67	$4,271,798 21
Bonds for circulation	759,000 00	568,000 00	568,000 00	701,000 00	739,000 00
Bonds for deposits...	350,000 00	350,000 00	350,000 00	350,000 00	350,000 00
U. S. bonds on hand..	....	142,000 00	149,500 00	11,500 00	375,050 00
Other stocks and b'ds	176,392 19	201,033 00	185,496 54	180,959 20	208,501 67
Due from res've ag'ts..	477,131 12	308,629 50	490,672 69	1,013,812 86	1,024,879 08
Due from nat'l banks	178,221 85	165,053 72	209,194 84	339,829 16	271,171 59
Due from State banks	109,982 75	139,175 29	158,825 99	425,573 37	449,426 17
Real estate, &c	162,599 20	198,899 70	197,724 70	212,527 05	248,029 90
Current expenses....	32,636 53	36,729 56	26,374 51	39,529 98	33,232 11
Premiums paid	4,000 00	4,000 00	4,000 00	5,736 61	5,955 92
Cash items	200,326 37	161,392 19	153,320 83	225,607 83	368,469 72
Clear'g-house exch'gs	....	....	....	....	....
Bills of other banks..	125,522 00	142,959 00	141,646 00	122,800 00	163,628 00
Fractional currency .	2,611 27	2,051 57	2,225 84	2,829 11	3,307 64
Specie	317,946 44	345,057 40	238,534 10	338,700 05	306,722 36
Legal-tender notes ..	309,032 00	214,946 00	276,328 00	238,433 00	261,401 00
U. S. cert's of deposit	....	....	....	....	....
Due from U. S. Treas.	40,827 76	27,124 78	27,222 98	35,595 00	41,353 10
Total	6,923,503 94	6,570,766 61	6,723,824 36	7,735,431 49	9,127,526 47

*by States and reserve cities—*Continued.

CITY OF ST. LOUIS.

Liabilities.	DECEMBER 31.	MARCH 11.	MAY 6.	JUNE 30.	OCTOBER 1.
	5 banks.	5 banks.	5 banks.	5 banks.	5 banks.
Capital stock.........	$2, 650, 000 00	$2, 650, 000 00	$2, 650, 000 00	$2, 650, 000 00	$2, 950, 000 00
Surplus fund........	770, 557 94	770, 557 94	770, 557 94	750, 560 37	553, 181 29
Undivided profits ...	138, 786 17	281, 853 30	313, 728 70	258, 034 01	286, 476 75
Nat'l bank circulation	769, 790 00	773, 690 00	770, 490 00	762, 390 00	1, 176, 190 00
State bank circulation					
Dividends unpaid....	89, 939 68	9, 796 18	24, 159 18	72, 926 18	12, 861 68
Individual deposits...	5, 353, 534 41	5, 302, 199 83	6, 016, 700 05	5, 586, 302 62	5, 955, 254 53
U. S. deposits........	131, 318 34	95, 345 85	140, 363 77	149, 397 12	115, 620 23
Dep'ts U.S.dis.officers					
Due to national banks	2, 394, 821 25	2, 472, 070 53	2, 478, 601 67	2, 631, 141 01	2, 172, 938 22
Due to State banks...	3, 363, 928 21	4, 101, 682 41	4, 545, 555 97	4, 768, 301 40	4, 026, 991 09
Notes re-discounted..	324, 876 26	113, 000 00			285, 382 75
Bills payable........	301, 500 00				450, 000 00
Total	16, 289, 082 26	16, 660, 196 04	17, 710, 157 28	17, 629, 142 71	17, 984, 896 54

KANSAS.

	12 banks.	12 banks.	12 banks.	12 banks.	13 banks.
Capital stock	$875, 000 00	$875, 000 00	$875, 000 00	$875, 000 00	$925, 000 00
Surplus fund........	194, 050 00	212, 460 00	212, 460 00	214, 460 00	225, 210 00
Undivided profits....	146, 505 32	106, 211 47	118, 908 43	121, 737 63	141, 793 38
Nat'l bank circulation	638, 980 00	557, 980 00	602, 980 00	602, 980 00	679, 460 00
State bank circulation					
Dividends unpaid.....				1, 500 00	
Individual deposits...	2, 461, 927 85	2, 358, 463 09	2, 548, 217 88	2, 692, 438 70	3, 239, 286 86
U. S. deposits........	61, 479 79	119, 082 25	150, 484 84	156, 737 32	142, 426 91
Dep'ts U.S.dis.officers	217, 544 16	170, 192 20	150, 816 65	130, 445 01	203, 848 65
Due to national banks	65, 087 11	18, 157 20	18, 599 21	20, 213 71	20, 014 12
Due to State banks...	170, 886 99	227, 642 34	206, 124 19	239, 944 99	209, 859 53
Notes re discounted..	17, 913 77	2, 546 00	2, 346 00	8, 473 50	69, 900 73
Bills payable........		10, 000 00			15, 000 00
Total	4, 849, 374 99	4, 657, 734 64	4, 885, 937 20	5, 063, 930 86	5, 871, 800 18

NEBRASKA.

	10 banks.	10 banks.	10 banks.	11 banks.	12 banks.
Capital stock	$850, 000 00	$850, 000 00	$850, 000 00	$850, 000 00	$910, 000 00
Surplus fund	247, 600 00	250, 100 00	250, 500 00	250, 500 00	294, 000 00
Undivided profits....	222, 600 26	189, 242 14	173, 608 83	204, 750 99	198, 893 84
Nat'l bank circulation	683, 100 00	511, 150 00	509, 750 00	584, 650 00	665, 050 00
State bank circulation					
Dividends unpaid	1, 622 50	4, 122 50	1, 234 00	2, 500 00	5, 000 00
Individual deposits...	3, 601, 377 48	3, 633, 732 71	3, 742, 746 37	4, 542, 091 45	5, 242, 391 78
U. S. deposits........	66, 919 99	55, 941 08	141, 408 21	104, 940 95	118, 647 64
Dep'ts U.S.dis.officers	258, 224 60	206, 375 87	153, 738 07	211, 313 60	106, 085 00
Due to national banks	350, 473 71	292, 337 40	298, 643 05	469, 344 87	651, 872 38
Due to State banks	345, 371 38	334, 056 40	420, 336 90	515, 340 53	728, 085 83
Notes re-discounted..	287, 214 02	252, 708 51	181, 858 93		117, 500 00
Bills payable........					
Total	6, 923, 503 94	6, 570, 766 61	6, 723, 824 36	7, 735, 431 49	9, 127, 526 47

Abstract of reports since October 1, 1880, arranged

COLORADO.

Resources.	DECEMBER 31. 14 banks.	MARCH 11. 14 banks.	MAY 6. 14 banks.	JUNE 30. 15 banks.	OCTOBER 1. 17 banks.
Loans and discounts	$5,222,431 10	$5,628,576 36	$6,172,711 03	$5,929,311 16	$6,510,663 31
Bonds for circulation	940,000 00	940,000 00	940,000 00	980,000 00	1,130,000 00
Bonds for deposits	200,000 00	200,000 00	200,000 00	200,000 00	200,000 00
U. S. bonds on hand	52,400 00	288,100 00	52,450 00	97,800 00	52,400 00
Other stocks and b'ds	649,499 09	745,485 94	603,702 85	593,723 75	656,132 37
Due from res've ag'ts	2,551,048 10	1,780,924 18	1,625,009 20	2,571,414 08	2,689,832 88
Due from nat'l banks	806,955 09	533,433 73	435,588 35	597,558 18	767,701 48
Due from State banks	396,898 33	498,911 14	557,628 39	682,553 35	619,259 72
Real estate, &c	148,009 45	179,836 15	171,050 10	176,678 40	175,620 43
Current expenses	58,865 51	66,619 05	42,781 43	25,075 50	46,877 04
Premiums paid	5,000 00	2,500 00	2,500 00	7,710 00	16,993 00
Cash items	166,808 32	101,703 62	247,662 52	186,890 45	210,350 81
Clear'g-house exch'gs					
Bills of other banks	218,529 00	195,686 00	197,303 00	267,434 00	240,438 00
Fractional currency	1,382 41	2,430 90	1,437 41	1,446 36	1,211 95
Specie	290,074 64	397,637 59	289,733 84	306,733 05	655,825 50
Legal-tender notes	739,167 00	609,110 00	727,943 00	773,446 00	626,903 00
U. S. cert's of deposit					
Due from U.S. Treas	76,567 21	68,983 67	58,667 87	74,552 27	75,072 37
Total	12,523,635 25	12,239,938 33	12,326,828 99	13,472,326 55	14,674,981 86

NEVADA.

	1 bank.	1 bank.	1 bank.	1 bank.	1 bank.
Loans and discounts	$107,545 15	$116,696 52	$137,533 62	$156,941 22	$181,229 89
Bonds for circulation	40,000 00	40,000 00	40,000 00	40,000 00	40,000 00
Bonds for deposits					
U. S. bonds on hand					
Other stocks and b'ds		1,679 94			8,008 14
Due from res've ag'ts	5,058 21	1,470 31	1,948 75	1,297 40	2,309 43
Due from nat'l banks			100 00		
Due from State banks		552 01	1,515 91	2,269 47	1,791 16
Real estate, &c	3,288 84	3,308 34	3,308 34	3,308 34	3,353 34
Current expenses		1,618 25	2,972 73		2,399 76
Premiums paid	3,225 00	3,225 00	3,225 00	3,225 00	3,225 00
Cash items	490 00		120 85	510 00	
Clear'g-house exch'gs					
Bills of other banks		2,355 00	170 00	520 00	1,935 00
Fractional currency					
Specie	46,923 98	50,912 13	48,507 68	26,033 53	40,207 69
Legal-tender notes	244 00	1,343 00		782 00	2,519 00
U. S. cert's of deposit					
Due from U.S. Treas	1,800 00	1,800 00	1,800 00	1,800 00	2,200 00
Total	208,575 18	224,960 50	241,202 88	236,687 05	289,178 41

CALIFORNIA.

	10 banks.	10 banks.	10 banks.	10 banks.	10 banks.
Loans and discounts	$3,329,936 81	$3,310,627 87	$3,302,558 75	$3,598,806 21	$4,195,237 53
Bonds for circulation	1,114,000 00	1,114,000 00	1,167,000 00	1,167,000 00	1,214,000 00
Bonds for deposits	50,000 00	50,000 00	50,000 00	50,000 00	50,000 00
U. S. bonds on hand	53,500 00	105,400 00	40,100 00	70,250 00	106,200 00
Other stocks and b'ds	161,945 36	159,854 92	183,653 19	178,627 05	193,667 07
Due from res've ag'ts	328,972 63	315,320 95	388,706 54	450,050 90	469,465 88
Due from nat'l banks	59,257 38	16,175 08	85,039 00	16,766 33	8,951 53
Due from State banks	588,030 27	312,618 65	518,574 00	410,628 23	606,747 53
Real estate, &c	280,364 44	288,225 19	325,744 19	299,240 17	309,550 01
Current expenses	6,529 15	25,305 46	38,110 25	24,705 68	41,689 95
Premiums paid	13,033 22	18,165 47	18,641 89	23,088 80	31,689 47
Cash items	75,756 70	30,803 34	45,867 98	45,502 13	45,915 33
Clear'g-house exch'gs					
Bills of other banks	23,044 00	10,337 00	38,045 00	64,987 00	84,625 00
Fractional currency	8 07	100 65	58 28	9 50	28 70
Specie	843,954 12	1,041,790 79	1,027,966 69	952,978 33	801,729 04
Legal-tender notes	10,211 00	8,554 00	9,701 00	13,441 00	15,782 00
U. S. cert's of deposit					
Due from U.S. Treas	39,130 00	39,130 00	40,615 00	41,265 00	41,030 00
Total	6,977,633 15	6,859,479 37	7,280,381 76	7,407,347 23	8,216,109 04

by States and reserve cities—Continued.

COLORADO.

Liabilities.	DECEMBER 31. 14 banks.	MARCH 11. 14 banks.	MAY 6. 14 banks.	JUNE 30. 15 banks.	OCTOBER 1. 17 banks.
Capital stock	$1,070,000 00	$1,070,000 00	$1,070,000 00	$1,190,000 00	$1,276,800 00
Surplus fund	320,000 00	333,000 00	358,300 00	409,300 00	468,000 00
Undivided profits	247,787 47	283,436 71	310,873 12	302,010 87	324,797 00
Nat'l bank circulation	846,000 00	834,900 00	836,100 00	869,700 00	984,900 00
State bank circulation					
Dividends unpaid	5,000 00		1,080 00	15,855 00	505 00
Individual deposits	8,753,579 00	8,737,716 75	8,734,951 50	9,815 710 05	10,352,358 27
U. S. deposits	116,396 66	108,854 93	130,034 07	50,750 40	43,851 10
Dep'ts U.S.dis.officers	102,483 65	67,949 77	93,048 74	118,976 96	91,907 74
Due to national banks	506,057 57	390,286 74	274,742 97	255,896 10	560,915 85
Due to State banks	556,330 81	413,793 43	517,698 59	444,127 17	570,946 90
Notes re-discounted					
Bills payable					
Total	12,523,635 25	12,239,938 33	12,326,828 99	13,472,326 55	14,674,981 86

NEVADA.

	1 bank.	1 bank.	1 bank.	1 bank.	1 bank.
Capital stock	$50,000 00	$50,000 00	$50,000 00	$50,000 00	$75,000 00
Surplus fund		2,036 04	2,036 04	2,036 04	8,786 02
Undivided profits	4,996 75	2,223 25	5,256 52	6,277 08	6,033 38
Nat'l bank circulation	36,000 00	36,000 00	36,000 00	36,000 00	36,000 00
State bank circulation					
Dividends unpaid					
Individual deposits	85,592 80	101,295 70	100,233 45	97,168 47	114,237 18
U. S. deposits					
Dep'ts U.S.dis.officers					
Due to national banks	18,969 37	24,427 54	35,590 03	35,390 50	9,905 89
Due to State banks	13,016 26	8,977 88	12,086 84	9,814 06	39,215 94
Notes re-discounted					
Bills payable					
Total	208,575 18	224,060 50	241,202 88	236,687 05	289,178 41

CALIFORNIA.

	10 banks.	10 banks.	10 banks.	10 banks.	10 banks.
Capital stock	$1,750,000 00	$1,770,000 00	$1,770,000 00	$1,770,000 00	$1,800,000 00
Surplus fund	207,410 67	213,997 81	254,327 40	258,677 07	264,612 35
Undivided profits	177,507 73	177,022 87	210,238 64	221,375 91	221,067 17
Nat'l bank circulation	948,525 00	943,935 00	947,635 00	943,750 00	1,000,465 00
State bank circulation					
Dividends unpaid	13,542 67	3,237 09	3,166 51	13,298 26	12,733 47
Individual deposits	3,720,520 62	3,403,520 55	3,815,430 44	3,825,006 33	4,490,034 54
U. S. deposits	9,865 69	6,480 82	4,678 36	20,652 75	2,291 26
Dep'ts U.S.dis.officers					143 20
Due to national banks	4,045 60	98,175 13	59,071 44	38,908 19	52,691 63
Due to State banks	146,206 17	243,110 10	165,833 97	280,678 72	282,070 42
Notes re-discounted					
Bills payable			50,000 00	35,000 00	90,000 00
Total	6,977,633 15	6,859,479 37	7,280,384 76	7,407,347 23	8,216,109 04

Abstract of reports since October 1, 1880, arranged

CITY OF SAN FRANCISCO.

Resources.	DECEMBER 31. 1 bank.	MARCH 11. 1 bank.	MAY 6. 1 bank.	JUNE 30. 1 bank.	OCTOBER 1. 1 bank.
Loans and discounts	$2,253,094 83	$2,063,179 82	$2,045,354 75	$2,054,486 16	$2,280,902 79
Bonds for circulation	600,000 00	600,000 00	600,000 00	600,000 00	600,000 00
Bonds for deposits					
U. S. bonds on hand					
Other stocks and b'ds					
Due from res've ag'ts					
Due from nat'l banks	48,132 37	109,417,03	245,712 96	225,028 83	169,323 28
Due from State banks	131,157 95	125,702 61	156,988 75	185,011 73	183,930 34
Real estate, &c	12,539 77	12,039 77	11,617 81	11,117 81	10,367 81
Current expenses		812 60	751 40		33 00
Premiums paid	10,000 00	10,000 00	10,000 00	10,000 00	10,000 00
Cash items	430 70	919 35	639 35	338 10	230 30
Clear'g-house exch'gs	844 96	40,408 97	98,282 12	70,314 23	125,503 92
Bills of other banks	12,880 00	28,300 00	27,480 00	3,740 00	5,675 00
Fractional currency	15 37	14 34	7 65	66 11	9 48
Specie	759,330 00	675,700 00	736,870 00	1,108,200 00	1,183,730 00
Legal-tender notes	2,060 00	2,130 00	1,330 00	4,310 00	7,837 00
U. S. cert's of deposit					
Due from U. S. Treas					
Total	3,830,485 95	3,668,624 49	3,935,034 79	4,272,612 97	4,577,602 92

OREGON.

	1 bank.	1 bank.	1 bank.	1 bank.	1 bank.
Loans and discounts	$1,025,180 26	$939,418 59	$981,250 08	$862,594 74	$1,021,696 60
Bonds for circulation	250,000 00	250,000 00	250,000 00	250,000 00	250,000 00
Bonds for deposits	500,000 00	500,000 00	500,000 00	500,000 00	500,000 00
U. S. bonds on hand	4,700 00	4,700 00	15,350 00	90,950 00	153,400 00
Other stocks and b'ds	175,477 86	179,559 84	193,997 44	186,469 74	404,790 78
Due from res've ag'ts	63,810 46	113,526 82	135,754 48	467,623 26	198,066 54
Due from nat'l banks	4,454 13	8,577 65	8,457 60	19,142 39	5,423 87
Due from State banks	73,066 30	44,018 79	191,241 32	68,690 86	59,632 96
Real estate, &c					
Current expenses	15,239 57	4,785 25	9,852 30	15,179 80	6,993 55
Premiums paid	265 50		860 62	10,934 12	23,767 75
Cash items	803 82	1,059 68	1,068 58	1,725 81	1,486 81
Clear'g-house exch'gs					
Bills of other banks	37,500 00	4,400 00	5,500 00	24,100 00	3,800 00
Fractional currency					
Specie	250,954 12	386,713 16	354,212 09	323,481 14	347,143 01
Legal-tender notes	41,000 00	5,400 00	15,700 00	17,700 00	2,200 00
U. S. cert's of deposit					
Due from U. S. Treas	14,638 30	11,847 15	15,650 00	18,942 00	25,929 40
Total	2,466,090 32	2,454,006 93	2,678,894 51	2,857,533 86	3,004,331 27

DAKOTA.

	6 banks.	6 banks.	7 banks.	7 banks.	8 banks.
Loans and discounts	$888,275 56	$917,523 63	$997,120 06	$1,031,788 36	$1,173,782 50
Bonds for circulation	245,000 00	245,000 00	295,000 00	295,000 00	345,000 00
Bonds for deposits	50,000 00	50,000 00	50,000 00	50,000 00	50,000 00
U. S. bonds on hand	2,350 00	2,500 00	2,500 00		
Other stocks and b'ds	42,609 97	63,463 89	67,812 99	80,839 95	91,967 78
Due from res've ag'ts	130,704 00	113,601 40	137,664 18	92,445 40	176,122 43
Due from nat'l banks	206,016 35	168,510 17	207,082 10	249,265,26	416,498 27
Due from State banks	120,707 62	152,470 95	98,252 04	182,328 70	221,156 43
Real estate, &c	70,255 50	71,137 25	73,384 00	75,792 70	103,530 53
Current expenses	9,815 30	17,886 01	22,086 60	13,052 99	14,366 31
Premiums paid	4,865 63	4,865 63	11,415 63	11,415 63	6,315 65
Cash items	12,435 35	8,965 75	9,276 35	11,901 08	20,535 96
Clear'g-house exch'gs					
Bills of other banks	62,895 00	42,482 00	42,745 00	64,092 00	81,241 00
Fractional currency	543 32	218 53	244 05	141 74	197 79
Specie	83,989 42	87,600 90	81,486 60	93,963 43	90,683 62
Legal-tender notes	160,449 00	131,181 00	146,170 00	132,750 00	148,223 00
U. S. cert's of deposit					
Due from U. S. Treas	11,025 00	11,025 00	9,325 00	13,275 00	15,525 00
Total	2,101,937 02	2,088,432 11	2,251,564 69	2,398,052 33	2,955,446 55

by States and reserve cities—Continued.

CITY OF SAN FRANCISCO.

Liabilities.	DECEMBER 31. 1 bank.	MARCH 11. 1 bank.	MAY 6. 1 bank.	JUNE 30. 1 bank.	OCTOBER 1. 1 bank.
Capital stock	$1,500,000 00	$1,500,000 00	$1,500,000 00	$1,500,000 00	$1,500,000 00
Surplus fund	164,675 73	171,004 33	174,004 33	174,004 33	179,603 36
Undivided profits	78,039 41	70,636 21	65,848 03	95,026 38	91,592 51
Nat'l bank circulation	462,730 00	462,505 00	449,000 00	439,670 00	333,805 00
State bank circulation					
Dividends unpaid	873 50	633 50	2,065 50	378 00	1,342 00
Individual deposits	1,185,952 78	1,105,928 64	1,359,792 62	1,659,397 32	1,674,654 31
U. S. deposits					
Dep'ts U.S.dis.officers					
Due to national banks	220,367 08	227,289 60	163,617 29	153,148 38	189,851 74
Due to State banks	217,847 43	130,627 21	215,507 02	250,988 56	606,754 00
Notes rediscounted					
Bills payable					
Total	3,830,485 95	3,668,624 49	3,935,034 79	4,272,612 97	4,577,602 92

OREGON.

	1 bank.	1 bank.	1 bank.	1 bank.	1 bank.
Capital stock	$250,000 00	$250,000 00	$250,000 00	$250,000 00	$250,000 00
Surplus fund	50,000 00	50,000 00	50,000 00	50,000 00	50,000 00
Undivided profits	359,925 39	352,139 36	366,884 59	386,547 75	320,686 74
Nat'l bank circulation	221,090 00	221,990 00	221,390 00	217,290 00	223,090 00
State bank circulation					
Dividends unpaid	15,000 00				15,000 00
Individual deposits	1,033,231 27	1,052,590 69	1,226,396 15	1,392,907 20	1,582,907 96
U. S. deposits	137,948 66	108,668 00	203,690 77	232,944 41	172,905 65
Dep'ts U.S.dis.officers	316,899 54	320,243 95	278,325 40	268,188 56	228,303 93
Due to national banks	14,980 67		3,450 52	5,691 29	74,147 88
Due to State banks	67,014 79	98,374 93	48,757 08	53,964 65	87,289 11
Notes rediscounted					
Bills payable					
Total	2,466,090 32	2,454,006 93	2,678,894 51	2,857,533 86	3,004,331 27

DAKOTA.

	6 banks.	6 banks.	7 banks.	7 banks.	8 banks.
Capital stock	$425,000 00	$425,000 00	$475,000 00	$505,000 00	$575,000 00
Surplus fund	56,000 00	76,500 00	76,500 00	76,500 00	83,100 00
Undivided profits	122,550 36	125,591 03	139,452 82	156,711 80	168,592 30
Nat'l bank circulation	218,500 00	219,800 00	217,600 00	259,300 00	303,900 00
State bank circulation					
Dividends unpaid	230 00	1,570 00	530 00	530 00	1,140 00
Individual deposits	1,178,307 67	1,159,178 91	1,220,244 11	1,308,442 92	1,741,179 38
U. S. deposits	36,802 23	10,263 37	33,979 42	27,439 65	33,993 07
Dep'ts U.S.dis.officers	47,633 50	54,003 70	43,365 78	41,517 73	16,061 31
Due to national banks	280 01	521 05	519 00	1,219 99	2,262 69
Due to State banks	16,624 25	16,004 05	41,373 56	21,390 24	30,217 80
Notes rediscounted					
Bills payable					
Total	2,101,937 02	2,088,432 11	2,251,564 69	2,398,052 33	2,955,446 55

14 C C

Abstract of reports since October 1, 1880, arranged

IDAHO.

Resources.	DECEMBER 31. 1 bank.	MARCH 11. 1 bank.	MAY 6. 1 bank.	JUNE 30. 1 bank.	OCTOBER 1. 1 bank.
Loans and discounts.	$103,410 82	$111,865 91	$123,700 36	$126,745 85	$101,303 27
Bonds for circulation.	100,000 00	100,000 00	100,000 00	100,000 00	100,000 00
Bonds for deposits.					
U. S. bonds on hand.					100,000 00
Other stocks and b'ds	46,965 23	44,187 65	43,789 41	44,046 73	46,138 99
Due from res've ag'ts.					
Due from nat'l banks.	581 25	420 28	26,808 08	236 87	2,615 18
Due from State banks	89,539 32	67,011 39	71,077 15	73,185 40	80,365 50
Real estate, &c	7,000 00	7,000 00	7,000 00	7,000 00	7,000 00
Current expenses.	6,245 27	2,018 40	3,073 08	4,006 54	4,060 63
Premiums paid					17,437 50
Cash items	3,594 45	1,249 17	2,408 06	4,626 90	5,967 58
Clear'g-house exch'gs					
Bills of other banks.	16,207 00	12,200 00	13,400 00	21,500 00	20,865 00
Fractional currency					
Specie	12,500 00	19,871 00	12,970 00	25,540 50	18,173 00
Legal-tender notes	23,300 00	25,303 00	21,750 00	20,611 00	23,250 00
U. S. cert's of deposit.					
Due from U. S. Treas	4,500 00	5,800 00	3,600 00	4,500 00	6,683 50
Total	413,843 34	396,926 80	431,576 14	431,999 79	533,860 15

MONTANA.

	3 banks.	3 banks.	3 banks.	3 banks.	3 banks.
Loans and discounts	$1,169,141 41	$1,217,573 55	$1,256,354 08	$1,118,427 35	$1,301,066 39
Bonds for circulation.	180,000 00	180,000 00	180,000 00	180,000 00	180,000 00
Bonds for deposits.	200,000 00	200,000 00	200,000 00	200,000 00	200,000 00
U. S. bonds on hand.					
Other stocks and b'ds	63,413 93	2,931 42	4,007 42	115,842 71	116,455 00
Due from res've ag'ts.	52,758 05	18,921 80	33,502 87	19,810 14	63,095 61
Due from nat'l banks.	3,798 60	48,894 03	35,424 95	31,731 37	34,981 98
Due from State banks	34,537 71	20,698 19	50,919 81	109,179 17	84,050 97
Real estate, &c	38,344 76	38,473 93	41,953 15	48,940 05	47,534 47
Current expenses.		9,091 69	14,298 88		11,501 11
Premiums paid	18,500 00	18,608 57	4,757 57	4,500 00	4,111 75
Cash items	8,885 71	3,470 01	7,972 94	44,208 39	37,297 63
Clear'g-house exch'gs					
Bills of other banks.	11,115 00	12,971 00	11,988 00	18,934 00	15,340 00
Fractional currency.	46 00	41 89	102 00		77 56
Specie	54,043 15	59,297 38	63,562 94	37,594 32	43,397 55
Legal-tender notes	60,800 00	70,000 00	63,200 00	80,500 00	81,150 00
U. S. cert's of deposit.					
Due from U. S. Treas	8,616 27	7,360 95	8,514 80	9,214 80	8,566 05
Total	1,904,000 59	1,908,334 41	1,976,619 41	2,018,382 30	2,228,626 07

NEW MEXICO.

	4 banks.	4 banks.	4 banks.	4 banks.	4 banks.
Loans and discounts	$634,471 47	$772,936 94	$804,295 29	$764,716 14	$722,051 61
Bonds for circulation	400,000 00	400,000 00	400,000 00	400,000 00	400,000 00
Bonds for deposits	160,000 00	160,000 00	160,000 00	160,000 00	160,000 00
U. S. bonds on hand.			400 00	400 00	400 00
Other stocks and b'ds	1,051 68	4,873 52	8,557 47	11,198 78	6,351 57
Due from res've ag'ts	117,377 36	97,526 51	179,095 52	176,654 60	243,067 24
Due from nat'l banks.	151,438 07	188,532 86	167,490 75	188,807 08	345,076 25
Due from State banks	176,767 22	91,520 20	72,754 26	87,826 85	95,019 04
Real estate, &c	19,690 05	21,170 80	21,203 80	22,206 55	27,409 47
Current expenses.	7,895 01	9,615 17	11,464 90	10,353 55	15,394 15
Premiums paid	3,902 80	3,062 50	3,062 50	3,062 50	2,295 81
Cash items	4,545 85	5,643 36	5,378 25	17,655 89	3,996 27
Clear'g-house exch'gs					
Bills of other banks.	27,802 00	21,695 00	28,061 00	14,027 00	10,398 00
Fractional currency.	186 74	136 28	358 57	592 07	161 27
Specie	14,982 82	16,449 11	24,221 89	44,171 00	83,030 00
Legal-tender notes	113,433 00	108,864 00	108,192 00	69,025 00	81,147 00
U. S. cert's of deposit.					
Due from U. S. Treas	18,021 04	18,621 04	18,821 04	18,000 00	18,000 00
Total	1,851,565 11	1,920,647 29	2,013,557 32	1,988,607 01	2,213,797 68

by States and reserve cities—Continued.

IDAHO.

Liabilities.	DECEMBER 31.	MARCH 11.	MAY 6.	JUNE 30.	OCTOBER 1.
	1 bank.	1 bank.	1 bank.	1 bank.	1 bank.
Capital stock	$100,000 00	$100,000 00	$100,000 00	$100,000 00	$100,000 00
Surplus fund	20,000 00	20,000 00	20,000 00	20,000 00	20,000 00
Undivided profits....	19,834 33	3,951 72	9,258 79	20,316 50	9,875 12
Nat'l bank circulation	82,200 00	83,500 00	82,800 00	81,700 00	82,850 00
State bank circulation					
Dividends unpaid.					
Individual deposits...	191,268 30	189,175 68	219,517 35	200,983 29	320,169 05
U. S. deposits.					
Dep'ts U.S.dis.officers					
Due to national banks					
Due to State banks...	540 71				965 98
Notes re-discounted					
Bills payable.					
Total	413,643 34	396,926 80	431,576 14	431,999 79	533,860 15

MONTANA.

	3 banks.	3 banks.	3 banks.	3 banks.	3 banks.
Capital stock	$200,000 00	$200,000 00	$200,000 00	$200,000 00	$200,000 00
Surplus fund	30,000 00	40,000 00	40,000 00	40,000 00	40,000 00
Undivided profits....	159,983 28	165,975 90	189,830 45	189,824 19	229,199 20
Nat'l bank circulation	156,300 00	157,300 00	159,200 00	157,900 00	157,800 00
State bank circulation					
Dividends unpaid.					
Individual deposits...	1,016,783 87	1,030,416 93	1,059,544 37	1,160,256 09	1,239,504 25
U. S. deposits........	23,139 58	15,705 90	38,011 69	11,712 04	11,667 86
Dep'ts U.S.dis.officers	156,881 17	160,348 00	185,913 38	107,378 80	135,884 04
Due to national banks	26,502 57	44,278 08	64,258 75	12,643 18	106,151 15
Due to State banks...	32,983 23	50,523 33	26,422 77	78,667 70	48,419 57
Notes re-discounted..	101,426 89	43,786 27	13,443 00		
Bills payable........					
Total	1,904,000 59	1,908,334 41	1,976,619 41	2,018,382 30	2,228,626 07

NEW MEXICO.

	4 banks.	4 banks.	4 banks.	4 banks.	4 banks.
Capital stock	$400,000 00	$400,000 00	$400,000 00	$400,000 00	$400,000 00
Surplus fund	50,381 01	87,381 01	91,291 71	92,678 98	100,678 98
Undivided profits....	54,695 51	28,824 96	42,412 24	40,967 51	50,427 29
Nat'l bank circulation	355,127 00	355,877 00	355,917 00	355,107 00	352,437 00
State bank circulation					
Dividends unpaid....					
Individual deposits...	697,370 36	716,322 85	759,335 26	810,322 42	989,849 16
U. S. deposits	64,912 25	111,517 88	112,455 72	69,589 95	38,965 96
Dep'ts U.S.dis.officers	113,677 52	113,780 66	65,915 44	98,777 70	96,824 88
Due to national banks	13,748 95	5,695 06	24,482 92	11,878 39	77,521 47
Due to State banks...	101,652 51	101,247 87	161,747 04	109,375 66	107,092 94
Notes re-discounted...					
Bills payable					
Total	1,851,565 11	1,920,647 29	2,013,557 33	1,988,697 61	2,213,797 08

Abstract of reports since October 1, 1880, arranged

UTAH.

Resources.	DECEMBER 31. 1 bank.	MARCH 11. 1 bank.	MAY 6. 1 bank.	JUNE 30. 1 bank.	OCTOBER 1. 1 bank.
Loans and discounts	$287,392 21	$405,884 60	$303,789 18	$125,399 63	$358,704 64
Bonds for circulation	200,000 00	200,000 00	200,000 00	200,000 00	200,000 00
Bonds for deposits	100,000 00	100,000 00	100,000 00	100,000 00	100,000 00
U. S. bonds on hand					150,000 00
Other stocks and b'ds	135,344 17	122,900 00	131,400 00	142,700 00	174,325 00
Due from res've ag'ts	34,876 19	46,127 04	56,709 08	78,972 59	88,640 03
Due from nat'l banks	43,034 96	70,833 21	86,043 42	124,392 94	150,241 95
Due from State banks	28,472 78	24,555 10	26,606 76	35,963 95	41,508 64
Real estate, &c	40,000 00	40,000 00	40,000 00	40,000 00	40,000 00
Current expenses	2,956 76	9,861 15	5,114 40	7,485 08	14,875 16
Premiums paid					
Cash items	14,305 07	2,498 06	2,494 67	10,063 72	9,970 19
Clear'g-house exch'gs					
Bills of other banks	6,785 00	18,004 00	27,923 00	14,240 00	23,515 00
Fractional currency	123 00	18 50	75 70	106 00	94 00
Specie	149,267 00	72,280 75	143,257 65	140,259 30	141,530 15
Legal-tender notes	53,589 00	31,526 00	25,158 00	37,563 00	24,470 00
U. S. cert's of deposit					
Due from U. S. Treas	9,000 00	9,000 00	9,000 00	9,000 00	9,000 00
Total	1,105,146 14	1,153,468 41	1,247,571 86	1,366,146 21	1,526,873 86

WASHINGTON.

	1 bank.	1 bank.	1 bank.	2 banks.	2 banks.
Loans and discounts	$402,575 21	$437,637 95	$458,577 89	$523,935 16	$509,664 13
Bonds for circulation	150,000 00	50,000 00	50,000 00	80,000 00	130,000 00
Bonds for deposits					
U. S. bonds on hand					
Other stocks and b'ds	5,032 32	4,146 97	3,666 97	3,992 22	7,529 05
Due from res've ag'ts	31,630 30	10,963 72	62,173 23	67,098 56	23,303 87
Due from nat'l banks	13,520 97				83,674 37
Due from State banks	347 60		15,128 27	6,272 39	64,766 79
Real estate, &c	3,400 00	3,400 00	3,756 61	9,543 74	9,557 24
Current expenses		2,934 26	5,349 45	349 53	4,648 90
Premiums paid					
Cash items	977 70	95 68	208 14	198 12	770 81
Clear'g-house exch'gs					
Bills of other banks	804 00	525 00	2,420 00	3,741 00	
Fractional currency					
Specie	37,084 20	77,879 35	50,403 65	82,749 89	32,006 06
Legal-tender notes	12,000 00	11,000 00	9,149 00	12,915 00	19,940 00
U. S. cert's of deposit					
Due from U. S. Treas	6,750 00	2,250 00	2,250 00	3,600 00	5,850 00
Total	664,122 30	600,832 93	663,083 21	794,395 61	891,711 22

WYOMING.

	2 banks.	2 banks.	2 banks.	3 banks.	3 banks.
Loans and discounts	$376,255 75	$399,808 99	$384,434 20	$445,117 79	$730,433 29
Bonds for circulation	64,000 00	64,000 00	64,000 00	94,000 00	94,000 00
Bonds for deposits					
U. S. bonds on hand					
Other stocks and b'ds	24,278 07	31,452 41	33,939 84	46,174 79	58,456 24
Due from res've ag'ts	33,571 27	4,007 99	14,298 05	94,760 33	87,887 61
Due from nat'l banks	54,543 15	36,883 91	54,864 64	92,146 62	77,215 02
Due from State banks	2,257 20	2,034 06	286 01	4,468 10	9,107 20
Real estate, &c	19,798 45	19,798 45	19,798 45	24,853 02	28,856 94
Current expenses		4,852 62	7,431 84	8,847 85	17,870 47
Premiums paid				339 12	381 99
Cash items	6,879 95	6,193 61	4,190 09	7,158 67	54,684 25
Clear'g-house exch'gs					
Bills of other banks	15,727 00	2,159 00	17,060 00	23,847 00	16,374 00
Fractional currency	217 05	82 45	83 76	52 49	65 36
Specie	44,384 80	68,335 15	38,964 10	57,708 85	71,089 20
Legal-tender notes	50,206 00	38,279 00	47,108 00	44,923 00	54,950 00
U. S. cert's of deposit					
Due from U. S. Treas	2,972 00	2,880 00	2,930 00	4,230 00	4,230 00
Total	695,090 69	680,767 64	689,388 98	948,627 63	1,305,601 57

by States and reserve cities—Continued.

UTAH.

Liabilities.	DECEMBER 31. 1 bank.	MARCH 11. 1 bank.	MAY 6. 1 bank.	JUNE 30. 1 bank.	OCTOBER 1. 1 bank.
Capital stock	$200,000 00	$200,000 00	$200,000 00	$200,000 00	$200,000 00
Surplus fund	75,000 00	100,000 00	100,000 00	100,000 00	100,000 00
Undivided profits	17,527 80	45,367 84	31,212 70	40,738 55	53,896 46
Nat'l bank circulation	176,700 00	172,300 00	168,700 00	162,000 00	152,500 00
State bank circulation					
Dividends unpaid	258 00	216 00	1,578 00	366 00	354 00
Individual deposits	569,164 07	577,633 17	676,250 88	745,881 27	943,857 39
U. S. deposits	19,190 47	43,885 66	50,524 71	82,851 59	26,687 27
Dep'ts U.S.dis.officers	37,595 84	12,072 50	16,067 01	30,075 68	41,536 69
Due to national banks					
Due to State banks	9,709 96	2,013 24	3,238 56	4,233 12	8,042 05
Notes re-discounted					
Bills payable					
Total	1,105,146 14	1,153,488 41	1,247,571 86	1,366,146 21	1,526,873 86

WASHINGTON.

	1 bank.	1 bank.	1 bank.	2 banks.	2 banks.
Capital stock	$150,000 00	$150,000 00	$150,000 00	$200,000 00	$200,000 00
Surplus fund	30,000 00	30,000 00	30,000 00	30,000 00	30,000 00
Undivided profits	39,000 00	61,793 67	70,517 31	73,189 43	88,669 38
Nat'l bank circulation	135,000 00	45,000 00	45,000 00	72,000 00	117,000 00
State bank circulation					
Dividends unpaid					
Individual deposits	291,200 08	279,804 56	363,274 29	383,547 97	456,041 84
U. S. deposits					
Dep'ts U.S.dis.officers					
Due to national banks		4,278 01	1,291 04		
Due to State banks	18,922 22	29,955 79	3,000 57	35,658 21	
Notes re-discounted					
Bills payable					
Total	664,122 30	600,832 93	663,083 21	794,395 61	891,711 22

WYOMING.

	2 banks.	2 banks.	2 banks.	3 banks.	3 banks.
Capital stock	$150,000 00	$150,000 00	$150,000 00	$225,000 00	$225,000 00
Surplus fund	50,000 00	50,000 00	50,000 00	50,000 00	50,000 00
Undivided profits	9,872 43	23,039 38	32,375 30	28,273 22	48,065 98
Nat'l bank circulation	54,900 00	55,400 00	53,600 00	84,100 00	83,350 00
State bank circulation					
Dividends unpaid	9,900 00				
Individual deposits	411,612 90	386,670 57	369,977 40	553,227 32	856,004 48
U. S. deposits					
Dep'ts U.S.dis.officers					
Due to national banks	2,715 46	15,532 61	30,591 48	5,447 01	30,261 60
Due to State banks	6,089 00	125 08	2,844 80	2,580 08	12,919 51
Notes re-discounted					
Bills payable					
Total	695,090 69	680,767 64	689,388 98	948,627 63	1,305,601 57

INDEX.

Page.

SUBSTITUTES FOR MONEY—Continued.

Tables showing the proportion which the receipts of the banks in each of the four principal cities, in the other reserve cities, and in all other banks bear to the total receipts 18

Recapitulation of the information given in table 18

Total receipts and proportion of checks and drafts of the States and Territories on June 30 and September 17 18

Table showing the same 19

Proportion of receipts representing legitimate business 19

Proportion of checks which pass through the clearing-house 20

Checks settled by transfers on books of the banks 20

Establishment of the London and New York clearing-houses 21

Membership of the assistant treasurer United States in New York clearing-house 21

Use of checks and drafts almost indispensable in banking business 21

Use of checks and drafts in France 21

Extract from Victor Bonnet on the same 21

Proposition of Bank of France to increase their use in that country 21

Extract from report of Bank of France on the same subject 21

Total number of banks and bankers in the United States 22

Mode of doing business 22

Effects of these methods and absurdity of the per capita theory in reference to circulation . 22

Necessity of a true measure of value in large as well as small transactions 22

Reference to Mr. Pownall's paper read before the London Bankers' Institute, Oct. 19, 1881.. 22

Table compiled from same, showing proportion of checks, coin, and notes in London, Edinburgh, Dublin, and country banks in 261 places, with New York city included for the purposes of comparison 22

Proportion of checks used in country districts in England, less than that used in corresponding districts in the United States 22

Extracts from Mr. Pownall's paper 23

TRANSACTIONS OF THE NEW YORK CLEARING-HOUSE 23

Average daily balances 23

Total amount of settlements during the year 24

Table showing yearly transactions of New York clearing-house for 28 years 24

Clearing-House transactions of the assistant treasurer at New York 24

Reference to clearing-house table in appendix 24

DISTRIBUTION OF COIN AND PAPER CURRENCY 24

Net imports of gold and estimated gold production since resumption on January 1, 1879 ... 25

Standard silver dollars coined during the past year 25

Tables showing coin and currency in the country on resumption day, and on November 1, 1879, 1880, and 1881 25

Increase during the year shown in the foregoing table 25

Tables showing gold, silver, and currency in the Treasury, and in the banks—State and national—on resumption day, and on November 1, 1879, 1880, and 1881 25

Tables showing the gold, silver, and currency in the country outside of the banks and Treasury on the same dates 26

Increase of gold and paper currency in the Treasury, and in the banks during the year ... 26

Issue of silver certificates, and amount outstanding on resumption day, and on November 1, 1879, 1880, and 1881 26

Total amount of silver dollars coined to November 1, 1881 26

Amount in the Treasury 26

Amount represented by silver certificates in circulation 26

Amount in the hands of the people 26

Increase since date of resumption of gold, silver coin, and paper currency outside of the Treasury and the banks 26

INTEREST-BEARING FUNDED DEBT OF THE UNITED STATES, AND AMOUNT HELD BY THE NATIONAL BANKS 26

Bonds continued at 3½ per cent., by the Secretary of the Treasury 27

Interest saved by the continuance and payment of bonds 27

Tables showing the interest-bearing funded debt of the United States on August 31, 1865, and on July 1, on each succeeding year, and on November 1, 1881 27

Tables showing the amount of United States bonds held as security for circulation on July 1 of each year from 1865 to 1881, inclusive, and on November 1, 1881, including those continued at 3½ per cent 28

United States bonds held by banks organized under State laws, as ascertained by reports made by State officers 28

INDEX. 217

Page.

INTEREST-BEARING FUNDED DEBT OF THE UNITED STATES, AND AMOUNT HELD BY THE NATIONAL BANKS—Continued.

Amount of such bonds held by the same banks in 1880 and 1881, arranged in geographical divisions of the country ... 29

Amount of same bonds held, as shown by reports made to the Commissioner of Internal Revenue, by State banks, private bankers, trust companies, and savings banks on May 31, 1879, 1880, and 1881, in different sections of the United States ... 29

Total amount of United States bonds held by all banks and bankers in the country, including national, in 1880 and 1881, with tables ... 30

LOANS AND RATES OF INTEREST ... 30

Classification of the loans of banks in New York, Boston, Philadelphia, and Baltimore in October, 1879, 1880, and 1881 ... 30

Classification of the loans in New York City for the last 5 years ... 31

Loans, capital, surplus, net deposits, specie, and paper money in the banks of New York City, other reserve cities, and the States and Territories in the Union on October 1, 1881 . 31

Increase of ratio of loans to capital and net deposits ... 31

Proportion of cash to net deposits on Oct. 1, 1879, 1880, and 1881 ... 31

Extract from report for 1880, commenting on the constant demand for bank accommodations . 31

Ratios of loans to means of banks for the past three years, in New York City, other reserve cities, and in the States and Territories ... 32

Ratios of cash to net deposits for same year ... 32

Extract from former reports showing necessity of checking unhealthy speculation ... 32

Reserve in New York City below the limit ... 32

Reserve in other reserve cities ... 33

Tendency to a rapid increase in loans and deposits, and a decrease in reserve, since resumption day ... 33

Business of banks rapidly expanding—the result, in part, of the large importation of gold and the issue of silver certificates ... 33

Decrease in bonds held by the national banks since 1879 ... 33

Attention of Congress called to section 5200 of the Revised Statutes, placing restrictions on loans upon collateral or on other than business paper ... 33

No adequate means of enforcing the law ... 33

Amendment suggested ... 33

Recommendation as to loans on other stocks and bonds ... 33

Rates of interest in New York City ... 34

Rates in Banks of England and France on call loans and commercial paper ... 34

Changes in rate of discount of the Bank of England during the year ... 34

Changes in rate of Bank of France ... 34

DUTIES OF DIRECTORS AND EXAMINERS ... 34

Laws relating to duties of directors ... 34

By-laws regulating their duties ... 35

Employés of banks under supervision of directors ... 35

Directors responsible for safety of funds committed to their care ... 35

Restrictions imposed by the National Bank Act, which it is their duty to observe ... 35

Government imposing these restrictions, does not become the guardian of the banks, or in any way responsible for the management of its funds ... 35

Duty of examiner to ascertain whether the officers of the bank and its directors comply with the law ... 35

Directors elected by the stockholders ... 36

Examiners' knowledge of the habits and characters of the employés of banks limited ... 36

What constitutes full and complete examination of a bank ... 36

Necessity for periodical examination of affairs of bank by committees appointed by the board of directors ... 36

Reports made by the banks to the Comptroller five times in each year enabling each stockholder to observe the condition of the bank ... 36

Directors have more opportunity to detect embezzlement than government examiners ... 37

Government examinations usually made only once a year ... 37

If both government examiners and directors perform their duties, almost absolute security is assured ... 37

Effects of government examinations in preventing impairment of capital stock, and the declaration of dividends not earned ... 37

Failures exceptional ... 37

Failure of The Mechanics' National Bank of Newark ... 37

Amount which it is estimated depositors will get on their claims ... 37

Government examination of this bank ... 37

15 C C

TABLES CONTAINED IN THE APPENDIX.

INDEX. 221

Page.

State banks, trust companies, private bankers, savings banks, with the average amount of their capital, deposits, and investments in United States bonds, for the six months ending May 31, 1880 102
Similar table for the six months ending May 31, 1881 104
Lawful money reserve of the national banks as shown by the reports of their condition at the close of business, on October 1, 1881 106
Table of the lawful money reserve of the national banks as shown by their reports from October 1, 1875, to October 1, 1881 108
Table of the liabilities of the national banks, and the reserve required and held at three dates in each year, from 1878 to 1881 110
Average yearly deposits, circulation, and reserve of the national banks in New York City, as reported to the New York clearing house, for the months of September and October in each year from 1874 to 1881 111
Amount and rate of taxation, United States and State, of the national banks, for the year 1867.. 112
Similar table for the year 1869 113
Similar table for the year 1874 114
Similar table for the year 1875 115
Similar table for the year 1876 116
Similar table for the year 1877 117
Similar table for the year 1878 118
Similar table for the year 1879 119
Dividends and earnings of the national banks, arranged by geographical divisions, for semi-annual periods from September 1, 1872, to September 1, 1881 120
Abstract of reports of dividends and earnings of national banks from September 1, 1880, to March 1, 1881 122
Similar table from March 1, 1881, to September 1, 1881 123
Table by States and reserve cities of the ratios to capital, and to capital and surplus, of the dividends and earnings of national banks, from March 1, 1877, to September 1, 1881 124
Number and denominations of national-bank notes issued and redeemed, and the number of each denomination outstanding on November 1, in each year, from 1869 to 1881 126
Table showing by States, the amount of national bank circulation issued, the amount of legal tender notes deposited in the United States Treasury to retire national-bank circulation, from June 20, 1874, to November 1, 1881, and amount remaining on deposit at latter date 127
Statement of the monthly increase and decrease of national-bank circulation, from November 1, 1878, to October 31, 1881, to which is added the preceding yearly increase since January 14, 1875 128
Clearings and balances of the banks in New York City for the weeks ending at various dates. 129
Taxes paid by State banks, savings banks, trust companies, and private bankers on their average capital and deposits, for the six months ending November 30, 187 130
Similar table for the six months ending May 31, 1877 131
Similar table for the six months ending May 31, 1878 132
Similar table for the six months ending May 31, 1879 133
Similar table for the six months ending May 31, 1880 134
Similar table for the six months ending May 31, 1881 135
Table by geographical divisions, of the number, average capital and deposits, of State banks, private bankers, and trust and loan companies, and of savings banks with and without capital, for the six months ending November 30, 1875 136
Similar table for the six months ending May 31, 1876 136
Similar table for the six months ending November 30, 1876 136
Similar table for the six months ending May 31, 1877 137
Similar table for the six months ending May 31, 1878 137
Similar table for May 31, 1878, giving private bankers separately 137
Similar table for May 31, 1878, combining State banks, private bankers, savings banks, and trust and loan companies, and giving, in addition, the number, capital, and deposits of national banks on June 29, 1878 138
Table, by geographical divisions, of the number, average capital and deposits, of State banks and trust companies, private bankers, and savings banks with and without capital, for the six months ending May 31, 1879, the private bankers being given separately 138
Similar table, in which the State banks, savings banks, private bankers, &c., are combined, giving, in addition, the number, capital, and deposits of the national banks on June 14, 1879.. 138
Tables similar to the last two, for the six months ending May 31, 1880 139
Tables of the resources and liabilities of State banks in different States, at various dates 140
Aggregate resources and liabilities of State banks from 1877 to 1881 142
Resources and liabilities of trust and loan companies in different States at various dates 142
Aggregate resources and liabilities of trust and loan companies from 1877 to 1881 143

16 C C

www.ingramcontent.com/pod-product-compliance
Lightning Source LLC
Chambersburg PA
CBHW021942220326
41599CB00013BA/1490